The Canadian Handbook of Flexible Benefits

The Canadian Handbook of Flexible Benefits

Robert J. McKay
Editor
Hewitt Associates

Third Edition

National Library of Canada Cataloguing in Publication Data

Library and Archives Canada Cataloguing in Publication

   Canadian handbook of flexible benefits/Robert J. McKay, editor. – 3rd ed.

Includes bibliographical references and index.
ISBN 978-0-470-83825-9

   1. Cafeteria benefit plans–Canada–Handbooks, manuals, etc. 2. Cafeteria benefit plans–Law and legislation–Canada–Handbooks, manuals, etc. I. McKay, Robert J.
HD4928.N62C36 2007   658.3'250971   C2006-904108-3

Production Credits:
Cover design: Natalia Burobina
Typesetter: Aptara Inc., New Delhi, India
Wiley Bicentennial Logo: Richard J. Pacifico
Printer: Tri-graphic Printing Ltd.

John Wiley & Sons Canada, Ltd.
6045 Freemont Blvd.
Mississauga, Ontario
L5R 4J3

Printed in the United States of America
12

Contents

Foreword

As the baby boomers reach retirement age, Canadian organizations are facing increased challenges with respect to attraction and retention. Generation X, the successors to the baby boomers, are far fewer in number, leaving an inadequate supply of employees — skilled or otherwise — to meet demand. To supplement the new generation, employers will need to look to other available human capital resources, such as retirees, immigrants, "virtual" employees in other countries, and disabled workers.

At the same time, health care costs continue to rise. In addition, employers face the possibility of having to pick up the coverage for medical services that may be offloaded from provincial plans. Organizations are attempting at least to contain future benefit cost increases, if not reduce overall expenses.

How does an employer provide benefit plans that can help attract and retain employees and accommodate the needs of a diverse workforce, while not driving up costs? Clearly, offering a "one size fits all" benefits program is not going to meet all employee needs any more than providing an overly rich plan will manage costs. The cost-effective solution is to enable workers to choose benefit options that give them only the coverage they need and want: flexible benefits.

And the time is right to call on flexible benefit programs to help meet these challenges. Many of the changes that flexible plans have undergone since the last edition of this book have focused on overcoming difficulties with employee communication and administration. Considerable progress has been made in facilitating both employee understanding of "flex" and handling of enrolment and record-keeping, particularly with the advent of online capabilities.

With solutions available for these issues and flexible benefits now an option for more organizations, including those with smaller employee populations, it is time for the next evolution of flexible benefit plans. These programs will offer "super flexibility," with options available to meet the widely divergent needs of tomorrow's workforce.

In addition to using flexible benefits to ease attraction and retention challenges and contain cost increases, employers are looking to these programs to meet other objectives:

- **Promote wellness**. The program may offer additional funds for employees who adopt a healthy lifestyle (e.g., regular exercise, annual medical check-up). In addition, benefit options may include fitness memberships and wellness accounts.

- **Provide retiree coverage**. With increased retiree longevity, employers that provide retiree health care benefits are looking at substantial, ever-escalating expenses. Retiree flex can help to keep costs in check.

- **Offer tax-effective compensation**. Recent tax rulings have established that some employees may be able to defer all or part of their bonus to a health spending account or convert it to pre-tax dollars.

- **Increase employee appreciation of total compensation**. Employees who are actively involved in choosing their benefits should have a better understanding of the value of these benefits compared with employees in traditional plans.

Flexible benefit plans are just that — flexible. They provide the wide range of options that different employees are looking for and also meet a variety of employer goals. In addition, the features of a flexible plan may be redesigned as objectives or staffing needs change.

When it comes to shifting demographics, decreases in provincial coverage, and rising health care costs, Canadian organizations must adapt their human resources programs and practices in order to ensure business success. Part of the solution may well lie in providing a flexible benefits plan.

Sarah J. Beech

Toronto, Ontario
April 2007

Editor's Note: Ms. Beech is Managing Principal, Consulting, for Hewitt Associates in Canada. She has consulted on the design and implementation of many flexible benefit plans.

Preface

"So what's new in flex?"

This simple question from a new Hewitt associate started the process towards the publication of this third edition of *The Canadian Handbook of Flexible Benefits*.

The answer to "what's new?" was remarkable. Since we published the second edition of the *Handbook* over ten years ago, the Internet has become commonplace, income tax implications of flexible benefits have been clarified, the Canada Revenue Agency has provided very favourable rulings on proposed plan features, the scope of flex has expanded dramatically, new benefits have been introduced, technology has simplified enrolment and administration, outsourcing is now a viable option, retirees now participate in flex plans, and much more.

And flex has moved beyond North America to Europe, Asia, South America, and Australia.

But the main change is that flex is no longer an experimental approach for leading-edge or early-adopter organizations. It is now the norm, used by over 40 per cent of major employers.

By the end of the conversation with the new associate, it was obvious that a new edition of the *Handbook* was long overdue.

This third edition involved a major rewrite of the entire text to incorporate all the changes described above (and many more not listed). And the focus of the *Handbook* has broadened from being a guide for introducing new plans to also providing insight and direction on maintaining existing plans. In addition, the *Handbook* is expected to be a valuable resource for employers with non-flexible programs looking for detailed information on topics as diverse as prescription drug formularies, retiree benefit issues, communication approaches, and outsourcing alternatives.

This book is intended to be useful to both the novice and the expert in employee benefit matters. Within the text are answers to some of the most frequently asked questions about flexible programs. For example: What alternatives exist for the design of a flexible program? In which benefit areas is choice-making most often introduced? How can the cost impact of a flexible program be measured?

Also included is detailed treatment of the more technical activities involved with the implementation and maintenance of a flexible program — the pricing of benefit options, establishing the administrative apparatus for individual elections, and ensuring that the plan meets Canada Revenue Agency requirements.

This book is organized in eight parts. *Part One* provides an overview of flexible benefits, including discussion of the major forces influencing the growth and development of flexible programs, a review of the alternatives available for flexible program structure, and a summary of the steps involved in starting a program.

Part Two focuses on the design of flexible programs. The section is organized by benefit area — health (including supplemental medical, prescription drugs, vision, and dental); death and disability coverages; flexible expense accounts; vacation and other time-off-with-pay arrangements; retirement options; and newer emerging benefits.

Part Three concentrates on the legal and regulatory environment. Included is the background on the legal and tax frameworks for employee benefits and how they apply to flexible programs. This section also looks at potential discrimination issues connected with provincial human rights legislation.

Part Four examines the structure and financing of flexible programs in terms of options and prices. Also included is a discussion of the insurance and risk aspects of flexible program choices.

Parts Five and *Six* explain the steps involved in communicating and administering flexible benefit programs.

Part Seven focuses on the experience under flexible programs and includes case studies of seven organizations that have introduced flexible benefits to their employees.

Part Eight looks at flexible benefits around the world.

Following Part Eight is an *Appendix* containing reprints of relevant government publications and a *Glossary* is also provided for readers who are unfamiliar with benefit terminology.

Key revisions in this third edition include:

- Broadening the focus to include maintenance of existing flexible programs in addition to implementing new plans;
- Significantly expanding the heath care discussion to reflect numerous changes in prescription drug benefits, including a discussion of alternative types of formularies;
- Adding a chapter on retiree flexible benefit programs;

- Expanding the flexible accounts discussion to include personal and perquisite accounts in addition to health spending accounts;
- Adding a "Provincial Issues" section in a number of the design chapters to discuss special considerations in Quebec, Alberta, British Columbia, and Nova Scotia;
- Expanding the range of range of flexible structures to include simplified designs and total compensation designs;
- Revising the pricing discussions to incorporate net pricing approaches in addition to traditional, credit-based structures;
- Updating the legal discussion to reflect Canada Revenue Agency's *Interpretation Bulletin (IT-529)* on flexible benefits;
- Revising the flexible pension chapter to incorporate Canada Revenue Agency's newsletter plans;
- Updating the administration chapters to reflect new technologies and Web-based enrolment;
- Discussing new administration alternatives, including outsourcing, co-sourcing, and multi-process outsourcing;
- Updating the communication section to cover online communication and the linkage to automated enrolment systems;
- Adding new case studies covering topics such as fixing an existing flexible plan, introducing flexible benefits at a smaller employer, and using flexible benefits to merge two programs;
- Writing a chapter on international flexible benefits describing flexible programs in eight countries in North and South America, Europe, Asia, and Australia; and
- Adding more than fifty glossary terms, including *multi-process outsourcing*, *dynamically frozen formulary*, and *perquisite account*.

It should be noted that throughout this book, the text refers to *flexible benefits*. Some readers may question whether the reference ought to be *flexible compensation*. The term *flexible benefits* was chosen because it has become the accepted term in Canada.

In fact, the term *flexible compensation* does more accurately describe the scope of flexible plans. Benefits represent a form of compensation, even though they are provided to the employee indirectly in the form of employer contributions for medical or other coverage, pension benefits, and the like. Moreover, given the significant sums involved — approaching 40 per cent of payroll in some organizations — the direction today is toward increased recognition of employee benefits as a component of total compensation. Finally, choice-making programs further blur once-distinct lines between benefits and compensation, as employees often are able to convert unused benefits to cash, or conversely, to divert a portion of pay to the purchase of benefits.

The updating of this book represents the collective efforts of many members of Hewitt Associates. These contributors were invaluable in sharing both their technical knowledge and practical insights into the many aspects of the operation of a flexible benefit program. Kelly Higgins and many others in the research practice at Hewitt were invaluable in assisting the various contributors. A special thanks to Diane Duncan, Elizabeth Ng, and especially Betty Wong who bore most of the burden of preparing the manuscript.

ROBERT J. MCKAY

Toronto, Ontario
April 2007

About the Editor

Robert J. McKay is an actuary and principal with Hewitt Associates in Toronto. Hewitt Associates pioneered the concept of flexible benefits in Canada and the United States, and is one of the world's largest consulting firms specializing in the design, financing, and delivery of employee benefits, compensation, and other human resource programs.

Over the past 25 years, Mr. McKay has designed and implemented flexible benefit plans for a wide variety of employers in both Canada and the United States. He is a frequent speaker on the topic of flexible benefits and is acknowledged as Canada's leading practitioner in the field.

Contributors

Sarah J. Beech	Managing Principal and Benefits Consultant
Linda M. Byron	Benefits Actuary
Timothy W. Clarke	Benefits Actuary
Cathy M. Course	Benefits Actuary
Roy A. Dawson	Benefits Consultant
Timothy J. Hadlow	Benefits Consultant
Todd J. Mathers	Listening Consultant
Marcia A. McDougall	Public Relations
Robert J. McKay	Benefits Consultant
Kimberly McMullen	Communication Consultant
Ellen Mole	Legal Consultant
Lucie Paquet	Benefits Consultant
Stephen D. Pibworth	Legal Consultant
Jean-François Potvin	Administration Consultant
Jeff Queen	Benefits Consultant
Mark S. Rowbotham	General Counsel and Legal Consultant
John C. Tompkins	Benefits Consultant
Philip Yores	Executive Compensation Consultant
Christopher J. Westcott	Benefits Consultant

International Contributors

Thais H. Blanco	São Paulo, Brazil
Susan M. DeGregorio	Pittsburgh, U.S.A.
Katie Heath	Hemel Hempstead, U.K.

Lucy Liu   Shanghai, China
Maureen J. Mersch   Lincolnshire, U.S.A.
Tibor Parniczky   Budapest, Hungary
Nerida J. Seccombe   Melbourne, Australia
Alexander van Stee   Amsterdam, The Netherlands

Part One

Overview

One

Origins and Objectives

The debate is over. Flexible benefits are here to stay. Companies such as the Bank of Montreal, DaimlerChrysler, IBM, Imperial Oil, Manulife Financial, Telus, and Wal-Mart have flexible benefit structures. In fact, over 40 per cent of major Canadian employers provide flexible benefits for their salaried, full-time employees, and this number is expected to grow significantly, perhaps doubling, in the next ten years. A 2005 survey by Hewitt Associates revealed that only 15 per cent of employers are not interested in providing a flexible benefit plan. The survey also revealed that 100 per cent of employers with flexible benefit plans felt they had made the right decision in introducing a flexible plan. If they had to make the choice again, every respondent would still choose to implement flexible benefits.

Many employers also extend their flexible benefit plans to hourly employees, part-time employees, and retirees. The only sector of the workforce that has not seen dramatic flexible benefit inroads is unionized groups of employees.

The first Canadian flexible benefit plans were introduced in the mid-1980s and, for the first decade or so, the concept of flexible benefits was viewed as a leading-edge approach to delivering benefits and compensation. Proponents touted employee involvement in compensation and benefit decisions as the wave of the future. Detractors proclaimed the notion suitable for academic discussion, but unfit for practical application. Until the mid-1990s management held back, uncomfortable with an idea that was both novel and innovative.

A key driver behind the accelerated growth of flexible plans since the mid-1990s has been the significant change in the Canadian health care arena that put pressure on the costs of employer-sponsored health care plans. As reported by the Canadian Institute for Health Information (CIHI), national health expenditures increased from about $500 per capita in 1975 to $2,200 in 1990 and reached almost $4,100 by 2004. CIHI also reported that spending on prescription and non-prescription drugs increased from $4 billion in 1985 to $21.8 billion in 2004.

The increase in expenditure applies to services paid for by the provincial plans as well as those paid for by individuals and by insurance companies. For example, CIHI reports that in 1975 the cost of prescription drugs not paid for by governments was less than $1 billion. By 2005 this exceeded $10 billion.

This trend is expected to continue, with health care costs expected to rise much faster than the Consumer Price Index. If the spending on drugs continues increasing at 10 per cent per year, the total cost will reach $39 billion by 2010 and $62 billion by 2015.

Paralleling this health care transformation is the change taking place within employer-sponsored benefit plans. Increased benefit costs are challenging employers to keep benefit plans affordable, yet still provide adequate health care coverage that meets the diverse and changing needs of employees. Flexible benefit plans offer an innovative approach that can help Canadian organizations manage in this challenging environment and have, therefore, moved to the forefront of benefit delivery systems. Employers regard flexible benefit plans as an effective method of controlling rising health care costs while providing an opportunity for employees to respond to their own unique health care needs. What was once regarded as unfit for practical application has evolved into the preferred choice of many organizations.

Figure 1.1 illustrates the dramatic growth of flexible benefit programs among Canadian organizations over the past twenty years. The growth has been particularly rapid since the mid-1990s. During that twenty-year period, flexible benefit structures have evolved to encompass a wide range of different approaches. While the credit-based pricing model used by the flexible benefit pioneers is still common, many employers have adopted simplified net pricing plans that do not explicitly provide employees with a pool of company credits to spend. Others have gone beyond the earliest designs by adopting a total compensation approach allowing employees to trade off between a flexible benefit plan, a retirement savings plan, and performance bonuses.

Figure 1.2 shows the prevalence of flexible benefit plans in various industry sectors. Well over 50 per cent of organizations in the insurance, banking, energy, oil, and personal products sectors now provide benefits through a flexible plan.

The concept of choice has existed within benefit programs for many years. For instance, employees have long had the opportunity to purchase supplemental life insurance beyond employer-provided levels, or to pay higher contributions for more valuable medical coverage. The essential difference between that type of choice and the creation of a flexible benefit choice-making program is that with the latter, employees have the opportunity to determine (within certain limits) how employer dollars for benefits are spent on their behalf. Conceptually, a flexible approach recognizes that a certain portion of total compensation will be provided by the employer in the form of employee benefits, but how that pool of funds is spent — in terms of types and levels of benefits — is essentially up to the individual to determine.

Figure 1.1
Prevalence of Flexible Benefit Plans Among Major Canadian Employers

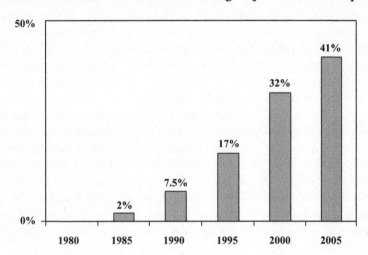

Source: Hewitt Associates

Figure 1.2
Prevalence of Canadian Flexible Benefit Plans by Industry

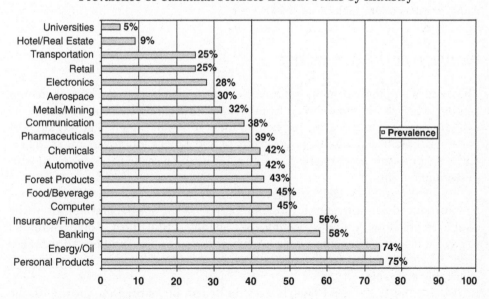

Source: Hewitt Associates

§ 1.1 ENVIRONMENT FOR FLEXIBLE BENEFITS

Interest in flexible benefits originated in the early 1980s when, in response to a mature employee benefits environment, a number of changes occurred. The demographics of the workforce had changed dramatically from decades earlier when benefit programs were in their infancy. At the same time, major employers in the United States successfully introduced flexible programs, in part because a recession focused their attention on finding ways to control costs. Meanwhile, the same pressures that led to a fundamental rethinking of benefit programs stimulated developments on two other fronts. First, in Ottawa, advance rulings by the Canada Revenue Agency (CRA) on a number of proposed flexible benefit plans enhanced the ability of employers to offer their employees choice. The CRA expanded on these rulings and further clarified the tax issues in 1998 when it issued an Interpretation Bulletin (*IT-529*) covering Flexible Employee Benefit Programs. Second, developments in automated enrolment and administration systems, and the emergence of outsourcing have made it much easier for employers to administer programs with choices.

The last decade has seen corporate reorganizations, rationalizations, and reengineering, in addition to escalating health costs — all of which have influenced the decisions made by employers in order to survive in the current competitive and challenging environment. Flexible benefits offer employers an opportunity to control benefit costs while still meeting the diverse needs of their employees.

Understanding the environment for flexible programs makes it easier to see that these programs developed as a rational response to complex, emerging issues, rather than as a gimmick of the 1980s.

EVOLUTION OF EMPLOYEE BENEFITS

The roots of employee benefits in Canada can be traced back to the late nineteenth century, when the country shifted from an agricultural to an industrial society. As workers migrated to cities and left behind the traditional extended family support system, people began looking to government and private employers for social security. Prior to this time, the responsibility for meeting security needs rested with individual families.

By 1900, the federal civil service, railways, and a few large financial institutions had introduced pension plans for their employees. That was the first step along the path in establishing employee benefits for Canadians. Still, most people continued to pay for health care as they needed it, whereas those who could not afford these services were provided free wards in hospitals, public clinics, sanatoriums, and charitable hospitals.

During the 1920s and 1930s, interest in benefit plans began to grow with the introduction of the *Old Age Pensions Act* (1927), and a proposal by the Canadian

Medical Association for a national health insurance plan. However, the Depression of the 1930s halted most efforts by private companies to introduce employee benefit plans. As the economy revived during the Second World War, employers once again began introducing benefit plans. Most plans were contributory, since the government considered that type to be less inflationary. Later, in 1945, the federal government proposed a comprehensive health insurance plan, but postponed it because the provinces would not transfer certain taxing authority to the federal government.

Public Health Care

The present health care system in Canada had its beginning in the *Hospital Insurance and Diagnostic Services Act* of 1957 and the *Medical Care Act* of 1966. Under these acts, provinces complying with established federal standards became entitled to annual subsidies from the federal government amounting to approximately one-half the cost of providing hospital and medical benefits. Hence, the birth of the present health care system and the ensuing balancing act, where the provinces control the health care system, but where the federal government provides funding if the provinces comply with federal conditions.

The *Hospital Insurance and Diagnostic Services Act* required that the provinces satisfy four conditions:

- The health insurance plan had to be administered on a not-for-profit basis by a public authority appointed by the government of the province.
- No minimum residence requirement or waiting period in excess of three months was allowed.
- Provinces were required to provide insured services on uniform terms and conditions to all residents.
- The percentage of insurable residents had to be at least 90 per cent at the start of the plan and 95 per cent after three years.

By January 1961, all the provinces had established hospital insurance plans, and by April 2 of the following year, all had medical care plans.

The *Canada Health Act* of 1984 replaced both the *Hospital Insurance and Diagnostic Services Act* and the *Medical Care Act*. The government had become concerned that the principles of the medical care legislation were being eroded. The new act re-established the purpose of the legislation and the responsibility of the federal government as outlined in Figure 1.3 on page 6.

Physicians are predominantly paid on a fee-for-service basis. The payment schedule is negotiated each year between the provincial government authority and the physicians' organization. Likewise, hospitals negotiate their operating budgets each year.

Figure 1.3
The Five Principles of Medicare

- *Universality*: All eligible residents of a province must be entitled to coverage by public health insurance under uniform terms and conditions. Individuals moving to a province may be subject to a waiting period of up to three months.
- *Accessibility*: Insured health services must be reasonably accessible to all insured persons. Financial impediments such as user fees are, therefore, prohibited.
- *Portability*: The public insurance plan must cover eligible residents while they are temporarily absent from the province. In addition, when an insured individual moves from one province to another, the original province must continue coverage during any waiting period imposed by the new province.
- *Comprehensiveness*: Medically necessary hospital and physicians' services must be covered by public health insurance.
- *Public Administration*: The public insurance plan must be operated on a non-profit basis and be accountable to the province.

Source: Health Canada

By the early 1980s, the federal government found that its universality principle was eroding, because some hospitals were charging extra user fees for hospital beds, and some physicians were extra-billing above the scheduled fees. As a result, the *Canada Health Act* outlawed extra-billing and user fees. It also reiterated the principles of the *Hospital Insurance and Diagnostic Services Act*, extended coverage to 100 per cent of a province's residents, and ensured portability between provinces.

Today, provincial governments administer the health insurance plans and are responsible for any costs beyond those subsidized by the federal government. Provincial funding arrangements vary, and include premiums and taxes charged to residents, employer payroll taxes, and financing from general tax revenues.

The Canadian health care environment is by no means static. In recent years cost pressures, concern about increased health care utilization due to an aging population, and difficulty in maintaining a high-quality health care system, have led to:

- A 2005 Supreme Court decision, *Chaoulli v. Quebec*, which may change how some health services are delivered under provincial plans. Dr. Chaoulli successfully argued that a one-year wait for a hip replacement for one of his patients violated the Quebec *Charter of Human Rights and Freedoms*. The Supreme Court agreed that lack of timely health care violates an individual's right to life and security as guaranteed by the Charter.

  The implications of this decision will depend on how provinces react. If they successfully reduce wait times and provide adequate quality of care, then the ruling could become irrelevant. On the other hand, if governments cannot reduce the wait times, then private solutions will be allowed where public care is inadequate.

- Nova Scotia amended its Pharmacare plan in 1995 to eliminate provincial drug coverage for residents age 65 and over who are members of employer-sponsored prescription drug plans. To prevent employers from cancelling their medical plans for Nova Scotia retirees, the legislation requires employers to provide prescription drug coverage in Nova Scotia if they provide it in other provinces.
- British Columbia went farther than Nova Scotia by introducing an income-based deductible for prescription drugs which significantly reduces or eliminates prescription drug benefits for many residents age 65 and over.

The effect of these and similar changes elsewhere has been to transfer costs from the public plans to employer-sponsored health care plans and to individuals.

Public Pensions

The *Old Age Security (OAS) Act* of 1952 introduced a basic flat-rate benefit to most residents. The Canada Pension Plan (CPP) — and in Quebec, the Quebec Pension Plan (QPP) — of 1966 began providing an earnings-related benefit to people who contributed to the plan during their working lives. The retirement pension from the CPP or QPP is equal to 25 per cent of the contributor's adjusted average earnings. The program also provides disability pensions, survivor's pensions, orphan's benefits, and death benefits. In addition, the Guaranteed Income Supplement, payable under the *Old Age Security Act*, supplements retirement income if an individual's pension falls below a specified threshold. All federal programs are then supplemented by various provincial guaranteed income plans to assist low-income pensioners.

Employer Plans

Canada experienced a major shift in responsibility for security and health care needs in the post–Second World War period. Canadians came to view security benefits and health care as fundamental needs and rights, like education.

They were willing to meet those needs collectively and pay for them through taxes. The result is that, today, the lion's share of these needs are met through government programs. Private employers offer a variety of benefits, but most of these supplement government programs. The most notable exceptions are dental care and group life insurance.

The result of these changes was a major shift in responsibility for security from the individual to the government and to the employer, resulting in the widespread availability of employee benefit coverage. By the 1970s, large corporations typically provided a final-average-pay pension plan, with many also offering a supplemental savings plan. Medical coverage included semi-private hospital accommodation and major medical coverage, with a small deductible and 80 to 100 per cent co-insurance. Company-paid life insurance provided at least one year's salary.

Long-term disability benefits replaced 60 per cent of pay, inclusive of Canada or Quebec Pension Plan (C/QPP) benefits.

Today, the configuration of employee benefit programs is even more complete. Among 432 major employers surveyed in 2005, the prevalence and characteristics of benefit programs for salaried employees included:

- 48 per cent maintain a defined benefit pension plan for all salaried employees that typically bases benefits on the employee's highest five-year earnings and requires no employee contributions. An additional 16 per cent of employers maintain a defined benefit plan for a grandfathered group of employees hired before a specified date.

    The prevalence of defined benefit plans in Canada and other countries has declined significantly over the past decade. In 1995, 83 per cent of major Canadian employers provided defined benefit pension plans for their salaried employees. This global decline is expected to continue in the next decade.

- 80 per cent offer one or more defined contribution vehicles that enable the employee to accumulate capital, usually as a primary or secondary source of retirement income. The most common defined contribution arrangements include company savings plans (82 per cent of employers offering a defined contribution plan) that typically match either 50 cents or a dollar for each dollar contributed by the employee up to certain limits; deferred profit sharing plans (8 per cent of employers); and money purchase pension plans (almost 50 per cent of employers offering a defined contribution plan).

    Paralleling the decline in the prevalence of defined benefit plans has been an increase in defined contribution programs. In 1995 only 61 per cent of employers offered a defined contribution plan for salaried employees.

- 100 per cent of the surveyed employers provide supplemental medical coverage. Almost a third of plans have deductibles, generally $100 or less. Employees also generally pay up to 20 per cent of the remaining costs through the co-insurance feature in the plans. Employee premiums are required in less than 30 per cent of the plans.

- In addition, 99 per cent of employers provide dental coverage, and 89 per cent provide vision care.

- Group life insurance is universally provided, with one to two times annual pay typically provided on a company-paid basis, and as much as four to five times annual pay provided in total from company-paid and contributory coverage. In addition, 88 per cent of the surveyed companies make life insurance for dependants of an employee available.

- Disability coverage is also universally provided. On short-term disability, typical practice is to continue all or a portion of salary for some period of time, such as six months, before commencement of long-term disability benefits. In the event of a prolonged disability, companies typically replace 60 per cent or more of salary, inclusive of Canada or Quebec Pension Plan disability benefits, with the income usually continuing until retirement.

- All companies provide paid vacations and holidays. Vacation time usually relates to the employee's length of service — for example, two weeks off after one year and three weeks after three years, grading up to five or more weeks after twenty years of service. In addition, most companies provide ten to twelve paid holidays per year.

CHANGES IN DEMOGRAPHICS

The changing demographics of the workforce are well documented. According to the Conference Board of Canada, as baby boomers age, the percentage of people over the age of 65 is expected to increase from 13 per cent in 2005 to 22 per cent by the year 2025. With the greying of the population, there will be a shift in the needs of society from acute to non-acute types of medical services, with greater demands for long-term and elder care programs. The aging of the population also brings with it a higher level of health care expenditures.

The aging population will put pressure on government, employers, and employees, through increased costs for post-retirement health care plans and higher Medicare costs.

Coupled with the changing demographics is a rising life expectancy for Canadians when compared to other countries. In 2002, the life expectancy at birth for Canadian females was 82.2 years and 77.2 years for Canadian males versus 79.9 for American females and 74.5 years for American males. Interestingly, Japan has one of the world's highest life expectancies and lowest infant mortality rates and yet, as indicated in Figure 1.4, has one of the lowest levels of spending on health care worldwide. Based on this data, the level of health care spending is not directly correlated with the general level of health of the respective populations.

Figures 1.5 and 1.6 on page 11 illustrate other well-documented changes in Canadian society that have occurred over the past thirty years. Figure 1.5 illustrates the dramatic change in the age profile of the Canadian population due to declining birth rates and rising life expectancy. In 1976, about 47 per cent of Canadians were under age 25 and only 8 per cent were over age 65. By 2026 the under age 25 group will comprise only 26 per cent of the population while those over age 65 will make up 21 per cent. Figure 1.6 on page 11 shows the significant increase in the percentage of women in the workforce in all age groups that has occurred over the past thirty years.

Demographic trends help define the challenges that will face employers and employees — including child care, flex time, job sharing, dual careers, and the development of appropriate benefit coverage options and subsidies. The era when an employer could design a single benefits package to be appropriate for all employees is long gone.

Greater diversity in the workforce has created significant pressure on employers to recognize and accommodate the variety in employee needs for benefits — both today and tomorrow, as those needs change over time. According to a 2005

Figure 1.4
Health Expenditures in Selected OECD Countries, 2004

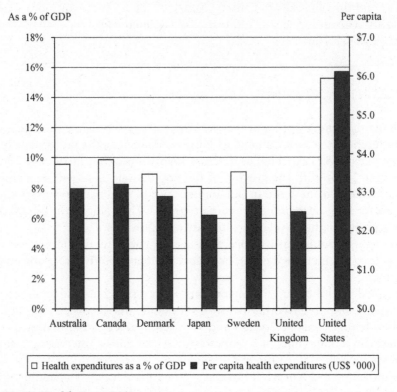

Source: OECD Health Data: 2006

survey of employers providing flexible benefits for their employees, "meeting diverse employee needs" was the most frequently cited objective of the flexible benefit program.

For example, child care represents one of the newer areas of need for many employees. Fewer households today — whether supported by one income or two — have the family network in place to care for young children. As a result, many employers are feeling increased pressure to "do something" to accommodate the needs of working parents. However, under sustained pressure to control benefit costs, few have been willing to shoulder the entire obligation for another new — and expensive — coverage area.

Related to the issue of diversity within the workforce is growing recognition that the needs, priorities, and values people have for benefits change over time. Benefits are intended to create a sense of security — something that is harder and

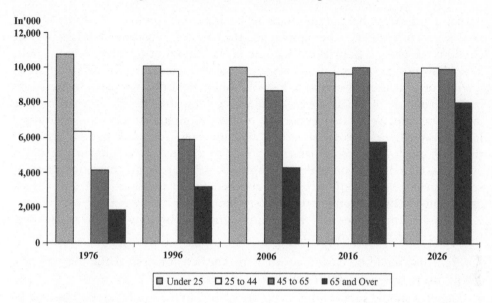

Figure 1.5
Age Distribution of Canadian Population

Source: Statistics Canada

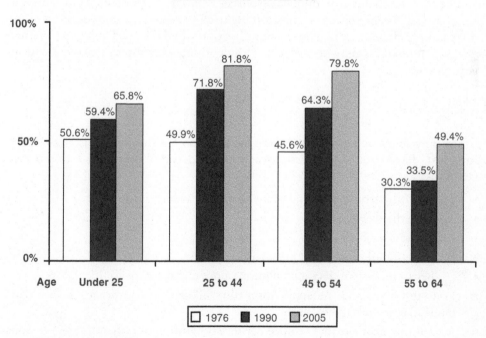

Figure 1.6
Women in the Workforce

Source: Statistics Canada

harder to provide in light of the changing business environment. Traditionally, the need for security tends to be high during the child-rearing years, but less so once children are grown. Retirement income is an important priority — but usually later in a working career. Life events such as marriage, saving for the purchase of a home or education of children, loss of employment by a spouse, are occasions for re-evaluation of benefit coverage. In effect, these differences set up a "moving target" for employee benefit programs to meet. Coupled with this moving target for employee benefit programs is the challenge employers face as well, knowing that their employees' needs, fears, and goals are constantly changing in light of the circumstances that surround them. Employers will be regularly challenged as they seek to provide responsive programs and benefits that address their employees' specific needs and respond to their life cycles.

Planning approaches for "reinventing" employee benefits used by many organizations focus on two major themes:

- Benefits should be customer-oriented. The "customers" of the benefits programs in this case are the covered employees.
- Benefits should support the corporate reality. In the future, employees will be less and less able to rely on their employers for security. Rather, they will be charged with the responsibility of developing their own careers and destinies.

Another issue arising out of the change in demographics is an increase in the number of households with duplicate sources of employee benefits. Many employers — as well as employees — question the usefulness of two sources of coverage (for example, dental), or high levels of protection when the need for such coverage may be minimal (as may be the case with death benefits for households with no dependants).

RISE IN COSTS

As the prevalence of benefit plans has grown, so too has the cost. Employer health care costs have risen significantly over the last decade because of a number of factors:

- Cost-shifting from provincial plans to private health plans;
- Aging of the workforce;
- Increased use of services;
- Introduction of higher-cost prescription drugs;
- Higher frequency of disability claims (more cognitive disabilities);
- Premium taxes and the application of retail sales tax to private health care plans in some provinces; and
- Accounting changes that require earlier recognition of postretirement benefit costs.

Changes to public health care coverage that have an influence on employers' benefit plans and the health care arena in general include:

- Limits on out-of-province emergency medical services;
- Fewer hospital beds because of hospital downsizing and restructuring, resulting in a reduction in the length of hospital stays;
- The removal of many non-essential medical services from provincial health plans; and
- The transfer of some postretirement prescription drug coverage onto the private sector in several provinces.

Higher rates of utilization and the aging population, in addition to the rising cost of medical services, are driving the escalation in health care costs. Simply stated, more people are making more use of more medical services. As a result, high growth rates have occurred in annual expenditures for health care.

One example of these escalating costs is the average cost of prescription drugs for members of group insurance plans. According to ESI Canada, the average annual prescription cost per claimant increased from $329 in 2000 to $524 in 2004. This 59.3 per cent increase was due to:

- A 17 per cent increase in the average annual number of prescriptions per individual (from 8.8 to 10.3);
- A 41 per cent increase in the average ingredient cost per prescription (from $30.52 to $43.00); and
- A 9 per cent increase in the typical dispensing fee (from $6.98 to $7.62).

The combined effect of these spiralling costs is larger health care bills for government and employers. Although few employers will be able to exert much control over external factors such as the cost of medical technology, many will be attempting to influence internal factors such as utilization. Influencing utilization through plan design and employee communication, for example, holds significant potential for helping to curb the rate of escalation in an employer's health care costs.

ECONOMIC UNCERTAINTY

It is apparent that how and where work gets done is changing as a result of competition for business and global alternatives for talent. Companies face intense competitive pressures — both foreign and domestic. Canadian operations of global companies face cost pressures from other, lower-cost locations of their own organization. Developments in technology and communication have enabled outsourcing and global sourcing to become viable. These changes mean that no business can afford to be complacent. Among other things, employers must develop benefit delivery systems that are nimble — that can respond to an employer's circumstances, and can allow employees to control or mitigate the impact of employer cutbacks. At the same time, employers will seek to avoid programs that create a sense of entitlement among employees; that sense of entitlement can be an obstacle to good employee relations during difficult economic times.

SHIFTING RESPONSIBILITY TO EMPLOYEES

Over the last decade many employers have shifted decision-making responsibilities to employees across a broad spectrum of areas. The movement to empower employees, so that they have greater authority to exercise control over manufacturing processes, customer service, and all other aspects of their employers' businesses, has spread to the area of benefits. The growth of flexible benefit plans, group RRSPs, and other defined contribution plans (with employees controlling both the amount and investment direction of their savings), and the expected expansion of health care cost containment initiatives, are all manifestations of this trend. As employers and employees grow more comfortable with the shift of responsibility to employees, the practice will continue to expand. Future cutbacks in provincial health care plans will accelerate this process, since employees and employers will be required to assume more responsibility for health care — from preventive, treatment, and delivery perspectives.

REGULATORY ENVIRONMENT

The framework of laws and regulations for employee benefits was in place for many years before the advent of flexible benefits, and so did not address the tax issues surrounding employee choice. Because the tax treatment of flexible plans was unclear, Canadian flexible benefit plans developed slowly until the mid-1990s, when the Canada Revenue Agency (CRA) provided long-awaited guidance. This guidance, in the form of an *Interpretation Bulletin on Flexible Employee Benefit Programs* (*IT-529*), plus a number of advance income tax rulings for specific plans, significantly enhanced the viability of flexible programs.

    The Interpretation Bulletin clarified that constructive receipt does not apply to properly designed flexible benefit programs. Constructive receipt is a doctrine developed through British and Canadian court rulings, whereby individuals are taxed on employer expenditures, if they could have taken the payment in cash, but elected not to do so. Canada Revenue Agency confirmed that members of flexible benefit plans are not taxed on employer contributions to flexible plans (typically called flexible credits) merely because one of the options — cash — is taxable. Instead, each individual is taxed based on how he or she elects to use the credits.

This is illustrated later in this chapter, where an employee is given the choice of spending flexible credits on group life (taxable), or on other benefits such as health care (non-taxable except provincially in Quebec). Because no section of the act deals specifically with flexible benefit plans, this confirmation was crucial to the growth of such programs in Canada. This evolution differs from what happened in the United States, where two changes had significant impact on the environment for flexible benefits.

The first change in the United States involved a legislative amendment to the Internal Revenue Code to permit choice making in benefits involving taxable and non-taxable options. It was the *Revenue Act of 1978* that created the "twin pillars" of flexible benefits — Section 401(k) and Section 125. Section 401(k) permitted trade-offs between cash and deferral of compensation into a retirement income vehicle. Section 125 permitted choice making between taxable and non-taxable benefits. Psychologically, the legislation had a major impact on the growth of flexible programs, in that a previously "grey area" within the tax code was clarified, providing a firm legal basis for choice-making programs. The increased prevalence of flexible benefits in the United States provided a stimulus for the development of flexible programs in Canada. *Canada Revenue Agency Interpretation Bulletin IT-529* is very similar to Section 125, as it permits employees to choose between taxable and non-taxable flexible options without the doctrine of constructive receipt applying.

The second change in the United States arose through regulation. In 1981, the IRS issued implementing regulations for Section 401(k) arrangements. Included within the regulations was a key provision permitting individuals to defer a portion of their salary into a retirement income vehicle. Shortly after release of the Section 401(k) regulations, salary reduction also came to be used for the purchase of other employee benefits. In effect, employee contributions for benefits were treated as employer payments, and escaped federal income and most state and local taxes. The result was that, for the first time, employees had a tax-efficient means of paying for benefits. Later, the *Tax Reform Act of 1986* confirmed, through legislation, the use of salary reduction for benefit purchases. Unfortunately, the Canadian tax authorities did not embrace the approach of using salary reduction to pay for certain benefits, thereby avoiding income tax. IT-529 specifically states that employees will be taxed on the amount of any salary reduction, except in certain circumstances.

ADMINISTRATIVE SOLUTIONS

Another factor affecting the growth of flexible benefits was the development of automated solutions to handle day-to-day flexible program operation. Although aspects of conventional employee benefit administration have been automated for many years, accommodating choice-making programs, with individual elections,

annual re-enrolments, and often special claims and payment record-keeping requirements, placed new demands on administrative systems and procedures.

Until the early 1980s, the obstacles associated with administering a flexible
program were largely viewed as insurmountable — unless an employer was willing
to commit significant resources to the design and programming of an internal system. Eventually, however, demand led to the proliferation of automated solutions
developed specifically for flexible program administration. Today, plan sponsors
can choose from administration alternatives ranging from installing software and
managing all administrative aspects internally (insourcing) to accessing third party
software (cosourcing) to retaining a third party to handle all administration responsibilities, including interaction with plan members (outsourcing). Many consulting firms, insurers, third-party administrators, and software vendors provide
administration services to meet the needs of both large and small organizations.

§ 1.2 EVOLUTION OF FLEXIBLE BENEFITS

The first flexible benefit programs were introduced in the United States in the early
1970s under relatively unusual circumstances. In 1973, a West Coast division of
TRW, Inc., adopted a choice-making arrangement with the primary purpose of
meeting diverse employee needs. The division employed a large group of highly educated engineers and technicians who wanted more control over benefit decisions.
TRW implemented a program that permitted employees to opt up or down from
previous life and medical coverage. If the employee chose less valuable coverage,
the difference was paid in cash. If the employee elected more valuable coverage,
the difference in price was paid through payroll deductions.

At about the same time, Educational Testing Service (ETS) in Princeton, New
Jersey, adopted a different type of flexible approach. A benefit study indicated that
ETS lagged behind other organizations in the competitiveness of their program.
The organization decided to enrich its program — but allow employees to decide
individually how the new funds should be spent on various benefit options.

These early social experiments proved tremendously successful. Employees
appreciated the opportunity to make benefits more useful and the employers received high marks (and considerable outside interest) for innovating on essentially
a new frontier. However, both situations were pigeonholed as small and unique employee environments. Not until 1978, when American Can Company implemented
a flexible program, did the barrier to the broader business community open.

American Can's primary interest in using flexible benefits was to find a means of
slowing the rate of growth in benefit costs and breaking a lock-step link with union-
driven benefits. In addition, the company was in the process of diversifying its
business and needed to be able to compete more effectively for talented employees.
American Can set up a program that carved the existing package into two pieces.
The first layer represented a cutback to a core level of benefits uniformly applicable

to all employees. The next layer provided the flexible benefit options. Employees could arrange the flexible options to suit individual circumstances.

The American Can experience represented a breakthrough in several ways. First, the company demonstrated that a flexible approach could work in a large company environment. Second, their experience showed that an existing program could be split so that choice making need not be an add-on or require additional employer funding. Finally, American Can introduced the concept that a flexible approach contained the potential to control future increases in benefit costs. By dividing an existing program into core and options segments, some of the built-in escalation in benefit costs could be curbed. If the cost of the flexible options increased, the company could make a conscious decision to add more money or pass along the cost to employees in the form of higher price tags.

The Canadian breakthrough into flexible benefits occurred when Cominco, a major West Coast mining company, introduced a flexible benefit plan for its 2,000 salaried employees in March 1984. Like American Can, Cominco split its flexible benefit package into a core level of benefits provided to all employees and several levels of options providing benefits greater than the core. The cost savings anticipated by Cominco, because the core benefits were not as rich as the previous program, were given back to employees as flexible credits. Employees received sufficient credits to buy back their previous program if they wished. Employees who wanted more coverage could supplement their credits through payroll deductions. Employees needing less coverage could direct excess flexible credits to the Cominco savings plan or could take them in taxable cash.

There were two major reasons why Cominco pioneered flexible benefits in Canada. First, Cominco wanted an attractive, innovative benefit package to appeal to the varying needs of its diverse employee group — employees ranging from corporate staff in Vancouver to salaried employees at Cominco's remote mines in Western Canada, including its Polaris mine located in the Northwest Territories, less than 100 kilometres from the magnetic North Pole. Second, Cominco wanted to reward its staff employees, who had borne the brunt of salary freezes in the early 1980s. The communication campaign for Flex-Com, as the Cominco program was called, emphasized that "flex" was a special privilege only extended to salaried employees.

Flex-Com was extremely well received, and more than 75 per cent of employees chose a different plan than they had had before the introduction of flexible benefits.

Other Canadian flexible pioneers include:

- 1980 — Hewitt Associates developed Canada's first health spending account.
- 1988 — American Express Canada, Inc., introduced the first flexible benefit plan in the financial sector. "Express Yourself" was also the first plan in Canada to use the net contributing pricing structure, instead of the credit-based approach. (See § 2.2 for a discussion of these approaches.)

- 1989 — The union representing Rocanville, Saskatchewan, hourly rated employees of PotashCorp, the world's largest producer of potash, negotiated a flexible program for its members. This was the first plan covering unionized employees and it followed the successful introduction of flexible benefits to staff employees.

- 1989 — BP Canada was the first employer to merge two traditional benefit plans using flexible benefits for the new program.

- 1989 — Prudential Insurance Company of America introduced the first flexible program at an insurance company. This was a crucial development, as Prudential, followed by other life insurance companies, used its own flexible benefit plan to learn about the underwriting and financial issues concerning flexible benefit programs. The insurance industry then used this knowledge to offer their services to clients who were introducing choice-making plans.

- 1991 — Husky Oil introduced Canada's first flexible pension program. This followed the adoption of a flexible benefit plan several months earlier.

- 1995 — DuPont Canada Inc. rolled out Canada's first flexible program for retirees.

- 1995 — Imperial Oil offered employees a choice between two managed care medical options, incorporating features such as managed drug formularies, and two traditional options without the cost management features.

- 2000 — AstraZeneca allowed employees to direct a portion of their savings plan match to the flexible benefits plan. This is now known as the Financial Security Approach. (See § 4.1 for a discussion of this approach.)

- 2004 — an employer obtained an advance income tax ruling allowing employees to direct a portion of their performance bonus to the Health Spending Account (HSA) in certain circumstances. (See § 12.4 for a discussion of the tax issues.)

- 2006 — an employer obtained an advance income tax ruling allowing employees to direct a portion of their performance bonus to their flexible credit pool in certain circumstances. (See § 12.4 for a discussion of the tax issues.)

§ 1.3 KEY PURPOSES FOR FLEXIBLE BENEFITS

The major movement toward flexible benefits in the 1980s and 1990s was born of the desire to meet diverse employee needs while at the same time containing benefits costs. Today these remain the two key objectives, as shown in Figure 1.7.

Figure 1.7 also reveals that the goal of containing benefit costs has increased significantly in importance as flexible benefits have moved from the early experimental years to the current mature stage.

Other objectives of flexible benefit programs include delivering compensation in a tax effective manner, attracting and retaining employees, and harmonizing two or more benefit programs.

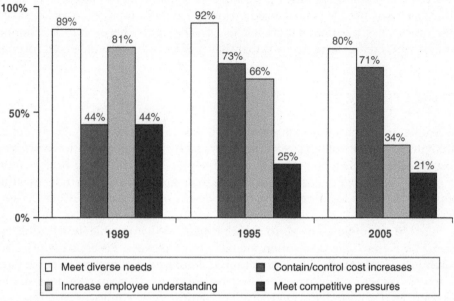

Figure 1.7
Advantages of Flexible Benefits; Employer Perspective

Source: Hewitt Associates

APPEAL TO DIVERSE EMPLOYEE NEEDS

Fundamentally, the use of flexible benefits is an alternative delivery mechanism for compensation and benefits. Under a conventional program, an employer provides a package of benefits to all employees. Little discretion exists for the individual to select, shape, or rearrange coverage levels to suit individual needs or circumstances.

In contrast, the distinguishing characteristic of a flexible approach is the opportunity for the individual to make choices about the use of employer-provided benefit funds. Under a flexible program, the employee decides among types of benefits and levels of coverage. In addition, the employee determines the form of compensation in terms of whether to spend the employer contribution on benefits, to receive some portion of the allocation in cash, or to save some or all of the allocation for use at a later date (such as retirement). In effect, a flexible approach recognizes the different needs employees have for benefits at different points in time.

But the appeal of a flexible program is not all on one side; the employer gains from the process as well. From the employer perspective, choice making is an opportunity that employees appreciate, which leads to higher rates of satisfaction with a benefit program, even in the absence of higher employer contributions for benefits or the introduction of new plans. Moreover, benefit options generally must include some recognition of "price" for employees to review and compare in making choices. Assigning a price tag to a benefit tends to give it a value that employees may not have recognized previously. Finally, in order to make choices, employees must understand their benefits. The process of becoming more familiar with benefits creates an active — rather than passive — interest in benefit coverage.

CONTROL BENEFIT COSTS

A flexible approach allows an employer to set in place a more clearly defined mechanism for controlling costs over the long term. With a conventional program, cost management can be achieved, but largely in terms of cutting back coverage or passing along higher costs to employees. A flexible approach introduces a third option — namely, allowing employees to trade off among coverages. Consider some examples:

First, if an employer needs to reduce benefit costs immediately, a flexible program can be introduced to soften the blow to employees. Perhaps the prior rich coverage is made available as an option, if employees are willing to pay a larger proportion of the cost or to accept lower benefits in another area. Perhaps another, less rich, level of coverage is made available at little or no employee cost. Instead of a unilateral decision either to reduce coverage or to increase contributions, the employer allows individual employees to decide how the necessary cost-containment efforts will affect them.

Second, a flexible program can provide employees with incentives to select lower levels of coverage — even in the absence of a reduction in employer contributions. Medical and dental plans that require more employee cost-sharing in the delivery of services (for example, deductibles and co-insurance amounts) tend to experience lower utilization. When the employee must pay a higher proportion of the cost of services, smarter health care utilization tends to result.

Third, the rise of managed care initiatives in Canada provides another means for employers to control health care costs. Managed health care programs originated in the United States in the 1980s, when health care costs were escalating rapidly. A managed health care program is a co-ordinated, pro-active effort to control rising costs while continuing to meet a high standard of service. Often plan sponsors intervene with health care providers in an effort to control costs. To be successful, managed care programs must operate as a partnership with all health care providers — doctors, pharmacists, and dentists. Greater emphasis is placed on employee involvement and educating employees to better understand how they can take action that will contribute to cost savings yet still receive quality care. Because prescription drugs are the largest component of most supplemental medical plans in Canada, many of the managed care initiatives involve attempting to change employee behaviour when purchasing prescriptions. These initiatives include mandating generic substitutions, introducing restricted drug formularies, and placing limits on reimbursement of dispensing fees. Sections 5.6 and 5.10 discuss managed care approaches for prescription drugs in detail.

Finally, a flexible approach allows the employer to separate decisions on the *cost* of benefits from decisions on the *form* of benefits. The employer determines each year how much funding the benefit program will receive. Employees then determine how that amount should be allocated among the various options available to them.

This enables the employer to avoid the automatic, inflation-driven escalation characteristic of conventional programs. In effect, the employer has introduced a defined contribution approach to paying for coverage. For example, if the cost of medical options rises faster than the employer's willingness to spend, employer contributions to the program can be held at a predetermined level. In this case, employees will be required either to pay more for the same level of coverage or to select a lower-valued option. Again, the employer keeps costs at acceptable levels while individual employees determine how limitations on the benefit dollar will affect them.

DELIVER COMPENSATION TAX-EFFECTIVELY

Tax efficiency can be introduced into a flexible program to take advantage of differing treatment of benefit plans under the *Income Tax Act*. Section 18(1)(a) of the act specifies that employer contributions for medical and dental plans are tax-deductible to the employer, while Section 6(c) states that the contribution is not taxable income to the employee. Since 1993, residents of Quebec have been taxed on the value of these benefits for purposes of Quebec income tax.

On the other hand, the cost of any company-paid group life coverage is a taxable benefit to the employee, while any benefits are paid tax-free to the beneficiary. Company-paid long-term disability (LTD) coverage is treated in the opposite manner to group life. When the employer pays the premium, benefit payments are taxable income to an employee who becomes disabled. However, the employer premium payment for LTD coverage is not taxable to the employee. By allowing the employee to decide which benefits to purchase with employer dollars and which to purchase with payroll deductions, a flexible plan can permit an individual to tailor benefits to meet his or her tax needs.

The situation can best be illustrated by an example. The ABC company provides company-paid LTD (60 per cent), medical, dental, and group life benefits (two times annual pay) and would like to offer some choice in its program. Consider an employee, Pat Doe, earning $75,000 per year. Assuming that the cost of group life coverage is $3.60 per year per $1,000 of benefits, Pat has a taxable benefit equal to the cost of $150,000 of insurance. The taxable benefit equals $3.60 × 150 or $540. So Pat pays $216 tax on this $540, assuming a marginal rate of 40 per cent.

ABC can introduce choice into the program with or without using a flexible structure. Without the flexible benefit framework, ABC could offer Pat the ability to purchase more medical and dental benefits through payroll deductions. Assuming the richer supplemental medical plan costs $340 per year more than the current plan, while the richer dental plan costs $200 more per year, ABC would collect $540 out of Pat's pay to cover the additional cost of the coverage. Since these contributions are after tax, Pat would have to earn $900 to pay the premiums. So under non-flexible choice making, there would be two tax consequences — Pat would purchase the optional medical and dental benefits with after-tax payroll deductions and would pay tax on the group life premiums.

How can a flexible benefit structure improve Pat's tax situation? The answer is by reversing who purchases the coverage, Pat can maximize the tax-effective use of ABC's benefit expenditures. A flexible plan could allow Pat to pay the $540 cost of group life through payroll deductions and direct ABC's savings of $540 to buy upgraded medical ($340) and dental ($200). Pat is still paying $540 in payroll deductions; however, ABC's expenditure no longer generates a taxable benefit for Pat. This is summarized in the following table:

Tax Consequences

Benefit	Non-Flexible Program	Flexible Program
Medical	Pat pays $340 cost with after-tax payroll deductions	ABC pays $340 cost with pre-tax credits (no taxable benefit except provincially in Quebec)
Dental	Pat pays $200 cost with after-tax payroll deductions	ABC pays $200 cost with pre-tax credits (no taxable benefit except provincially in Quebec)
Group Life	ABC pays $540 cost (Pat pays $216 tax on taxable benefit)	Pat pays $540 cost with after-tax payroll deductions
Summary	ABC pays $540 Pat pays $756 ($540 in premiums plus $216 in income tax)	ABC pays $540 Pat pays $540

So Pat pays $216 less tax under the flexible benefit structure for exactly the same coverage.

Another tax advantage is available in long-term disability. If Pat becomes disabled, the 60 per cent benefit will be taxable income because ABC paid the LTD premium. Under a flexible benefit plan, Pat could be given the choice of maintaining a company-paid LTD plan or paying the premium with after-tax payroll deductions. In the latter case, the 60 per cent benefit would be tax-free if Pat became disabled. Pat could direct the LTD premium that ABC would otherwise have paid to purchase another benefit such as additional vacation.

In the 1990s, a number of organizations introduced programs with a feature allowing employees to convert taxable salary into non-taxable benefits. Employees at these companies saw a 2 or 3 per cent reduction in their taxable salary with a corresponding 2 or 3 per cent of salary in non-taxable employer contributions to health and dental benefits. These plans allow employees to take their employer contribution in taxable cash if they elect not to use it on health and dental coverage.

Employers considering such an approach should be aware that Canada Revenue Agency believes that some of these arrangements may violate the *Income Tax Act* and has stated that, in these cases, it will tax the entire 2 or 3 per cent amount for all employees. In particular, Canada Revenue Agency's publication, *IT-529*, states that "the conversion of any portion of the employee's salary to flex credits will result in an income inclusion of the amount of salary so converted." Fortunately, there are two acceptable methods of restructuring a compensation package to convert taxable cash into non-taxable benefits. The first method, described in *IT-529*, permits a reduction in salary or wages and a corresponding increase in pre-tax flexible credits upon the expiry of a former employment contract. Second, Canada Revenue Agency has recently issued several advanced income tax rulings permitting performance bonuses to be converted into employer contributions to health care and other benefits if certain conditions are met. These issues are discussed in Chapter 12.

ATTRACTING AND RETAINING EMPLOYEES

Organizations implementing flexible programs tend to be regarded as "innovative," "responsive," or "leading-edge" employers. Indeed, many companies view flexible benefits as a means of differentiating themselves, particularly in markets where there is strong competition for highly qualified employees.

To some extent, as well, flexible programs have moved sufficiently into the mainstream of employee benefits to set the standard for "competitive practice." Increasingly, flexibility is being regarded as a "benefit" — the lack of which can work to lower the perceived value of even a generous conventional program.

HARMONIZING BENEFIT PROGRAMS

Flexible benefits provide a mechanism for combining benefit programs of merged or acquired organizations. Instead of continuing separate programs (thereby facilitating ongoing comparison of the different structures) or merging programs into a whole (which often leads to "cherry picking" the richest plans from each entity), a flexible approach allows the employer to offer benefit options that may resemble, but not duplicate, prior coverage. That way, employees can come close to reconstructing earlier coverage without saddling the employer with a prior program.

§ 1.4 EMERGING OBJECTIVES FOR FLEXIBLE BENEFITS

The objectives described in Section 1.3 will remain important long into the future. But some newer objectives are emerging today that will expand the uses for flexible benefits. Consider these possibilities:

- Facilitating company cost variations by geographic location or business unit. Even companies with a common benefit structure across the organization may want to introduce company cost variations. The reason may be to reflect differences in cost by geographic location or differences in acceptable overhead among various lines of business within the organization. For example, a diversified company may need to maintain lower compensation costs in labour-intensive operations (such as restaurant operations), but have a competitive need to maintain high benefit levels in other businesses. Such an employer may be able to maintain an identical flexible program for all business units, while varying the flexible credit allowance (or option price tags) based on the business unit's cost constraints.

- Varying benefit contributions based on business performance. Many organizations need to minimize their fixed costs, while being able to tolerate greater fluctuations in variable costs. Their inclination would be to spend labour dollars in ways that will motivate employees to be more productive. These management needs have resulted in revisions to direct pay systems — more emphasis on incentives, such as bonuses and restructuring of salary programs, so that performance becomes a more important factor. To a certain extent, fixed cost constraints have also affected the retirement area, with many employers shifting money away from defined benefit pensions and into defined contribution vehicles that do not represent the permanent, fixed commitment of a traditional pension plan.

  A few employers also are exploring the use of flexible benefits to allow variations in the funding of benefit plan coverage based on company performance. Certainly no one is suggesting that an employee's entire benefit allocation should be subject to the vagaries of profitability. However, some employers are investigating the possibility of providing a fixed credit amount that will purchase a safety net of coverage, as well as providing an additional variable contribution determined each year based upon business performance. Employees could use the variable amount to purchase benefits, defer the amount into a tax-favoured savings plan, or take the amount as taxable cash.

- Reducing compensation inequities. Most organizations currently pay some employees more than others through the benefit program. For example, employees who cover dependants in a group health plan typically receive more value, in the form of a higher employer subsidy, than employees with no dependants. Moreover, older employees receive more value from a life insurance program than younger employees. To some organizations, these additional subsidies are appropriate and consistent with financial security goals for employees. Others, however, have concluded that this differentiation by employee — driven not by performance or service, but by the life circumstances of the employee — is no longer appropriate.

These latter employers are using flexible benefits to reduce or eliminate differences in treatment among employees, either immediately upon introduction of the program or gradually over a period of years. The objective is to equalize employer-provided contributions for benefits, regardless of the employee's age or number of dependants. Two additional forces have encouraged the movement to equality. First, employers wishing to control costs have questioned the traditional practice of providing extra money or benefits to dependants. Second, pressure for equal treatment for same-sex and other non-traditional family units, such as single employees with dependent parents, has caused a re-examination of benefit subsidies.

- Encouraging a total compensation perspective. Such motivations as changing the fixed nature of employer contributions for group benefits, introducing performance-based contributions, maximizing employee perceptions of benefits, and reducing compensation inequities often reflect a more fundamental objective: to promote a total compensation perspective among employees, so benefit dollars appear more similar to direct pay and therefore more "real" to employees. By expressing employer contributions for benefits as dollars and allowing employees to decide how those dollars are to be spent, the line between direct pay and benefits becomes less distinct. Employees see their compensation as one amount in pay and another in flexible credits, plus any other non-flexible benefit amounts — the entirety of which represents total compensation.

  From management's perspective, the total compensation viewpoint also reinforces the concept that benefit costs, like direct pay costs, can and should be controlled.

- Rewarding specific employee actions. Some employers are becoming interested in using flexible benefit plans as vehicles for reinforcing value systems. These employers are incorporating features into the flexible plan to encourage employees to engage in desirable conduct and to penalize employees who engage in undesirable conduct. This differs from the historical approach of providing relatively uniform funding and reimbursement levels for all employees — with differences only based on criteria such as family or employment status. This trend has already emerged in the area of health benefits in the U.S., and certain aspects are being incorporated in a growing number of Canadian flexible benefit plans.

  For example, some Canadian employers reward desirable conduct by providing additional credits for supplemental medical coverage for employees who meet various health-related criteria established by the employer. These criteria may include employee representations that they do not smoke, requirements that the employees undergo various health-related tests (choles-terol, high blood pressure), and a pledge to undertake regular fitness activities.

On the other hand, some U.S. employers penalize risky conduct by reducing reimbursement levels for certain types of claims, such as injuries incurred while driving under the influence of drugs or alcohol. These employers believe that employees or dependants who take personal risks should bear some of the responsibility for the treatment costs of any resulting injuries. That is the basis for imposing additional deductibles for certain preventable health conditions or accidents.

Although these are limited examples, it is likely that this practice will grow. Employers must allocate available benefit dollars among their employees, and one way is to encourage employees to take action that will benefit both the employee and the employer.

Two

Elements of Flexible Benefits

§ 2.1 INTRODUCTION

All flexible plans involve opening up benefit and compensation programs to individual choice. However, the degree of flexibility offered varies substantially, depending on the type of program adopted. For example, a program allowing employees to purchase optional benefits with payroll deductions provides limited flexibility. More choice can be provided with the addition of a health spending account, which offers employees the opportunity to pay for certain medical expenses on a tax-efficient basis. In contrast, a full flex program that permits employees to decide among types of benefits, levels of coverage, and forms of compensation (cash, savings, or benefit purchase) provides the highest degree of flexibility. In practice, however, the different approaches overlap, with many employers combining some or all of these elements.

§ 2.2 CHOICE-MAKING

In General

The earliest flexible benefit plans in Canada and the United States were based on one particular model, now known as "full flex." Employees were given a range of options and asked to create a package to meet their needs by selecting one option from each benefit area. Employees paid for the selected options by spending company-provided flexible credits, supplemented, where necessary, by employee payroll deductions. Flexible benefit programs have evolved since that time to include a wide range of different models. At one end of the spectrum, the plans

with the most flexibility offer employees a wide range of choice, utilize an explicit credit-based pricing structure, and allow employees to renegotiate part of
their compensation package in exchange for additional tax-efficient flexible credits. Simpler plans, on the other hand, provide limited choice and use a net pricing
structure instead of price tags and credits.

In examining the various flexible structures, it can be helpful to look at the
breadth of choice provided to employees, the source of the funds to pay for the
choices, and the pricing structure used to present the plan to employees.

Breadth of Choice

In allowing employees to trade off among benefits, employers can create ways to
manage costs, incorporate cost control features, accommodate diverse employee
needs, offer greater variety in benefits, and increase the perceived value of benefit
expenditures. The broadest flexible benefits programs allow employees to make
benefits choices in many areas, including health care, disability, life insurance, and
vacation. Table 2.2 on page 32 shows the prevalence of various benefit coverages
under Canadian flexible benefit plans.

In recent years, many employers have introduced simplified flexible plans that
provide employees with meaningful choices while avoiding some of the complexities of broader, full flex plans. One simplified approach is to limit choice to the
health care area. These plans offer choices in medical and dental coverage, frequently supplemented by a health spending account. Another simplified structure
is known as the modular approach. Here, employers offer the employee a number
of modules or packages, each of which includes specific coverages in several benefit
areas, such as medical, dental, long-term disability, and life insurance. Employees
are typically asked to select a core, moderate, or rich module. The core module
normally generates a contribution to a health spending account or is available at
no cost to employees, while the rich module frequently requires employee payroll
deductions.

Source of Funds (Where the Money Comes From)

Although the approaches used to introduce flexible benefits vary considerably from
one employer to another, conceptually, the funds used to drive a choice-making
system are either pre-tax employer credits or after-tax employee payroll deductions. Pre-tax credits are generated in one of three ways: rearrangement of existing
benefit dollars, introduction of new employer money, or a renegotiation of direct
pay.

- **Rearrangement.** Rearranging employer benefit subsidies is useful when current benefits are more valuable than all employees need (or the employer can
  afford to support). The employer may offer lower or core levels of benefits,

or even permit employees to waive coverage entirely in some areas. All, or a portion, of the difference in value between pre-flex benefit levels and the core benefit levels, can be used to provide the funds or flexible credits for employees to construct a new program.

- **New employer money.** The second source of credits is the introduction of new employer money to provide additional funds in a flexible program. While most employers are not interested in increasing their benefit expenditures, a number of employers have added flexible credits to a plan for non-bargained employees coincident with signing a new collective agreement with a union. In this way, the employer pays the same cost for the non-bargained employee as negotiated with the union, but provides more economic value to the employee — because the credits have tax advantages and they allow employees to select benefits to meet their individual needs.

  Employers need not lock in to an allocation of additional employer dollars each year. A profit-related or gain-sharing technique can be used to provide additional flexible credits based on financial performance of the employer. Such an approach reduces fixed costs, because additional allocations are made only in years when the allocation can be justified by performance.

- **Renegotiation of compensation.** In the United States this is referred to as salary reduction and is sanctioned by Section 125 of the Internal Revenue Code. Section 125 allows an employee to elect to take a reduction in taxable pay for a corresponding increase in non-taxable flexible credits, thereby reducing his or her income-tax liability. In Canada, direct salary reduction is not tax effective, because Canada Revenue Agency has ruled on multiple occasions that, where an employee reduces salary to increase the flexible credit allocation, the amount of reduction must be included in the employee's income. However, there are some exceptions to this rule. For example, employees may be able to exchange bonuses and other forms of contingent pay for additional pre-tax credits. The tax advantages of using credits instead of payroll deductions are described later in this chapter.

Financial Structure (How Employer Money Is Spent)

Two financial structures have evolved for flexible plans: an explicit pricing approach known as credit-based pricing and an implicit approach known as net pricing.

- **Credit-based pricing.** The terms "credits and price tags," "full flex," and "cafeteria plan" are often used interchangeably to describe a plan where employees pay for benefit coverage with a combination of employer-provided flexible credits and after-tax employee contributions. A pool of credits is created, from which employees can purchase benefits tailored to meet their own needs. The benefits all come with a "price tag," and each employee spends the credits to purchase benefits. Any leftover credits are generally allocated to the employee in the form of taxable cash, a contribution to a Registered Retirement Savings Plan, a health spending account, or a taxable personal account.

Credits can be calculated in several ways: a percentage of the employee's pay, a flat-dollar amount, or a combination of these two approaches. Flat-dollar allocations have the advantage of not growing automatically with increases in pay or inflation, and any change in the flat-dollar allocation can be communicated as a benefit improvement. Sometimes a credit formula is based on service.

• **Net contribution pricing.** Under net contribution pricing, often referred to as net pricing, employers do not utilize the credit-and-price-tag structure. Instead, employees are offered choices and see their net cost or net credit for each choice (this equals the price tag minus credit, but the specific amounts are not shown). The costs are paid either using employee payroll deductions or employer pre-tax contributions created by choosing a low level of coverage in another benefit area. Any amounts left over can be allocated as outlined under "credit-based pricing."

The earliest form of net contribution pricing was the "opt-up-or-down" structure, which allowed employees to reduce or increase coverage levels in various benefit areas. When employees chose coverage levels lower than the previous employer-paid levels, employer funds were generated for them to use in other benefit areas. Election of higher coverage in one area required either trading down in another benefit area or increasing employee contributions.

PRE-TAX FLEXIBLE CREDITS VERSUS AFTER-TAX PAYROLL DEDUCTIONS

Flexible credits are more powerful than payroll deductions. Payroll deductions are taken off an employee's pay after tax has been withheld; so to contribute $100 to buy a benefit with deductions, the employee might have had to earn $150 or $175 or more. Flexible credits, on the other hand, are not taxed until they are spent, and their tax treatment depends on how they are spent. For tax purposes, flexible credits are treated as employer benefit premiums, not as employee earnings. Therefore, they are taxed according to how they are used by the employee. For example, credits used to purchase supplemental medical or dental benefits are not taxed (except provincially in Quebec). This is because any employer contribution to a private health services plan, such as supplemental medical or dental, is not considered income to the employee. In addition, the credits are a tax-deductible business expense to the employer. The net result is that the employee can purchase $100 of coverage with $100 in credits, which is more advantageous than purchasing it with $100 of payroll deductions.

The tax advantage of flexible credits does not apply to all benefits; for example, any credits used to purchase life insurance produce a taxable benefit to the employee. Nor does the tax advantage apply to the same degree to Quebec

Table 2.1
Income Tax Treatment of Flexible Benefits and Credits

Benefit Type	Employer Contribution Tax-Deductible	Tax Treatment of Employer Contributions (Including Flexible Credits) to Employee	Tax Treatment of Benefit Payouts
Supplemental Medical	Yes	No taxable benefit*	Not taxable
Dental	Yes	No taxable benefit*	Not taxable
Vision	Yes	No taxable benefit*	Not taxable
Health Spending Account	Yes	No taxable benefit	Not taxable**
Employee Group Life	Yes	Cost of coverage taxable benefit to employee***	Not taxable
Accidental Death and Disability (AD&D)	Yes	No taxable benefit*	Not taxable
Dependant Life	Yes	Cost of coverage taxable benefit to employee	Not taxable
Long-Term Disability	Yes	No taxable benefit	Taxable income
Cash	Yes	N/A	Taxable income

*For employees residing in Quebec, the value of medical, dental, vision, and AD&D benefits purchased with flexible credits is subject to Quebec income tax. These benefits do, however, remain free of federal tax. So there is still value from a tax perspective for a Quebec employee, but not to the same extent as for employees in other provinces.
**Again, the rules are different for Quebec employees, as benefit payments from a health spending account are considered taxable income to the employee for Quebec income tax purposes.
***A death benefit of up to $10,000 may be paid by the employer with no tax consequences to the employee or beneficiary.

employees; the value of medical and dental coverage is taxable income for Quebec income tax purposes. Chapter 12 discusses the tax treatment of flexible benefits and credits in detail. Some of the main points concerning tax treatment are summarized in Table 2.1.

The different tax treatment of benefits offers major opportunities for employees under a flexible plan. For example, an employee participating in a 60 per cent employer-paid long-term disability benefit before the introduction of flexible benefits might prefer to pay the premium using after-tax payroll deductions under a flexible program and direct the employer contribution to purchase an improved dental plan. In that way, any long-term disability benefit payout would be tax-free to the employee. And the employer contribution used to purchase extra dental coverage is not taxable to the employee (or is subject only to Quebec income tax for a Quebec employee).

Making the best use of the opportunities presented by the different tax treatments involves meeting a number of challenges. Employees must be educated in the subtleties of the *Income Tax Act* as it applies to benefits. This requires an extensive communication effort. Alternatively, the flexible program may not allow employees to choose their payment method; instead, the plan would unilaterally allocate employer flexible credits to pay for specific benefits. This simplifies both the administration and the communication of the plan. In any event, the administration of the program is complicated by tracking benefits purchased by two types of dollars — employer flexible credits (which can be tax-free or taxable depending upon allocation) and after-tax employee payroll deductions.

AREAS OF CHOICE

Certain benefits accommodate choice-making better than others. Defined benefit pension plans represent an area where choice-making is not easily introduced, because the value of any benefit trade-off varies significantly with the age and pay of the employee. Still, as will be discussed in Chapter 10, some employers have introduced a measure of choice-making in the retirement area. In these cases, the choice-making retirement program is separate from the flexible benefit program.

As shown in Table 2.2, the areas that most readily accommodate choice-making include indemnity plan coverages (health care, group term life insurance, and

Table 2.2
Benefit Areas Offered

Type of Benefit	Part of Flexible Program
HEALTH CARE	
Supplemental medical	84%
Dental	86%
Health spending account	90%
GROUP LIFE	
Employee life	70%
Survivor's income	10%
Spouse's life	66%
Children's life	64%
Employee AD&D	62%
Spouse's AD&D	48%
Children's AD&D	45%
DISABILITY	
Short-term disability	15%
Long-term disability	58%
OTHER	
Vacation buying	20%
Vacation selling	7%
Defined contribution pension/RRSP	48%
Defined benefit pension, flexible account	6%

Note: The percentages do not total 100 per cent due to multiple choices offered.
Source: Hewitt Associates 2005 Survey of Employer Attitudes toward Flexible Benefits.

disability), and time off with pay. Each of these areas, however, presents unique challenges.

In health care, most employers structure options around a supplemental medical plan, with differences occurring mainly in areas such as the deductible, co-insurance, prescription drug cost management features, and maximum payment amounts. Items such as covered expenses are usually kept fairly constant from option to option.

Key issues to settle in medical and dental benefits include the appropriate levels of deductibles, co-insurance and out-of-pocket limits, the minimum level of required coverage (if any), the inclusion of cost-containment initiatives, and the degree to which employer subsidies of dependent coverage should continue.

Within group-term life insurance, there are several key considerations related to the degree of choice to be offered. For example, in addition to deciding what total amounts of insurance to offer, an employer must also decide the increments of coverage (for example, multiples of $10,000 or multiples of pay). Existing practice, as well as administrative convenience, will usually influence this decision. Moreover, the employer must decide the pricing approach to be used — age-gender-and-smoker-related (which reflects true cost) or a flat rate for all employees.

Finally, a decision also must be made as to whether or not an employee may pay for coverage with before-tax dollars, recognizing that employees are taxed on the value of any coverage paid for either directly by the employer or indirectly through flexible credits. It may be simpler to require all life insurance coverage to be purchased with after-tax payroll deductions.

Structuring appropriate levels of choice in the long-term disability area can be challenging as well. Many flexible plans offer several alternative pay replacement levels, benefit duration periods, or options that provide an inflation-protected benefit. The key issues in the disability area include the appropriateness of letting employees waive coverage (very few employers allow employees to opt out), the impact of employer versus employee contributions on the taxability and resulting adequacy of disability income, and the most appropriate levels of pay replacement, if options are offered.

Finally, the area of time off with pay will require some special decisions. About 25 per cent of employers with flexible benefit plans include vacation time as a choice area within a flexible program, offering employees either or both of the buying and selling aspects of a vacation choice. Most organizations limit the choice to a one-way decision. For example, some organizations limit employee choice to the selling of vacation days only, that is, receiving more pay in return for fewer vacation days. Within these organizations, concern often centres on the potential for scheduling conflicts when employees are permitted more time off. Other employers offer employees only the choice of buying vacation days, that is, receiving less pay in return for more vacation days. Existing carry-over policies, staffing considerations for employees taking additional days off, and the potential impact on cash flow are key influences on decisions to include buying and/or selling of vacation time. As with most areas of flexible benefits, there are no right or wrong approaches. Each design area needs to be evaluated against the employer's particular circumstances and environment.

In terms of the overall design of a flexible benefit program, many employers initially are tempted to restrict the types and levels of choice offered as a means of simplifying decisions for employees or managing the financial stability of the program. Experience shows, however, that employees feel comfortable with even the most complex flexible programs, provided the choices are communicated well. Conversely, even the simplest program can generate confusion if the communication effort is slighted. So although there are often good reasons to restrict choice — to provide minimum levels of protection or to minimize adverse selection — concern about employee understanding of a flexible program need not dictate the degree of choice available.

SPECIAL CONSIDERATIONS

Two topics related to choice-making have yet to be discussed: adverse selection and waivers of coverage. Like other aspects of choice-making, these two topics are complex and will be dealt with in greater detail in later chapters. To round out this discussion, however, brief mention will be made here.

Adverse Selection

All voluntary benefit plans contain an element of employee selection. Employees participate because they know they will use the benefit (such as dental), or because they know they will need the benefit if an unforeseen event occurs (medical emergency, death, or disability).

Adverse selection occurs when employees can accurately anticipate their use of benefits and choose the option that provides the most coverage at the least cost. For example, an employee facing orthodontic expenses for a child knows that the highest level of dental coverage is a good buy, even if the benefit price tags are high. In most situations, however, employees cannot accurately project all of their benefit use, particularly for a family. In fact, many employees will choose the highest available level of medical and dental coverage just in case a major expense occurs, in other words, as insurance protection.

The potential for adverse selection can be controlled through the design of a flexible program. Various techniques enable employers to offer a wide range of choices without running much risk of greater-than-expected claims. These techniques will be discussed at length in Chapter 16. In brief, however, the approaches include:

- Restricting the employee's ability to increase or decrease coverage levels dramatically from one year to the next;
- Subsidizing the price tags for certain options to encourage broad participation;
- Providing a less-than-full-value rebate to employees waiving coverage;
- Grouping coverages for more predictable expenses (for example, vision care) with less predictable expenses (for example, other supplemental medical); and
- Encouraging use of health spending accounts as an alternative to insuring more predictable types of expenses (for example, vision, dental).

Each of these techniques can help control adverse selection. The price of utilizing some of these techniques, however, is reduced choice-making for the employee. The practitioner needs to recognize that the objectives of maximum flexibility in choice-making and elimination of adverse selection are often in conflict.

Waiving Coverage/Opting Out

Some plans allow employees to elect no coverage in certain benefit areas, which constitutes a waiver of coverage. This is frequently referred to as opting out. Whether opting out is allowed, and in which benefit areas, is a matter of employer discretion — and different employers will decide the issue in different ways. Some will refuse to allow employees to elect coverage below certain minimum core levels. Others will permit waivers only in certain benefit areas. Still others are comfortable allowing employees the complete freedom to opt out entirely. Plans allowing opting out in all benefit areas are very rare in Canada and are often referred to as cafeteria plans; however, the term "cafeteria plan" is also frequently used interchangeably with the term "flexible benefit plan."

Employers often are more concerned about employees going without supplemental medical, life insurance, and disability income benefits than going without dental coverage, for example. However, experience has shown that employees who waive supplemental medical coverage are not going bare. Instead, they typically have health coverage from another source, such as their spouse's employer. And even if they do not have other supplemental coverage available, they still are covered for most major expenses through their provincial health plan. Employers who want to allow opting out of medical benefits, but also want to ensure their employees have heath care protection, may require employees who opt out to demonstrate that they have access to coverage from another source.

Like adverse selection, restrictions on an employee's ability to waive coverage can often conflict with the objective of providing maximum flexibility through choice-making.

§ 2.3 HEALTH SPENDING, PERSONAL, AND PERQUISITE ACCOUNTS

In addition to offering a range of choices in benefits such as life insurance and health care, many employers also provide employees with one or more accounts that can be used to reimburse eligible expenses. In fact, the simplest flexible plans comprise a traditional, no-choice benefit plan supplemented by an account.

Three types of accounts may be included in a flexible plan: a health spending account used to reimburse eligible health care expenses; a personal account used to reimburse non-health care expenses; and a perquisite account used to reimburse executives who purchase perquisites from a list established by the employer.

HEALTH SPENDING ACCOUNTS

In General

A health spending account (HSA) is an individual employee account that provides reimbursement of eligible health care expenses. At the start of the plan year, the employee decides whether or not to establish an account and how many flexible credits to allocate to it. When an eligible expense is incurred, the employee submits a request for reimbursement to the administrator, who issues payment from the account. In some net pricing plans, the HSA balance is linked to the medical and dental choice. For example, the lowest medical option may be packaged with a $500 direct allocation to the HSA.

Health spending account reimbursements represent non-taxable income to the employee in all provinces except Quebec, just as though he or she had been reimbursed for a medical claim under a traditional supplemental medical plan. In Quebec, such reimbursements are treated as taxable income for Quebec income tax purposes. The only funds that can be directed tax-free to an HSA are employer-provided funds. As discussed earlier in this chapter and in detail in Chapter 12, Canada Revenue Agency prohibits employers from structuring plans where the employee's salary is reduced by 2 per cent, say, in exchange for a 2 per cent contribution to the account. Despite clear direction from Canada Revenue Agency on this issue, a number of major employers have elected to structure their plans in this manner.

A significant consideration with a health spending account is that expenses must be anticipated very carefully. Under the Canada Revenue Agency rules for health spending accounts, any monies left on deposit at year-end can be rolled forward into next year's account — they cannot be cashed out. At the end of the second year, any unused funds must be forfeited. (An alternative approach is to design an account that requires forfeiture at the end of each year but allows the roll-forward of claim amounts that have not been fully reimbursed in the current year. These approaches are discussed in detail in Chapter 7.)

Despite the need to plan carefully, health spending accounts represent a versatile and popular element in flexible benefit programs. Employers offering a choice-making program often include a health spending account as another benefit option. But an account can also be adopted on a stand-alone basis in the absence of any other choices within an employer's benefit program.

The popularity of this element of a flexible program is attributable to several motivations, including:

- Expanding the types of benefits offered to employees with little or no additional employer cost (such as adding vision care);
- Adding additional employer contributions in a way that can benefit all employees rather than just those using a particular benefit feature (e.g., increasing a paramedical maximum);
- Encouraging employees to self-insure predictable or budgetable expenses that are subject to adverse selection (such as dental care); and
- Delivering compensation tax effectively.

Sources of Funds

Health spending accounts attached to a flexible benefit program are more apt to be funded from two sources — direct employer contributions and/or flexible credits freed up from trade-offs in other benefit areas. In contrast, stand-alone accounts are funded by employer contributions only.

Deposits can be spread proportionally throughout the year. This avoids a major drain on the employer's income at any one point during the year. Or, they may be deposited in blocks (for example, at the end of each quarter or at the beginning of the year to reduce the record-keeping effort and provide greater flexibility for employees).

Types of Benefits

Under a health spending account, employees can be reimbursed for health-related expenses not covered by the employer's (or another employer's) medical and dental plans. In general, any health-related expense that could be used to meet requirements for a tax credit on an employee's income tax return is eligible for reimbursement. For example, deductible and co-insurance amounts may be reimbursed for both supplemental medical and dental benefits, along with the cost of procedures not covered by the underlying medical and dental plans. These might include drugs that have been prescribed but are also available over the counter, vision care expenses, and orthodontic work.

Mechanics of the Process

The mechanics of the election/enrolment process and the reimbursement of expenses are fairly straightforward. These are essentially governed by Canada Revenue Agency requirements.

Employees decide whether or not to allocate funds to the account prior to the beginning of a plan year. These funds may arise from either of the sources identified earlier.

Once made, the elections cannot be changed for any reason during the year, unless the employee has a change in family status. Addition or loss of a dependant and a change in a spouse's employment status are examples of family status changes that generally would allow an employee to change elections during the year.

With the election in place, the employer creates individual book accounts for the health spending accounts of those employees who have elected to participate. No formal segregation of assets takes place, and no monies are deposited in trust. Instead, the accounts are carried on the books of the employer, who tracks both debits (reimbursements) and credits (accruals). Typically, an insurance carrier or other third party administrator provides health spending account adjudication, payment, and reporting services.

When an employee incurs an eligible expense under the account, the employee completes a reimbursement claim form and submits it, along with a copy of the bill or proof of payment (such as a receipt or explanation of benefits form from an insurer), to the plan administrator for reimbursement. The administrator reviews the claim and reimburses the employee.

After the end of the year, employers typically allow employees a few months to submit claims incurred during the prior plan year. Once this process is completed, all unused deposits are either forfeited or forwarded to next year's account, depending upon the design of the plan. (In practice, most employees take care to estimate expenses with enough precision to avoid forfeiture or forwarding of account balances.) Disposition of forfeitures is a matter of employer discretion. Some reallocate funds to participants on an average per capita basis (that is, unrelated to the employee's actual amount of forfeiture). A few have adopted practices unrelated to the benefit program, such as donating the funds to charity. Most use forfeitures to reduce employer benefit costs in the following year.

PERSONAL ACCOUNTS

A personal account is used to reimburse employees for specified expenses that are not eligible for payment under a health spending account. The employer determines the list of eligible expenses, which frequently includes items such as:

- cellular telephones
- computer hardware/software

- financial counselling
- fitness club
- fitness equipment
- Registered Education Savings Plans (RESP).

Personal accounts are funded using excess credits that the employee does not spend on other benefits and does not wish to direct to a health spending account. Employers create personal accounts when they are not comfortable allowing employees to take unused credits as taxable cash or when the intent is to complement other employer initiatives, such as employee wellness.

Deposits to personal accounts generate a taxable benefit when they are made. Because of this, the "use it or lose it" rules of health spending accounts are unnecessary, and any unused account balance can be rolled forward from one year to the next.

A variation of the personal account is a wellness account, in which the list of eligible expenses is designed to reinforce employer wellness initiatives. Eligible expense items under a wellness account typically include:

- fitness club memberships
- personal trainer fees
- exercise equipment for the home.

Occasionally, expenses for sports activities may also be included (e.g., registration fees for classes such as yoga, self-defence, or hockey leagues). There is no restriction on what employers can include as eligible expenses in a wellness account, since all amounts reimbursed to employees are taxable under Canada Revenue Agency rules.

PERQUISITE ACCOUNTS

A flexible perquisite program is essentially a discretionary personal spending account for executives. Participants are provided with an allowance which they use to purchase perquisites from a list of available choices. They can spend all of their allowance on one item or spread it among several. The employer determines the key plan features, namely the amount of the allowance for each executive and the type of perquisites that are available. Similar to flexible benefit programs, an employer may provide core perquisites with some portion allotted for flex choices — the key is flexibility.

Employer objectives for introducing a flexible perquisite account are very similar to the reasons employers introduce flexible benefit plans and include:

- tailoring the programs to the needs of each executive;
- reducing the burden of administration by simplifying the execution of the plan;

- assisting with cost control (both corporate and personal) by establishing limits and guidelines; and
- communicating the value of perquisites for executives.

The available choices in a typical perquisite account might include:

- cellular telephones
- club memberships (country, luncheon, or health and fitness)
- company car (lease or purchase)
- business-class air travel
- home computer
- home fax
- home alarm systems
- executive medical exams
- parking
- personal trainer
- professional service fees (retirement/financial planning, tax preparation).

The tax consequences of payments from the account depend on the nature of the specific perquisite. Some payments, such as reimbursement for an executive medical examination, are tax-free except in Quebec. Others, such as individual financial planning, are normally considered a taxable benefit to the executive. The taxability of many items, such as cellular telephones, depends on the business need and usage.

Most organizations with perquisite accounts calculate the allowance as a flat amount based on the executive's position. However, in an incentive-driven environment, the allowance may be increased or decreased based on individual and corporate performance criteria.

Policies must be developed to deal with situations where the allowance has been under-spent in a given period (usually annually). For allowance amounts that are not completely exhausted by year-end, some alternatives include a carry-over provision so that the executive can "save-up" the perquisite allowance, a cash distribution, a deferral into a group RRSP, or forfeiture of the amount.

Three

Starting and Maintaining a Flexible Program

The impetus to investigate flexible benefits can originate within an organization in a number of ways. Business conditions might be such as to require a cutback in employee benefit costs or significant levelling of the rate of escalation in costs. Employees may have lobbied the employer for greater involvement in benefit decisions or for expansion of the existing program into new benefit areas. Employers may want to reduce the entitlement mentality of their employees. A benchmarking analysis might have revealed disparities in the current program significant enough to warrant management concern over trailing competitive practice. The employer may be having trouble recruiting employees in a competitive labour market. Whatever the motivations, the next step involves determining whether or not a flexible program would meet the needs of the organization, and if so, what type of program would make the most sense, and then developing a strategy to implement the program.

The purpose of this chapter is to provide a framework or model for organizing the start-up effort and to preview the steps involved in implementing a flexible program. The chapter also addresses what activities are required to maintain a plan once it has been implemented. Finally, it reviews the steps which should be undertaken to refresh a flexible plan that no longer meets the needs of the organization or of its employees.

Many of the functions discussed in this chapter are technical or substantive in nature and are dealt with at length in subsequent chapters of this book. This material focuses on the process for launching and maintaining the plan and revitalizing it when it no longer meets its goals.

§ 3.1 OVERVIEW OF THE PROCESS

One of the few universal truths about a flexible benefit project is that it is usually broader in scope and reach than almost any other modification an organization might make to the structure and nature of compensation and benefits. As a result, most organizations set high expectations for the outcome of a flexible program — and expect to achieve them, or few would commit the energy and resources needed to set a program in place.

The complexity of the undertaking stems largely from the multidisciplinary nature of the effort. For example, employees are asked to make decisions in areas where they previously had little involvement, so communication plays a more extensive role than it would in almost any other type of benefit change. The choice-making mechanism requires tracking of individual elections and/or accounting for the flow of funds under health spending and personal accounts. So administrative considerations exert considerable influence on the feasibility and type of flexible program an employer decides to adopt. In many organizations, a decision to go with a flexible approach hinges on cost considerations, so that, in a sense, a flexible program is more price-sensitive than a conventional program. Careful attention is paid to establishing the financial structure of a flexible program to achieve the organization's objectives in the first and subsequent years of operation.

Figure 3.1 provides a model of the process many organizations have followed for moving a flexible program from inception through implementation. Most organizations find it useful to divide the development process into two phases. One is creating the preliminary design, determining its feasibility, and generally planning the steps involved in an implementation. The other is actually executing the plan: finalizing the program design and cost structure, developing the communication materials, building an administration system or selecting a vendor to handle the administration, and otherwise readying the program for first-time enrolment of employees.

Although Figure 3.1 separates the various activities into distinct stages, in reality many of the steps overlap. For example, design of the program rarely occurs independent of the pricing of options. The primary purpose of the figure is to illustrate the different types of functions that need to be performed to launch a program; only secondarily is it to show the progression or order of the various steps.

The time frame for implementing a flexible program varies by employer. A very few organizations have installed full choice-making programs in as short a period as four months. In general, however, implementation time schedules range from six to twelve months. The systems effort is usually the most time-consuming aspect, with an average of six months required for implementation of administrative software. (Longer time frames are usually required for internal development of an administrative solution.) Employee communication ranks next, with an average of two to four months needed for development of communication materials. After development, most organizations allow about four weeks for enrolment of employees.

Figure 3.1
Steps in Starting a Flexible Program

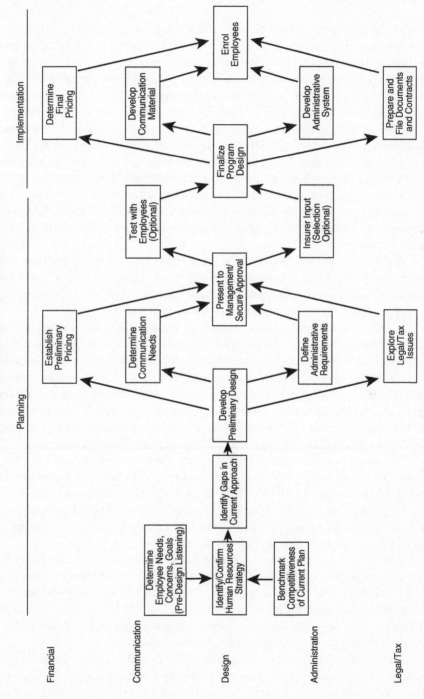

§ 3.2 GETTING STARTED

One of the first steps an organization usually takes is assembling a project team for development and installation of the program. The core team normally consists of a project leader and others from within human resources or the benefit department. An effective step to take early in the process, however, is expansion of the team to include input or representation from other parts of the organization that will be most affected by a flexible program. In some cases, this involves primarily staff roles — namely, systems or internal administration, corporate communication (sometimes also including training or public relations), finance, legal counsel, and so forth. In other cases, the project team includes line managers to add perspective and another view of benefit and compensation issues.

There are several reasons for seeking early input from these other areas.

One is to bring to the surface any constraints or limitations that could hamper or impede development of the program later on, particularly in the area of administration.

Another reason is to broaden the knowledge base for decisions that will need to be made about a flexible program. Participation from those closest to a particular issue will yield better and more informed judgments on the numerous aspects of a flexible program where few right or obvious answers exist.

Finally, expanding the composition of the project team promotes consensus-building along the way and a sense of ownership or responsibility for the outcome. Involvement in the process produces not only better decisions, but a broader group of people who understand the reasons and rationale underlying the decisions. That shared understanding will help increase the sense of purpose people feel when carrying out the developmental tasks required to unveil a new program — and will produce substantial dividends when many of these same specialists are called upon later to explain the merits of the new approach to employees.

No magic combination exists for either the size or composition of the project team. In general, a two- or three-person team may be too small to assure adequate input, while a group of 15 to 20 may impede effective decision making.

Depending on the size of the organization, six to eight members may constitute a workable project team — large enough to ensure breadth of perspective, while small enough to facilitate decision-making.

Within the special project team, it often makes sense to combine doers and decision-makers. For example, an overall project leader might have day-to-day responsibility for co-ordinating the specialized tasks that need to be performed and for keeping the team on its assigned time schedule. Meanwhile, senior decision-makers would be freed to concentrate on policy issues or to steer the process through appropriate channels within the organization.

Many organizations also bring in individuals from outside the employer (or the benefit area), both in the preliminary planning and later stages of implementation. The role performed by such an individual may be that of serving as a technical resource (for information on what can be done, how other organizations have handled a similar matter, the impact of particular decisions, etc.); as a process facilitator (to identify key issues, bring the project team to consensus, etc.); or as an organizer (to scope out what needs to be done, advise on efficient means of accomplishing a particular task, etc.). This type of assistance may come from an independent consulting firm, a brokerage or insurance company consultant, or even from another internal person operating in the capacity of advisor or consultant.

§ 3.3 PLANNING THE PROGRAM

The sample framework described here for planning the program includes:

1. Understanding the current situation (identifying/confirming the human resource strategy; determining employee needs, concerns, and goals; and measuring the competitive position of the current program);
2. Identifying gaps or shortcomings in the current programs by evaluating the information collected in (1);
3. Determining the preliminary design (benefit areas to be included, development of specific options, decisions on the financial structure and overall cost impact);
4. Analysing the implementation effort (required tasks, potential constraints, likely alternatives, budget and staffing requirements);
5. Exploring legal and tax issues;
6. Securing management approval to proceed;
7. As an optional but often useful step, testing the proposed program with a sample of employees; and
8. Seeking input from the insurance carrier.

Although the model incorporates all of these steps under the planning phase of the program, in some instances the steps are viewed as covering two phases: preliminary design (including management approval and employee testing) and planning for implementation.

Regardless of how the effort is categorized or how formal or informal the process is, the following steps are generally taken when planning a flexible benefit program.

UNDERSTANDING THE CURRENT SITUATION

As a means of establishing the groundwork for the flexible benefit study, many organizations incorporate one or more of three substeps:

- identify/confirm the human resource strategy;
- determine employee needs, concerns, and goals; and
- measure the competitive position of the current program.

Identify/Confirm the Human Resource Strategy

It is common for organizations to develop human resource strategies which, among other things, set the direction for the benefit program. For example, these strategies can establish the desired competitive position or address other issues such as empowerment, responsibility, matching benefits and rewards to individual needs, being an employer of choice, or creating a common benefit plan from different programs as a result of a merger. Identifying and confirming these strategies provides the high-level framework for the ensuing flexible benefit design.

Determine Employee Needs, Concerns, and Goals

Where the scope of the flexible benefit project is quite broad, many organizations have found it useful to collect employee input by means of surveys or focus groups. The purpose of this step is to identify employee needs, concerns, and goals rather than comments on or criticisms of specific benefits. In this way, the flexible benefit plan can be designed to specifically handle those issues, rather than being a mere rearrangement of the current life, health, and disability benefits.

Measure Competitive Position

It is often important to have a benchmark measure of the current plan's competitive position. An organization may have fallen behind its comparator group and want to use the flexible benefit plan to improve its position. Alternatively, cost reduction may be the objective, but not so extreme as to compromise the desired competitive position identified in the human resource strategy. This initial competitive measurement can then be used later to test the impact of the new flexible benefit plan. Such a review would also identify any trends within the industry or comparator organizations.

GAP ANALYSIS

At this point, the information concerning the current situation is analysed to identify any gaps, or shortcomings, in the current program. This process can be aided by developing a matrix to compare the competitive position and human resource strategy objectives against the employee input. The results can then be applied to each benefit area during the design phase. The gap analysis will also help identify any changes or modifications that might be required in the human resource strategy to address issues that emerge from the employee needs, concerns, and goals data. Armed with this information, development of the preliminary design can begin.

DEVELOP PRELIMINARY DESIGN

Each organization is unique. Organizations vary by the size and characteristics of the employee workforce, the provisions of the current benefit program, the objectives for exploring a flexible benefit program, the financial and administrative constraints, and the current employee relations environment. Combined with the results of the gap analysis, all of these differences come together as input into designing a program that will be the best fit for that organization. In the same way that no two traditional benefit programs are exactly alike, no two flexible programs are identical.

The project team can use a number of approaches to narrow down the choices among the wide range of available design alternatives and, ultimately, to determine the most appropriate program design. An approach that has worked well for many firms involves three components: data collection, objective setting, and development of design and pricing. Following this progression produces an approach that has a high likelihood of reflecting the uniqueness of the organization, its attitudes, and its employees, and of meeting the organization's objectives (i.e., being viewed as successful by management and employees).

Collect Data

The data collection substep ensures that the project team knows as much as it can before starting to design the program. Although what is needed and what level of depth is required will vary considerably, the following list may be helpful:

- employee data (number, types, demographic characteristics)
- current benefits (types, eligibility requirements, benefit levels, employee contributions)
- current benefit costs (costs by benefit area — per employee, as a per cent of pay, per $1,000 of coverage)
- health care costs broken down by type of service (drugs, hospital, vision, out-of-Canada); by division, by status (active, retiree under age 65, retiree over age 65)
- number of employees participating in, and opting out of, current benefits
- flexible benefit approaches and issues (what can be done, what others are doing, etc., in order to bring the project team to a common level of knowledge).

Set Objectives

The design process is typically streamlined by identifying to begin with how management views certain key issues. Examples of the types of issues helpful to identify, discuss, and reach consensus on can include:

- What are the primary objectives for considering the implementation of a flexible benefit program?
- What are the financial goals and/or constraints for the program?
- What employee groups should be included (active, bargaining, retirees)?
- How should responsibility for the financial security of employees be allocated between the organization and the employee?
- What minimum level of coverage (if any) should be required for employees in each benefit area?
- Should benefits be viewed primarily as a source of protection or as a part of total compensation?
- Should (or must) the current plan be maintained as an option in each benefit area?
- What concerns or problems exist with the current benefit plans (from the employer and employee perspective)?

Develop Design

With the foundation of knowledge gained from the data-collection stage and the objective-setting process, the project task force is prepared to develop alternative design approaches, consider the relative merits of each, and select the design that best fits the organization.

The types of decisions which need to be made in this stage include:

- Which general structure should be used?
  - The full flex approach, where the employee creates a unique benefit plan from a wide range of options;
  - A simplified approach, such as a modular plan, where the employee chooses from three or four packages or modules. Each module contains a predetermined level of medical, dental, life, and possibly disability benefits;
  - A health spending account; or
  - A combination of the above approaches.
- Which benefit areas should be opened to employee choice?

supplemental medical	spousal life	pension
dental	accidental death	vacation
vision	short-term disability	home and auto
employee life	long-term disability	other

- What range of choice is appropriate (from low option to high option)?
- How many options should be made available?
- Which design features should vary among the various options?
- Should a health spending and/or a personal account be introduced?
- Should cash be an option for unused employer contributions?

The project team will generally be able to reach a consensus on most issues, but it may decide to leave open one or two difficult decisions for additional input from a group such as senior management. For example, should employees be permitted to opt out of supplemental medical? Should vacation choices be incorporated into the program? Or, should cash be an option?

Develop the Financial Structure

Once the basic design structure of the flexible program has been determined, an organization needs to analyse the expected impact on employer and employee costs by developing the preliminary pricing structure and estimating the expected costs.

The first step is to select the appropriate financial model; either the credit-based approach or the net contribution pricing structure. If the credit-based model is chosen, the next steps are to develop the approximate level of flexible credits, the approach for allocating these credits to individual employees, and the price tags to be charged to employees for the various options. Similarly, if net contribution pricing is being adopted, the next step is to calculate the total employer subsidy and then determine how this subsidy will be allocated to individual employees. This subsidy is subtracted from the total option cost to produce the net price for the option.

The desired short-term impact on employer costs will typically be addressed in the objective-setting phase. Often, the objective is to maintain the same level of cost which would have been produced by the prior program in the initial year of the flexible program, but gain added control over the rate of increase in future years. In some programs, the objective is to produce an immediate short-term saving in benefit costs. This may be defined as a specific dollar amount, a specific percentage of supplemental medical costs or overall benefit costs, or a certain amount of saving resulting from a particular aspect of the new program. Pricing decisions, in combination with other aspects of the program, will determine the resulting impact on the organization's costs.

The intended impact on employee costs will also help dictate the decisions on option pricing. In some situations, all employees must be allowed to buy back their previous coverage with no change in net contributions (prices less credits). In other cases, prices are being modified — for example, to move from a flat-rate basis to an age-related basis in group life, or to increase medical contributions — thereby creating an expectation that the implementation of the new program will create some winners and losers among employees. Geographic issues may also be addressed at this point. Utilization under supplemental medical plans varies by province, due to the differing provincial medical plans. There can also be provincial differences in dental plan utilization. In addition, certain provinces charge retail sales tax on benefits, and premium taxes also vary by province. Moving from a common pricing basis, which most traditional benefit programs follow, to a geographic basis can create winners and losers, especially when dealing with tax issues. An analysis of these winners and losers under alternative credit and pricing strategies is typically an important aspect of decision making in this area.

ANALYSE IMPLEMENTATION EFFORT

Before most organizations are prepared to adopt flexible benefits, the effort required to implement the program must be understood. The two major implementation activities are employee communication and plan administration.

Determining Communication Needs

Introduction of any flexible benefit program requires explaining the decisions employees will be asked to make. However, the context of the basic communication message (concept and mechanics of choice-making) will be influenced by the specific circumstances of the employer. For example, is the new flexible program primarily a good news message for employees — that is, nobody loses under the program, employer costs will remain the same at least in the first year, and/or significant new benefit opportunities are being incorporated? Or does the flexible program represent a vehicle for accomplishing certain other employer objectives, such as some immediate reduction in costs, or phase-out of dependant or other subsidies?

Most flexible program introductions contain elements of each; however, the relative proportions of each will have a critical influence on the tone, themes, and messages used in the communication effort.

Particularly where cost management is one of the primary objectives for the new flexible benefit plan (through option designs, pricing strategy or both), advance communication of how and why employee behaviour change is needed can be important to the success of the program. In the past, organizations have typically not communicated well with employees on the cost of benefit programs. Therefore, the launch of the new flexible benefit plan can be assisted by supplying some early information to employees that will place the new plan in a proper context.

This contextual backdrop will have been established largely in the preliminary design and financial structuring discussions, but the viewpoint reflected at that stage will have been primarily that of the employer. The next step involves working with the tentative program design and structure to gauge how the program will play with employees.

Here environment plays a critical role. For example, have employees been lobbying for changes in benefits, so that even a cutback in certain areas would be viewed as a reasonable trade-off for the opportunity to exercise choice elsewhere in the program? What is the general mood or trust level concerning the employer? For example, have employees experienced changes in other areas so that the timing of a flexible program implementation might raise suspicions? What are employee perceptions of the business conditions of the employer, and how might these perceptions influence the packaging or look of communication materials?

Once the context has been established, the specifics of the communication effort need to be defined at least in enough reasonable detail to develop preliminary budgets for implementation. Also, the project team needs to focus on the assignment and staffing of communication responsibilities: how much and which elements of the communication effort can be accomplished internally? In terms of developing the preliminary communication plan, consideration should focus on the following kinds of issues:

- Types of communication channels through which to reach employees (Internet, intranet, newsletters, booklets, audiovisual presentations, mailings to the employee's home, call centre, etc.);
- Quantity and quality of communication materials;
- Characteristics of the workforce or environment that might require special attention (for example, diverse education levels, English- and French-speaking employees, work areas with limited space for storing materials);
- Logistics of distributing and receiving communication materials; and
- Timing of the release of information to employees, including the staffing of training sessions, automated enrolment processes, benefit hotlines, and so forth.

It also may be helpful to review communication samples from other organizations where flexible programs have been introduced. However, although useful for the gleaning of ideas, few prototypes exist for adoption by other organizations. Every flexible program is different — the communication materials will reflect those differences as well as the unique environment of the particular employer introducing the program.

Defining Administrative Requirements

Basically, the objective of this step is to determine what needs to be done to administer the flexible program and to identify how administration will be accomplished. Much of the project team's effort in this area will focus on information-gathering: assessing current capabilities, defining new requirements of the flexible program, and evaluating alternatives for handling administration.

In this regard, it is often most useful to begin with an audit of existing systems and procedures. How well (or poorly) is benefit administration currently accomplished? What is the capability of existing payroll and human resource information systems? What computer and people resources presently are available? Part of the audit process might also involve uncovering any plans for upgrading or modifying existing systems and procedures. Looking forward a few years may aid the project team in evaluating whether any present constraints are likely to pose a temporary versus more permanent barrier to either the design or the administration of the flexible program.

Next, most organizations develop a checklist of administrative requirements. The focus here is on identifying which procedures and tasks already are being performed, as well as what new requirements will be needed to accomplish flexible program administration, such as calculating individual net prices, or processing health spending account contributions. Definition of systems requirements establishes criteria for determining what direction to take for flexible program administration.

A subsequent step usually involves evaluating externally developed administrative solutions. Here the project team is concentrating on narrowing the range of possibilities: internal development, installation or co-sourcing of a software package, third-party administration, or full outsourcing. In addition, a number of payroll/HRIS systems have flexible benefit modules available.

Even if an organization has the internal resources and capability to develop its own system, a review of the systems alternatives available on the outside may be a useful part of the process. Flexible programs require unique and specialized knowledge within the area of benefits and human resource information management. So interviewing technical specialists from provider organizations often will yield helpful information.

The adoption of flexible benefit outsourcing has grown rapidly since the late 1990s. Employers now have a wide range of options for outsourcing the routine plan transactional activities (enrolment, record-keeping, etc.), the participant inquiry services (coverage, eligibility questions, etc.), and the third-party plan management (interaction with benefit carriers and payroll). Approximately half of employers with flexible plans outsource the transactional activities to an insurance company or other third-party provider, while a third now outsource the participant inquiry function. And more than a quarter of organizations also outsource the third-party plan management activities.

Another step involves exploring staffing considerations and planning the training of flexible program administrators. Depending on the type of flexible program under consideration, the administrative workload may be handled with existing resources or may require some additional staffing. Either way, however, the people responsible for administering the program on an ongoing basis will need training in the requirements and operation of the new system.

Once these steps have been completed, the project team will be in a reasonably good position to determine the magnitude of the effort and costs involved in implementing an administrative system. At this point, however, the cost figures remain preliminary, because finalization of certain details of the program design may yet influence the ultimate cost of administration.

EXPLORE LEGAL AND TAX ISSUES

As soon as the preliminary design has been established, some organizations involve their legal counsel or tax experts to research, investigate, or confirm any legal issues. No specific legislation or regulations exist concerning flexible benefit programs. The legal guidance for these plans comes from sections of the *Income*

Tax Act dealing with employee benefits and the corresponding Canada Revenue Agency Interpretation Bulletins, particularly *IT-529* on Flexible Employee Benefit Programs (also Quebec employer information materials on matters such as the treatment of taxable benefits). Employers may also wish to review the Canada Revenue Agency opinion letters on the topic. These letters set out responses to specific and hypothetical situations presented to Canada Revenue Agency by employers seeking clarification in "grey" areas.

It should be noted that the Interpretation Bulletin and the letters represent Canada Revenue Agency's opinion as to how it would interpret the *Income Tax Act* and Regulations. To date, no employer has challenged Canada Revenue Agency's position on these issues and the agency has not challenged any employer on the structure of its flexible plan. As a result, an organization's legal counsel may want to seek additional guidance or input from outside lawyers specializing in employee benefit issues.

PRESENT TO MANAGEMENT/SECURE APPROVAL

By this point in the process, the project team has completed the staff work necessary to enable management to make an informed go/no-go decision.

How formal or informal the decision-making process is depends on the organization and the extent of management involvement in the developmental phases of the program. Although a flexible program is not generally viewed as requiring approval of the board of directors, most organizations take measures to inform at least the compensation committee of the board of the status of a flexible program undertaking.

One of the reasons formalized management approval occurs at this stage of the process (rather than earlier) is to minimize the possibility of making decisions based on insufficient information. The project team needs to make sufficient progress in the areas identified earlier to provide management a complete picture of the issues involved — impact on employer cost, impact on employees, time frame, administrative ramifications, and so forth. Also, until this point, the project team has committed largely time (rather than significant dollars) to determining the feasibility of a flexible program. From this point forward, the organization usually will be committing hard dollars to the implementation effort, and the budgets usually need to be established and approved in advance.

In presenting the program to management, organizations typically include information on the following:

- gaps in the current program
- objectives for the new program
- business justification for moving to flexible benefits
- scope and design of the flexible program
- cost/benefit analysis

- communication considerations
- administrative and systems considerations
- legal and tax issues
- timetable for implementation
- implementation budgets and costs.

TEST WITH EMPLOYEES (POST-DESIGN LISTENING)

While not a mandatory step in a flexible program implementation, many organizations find it useful to gather employee input at this stage. Some of the reasons for pretesting a program with employees include the following:

- To collect employee reactions and attitudes toward the concept of flexible benefits and the specifics of the particular flexible program design;
- To test the types of choices employees will be likely to make, and as a result, identify whether assumptions about option pricing, adverse selection, and so forth, are on target;
- To identify any differences in attitudes or information needs among employee subgroups;
- To test the content or approach to be used in the communication effort; and
- To build some employee ownership into the flexible program.

INSURANCE COMPANY INPUT

At this point, depending upon the plan design and the current insurance arrangements, it may be appropriate to seek input from the organization's insurer(s). This may entail providing the current insurer with information on the proposed design, or it may involve selecting a new carrier by obtaining financial and administrative input from a number of insurers.

Unlike the early years of flexible benefit development, all major Canadian group insurance companies now have substantial experience with flexible benefit plans. In fact, all of the major group carriers first implemented flexible benefit plans for their own employees as a means of familiarizing themselves with the issues with which their clients would be dealing.

Areas that should be tested with insurers at this stage include long-term disability designs (particularly underwriting constraints that may affect adverse selection control features) and medical plan designs that incorporate managed prescription drug benefits. (This is because all of the insurers use third-party networks for drug plan adjudication and there may be some issues around transferring plan information to track combined deductibles and other plan limits.) If an organization wishes to evaluate other insurers' capabilities or to consolidate the number of insurers to achieve administrative efficiency, a request for proposal (RFP) should be conducted to allow sufficient time for transition to the new carrier. There will be considerable activity involved in the implementation of the new flexible benefit plan, and most organizations find it helpful to establish insurance arrangements before launching into the implementation phase.

§ 3.4 IMPLEMENTING THE PROGRAM

The following framework or model focuses on completing the steps to install a flexible program: finalizing the program design and financial structure, developing communication and enrolment materials, building or implementing an administrative system, developing day-to-day operating procedures, and completing the necessary legal documents or insurance contracts.

Note that one of the most important steps the project team can take is to assign responsibilities and completion dates for each of the various tasks and then monitor progress against the overall time schedule. All of the different subgroups will be working on separate tasks within the implementation effort, but the whole needs to come together at the end for enrolment of employees. Co-ordination becomes critical, because not one of the subgroup's undertakings is an optional part of the implementation. Delay (or derailment) of any one of the independent tasks will affect (or postpone) the outcome of the entire project.

FINALIZE PROGRAM DESIGN

The preliminary program design might undergo some changes (either modest or substantive) as a result of management input received during the approval stage or as a result of employee feedback if the program was tested with employees.

Irrespective of these changes, however, the preliminary design needs to be brought to a finer level of detail. This level of detail generally is not required earlier in the process (to evaluate the overall impact on employer or employee costs, administrative requirements, and so forth), but it is necessary at this point to develop the administrative system and employee communication materials. Here the project team will be concentrating on issues such as the following:

- How (if at all) will pay changes during the year affect coverage amounts and/or employee contributions?
- What is the minimum claim amount that can be submitted for the issuing of a reimbursement cheque from the health spending account?

- When does an employee transferring from one division to another become eligible to make elections?
- How long does coverage continue after an employee terminates?
- What choices are available upon a change in status?
- How will employees on leave of absence be treated?

DETERMINE FINAL PRICING

The option price tags and flexible credit allowances (in plans using credit-based pricing) or the option prices (in plans adopting net contribution pricing) developed for the preliminary design may have been based on limited cost data or tentative decisions on allocation methodology as a way to minimize the investment of time and effort required in the early stages of developing the program.

However, once the program has been approved and final design decisions made, it is typical practice to re-evaluate the pricing structure.

Additional (and more current) experience data may be available. Given the passage of time, an organization's insurer or third-party administrator may be able to produce a better breakdown of recent claims. The new data will be helpful for taking a second look at the impact of the proposed financial structure.

In many cases, the prices for certain options will be identical to the rates charged by the carrier. However, a change in carriers usually will result in some last-minute pricing changes.

DEVELOP COMMUNICATION MATERIAL

The reason for developing communication material is essentially twofold: to help employees understand the nature of the flexible program and options available to them; and to enrol employees in the program — preferably with as few errors as possible. To accomplish these goals, different types of communication materials are needed.

One type of material is largely informational. This category includes announcement brochures, special newsletters, articles in employer magazines or newspapers, meeting presentations, and descriptive booklets or online handbooks.

Another type of material concentrates on getting employees enrolled in the flexible program. Enrolment material generally includes a booklet describing the program, along with an electronic election form to enrol employees in the program. Most election forms allow employees to change their election up to the enrolment cut-off date and it is often suggested to employees that they model various "what-if" scenarios before making a final decision. Enrolment systems typically provide employees with personalized online statements showing available options, option price tags, and credit allowances (if any). To conclude the enrolment process, most organizations provide printed or online confirmation statements recapping employee elections before the options become effective.

How elaborate the communication effort is depends on the organization and the circumstances surrounding the flexible program introduction. Some organizations choose to create a splash with the new program, complete with a name and special logos, high-quality graphics and paper stock, and interactive online planning tools. Others adopt a more low-key approach.

Regardless of production values, most organizations find that communicating by means of a variety of media is necessary to ensure a high level of employee understanding. Combinations of print and online communications, face-to-face meetings, multi-media shows, video, and other electronic communications are frequently employed.

A different aspect of the communication process is aimed at meeting leaders and flexible program administrators. These people usually are involved in employee meetings or other one-on-one interfaces with employees. It is often most helpful if they can have training programs available to them, meeting leader guides and so forth, to prepare them for the roles they will play in the unveiling and eventual operation of the flexible program.

DEVELOP ADMINISTRATIVE SYSTEM

Procedures and record-keeping systems will need to be developed to handle administration of the program. The degree to which the system is automated depends on the size of the employee group, the nature and structure of the program, and the computer and personnel resources available. In general, administrative systems and procedures need to be able to accomplish the following:

- Determine participant eligibility;
- Compute flexible credit allowances and option price tags (if credits and prices are part of the design) or the option prices (in net pricing plans);
- Enrol employees in their benefit choices (including editing employee elections);
- Produce confirmation statements;
- Process interim coverage for new employees (if appropriate), and coverage changes for employees with a change in family status during the year;
- Report to payroll and insurers/administrators (payroll deductions, taxable benefit calculations, eligibility information); and
- Report to management on various aspects of the program, such as use of flexible credits or payroll deductions, enrolment in each benefit area, utilization by coverage category, and so forth.

To avoid any last-minute surprises, most organizations work into the implementation timetable a period for testing the administrative system before the initial enrolment. That way, any potential problems can be corrected before the flood of first-time enrolments.

PREPARE DOCUMENTS AND CONTRACTS

No formal legal document is required to establish the flexible program. However, depending on the design of the program, it may be necessary to modify other plan documents. The savings plan, for example, may need to clarify that unused employer contributions may be transferred into the plan. Insurance contracts and administrative service agreements will have to be developed, in the case of a new insurance carrier, or extensively rewritten, in the case of an existing carrier.

§ 3.5 ENROLLING EMPLOYEES

At this point, everything the project team has worked so hard to accomplish will come together. Employees will understand the new flexible program and make choices based on their own individual needs. The administrative system will record the elections and be ready to handle the activities involved in ongoing administration. And the project team will feel a tremendous sense of accomplishment over a job well done.

After the pace of the initial enrolment has subsided, the project team usually reassembles for a debriefing. The purpose is to incorporate any lessons learned from the first enrolment into planning for subsequent years. This might involve identifying areas on the election form where employees or administrators had difficulty entering elections, or uncovering common themes in the questions employees asked about the program that might be addressed in subsequent communications. It might also involve re-evaluating any options that were elected by only a very small percentage of employees, and generally looking for ways to streamline or improve any aspect of the flexible program's operation in later years.

§ 3.6 MAINTAINING A FLEXIBLE PROGRAM

Following the launch of a flexible benefit plan, the implementation team is disbanded and the individuals move on to other projects or return to their regular activities. While the effort required to maintain a flexible plan is much less than the implementation effort, resources must be allocated to manage the plan so it continues to meet the objectives established at the beginning of the process.

Some of the maintenance activities, such as repricing, are normally undertaken once a year, while others, such as benchmarking, may only be required every two or three years. A few activities need to be undertaken only once every five years or so.

ANNUAL ACTIVITIES

Most annual activities, including a financial review, plan repricing, and employee communication, are a necessary part of preparing for the annual re-enrolment of plan members.

Financial Review

The financial analysis of a flexible benefit plan is considerably more complex than a review of a traditional plan. In the latter case, the actual plan costs for the past year are compared to the expected costs. Next, the premiums for the upcoming year are estimated by adjusting for any variance between the prior year's actual and expected costs and then adding any anticipated increases for the upcoming year.

For a flexible plan, the goal is also to compare the actual and expected costs; however, the results will almost certainly differ by option. Frequently the lowest options perform better than expected, because the lower users tend to select these options, while the most valuable options perform worse than expected. Another complicating factor is that the financial analysis must isolate the impact of inflation and utilization increases from the impact of adverse selection so as to determine the underlying change in the cost structure. A review of the health care claims by service (vision, drugs, paramedical, etc.) and option is useful for understanding why the actual costs differed from the expected costs.

For flexible programs, the trend rate, or anticipated cost increase for the coming year, will frequently differ by option. Options with cost management features, such as prescription drug formularies and benefit maximums, will normally have a lower trend rate than plans with few cost management features.

Repricing

Prior to the re-enrolment window, the plan sponsor should review the financial analysis and decide on the pricing for the upcoming year. Some employers have a stated policy on how cost increases are to be shared with employees; for example, any increases may be shared 50/50 with employees. Or the company may absorb any increase up to, say, 4 per cent, with the employees picking up the excess. Other employers decide each year on the cost sharing, basing their decision on factors such as the magnitude of cost increases, company performance, and competitive practice.

Once the cost increases have been determined and the cost sharing approach established, the plan sponsor must decide whether to apply the same changes across all options or to have different rates of increase by option. For example, if the lowest options had the best financial experience, the employer may decide to leave their pricing unchanged and have the entire increase borne by employees electing the highest options.

Another important step in repricing is to estimate the projected enrolment in each option for the coming year. A review of the enrolment trends over the previous three years is the best predictor of future enrolments. However, any estimate based on prior enrolment patterns will need to be adjusted if there are design and pricing changes planned for the next plan year.

Communication

Re-enrolment communication normally focuses on changes since the last enrolment (including pricing) and how to re-enrol. Both topics are frequently reflected in an online enrolment/administration system, in which case the employer would simply notify employees of the dates of the re-enrolment window and provide a link to the appropriate Web site. Some employers supplement this with a printed summary of the changes and enrolment instructions for the upcoming year, but this is becoming less common as employers move to a fully Web-based enrolment/communication system.

BIENNIAL OR TRIENNIAL ACTIVITIES

Every two or three years, plan sponsors should conduct a minor review of the plan design and its delivery in case any "tweaking" is appropriate to optimize performance. The following activities could be conducted simultaneously or independently.

Plan Design Benchmarking

Most employers establish a competitive target for their benefits program as part of their overall total compensation philosophy. The goal is frequently expressed as a percentile. For example, the target competitive position may be the 50th percentile (meaning 50 per cent of plans in the comparator group should rank the same as or below the sponsor's plan) or the 75th percentile (75 per cent of plans should rank the same as or below the sponsor's plan).

The steps in benchmarking the plan design include:

- Determine the benchmarking methodology. The most common approach is to calculate the relative value of the plan sponsor's program compared to the plans of the comparator group. The relative value measures the employer's relative cost if all of the employers had identical workforces (i.e., same demographics, salary increases, mortality, etc.) and experienced exactly the same plan usage (i.e., the same rates of disability, use of vision care, etc.). The relative value approach neutralizes all factors influencing cost except for the plan design.

- Select the comparator group. Typically companies in the same industry and those located in the same geographical area are selected.
- Solicit agreement to participate and collect design and pricing details from the comparator group.
- Prepare the benchmarking analysis (this is typically prepared by a benefit consulting firm that has an established methodology and database of plan design information).
- Review the results.
- Decide on any changes, based on the results.

Plan Design Review

The structure of a flexible benefit plan allows frequent design changes in the various options. For example, if the benchmarking study indicates that dental benefits are no longer competitive, the sponsor could increase the maximum reimbursement in the richest dental option. The employer could pay for the improvement by providing additional credits or by keeping the net price unchanged, depending on the pricing structure being used in the plan. Or, the cost could be paid by employees electing the option. In addition to modifying existing options, new coverages such as home and auto insurance could be added.

Any changes or clarifications in the tax basis of flexible plans, announced by the Canada Revenue Agency, may provide an opportunity to improve the plan and broaden its appeal.

Insurance Carrier Benchmarking

The plan sponsor should review the insurance carrier fees (retention charges) to ensure they remain competitive. A benefits consultant or broker should have information on competitive fees currently being charged by all carriers for similar programs.

ONCE EVERY FIVE YEARS

Once every five years or so, the plan sponsor should review all of the key design, financial, and delivery aspects of the flexible benefits plan.

Insurance Marketing

Employers sponsoring traditional or flexible benefits plans may wish to consider putting the insurance arrangements "out to market" to ensure that the best insurance carrier is in place to deliver the program. Since changing insurance carriers is a major undertaking, employers should only consider marketing their coverage if they are unhappy with the service, technology, rates, or fees charged by their incumbent insurer.

A marketing involves:

- Interviewing all HR staff dealing with the carrier.
- Reviewing feedback from employees on the carrier's performance.
- Preparing a request for proposal (RFP) outlining the plan requirements, insurance arrangements, selection criteria, and employee demographic information.
- Distributing the RFP to the potential carriers.
- Evaluating the responses to the RFP.
- Selecting the insurance carrier.
- Implementing changes (if a new carrier is selected).

Major Design Review

The sponsor should review all of the design and pricing elements as part of the five-year review. The number of options and the features of each option (deductibles, maximums, co-payments, covered expenses, etc.) would be reviewed and modified where needed. The price tags and credits, or the net cost, for each option would be adjusted to reflect any design changes and any rebalancing of the plan's financial structure. The only element that would not likely change is the overall structure of the plan; such a change would more likely occur during a complete program overhaul, as discussed in Section 3.7.

Administration and Communication Review

With the rapid changes in administration solutions and communication approaches due to technology advancements, employers should review how their plan is administered and communicated at least once every five years. For example, five years ago many plans used a combination of paper and stand-alone enrolment tools during the annual enrolment window. Today, the vast majority of organizations are eliminating paper and moving to Web-based solutions that support year-round administration activities. These solutions are also the primary source of program information for employees.

§ 3.7 REVITALIZING AN EXISTING FLEXIBLE PROGRAM

Occasionally, a flexible benefit plan will need a complete overhaul. This is less likely to be the case where the plan sponsor has actively maintained the plan, as described in Section 3.6.

The employer may need to overhaul or revitalize the plan if:

- The plan design or pricing was not reviewed on a regular basis and the plan no longer meets the original objectives.
- The objectives have changed since the plan was implemented. For example, cost containment may have been a low priority when the plan was introduced but has become the key priority now. This change in focus may require that the design and pricing be thoroughly revisited.
- The sponsoring organization merges with another company and a new plan must be developed.
- The plan is lacking excitement and needs to be refreshed so as to attract and retain employees.
- New technology and communication approaches are being introduced and the company wants to revitalize the plan design at the same time in order to make the largest impact.

There are three steps to determining the magnitude and nature of the changes needed to revitalize a flexible benefit plan. They are updating the plan objectives, reviewing employee feedback, and preparing a gap analysis comparing the exiting flexible plan to the desired state.

REVISITING PLAN OBJECTIVES

The original plan objectives should be reviewed and modified where necessary so that they reflect the current views of management. Undoubtedly, many relevant factors and considerations will have changed, such as:

- The programs provided by competitors.
- Global competition and the impact on total compensation.
- Employee demographics.
- The plan's financial constraints.
- Employer priorities among the competing goals of cost containment, meeting diverse needs, attracting and retaining employees, and so forth.
- Administration technologies and communication approaches.
- Insurance carrier capabilities.
- Available cost containment features.

In addition, the current management team may be different from the team that implemented the program. The new team may have different priorities and perspectives.

The new statement of objectives will be a key factor in analysing the gaps between the current and desired programs.

REVIEWING EMPLOYEE FEEDBACK

Another consideration for the gap analysis is understanding employee perspectives concerning the program. Does the plan meet their needs? Is it considered too complex? Too narrow in scope? Do employees believe it is competitive? Does the plan help attract and retain employees? What changes would make it more useful to employees? Which demographic groups are most positive about the plan? Which are most negative?

Employers can get answers to these questions through employee surveys or focus groups. Or they may already know the answers from previous employee listening initiatives. Additional perspectives can be collected from individuals dealing directly with employees on benefits issues, such as staff in an outsourcing call centre.

CONDUCTING A GAP ANALYSIS OF PLAN DESIGN, FIANANCING, AND DELIVERY

Based on the updated objectives and current employee perspectives, the employer can identify the shortcomings or gaps in the existing flexible program.

REVITALIZING THE PLAN

The steps in closing these gaps to revitalize the program parallel those necessary to implement a new program. They include redesigning and repricing the plan, modifying the communication approach, and making any required administration changes. Although the steps are similar to those needed to implement a plan, the effort will normally be much less than would be needed for a new plan, since many aspects of the current plan can almost certainly be reused.

Four

Plan Structure and Eligibility

The purpose of Part Two is to provide a benefit-by-benefit guide to the design of a flexible benefit program. Regardless of the components of the program, however, an organization ultimately will need to decide on the overall structure of the flexible benefit plan, which employee groups are to be covered under the plan, and what, if any, special requirements should apply for certain groups.

§ 4.1 PLAN STRUCTURE

Today's flexible benefit plans span a wide spectrum of structures, with the original core-plus-credits type falling somewhere near the middle of the range. The key reason for the appeal of flexible programs is that no single benefit package is right for every employee. The same rationale applies to the structure of flexible plans; the configuration that suits company ABC may not meet the needs of company XYZ.

The essence of a flexible benefit plan is the ability of participants to make choices as to how some of the employer's benefit expenditures are spent. Provided a benefit program contains some element of choice in how to spend employer benefit dollars, it can be described as "flexible."

Figure 4.1 on page 66 illustrates the full spectrum of flexible benefit structures.

The traditional plan at the left of the spectrum provides no choice for employees in how to spend employer benefit dollars. However, it may allow employees to buy some additional coverage using their own payroll deductions. A traditional plan tends to appeal to smaller employers, to more paternalistic organizations, and to companies where benefits are relatively unimportant in attracting and retaining employees. Many plans for unionized employees also fit into this category.

Figure 4.1
The Spectrum of Flexible Benefit Structures

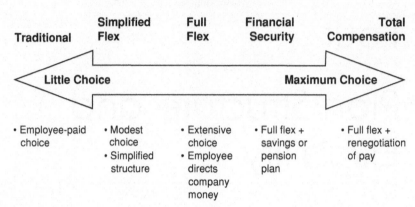

More choice for employees is added as you move along the spectrum to the right until you reach the total compensation approach, offering maximum choice. There is also a fundamental shift in philosophy as you progress along the spectrum. Towards the left of the spectrum, benefits and compensation are seen as distinct elements; towards the right, they are viewed as part of the whole compensation package.

SIMPLIFIED FLEX

Many newer flexible benefit plans give employees some choice in how to spend employer money but do not incorporate some of the more complex features of "core plus credits" flexible plans. These fall between traditional, no-choice plans and full flex programs on the spectrum. Types of simplified flexible benefit plans include the following:

Health Spending Account Only

Undoubtedly, the simplest flexible benefit plan is one that provides a health spending account on top of a traditional benefits program. In most provinces (Quebec is the only exception), employees can use the employer-provided funds in their health spending account to receive tax-free reimbursement of health care expenses. Since this arrangement allows employees to direct employer dollars to pay for their unique health care needs, it meets the definition of a flexible benefit program.

Modular

Under a modular flexible benefit plan, benefits are grouped together in a package and employees choose among the different packages. For example, life insurance, disability insurance, and health and dental coverage might be grouped together in three packages depending on the level of coverage — high, medium, and low. Employees choose the package that best suits their needs. However, they do not make separate choices for each benefit as they would under a full flex plan.

Health Care Only

This type of simplified plan allows employees to direct employer money within health care choices only. This is simpler than a full flex plan but still offers employees a wide range of choice in a very important benefit area.

Net Contribution Pricing

As discussed in Chapter 2, net pricing refers to flexible plans that do not utilize a credit and price tag financial structure. Instead, employees are shown the net cost of each option (equal to the price tag less the credit of the full flex approach). Where the net cost is negative, the amount is frequently directed to a health spending account.

Net pricing plans are becoming the most popular type of simplified flex plans, as they can provide the same range of choice to employees as full flex plans without some of the communication and administrative complexities of full flex. The downside of net pricing plans is that the plan sponsor has less control over future cost increases. Under a full flex plan, the employer can make a separate decision on changes in price tags and credits (and as such, can communicate the realistic or true cost of the benefit), whereas in a net pricing plan only the employee net cost changes from year to year. Nevertheless, net pricing plans are now the norm for flexible plans in the United Sates.

Appeal of Simplified Flex

Simplified flexible plans generally appeal to smaller organizations, to those that want to "keep it simple," and to those that consider themselves administratively challenged. Organizations that provide a relatively low level of employer-paid benefits also find this approach appealing, as there may not be enough funding available to make the full flex approach viable. This type of structure may also serve as an "entry point" for organizations seeking to move further along the design spectrum, but slowly.

FULL FLEX

The earliest flexible benefit plans were full flex programs, often called "core plus credits" or "cafeteria plans." These plans normally provide significantly more

Figure 4.2
Structure of a Full Flex Plan

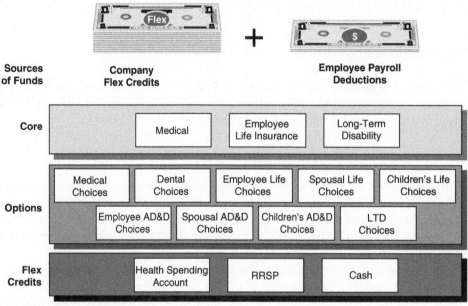

AD&D: Accidental Death and Dismemberment

choice than simplified flex plans, as well as offering significant tax advantages to employees.

Under a full flex plan, employees choose from a range of options in several benefit areas. The lowest option (core) is the minimum level of coverage that is permitted by the employer in each benefit type — this may be no coverage for some benefits, such as dental. A full flex plan generally includes a health spending account as one of the options.

Employees pay for options with a combination of pre-tax employer-provided credits and after-tax payroll deductions. Credits that are not needed to pay for the options may be directed to the health spending account or a personal account. Some employers allow their employees to withdraw unused credits as cash from the plan.

A typical full flex plan is shown in Figure 4.2.

Appeal of Full Flex

Full flex plans typically appeal to organizations that have larger populations, want to encourage employee self-service, have rich benefits programs (the richer the program, the more employer money available for employees to use), and are trying to balance the competing goals of cost management and employee attraction and retention.

FINANCIAL SECURITY

A financial security plan combines a full flex plan with a pension or group savings plan.

The most common financial security plan allows employees to exchange part or all of their group savings plan match for additional pre-tax credits in a flexible benefit plan or a deposit to their health spending account. The portion of their matched funds that is not redirected to the benefit plan is deposited in the savings plan group RRSP (or after-tax account for employees with no RRSP room). And funds can go the other way, too. If employees don't spend all of their employer-provided flex credits on benefit choices, they may deposit them in the group RRSP or in their after-tax account.

The link between a savings plan and a flexible benefits plan is illustrated Figure 4.3.

Appeal of the Financial Security Approach

Financial security plans are very similar in appeal to full flex plans. The differentiators are that organizations who want to be at this point on the spectrum are looking for maximum tax effectiveness along with maximum choice for their employees. They view their retirement and group benefits as one integrated program.

Figure 4.3
Financial Security Flexible Benefit Structure

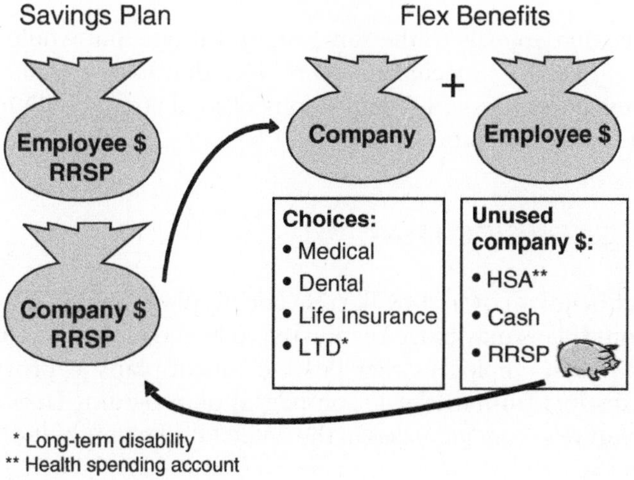

* Long-term disability
** Health spending account

For many organizations, a financial security plan is the natural next step beyond a full flex plan.

TOTAL COMPENSATION

The philosophy behind a total compensation plan is that salary and benefits should be interchangeable; the employer provides a total compensation package and the employee selects what portion should be taken as pay and what portion as benefits. Such plans combine all of the features of full flex or financial security structures with the employees' ability to allocate direct compensation elements to the plan. Many U.S. benefit plans fall into this category because of the favourable tax legislation there that allows employees to purchase certain benefits using pre-tax salary reduction.

In Canada, the Canada Revenue Agency (CRA) rules on salary reduction are much more restrictive than those in the U.S. Nevertheless, a number of employers have moved toward the total compensation end of the spectrum in recent years. (The CRA rules state that salary and vacation cannot be converted to flex credits without including the amount in income for tax purposes, unless the changes result from a collective bargaining agreement or a contract of employment is renegotiated upon expiry and the new contract provides for a decrease in salary and the introduction of flex credits.) However, CRA will allow employees to exchange part or all of a performance bonus for additional flex credits in certain circumstances. Chapter 12, "Taxation of Flexible Benefits," discusses this issue in detail.

Moving to a total compensation structure requires careful design planning to ensure that tax-effectiveness opportunities are maximized.

Appeal of Total Compensation

Total compensation appeals to the same organizations that would find financial security plans attractive. Specifically, employers that have a goal of maximizing tax effectiveness and those with a philosophy of total compensation would like to be at this end of the spectrum.

FUTURE TOTAL COMPENSATION PLANS

As the types of benefits covered by flexible benefit plans continue to increase, the structure of some plans may move beyond the right end of the spectrum. Currently, employees and most employers view flexible benefit plans as programs that are separate and distinct from the basic compensation program. Thus, pay increases are viewed separately from increases in the financial elements of the flexible benefit plan.

This perspective is beginning to erode. Employers recognize that both benefit and salary costs are payroll expenses — both are components of employees' total compensation. In coming years, employers may restructure their traditional and flexible benefit plans to communicate the relationship of these components to employees. Under this restructured approach, employees would receive a total compensation amount composed of base compensation, any incentive or variable pay, and an amount that represents the employer subsidy for benefits. In turn, this total amount would be "spent" on mandatory benefits (such as statutory benefits or any employer-required coverage), and on any elective benefit coverage selected by the employee. As a result, the current distinction between pay and benefit dollars would be eroded as dollars flowed more freely across categories.

This approach would hold a number of attractions for employers:

- Each paycheque becomes a benefit statement. Rather than seeing only the cash component of each paycheque, the employee sees the total value of all compensation and benefits.

- The employer is better positioned to manage the cost of benefit increases. Currently, employees view their compensation increases separately from increases in costs under the flexible benefit plan. If employee prices increase more than employer subsidies, employees may focus on their "loss" under the flexible benefit plan, without considering the relationship of these changes to compensation increases. Under a total compensation approach, the entire compensation package increases at a specified, visible rate. In effect, the total compensation approach reinforces the ability of employers to use flexible benefit plans to separate the cost of benefits from the level of employer subsidy for benefits.

- The employer can move from subsidies that relate to the cost of coverage to more visible rewards that reflect organizational values and goals. Credits for service, educational achievements, performance, and positive health habits may be used to reallocate some portion of the pay-based and family-status subsidies prevalent today.

- The employer's ability to use variable pay credits as a part of the total compensation package is significantly enhanced. This variable pay can be based on a number of factors, such as corporate or individual performance. Using a total compensation approach makes it easier for employees to evaluate how much of their variable pay to spend on benefits and how much to take as cash.

- The use of employer subsidies can be leveraged through the use of group purchasing, payroll deductions, convenience benefits, financial planning tools, and other sources of value. These strategies are essential if employers are to improve total compensation value while managing costs.

Table 4.1
Ability of Various Flexible Benefit Structures to Achieve Objectives

Plan	Employee Choice	Employee Tax Advantages	Ease of Administration	Employer Cost Control	Employee Understanding of Benefits
Traditional	★	★★	★★★★★	★	★
Simplified Flex	★★★	★★★	★★★	★★	★★★
Full Flex	★★★★	★★★★	★★	★★★★	★★★★
Financial Security	★★★★★	★★★★★	★	★★★★★	★★★★
Total Compensation	★★★★★	★★★★★	★	★★★★★	★★★★

COMPARING FLEXIBLE PLAN STRUCTURES

Table 4.1 compares the range of flexible structures and their ability to achieve certain goals.

As illustrated, each structure achieves these goals to varying degrees. Every organization must decide on the relative importance of each goal in order to assess which structure is most appropriate.

§ 4.2 TYPES OF COVERAGE CATEGORIES

For many organizations, the coverage and eligibility determination will largely represent an extension of practices in place before the flexible benefits plan was introduced. For example, if all employees were originally covered under a common, non-flexible benefit program, the flexible program typically would cover the same employee group. Similarly, groups excluded from previous coverage (such as part-time employees) or covered under separate arrangements (such as members of a collective bargaining unit, or retired employees) would likely remain outside the flexible program.

For other organizations, different issues may arise. Large or diverse organizations may already operate multiple employee benefit programs based on cost or other considerations relating to the different business units or operating entities. In these instances, coverage decisions might be influenced by the type of benefits or the financing structure already in place.

There also may be other considerations, such as the employee relations environment or the compatibility of administrative systems and procedures.

A separate issue for flexible programs is coverage of new employees — those who join an organization sometime before the next annual enrolment. Most organizations allow new employees to participate in the flexible plan as soon as they join the organization. The remaining employers have a waiting period before eligibility for flexible program participation begins.

This section examines the issues relating to coverage of different employee groups under a flexible program.

SALARIED EMPLOYEES

Flexible benefit programs originated within the salaried employee population. To date, almost all Canadian flexible benefits programs cover full-time salaried employees. In general, few employers impose eligibility restrictions on active employees other than that they must be regular, full-time salaried employees. (See also the later discussion of coverage for new employees in Section 4.3.)

Occasionally, however, organizations impose eligibility requirements by employee group or by benefit area. For example, a one-year waiting period might apply for long-term disability coverage for certain employees, such as those outside management ranks. All other flexible program choices would be available, but disability coverage as an option would not be available until an employee satisfied the service requirement.

HOURLY NON-UNIONIZED EMPLOYEES

Flexible benefit programs for hourly employees are much more prevalent for a non-union workforce than for a unionized group. The employers who do sponsor flexible programs for this group are typically those whose non-union employees were previously covered under the same program as salaried employees. In this case, the hourly group is normally covered under the flexible plan when it is introduced. Based on the results of a 2005 survey by Hewitt Associates, 80 per cent of employers with flexible benefit plans include full-time, non-bargaining hourly employees in the plan, while an additional 14 per cent anticipate extending coverage to this group at a future date.

HOURLY UNIONIZED EMPLOYEES

Flexible benefit programs have been much slower to emerge within the hourly unionized workforce for several reasons. One reason is the strong influence of the collective bargaining process on the determination (or shaping) of benefits for hourly unionized employees. Flexible benefits have been pegged within the labour environment as essentially a technique for shifting a greater proportion of the cost of benefits (particularly supplemental medical and dental) to employees. Recognition that the primary thrust of flexible programs among salaried employees is to permit the tailoring of benefits to individual needs has been slow to gain union acceptance.

Another factor is deep-seated union concern about the ability of members to make benefit decisions. A perception often exists that benefit decisions are more complicated than other personal financial decisions an employee might make, and that the penalty for a wrong election is severe (for example, high medical expenses should the employee waive coverage). In general, familiarity with risk-reducing features such as stop-loss limits and core coverage is low.

To some extent, the concept of flexible benefits, with its emphasis on individual determination of benefit needs, also runs counter to the basic principle of collective bargaining. Providing choices to individual members has the potential to diminish the role of the union. While certainly not an overt consideration, shades of this reasoning may underlie general labour reaction to choice-making approaches. (In reality, bargaining on employer contributions to a flexible program, in terms of credits and prices, would be little different from negotiating benefit schedules and flat-dollar amounts, for which a union currently is able to "take credit" with constituents.)

The first plan for unionized employees in Canada was introduced in Saskatchewan in July of 1990. The union representing employees at the Rocanville mine of the Potash Corporation of Saskatchewan Inc. negotiated a flexible benefit plan patterned after the successful plan covering salaried employees.

Since then, some other organizations have negotiated some form of flexible program with various unions. All of the situations have been unique. In general, however, the bargaining situations included the following kinds of elements:

- The flexible program was implemented first for salaried employees and was a popular program.
- The employer demonstrated to the union that an active effort was under way to control health care costs beyond introducing a flexible program.
- The flexible program retained the pre-flex plan as an option, with employer-contributed credits sufficient to purchase this pre-flex option, at least in the first year, at the same employee cost (if any).
- The flexible program provided union employees substantially the same benefits as salaried employees.
- A particularly attractive option was "bundled" with the flexible program.
- Some equitable solution was agreed upon for the sharing of any cost increases or reductions in subsequent years.

Union issues should be addressed early in the design process and a strategy developed for how, if ever, they will be incorporated into the program.

Generally, plans are designed for the salaried population. The design is then examined to see how it would apply for union employees. Including a labour relations representative on the design team can help ensure that there are no "deal breakers" in the design.

One of the key considerations for bargaining flexible benefits is how to handle the financial aspects of the plan for a multi-year contract. Most unions are uncomfortable giving management full discretion over how much credits and price tags will rise each year (assuming a credit-based pricing approach is used) or how the net price will increase (assuming net contribution pricing). In practice, several approaches have been used:

- The credits and price tags or the net price remain fixed over the life of the contract (in effect, the employer picks up all of the inflationary cost during the term of the contract).
- The credits and price tags or the net price are determined up front for each year during the contract period.
- The credits and price tags or the net price are increased each year according to some indices (CPI, for example). The same index can be used for both credits and prices or separate indices can be used (e.g., tie credits to CPI, but tie prices to medical inflation). Often, putting a cap on the annual increase or on the maximum total increase during the contract will make the union more comfortable with an indexed approach.
- Credits and price tags or the net price are bargained each year.

PART-TIME EMPLOYEES

Part-time employees represent a growing segment of the workforce: part-time employment participation increased from 10 per cent in 1976 to 19 per cent in 2003. About 3 million people work part-time and the majority of these are women. The highest concentration of part-timers is found in the retail, food services, education, and health care sectors.

Part-time benefits vary substantially among employers. In industries where part-time employees comprise a significant portion of the regular workforce, part-timers generally are extended benefit coverage, but only infrequently at the same level of employer subsidy as the full-time employee population. In other industries where part-time employment is less common, few, if any, benefits are provided.

Another important consideration in part-time employee benefit coverage is the number of hours worked. Part-time employees working at least 30 hours a week typically receive benefits, while employees working fewer than 15 or 20 hours generally receive no benefits beyond provincially mandated coverage, such as vacation and pensions. For employees working between 15 and 30 hours per week, benefits coverage is dependent on factors such as industry and location. Saskatchewan was the first and so far only province to introduce mandatory benefit coverage for part-time employees who work an average of 15 hours a week or more for a minimum period of six months. Paid sick leave, disability insurance, and vision care are not included in the required benefits.

Ninety-one per cent of employers with salaried part-time employees include some part-timers in the flexible benefit program, as do 72 per cent of employers with hourly, non-union part-time employees.

Most employers that include part-time employees under the program provide the same benefit options but frequently provide a lower employer subsidy (i.e., fewer credits) to part-time employees or charge higher price tags for benefit options. In some cases the employer offers fewer benefit areas to part-time employees. Some employers use more than one of these approaches.

Where the level of employer subsidy is based on hours of employment, an issue sometimes arises over the determination of hours worked. Most employers use scheduled, rather than actual, hours for determining the employer subsidy. However, inequities could result when actual hours vary substantially from scheduled hours of employment — either significantly higher or lower. Some employers have remedied the problem by using an alternative definition, such as actual hours of employment during the previous quarter.

RETIRED EMPLOYEES

Flexible benefits for retirees is becoming more popular in Canada. In 1994, 20 per cent of employers with flexible benefit plans reported covering retirees under their flexible benefit program. By 2005 this had increased to 36 per cent, with a further 13 per cent of employers planning to add retirees to the flexible plan at a future date. The remaining employers either cover retired employees under a separate non-flexible retiree arrangement or provide no retiree coverage.

Approaches to flexibility for retirees include constructing a flexible program that is comparable to the employee plan (usually providing health benefits or health and death benefits only) or permitting the employee to make a one-time election of pre-retirement flexible program coverage and allowing that coverage to remain in force throughout retirement. Another approach that is gaining acceptance is to provide a health spending account to retirees, combined with catastrophic medical coverage.

There are a number of reasons why many employers have not offered flexible options to retirees. These include:

- A belief that retirees are more homogeneous than active workers and that their needs do not vary significantly. (In fact, the demographic and lifestyle differences among retirees can be even more dramatic than among active employees. For example, the benefit needs of a 55-year-old retiree with a working spouse and children in university are very different from those of an 80-year-old widow or widower living in Florida for six months of the year.)

- Difficulty in communicating with retirees. The communication approaches used for active employees, such employee meetings or intranet Web sites, cannot easily be used in a retiree program.

- The sense among employers that some of the key motivations for introducing flexible benefits to the active workforce do not apply to retirees. Specifically, increasing employee awareness of benefits, attracting and retaining employees, and being competitive are not applicable to retirees.

- A greater concern about adverse selection, because retirees with chronic diseases would elect options with maximum medical coverage. This would drive up costs in future years.

Despite these reasons, flexible benefit plans for retirees are being implemented by more organizations today. The impetus comes from several directions, including:

- Flexible benefit plans have a good track record for active employees; as employees retire, they pressure their employers to continue offering choice.

- The increasing cost of retiree benefits encourages employers to adopt a defined contribution funding approach whereby employers agree to pay a specified number of dollars per retiree. Any additional costs would be paid by the retiree. Under this approach, future inflationary increases in health care costs are not factored into the post-retirement liabilities (CICA 3461 in Canada and FAS 106 and 112 in the United States), substantially lowering the employer's annual expense.

    Retiree medical costs have increased even faster than active employee costs in some cases, as people live longer and technology keeps advancing. The possibility that provincial health insurance plans will try to pay less of the medical bills for the elderly is also a concern that has encouraged some employers to limit their future liabilities through flexible programs. As an example of provincial cutbacks, some provinces that pay for prescription drugs for residents over age 65 are beginning to share the cost with seniors, which shifts costs back to the private sector when insurance is available.

- "Retiree flex" allows employers to reward career employees by providing them with a greater company subsidy than employees who retiree with relatively short service. Under some plans, employees accrue retiree supplemental medical, dental, and life insurance benefits over their careers, in much the same way they earn pensions. To accomplish this, the employer ties its subsidy to service at retirement and grants each retiree $50, say, in credits for each year of service.

- As employers cut back their contributions to retiree health care for all employees or for selected groups (e.g., short-service retirees), the need for choice increases. Retirees can then choose more limited coverage at a lower cost or more extensive coverage at a higher cost.

There are a number of considerations for employers in implementing new benefit programs for retirees. An important Supreme Court case, *Dayco (Canada) Ltd. v National Automobile, Aerospace and Agricultural Implement Workers' Union of Canada*, led to the conclusion that retiree benefits accrue during the life of a collective agreement and vest at retirement. In the absence of a clear statement in writing to retirees at the time they were active, the employer's ability to terminate or substantially change retiree benefits may be limited. For this reason, many employers carefully examine whether a "promise" was made to current retirees before changing their programs.

§ 4.3 COVERAGE FOR NEW EMPLOYEES

Until recently, many employers were uncomfortable with allowing new employees to make flexible benefit choices immediately upon employment — especially choices that were irrevocable until the next enrolment or a change in family status. These employers were concerned that new employees would have to evaluate their choices and make decisions without the same level of support provided to existing employees at the annual enrolment.

Today most employers have done away with a waiting period and permit immediate participation in the full choice-making program. The widespread use of outsourcing combined with Internet-based modelling and enrolment systems have provided new employees with the same information, support, and tools available to all employees. Many employers feel that it is a competitive advantage to have employees participate as soon as they join the company. For the remaining employers, the waiting period ranges from 30 days up to the date of the next annual enrolment. During the waiting period, a fixed package of benefits may be provided.

§ 4.4 COVERAGE BY BUSINESS UNIT

In general, most organizations cover all employees under a common flexible program structure, except where it is more appropriate to develop separate programs, such as union-negotiated arrangements. In addition, the culture of an organization most likely will influence the appropriateness of developing different flexible programs for separate employee groups, or excluding certain groups from coverage.

In some organizations, a flexible approach provides the opportunity to unify benefit structures across business units or entities. This can reduce or minimize the cost and administrative effort involved in operating separate programs or enhance the ability to transfer employees among operations.

Coverage decisions occasionally hinge on the compatibility and flexibility of administrative systems and procedures. (For example, in a case where groups of employees are on different payroll systems, the administrative system for the flexible program must be able to accept multiple sources of employee data and produce output for these same employee groups.)

Conceptually, however, what the employer is doing is creating a common flexible program "umbrella" for all employee groups. Under the umbrella program, certain design specifics may vary. For example, a largely white-collar business unit may include vacation buying, while a manufacturing unit, because of the high cost of hiring replacement labour, may not include it.

The pricing structure might be set up to reflect geographical differences or the cost structure of the business unit. The essential framework, however, is in place to cover all employees across the organization under a common benefit structure.

Part Two

Design

Five
Health Care

§ 5.1 INTRODUCTION

Choice in health care benefits is usually a cornerstone of a flexible benefit program — a "natural" for employee choice-making. Health benefits are among the most visible, positively perceived, and frequently used of all employee benefits. The high cost (and value) of health care benefits, as well as concern over the potential for large unexpected expenses, means that employees will seriously consider which choices are best for them. The frequent availability of coverage through alternative sources, particularly the spouse's employer, dramatically increases employee interest in choices.

Before analysing how health care benefits can be incorporated into a flexible benefit plan, it is necessary to review how employer-sponsored health benefits coordinate with Canada's universal health care system. Each province and territory has a health insurance plan providing 100 per cent payment of most medical and hospital services for individuals who have been residents for at least three months. Although the provincial plans differ in some details, they all pay for the following services:

- Physicians' and surgeons' fees
- Hospital room and board at ward rates
- Hospital miscellaneous expenses
- Expenses incurred outside the province, up to the same amount that would have been paid in the province.

Several provinces also pay for certain dental expenses.

Supplemental medical plans "top up" the benefits provided under the provincial health insurance plans. According to *Hewitt Associates Spec Book*™, 100 per cent of major employers provide supplemental plans to their employees.

Supplemental plans generally cover services such as:

- hospital room and board at semi-private and, in some cases, private rates
- prescription drugs
- private duty nursing
- emergency medical expenses incurred outside Canada in excess of the amount paid by the provincial health insurance plan
- medical devices and equipment such as wheelchairs, artificial limbs, and orthopedic shoes
- ambulance services.

Most supplemental medical plans pay 100 per cent of semi-private hospital expenses and reimburse other eligible expenses at 80 to100 per cent of expenses in excess of the deductible, if any. Deductibles are generally very low; the most common deductible is $25 per individual and $50 per family per year. The majority of plans have no overall maximum payment. However, plans often have internal maximums that apply to certain services, such as private duty nursing ($5,000 or $10,000 per person per year) and vision care ($150 every twenty-four months).

A growing number of plans cover prescription drugs within the supplemental medical plan, but with a separate deductible (with many plans using between $1.00 and $9.00 per prescription) and/or differing reimbursement levels (a common arrangement being a higher level for supplemental medical and a lower level for prescription drugs). Also emerging is greater prevalence of two-tier reimbursement levels for prescription drugs (for example, 80 per cent for brand name drugs and 100 per cent for generic-equivalent drugs). Many plans also include separate out-of-pocket limits for prescription drug expenses, independent from the out-of-pocket expenses for other major medical services.

All the attention paid to health care in the past several years reflects the state of transition within the industry and in the approaches employers are utilizing to provide health care benefits to employees. Several developments demonstrate this transition:

- Consistently high cost increases over the last ten-plus years have grabbed the attention of employers and forced more active involvement in attempting to improve the management of medical and dental costs. Figure 5.1 shows that medical costs have risen at over four times the rate of general inflation, and dental costs have risen at almost three times the rate of inflation.
- Alternative health care delivery systems, such as restricted drug formularies, are now being offered by most major insurance companies through pharmacy benefit managers (PBMs).

These and other factors highlight the fact that a great deal is happening in the health care benefit arena quite apart from the trend toward flexibility. Often it is extremely difficult to separate the design of health care choices from many of the

Figure 5.1
Health Care Cost Increase

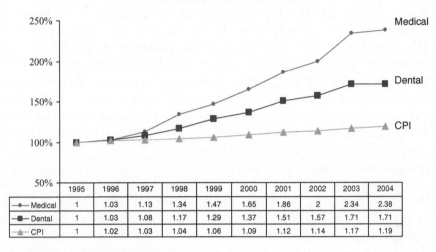

	1995	1996	1997	1998	1999	2000	2001	2002	2003	2004
Medical	1	1.03	1.13	1.34	1.47	1.65	1.86	2	2.34	2.38
Dental	1	1.03	1.08	1.17	1.29	1.37	1.51	1.57	1.71	1.71
CPI	1	1.02	1.03	1.04	1.06	1.09	1.12	1.14	1.17	1.19

Source: CLHIA and Statistics Canada

other design challenges facing employers. In fact, introduction of a flexible program is usually viewed as an opportunity for an organization to step back from the day-to-day operations and rethink overall employee benefits strategy (whether specific to flexibility or not) in health care. Frequently, a number of changes unrelated to a flexible approach are packaged with the introduction of choice-making in health care.

§ 5.2 OBJECTIVES FOR CHOICE-MAKING IN HEALTH CARE

The objectives an employer has for health care choices typically are consistent with those that apply to the overall flexible benefit program. Frequently, the major objectives relate to appealing to diverse employee needs and controlling benefit costs. Although these and other objectives were discussed in Chapter 1, some aspects of each are particularly applicable to health care benefits.

- **Appeal to employees.** Providing an employee with choices in health care recognizes that a single plan cannot best meet everyone's needs. There is a diversity of needs within any workforce, relating to the number and characteristics of dependants, the availability of coverage from other sources, anticipated utilization, financial resources (to pay premiums and claims), tolerance for risk, and so forth. Moreover, the needs of an individual are likely to change over time. Providing choices to employees responds to this diversity and gives employees greater control, with the net result being enhanced awareness and perhaps greater appreciation of the coverage.

- **Control benefit costs.** The employer's objective to control or manage benefit costs is usually strongest in health care, because costs have typically escalated much more rapidly there than in other benefits. In addition to seeking greater control over future cost increases, an organization may wish to find ways of encouraging more cost-efficient employee utilization of health care services (either less expensive providers or fewer unnecessary services).

- **Deliver tax effectiveness.** Within the health care portion of a flexible benefit program, tax efficiencies for the employee arise in two ways: either through the use of company-provided flexible credits to purchase enhanced coverage or through freeing up company funds and directing them to a health spending account when purchasing reduced coverage.

- **Merge different programs.** When two companies or two programs within a single company are being merged, it can sometimes become a very sensitive issue to require one group to give up their medical plan and move to the other group's plan. Under a flexible program, both plans may be left as options as a way of smoothing the transition.

- **Emphasize value.** Many employers believe that employees do not fully understand or appreciate the real value (cost) of their health care benefits. Through giving employees choices and presenting them with the prices of each option, it is possible to enhance employee appreciation of the true value of these benefits.

§ 5.3 TYPES OF HEALTH CARE CHOICES

Choices can be provided in any health care benefit area. Over 80 per cent of plans offer choices in medical and dental. Although the subject is covered in depth in Chapter 7, it should be noted that 90 per cent of flexible benefit programs include a health spending account that provides for pre-tax reimbursement of medical, dental, and vision expenses not covered by an employer's other plans.

A recent survey of organizations that offer choice-making programs yields the following table, which illustrates the prevalence of choices in company-sponsored health care plans:

Benefit Area	Per Cent of Employers
Medical:	84%
Dental:	86%
Health spending accounts:	90%

Source: *Hewitt Associates 2005 Survey of Employer Attitudes Towards Flexible Benefits*.

It is worth noting that the prevalence of health spending accounts has grown from 72 per cent to 90 per cent in the last ten years.

SUPPLEMENTAL MEDICAL

The most common reasons that employers provide choices in supplemental medical include costs that are rising more rapidly than other employer-provided benefits; concern about costs shifting from provincial plans; supplemental medical is highly visible; and a substantial percentage of employees may have the opportunity to be covered under a working spouse's supplemental plan.

In terms of design characteristics, a choice of two to four supplemental medical plans generally is offered to employees. The primary variations in the options are the size of deductible, the co-insurance level, and the services covered. Employees may be allowed to select no coverage as an option, although a minimum or core level of coverage is required in about a third of programs.

While many employers include cost containment features in all plan options (e.g., co-insurance, maximums, deductibles), a number of flexible programs have created a structure that includes a choice between two types of supplemental medical options — traditional indemnity and cost containment plans. The focus of cost containment options is to control the costs of health care by motivating or requiring the employee to use the most cost-effective service available. In effect, employees participating in a cost containment option become smart shoppers looking for the best service at the least cost. Indemnity plans, on the other hand, pay 80 to 100 per cent of a procedure so the incentive for an employee to shop around is low (in an 80 per cent plan) to nonexistent (in a 100 per cent plan). Some employers who offer a choice between cost containment and indemnity plans have told employees that in the future, the employer will base its subsidy on the cost increases in the cost containment plan. Additional costs incurred by employees in the indemnity plan will be picked up by employees electing it. For example, one major employer will pick up 50 per cent of cost increases in the cost containment plan. Employees in the more expensive traditional plan receive the same dollar subsidy as those in the cost containment plan. Over time, their costs are expected to rise significantly faster than those of employees electing the cost containment options.

PRESCRIPTION DRUGS

Historically, prescription drug coverage has been considered the primary element in supplemental medical or health insurance benefit plans. However, in recent years, some employers have sought to add flexibility to their benefit programs by offering separate choices for medical and prescription drug coverage.

Under this type of structure, an employer might offer a range of options for prescription drug coverage, and a separate range of options for other medical coverage. If such a de-linking of medical and drug coverage is undertaken, this places additional pressure on pricing the program properly, as the greater degree of choice offered will increase the opportunity for employees to adversely select against the plan. Specific techniques to handle this adverse selection through both plan design and pricing are discussed in Chapter 16.

A cost containment approach, discussed later in this chapter, is to create separate choices for prescription drugs and supplemental medical. The purpose is to incorporate cost containment approaches in the prescription drug options, while maintaining a more traditional approach for other medical services, such as hospital, vision, and paramedical practitioners. This allows the employer to focus cost containment initiatives on the element that has sustained the greatest cost increases and represents the largest portion (typically 60 to 80 per cent) of medical plan costs.

DENTAL

In the majority of situations, dental plans offer a choice of two or three plans — with the plans providing different coverage levels across all types of expenses (diagnostic and preventive, restorative, reconstructive, orthodontic, and so on) — or one plan having a different emphasis in coverage (such as substantial coverage for diagnostic and preventive services, but little or no coverage for major services). In some plans the employee is offered a yes or no choice — either to elect dental or take no dental coverage at all.

VISION

It is relatively infrequent to have vision benefits as a stand-alone option within a flexible program. When provided as an option under a program, vision is most often combined with a supplemental medical selection, primarily to minimize the potential for substantial adverse selection. Alternatively, it may be excluded from the supplemental medical plan altogether and covered under a health spending account.

PROVINCIAL HEALTH INSURANCE PREMIUM REIMBURSEMENT

Employers operating in Alberta or British Columbia sometimes include provincial health insurance plan premium reimbursement under their flexible plans. These two provinces have the only remaining employee premiums for provincial coverage. All other provinces fund their programs out of general revenue and/or an employer payroll tax. In the case of Ontario, an additional employee "premium" based on taxable income is collected through the income tax system.

In 2007, the Alberta and BC monthly premiums were:

	Single	Couple	Family
Alberta	$44.00	$88.00	$88.00
British Columbia	$54.00	$96.00	$108.00

For couples and families, one spouse, but not both, elects to pay the premium.

Although this is an employee premium, the majority of large employers reimburse all or part of the premium as an employee benefit. Employers who do reimburse the premium can offer two choices under the flexible benefit plan:

Option 1: Have the company pay the premium; or
Option 2: Have the spouse's employer pay the premium (if the spouse's employer is among those that do pay). Employees who elect this opt-out option will receive extra flexible credits that can be used to purchase other benefits. Typically, the credit given to employees will be less than the actual premium, producing a potential employer cost saving.

However, since there are only two provinces with premiums, most national employers handle the provincial premiums outside of the flexible benefit plan structure.

§ 5.4 GENERAL HEALTH CARE DESIGN CONSIDERATIONS

Many design considerations relate specifically to medical, prescription drugs, dental, or vision. However, a number of design issues cross the full spectrum of health care benefits. Such issues include the determination of the sources of coverage, the coverage tiers, whether employees should be allowed to opt out of coverage, the sources of funds to pay for the benefits, the relationship with a health spending account, and the overall appeal or attractiveness of the options to employees. The general considerations that cross health care areas are addressed in this section, with greater detail provided later in each of the specific benefit design sections.

SOURCES OF COVERAGE

The principal sources of health care coverage are indemnity plans and cost containment plans.

1. **Indemnity plans.** Traditional employer-sponsored plans are the primary source of supplemental medical, prescription drug, dental, and vision coverage for most organizations. These plans may be fully insured, partially insured, or self-insured, but in any event the company determines the coverage levels to be provided, and the participant generally determines which service providers (hospitals, pharmacists, dentists, and so on) are to be utilized.

2. **Cost containment plans.** A cost containment plan is a health or dental plan that has some limitations on which providers or services employees may use. The limitations are generally of two types — either an outright restriction on which covered services will be reimbursed, or an incentive through greater reimbursement to select a cost-effective procedure or service.

   The first attempt at introducing a cost containment feature in Canada was through dental capitation plans in the 1980s. A capitation plan is a dental plan sponsored by an organization that, for a fixed prepaid monthly fee, provides a broad range of dental care services as needed by the participant. These services are provided by a specified group of dentists. Such organizations are sometimes referred to as dental maintenance organizations (DMOs). Despite an extensive marketing effort by the insurance industry, capitation dental plans never caught on in Canada. The main reason for this failure was timing — in the mid- to late 1980s, when these plans were introduced, cost containment was not a major concern of many employers. A second factor contributing to their failure was the dental profession, which, in large part, objected to the capitation principle on the grounds that employees lost their freedom of choice. Another concern of dentists was that the capitation initiative would have reduced their earnings if it had become popular.

Although several attempts have been made periodically by dentists to create networks, the approach has not been demanded by employers or insurers and as a result has continued to languish as a method of dealing with dental cost management, despite annual inflationary cost increases of 5 per cent or so on average over the last ten years.

The most prevalent cost containment feature in Canada is the use of restrictive formularies for prescription drugs. This and other cost containment features will be discussed later in this chapter.

3. **Health spending accounts.** HSAs are discussed extensively in Chapter 7; they should be considered a third source of health care coverage because an HSA reimburses the participating employee for certain health care expenses. Moreover, an employee's decisions on health care options are likely to be influenced by the existence of an HSA as a pre-tax source of reimbursement for out-of-pocket expenditures.

In most cases, indemnity plans and an HSA will be incorporated as sources of coverage within a flexible benefit program. Cost containment options are being included in an increasing number of plans.

SOURCES OF FUNDS

It is quite rare for health care options to be paid either fully by the plan sponsor or completely by the employees. Generally, the employer will provide a significant subsidy, and the participating employee will pay the additional cost required to select the desired options. The employer's subsidy may differ for medical and dental; it may vary by the number of family members covered and it may be the same as or different from the subsidy in the pre-flexible program. Determining the plan sponsor's subsidy and how that subsidy is reflected in the pricing structure is covered in Chapter 14.

In nearly all flexible programs using credit-based pricing, any employee contributions for health care benefits are paid on a pre-tax basis using employer-provided flexible credits. Where credits are not sufficient to buy the desired level of coverage, they can usually be supplemented by trading off other benefits. Paying for health care benefits in this manner does not generate a taxable benefit except provincially in Quebec. Nor does it change the tax-free treatment of benefit payments.

OPTION ATTRACTIVENESS

The detailed design considerations relating to each type of health care benefit will be covered in the next sections of this chapter. However, after all of the individual health care options are designed, it usually makes good sense to review the overall design from the employee's perspective. For example, the options should be attractive to employees.

In general, simplicity in option design strengthens a positive employee response. There are sufficient complexities within a flexible program without introducing health care options that have a great number of minor and difficult-to-understand differences. A parallel structure among the options with only two or three key elements varying (such as deductibles, co-insurance and out-of-pocket maximum limits) can enhance employee understanding and appeal. If practical, it is beneficial to have this parallelism apply not only within a benefit area, such as supplemental medical, but across all health care options. For example, it may be appropriate for a program with a four-tier pricing structure in medical to use a four-tier structure in dental as well, even though the dental prices alone might not seem to justify so fine a breakdown of employee contributions.

The options also should be reviewed to ensure a reasonable spread of employee value and cost. If there are many options with only minor differences in provisions and prices, employees may struggle with adequately differentiating between the options. If there are few options with wide gaps between them, employees may feel uncomfortable with moving away from their comfort zone of current benefits. A reasonable middle ground should be struck.

An organization may have an objective of encouraging employees to select certain options — for example, a medical option with a deductible and co-insurance instead of the prior no-deductible, 100 per cent co-insurance medical option. This can be aided by adding certain attractive features to the preferred option (e.g., higher maximum plan payments), by subsidizing the prices of that option, or by the manner in which the program is communicated (including how the options are named).

Although certain options may not appeal to a broad group of employees and, therefore, participation is anticipated to be low, keeping these options may be very appropriate. Some options may be important because they meet the needs of a small, but significant, subgroup of employees. For example, a medical plan designed with very low co-insurance may be just the right fit for employees covered under their spouse's medical plan so that they can combine coverage at low cost and avoid duplication of coverage. This type of option is often called a co-ordination option.

During the election process, employees will, to varying degrees, scrutinize the option features and the price differentials to determine which option best meets their needs. The employer should anticipate this employee scrutiny and test the design and pricing to ensure that the options make sense. Options with higher price tags should provide extra coverage commensurate with the added cost.

OPT-OUT CHOICE

The issue of whether employees should be permitted to opt out of health care coverage has the potential to be one of the most emotionally charged subjects in the design of a flexible benefit program. Whether or not it actually becomes a major issue is often based on either philosophical issues or pre-flexible program practices.

For instance, many organizations currently have contributory supplemental medical plans with a small monthly contribution for employee coverage and a higher contribution level if dependants are covered. In such an environment, a small percentage of employees typically decide not to pay the contribution, however modest, and therefore, effectively opt out of medical coverage. Presumably, these employees — or almost all of them — have supplemental medical coverage from another source, although the employer usually has no verification of other coverage. An employer with this type of situation may be uncomfortable with employees forgoing coverage under a flexible program, but in reality, that bridge has already been crossed and minimum supplemental medical coverage usually is not required.

In other situations, waivers of coverage may not be permitted. This occurs frequently when the prior medical plan was non-contributory for all employees and their dependants. In such a case, neither employee nor employer is accustomed to choice and both may be particularly wary of an opt-out alternative. The mandatory nature of provincial health insurance plans, however, minimizes this problem. Even if employees opt out of the supplemental program, they are still covered for most medical expenses through the provincial plan. Because of this, most flexible benefit plans (64 per cent) permit opting out of supplemental medical. In some of these cases, they communicate the provincial program as the core.

Although the concern over an employee electing to forgo medical coverage is usually related to the potential for a large uninsured claim, different issues arise in the area of dental, because a catastrophic dental claim is extremely unlikely. If an organization has a significant concern over employees opting out of dental coverage, it usually is related to the potential for adverse selection and the ability of an individual to defer necessary dental treatment from a period without coverage to a period with coverage. This type of manipulation will lead to higher rates for all plan participants. Most employees and plan sponsors view this as unfair to participants who remain in the plan year after year. Requiring a minimum level of coverage may reduce the individual's ability or incentive to select against the plan. (See Chapter 16 for a discussion of adverse selection issues.)

If, under a flexible benefit program, an employee is allowed to opt out of health care coverage, three significant issues need to be addressed.

First, should the employee be required to provide some evidence of other coverage, particularly for supplemental medical? Due to administrative considerations, most employers simply rely on an employee's own word that they have appropriate coverage elsewhere. Sometimes this process is as simple as signing a statement on the annual enrolment form or checking a box on an online enrolment tool, while in other cases, more extensive documentation is required.

Second, should some restrictions be placed on the options that are available during subsequent enrolments? Although re-enrolment restrictions reduce the potential for adverse selection, they also diminish the attractiveness of the no-coverage choice for an employee who is uncertain about what may be needed in future years. Such restrictions have been utilized by the majority of flexible benefit plans in the several years following their introduction. However, many employers with more established plans have reduced or eliminated their selection restrictions, as experience has shown that the percentage of employees changing options each year tends to stabilize as a plan matures. In a recent survey, 68 per cent of employers with a flex plan older than one year indicated that the number of employees changing options stays about the same at each enrolment.

Third, if the flexible program provides credits to employees, how many credits should be given to an employee opting out of medical? Out of dental? The amount should be sufficient to make it worth considering for employees with other coverage, but not so high as to exceed the expected reduction in claims for those who opt out. (In general, those who are in a position to consider dropping health coverage are likely to already generate lower-than-average claims costs. For more complete discussion of credit determination, see Chapter 14, "Pricing.")

HEALTH SPENDING ACCOUNTS

A health spending account (HSA) provides reimbursement of health care expenses not paid by an employee's choice of medical, prescription drug, dental, or vision options. The existence of an HSA may not have a major effect on the design of the health care options, but there may be certain decisions that are influenced by the HSA.

The most dramatic example might be the elimination of vision care and its replacement by an HSA deposit. This might be appropriate in a situation where the vision benefits are so low as to be viewed by employees as more of an irritant than a significant benefit, and where the administrative expenses are disproportionately high relative to the benefits provided.

In other situations, employee pressure for increases in certain special benefits may be better handled by adding an HSA than by increasing benefits under the health care options. This is particularly true for quite predictable benefits that are very important to a subgroup of employees, but of minimal interest to the vast majority of employees. A prime example is orthodontia, which is usually paid at 50 per cent, up to a specified dollar limit under the dental plan. The uninsured 50 per cent and any amount over the lifetime maximum could be paid out of the HSA.

DEFAULT COVERAGES

In the initial year of a flexible program, all employees are encouraged and expected to actively enrol in the flexible benefit program, indicating their coverage choices. Reminder notices and contact with supervisors should produce close to a 100 per cent response. However, it is usually necessary to assign default coverages for employees who simply fail to enrol.

The default coverage could be any option, but might be determined as the option closest to the employee's prior coverage, the non-contributory option (if one is available), the lowest option, or no coverage. The default with respect to the family members covered might be the coverage category in effect most recently or employee-only coverage. However, employee-only coverage as a default is most often the case, due to administrative considerations in transferring dependant coverage history from the prior plan records. Many plans still do not require "positive enrolment" — whereby employees declare their eligible dependants up front — and therefore from default coverage as they have no claims history non-claiming dependants may be omitted. In subsequent years, the default coverages most often duplicate the prior year's election (regarding both type of option and covered dependants).

Decisions as to default coverages (what they should be and whether they should be explicitly communicated to employees) typically reflect the employer's attitudes toward responsibility for protecting employees versus providing employees with additional incentive to actively enrol.

CHANGING THE NUMBER OF OPTIONS OVER TIME

Once a flexible benefit plan has been operating for several years, consideration needs to be given to the enrolment in each of the options, changing employer and/or employee needs, and competitive issues. Also, in some cases, the original plan may have taken a modest approach to choice-making in order to slowly introduce employees to the concept. After a few years, many employers and employees are ready for even more flexibility.

In a 2005 survey conducted by Hewitt Associates, about half the respondents indicated that they had changed the number of options since they originally launched their plan. Most, about 60 per cent, indicated they had increased the number of options. The reasons given for the changes included:

- to better meet employee needs (67 per cent),
- keeping up with competitive practice (42 per cent),
- expanding as new benefits are offered through providers (28 per cent), and
- re-aligning with business goals and objectives (19 per cent).

(Note that the numbers do not add up to 100 per cent because many employers indicated more than one rationale for change.)

One of the chief advantages of a flexible benefit plan structure is the ability to adjust the plan designs and add to or change the choices available to employees as cost, coverage, and competitive and administrative opportunities change.

COVERAGE TIERS

The majority of health care plans have some features that reflect the number or types of individuals covered under the plan, in either program design or pricing, or both. When designing health care options, it is important to consider these features and whether every option should use the same approach.

The most common plan design features that relate to the number of individuals covered under an employee's election are family maximums on deductibles and out-of-pocket maximum limits. For example, a supplemental medical plan may have a $50 annual deductible for an individual, but may provide that after three members of a family have each incurred their $50 individual deductible (or alternatively, after all family members in total have incurred $150 in deductibles), no more deductibles will be charged to the family that year. Such a plan may also have a family out-of-pocket limit (the maximum paid by the employee in a year), which is three times the individual out-of-pocket limit. For example, once the individual or family has satisfied the deductible, co-insurance charges on remaining expenses will not exceed $250 per person or $750 per family.

Family maximums on deductibles and out-of-pocket limits — especially those that are three or more times the individual amounts — usually add very little to the cost of an option (frequently, less than 1 or 2 per cent). Often, the added security provided through these family limits will significantly exceed the incremental cost. This comfort factor may be particularly important in a flexible option with a large deductible and a high out-of-pocket limit. Even though the advantage is more significant in high-deductible plans, typically all supplemental medical options within a flexible program will have parallel features in this area.

On the pricing side, the family-coverage issue is of greater significance. Although it is rare for a contributory plan to use a one-tier pricing approach, a completely non-contributory plan effectively has a one-tier price structure — the

same price regardless of number or type of dependants. Plans with very low employee contributions have often utilized a two-tier pricing approach — one cost for
employee-only coverage and a higher cost for family coverage, regardless of the
number of dependants. As employee contributions for family coverage increase,
the incentive grows to subdivide the family category to reflect the expected cost
impact of varying the numbers or types of dependants. Subdividing by size of the
family unit also helps minimize equity concerns in terms of the employee covering only one dependant paying the same amount as an employee covering several
dependants. In these situations, three- and four-tier pricing approaches are most
common. The most typical breakdowns include:

- Employee-only, family
- Employee-only, employee-plus-one, employee-plus-two-or-more dependants
- Employee-only, employee-plus-spouse-or-children, employee-plus-spouse-
  and-children
- Employee-only, employee-plus-spouse, employee-plus-children, employee-
  plus-spouse-plus-children.
- Employee-only, employee-plus-one, employee-plus-two, employee-plus-three-
  or-more-dependants.

The approaches that distinguish between types of dependants (spouse versus children), rather than simply the number of dependants, tend to favour single parents
with more than one child, by allowing them to pay less than the full-family rate.
This approach may also be somewhat more equitable in that an average child tends
to generate lower claims than an adult, especially for medical benefits.

A more extensive discussion of pricing issues by family status is included in
Chapter 14.

CO-ORDINATION WITH OTHER PLANS

All health care plans, whether flexible or not, need to have clearly defined rules that
outline what is paid in the event that an individual incurring claims is covered by
two employer plans. One of the plans will be primary (i.e., paying first) and the
other will be secondary (i.e., paying second). When only one plan is involved (or
the plan is the primary payer), the benefits to be paid are clear, that is, whatever
the primary (or only) plan normally would provide. When two employer plans are
involved, the issues become more complicated. Which plan is the primary versus
the secondary payer? And what benefits will the plan pay, if it is determined to be
secondary?

In Canada, the Canadian Life and Health Insurance Association (CLHIA), to
which about 95 per cent of insurers belong, has published guidelines for the co-
ordination of claims when an individual is covered by more than one group insurance plan. Under the CLHIA guidelines, the employee's claims go to the employer's

plan first, then to the spouse's plan as second payer. For dependent children, the plan covering the parent with the earlier birthday in the calendar year is the primary payer.

Traditionally, co-ordination has meant that employees with dual coverage could receive up to 100 per cent payment of covered expenses. A secondary plan was required to pay its regular benefits, but to no more than the amount necessary to pay the full amount of the claim in combination with the primary plan. The situation is in direct conflict with the goals most employers have for encouraging employees to reduce medical utilization, and is often believed to be unfair to other employees with only one source of coverage. As a result, some self-insured plans ignored the traditional approach to co-ordination of benefits and provided less-than-full payment in duplicate coverage situations through alternate methods of co-ordinating payments between plans.

Employers in the United States have been aggressive when it comes to dealing with co-ordination of benefits. One of the common co-ordination techniques used in the United States is known as maintenance of benefits or benefits-less-benefits. Under this approach, the deductibles and co-payment amounts are preserved when the plan is secondary, because the secondary plan defines its payment as the difference between what it would normally pay if it were the sole plan, and what the other plan actually pays. Thus the covered individual does not receive full payment from the combination of the two plans.

Consideration of a maintenance of benefits (or some other intermediate) approach to handling two-plan coverage is particularly appropriate when introducing a flexible program with choices in health care. Under the traditional co-ordination of benefits method, the individual covered under two plans would often receive full payment of any claim, regardless of the option selected. On the other hand, the maintenance of benefits approach would retain a difference in payments between the options when the flexible program is secondary (as is the case in the absence of another plan) and avoid providing full payment of the total claim (as is also the case in the absence of another plan). With more two-income families and double-digit increases in supplemental medical plan costs, Canadian employers may also want to consider alternatives to 100 per cent payment of covered expenses.

A few Canadian employers introduced this approach several years ago but others have not followed suit, in part because it is seen as being against the intent of providing 100 per cent coverage when co-ordinating between two plans. As a result, insurance carriers' claims systems have not been adjusted to accommodate a modified co-ordination of benefits approach, so it is still rarely seen in Canada.

Instead, a plan design approach to co-ordination that has become quite popular is the "Co-ordination" option. Since co-ordination is limited to a maximum of 100 per cent, but many plans provide at least 75 per cent coverage, combining two such 75 per cent plans results in an employee being "overinsured." Under the co-ordination approach, the co-insurance level is 20 to 25 per cent. This is intended to dovetail with another employer's plan that might provide 80 per cent or 75 per cent coverage. In combination, the employee obtains 100 per cent coverage with minimal or no overinsurance. Additionally, the price tag for this coverage is quite low due to the low level of reimbursement, which means an employee will often have excess credits remaining to deposit in a health spending account to provide for any additional expenses not fully covered, or covered at all, by either plan.

EMPLOYMENT OF COUPLES

Sometimes, a significant number of married couples work for the same organization. When both spouses are employed at the same organization, the supplemental medical and other health care plans need to specify any special rules. For example, can an employee be covered both as an employee and as a dependant? Should one employee elect family coverage and the other elect no coverage? Do the same co-ordination of benefits provisions apply to an individual covered twice under the plan, as would apply to an individual covered by different employer plans?

These issues have typically been resolved under the prior health care plans, and often parallel decisions are appropriate when moving into a flexible program. The subject should be re-addressed, however, particularly if there are significant changes in pricing (to either level or structure of employee contributions) or co-ordination of benefit provisions (which may eliminate any incentive to be covered twice by the same plan).

If the flexible program specifically identifies credits for employees from the medical plan, and these credits vary by family status or number of covered dependants, this issue becomes more complex. Do both employees receive the same credits they would have received had their spouse been employed elsewhere? This may seem to be the most equitable (especially to employees), but could significantly increase the organization's cost, because both employees do not receive the full medical value in a traditional plan. Should each employee be allowed to cover himself or herself and only one be allowed to cover the children? Can the organization even adequately identify where these situations exist? In these situations, a balance must be struck between cost and equity as well as administrative considerations.

BUILD YOUR OWN PLANS

A trend beginning to emerge in the United States that could ultimately be reflected in Canadian flexible benefit plan design is known as "build your own plan." Essentially, this approach allows employees to select various levels of coverage for various types of services. Originally called "cafeteria" plans by many, this approach goes even farther, by allowing employees to select among various vendors the level of deductible, co-insurance, and often the applicable maximums. The ability of online enrolment tools to swiftly calculate and show the costs associated with an employee's choices has enhanced the appeal of this approach. A comparable example might be how individuals currently choose their home or automobile insurance from a variety of insurers, selecting the level of deductible, as well as the type and level of coverage.

§ 5.5 DESIGN OF SUPPLEMENTAL MEDICAL

IN GENERAL

For the same reasons that supplemental medical is usually considered the best candidate for choice-making within a flexible benefit program, the design of supplemental medical choices is typically the most time-consuming aspect of developing the flexible program. There are numerous challenging issues surrounding the development of medical choices: for example, how many should there be, in what ways should they differ, and how should adverse selection be minimized? Decisions on these issues are most often complicated by other medical design changes also under consideration: for example, the addition of vision coverage, an increase in deductible levels, and introduction of cost management features. The pages that follow address the considerations applicable to these design issues, with an emphasis on those aspects that are unique to or accentuated by the introduction of medical choice-making.

STRUCTURE OF OPTIONS

Detailing the design features of each supplemental medical option usually begins with an outline of the basic structure of medical choices. How many options should be made available to employees? Will the current plan be offered as an option? What will be the lowest option? How will the supplemental medical options differ?

Most often, the lowest plan option is viewed as a catastrophic-protection or safety-net option. An individual covered under this option would have virtually no protection from the higher-frequency, low-cost claims. But in the event of a major unexpected medical problem generating a large claim, such as a large prescription drug claim or an out-of-Canada expense, this option would serve to protect the individual from high expenses.

High Option

Employees often have a love-hate relationship with their supplemental medical coverage. While they may sometimes complain about what the plan fails to cover and how long it takes to get a claim paid, they tend to react with great concern if the plan is cut back or restructured. And if the current plan is seen by management as being inefficient or encouraging over-utilization of medical services, one objective of the flexible program may be to move away from that plan.

If the existing medical plan is not viewed as an appropriate long-term choice, the issue of whether it should be maintained as a flexible option can be difficult. Keeping the current plan as one of the options can help smooth the transition to the flexible program and soften any employee concerns that might arise. This may be especially important for an organization that has undergone a great deal of turmoil or whose employees are particularly suspicious or where other employee groups (such as union employees) are covered under a similar supplemental medical plan. On the other hand, a flexible benefit plan is a way for an employer to signal a change and design a new plan that better meets company and employee needs for the foreseeable future. An added advantage of not including the current plan as an option comes in the communication of the plan: employees cannot simply take the easy way out and just choose what they had before — instead they must consider each of the options to decide what is best for them.

If the claims experience under the options will be used to set prices in future years, it is quite likely that the high option will become more and more expensive relative to the other options, thereby eventually pricing itself out of existence. If the gradual increases serve to move employees into more cost-effective options, then the elimination of the pre-flexible plan can be made in a future year without disrupting many employees. However, this approach may simply serve to defer employee reaction that might have been dealt with satisfactorily in the first year. Deciding which strategy is preferable (immediate elimination or gradual elimination through pricing) is fundamentally a judgment call that needs to be made by each organization.

The bottom line for most flexible programs is that the current medical plan, or a design very similar, is almost always offered as one of the initial supplemental medical options. Occasionally, some tinkering is necessary to make it parallel to the other options or to modify certain features for cost-management purposes.

Often employees welcome an option that is even richer than the existing plan, and are willing to pay the added cost. This is particularly true where the current plan has significant employee co-payments through co-insurance and deductibles, or does not cover certain expenses, such as vision, at adequate levels. However, if offered, such an option typically will result in high claims experience and ultimately higher prices in subsequent years. Therefore, the plan designers must weigh the employee demands for a top-notch medical plan against the potential negative reaction when prices rise in the future.

Determining the level of coverage that is appropriate for the high supplemental medical option will usually be based on a number of considerations, including:

- Provisions of the pre-flexible supplemental medical plan
- Medical benefits for other employee groups within the organization
- Employee relations environment
- Employer financial objectives and/or cost-sharing goals
- Competitive practice.

Low Option

In many situations, the low supplemental medical option is defined by whether employees should be allowed to opt out of medical coverage. If employees are allowed to waive coverage, the lowest option is no coverage. If not, the provisions of the low option need to be established.

Defining the level of expense that a typical employee could absorb in this type of situation is quite subjective. However, the considerations include:

- What portion of the employee group is likely to have coverage available through a working spouse? This is probably the subgroup with the lowest need for protection.
- How much can the typical employee afford to pay in supplemental medical expenses in a particular year? Although this may be difficult to define, the answer is largely a function of pay level. An investment banking firm with an average income of $100,000 will likely come to a very different conclusion from a retailer with an average pay of $35,000.
- What responsibility does the organization assume to protect employees from the risk of making poor decisions? If concern is high, the spread between the highest and the lowest options should be narrowed.

Typically, employers take two approaches to designing the lowest available option: a "catastrophic" design and an "out-of-Canada" design.

- Catastrophic design: The catastrophic design has a substantial up-front deductible (often $500 or more), 80 per cent or lower payment of remaining expenses, and a high out-of-pocket limit (sometimes as high as $1,000 or more). In some cases, the deductible may be lower (for example, $100 for a relatively low-paying organization) or substantially higher (for example, $1,000 for a high-paying organization that almost decided to allow employees to opt out completely).

   Most often the option has family deductible and out-of-pocket limits of two or three times the individual amounts. However, as the individual deductible and out-of-pocket limits become larger, organizations sometimes reduce the family maximum to minimize some of the risk involved. At the extreme, for a very large deductible option (for example, $1,000), the deductible and out-of-pocket limit may be per family amounts. This adds very little extra cost to the option because it is unlikely that a family selecting such a low option would have more than one individual with very large expenses in a single year.

   It is up to the employer to determine what level of employee out-of-pocket expense is to be considered "catastrophic." In some cases, $1,000 can be a substantial expense for a lower-paid employee, while in other cases, $5,000 or more may be deemed appropriate. Care must be taken over time to index the deductibles and limits so that they maintain their relationship to inflationary cost increases; otherwise the employer's share of the option's cost will increase.

- Out-of-Canada design: The out-of-Canada design provides coverage only for emergency expenses incurred while outside Canada or, in some cases, also while outside the employee's province of residence. The rationale behind the design is that emergency expenses incurred while travelling, particularly in the United States, can be extremely expensive for an individual, and provincial health care plans provide modest coverage at best for such expenses (see Section 5.12 for more on provincial coverage outside Canada). However, the cost of providing insurance coverage for this risk is relatively low, which translates into a low price tag for the option.

   By having an option that covers these expenses at a minimum, employers do not have to be concerned that employees will forget to purchase individual travel coverage, and employees will have protection against claims that can be "catastrophic."

In designing the low option plan, consideration should be given to the level of subsidy the company will make toward the flexible plan. If a fixed dollar amount will be provided to all employees, often the low option will generate cash back to the employee who elects to opt down. If the company has a substantial number of employees who are not participating in the pre-flexible plan, offering this "cash back" incentive will create an immediate cash outlay to each of these individuals as well as providing coverage that may be duplicative. The design of the low option, therefore, should be revisited for consistency with the company's financial objectives once a pricing strategy is selected. Chapter 14 explores this subject in greater detail.

Other Options

Once the highest and the lowest supplemental medical options are defined, other options can be created to fill in between the extremes. How much filling in is appropriate depends a great deal on how wide the gap is. If the richest plan is the prior high-value medical plan and the lowest option is no coverage, there is a wide gap. In that case, a greater need exists for intermediate options. By contrast, if the highest and the lowest options both provide 80 per cent coverage with deductibles of $0 and $100 respectively, less need exists for intermediate options.

   Today, in a typical situation, employees are offered three or four choices, with all the options structured in a fairly parallel manner in terms of reasonable progression in deductible amounts, co-insurance percentages, and out-of-pocket maximum limits. Sometimes, however, the options also differ in terms of which expenses are covered. Frequently, certain expenses that are covered under the highest level option, such as semi-private hospital coverage and vision care, are excluded from the lower options to help differentiate them from the other plans.

Many flexible programs introduced in recent years include one or two cost containment options. These options contain features to help reduce the overall cost of health care benefits, by either giving the employee an incentive to elect the lowest cost procedure or service, or including a disincentive for using the expensive elements. Typical cost containment features are discussed in Sections 5.9 and 5.10.

If the prior supplemental medical plan is maintained as the high option, but the organization wishes to encourage employees to select or at least seriously consider the lower plan options, placing higher lifetime maximums or lower out-of-pocket limits on the lower options could help to accomplish that result. In practice, however, different lifetime maximums on the options may not be particularly meaningful under a program in which employees have the opportunity to make annual changes in their coverage choices.

Another consideration is whether or not to include any out-of-pocket maximum protection and, if so, at what level. Some plans provide no out-of-pocket maximum limit at all — employees continue to pay their share of the co-insurance no matter what their claim level is — while others provide out-of-pocket maximum in only one or two of the options. This is particularly true where the highest option provides 100 per cent co-insurance. If employees want full protection, they must take the highest option, and pay the highest price tag. Similar to the considerations under the low option catastrophic plan, regular indexing of the out-of-pocket maximum limits is important due to the erosion caused by high medical cost inflation.

An example of a fairly common supplemental medical option structure is illustrated in Example 5.1 below.

Example 5.1
Typical Supplemental Medical Options

Option	Deductible (Individual/ Couple/ Family)	Plan Payments	Out-of-Pocket Limit	Hospital	Vision
Premium	None	90%	$250/$500/ $750	Semi-private/ private	$200
Standard	$50/$100/ $150	80%	$500/$1,000/ $1,500	Semi-private	$150
Cost Containment	$50/$100/$150 (plus $5 per prescription)	80% (80% formulary; 40% non-formulary drugs)	$500/$1,000/ $1,500	Semi-private to $150/day	$150
Co-ordination	None	20%	None	Not covered	$150
Catastrophic	$1,000/$1,000/ $1,000	80%	$2,000/$2,000/ $2,000	Not covered	Not covered

§ 5.6 DESIGN OF PRESCRIPTION DRUGS OPTIONS

When designing a flexible benefit plan, prescription drug benefits are frequently considered separately from other supplemental medical coverages. This is true whether the flexible plan provides stand-alone prescription drug options or integrates them with the supplemental medical options. Prescription drugs are considered separately because the issues are unique, the cost impact is substantial, and drugs are administered separately from the other coverages. The issues discussed in this section apply to all prescription drug coverages, whether or not they are offered as stand-alone options.

DESIGN CONSIDERATIONS

Pharmacists generally price prescription drugs based on several components. The three key ones are the cost of the ingredient, the ingredient mark-up, and the cost of dispensing. The cost of the ingredient and the mark-up on the ingredient are, in many cases, regulated by the federal and provincial authorities. However, the dispensing fees can vary dramatically from pharmacy to pharmacy.

In Ontario some pharmacists charge in the $10 to $13 range, while others, particularly firms using their pharmacy operations as a loss leader, charge as little as $2 or $4. Those at the higher end claim that they are offering a much higher level of professional service than those that discount their fees.

Because of this variation, a number of employers have built features into their plans to encourage employees to shop for the lowest-cost pharmacy. Some of the features commonly used include:

- Reimburse a percentage (e.g., 50 per cent) of the dispensing fee to encourage employees to shop for the lowest-cost provider.
- Cap or limit amount they will reimburse towards the dispensing fee component of the price. For example, one plan reimburses 80 per cent of prescription ingredient costs without limit plus 80 per cent of the dispensing fee, up to $5.
- Provide no coverage for dispensing fees. In some organizations this may be communicated to employees as a deductible or co-pay with each prescription equal to the amount of the dispensing fee.

These features are easy to introduce in provinces such as Ontario, where the pharmacy is required to post the dispensing fee in the store and to separately identify the amount on the receipt. In other provinces, however, where there is no separate identification on the receipt, this feature may require the use of a drug card with an electronic data interchange (EDI) feature. By using the card, the administrator instantly knows the dispensing fee charged by the particular pharmacy.

FORMULARY VARIATIONS BY OPTION

In most cases, when a company introduces a drug formulary (list of drugs paid by the plan) within either an existing flexible benefit program or as part of a new plan, it introduces the drug formulary into all plan options. Given the complexity involved with a new drug formulary, most companies desire to simplify the program for employees as much as possible, which means using the same formulary structure across the options, using differences in deductibles, co-pays, or co-insurance to differentiate the plan options.

In some cases, though, companies have designed flexible benefit plans using a drug formulary in most options, but omitting it in a specific plan option. The two circumstances where these non-formulary options are successful in a plan utilizing a drug formulary are:

- Not including the formulary in a co-ordination of benefits plan option (e.g., a plan option which provides only 20 per cent reimbursement). In this case, since the employer plan is the secondary coverage used by the employee, this coverage will not generally drive the decision about what drugs the employee receives. In addition, since formulary information is less likely to be available to the plan member at the point of sale, it makes it more difficult for employees to understand what the plan would pay for a given drug, or what alternatives might be available.

- Some plans have excluded the formulary from their highest medical or drug option. In this case, the employer's rationale is to ease the introduction of a formulary by continuing to offer one option with broader coverage not restricted by the formulary. Generally in this situation, the long-term employer funding level is tied to the plan option with the formulary, meaning that as the cost of the non-formulary option increases faster than the other options, the price employees need to pay to participate in this option will also increase. In this way the company is able to balance its need to control costs by funding the formulary option, while allowing employees to pay for the flexibility of a non-formulary option.

Section 5.10 provides additional background on formularies currently in use in Canada.

Coverage for Non-Formulary Drugs

One of the most challenging decisions when designing flexible benefit options containing prescription drug coverage is how to reimburse non-formulary or non-preferred drugs.

Under the provincial plans and some supplemental plans, formulary drugs are reimbursed at one level, while non-formulary drugs can be treated in one of three

Example 5.2
Typical Prescription Drug Option

	Option 1	Option 2	Option 3
Formulary	N/A	All drugs legally requiring a prescription	Managed therapeutic formulary
Co-insurance	No coverage	20%	Formulary @ 80% Non-formulary @ 50%
Dispensing Fee	N/A	20%	80% to $5

	Option 4	Option 5
Formulary	Managed therapeutic formulary	All drugs legally requiring a prescription
Co-insurance	Formulary @ 100% Non-formulary @ 70%	100%
Dispensing Fee	100% to $5	100%

general ways:

- Reimbursed at a significantly reduced level (e.g., half of the formulary drug);
- Reimbursed in certain circumstances (e.g., through an exception process); or
- Not reimbursed at all.

An example of a prescription drug plan incorporating the features described above is illustrated in Example 5.2.

§ 5.7 DESIGN OF VISION CARE

Most of the organizations with flexible programs include vision choices in at least one of the options under the program. Where a choice does occur, it is generally part of supplemental medical. It is unusual to create a stand-alone vision care plan, due to the risk of adverse selection.

If there is existing vision coverage that is generating concerns over the value provided relative to the expense and administrative effort, there is an alternative to maintaining the status quo. The employer terminates the vision plan, converts the employer contribution into flexible credits, and positions the health spending account as an alternative means of covering these expenses.

Vision care preferred providers have developed to provide discounts from normal retail charges. Discounts on materials (lenses and frames) can be substantial, sometimes approaching 50 per cent of retail cost.

A recent development triggered by reductions in provincial plan coverage is to introduce a separate maximum for eye exams in order to provide coverage for those who wish to monitor their visual health, but who do not require vision correction.

§ 5.8 DESIGN OF DENTAL

IN GENERAL

Almost 90 per cent of the organizations with flexible benefit programs include dental choices as an element of the program. The attractions for the employer and for the employee are quite similar to the ones that make supplemental medical the most prevalent area for choice-making. The plan design process is typically less complex for dental benefits than for medical benefits, and for this reason is often used as the first benefit for decision-making during enrolment, so that employees can more readily understand the choice-making process.

Although cost increases in dental have been below those associated with medical plans, as shown in Figure 5.1 on page 87, nevertheless the increases are in excess of general inflationary trends.

DENTAL FEE GUIDE

Part of the reason for the cost increases is that dental services are typically priced based on the *Canadian Dental Association Fee Guide*. This is a guideline for practising dentists to use in pricing their services, and, in most cases, is followed by the employer. Each year the fee guide is updated to take into account the changes in the mix of services in dental treatments as well as operating costs in dental practices. Figure 5.2 below shows the changes in the fee guide over the last five years.

Figure 5.2
Dental Fee Guide Increases from 2002 to 2006

Province	2006	2005	2004	2003	2002
Alberta	n/a	4%	4 to5.5%	3.8%	n/a
British Columbia	3.5%	3.4%	4.5%	3.3%	2.3%
Manitoba	3.5%	3.5%	3.2%	3.3%	3.6%
New Brunswick	2.6%	3%	3%	3%	3%
Newfoundland	3.7%	3.2%	1.6%	3.9%	3%
Northwest Territories and Nunavut	3.4%	3.2%	6%	3.1%	2.1%
Nova Scotia	3.2%	3.3%	3.4%	3.9%	2.6%
Ontario	3.6%	2.6%	4%	3% to 4%	2.5% to 3%
Prince Edward Island	2%	2.1%	1.8%	2.9%	n/a
Quebec	4.8%	2.8%	3.9%	2.5%	3.4%
Saskatchewan	4.9%	4.1%	5.7%	4.1%	3.4%
Yukon	3.4%	3.4%	4.9%	4%	3%

Each province has its own dental association; however, in general, the Canadian Association's fee recommendations are adopted by the provincial fee guides. The exceptions are Quebec and Alberta. In Alberta, the fee guide was abandoned by the Alberta Dental Association in 1998, allowing dentists to charge whatever the market would bear. Since that time, insurers have maintained a *de facto* fee guide for Alberta services. For further discussion of this topic, see Section 5.11, "Provincial Issues."

STRUCTURE OF OPTIONS

The design decisions in dental planning relate primarily to the number and type of options to be made available to employees.

Types of Options

As discussed earlier, employees are frequently allowed to opt out of dental coverage within flexible programs, because the risk to the employee of doing so is modest. In such a program, the lowest option has already been defined as no coverage.

Usually, the organization introducing the flexible program already has a dental plan in place that is operating with reasonable success, and the employer is experiencing little pressure to modify it. When this is the case, it is often an easy decision to maintain the existing dental plan as an option.

In some cases, the employer provides two options in dental, the current plan or no coverage. This is essentially a yes or no choice. However, if there are concerns about the current dental plan, these might be addressed in one of three ways under the flexible program:

- Modify the existing plan. For example, the existing plan might be quite satisfactory except that the annual maximum is less than competitive, or the employer wishes to limit the reimbursement of recall exams to once every twelve months. Either change could be made with essentially the same plan offered under the flexible program.
- Add one or two options. Possibly the existing plan provides maximum benefits or a dental fee guide that have not been updated in some time, or simply pays benefits that are lower than many employees believe are competitive. In such a case, the current plan could be maintained as an option and a new plan introduced that meets the need for increased coverage. Or the current plan might have a high level of employee contributions, in which case a lower coverage option (with no or lower employee contributions) might be added.
- Drop dental coverage. If a plan has generated a great deal of employee dissatisfaction (either due to low benefit levels or poor claims handling), and if the plan sponsor is concerned over the level of administrative cost and effort to maintain the plan, one alternative might be to terminate the dental plan,

convert the prior company cost into credits for employees, and simply allow employees who expect to have dental expenses to use these credits in a health spending account. Those who do not expect significant dental expenses could use their credits for other purposes.

Alternatively, one option may be designed to emphasize diagnostic and preventive expenses with marginal (or no coverage) for major expenses. This may be a replacement for the no-coverage option in order to encourage continuing visits to the dentist for exams, X-rays, and cleanings.

There are both broad and detailed design issues that need to be addressed when designing a new dental plan or creating additional options. These include size and type of deductible, whether the deductible should be waived for certain types of expenses, plan payment levels for various types of expenses (diagnostic and preventive, accidental dental, restorative, major, orthodontic, etc.), which annual fee guide will apply (e.g., current, one-year lag, two-year lag), and maximums (annual and lifetime). These are important subjects for the design of dental plans generally, but they will be addressed here only in the context of choice-making programs.

If alternative dental plans are to be offered, the alternatives can be designed to provide higher (or lower) coverage across most types of expenses. The differences in benefits and prices should be sufficient to provide employees with meaningful choices.

Often the across-the-board differences in benefit levels do not apply to orthodontic benefits. Orthodontic expenses are substantial, generally quite predictable, and typically somewhat deferrable. Plan benefits for orthodontia are also usually subject to a separate lifetime maximum, such as $2,000 or $2,500. To reduce the potential for employee manipulation (that is, making a selection based on what is known to be an upcoming expense), and because of the problems associated with different lifetime maximums under a program with choices, all dental options could have the same lifetime orthodontia maximum.

Number of Options

The predictability of dental expenses makes it important to achieve a high level of participation in each plan option so as to minimize adverse selection concerns. Adequate participation is achieved partially by minimizing the number of plans, but also by pricing approaches and restrictions on changes in coverage. Therefore, plans rarely offer more than three or four options.

SPECIAL DENTAL CONSIDERATIONS

Co-ordination with Other Plans

As is the case with medical, dental plans need to be structured to co-ordinate with other employers' plans. But the scope of the issue is narrower in dental, for several reasons. First, situations with duplicate coverage are less frequent. Many smaller employers do not provide dental insurance to their employees, and those that do often require contributions for participation. Second, for many claims, each plan may pay less than 50 per cent of the submitted claim, due to deductibles, employee co-payments (which may be as high as 50 per cent for major expenses), and expenses exceeding the applicable fee guide. So, the total coverage does not often exceed 100 per cent — the point at which most traditional co-ordination of benefits provisions become effective.

As discussed for supplemental medical plans, a "co-ordination" option also works well for dental as most employer plans do not provide 100 per cent coverage for most dental expenses.

Anticipatory Behaviour

Under a flexible program, the communication with employees usually starts at least three months before the new benefits become effective. Changes in benefits being provided by the plans may encourage an acceleration (if benefits are being reduced) or a deferral (if benefits are being increased) of visits to the dentist. This may not be a significant problem, but probably merits consideration, both when designing the options and when discussing the timing of the communication steps. In many cases, this situation can be dealt with by carrying forward employees' claims histories from the prior plan, rather than making a fresh start with new limits under the new designs.

Adverse Selection

As we have seen, the opportunity for an employee to select against the plan is much greater in dental than in medical. The impact of this adverse selection can be moderated by effective plan design, pricing, and restrictions on changes.

§ 5.9 HEALTH CARE COST CONTROL

Over the last ten years, health care expenditures have risen significantly faster than other payroll costs. The forces driving the rapid escalation in costs include new technology, cost shifting from provincial to employer plans, and increased utilization of services — none of which is expected to diminish in the near future. As a result, employers continue to look for new ways to provide health care benefits, while slowing the overall rate of escalation in costs, or even reducing the company's share of the total cost. While a flexible program can help an employer gain control over its share of costs, the mechanism of choice-making alone is limited in its capacity to slow the rate of increase. The purpose of this section is to explore in further detail the potential to control health care costs through a flexible program, and to explain ways of incorporating cost containment in a flexible program design.

GENERAL COST-SAVING CHARACTERISTICS OF FLEXIBLE PROGRAMS

A flexible program helps employers control both the rate of increase and the absolute level of their share of medical (as well as other benefit) costs in several ways. These include reducing pressure to add new employer-paid benefits, slowing the rate of increase in health care costs, shifting a greater share of costs to employees, and reducing duplicate coverage for dependants.

Reduced Pressure for New Benefits

One of the clearest ways to illustrate how flexible programs operate to reduce pressure to add new benefits is with vision care. Typically, employers were adding to vision benefit limits at company expense. When health care costs began to soar, this trend slowed down. Now, some employers with flexible programs simply introduce health spending accounts as a vehicle for reimbursing vision care expenses. Employees are given the opportunity to fund the account by opting down or away from other benefits. In this way, these employers avoid accepting full responsibility for funding vision benefits (thereby saving anywhere from $50 to $100 per employee per year), while still being responsive to the segment of the employee population interested in vision care. In effect, these companies save money by avoiding spending on benefits that would be appreciated by only a portion of the workforce.

In the future, innovative benefit areas under consideration might include long-term care (e.g., nursing home coverage) and critical illness insurance. Both face the same stumbling blocks as vision — employer reluctance to increase benefit costs and appeal to only narrow (albeit sometimes vocal) segments of the workforce. Employers with flexible programs, however, can more easily introduce these types of benefits under the umbrella of choice-making. While government requirements restrict the choices that may be provided on a tax-favoured basis, it is not uncommon for employers to offer, as part of the overall flexible program, additional options paid for by the employee through after-tax payroll deductions.

Lower Rates of Increase in Supplemental Medical Costs

Choices in the medical area can slow the rate of increase in health care claims, but usually not dramatically. Cost increases are moderated because employees who shift to medical options with greater cost sharing are more deliberate in their use of services as a result of participating in the "purchase" of services. However, the magnitude of the impact on claims is limited by three factors. First, typically less than half of employees shift away from the highest option available in the first few years of program operation (unless the pricing structure forces the issue). Therefore, utilization savings occur for only a portion of the workforce. Moreover, the profile of the employee most likely to opt down (or out) is not the high utilizer of plan benefits. The relatively small percentage of individuals that drives the majority of a company's claims in a given year will most likely be enrolled in the richest medical option. This often will hold true even when option pricing makes the high option plan a poor economic choice. Second, since employers' plans are supplemental to the underlying provincial coverage, the ability of employers to influence utilization is limited. For example, there is little an employer can do to reduce the length of a hospital stay, as long as the province fully pays for ward accommodation. Third, when an employee "opts down," the full impact on utilization is felt in the first year. No further decreases are likely to occur from year to year, until the employee moves to an even lower option. In fact, fixed-dollar deductibles and out-of-pocket limits have diminishing influence on utilization over time, because a greater share of expenses will exceed any given fixed-dollar amount. For example, if 70 per cent of individuals have expenses under $500 this year, then only about 65 per cent will likely fall under that amount next year, as a result of inflation and increased utilization.

Ultimately, employees and their covered dependants make the decision to see a doctor, submit to tests or treatments, take prescription drugs, or enter the hospital. Annual communication with employees concerning flexible choices offers employers a significant and regular opportunity to educate employees on appropriate use of health care services. Well-communicated information to employees on their importance, responsibility, and rights in this process can affect utilization.

Greater Cost Sharing with Employees

A flexible program can slow the rate of employer cost increases by simply shifting costs to employees (e.g., increasing deductibles and out-of-pocket limits for existing options, limiting the rate of increase in flexible credits, or increasing the price tags for the options). Simply stated, for credit-based pricing:

$$\text{employer costs} = \text{claims} + \text{expenses} + \text{credits} - \text{price tags}$$

To the degree that an employer limits the rate of increase in claims (through benefit provisions, cost management programs, and education) or credits, or increases price tags faster than overall inflation in medical, flexibility can successfully slow the rate of employer cost increases. However, employee relations concerns will limit the willingness of many employers to shift costs significantly, particularly at the outset of a flexible program.

For plans using a net pricing approach:

$$\text{employer costs} = \text{claims} + \text{expenses} - \text{prices}$$

The ability to control costs through pricing for net pricing plans is less than for credit-based plans, because credit-based pricing offers two pricing levers that can be used to manage costs — credits and price tags; while net pricing only has one lever — prices.

Less Duplicate Coverage for Dependants

Flexibility can help an employer slow the rate of increase in dollars spent per employee by encouraging employees to waive duplicate coverage for dependants. Employers who have traditionally provided coverage at low or no cost to employees often want to continue to do so, if employees truly need the coverage. But many employers are no longer willing to bear the full burden of covering dependants when another employer is simply shifting its own fair share of the cost by pushing employees out of its own plan through relatively high contributions for employee and dependant coverage. Employers can avoid this "dependant shifting" by introducing or increasing employee contributions, but many are reluctant to hurt employees who truly need family coverage. A flexible program helps them accomplish the same thing without "takeaways," by introducing flexible credits for those who do waive duplicate dependant coverage, provided the credits do not over-compensate employees for the trade-off. Alternatively, an option design that provides a low level of coverage that can be combined with another employer's higher level of coverage can serve to move employees with dependants to a low-cost, low-level option and out of the higher options with more coverage.

COST SAVINGS THROUGH COST CONTAINMENT PLAN DESIGN

While flexible programs help address cost issues for a wide range of benefits (e.g., life, disability, vacation), they are not the sole answer to controlling costs. The cost of health care services is likely to continue to increase faster than inflation or wages, even when flexible options are available in the medical area. Cost increase factors include new technology, increased utilization due to an aging workforce, new drugs, increased numbers of retirees, and provincial cost shifting, as well as general price inflation; all these factors affect employers with flexible medical options just as they do employers with traditional plans.

Flexible programs address cost management by maximizing value to employees through offering choice, while at the same time controlling employer dollars. In addition, cost containment in the medical area focuses on savings through tight management of both employee utilization of services and provider costs. Earlier versions of this book had predicted that health care cost management tactics would become much more aggressive in the latter half of the 1990s, but as of the mid-2000s that has not been the case. Employers and employees absorbed the majority of cost increases over the last decade, while keeping plan design structures intact overall. In part, this is because the delivery of health care services in the Canadian marketplace has not yet changed to provide appropriate incentives to implement more effective cost containment initiatives.

Cost containment arrangements vary significantly among plans and employers. At one extreme, a few employers are designing medical plans to direct all employees to a network or limited list of providers or services through strong financial incentives. These employers expect to save on health care expenses because all employees are brought into a single risk pool, preferential provider prices are negotiated, and use of services is tightly monitored. Those employees who choose to use providers not on the preferred list incur large deductibles and high co-insurance amounts.

DESIGNING A FLEXIBLE COST CONTAINMENT PLAN

The issues involved in introducing cost containment differ for employers with existing flexible programs, in that revision to options to incorporate cost containment elements needs to be accomplished with as little disruption to the existing program as possible. In this regard, design decisions typically focus on a few key issues: number and mix of options, structure of the cost containment elements, and incentives to use the preferred providers.

Number and Mix of Options

Specific cost containment features are still quite new to Canadian supplemental medical plans. Therefore, to help ensure acceptance of these features in a flexible program, many employers have elected to include both traditional indemnity plans and one or two cost containment options in their program design. This leads to flexible supplemental medical plans containing four, five, or even six options. Over time, as employees become comfortable with the cost containment features, it is likely that employers may eliminate one or all of the indemnity plans. Other employers have taken the approach of separating the prescription drug options from the supplemental medical options, which results in even more choices for employees.

Structure of the Cost Containment Elements

The cost containment elements are typically included in options that are not as rich as the current indemnity plan. However, employers often try to duplicate as many features as possible (maximums and deductibles, for example) in the cost containment plan to help employees see that it is not a major change from the current plan. Some employers actually include some improvements in the cost containment plan (such as greater vision coverage) under the rationale that the current plan is being frozen and all future improvements will be made to the cost containment plan. This serves as an incentive for employees to elect the new plan. In situations where the drug plan has been separated from the supplemental medical plan, the resulting drug plan choices often all contain cost containment elements, while the medical options retain a more familiar indemnity plan structure.

Incentives to Use Preferred Providers

To be effective, a supplemental medical plan must either include incentives to use the cost containment features or disincentives from using the traditional plan features. Typically, these incentives are a higher reimbursement level for using preferred provider elements. The plan sponsor may also motivate employees into electing a plan with cost containment provisions by the pricing of the options. In effect, the employer may subsidize the cost containment plan to encourage employees to select it. A challenge to this approach is assembling, negotiating with, and managing the group of preferred providers. In the case of vision care, several large group insurers have arranged for reduced costs for their plan members. However, in most other situations, it has been left up to the employer to create the preferred provider network.

Another issue in creating a provider network is often a political one, wherein certain providers are existing customers of the employer's own business. It can be challenging to negotiate preferred arrangements and/or run the risk that the customers might be offended.

A number of years ago a major financial institution introduced a preferred dental network option in a flexible plan. The option was withdrawn within a few weeks after disgruntled dentists mailed their cut up credit cards to the marketing department of the institution.

Insurer/Administrator Issues

In developing a cost containment plan design, it is important to understand the limitations of the insurers and administrators. While a best practices plan design may include some features (deductibles or out-of-pocket maximum limits, for example) that apply to medical and dental together, the administrative limitations of the providers may make this impossible to implement. Even within the supplemental medical options, there will likely be problems in incorporating certain design features. This occurs because many insurance companies use a third party to administer and adjudicate the prescription drug benefits for their clients. Unless the claims systems for the third party ties in directly with the systems of the insurer, it is very difficult to have a deductible that applies to all supplemental medical expenses, including drugs.

Wellness Initiatives

In an effort to focus attention on prevention, more employers are introducing workplace wellness initiatives to help reduce the number, and hence cost, of health

care claims. These initiatives include reimbursement of health club dues or provision of on-site facilities; health fairs; online health-risk assessment tools; vaccina-
tion programs; general educational sessions such as lunch-and-learns; or bringing
outside groups such as weight management, back care, or disease management
organizations into the workplace to educate employees. For example, in a 2005
survey conducted by Hewitt Associates, 37 per cent of respondents indicated that
they include fitness memberships in their benefit program today and a further 19
per cent expect to add coverage within three years.

Some employers have also tied wellness initiatives to their flexible benefit program through the application of credits. In these cases, additional credits are provided to reward people for engaging in specified healthy behaviours such as not
smoking, exercising regularly, or having an annual health test. These additional
credits can then be used to purchase coverage or features under the flexible benefit plan. In other cases, employees can utilize any excess credits arising from the
benefit plan elections in a wellness account under which health-related services or
equipment are an eligible (although taxable) expense, for example, home exercise
bicycle or personal trainer fees.

COMMUNICATION

The preceding sections provide an overview of the elements and characteristics of
cost containment programs. An important element in successfully merging cost
containment into a flexible benefit program is clearly communicating plan provisions and their implications to employees.

Choice plans require more work from employees than traditional plans. Cost
containment options further complicate the decision-making process. As a general rule, the fewer moving parts there are, the easier it is for employees to understand the program. If employees do not understand the alternatives, they are more
likely to maintain the most expensive coverage available ("just to be safe") and
defeat the objective of maximizing employee appreciation of benefits. Every effort
should be made to make plan provisions easy to understand through clear, concise
summaries.

§ 5.10 COST CONTROL FOR PRESCRIPTION DRUG BENEFITS

The highest cost element of most supplemental medical plans is prescription drugs.
In a typical plan, prescription drug costs range from 60 to 80 per cent of the total
supplemental plan cost, and the rate of inflation on these costs is among the highest
of all health care services. Reasons for the high cost increases include new, high-
cost drugs being introduced; the aging workforce (the number of prescriptions and
the cost per prescription tend to increase with age); drugs being created to treat

conditions for which drug therapies were not previously available; and steadily rising professional charges by the pharmacist (the dispensing fee).

Plans are attempting to deal with the rising prescription drug costs by introducing a number of cost management features. These include restricting which drugs a plan will cover by using a formulary, or list of best practice drugs; including a drug utilization review (DUR) element in the administration of the plan; requiring prior authorization of certain drugs; utilizing step-therapies to ensure the lowest-cost drugs are used first; and limiting how much the plan will pay towards the dispensing fee element of a drug claim.

A much anticipated drug cost management technique promoted in the mid-1990s was mail order or direct delivery pharmacy. However, the expected reduction in professional fees and/or ingredient fees never really materialized, due to restrictions on sending prescription drugs via Canada Post and more aggressive pricing competition among pharmacies. By the mid-2000s, mail order pharmacy accounted for less than 1 per cent of the total prescription drug market in Canada. Even in the United States, mail order prescriptions represented only about 7 per cent of the total market in 2005.

Prescription drug formularies are not new to Canada. The provincial drug benefit plans have been using the concept for many years to limit which drugs are covered under the province's plan. Simply stated, a formulary is a list of approved prescription drugs.

The overall goal in developing a prescription drug formulary is to produce a list of high-quality, effective, and cost-efficient drugs. The ultimate objective is to balance the cost containment or cost control objectives of the company with the desire of employees and employers that employees have access to the health care treatments they need.

Most of the major insurance carriers manage their own set of formularies, either through in-house resources or third-party pharmacy benefit managers. While similarities exist among the decision processes at all these companies, there is no standard formulary in use across the country at the present time. This significantly reduces the effectiveness of this approach, because physicians, pharmacists, insurers, third-party administrators, and employees have to deal with different formularies through different supplemental medical plans.

USE OF PRESCRIPTION DRUG CARDS

For many of the newer or more innovative plan designs, key elements of the program work best when the employee has price and coverage information available at the point of sale. In order to provide this information, most employers who implement formularies, procedural limitations, or dispensing fee limitations use a prescription drug card.

Use of these cards allows the pharmacist to both inform the employee of the financial implications of the purchase, and educate the employee at the point of sale about the alternative products that might be available at a reduced cost.

In the late 1980s and early 1990s, when drug cards were first introduced, there was significant anecdotal evidence that the presence of a drug card substantially increased the cost to the plan, due to:

- Shifting costs from spouses' plans without a card;
- The elimination of the cash effect, where individuals might forgo having a prescription filled because they do not want to pay the cash up front, even though they know they would be reimbursed at a later date; and
- The elimination of the "shoebox effect," whereby employees would forget to submit small prescription drug claims for reimbursement. An electronic card eliminates the shoebox effect and, therefore, increases costs to the plan.

However, with the use of positive enrolment, and continuing increases in drug costs, the cost impact of implementing a drug card has dropped substantially. Most now estimate that the ongoing impact of drug card implementation is approximately 5 to 10 per cent.

It is worth noting that although the increase in claims incurred due to the addition of a drug card is small, there is also a cash flow/timing element to be considered. With the addition of a drug card, the lag time between when claims are incurred and when claims are paid is eliminated. In the case where this lag was one month on a reimbursement basis, elimination of this lag means that thirteeen months of claims were paid in the first plan year under a drug card. This 8 per cent increase is not actually an increase in claims, but a decrease in the lag time for claims payment.

TYPES OF FORMULARIES

As prescription drug costs have continued to escalate in Canada in recent years, a number of different approaches to designing prescription drug formularies have been tried, with varying degrees of success.

As mentioned previously, the exact formulary lists vary by insurance provider, based on the decisions made by their pharmacy review boards, but in general formularies can be grouped into the following five categories.

Mandatory Generic Substitution Formularies

The least invasive, and therefore easiest to implement, of the formulary types, requires pharmacists to substitute generic drugs where available when an equivalent brand name drug has been prescribed.

Since the active ingredient in the generic and the brand are identical, these generic substitution plans are easiest to communicate to employees. Employers are able to communicate to employees that they will get exactly the same medical ingredient that was prescribed to them by their doctor, in the least expensive form, if a generic is available.

Logistically, this type of plan is also very easy to implement, because pharmacists are allowed to make these substitutions at the pharmacy without first contacting the prescribing physician.

Though this is the easiest formulary to implement, it is the formulary with the smallest impact on plan costs. Because in many provinces pharmacists already automatically substitute generics for brands when they exist, and because most of the prescription drugs driving employer costs are single-source drugs (i.e., drugs that retain patent protection and therefore have no generic equivalent), the cost saving to employers is quite low, often no more than 1 to 2 per cent of prescription drug costs.

Exclusions by Class Formularies

As employers attempt to balance their objective of providing medically necessary health care benefits at a reasonable cost, the medical necessity of certain classes of drugs is called into question.

Classes of drugs such as those used to treat obesity, erectile dysfunction (ED), male pattern baldness, infertility, smoking cessation, or cosmetic problems (e.g., Botox) are not considered medically necessary by some employers. These classes of drugs are sometimes referred to as "lifestyle" drugs, and when categorized as such may be removed from the list of drugs covered by a formulary.

While these drugs do not represent a significant portion of employer drug costs today, employers adopting these types of exclusions view their decision as both saving cost in the short term, and protecting against a potential increase in prevalence of these types of products over the longer term.

Frozen Formularies

In attempting to meet both the objective of long-term cost control and the objective of not reducing existing coverage for employees, some companies have implemented frozen formularies. The concept of a frozen formulary is that all prescription drugs available as of a given date will be eligible for reimbursement in the future. However, new drugs released after that date will not be eligible under the plan. In this way, employers can communicate to employees that no coverage has been removed with this initiative, even though future enhancements have been eliminated.

The challenge with a strictly frozen formulary is that it does not adapt to changes in drugs available that employees would reasonably expect to be included, for example:

- If Drug X was available in 5 mg and 10 mg dosages prior to the frozen date, and then a 20 mg dosage is released later, this new dosage would not be added.
- If a generic to Drug X is released at 50 per cent of the cost of the brand name, this new lower-cost drug would not be added to a strictly frozen formulary.

For these reasons, a variation known as a dynamically frozen formulary has evolved. In this variation, the only new drugs added after the freeze date are line extensions (e.g., new dosages) and generics. Another form of dynamically frozen formulary also adds new breakthrough drugs that are shown to be cost effective and have no equivalent already on the formulary.

Managed Therapeutic Substitution Formularies

Two drugs are of the same therapeutic class if they have different active ingredients but can be substituted for one another to provide the same clinical outcome. Under a formulary with therapeutic substitution, the eligible drug is the lowest-cost drug with comparable clinic outcomes in a therapeutic class.

Depending upon the make-up of the formulary, the expected savings under the supplemental medical plan can be as high as 20 to 30 per cent. The expected savings for a particular plan can be estimated by the insurer or administrator by reviewing the actual drug claims incurred by the plan over the past few years.

The savings are generally significantly less than 20 to 30 per cent, due to two specific design decisions frequently made to soften the impact on employees.

- **Second tier co-insurance**. The potential saving of 20 to 30 per cent is based on the assumption that non-preferred drugs will not be reimbursed at all. In this case, employees are forced to either switch to a product that is on the formulary, or to pay the entire cost of the non-preferred drug.

  In practice, most companies implement the formulary with the objective of providing a financial incentive to purchase preferred drugs, but also provide some financial support for the purchase of non-preferred products.

  Common structures that employers might consider include:
  - 90 per cent co-insurance for preferred drugs, 50 per cent for non-preferred
  - 80 per cent coverage up to a $500 out-of-pocket maximum for preferred drugs, 60 per cent for non-preferred drugs with no out-of-pocket maximum
  - 90 per cent coverage for all drugs, with an annual limit of $500 for non-preferred drugs, or drugs in certain classes (e.g., erectile dysfunction or infertility)
  - $5 co-pay for preferred drugs, $15 for non-preferred drugs

The exact structure will need to balance the employer's conflicting objectives of long-term cost savings and minimizing the impact of the change on employees.

- **Grandfathering**. When a therapeutic formulary is implemented, one of the key issues to address is grandfathering.

Depending on the grandfathering approach taken, the company's first year cost savings could be as much as the full 20 to 30 per cent (if there is no grandfathering) or as little as 1 to 2 per cent (where there is full grandfathering of all drugs being prescribed to current employees). Typically, the majority of the grandfathering impact is eliminated over five to seven years, due to employee turnover and changing drug treatments, at which point the full cost savings is achieved. Please see page 124 for a complete discussion of grandfathering.

Based on Provincial Formularies

Several years ago, when formularies were becoming popular, some employers elected to use the provincial formularies for their employees. The advantage was that they were widely known and understood by doctors and pharmacists. The disadvantage was that they were developed based on the needs of an older, non-working population and did not always meet the needs of a younger, working group.

The prime consideration for inclusion on a provincial formulary is cost effectiveness of the prescription for the formulary's target population, namely seniors. For a group of employees, however, it may be cost effective for the plan to cover a more expensive drug that returns the employee to work faster than a less expensive prescription. This difference in goals makes a strict definition based on a provincial formulary difficult to apply effectively to a working population.

A second concern over the use of a provincial formulary is the degree of difference in the formularies used by various provincial governments. While there may be some logic to employees in one province of using the formulary of their own provincial government, it is challenging to explain to employees in Alberta why their reimbursement is based on the Ontario government formulary.

For these reasons, although originally popular, employer formularies based on provincial formularies have declined in recent years as other types of formularies more tailored to a working population have been developed.

FORMULARY IMPLEMENTATION

Drug Card

As mentioned above, administration of a formulary may require employees and their families to use a prescription drug card. This is used by the pharmacist for identification and to facilitate the drug utilization review discussed later in this section. While a drug card may lead to lower administration costs due to the elimination of paper claims forms, the utilization of the drug plan by employees may be 5 to 10 per cent higher with a card than without. A number of steps can be taken to reduce the extra costs of a card but these steps likely will not eliminate the costs completely.

Grandfathering

When implementing a drug formulary, employees will have the strongest negative reaction where the formulary impacts medications that employees are already taking. Employees are generally willing to accept the concept of a formulary for drugs they might be prescribed in the future. However, when implementing a formulary means that someone must change his or her existing medication or suffer financial penalties, employees are far less positive.

In order to ease the implementation process, many employers provide some level of individual drug grandfathering to employees. Generally, the grandfathering consists of two elements:

- Which drugs will be grandfathered:
  - All drugs the employee has recently taken (e.g., last six to twelve months)?
  - Recently prescribed maintenance drugs only?
  - Drugs in specific classes?
  - Only those drugs specifically requested by the employee (a type of exception processing)?
- For how long they will be grandfathered:
  - A specified period of time to ease the transition (e.g., six or twelve months)? or
  - For as long as the member remains in the plan?

When considering what grandfathering approach to use, the employer is trying to balance its desire to implement a new plan and achieve cost savings with the desire for a positive employee perception and employee health outcome from the transition.

Communication

Even where a plan sponsor is introducing a formulary designed for a working population and the exception process is quite limited, success is not guaranteed. A critical element is communication to employees, their physicians, and pharmacists. A number of employers go as far as providing employees with a letter describing the formulary to give their physician. Employees may also be given a list of drugs reimbursed for the employee in the prior year. The listing indicates which drugs are on the formulary and which are not. For those that are listed, a generic or therapeutic substitution is indicated, if available. The listing helps employees decide whether to select the cost containment option under the flexible plan or retain the traditional option. The cost containment option in these programs contains a formulary, while the traditional plan reimburses all drugs which require a prescription.

MANAGING DRUG COSTS THROUGH PROCEDURAL LIMITATIONS

In addition to limitations in the specific drugs that are covered under the plan by use of a formulary, and the coverage offered within the various flexible benefit options, there are several other tools available to help companies manage which employees will have access to which drugs. These tools can be used in combination with the various drug formularies, although some combinations of formularies and processes work more effectively than others.

Exception Processes

First, the plan might include an exception process to allow an employee to bypass the formulary because of a unique situation. In one case, an employer found that almost all of the potential savings disappeared due to a liberal exception policy. At the other extreme, another employer considers exceptions only where the individual is currently taking a prescription drug on which he or she has been stabilized and going off the drug would cause a life-or-limb-threatening condition.

Exception processes are usually more attractive to companies in theory than in practice. In theory, the concept that employees can have access to non-formulary drugs in particular circumstances is both appealing to the company and a selling point for employees to become comfortable with the concept of a formulary.

However, in practice, the details of an exception process raise many questions:

- Who will make the determination if an exception is valid? Most employers do not want to make these decisions directly, and therefore their insurer or prescription drug benefit manager (PBM) is asked to make these decisions.
- What criteria should be applied? Is a simple doctor's note requesting the drug sufficient, or does detailed medical evidence need to be provided?
- How do you communicate this process to employees?

Although the adjudication systems today are capable of handling individual drug exceptions on an automated basis, many employers have moved away from exception processes in recent years.

Prior Authorization

Recognizing that there are some drugs that are valid and valuable in certain circumstances, but not in others, companies and their insurers have moved toward building a formalized and consistent process for determining who is allowed to have which drugs, and under what circumstances.

Prior authorization processes usually work with a specified list of drugs, and allow a process as follows:

- Prior authorization drugs are not covered without approval by the PBM. Approval is obtained by the employee and doctor filling in a brief form either prior to or after the prescription has been filled. The approval form will usually ask questions regarding:
  - Nature of the condition for which the medication is prescribed
  - Key diagnostic information (e.g., blood pressure, weight, etc.)
  - What other treatment protocols were previously tried.
- Provided that the condition that is being treated is medically necessary and that appropriate treatment protocol is being followed, the prescribed medication will be reimbursed by the plan.

Implementing a prior authorization process on certain medications can potentially save cost to the employer through both a reduction in the number of prescriptions (in the case of medications being prescribed that were not medically necessary), and through employees switching their prescriptions to more appropriate, and potentially lower-cost, items.

Prior authorization is often a good fit when a plan has a drug formulary, as it enables an employee who goes through the prior authorization process to get a non-formulary drug reimbursed at the formulary level.

Maintenance Prescriptions

Dispensing fees are a substantial portion of the cost of prescription drugs. For maintenance medications (prescriptions that a person takes on an ongoing basis) an employer can potentially reduce its drug plan costs by encouraging members to get larger supplies of medications with each prescription.

Where appropriate, plans that recommend maintenance prescriptions will prompt the pharmacist to offer an employee a longer supply (e.g., 90 days rather than 30 days) each time they fill the prescription. In reducing by as much as two-thirds the number of dispensing fees paid on maintenance drugs, employers can achieve cost saving regardless of the use or absence of a drug formulary.

Trial Prescriptions

One of the areas that has been identified as a cost within existing benefit plans is unused medications. Specifically, when an individual has been prescribed a drug for the first time, in a portion of the cases, the individual suffers from side effects of the medication and does not complete the prescription as filled. In these cases, the unused medication cannot be returned and is, in effect, a wasted expense by both the individual and their benefit plan.

A trial prescription program attempts to reduce this wastage by encouraging employees who are prescribed a drug for the first time to take a smaller amount (e.g., seven days instead of 30 days) when initially picking up the prescription. A member who reacts well to the new medication and wishes to have the remainder of the prescription filled can return to the pharmacist after the initial supply runs out and receive the remainder.

While the use of a maintenance prescription program is universally agreed to be a mechanism for reducing drug plan costs, the cost/benefit analysis on trial prescriptions is still uncertain. The savings in drug ingredient cost in those cases where medicine would have been wasted is offset by having to pay the pharmacist an additional fee to dispense the medication twice.

DIRECT DELIVERY (MAIL ORDER) PHARMACIES

Direct delivery pharmacies are a form of preferred provider designed to be a low-cost alternative to traditional retail pharmacies. The concept was developed and has matured in the United States, where the employee contacts the provider, who sends the prescription by express mail.

However, in Canada, there have been several substantial barriers to successful implementation of mail order pharmacy benefits:

- Federal legislation prohibits prescriptions being sent by mail, so here the prescriptions are sent by courier. The additional courier charges largely offset the reduction in dispensing fees paid by the plan or the employee.
- Competition among pharmacies has resulted in some pharmacies providing delivery.

As a result, there have not been sufficient cost savings available through mail order programs to make this a viable option for most employers.

§ 5.11 PROVINCIAL ISSUES

Organizations with employees in Quebec and Alberta need to reflect special consideration for these employees.

QUEBEC DRUG PLAN

Under provincial law, all Quebec residents must have prescription drug coverage. Employers that offer coverage for medical, dental, or disability benefits must also offer prescription drug coverage that meets legislated minimum coverage requirements.

An employee who has coverage offered through a private plan must enrol in the plan unless he or she can prove to the employer that coverage is available under another private plan (for example, a spouse's employer plan). Only individuals who do not have access to any private plan can obtain their prescription drug coverage through the government plan, which is administered by the *Régie de l'assurance maladie du Québec* (RAMQ). The exception is persons age 65 and over. They are automatically covered under the government plan, but can choose instead to be covered under a private plan. The private plan can be either the first payer or a supplemental plan, depending upon the type of private plan available to the individual.

Minimum prescription drug coverage requirements are subject to change every July 1 and dictate a threshold percentage of reimbursement for all drugs listed on the formulary (71 per cent since July 1, 2006) and the maximum out-of-pocket expense an adult plus dependent children can incur in a year ($881 since July 1, 2006). Another requirement is to cover all drugs listed on the RAMQ formulary.

It is important for a flexible benefit plan that provides choice in prescription drug coverage to have at least one option that meets the government's minimum coverage requirements.

In any event, insurers operating in Canada can adjudicate claims in accordance with the rules for Quebec residents even if the plan option coverage does not meet all of the minimum requirements. For example, if the plan covers prescription drugs at 70 per cent, insurers have the administrative capability to reimburse at the 71 per cent minimum requirement for drugs listed on the RAMQ formulary for Quebec residents.

Communicating to Quebec employees their obligation to take the government-mandated minimum (or better) coverage offered to them unless they have coverage under another private plan is important, since it is the employer's responsibility to ensure that employees, spouses and dependent children are covered for prescription drugs. Individuals in Quebec are required to report the source of their prescription drug coverage and that it meets the government's minimum requirements when completing their personal income tax returns each year. While employees are responsible for taking the coverage offered to them and their dependants, employers have the obligation to provide at least the minimum level of coverage for all Quebec employees and to verify that those declining coverage are in fact covered by another plan.

ALBERTA DENTAL FEE GUIDE

Each year most provincial dental associations establish guides that provide suggested fees for dentists to charge for all dental services. In order to determine a reasonable and customary fee for each dental procedure, benefit plans rely on the provincial dental association guides. The exception is the Alberta Dental Association (ADA), which has not published a fee guide since 1997, when it allowed its member dentists to determine their fees on their own. This created a challenge for insurers, since there was no longer a basis upon which to adjudicate dental claims in Alberta. As a result, the Canadian Life and Health Insurance Association of Canada (CLHIA), along with many Canadian insurers, now produces their own common *Dental Reimbursement Guide for Alberta* on an annual basis.

Effective February 1, 2005, reimbursement levels for dental services in Alberta are determined by each insurance company, using data compiled by the CLHIA. Each insurer analyses this data and determines its reimbursement schedule. This ultimately will create differences in reimbursement levels by insurer.

§ 5.12 PROVINCIAL HEALTH INSURANCE PLANS

OVERVIEW

All ten provinces and three territories sponsor health insurance for their residents with hospital and medical insurance plans. The plans came into existence as a result of the federal *Hospital Insurance and Diagnostic Services Act* of 1957 and the federal *Medical Care Act* of 1966. The agreements specified that the federal government would pay approximately 50 per cent of the cost of the plans.

In 1984, the *Canada Health Act* replaced these statutes and set out the current prerequisites for federal contributions to provincial health service plans. Provinces complying with the *Canada Health Act* are entitled to a transfer of federal tax revenues and a per capita cash payment that escalates with the growth in the gross national product (GNP). Since the cost of health care services has increased faster than the increase in the GNP, federal support has slipped from the initial 50 per cent.

The *Canada Health Act* establishes the following criteria for federal–provincial co-operation:

- **Universality.** The plan must entitle all residents in the province to all insured services on uniform terms and conditions. Exceptions to this include members of the Canadian Forces covered under the *National Defence Act*, and Royal Canadian Mounted Police officers of rank covered under the *RCMP Act*.
- **Accessibility.** Insured health services must be available on uniform conditions and on a basis that includes no direct or indirect impediments to reasonable access.
- **Portability.** When a person takes up residence in another province, coverage must continue during the minimum waiting period of the new province. Insured persons temporarily absent from their home province must be eligible

for coverage at the rate payable by the plan of the host province; where the services are provided outside Canada, coverage shall be at the rate payable for similar services provided in the province. In cases of referral, where services are unavailable in Canada, prior approval from the provincial authorities is generally required.

- **Comprehensiveness.** The plan must insure all medically necessary services provided by doctors, hospitals, and dentists.
- **Public administration.** The plan must be administered on a non-profit basis by a public authority appointed by and accountable to the government of the province.

Extra billing and most user charges are prohibited. The *Canada Health Act* provides for a reduction in federal funding in the event of extra billing or prohibited user charges.

CONTROL STRUCTURE

There are essentially three areas of control in the health care system: the federal government, the provincial government, and the medical profession.

Federal Government

The federal government controls the supply of medical practitioners by:

- limiting the number of immigrant doctors
- setting regional quotas of specialists
- offering practice incentives for underserved areas.

Provincial Governments

Provincial governments regulate the supply of facilities and expenditures and they set quality controls. Provincial health ministers have the following responsibilities under the hospital insurance plans:

- setting the annual operating budgets of hospitals
- controlling all hospital residency training
- setting ceilings on the number of specialists in training
- controlling the supply of beds, equipment, and new services
- conducting quality inspections
- monitoring utilization and costs.

Under the medical insurance plans, the health minister and a commission share the following responsibilities:

- negotiating fee schedules and income ceilings
- conducting claims reviews
- constructing profiles of procedures performed by each physician
- verifying physicians' billings
- recommending physicians for prosecution.

Medical Profession

The medical profession regulates medical quality, expenditure, and fraud controls through the health professions board and the College of Physicians and Surgeons. As such, it is responsible for:

- medical licensing and discipline
- standards, inspection of doctors' office records, and practices
- investigating complaints over fees.

FUNDING

The provincial governments are responsible for any costs remaining after the federal subsidy.

In Prince Edward Island, Nova Scotia, New Brunswick, Saskatchewan, the Northwest Territories, Nunavut, and the Yukon, the hospital and medical plans are funded by general operating revenue alone.

The other six provinces collect additional funds beyond general operating revenue. Four provinces levy a payroll tax on employers:

- Newfoundland — 4 per cent of payroll between $600,000 and $700,000 or 2 per cent over $500,000 if payroll exceeds $700,000.
- Ontario — 1.95 per cent of payroll in excess of $400,000 for private sector employers; 0.98 to 1.95 per cent for public sector; plus Ontario Health Premium based on taxable income in excess of $20,000. The maximum annual premium, for taxable income above $200,600, is $900.
- Quebec — 2.7 per cent of payroll if $1 million or less, 2.7 per cent to 4.26 per cent of payroll if between $1 million and $5 million; 4.26 per cent of payroll if more than $5 million.
- Manitoba — 4.3 per cent of payroll between $1 million and $2 million; 2.15 per cent of total payroll if over $2 million.

The provinces of Alberta and British Columbia require residents covered by the plan to pay premiums. Special exemptions are made for low-income residents in both provinces. In early 2007, monthly premiums in these two provinces were as follows:

- Alberta
  - Single: $44
  - Family: $88
- British Columbia
  - Single: $54
  - Individual plus one dependant: $96
  - Family: $108

COVERAGE RULES

Eligibility

All residents, regardless of health, age, or financial status, are eligible for benefits. This is a prerequisite under the agreement between the federal and provincial governments. A "resident" means a person lawfully allowed to be and remain in Canada, who is ordinarily present in the particular province or territory. By definition, this excludes tourists, transients, and visitors.

Coverage is compulsory in some provinces and not in others. However, all provinces require individuals to enrol or register in the program.

Effective Dates of Coverage

The normal residency period that must be established in each province is three months for persons moving from province to province in Canada. A person leaving one province to establish residence in another province is usually covered for the three-month period by the plan in the province of prior residence.

Students attending school outside their home province are generally considered to be residents of their home province for purposes of their health services plan.

People establishing residence in a province, who previously lived outside Canada, are normally considered residents on the date of their arrival. In British Columbia and Ontario, however, there is a three-month waiting period. The spouse and dependent children of a resident are insured as a family unit. The head of the family is required to register all members of the family.

Age limits on dependent children vary somewhat. However, most provinces define dependent children as under age 19 or under age 21 if they are full-time students. Handicapped dependants are eligible with no age limit.

A detailed and up-to-date description of the types of medical services provided under each program by province can be found at www.hewitt.com/provhealthcare.

DENTAL

The range of dental services provided to eligible residents varies from province to province. In provinces where senior citizens are beneficiaries of the program, the dental plan provides coverage for major restorative services such as dentures. In provinces where children are the beneficiaries, the emphasis is on preventive and basic restorative services.

A detailed and up-to-date description of the types of dental services provided under each program by province can be found at www.hewitt.com/provhealthcare.

OUT-OF-PROVINCE COVERAGE

All provincial plans provide coverage for residents in need of emergency care and treatment while temporarily absent from their home province. "Temporarily absent" is normally defined as absence for up to one year. The plans usually pay expenses whether they are incurred inside or outside of Canada. When a resident leaves his or her province and relocates to another province, home-province coverage is continued for two months after the month of arrival in the new province, plus, in some cases, time spent in transit. Coverage in the new home province commences three months after arrival. Some provinces also continue coverage for up to three months when residents leave the province to establish permanent residence outside Canada.

Out-of-province medical expenses incurred while temporarily absent are generally paid at the host province rate. Out-of-province hospital expenses incurred while temporarily absent are generally paid in accordance with the standard interprovincial schedule. Outside Canada, dollar limits based on home rates are usually applied.

Note that out-of-province coverage generally applies only to emergency treatment required when a resident is absent from the province. Elective treatment received outside the province is either not covered, or covered at lower rates than the rates that apply in the event of an accident or unexpected illness.

CO-ORDINATION OF PRIVATE INSURANCE WITH PROVINCIAL PLANS

Generally speaking, private insurance cannot duplicate provincial plan coverage. Some provinces specifically prohibit private insurers from providing benefits covered by the provincial programs. In others, although no prohibition exists, a resident is not able to receive duplicate reimbursement.

On the other hand, services over and above those provided by the provincial plan can usually be insured. Examples of this are the differential between semi-private or private accommodation and ward-level coverage in a hospital. One major exception to this rule is that the cost of physicians' services above the provincial fee guide cannot legally be insured in most provinces.

Six

Death and Disability

§ 6.1 INTRODUCTION

Death and disability coverages often are included as choice areas within flexible programs. These benefits are not as highly utilized or as visible as supplemental medical and dental benefits, but they do serve a valuable function: providing protection to employees and their dependants from loss of income due to death, accident, injury, or illness. Because death and disability premiums are not escalating as rapidly and consistently as medical and dental premiums, cost control usually is not as critical a design consideration. However, a host of other factors create other kinds of design challenges for the structuring of death and disability benefit options.

Designing choices in death benefit coverage can become complex because of the many types of group life insurance available. In addition to deciding what form or forms of death benefits to offer, an employer will need to address various other issues. For example, what levels of coverage should be made available? How should the options be priced? Who should pay for the coverage?

Answers to these questions are not always easy or obvious. The design of death benefit choices must take into account the employer's objectives and employees' needs, as well as tax requirements.

Although the design of disability benefit choices often is viewed as less complex than that of other benefits, there are a number of issues unique to disability. For example, in the area of short-term disability, the primary issue is whether to offer choices at all, given the extent of coverage already provided through an employer's underlying sick leave or salary continuation program. In long-term disability benefits, a major design issue relates to determining the appropriate level(s) of pay replacement to ensure that the choices are distinct and different, and yet provide an adequate, but not excessive, benefit amount to employees. Another consideration is whether or not to use flexible credits for pre-tax premium payment, in light of benefit taxation rules.

§ 6.2 DEATH BENEFITS

Group life insurance is a natural benefit area to include in a choice-making program, because death benefit needs vary greatly over an employee's lifetime. For example, the needs of a middle-aged employee with a spouse at home, children, and a mortgage will be much greater than those of a young employee without a spouse. In contrast, an older employee nearing retirement with neither children to support nor mortgage payments — but drawing a career-high income — will have other needs again.

In addition, an employee may have various sources of death benefits outside the group life plan, such as the Canada/Quebec Pension Plan, retirement plans, creditor insurance on a mortgage or other loans, and individual life insurance policies. Providing choices in group life enables employees to select the level of coverage that best meets their individual needs and co-ordinates with other sources of coverage.

TYPES OF GROUP LIFE INSURANCE

Group term life insurance is the only form of life insurance typically included in a flexible program. Whole life and universal life policies are generally not included, because these forms of insurance allow cash value buildup and, therefore, do not receive the same tax treatment as group term insurance. A few employers, however, offer whole life or universal life (on a group or individual basis) within the flexible program, as long as the coverage is purchased with after-tax payroll deductions — not flexible credits.

EMPLOYEE LIFE INSURANCE

Employee life insurance provides a lump-sum benefit to a designated beneficiary upon the death of the employee. The primary intent is to ease the financial strain on a family resulting from the loss of an income provider. The cost of any employer-paid coverage is a taxable benefit for employees while the benefit is paid tax-free to the beneficiary. The one exception to this rule is that employers may self-insure and self-administer a death benefit of up to $10,000 that is tax-free to the beneficiary and does not generate a taxable benefit to the employee.

A benefit purchased with employer funds (typically by using flexible credits) is considered an employer-provided benefit and therefore taxable, subject to the possible $10,000 exemption described above.

In a typical flexible program structure, an employer provides a certain core level of coverage and offers various options to supplement basic coverage amounts. Levels of coverage typically are based on multiples of annual pay (such as one times pay, two times pay, and so on), although occasionally flat-dollar amounts (such as $25,000, $50,000, and so on) are offered. Many employers place a dollar cap on the total benefit payable; usually this is a requirement of the insurance company underwriting the benefits.

Employers may charge all employees a flat rate per $1,000 of coverage or assign risk-related rates, which better reflect the true cost of the coverage. For example, older, higher-risk employees may pay more than younger, lower-risk employees. Some plans also consider gender and smoker status in setting the rates, with males paying more than females and smokers paying more than non-smokers.

Accidental Death and Dismemberment

Accidental death and dismemberment (AD&D) coverage provides additional benefits if an employee's death occurs as the result of an accident. The plan also pays benefits — usually stated as a percentage of the policy's face value — in the event of accidental dismemberment. Some plans provide benefits only in the event of accidental dismemberment.

A few employers structure AD&D coverage in exactly the same way as employee life insurance, so the benefit for an accidental death is double the benefit paid for death by other causes. In these cases, the cost of employee life and AD&D coverage may be bundled into a combined rate. Most often, however, employers construct a separate AD&D plan with different levels of coverage and separate premiums. AD&D coverage is typically quite inexpensive, and the cost does not vary by age, gender, or smoker status. So unless AD&D is tied to employee life (and the combined rate is age/gender/smoker graded), AD&D is priced as a flat amount per $1,000 of coverage, applicable to everyone.

Dependant Life Insurance

Dependant life insurance provides a lump-sum benefit to a beneficiary (typically the employee) upon the death of a spouse or child. Coverage for a spouse and children may be packaged as one election or offered separately as independent options. The coverage usually is offered in flat-dollar amounts, typically providing higher benefits for a spouse (say, up to $200,000) than for a child (for example, up to $30,000). Until recently, the coverage amounts available for dependant life were generally much lower than for employee life. This was due to the belief that the death of a dependant generally had less impact on a family's financial status than the death of the employee.

However, many flexible programs offer significant amounts of spouse's group life insurance — up to $500,000 or even more in some cases. This level of benefit can meet the needs of many types of employees. For example, the "traditional" male employee with a wife and children at home might purchase $200,000 of spouse's life insurance to pay for child care if his wife died. A two-income family would also find large amounts of spouse's insurance attractive if the spouse does not have coverage through an employer or the premium is less than the cost of employee insurance offered by the spouse's employer.

Dependant life usually is available on a contributory basis only. The cost for spousal coverage is generally a graded rate (often based on the age of the employee or spouse and the gender and smoker status of the spouse) per $1,000 of coverage. Employers providing children's life coverage or a modest level of spousal coverage usually base the cost on a flat-dollar amount per $1,000 of coverage (normally charging one rate regardless of the number of children covered).

Survivor Income

Survivor income plans are designed to provide a continuing stream of payments (usually paid monthly) to an employee's surviving spouse and/or child(ren). Survivor income benefits may be based on a percentage of the employee's pay (such as 25 per cent of salary) or may provide a flat-dollar amount (such as $500 per month). The plan often provides one amount for a surviving spouse, plus another amount for children.

Twenty-three per cent of employers offering survivor income benefits provide coverage on a contributory basis. Where the employee is required to contribute, premiums usually are based on pay, age, or a combination of pay and age.

DESIGN CONSIDERATIONS

Designing group life insurance options within a flexible program requires consideration and analysis of various factors — including an employer's objectives, the needs of employees, and income tax requirements. Coverage provided under a prior plan also is a consideration in terms of evaluating whether to continue or modify current practice.

Areas of Choice

A fundamental design decision is whether to offer group life insurance in a flexible program. Since employers typically offer some degree of choice in existing employee life plans, most flexible programs include employee life insurance as a choice-making area. In cases where the employee life insurance choices did not previously exist, many employers view introduction of a flexible program as an opportunity to offer group life choices, because employees generally perceive choice-making as a benefit enhancement. Many employers also offer choices in AD&D (62 per cent) and dependant life (66 per cent). Almost half of employers offer dependant AD&D. These benefits are popular with employees and often can be included as options in a flexible program at little or no employer cost.

Inclusion of AD&D within a flexible benefit program enjoys certain tax advantages. Under the *Income Tax Act*, AD&D is treated as a non-taxable accident and sickness benefit; therefore, any company-paid coverage is not included in the employee's taxable income. In a ruling on a proposed flexible program, Canada Revenue Agency confirmed that this same favourable tax treatment extends to spousal and children's AD&D. However, in Quebec, the cost of company-paid AD&D coverage is a taxable benefit for Quebec income tax purposes.

Employers may not subsidize dependant life coverage on a non-taxable basis — any company-paid coverage generates a taxable benefit to the employee equal to the employer's cost. This includes any employer-provided flexible credits that the employee directs towards the cost of dependant life. As a result, some employers offer dependant life coverage choices on an after-tax payroll deduction basis only.

Very few flexible programs offer survivor income choices. These plans tend to be moderately expensive and often difficult to price, because benefits usually are payable for an indefinite period of time (for example, until the spouse's death or remarriage). Moreover, survivor income plans have not been as popular with employees as other types of life insurance, probably because the payment mechanism (a portion of the employee's earnings paid out over a period of time) is more difficult to understand and holds less appeal than a lump-sum life insurance payment.

Structure of Options

Some of the key issues employers need to address in determining the structure of death benefit options are discussed next.

(i) **High option.** Determining the high death benefit option usually is a function of various factors. These include employee needs and the presence of other death benefits, such as survivor income plans and pension plans. In addition, underwriting considerations will affect the maximum benefits permissible in a flexible program. (For more complete discussion of this issue, see Chapter 17.)

  For employee life and AD&D, a high-end option of four, five, or six times pay is usually considered adequate to meet almost all employees' needs. Separately, some employers impose an overall plan maximum (in terms of a dollar limit), usually for underwriting reasons.

  For dependant life, employers usually limit the "richest" option to $200,000 or $500,000 for spouse coverage, and $20,000 or $30,000 for children.

  For survivor income, the high-end option usually is no greater than 50 per cent of the employee's annual pay for the surviving spouse, plus an incremental amount such as 5 per cent of pay per child, to a maximum of 15 per cent of pay for children.

(ii) **Low option.** The fundamental issue related to the lowest death benefit option is whether to require employees to take a minimum level of protection, or to allow employees to opt out of coverage completely. Most employers feel a sense of obligation to ensure that all employees have at least a core level of life insurance. Few plans allow employees to opt out of coverage completely. Common minimum benefit amounts are one times annual pay or a flat amount such as $25,000. Minimums may be based on estimated burial expenses, competitive practice, past benefit levels, or a combination of these factors.

Since AD&D, survivor income, and dependant life generally are supplemental death benefits (with little or no company subsidy), employees typically have the option to decline coverage.

(iii) **Increments of coverage.** Common practice for employee life, and usually AD&D, is to establish incremental levels of coverage based on multiples of annual pay, rather than flat-dollar amounts. Tying coverage to pay is based on the premise that life insurance is generally intended to replace the employee's income, so the level of coverage should bear some reasonable relationship to an employee's earnings. Among employers with options offered as multiples of pay, the most common increment of coverage is a full multiple of pay — such as one times pay, two times pay, and so forth. In some cases, employers also offer half multiples — for example, 0.5 times pay, 1.5 times pay, and so forth. This is frequently found where the plan's rules allow the employee to increase coverage one level a year without medical evidence. The half multiple reduces the insurer's risk.

Only a minority of employers base levels of employee coverage on flat-dollar amounts, with the most common increments being $10,000 or $20,000. Employers who use flat-dollar amounts believe they allow employees to choose a benefit level that precisely meets their needs.

Dependant life is almost always offered in flat-dollar increments, usually at lower levels than employee life. Survivor income typically is offered in increments of the employee's pay, such as 10 per cent to 50 per cent, sometimes to a flat-dollar maximum on the monthly benefit payable. Less frequently, the increment is a flat-dollar amount (such as $100 to $1,000) payable monthly.

(iv) **Number of options.** An employer may offer any number of options to employees. Conceptually, the employer's goal is to offer enough choices to provide a reasonable degree of flexibility to employees, but not so many choices as to cause confusion or unnecessary administrative complexity.

Generally, the number of options offered is a function of other decisions concerning the range of options — such as the spread between the highest and lowest levels of coverage, the increments of coverage, and the ease of plan administration.

Source of Funds

(i) **Employee life insurance.** The funding of employee group life options in a flexible program often mirrors the funding approach used for the prior basic-plus-optional group life plan. In other words, under a flexible program, an employer typically funds a basic level of coverage — either by attaching a $0 price tag under a net pricing structure or by providing employees with enough credits to purchase the basic coverage under the core-plus-credits approach. Employees have the option of purchasing additional levels of coverage using remaining flexible credits or their own contributions.

Another design issue related to funding is whether to permit employees to use flexible credits to pay the group life premium either to supplement after-tax payroll deductions or to replace the deductions. Under *Income Tax Act* Section 6(1), the cost of employer-provided group life insurance is considered taxable income to the employee, although employers may self-insure and self-administer a $10,000 death benefit on a tax-free basis. Coverage paid with employer flexible credits is considered employer-provided. Thus, allowing employees to pay for amounts other than the $10,000 death benefit with credits creates a taxable benefit. As a result, some employers have concluded that group life insurance should only be purchased using payroll deductions. Others have permitted credits to be used to purchase group life. In these cases, the employer frequently requires that employees spend credits in areas such as medical, dental, and health spending accounts first, since these credits do not generate a taxable benefit. If any credits are left over, they can then be spent on group life insurance.

Depending on the structure of the plan, certain employees will notice a tax saving by purchasing group life with flexible credits, while others will notice a tax disadvantage. This complication occurs because, under employee optional life insurance, the employee pays tax based on a taxable benefit calculation as prescribed by Canada Revenue Agency. The taxable benefit is the "cost" of company-paid life insurance, and the cost is based on the average premium rate paid by the company. Employees whose actual premium is higher than the average cost will reduce their taxes by paying with credits, while those with a lower premium will see a tax increase. This is illustrated through the following example:

Assume the average cost for company-paid basic and optional life insurance at a company is $0.25 per month per $1,000 of coverage, based on all participating employees. Consider an employee — a 50-year-old male smoker — who purchases $100,000 group life insurance at a monthly premium rate of $0.60 per $1,000 or $60 per month. This individual pays $720 per year for the coverage. If the benefit is purchased with payroll deductions, he would need to earn $1,200 — assuming a 40 per cent tax bracket — to pay the premium of $720. If, on the other hand, he pays the premium with $720 in flexible credits, his taxable benefit is $25 per month ($0.25 per $1,000 average cost times $100,000), or $300 per year. His tax would be $120 (40 per cent of $300), so he is much better off using credits instead of deductions.

On the other hand, a young, female non-smoker, with a premium of $0.05 per month per $1,000, would be much better off using deductions. For the same coverage as in the previous example, her premium would be $5 per month or $60 per year. If the coverage were purchased with credits, the taxable benefit would still be based on the $0.25 average cost and would be $25 per month or $300 per year.

The above description applies to policies deemed to be group term life insurance as defined in Section 248(1) of the *Income Tax Act*.

Canada Revenue Agency has ruled that if optional employee life insurance coverage is included under the same policy and contract as optional spousal and/or children's life insurance, then the coverage is not considered group term life insurance under the *Income Tax Act*. In this case, the taxable benefit is not calculated based on the average cost of insurance. Instead, the taxable benefit for any company-paid life insurance (including insurance purchased with credits) is based on the actual cost of the coverage, as the benefit falls under the general income tax provisions for taxable benefits from employment. In practice, this means that the taxable benefit for any optional life insurance paid for with flexible credits can be based on the actual risk-related rates, rather than the average rate. In the above example, this would mean the following:

- The 50-year-old male would pay $720 in payroll deductions or could use $720 in flexible credits and receive a $720 taxable benefit.
- The younger female would pay $60 in payroll deductions or could use $60 in flexible credits and receive a $60 taxable benefit.

Employers considering allowing coverage to be purchased using flexible credits should review their plan and funding structure to determine which rules apply, and to decide whether changes are appropriate before making a decision.

(ii) **Dependant life insurance.** Dependant life typically is paid for solely by the employee. Here again, the issue is whether to require after-tax premium payment using deductions or allow pre-tax payment through credits.

Dependant life falls under Section 6(1)(a) of the *Income Tax Act*. Therefore, the value of all employer-provided dependant life (which would include coverage paid for with flexible credits) is taxable to employees. Since the cost of dependent life is relatively inexpensive and there are no major tax advantages to using flexible credits to purchase dependant life benefits, some employers simply require that employees pay the contributions in after-tax payroll deduction dollars.

Option Pricing/Credit Allocation

The primary design issue facing employers in the area of pricing group life options is whether to charge a flat rate to all employees, or graduated rates based on age and other risk factors. Although prior practice will have some bearing on the decision, other design objectives may make it appropriate to consider a change.

For employee life, risk-graded rates reflecting age and possible gender and/or smoker status are much more consistent with actual cost than flat rates for all employees, considering the relationship between the factors and the probability of a claim. Moreover, employers run the risk of adverse selection under a flat-rate scheme, since a flat rate typically is less expensive for older male smokers (which encourages plan participation) and more expensive for younger female non-smokers (which provides an incentive to seek coverage elsewhere).

In situations where risk-graded rates represent a departure from prior practice, employers need to be sensitive to what might be perceived as a "take-away" by some employees. In these cases, employers may want to consider offering the lowest level of coverage (such as one times pay) to all employees at a flat rate, and price higher coverage options on a graded basis. This dual price structure adds an element of complexity from both a communication and an administration perspective, but may be appropriate in some situations.

Credit allocation for a graded pricing structure is another design issue when credits are based on a cutback from prior coverage levels. Employers who provide all employees the same per cent of pay credit allocation, in essence, make lower-cost employees (who pay less for coverage) winners, and higher-cost employees (who pay more) losers. Another alternative is to age-grade the credit allocation structure so it correlates directly with the pricing structure. This approach may raise a question about equity (since older employees receive more credits than younger employees), but it does eliminate the concern over winners and losers. Some employers partially address the equity issue by narrowing the spread — making age differences in the credit allocation less extreme than age differences in the prices. Theoretically, employers could grade the credits to reflect gender and smoker status. However, few, if any, employers would want to allocate more credits to smokers and males than to non-smokers and females. (See Chapter 13 for a complete discussion of the relevant human rights issues involved.)

In general, graded rates based on the dependant's age, gender, and smoker status are impractical for smaller amounts of dependant life — especially covering children. Most employers, however, grade the rates for spouse coverage based on the spouse's or employee's age and, if appropriate, the spouse's gender and smoker status, especially when substantial amounts of coverage are available.

Enrolment/Re-enrolment Restrictions

Most employers attempt to limit the potential for adverse selection in life insurance by implementing enrolment and/or re-enrolment restrictions. This can be accomplished by placing restrictions on first-year elections if employees elect higher than previous levels of coverage. For subsequent enrolments, most employers place restrictions on an employee's ability to elect more coverage. Some employers allow the employee to increase one level of coverage with no evidence, while the majority require proof of insurability for any increase. (See also Chapter 17, "Insurance Considerations.")

§ 6.3 DISABILITY BENEFITS

Disability income plans protect employees against the loss of income due to illness or injury. Disability benefits — particularly short-term disability — are not as commonly included under flexible programs as many other group benefits, such as supplemental medical, dental, and life insurance. About 60 per cent of flexible plans offer choices in disability to expand the scope of choices offered, to provide benefits on a more tax-efficient basis, to offer cost-of-living protection, or to fill in any gaps in other employer-provided coverages.

TYPES OF DISABILITY COVERAGE

Both short-term and long-term disability income benefits may be offered under flexible programs.

Short-Term Disability

Short-term disability (STD) options are designed to replace a portion of a sick or injured employee's income after expiration of a company's underlying sick leave or salary continuation benefits (such as 30 or 60 days), but before commencement of long-term disability benefits (usually 17 weeks or six months). Many sick leave or salary continuation plans provide full or partial pay replacement for an extended period of time, often related to the employee's length of service. Occasionally for shorter-service employees, however, a gap in coverage may exist.

Options in short-term disability may be intended to allow employees to fill in the gap or to top up or reduce coverage, usually on an employee-pay-all basis. Benefit amounts typically match the levels of pay replacement offered under options in the long-term disability area.

Long-Term Disability

Long-term disability (LTD) plans provide income to employees unable to work for an extended period of time as a result of illness or injury. LTD benefits typically commence after a 17-week or six-month waiting period, and continue until retirement age or until the employee recovers. LTD benefits are designed to replace a portion of an employee's income — typically 50 to 70 per cent — and are generally integrated with benefits from other sources, particularly the Canada/Quebec Pension Plan and Worker's Compensation.

DESIGN CONSIDERATIONS

As with other benefit areas, offering disability choices in a flexible program requires consideration of a variety of factors based on employer objectives and employee needs.

Areas of Choice

A fundamental decision in the design of a flexible program is whether or not to include choices in disability.

Short-term disability represents an emerging coverage area under flexible programs. Very few flexible programs offer STD choices. Typically, the chief design consideration on whether to include short-term disability choices under the flexible program relates to the employer's existing sick leave or salary continuation practices. If the employer already provides full or partial pay replacement to employees for the entire LTD waiting period, the need for STD choices may be absent. However, if salary continuation or sick leave benefits are service-related or dependent upon an employee's employment classification (such as hourly, salaried, and management), STD choices may represent an appropriate choice area under a flexible program. A few employers who offer substantial salary continuation benefits allow employees to elect a lower level of coverage and use the credits elsewhere.

Long-term disability benefit choices are offered in almost 60 per cent of flexible programs. For employers with contributory LTD coverage prior to the introduction of flexible benefits (which employees could decline to take), inclusion of LTD under a flexible program represents an extension of current practice. For other employers with non-contributory coverage, inclusion of LTD under the flexible program may provide employees an opportunity to upgrade existing benefits on an elective (versus company-paid) basis. As an alternative, they may elect lower coverage, or none at all, and use the savings for other choices.

Structure of Options

Following are key issues employers need to address in determining the structure
of options in the area of disability.

(i) **High option.** Generally, 70 per cent pay replacement is the highest LTD benefit
option made available. Replacement of more than 70 per cent of pay may
create insufficient incentive for an employee to seek rehabilitation and return
to work. If the LTD plan is employee-paid, the high option would generally
be less than 70 per cent, because the payout is non-taxable. For STD, a high
option of between 70 and 100 per cent is usually provided.

Underwriting restrictions may dictate a dollar maximum on monthly benefits payable; this may cap the benefit received by employees at higher pay
levels.

Most insurers do not allow disabled employees to receive more than 85 or
90 per cent of their pre-disability income on an after-tax basis. This is implemented through what is often referred to in the insurance industry as an "all
source maximum" — the highest amount of benefit a disabled employee can
receive, including income from other sources, most often the Canada/Quebec
Pension Plan and Worker's Compensation.

This means that higher-income earners in a fully contributory plan (where
benefits are paid tax-free) may have their benefits capped. To reduce the communication challenges associated with capped benefits as a result of reaching
the all source maximum, fully contributory plan options are often tiered (providing lower percentages of pay replacement at higher levels of income). This
is intended to mimic the income tax brackets to produce an after-tax benefit
that will not exceed the all source maximum threshold. For example, a high
option for a fully contributory plan may provide a 70 per cent pay replacement to $2,000 of monthly benefit and 50 per cent pay replacement after that,
subject to any overall dollar maximum on the monthly benefit payable.

(ii) **Low option.** An employee's choice in STD benefits often is simply whether or
not to purchase coverage to fill any gap between the end of sick leave or salary
continuation and the beginning of LTD coverage. Thus, the low-end option is,
in essence, no coverage.

Among flexible programs offering LTD choices, only a few have no coverage
as the low-end option. An employer's decision about whether to allow employees to waive LTD coverage is often influenced by various factors. One is that
Canada/Quebec Pension Plan disability benefits provide, in a sense, a core
level of protection. So employees waiving coverage still have available at least
one alternate source of protection if a disability is serious enough to satisfy
C/QPP criteria. The potential duration of disability is another factor. Some
employers will allow employees over age 55 or 60 to opt out, as the potential duration the employee may receive disability payments is relatively short

compared to that for a younger employee. Another factor is an employer's sense of responsibility to provide all employees with some level of additional protection. In addition, concern over adverse selection (i.e., the likelihood that high-risk employees will be more inclined to elect coverage) also may cause an employer to require at least a minimum level of disability coverage.

Generally, 50 to 60 per cent of pay replacement is the minimum benefit option offered. Less than 50 per cent of pay replacement typically is viewed as too low to allow the employee to maintain an adequate standard of living. Moreover, at lower levels of pay replacement, a large proportion of the benefit typically would be eliminated through integration with government benefits, particularly at lower income levels. This would be of particular concern where employees had been contributing for coverage and then received little benefit from the LTD plan due to integration with C/QPP or other plans.

As in the high option, the lower options for fully contributory plans are often tiered to ensure that the after-tax benefit does not exceed the all source maximum.

(iii) **Number of options.** Unlike many other benefit areas included in a flexible program, most employers with disability options limit the number of choices, with fewer options (if any) offered for short-term disability than for long-term disability.

The typical objective of disability benefits is to allow an employee to maintain an adequate standard of living during a period of disability. The range of pay replacement generally considered appropriate for this purpose is relatively narrow.

For long-term disability, 50 to 70 per cent pay replacement is usually considered adequate. Although employers could offer multiple options within that range, the difference in cost (and benefit dollars) is fairly small. Some employers provide two clear-cut choices in LTD — options of one-half and two-thirds pay replacement. Other employers might provide a non-contributory core benefit with a relatively modest dollar maximum (such as $1,500 per month), or a low level of pay replacement (such as 50 per cent), or a low limit on covered pay (such as $2,000 per month), or no indexing of the benefit with inflation, and allow employees who are affected by these limits to select higher options (at their cost).

Although LTD plans only provide two or three levels of benefit, an increasing proportion of plans double the number of choices by allowing the employee to purchase an inflation-protected LTD benefit with a higher premium. An employee would, therefore, have two choices to make: first, what initial level of benefit is appropriate (say, 50, 60, or 70 per cent); and second, whether or not the benefit should be indexed. Few, if any, plans have full inflation protection. Instead, they protect the full increase in the Consumer Price Index (with some plans protecting a portion of the Consumer Price Index increase — such as 50 or 60 per cent) and limit the annual increase to, say, 5 per cent.

The cost-of-living increases normally occur once a year, starting 12 months after the first LTD payment. Some plans delay the cost-of-living adjustment (COLA) until two or five years after LTD payments begin, to limit costs.

Where STD is included in a flexible program, an employee's choices often parallel the pay replacement amounts available under the LTD plan. On the other hand, the choice may be to extend the duration of benefits to fill any gap between STD and LTD. Choices of this nature are especially important to short-service employees who may not have accrued enough days to cover the LTD waiting period.

Sources of Funds

Funding approaches for disability benefits vary.

For short-term disability, most employers continue to provide salary continuation to currently eligible employees on a fully company-paid basis. However, inside the flexible program, the options for employees with a gap in coverage usually are provided on an employee-pay-all basis.

For long-term disability, funding approaches differ. Basically, the approaches available include continuing to provide fully company-paid coverage, providing a core level of coverage and allowing employees to purchase higher coverage levels, or requiring employees to bear the full cost of coverage. Many employers choose to fund LTD under the flexible program at the same level, as would have been the case under the prior program.

A decision as to whether to use flexible credits or payroll deductions to purchase options under the program is often complicated. Under the *Income Tax Act*, benefits completely paid for by payroll deductions on an after-tax basis are non-taxable to an employee who becomes disabled. On the other hand, benefits attributable to flexible credits are treated as employer-provided and, therefore, are taxable when paid. Some employers require the use of credits for premium payment on the grounds that credits represent a more cost-efficient means of paying for the coverage, since the probability of disability occurring is relatively low and, therefore, the tax consequences of receiving disability benefits will affect relatively few employees. Moreover, in most cases, the marginal tax rate for employees receiving disability benefits is considerably lower than for active employees making contributions. This is due to the reduction in income from full salary to partial pay replacement.

Other employers take the opposite view. They believe their employees are better served by paying the premium with after-tax payroll deductions. In these cases, the benefit is received tax-free by disabled employees.

A third group of employers believes there is no right or wrong answer to the credit versus payroll deduction debate. So, they allow the employee to decide how to pay the premium and, therefore, whether or not the benefit would be taxable.

Some have argued that this complicates LTD choices so much that most employees will not understand the program — employees have two or even three choices to make (level of benefit, how to purchase it, and possibly whether or not to buy inflation protection).

Despite the skeptics, a number of flexible plans do give employees the choice of whether to pay premiums with flexible credits or with payroll deductions. These plans have been very successful, particularly as the use of enrolment technology simplifies plan administration and communication. For example, the Business Development Bank of Canada (BDC) implemented a flexible benefit plan where employees could pay LTD premiums with either flexible credits or payroll deductions. Prior to introducing flexible benefits in 2003, LTD was a company-paid plan. Now, more than a third of BDC employees elect the payroll deduction option and direct their LTD flex credits elsewhere. If any of these employees become disabled, their LTD benefit will be provided tax-free.

A plan offering the choice between payroll deductions and credits must carefully structure the insurance arrangements. No company contribution can directly or indirectly go to the employee-paid plan, or else Canada Revenue Agency would treat the benefit as taxable. Canada Revenue Agency has given written confirmation, however, that where the financial accounting is separate, employees can be given the choice as to how to pay for the benefit.

Option Pricing/Credit Allocation

Under a flexible approach, employers must decide how to price options and allocate credits, assuming the flexible plan has a credit-based financial structure. Typically, the credit allocation and price tags are expressed as a percentage of pay, since the benefits are based on pay. Employers who fully fund one disability option usually attach a $0 price tag to the option under a net pricing approach or provide flexible credits equal to the cost of the coverage if they utilize a credit-based pricing structure. Option price tags usually represent the expected true cost of disability coverage based on insurance carrier rates. Since the range of coverage is limited to 50 to 70 per cent pay replacement, the difference in the cost of various options is usually modest. Although not a common practice, some employers use age-graded prices, since the probability of a long-term disability varies substantially by age.

For the same gross disability benefit, it is likely that the insurance carrier rates and the option price tags will be higher for fully employee-paid plans than those paid partially or fully by the employer. LTD premiums for a fully contributory plan providing a benefit that is not taxable may be 5 to 10 per cent higher than the premiums for a similar plan where the benefit is taxable. The rationale is that adverse selection may be greater for employee-paid plans, since the after-tax benefit is higher and employees are more acutely aware of the plan costs.

The cost of adding inflation protection to an LTD benefit is also relatively modest. A 5 per cent cost-of-living feature might increase LTD premiums by 15 to 20 per cent.

Enrolment/Re-enrolment Restrictions

On initial enrolment, some employers allow employees to choose any LTD option. The majority of employers, however, require proof of insurability if the employee elects higher coverage than under the prior program.

On re-enrolment, most programs require evidence of insurability from employees who wish to increase the level of coverage. The purpose of this requirement is to limit exposure to adverse selection. Evidence is not generally required to add cost-of-living features.

§ 6.4 PROVINCIAL ISSUES

ALBERTA REQUIREMENTS FOR SELF-FUNDED DISABILITY BENEFITS AND LIFE INSURANCE PLANS

In 2003, Alberta passed Bill 12, the *Financial Sector Statutes Amendment Act* ("Bill 12"), which imposes requirements on plan sponsors of self-funded plans. The intent of the legislation was to protect employees from the loss of benefits if their employer went bankrupt. As a result, self-funded life insurance is no longer a viable option for the portion of any plan that includes Alberta employees or residents.

Bill 12 and the associated regulations appear to apply to all death benefits. However, according to the Deputy Superintendent of Alberta Finance, which administers the *Insurance Act*, Bill 12 is meant to allow death benefits of up to $10,000 to be provided on a tax-exempt basis under the *Income Tax Act*, but is meant to forbid any other self-funded life insurance or death benefits.

Bill 12 permits self-funded (ASO) plans which provide short- or long-term income replacement benefits due to disability, sickness, or disease, provided that no death benefit is payable. The rules apply to any entity (employers, associations, or trusts) with plan participants who are employed in or are resident in Alberta. Any provider of an ASO disability plan not meeting these terms — for example, by continuing to provide a death benefit — could be subject to an administrative penalty of up to $10,000 per occurrence.

In addition, ASO disability plan sponsors have an obligation to communicate with plan members in specified ways at specified times.

- **Content.** Plan sponsors are now obligated to disclose to plan members that the benefits provided under the ASO disability plan are not underwritten by an insurer, and that benefits would be payable from the sponsor's net income or retained earnings. The intent is to put employees on notice that there is some risk of non-payment, and that they may wish to seek their own insurance coverage.

- **Timing.** Disclosure is required "prior to or at the time that the benefits are offered." This could be done at the time of initial enrolment for new hires and at the time of annual enrolment for flexible benefit plans. Meeting the disclosure requirement may be as simple as updating plan documentation on any benefits information that is accessible to employees.

- **Recipients.** The fact that Bill 12 applies to members of a self-insured disability plan who are resident in Alberta, even if not employed in Alberta, broadens the legislation's scope. For instance, an employee who works in British Columbia for a British Columbia employer, but who lives in Alberta, would be entitled to disclosure. So would a person who lives in Alberta but is covered by an employer's multi-provincial or Canada-wide self-insured disability benefits plan. Multi-provincial employers who often transfer employees in and out of Alberta may find it simpler to give notice to all new hires or new enrollees in all provinces.

Seven

Flexible Accounts — Health Spending, Personal, and Perquisite

§ 7.1 INTRODUCTION

A flexible account is an individual employee account funded by employer contributions that is set up to reimburse eligible benefit expenses — health care, executive perquisites, or personal benefits. For health care and personal accounts, employees decide whether to participate and how many employer dollars or credits to allocate to each account. Participation in perquisite accounts is typically automatic, based on the role of the individual executive. When an expense is incurred, the employee submits a request for reimbursement to the administrator, who verifies that the expense is eligible, checks that there are sufficient funds in the account, and then issues payment from the account.

THREE TYPES OF ACCOUNTS

A flexible account most commonly serves as a means of paying for health-related expenses. Where the employer wishes to reimburse both health and non-health expenses, separate accounts are set up to cover the health-related expenses (health spending account) and the non–health-related expenses (personal account). A third account may be set up for executive perquisites, although it is normally administered separately from the flexible plan.

If a health spending account is structured properly, these payments are not taxable to the recipient (except for provincial taxes in Quebec). Reimbursement of personal and perquisite expenses is taxable, unless the expense is specifically exempted under the *Income Tax Act*. These accounts can be attractive even where the benefits are taxable to employees, however, due to their inherent flexibility.

The flexible account concept provides considerable versatility to both the employer and the employee. Unlike indemnity plans, in which the employee is purchasing protection in case an event occurs, a flexible account exists to be used.

WHY FLEXIBLE ACCOUNTS ARE POPULAR

Flexible accounts represent one of the most versatile elements within a flexible benefit program. Companies offering a choice-making program can include a health spending or personal account, or both accounts, as a benefit option. And these accounts, particularly health spending accounts, can be adopted on a stand-alone basis in the absence of any other choices within an employer's benefit program.

Perquisite accounts are normally stand-alone programs, although they can be linked to a flexible benefits program by allowing the executive to direct some of the perquisite funds to a health spending or personal account.

Flexible accounts have become very popular, as they allow the employer to:

- Expand the types of benefits offered to employees with little or no additional employer cost (for example, orthodontia, laser eye surgery, and health clubs);
- Add a new benefit without subsidizing an expensive coverage area;
- Offer a benefit that might appeal to only a small segment of the employee population;
- Contain costs by establishing a defined company contribution toward benefits, while providing employees with flexibility over how the funds are spent; and
- Test the appeal of flexible benefits without committing to a broad-based, full-choice program.

Health spending accounts are the most common type of account, primarily due to their tax-favoured status. In addition to the advantages outlined above, health spending accounts can:

- Deliver compensation tax-effectively;
- Encourage employees to self-insure predictable or budgetable expenses that are subject to adverse selection (for example, vision care and basic dental care);

- Soften the impact of higher employee cost sharing through deductibles and co-payment amounts;

- Replace existing coverage: for example, a dental plan or post-retirement benefits. In these cases, all employees are treated equally, while the employer gains control over future cost increases as it determines if and when to increase its allocation to the account. (The use of flexible accounts instead of traditional indemnity plans for post-retirement is increasing in prevalence as employers struggle to manage these ongoing costs and accounting expenses.)

- Obtain the maximum value from health benefits for a Quebec employee. Since a Quebec employee is taxed on the value of medical and dental benefits, the tax on a health spending account is related directly to the benefits received. Contrast this to a traditional health insurance plan, where the taxable benefit value may exceed the benefit actually derived by the employee.

§ 7.2 HEALTH SPENDING ACCOUNTS

OVERVIEW

Under a health spending account, employees are reimbursed for health-related expenses not covered by provincial health insurance or any other health plans. To qualify for tax-favoured treatment, the account must be structured as a private health services plan. Coverage under the plan must, therefore, be for health care expenses that would otherwise have been eligible for a tax credit under the *Income Tax Act*, without reference to the 3-per-cent-of-net-income threshold specified in the act. Once these and other requirements discussed later in this chapter are met, payment of eligible expenses is deductible by the employer and is not taxable to the employee. Note that since a private health services plan is considered to be insurance, payments from these accounts are a taxable benefit under provincial income tax for Quebec employees.

The legal framework or set of rules within which a flexible benefit program must operate is discussed in Chapter 12. The main sources of reference are Canada Revenue Agency *Interpretation Bulletins* on flexible employee benefit programs (*IT-529*), the meaning of private health services plans (*IT-339R2*), employee fringe benefits (*IT-470R*), and medical expense and disability tax credit and attendant care expense deduction (*IT-519R2* (consolidated)). These publications are reproduced in the Appendix.

Expenses can be reimbursed for the employee and eligible dependents. The definition of dependant for health spending accounts can be expanded beyond the traditional dependants (spouse and dependent children) covered under medical and dental plans to include any dependant who is financially dependant on the employee as defined by the *Income Tax Act*. Additional dependants could therefore include elderly parents and financially dependent siblings.

Eligible expenses can include:

- deductible and co-payment amounts, plus benefits exceeding the maximum limits under the medical and dental plans;
- medical practitioners' fees, such as acupuncturists, chiropractors, and speech therapists;
- dental expenses;
- health care facilities, such as nursing homes and institutions;
- medical devices and supplies, including artificial limbs, walkers, and hearing aids;
- other expenses, such as ambulance service and seeing-eye dogs;
- payment of premiums to other insurers for the purchase of medical or dental insurance; and
- payment of premiums to Quebec and Nova Scotia for provincial prescription drug coverage. Note, however, that premiums for provincial Medicare in Alberta and British Columbia cannot be paid tax-free from a health spending account.

An extensive list of eligible expenses is contained in Section 7.8.

REQUIREMENTS FOR HEALTH SPENDING ACCOUNTS

As long as a health spending account meets Canada Revenue Agency guidelines, reimbursements are tax-free to the employee. In such cases, the account is considered a private health services plan and payments are treated the same way as a claim under a traditional supplemental medical or dental plan. The only exception is Quebec, where reimbursements are taxable income for Quebec income tax purposes.

Originally, Canada Revenue Agency indicated that health spending accounts would be treated as private health services plans as long as there was an element of risk to the operation of the accounts. This meant that funds held in health spending accounts were subject to a risk of loss, just as premiums paid for insurance coverage might never be recovered if the insured risk never occurs.

Over the years, the requirements were clarified and softened and now Canada Revenue Agency imposes two major requirements on health spending accounts: to incorporate insurance risk and to prevent abuse. First, employees must designate how much money will be allocated to their accounts only once a year. Second, the plan must require forfeiture of any unused account balances — two forfeiture or "use-it-or-lose-it" methods are acceptable under *IT-529*.

Annual Elections

An employee's election to allocate funds to a health spending account must be made in advance of the plan year and must be irrevocable. Therefore, if an employee allocates employer funds to his or her HSA, those amounts cannot later be withdrawn. They must be used within the HSA in respect of eligible expenses.

If there is a change in the employee's family status, such as marriage or divorce, the birth or death of a family member, or the spouse's loss of coverage or employment, an additional allocation to the account during the year would be acceptable. A reduction would need to be treated carefully to avoid having it appear as a retroactive change.

For employees hired mid-year, immediate enrolment is permissible. Most employers pro-rate the annual amount available, rather than giving access to the full annual amount.

An employee's annual allocation is an estimate of an amount sufficient to cover anticipated claims in the coming plan year. Employees can generally predict some expenses for the coming year, such as the amount they will need for basic dental care or the price of a new pair of eyeglasses. Certain other expenses, though, may be difficult to foresee when employees make their annual elections. Effective communication and planning tools to help employees predict expenses in a coming year can make the annual election requirement less onerous than it appears at first glance.

Rollover/Forfeiture

A major consideration with health spending accounts is that expenses must be anticipated carefully, or the employee will have an unused account balance at year-end. There are two ways of handling the forfeiture of year-end account balances to incorporate a risk element, according to *IT-529*. Plans can either employ a one-year rollover of unused balances or a one-year rollover of unpaid claims. The majority of plans roll over unused balances:

- **Roll over unused balances.** Funds in the account are used to reimburse eligible expenses incurred during the year. Any balance remaining at year-end is rolled over to the next year's account to reimburse expenses incurred in the second year. At the end of the second year any unused amounts from the first year are forfeited.

    Where unused balances are rolled over, any claims in the new year should be reimbursed from the remaining rollover amount to reduce the chance of any forfeiture at the end of the second year.

- **Roll over unpaid claims.** Like the roll-over-unused-balance approach, funds in the account can be used to reimburse eligible expenses incurred during the current year. In addition, unpaid claims from the prior year can also be paid from the current year's balance, as long as the participant allocated funds to the previous year's HSA. Any remaining funds in the account balances at the end of the year are forfeited.

Where unpaid claims are rolled over, any claims from the prior year should be reimbursed first, as any unpaid claims from the current year could be rolled over to the following year.

Health spending accounts must incorporate one, but not both, of these approaches in order to maintain their tax-free status. Note that unused balances cannot be paid out in taxable cash at the end of the year. CRA's view is that to permit cash out or longer rollover periods would violate the indemnity principle of an insurance plan, and thus disqualify the account as a private health services plan.

To illustrate how each approach works, consider how two different employees might be affected.

Roll Over Unused Balances

In the first case, Pat's plan permits the rollover of unused balances. Pat allocates $700 to the account in year 1 and $400 in year 2:

Date	Activity	Amount	Year 1 Remaining Balance	Year 2 Remaining Balance
Year 1				
January 1	Year 1 (account deposit)	$700	$700	n/a
March 10	Claim (medical deductible)	($25)	$675	n/a
June 26	Claim (glasses)	($250)	$425	n/a
August 8	Claim (dental check-up)	($150)	$275	n/a
December 31	Year-end		$275*	n/a
Year 2				
January 1	Year 1 Roll over	$275	$275	$0
January 1	Year 2 (account deposit)	$400	$275	$400
February 15	Claim (medical deductible)	($25)	$250	$400
June 15	Claim (dental check-up)	($155)	$95	$400
December 31	Year-end		$95**	$400***

*Pat would roll $275 over to next year.
**The $95 from year 1 is forfeited.
***Pat would roll $400 (the full amount contributed in year 2) to the third year.

Roll Over Unpaid Claims

In the second case, Rob's plan requires unused balances to be forfeited at year-end, but permits unpaid claims to be rolled over. In this example, Rob's claims in year 1 exceed his available balance by $100; therefore, in year 2, Rob makes sure to make an allocation large enough to at least cover the remaining claims amount from the prior year. Note that Rob cannot pay year 0 expenses from the year 1 account because he made no allocation to the account in year 0.

Date	Activity	Amount	Remaining Balance
Year 1			
January 1	Year 1 (account deposit)	$500	$500
February 8	Claim (dental bridge repair)	($350)	$150
October 28	Claim (glasses)	($250)	$0*
December 31	Year-end	–	$0
Year 2			
January 1	Year 2 (account deposit)	$500	$500
January 1	Claim (unsatisfied Year 1 claim amount)	($100)	$400
October 28	Claim (dental check-up)	($150)	$250
September 18	Claim (medical deductible)	($50)	$200
December 31	Year-end	–	$200**

*Rob would have received only $150 towards his $250 glasses claim, leaving $100 in uncovered claims for payment from next year's account.
**Rob's remaining $200 balance would be forfeited since all year 1 and year 2 claims have been covered.

AN EXAMPLE OF A HEALTH SPENDING ACCOUNT

Under an actual case example, employees are provided with flexible credits of $120. After completing two full years of service, an additional $120 is provided for each year of service, up to 10 years. An employee with 10 or more years of service, therefore, receives flexible credits of $1,320. The company-paid credits may be supplemented by credits generated from other benefits. For example, employees can direct the employer's LTD premium to the account and pay for LTD themselves with after-tax dollars. Prior to the beginning of the year, the employee elects how many credits should be directed to the account.

The plan does not pay the employee's bills for health care directly. Instead, it reimburses expenses incurred by the employee (and/or dependants) that are not reimbursed under any other employer-sponsored plan.

Health care expenses that may be reimbursed under the plan include:

- amounts not paid by the basic medical plan, such as the deductible and co-insurance
- premiums, deductibles, and co-insurance for other health, out-of-country-emergency health care, dental, or vision plans under which the employee or dependants are covered
- virtually all dental expenses (the employer does not have a traditional dental plan)

- prescribed drugs
- virtually all vision expenses (including laser eye surgery)
- hearing expenses
- psychiatric or psychological counselling
- transportation expenses to receive medical care
- miscellaneous expenses, including birth control pills, cosmetic surgery, and smoking cessation or weight-loss programs prescribed by a physician.

The plan operates on a calendar-year basis. At annual re-enrolment, employees can direct credits to the account. During the year, employees submit claims as they are incurred, as long as there is a balance remaining in the health spending account.

Any unused balances at the end of a year are carried forward to next year's account and then forfeited if still unused at the end of the second year.

§ 7.3 PERSONAL ACCOUNTS

Personal accounts are created using excess employer funds that the employee does not spend on other benefits and does not wish to direct to a health spending account. Employers introduce personal accounts when they are not comfortable allowing employees to take unused funds as taxable cash, or when they want to complement other initiatives, such as employee wellness.

A wide range of benefit expenses can be considered for reimbursement from personal accounts. Some employers restrict reimbursement to health/wellness/fitness-related items and label their accounts as "Wellness Accounts."

Others allow reimbursement for health, financial management, and lifestyle expenses, such as the following:

- child care/elder care
- financial counselling
- golf green fees
- gym memberships
- home/auto insurance
- legal counselling
- registered education savings plan
- services of a professional accountant
- sports equipment.

The most generous accounts reimburse any item, provided it is not illegal. Employees with these accounts have had items such as vacations or gas for personal use paid for.

TAX ISSUES

Unlike the tax-favoured status of health spending accounts, items reimbursed through personal accounts generally count as taxable income to the employee. To streamline administration of such accounts, the majority of employers tax the accounts based on the allocations rather than the reimbursements. Because the tax is taken off up front, any balance remaining in the account at year-end can be rolled over indefinitely and even cashed out at termination of employment.

There are two approaches commonly used to withhold the tax on personal accounts:

- Deduct the full amount of tax at the beginning of the plan year; or
- Deduct the tax in equal instalments throughout the year.

In both cases, the full "deposit" is credited to the account and the tax is handled through payroll.

AN EXAMPLE OF A PERSONAL ACCOUNT

In an actual case example, an organization wanted to provide additional uses for credits within its flexible benefit plan, so it created a personal account option.

Employees can choose to direct funds to the account as part of the annual flexible benefit plan enrolment. These funds come from the total company-provided flexible credits allocated for use by employees in the flexible benefit plan, and from amounts generated by selling vacation days. Employees may direct any amount from these sources to the personal account. Income tax on the allocation is withheld during the year.

Employees can access their full account balance at any time. The expectation is that employees will use their full accounts each year. Unused balances are simply carried forward to the next year — there is no use-it-or-lose-it rule, since contributions are taxed in the year they are made. However, the company does not pay any interest on personal account balances.

Employees submit claims up to the amount of their account balance to the administrator.

Eligible expenses include:

- a variety of wellness items (physical fitness, smoking-cessation programs (including programs for spouses))
- weight control, mental health (stress management, yoga, tai chi)
- St. John's Ambulance courses and CPR courses
- daycare/elder care expenses
- individual life insurance premiums (the company is a life insurance company).

§ 7.4 EXECUTIVE PERQUISITE ACCOUNTS

A perquisite account is a discretionary personal spending account for executives. Participants are provided with an allowance they can use to purchase perquisites from a list of available choices. They can spend their entire allowance on one item or divide it among several items. The employer determines the key plan features, such as the amount of the allowance for each executive and the type of perquisites that are available. Sometimes there is a specified list of items within a particular category, while in other cases choices are completely at the executive's discretion. The former approach allows the employer to direct the executive's choices within corporate policies, such as the type of company car that may be leased or purchased.

Executive perquisite accounts are becoming more popular in Canada. Employer objectives for introducing such an account are very similar to the reasons employers introduce flexible benefit plans and include:

- Each executive can choose the perquisites of most value to him or her;
- The employer's cost is limited to a fixed dollar amount;
- Administration can be reduced compared to a traditional perquisite program, since each executive makes his or her own arrangements and submits expenses to the company for reimbursement;
- Executives can maximize the tax-effectiveness of perquisites by choosing how to spend the money in the account (the tax treatment of the perquisite account dollars spent depends on the type of perquisite chosen);
- Communicating the value of perquisites for executives; and
- Treating executives in similar roles equally. (A traditional perquisite plan might pay for a golf club membership, which may of no value to a non-golfer. A perquisite account allows this executive to direct the funds elsewhere.)

The following items are eligible expenses in a typical perquisite account:

- Automobile
- Business attire
- Business-class air travel
- Cellular phone
  - business
  - personal
- Charitable contributions
- Child care
- Club memberships
- Elder care
- Entertainment expenses

- Financial counselling
- Health/fitness club
- Home computer
- Home security
- Legal counselling
- Newspaper/magazine subscriptions
- Optional life insurance
- Retirement counselling
- School fees
- Spouse travel if business-related
- Vacation travel

TAX ISSUES

The tax treatment of a perquisite account depends on the type of perquisite that is being reimbursed. For example, reimbursement of normal business attire would be taxable, while payment for retirement planning would normally be non-taxable.

Although Canada Revenue Agency has not ruled on perquisite accounts, it is likely that any unused amounts would have to be paid out or forfeited at year-end; otherwise, the plan could possibly be considered a salary deferral arrangement.

AN EXAMPLE OF A PERQUISITE ACCOUNT

An organization sponsored a traditional perquisite plan under which specified executives were entitled to benefits such as automobiles, parking, and health and social club memberships. The company converted to a perquisite account to simplify administration, provide more value to executives, and cap the company's costs.

Executives are provided with annual allocations according to the following schedule:

- Chief executive officer: $40,000
- Senior vice presidents and other direct reports to CEO: $30,000
- Vice presidents: $17,500
- Directors: $10,000

Individuals joining the executive group during the year receive a proportional allocation.

Executives submit claims up to their account balance to the company, which reimburses the executive. Any tax payable on the perquisite is withheld from the reimbursement. Any balances in the account at year end are forfeited.

On retirement, death, or termination (except for cause) of the executive, the account remains open for the balance of the year. Any remaining funds are then forfeited.

Eligible expenses include:

- Automobile
- Business-class air travel
- Charitable contributions
- Club memberships
- Financial counselling
- Health/fitness club
- Home security
- Legal counselling
- Retirement counselling

§ 7.5 ACCOUNT MECHANICS

Employees decide whether to direct funds to each type of flexible account offered by the company prior to the beginning of a plan year. Typically, a health spending account would be established, which may be supplemented by a personal account. These funds may arise from any of the sources identified below. Funds may not be transferred from one type of account to another during the plan year.

CREATION OF ACCOUNTS

With the elections in place, the employer creates individual book accounts for each flexible account in which the employee has chosen to participate. No formal segregation of assets takes place and no monies are deposited in trust. Instead, the accounts are carried on the books of the employer, who tracks both debits (reimbursements) and credits (accruals).

SOURCES OF FUNDS

There are many possible sources of company contributions to a flexible account. If accounts are being offered as a new benefit, an employer may have the resources to channel new money into the accounts. If the flexible accounts are part of a full-choice flexible benefit program, the plan design usually dictates how many credits each employee will be able to spend for the whole program. By choosing lower-cost options where available, employer funds are freed up and may be directed to the expense accounts. The employer need not make a specific allocation of funds to the account; each employee is expected to determine the mix of benefits and expense account amounts that best fits his or her particular needs. In contrast, stand-alone accounts are funded by direct employer contributions only.

Additional Sources for Health Spending Accounts

Recent rulings from Canada Revenue Agency permit a portion of a bonus to be allocated to an employee's health spending account. This can be very attractive for bonus-eligible employees as it allows them to significantly increase the available funds in the tax-free account. (Refer to Chapter 12 for a discussion of this ruling, including a summary of the required conditions.) Another source of additional pre-tax funds is the financial security structure described in Chapter 4. Under this approach, employees can choose to allocate all or part of their company savings plan match to the flexible account.

Some employers have introduced a health spending account as a way to ease concern over reduced health care benefits. Part of the employer's savings from adopting a less valuable medical plan might be contributed to employee accounts.

Communication Issues

How the employer contribution is communicated to employees is an important consideration in implementing an account. If there is no guarantee that employer contributions will continue at the same level in the future, or if the first year contribution is seed money, not to be repeated in future years, this should be made clear in the initial communication to employees. If the contribution is tied to savings in other parts of the benefit program, employees may expect information on how well costs have been controlled.

Timing of "Deposits"

Employer contributions and benefit trade-off dollars may be deposited at the start of the year, uniformly throughout the year, or in blocks (for example, at the end of each quarter) to reduce the record-keeping effort.

If the funds are allocated in full at the beginning of the plan year, the employer is at financial risk if an employee is reimbursed in full and then terminates. For this reason, some plans credit the accounts on a monthly basis. In these cases, reimbursements are only made up to the amount credited in the account and any excess claim is carried forward and reimbursed from future amounts credited to the account. Employees find accounts to be more valuable where access to the full balance is permitted at any time during the year, because reimbursement of a claim is not delayed or spread over the year.

PAYMENT OF EXPENSES

When an employee incurs an eligible expense under one of the accounts, he or she completes a reimbursement claim form and submits it, along with a copy of the bill or receipt or other proof of payment to the plan administrator for reimbursement. The administrator, after reviewing the claim for eligibility and availability of funds, reimburses the employee for the amount of the claim. The payment process is illustrated in Figure 7.1. Administratively, the plan may need to track separate balances if the year-end rollover of unused balances is permitted. The rolled-over balance needs to be tracked separately so that claims from the new year can be applied to it first, to minimize the chance of forfeiture at the end of the year.

Where a health spending account claim is to be submitted in conjunction with a regular medical or dental claim, the insurance carrier can usually accept one combined claim form to simplify the process. For example, consider an employee who purchases eyeglasses costing $500. If the medical plan pays $200, the employee could indicate on the medical claim form that any uninsured amount should automatically be paid from the health spending account. In this case, the employee would receive $500: $200 from the medical plan and $300 from the account, as long as funds are available.

END OF YEAR

After the end of the year, employers typically allow employees a month or two to submit health spending account claims incurred during the year. Once this process is completed, all unused deposits or accruals for active employees are either forfeited or rolled over to the next year, depending on the design of the plan. Any unused deposits or accruals for terminated employees are forfeited and revert to the employer. (In practice, most employees take care to estimate expenses with enough precision to avoid forfeiture.)

Disposition of forfeitures is at the employer's discretion. Funds could be reallocated to flexible account participants on a per capita basis (unrelated to the individual employee's actual amount of forfeiture) on behalf of the employer.

Alternatively, forfeitures could be used to reduce employer benefit costs in a subsequent year. A further possibility would be to donate the forfeited funds to a charitable organization on behalf of the employer.

Figure 7.1
Flexible Account Claims

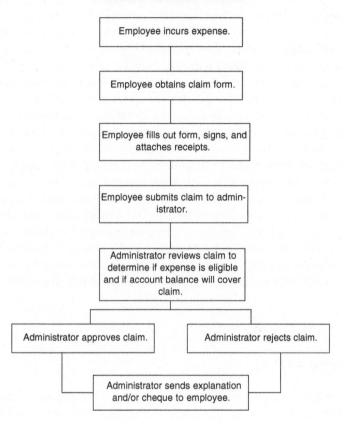

§ 7.6 DESIGN CONSIDERATIONS

TYPE OF APPROACH

Flexible expense accounts may serve as the cornerstone of a flexible benefit program or exist as another option within a broader choice-making arrangement. The appropriate flexible account design will depend on an organization's objectives.

The first decision the employer must make is whether or not to introduce a flexible account. The second decision is what type(s) of account(s) should be included.

An important consideration in whether or not to introduce an account is the amount of funds that could be directed to the account. If an employee could allocate only $100 or $200 at most, it may not be worth the administrative and communication effort to install an account. However, if the employee could direct $500, say, from other benefit areas and, possibly, from new employer money, then a flexible account would be an attractive, viable benefit plan. Also, internal administrative capabilities may be a consideration in whether or not to include an expense account, although this is a diminishing issue with the increased availability of third-party administrators and computerized administration packages.

Virtually all employers offering an expense account have a health spending account — these accounts are simple to understand, tax-effective, and complement the other health care plans sponsored by the employer. The growth of health spending accounts has been dramatic; 90 per cent of employers with flexible programs now include such an account in their program. Fewer employers provide a personal account; however, there is growing interest as flexibility increases.

The introduction of a stand-alone health spending account to replace medical benefit plans as a cost management feature has gained some attention. Through this approach, an employer can control its cost through the defined contribution nature of flexible expense accounts. However, in the absence of access to any other health or dental insurance, a stand-alone plan may cause concern among employees. See Section 7.7 for a more complete discussion of this approach.

IMPACT ON OTHER BENEFIT CHOICES

Health Spending Accounts

The tax advantage of paying for deductibles, co-payment amounts, and other non-reimbursed expenses on a pre-tax basis exists only through a health spending account. In a choice-making program, those employees who expect to have few expenses in a particular coverage area may be encouraged to choose a lower-cost option or opt out of a benefit entirely, if they know the expenses they do incur can be reimbursed from their account. For example, employees who anticipate minimal routine dental expenses may choose to opt out of a dental program entirely, using freed-up funds for another benefit package, while any dental expenses that do occur could be reimbursed through a health spending account. Another example would be where an employee decides to elect a low-value (high-deductible) medical care plan, using freed-up credits to purchase additional long-term disability coverage, while expenses toward the high deductible can be reimbursed from the health spending account.

Personal Accounts

The presence of an expense account covering expenses other than health care should have no direct effect on an employee's choices under the traditional benefit options. However, to the extent that the list of eligible expenses under the account is attractive, some employees may elect lower coverage in some of the traditional benefits to free money up for use in the personal account.

Perquisite

Most perquisite accounts operate independent of a flexible benefit plan. Therefore, the presence of an account should have no effect on an executive's flexible benefits choices. The exception is where the executive can direct perquisite funds to a health spending account. Because of the relatively large amount of funds available for perquisites, such an executive could direct significant funds to the health spending account, which could encourage him or her to select a lower medical or dental option.

FUNDING

A number of decisions must be made in determining how to fund flexible accounts. The employer must decide where the funds should come from (new money or dollars freed up from benefit trade-offs), how much is available, when it will be available, whether any limits should be imposed on accounts, and how to handle any forfeitures. Budgeting is relatively straightforward for employers, since the maximum expenditure is the total allocation to the accounts.

LIMITS

Another plan design decision is whether there should be any limits on how much an employee can allocate to the flexible account. A reason for placing a ceiling on contributions is to limit the risk of substantial individual forfeitures or rollovers. In practice, very few plans have a limit.

CHANGES DURING THE YEAR

Several events can potentially trigger changes to a flexible account. Changes in family status, terminations, retirements, and deaths all will occur during the plan year, and there are certain requirements to deal with these changes.

Health Spending Accounts

(i) **Family status changes.** As mentioned earlier, Canada Revenue Agency requires that contribution elections must be made annually in advance and be irrevocable. This is because of the need to maintain an element of insurance — to permit otherwise could enable employees to increase (or decrease) their contributions if a claim situation occurred (or didn't occur). However, Canada Revenue Agency permits an exception to this rule in the event of a change in family status. Typical events that qualify as a change in family status are a marriage or divorce, birth or adoption of a child, a dependant ceasing to qualify as a dependant, or a spouse's loss of coverage or employment. Election changes are acceptable in these instances, as the events are unrelated to situations where the individual needs to increase or decrease a spending account balance. Care must be taken, however, to ensure there is no element of retroactivity in an election change.

Permitting mid-year election changes can complicate administration. As a result, some employers prohibit any mid-year changes to the health spending account balance. This approach is justified on the basis that the longest an employee may have to wait following a family status change is less than 12 months, which typically does not create a hardship situation. This requirement is usually consistent with changes in coverage rules for other benefits in the flexible benefit plan.

To simplify administration, plans that do permit mid-year changes to health spending accounts often require that the employee not reduce the original allocation — the same amount or a greater amount can be allocated. Alternatively, a formula for pro-rating the new balance desired by the employee can be used. In the following example, the new coverage level for an employee switching from an original contribution of $600 at the beginning of the year to a $900 contribution midway through the year can be treated as follows in order to keep the plan within Canada Revenue Agency guidelines:

– Coverage on January 1 = $600 ($50 × 12)
– Coverage rate on July 1 = $900 ($75 × 12)
– Actual coverage in effect on July 1 = $750 ($50 × 6) + ($75 × 6)

In this example, expenses incurred before July 1 would be subject to the $600 coverage maximum; however, the total amount the employee may claim for the year is $750.

(ii) **Terminations.** Canada Revenue Agency requires that health spending account balances be forfeited upon termination. However, the termination date can be defined as either the end of the calendar year of termination or the actual date of termination.

Most employers are concerned that employees terminating mid-year will get more than their fair share of benefits from the health spending account, but do not want the actions of those terminating to drive the plan design for active employees. The primary concern is that terminating employees may collect more in benefits than their contributions would support prior to termination. For example, in plans where the full contribution is credited at the start of the year, a mid-year termination could enable the employee to spend the full year's account balance. This issue is best addressed through plan design whereby contributions are credited evenly throughout the year. In this way, employees have access only to the funds they have "earned." Upon termination, this accrued balance would be the only amount available and minimizes any potential "windfall." The degree of risk to employers from terminations will vary depending upon the demographics of the workforce. In assessing an employer's financial risk from mid-year terminations, consideration needs to be given to factors such as the annual turnover rate, the average rate of plan participation, and the average annual coverage level elected. These factors can then be used to estimate the added risk associated with terminations against the added flexibility and usefulness to employees from a plan design that permits access to the annual account balance any time in the year.

To overcome some of the abruptness of terminating the account when a mid-year termination occurs, some plans keep the account open until the end of the year. This requires additional administrative effort but provides greater flexibility to the terminating employee. While claims that were incurred both prior to and after the termination date may legally be paid from the account, most employers restrict payment to those incurred before termination.

(iii) **Retirements.** Mid-year retirements are generally treated the same way as terminations. In situations where there are no retiree benefits offered, or when there is no retiree expense account feature, employers are more likely to permit access to the account balance until the end of the calendar year of retirement.

When a retiree health spending account is available, whether as part of the postretirement benefit plan or on its own, Canada Revenue Agency permits the balance in the employee's account to be transferred to the individual's retiree health spending account in the year the employee retires. A retiree health spending account is subject to the same rules and conditions as an active employee's account.

(iv) **Deaths.** When an employee dies, the account balance is generally treated as if a termination has occurred. Extending access to the end of the calendar year is permitted and provides added flexibility to the surviving dependants in order to allow them sufficient time to submit any claims for themselves or the employee.

Personal Accounts

(i) **Family status changes.** Flexible programs typically adopt the same approach to handling family status changes for personal accounts as they use for health accounts. To do otherwise would likely cause administration and communication complexities.

(ii) **Terminations, retirements, and deaths.** In these cases, the balance in the account is normally paid to the former employee or beneficiary. Canada Revenue Agency restrictions on health accounts do not apply to the personal accounts, as the funds are normally taxable.

Perquisite Accounts

 (i) **Family status changes.** Since the allocation to an executive's perquisite account does not depend on family status, no changes are necessary to the allocation where the status changes during the year.

(ii) **Terminations, retirements, and deaths.** The approach varies from employer to employer and may even vary from executive to executive. In many cases, the balance in the account is paid to the former executive or beneficiary. However, other employers require that the balance be forfeited on termination (particularly for cause) and on retirement.

DISPOSITION OF FUNDS AT YEAR-END

Health Spending Accounts

The plan design must include a method of disposing of left-over funds in an employee's account at year-end. Of the two approaches described earlier (rolling over unused balances or rolling over unpaid claims), rolling over unpaid claims is easier to administer. If the forfeited funds revert to the employer, it is also generally the more cost-effective. However, employees generally prefer that the unused balances be rolled over, to reduce their risk of forfeiture.

Personal Accounts

Left-over funds are either rolled over to the next year's account (this is the common approach) or paid in cash to the employee. In either case, the employee is taxed on the funds in the current year.

Perquisite Accounts

Left-over funds are typically paid out or forfeited, to ensure that salary deferral rules do not apply to the perquisite plan.

§ 7.7 HEALTH SPENDING ACCOUNTS REPLACING TRADITIONAL HEALTH AND DENTAL PROGRAMS

With the growing emphasis on benefit plan cost management, employers have begun to look at replacing traditional medical and dental plans with health spending accounts. This is particularly true for dental plans, where the financial exposure for employees is less than in medical situations.

More recently there is growing appeal for replacing traditional indemnity insurance plans for postretirement benefits with a health spending account. Not only does this cap the inflationary cost of traditional plans, it also has a positive impact on postretirement benefit liabilities. These accounts may provide different levels of funding based on years of service or a straight contribution per retiree.

Health spending accounts are attractive for cost containment purposes because the employer contribution is fixed; they are tax-effective, provide flexibility, and are relatively simple to administer and communicate. The fixed contribution means the employer has control over the rate of growth of benefit costs. (This is not unique to accounts; it is a fundamental principle of all flexible arrangements.) Rather than being subject to high rates of medical inflation, the employer dictates when and how its contributions to the account will grow. The employer's contributions are tax-deductible and do not give rise to a taxable benefit for employees (except in Quebec). Employees have control over the use of funds in their account, free of such limitations as frequency limits (e.g., dental check-ups), co-insurance, or maxima (e.g., annual paramedical limits). Employees can even use their account balances to pay the premiums for individual medical and dental insurance. Employees can decide for themselves which expenses to cover (subject to Canada Revenue Agency requirements — see Section 7.8). Plan documentation is straightforward.

The drawbacks to relying exclusively on a health spending account to provide traditional medical and dental benefits include providing inadequate coverage for large expenses and creating inequities for some employees. By their very nature, the health spending account approach means that only a fixed amount of money is available to the employee, although the rollover feature can extend this somewhat. Unlike an insurance plan, which promises a benefit in the event of a claim (subject to certain limitations) in a significant medical situation, the employer's contribution to an account will be insufficient. In short, there is no real insurance protection. With the cost of medical expenses rising faster than general inflation and the increasing evidence of substantial government cost-shifting from provincial medical plans, employees' needs for insurance protection are increasing. The contribution basis can also create inequities. A flat contribution per employee to a health spending account usually means family employees receive relatively less benefit protection than single employees. A percentage of pay contribution, while equitable from a total compensation perspective, means lower-paid employees receive less coverage than higher-paid employees — but lower-paid employees often have a greater need for protection from health costs.

Combining the elements of both approaches through a flexible benefit plan structure — the fixed contribution feature of a health spending account and the defined benefit available from an indemnity plan — can represent a better way for employers to achieve both objectives of cost management and meeting employee needs, rather than simply replacing the insurance plan with a spending account.

§ 7.8 ELIGIBLE EXPENSES FOR HEALTH SPENDING ACCOUNTS

The usefulness of a health spending account is very broad. The eligible expenses are those that would be tax-deductible and are listed in the *Income Tax Act*, its regulations, and *Interpretation Bulletins*. Taxpayers can claim tax credits for eligible expenses for tax purposes for themselves, their spouses, or any dependants for whom they may be claiming a tax credit that year. This list is kept up to date and current on the government's Web site: http://www.cra-arc.gc.ca/E/pub/tp/it519r2-consolid/README.html IT519R2-CONSOLID Medical Expense and Disability Tax Credits and Attendant Care Expense Deduction.

In addition to deductibles and co-insurance amounts, the expenses covered by the account could include the following items, as long as no other provincial health insurance or private health care plan covers them.

PRACTITIONERS

Registered in the province where the expense occurred:

- Acupuncturists
- Chiropodists (or podiatrists)
- Chiropractors
- Christian Science practitioners
- Dental hygienists
- Dietitians
- Naturopaths
- Occupational therapists who are members of the Canadian Association of Occupational Therapists
- Osteopaths
- Physiotherapists
- Psychoanalysts who are members of the Canadian Institute of Psychoanalysis or of the Quebec Association of Jungian Psychoanalysts
- Psychologists
- Qualified speech-language pathologists or audiologists such as, for example, a person who is certified as such by the Canadian Association of Speech-Language Pathologists and Audiologists (CASLPA) or a provincial affiliate of that organization
- Therapeutists (or therapists).

DENTAL EXPENSES

- preventive, diagnostic, restorative, orthodontic, and therapeutic care.

FACILITIES

- Amounts paid to a nursing home for the full-time care of a patient who, due to a lack of normal mental capacity, will be dependent upon others for now and the foreseeable future.
- Payments to a public or licensed private hospital.
- Payments to a special school, institution, or other place for care, training, or use of equipment, facilities, or personnel, with regard to a mentally or physically handicapped individual. An "appropriately qualified person" must certify the individual and his or her special requirements.
- Remuneration paid for a full-time attendant, if the patient lives in a self-contained domestic establishment (for example, his or her home). A doctor must certify that the patient is likely to be dependent on others for his or her personal needs by reason of physical or mental infirmity that is of indefinite duration.
- Remuneration paid for a full-time attendant, or for the cost of full-time care in a nursing home, for a patient who has a severe and prolonged mental or physical impairment. The condition must be certified by a medical doctor or optometrist, where applicable. An impairment is considered severe and prolonged if it markedly restricts daily activities and can reasonably be expected to last for a continuous period of at least twelve months.

DEVICES AND SUPPLIES

- Artificial eye
- Artificial limbs
- Crutches
- Cloth diapers or disposable briefs for use by persons who are incontinent by reason of illness, injury, or affliction
- Device designed exclusively to enable an individual with a mobility impairment to operate a vehicle
- Device designed to assist a disabled individual in walking
- Device designed to be attached to infants diagnosed as being prone to sudden infant death syndrome in order to sound an alarm if the infant ceases to breathe
- Device designed to enable diabetics to measure blood sugar levels
- Device or equipment designed to pace or monitor the heart of an individual who suffers from heart disease
- Device or equipment, including a replacement part, designed exclusively for use by an individual who is suffering from a severe chronic respiratory ailment

or a severe chronic immune system disregulation, but not including an air conditioner, humidifier, dehumidifier, or air cleaner

- Device or equipment, including a synthetic speech system, Braille printer, and large print-on-screen device, designed exclusively to be used by a blind individual in the operation of a computer
- Device to decode special television signals to permit the vocal portion of the signal to be visually displayed
- Drugs, medications, or other preparations or substances prescribed by a medical practitioner or dentist and recorded by a pharmacist
- Electronic or computerized environmental control system designed exclusively for the use of an individual with a severe and prolonged mobility restriction
- Electronic speech synthesizer that enables a mute individual to communicate by use of a portable keyboard
- External breast prosthesis that is required because of a mastectomy
- Extremity pump or elastic support hose designed exclusively to relieve swelling caused by chronic lymphedema
- Eyeglasses or other devices for the treatment or correction of a patient's vision defect, as prescribed by a medical practitioner or optometrist
- Hearing aids
- Hospital bed, including attachments to it that may have been included in a prescription
- Ileostomy or colostomy pads
- Inductive coupling osteogenesis stimulator for treating non-union of fractures or aiding in bone fusion
- Infusion pump, including disposable peripherals, used in the treatment of diabetes, or a device designed to enable a diabetic to measure his or her blood sugar level
- Insulin
- Iron lung
- Kidney machines
- Laryngeal speaking aids
- Limb braces
- Mechanical device or equipment designed to be used to assist an individual to enter or leave a bathtub or shower, or to get on or off a toilet
- Needle or syringe
- Optical scanner or similar device designed to be used by blind individuals to enable them to read print

- Orthopedic shoe or boot, or an insert for a shoe or boot, made to order for an individual in accordance with a prescription to overcome a physical disability of the individual
- Oxygen tent or equipment
- Power-operated lift designed exclusively for use by disabled individuals to allow them access to different levels of a building, or assist them to gain access to a vehicle, or to place wheelchairs in or on a vehicle
- Rocking bed for poliomyelitis victims
- Spinal braces
- Teletypewriter or similar device, including a telephone ringing indicator that enables a deaf or mute individual to receive telephone calls
- Truss for a hernia
- Walkers
- Wheelchairs
- Wig made to order for an individual who has suffered abnormal hair loss owing to disease, medical treatment, or accident

OTHER

- Costs of acquisition, care, and maintenance (including food and veterinarian care) of a dog, if the dog is trained to guide a blind person or alert a profoundly deaf individual. In addition, travelling, board, and lodging expenses, while in full-time attendance at a training institution, are allowable.
- Costs of medical services and supplies outside the province of residence.
- Diagnostic, laboratory, and radiological procedures or services used for maintaining health, preventing disease, or assisting in diagnosis.
- Modifications to a home for a person who lacks normal physical development or is confined to a wheelchair.
- Premiums payable to another private health services plan (e.g., individual travel health insurance).
- Premiums payable to a provincial pharmacare plan.
- Physician block fees.
- On behalf of a patient who requires a bone marrow or organ transplant:
  - Reasonable expenses to locate a compatible donor and arrange for the transplant; and
  - Reasonable travel, board, and lodging expenses of the donor and the patient in respect of the transplant.

- Transportation by ambulance to or from a public or licensed private hospital for the patient.
- Transportation expenses paid to an individual who is in the business of providing transportation services to transport the patient and one additional person (if necessary, as certified by a medical practitioner), provided:
  - Equivalent medical services are not available locally;
  - The route taken is reasonably direct; and
  - The medical treatment sought is reasonable and the distance travelled is at least 40 kilometres.
- Reasonable expenses for private transportation if the patient has to travel a distance of over 80 kilometres and hired transportation is not readily available.
- Reasonable expenses for meals and accommodation for the patient and, if required, the accompanying individual, provided the conditions for transportation expenses are satisfied and the distance travelled is at least 80 kilometres.

§ 7.9 PROVINCIAL ISSUES

QUEBEC TAXATION

When a health spending account is structured as a private health services plan, it is not taxable to the employee under the *Income Tax Act*. However, these accounts are a taxable benefit under the provincial income tax for Quebec employees.

Typically, in a choice-making plan, the employee decides the amount of flexible credits to be allocated to the health spending account. This is considered an "individual" plan, since it is a unique and specific agreement between the employer and employee; therefore, the employee is taxed on the amount reimbursed in the given year, plus associated administration fees and taxes.

A taxable benefit should theoretically be deducted from an employee's pay throughout the year, based on estimated spending account payouts. However, Revenue Quebec does not require employers to withhold income tax from employees during the year because health spending account claims are typically relatively small and may be spread over two years with a risk of forfeiture of any remaining amounts. Therefore many employers report the taxable benefit only on the employee's Relevé-1 when the amounts are known following year-end.

Eight

Time Off with Pay

§ 8.1 INTRODUCTION

Benefit programs include several different variations of time off with pay, from vacation through holidays and sick leave to a variety of leaves of absence (such as jury duty and maternity leave). Some of these types of time off, such as vacation, tend to be taken largely at the employee's election. Most holidays are fixed on particular dates, although employers frequently allow a few holidays to float, leaving it to the employee's discretion when to take the days. Sick leave is intended to be used only when the employee is legitimately ill. Leaves of absence, on the other hand, although technically a type of time off, usually are excluded from a flexible program, largely because leaves tend to last an extended period of time and typically require management approval.

While many employers provide sick leave, the provisions most often are intended to cover only employee illnesses; that is, employees are required to use personal days, vacation days, or unpaid leave to care for sick family members — typically, children. Greater recognition of "work and family" issues in the workplace is generating considerable interest in the time-off area of flexible benefit programs.

Another emerging development in the area of time off with pay is the combining of all the different types of paid time off (excluding leaves) into a single umbrella category: personal days or personal time. The employee receives a specified allotment of days and determines how to use the time — whether for vacation or for illness, and sometimes even for holidays. The umbrella category also helps minimize the burden to employers of having to police the separate types of time off. The employee recognizes that excessive sick days erode the time available for vacation and vice versa.

Time off with pay is a popular option within flexible programs; 22 per cent of employers permit buying and 8 per cent permit selling of vacation days.

179

§ 8.2 OBJECTIVES FOR CHOICE-MAKING IN TIME OFF

One of the chief reasons employers include time off in a flexible program is that the trading of vacation time is popular with employees. In fact, time off typically ranks at (or near) the top of the list of benefit changes employees would like to see included in a flexible approach.

For example, buying usually holds considerable appeal for younger employees with shorter service, since vacation allotments usually relate to length of employment. Also, shorter-service employees are more likely to be part of a dual-income household where flexibility in matching vacation schedules is likely to be important. (For example, the employee might be eligible for two weeks, while the spouse may receive three to four weeks elsewhere.) These employees tend to be interested in trading other benefits (for example, supplemental medical when coverage is available through the spouse's employer) for additional time off. Buying of vacation time also may appeal to some longer-service employees who have sufficient vacation time for normal needs, but periodically might be interested in an extended vacation.

Proposals to management to include vacation buying can seem frivolous. Moreover, some managers will have legitimate concerns that increased vacation time will aggravate scheduling problems in areas with workforce shortages. Therefore, during the design process, it is often helpful to gather data on employee needs in the area of time off, particularly for unexpected emergencies such as care of sick children, and to emphasize to management that only a limited number of days will be available for this purpose.

In terms of financial impact, the purchase of time off is equivalent to allowing employees to take unpaid leave, but with less disruption to the income stream. (Also, the stress and conflict employees may feel when requesting unpaid leave is diminished.) Typically, the salary reduction taken to purchase additional time off is a level amount withheld from each paycheque throughout the year.

The opportunity to sell time off tends to appeal to older, longer-service, and often higher-paid employees. Frequently, these employees may be using only a portion of their scheduled vacation time and may be forfeiting the rest in organizations without carry-over provisions. Also, these employees tend to place greater priority on security coverages and may want to use the dollars freed from vacation time to pay for coverages in other areas, particularly in organizations implementing age-related premiums (for example, for life insurance).

Among organizations that permit both buying and selling, the buyers tend to be younger, shorter-service, and lower-paid employees. Conversely, the sellers tend to be somewhat higher-paid employees, most likely those with sufficient seniority to have extra unused days. The net effect of buying and selling between these two groups tends to come close to zero from the standpoint of cost.

Beyond offering a popular option to employees, employers often have other reasons for including time off in a flexible program. Other possible objectives include:

- **Expansion of vacation schedules.** When competitive or other pressures cause an employer to consider extending vacation (or other time-off programs), a flexible approach can enable liberalization without commensurate cost to the employer. An organization may offer employees the option to buy more time without a blanket increase in vacation days for everyone. If an employer wants to pay a portion of the cost, an extra contribution for all employees can be added to the flexible credit pool.

- **Paying for benefits.** Vacation selling can help an employee pay for benefit options selected under a flexible program. Selling five days of vacation time (1/52nd of a year) can add almost 2 per cent of pay to the credit total. This may be an attractive way to allow employees to expand the funds available for purchase of other benefits without a blanket increase in employer contributions. Note however that, as discussed later, Canada Revenue Agency considers vacation selling a taxable event, so any funds generated are considered taxable income to the employee (see Chapter 12). Some employers have reduced vacation time for all employees and provided equivalent pre-tax flexible credits in return. Employees can then choose to buy back the vacation time or use the credits available for other benefits. This is possible only where the vacation schedule is more generous than the provincial requirements.

- **Transition from a banking system.** Historically, many employers have allowed employees to bank unused vacation time for use at a later date. However, the potential for large, unfunded liabilities to accumulate on a company's books often makes vacation banking an unattractive system. To some extent, introduction of a flexible program, including the opportunity to buy or sell vacation days, may provide the motivation or rationale for cutting back or eliminating an existing banking system. As will be discussed later, the carrying forward of unused vacation time is considerably more difficult to accommodate under a choice-making program.

- **Accommodate time off to care for family members, especially children.** A number of factors have contributed to a growing interest among employers in accommodating the needs of employees with children, including the continued rise of two-income and single-parent households, a lengthening work week, and a shortage of daycare facilities (particularly when a child is ill). In some settings, employees have also expressed frustration over having to use vacation time to care for sick children — instead of having the time available for genuine vacation purposes. On the other hand, few employers have been willing to add to payroll costs at the expense of productivity by paying for sick child days as well as employee sick days. As a compromise, a number of companies have been willing to let employees purchase additional time off under a flexible program. This approach permits the employer to avoid the appearance of having employees give up vacation time to meet unexpected family emergencies, while allowing employees to preserve vacation for rest and relaxation.

§ 8.3 TYPES OF TIME-OFF CHOICES

Conceptually, an employer could allow choice-making in any time-off area. In practice, however, the buying and selling of time off is most common in the vacation area. Inclusion of holidays as an area of choice usually is more prevalent in industries that operate every day of the year (such as hospitals and airlines). Sick leave is only rarely included under a flexible program, except to the extent that an employer has consolidated (or intends to consolidate) the various types of time off into a personal leave or paid time-off umbrella. (See also Chapter 6 on disability benefits for discussion of short-term disability coverage under flexible programs.) Other special-purpose types of time off (such as leaves of absence) almost always are left outside flexible program structures.

VACATION

Vacation is the type of time off most frequently included in flexible programs. Typically, employers retain the pre-flexible vacation schedule and permit the buying of additional days beyond that point or the selling of days within the existing schedule. Key issues relating to designing a vacation option include:

- **Number of days.** Companies generally limit the number of days that may be traded, for several reasons. One reason is to limit the magnitude of the amount of soft-dollar expense from time off that can be converted into hard-dollar cost (i.e., converting unused days to taxable flexible credits or cash, if the plan permits). Another reason is that limiting the number of days that can be bought or sold to a set number helps minimize potential scheduling problems, particularly in situations where the employee would need to be replaced during the vacation.

- **Units of time.** Conceivably, organizations could permit the buying or selling of vacation in any increment of time. In practice, most organizations use days. Denominating time off in days — rather than a block of time, such as a week — offers employees greater flexibility, especially with the fairly high price of purchasing a full week of vacation (usually about 2 per cent of annual pay). On the other hand, blocks of time may be easier to track, particularly in organizations with non-standard work weeks (such as ten- or twelve-hour shifts). Denominating time off in units of less than a day is rare.

- **Pricing of time.** The pricing of time off raises issues relating to economics versus perception. From an economic standpoint, a case could be made that the value of a day of time is higher than the actual daily rate for buying purposes and lower for selling purposes. That is, both the cost of employee benefits and the value of unused vacation time currently donated to the employer (that does not allow vacation banking) should be factored into the arithmetic. Only rarely, however, are employers able to calculate the true value of time off with such precision — or convince employees of the logic of such an approach. As a result, most flexible programs price time off at 100 per cent of the daily rate of pay.

  Occasionally, a dollar maximum is placed on the price assigned to a day of vacation, especially for selling days, in order to limit the hard-dollar exposure from highly paid employees.

HOLIDAYS

The inclusion of holidays in a choice-making program usually is related on the employer's business. Some organizations operate every day of the year (for example, hospitals), so the buying or selling of holidays can be treated in much the same way as vacation time. In fact, at these organizations, vacation and holiday time frequently are treated as like entities and continue as such under a choice-making program.

At most organizations, however, practical barriers prohibit the inclusion of holidays. If an organization is closed on designated holidays (for example, national or provincial holidays), allowing sale of the day makes little sense. Many organizations make available additional floating days that employees may take largely at their discretion (much like vacation). It is the floating, rather than fixed, holidays that become eligible for trade under the choice-making program.

Floating days also may work well as options in an organization that wants to provide time-off flexibility but is constrained by a vacation banking system. Floating days usually are not subject to banking in the same way as vacation days. Outside the flexible program, the employer might retain banking of vacation days, while inside the program, only the floating days are available as a choice area.

PERSONAL DAYS

In general, few organizations include sick leave or initial illness days as a choice area within a flexible program. (Typically, sick leave policies provide full or partial salary continuation for a period of time, such as 30 days or a period related to the employee's length of service.) Companies tend to have more difficulty with the abuse of sick leave than almost any other benefit area. It is a difficult management problem to control, with major cost implications, when employees treat accrued sick time as though it were vacation.

Instead, some organizations have opted to consolidate vacation, holidays (all or only the floating days), and sick leave into an umbrella of paid time off. The idea is to move away from the traditional concept of special-purpose types of time off and into an environment that provides a total number of days with pay and permits employees to decide how to use those days — whether for vacation or illness. The total number of days off may remain the same, or the sick days may be reduced, but the point is to create awareness that only a certain number of personal days will be allotted each year. A flexible approach simply allows employees to buy or sell days above or below their specified allotment. This is an area where there has been substantially more uptake in the U.S. than in Canada, at least partly due to regulatory differences (i.e., in statutory minimum vacation time).

§ 8.4 REGULATORY RESTRICTIONS ON TIME-OFF CHOICES

Time off is unlike almost any other benefit area that could be included under a flexible program. Outside a flexible program, an employee who has earned time off often has a choice to take that vacation now or later or to carry over unused time, generally without application of any special rules. Canada Revenue Agency has stated, however, that offering this same choice in a flexible program could trigger special rules — namely, the prohibition against deferral of compensation except as allowed under Section 248(1) of the *Income Tax Act*.

CANADA REVENUE AGENCY'S POSITION

Canada Revenue Agency outlines its position concerning vacation buying and selling in *Interpretation Bulletin IT-529*.

Vacation Buying

According to *IT-529*, the flexible program must be structured so that any time off purchased with flexible credits or salary reduction cannot be carried forward from one year to the next. The rationale is that a carry-forward could create prohibited salary deferral — salary deferral through the buying of vacation does not fall under the permissible methods specified in Section 248(1) of the *Income Tax Act*.

Therefore unused days must either be cashed out within the year they are purchased, or forfeited.

A plan sponsor wanting to minimize the risk of a Canada Revenue Agency challenge could split vacation days into two types — regular and purchased days. Regular vacation should be used first. Purchased vacation would only be used after all regular vacation has been used. To prevent any employee from using a vacation-buying feature to build up large amounts of untaxed deferred compensation, the plan would require that any unused purchased vacation be cashed out at the end of the year.

For example, assume an employee is entitled to four weeks of vacation and the flexible feature permits the employee to buy five additional days. If that employee elects to buy a week, for a total of five weeks of vacation, then the employee's purchased days are the extra five days in excess of four weeks.

- If the employee uses all five weeks of vacation, no days are cashed out.
- If the employee uses only four weeks of vacation, the five purchased days cannot be banked — they must be cashed out.
- If the employee uses only three weeks of vacation, the five unused, regular days would be eligible to be carried forward for use in the subsequent year. However, the five unused, purchased days would still have to be cashed out.

Most companies encourage employees to use vacation days — whether regular or purchased — in the current year to avoid loss of unused vacation time. Alternatively, some organizations will cash out any unused purchased days before the end of the year. That way, the employee avoids being in the position of deferring compensation to a subsequent tax year.

Vacation Selling

According to *IT-529*, all amounts generated from vacation selling are taxable income to the employee. The amount credited to the plan is taxable in the year of sale. The Canada Revenue Agency considers that an employee's entitlement to vacation each year is a right that has value to that employee. Even in a situation where the employee must forfeit his or her vacation entitlement at the end of the year if not taken, the entitlement still has value if the employee can convert the entitlement to flex credits.

PROVINCIAL LABOUR STANDARDS

Labour Standards Acts or similar legislation can restrict vacation selling within a flexible program. Each province and territory has an act giving minimum vacation requirements for employees under its jurisdiction. For federally regulated industries, the *Canada Labour Code* contains similar requirements. The minimum vacation entitlements are summarized in Table 8.1.

Table 8.1
Minimum Vacation Entitlement in Each Province

Jurisdiction	Annual Vacation	Vacation Pay (as per cent of annual earnings)	Eligibility
Federal	2 weeks	4%	after 1 year
	3 weeks	6%	after 6 years
Alberta	2 weeks	4%	after 1 year
	3 weeks	6%	after 5 years
British Columbia	2 weeks	4%	after 1 year
	3 weeks	6%	after 5 years
Manitoba	2 weeks	4%	after 1 year
	3 weeks	6%	after 5 years
New Brunswick	2 weeks	4%	after 1 year
	3 weeks	6%	after 8 years
Newfoundland and Labrador	2 weeks	4%	after 1 year
	3 weeks	6%	after 5 years
Northwest Territories	2 weeks	4%	after 1 year
	3 weeks	6%	after 15 years
Nova Scotia	2 weeks	4%	after 1 year
	3 weeks	6%	after 8 years
Nunavut	2 weeks	4%	after 1 year
	3 weeks	6%	after 5 years
Ontario	2 weeks	4%	after 1 year
Prince Edward Island	2 weeks	4%	after 1 year
Quebec	2 weeks	4%	after 1 year
	3 weeks	6%	after 5 years
Saskatchewan	3 weeks	5.77%	after 1 year
	4 weeks	7.69%	after 10 years
Yukon Territory	2 weeks	4%	after 1 year

§ 8.5 DESIGN CONSIDERATIONS

TYPE OF APPROACH

One key consideration is whether to allow choices in the area of time off. As mentioned in Section 8.4, the banking of purchased time off under a flexible program is prohibited. Therefore, organizations with extensive banking arrangements already in place either would need to modify current practices or retain vacation banking outside the flexible program, while permitting more limited choices (such as floating holidays or purchase of additional non-bankable vacation days) within the flexible program.

Other considerations relate to the areas of scheduling (for buying) and hard-dollar cost (for selling). Allowing employees to buy extra time off raises the potential for scheduling conflicts — or greater costs if the employee who buys extra vacation must be replaced at a higher rate. As a result, most organizations are careful to communicate that purchased time off requires the same scheduling and co-ordination with management or supervisory staff as regular vacation. (In fact, some organizations require a supervisor's approval before the employee may purchase additional days.)

The selling of time involves conversion of soft-dollar expense to hard-dollar cost, particularly among employees who previously failed to use their entire allotment. In practice, however, most employers find that even among senior (higher-paid) employees, vacation remains a valuable benefit, so the amount of time actually sold has a relatively modest impact on costs. Further, where vacation buying is also allowed, more employees tend to purchase vacation time, so the net cost effect tends to be minimal.

For employers interested in offering flexibility in time off, the trend in recent years has been to combine opportunities, rather than to allow only buying or selling. The combined offering tends to mitigate the cost effect of allowing selling only and provides the broadest flexibility to employees.

AREAS OF CHOICE

Majority practice is to restrict time-off choices to vacation only. Sometimes employers will include holidays — usually only the days that float. The exception is industries that operate every day of the year, so that the trading of holidays represents a practical option. Sick leave is eligible for trading only to the extent that an organization already has converted to an umbrella time-off program that treats all time off as personal days, regardless of reason.

LIMITS ON CHOICE

Most programs place some limits on the trading of time off. Usually, the limits take the form of a maximum number of days that may be bought or sold — typically five days either way. Most organizations set a price for days bought or sold at 100 per cent of pay. Only a minority of organizations limit their exposure by capping the dollar amount on days sold (for example, actual pay to no more than $300 per day). Separately, most organizations require employees to take some vacation time (for example, a minimum of two weeks or the provincial standard, if greater) at least partly to restrict the potential for abuse in terms of allowing employees to cash out vacation and then use the time anyway.

DIFFERENT CALENDAR AND FLEXIBLE PLAN YEARS

Canada Revenue Agency's opinion that unused, purchased vacation days must be cashed out before the end of the calendar year is difficult or impossible to administer where the flexible plan year does not end December 31. For example, consider a flexible plan where employees select benefits for the period April 1 to March 31. Since the flexible year is only three-quarters completed by December 31, the plan administrator does not know which purchased days will be used by March 31. In this case, a reasonable application of Canada Revenue Agency's position would require that the unused, purchased days be cashed out by the end of the following calendar year. Another approach is to treat the plan year as the date that everything is based on, that is, cashed out or forfeited at the end of the plan year, ignoring the calendar year. Applying all within a fixed 12-month period is also a "reasonable application" of CRA's calendar year rules.

ADMINISTRATION OF CHOICES

To some extent, an organization's level of comfort with vacation choices may hinge on the systems and procedures already in place to monitor time-off recording. At issue is the potential for abuse — allowing employees either to cash out a portion of time off and use the days anyway, or to take more time than even an additional purchased allotment. Different organizations decide the issue in different ways. Some have adequate controls in place to monitor time reporting accurately. Some require the manager's approval before buying additional days. Others have only limited concern over the potential for employees abusing time-off policies, irrespective of controls. In any event, administration may loom as an issue that inclines an organization one way or the other on inclusion of time-off choices in a flexible program.

Because of Canada Revenue Agency's position that selling vacation time creates a taxable benefit, it is important to review the capabilities of the flexible benefit administration system to support this plan design. Modification may be required if the administration system forces vacation selling dollars into the non-taxable credit pool, a common feature of U.S.-developed administration systems.

§ 8.6 PAYING FOR PURCHASED VACATION

For administrative simplicity, most plans require employees to purchase vacation using either credits or payroll deductions. If payroll deductions are used, they have the effect of reducing gross earnings, i.e., they are a pre-tax salary reduction. CRA confirmed this treatment in IT-529 by describing vacation bought with payroll deductions as equivalent to unpaid leave.

Nine

Flexible Benefits for Retirees

§ 9.1 INTRODUCTION

For many years retiree benefits were an afterthought — companies typically continued their active employees' health coverages in retirement and offered limited life insurance. This approach has changed dramatically in recent years, as the majority of employers have either changed or are planning on changing their approach to providing benefits for their retirees.

According to a survey conducted by Hewitt Associates in December 2005, only 45 per cent of employers provide retiree benefit plans. The most common reasons why these employers sponsor retiree benefits are to provide competitive total compensation (76 per cent), to reward long-service employees (56 per cent), and to attract and retain employees (46 per cent). The most common reason why 55 per cent of employers do not have retiree plans is the fear of rapidly rising health care costs (82 per cent of employers without plans).

ENVIRONMENT FOR RETIREE BENEFITS

A number of factors have combined to cause employers to reconsider their retiree benefits strategy, including the aging workforce, the rising cost of health care, the accounting rules for recognizing retiree benefit liabilities on financial statements, and provincial downloading to private health care plans.

Canada's aging workforce, including "veterans" (those roughly age 60 plus) and "baby boomers" (those around ages 40 to 60), will be exerting significant pressure on retiree benefit plans in the coming years. The impact of the elimination of mandatory retirement in most provinces may slow some of the pressure, but sooner or later employers will be confronted with what to do about their retiree benefit plans.

Employees are retiring in greater numbers, in many cases retiring earlier and living longer, healthier lives than ever before. As a result, the retiree population is as diverse in needs as the active workforce — including the young retiree with dependent children, the retiree with a mortgage and a still-working spouse with medical coverage, the retiree working part-time on contract for a prior or other employer, and the elderly retiree requiring nursing home care. A single benefit program may not adequately meet the needs of a retiree population with a wide range of ages, health conditions, family situations, working circumstances, and financial situations.

In addition to dealing with the effects of the growing size and diversity of the retiree population, employers continue to struggle with the rising costs of retiree benefits and the challenges raised by the accounting impact of postretirement medical benefits. In 2000, the Canadian Institute of Chartered Accountants (CICA) adopted *Handbook Section 3461*, dealing with Employee Future Benefits. This section requires employers to recognize any retiree medical, dental, life insurance, and other benefits they provide to retirees. The section requires recognition of the cost for existing retirees and for employees who may retire and be eligible for these benefits in the future. Medical plan designs that provide high employer subsidies for retirees and/or incorporate extensive coverage leave the employer open to risk from high medical inflation and can produce a significant accounting expense. These accounting rules, and related plan costs, have forced many employers to re-examine the commitments made to current and future retirees.

Compounding the cost pressures on employer-sponsored retiree benefit plans is the reaction of various governments to their own, similar cost pressures: downloading of costs to retirees through cutbacks under the provincial plans; restrictions on access and coverage; and increasing cost sharing. Employer plans are then forced to make difficult decisions as to how the plan will, or will not, accommodate the government plan changes.

As employers have evaluated their retiree benefit programs, they have sought to balance employees' postretirement security needs with employers' financial constraints. However, for individuals who have already retired, employers have been reluctant to cut back benefits unilaterally (even when such reductions might be legally permissible).

Finally, the provision of retiree benefits is becoming a competitiveness issue. Employees increasingly are looking to employers to provide access to some form of retiree benefits at the same time that employers' retiree populations are growing exponentially. With extensive global competition, the cost and delivery of retiree benefits will be a major business factor.

REASONS FOR ADOPTING RETIREE FLEXIBLE BENEFITS

In addressing these issues, many employers have been attracted to the possibility of adopting some form of retiree flexible benefit program. A flexible benefits plan proves to be an attractive vehicle for a number of reasons:

- A large number of active employees are now covered by flexible benefit plans. These employees are generally receptive to the use of flexible benefits to provide their retiree benefits. This is particularly true for the increasing number of early retirees who leave their employers under restructuring programs that offer early retirement windows.

- The range of retiree medical needs and available alternatives continues to grow. Managed care and health spending account coverage are just some examples of the variety of solutions available to meet retiree medical needs. As the range of needs and alternatives grows, an employer's ability to design a single program and a single set of solutions diminishes. This range of alternatives further serves to make a flexible benefit approach attractive.

- Some employers are turning to a defined contribution approach for retiree medical benefits. Under such an approach, the flexible benefit plan can recognize length of service — for example, retirees can be provided with additional funding for each year of active service. The employer may leave it up to the retiree to decide how the credits are spent — on health spending account contributions, prescription drugs, dental coverage, or life insurance premiums.

- The defined contribution approach can also better deal with the objective of providing access to useful coverage to retirees, while at the same time managing the company's liabilities from both cash flow and accounting requirements. The employer can specify the rate at which it is willing to allow credits to increase over time (including no increase), independent of actual inflation rates.

- Some employers offer retiree life insurance benefits. These benefits may not be important to retirees, or may be a concern due to taxable benefit implications and, therefore, can be a potential source of credits to pay premiums under the retiree supplemental medical plan.

- In the case of existing retirees, a flexible benefit plan can allow the employer to offer retirees a choice between the existing plan and a new supplemental medical plan. The new medical plan may be beneficial to the employer, while the retiree flexible benefit program may contain incentives for retirees to select the new medical plan. For example, retirees might be given the opportunity to utilize a new health spending account. Or the new flexible benefit plan may offer enhanced benefits, such as vision or other coverage not available in the current plan. To many employers, providing retirees with a choice between retaining the current program and selecting a new flexible program is more acceptable than adopting unilateral changes.

As governments continue to struggle with cost pressures of their own and as they shift these costs to employers, employees, and retirees, it is unlikely that an opportunity for tax-assisted retirement health plan savings will emerge. As a result, the need for employees to contribute to their retirement savings plans (e.g., RRSPs) has never been greater. These funds will likely be needed to supplement the ever-rising cost of retiree benefits provided by both governments and employers.

§ 9.2 SPECIAL CONSIDERATIONS

The considerations for a retiree flexible benefit plan are quite similar to those discussed in this book for flexible benefit plans for employees. However, there are some elements that require additional consideration for employers when designing and operating a retiree flexible benefit plan, because of the unique nature of the retiree population. These issues include:

- Design structure: what type of structure makes the most sense for the retiree population? A full flexible benefit plan? A spending account plus catastrophic coverage? How should the plan supplement provincial health plans?

- Legal: does the employer legally have the right to make changes to existing retiree plans, in view of past promises? How can it preserve this right for the future?

- Financial: how much should the employer subsidize the plan, now and in the future? How can the plan be protected against adverse selection and ongoing cost challenges? How can the accounting cost implications be managed? Can an employer even afford to have a retiree benefit plan at all?

- Enrolment: what unique enrolment approaches are appropriate for a retiree group? Is annual enrolment, which is typical for employee plans, appropriate for retirees?

- Communication: how will enrolment opportunities, future changes to the plan design, and pricing changes be communicated?

- Administration: how will retirees make their elections at retirement and in the future? How will retiree contributions toward the cost of their elections be managed?

DESIGN STRUCTURES

Two approaches have emerged to offer flexibility for retirees: full flex plans and simplified flex plans.

The full flex retiree plan is similar in structure to full flex for active employees, with three exceptions:

- The retiree coverages are normally limited to health care and possibly life insurance;
- The retiree options are frequently different from the active plan options due to the different needs of retirees, the availability of provincial drug coverage in most jurisdictions, and the unique cost pressures of retiree medical; and
- The retiree re-enrolment rules may differ from the employee-plan rules.

Simplified flex plans are usually limited to health care and are designed to provide some protection for the retiree, while limiting the employer's long-term liabilities.

Section 9.3 discusses full flex and simplified health care plans in detail.

LEGAL CONSIDERATIONS

A key consideration for employers is whether or not the company can legally change the benefits of existing retirees, or if the new plan applies only to future retirees (perhaps subject to a reasonable notice period and to some grandfathering for employees nearing retirement).

A landmark case concerning an employer's ability to make changes to retiree benefits was the 1993 decision of the Supreme Court of Canada in *Dayco (Canada) Ltd. v. National Automobile, Aerospace and Agricultural Implement Workers' Union of Canada*. Although the *Dayco* case dealt with union-negotiated benefits, the principles are broadly applicable. In *Dayco*, the company discontinued benefits to retirees upon the expiry of the collective agreement. The Supreme Court of Canada held that, depending on the wording of the collective agreement, the promise to provide benefits to retirees can survive the expiration of the agreement. The Court held that the right to retirement benefits can vest upon retirement and any reduction in those benefits can be grieved by the union.

The 1995 decision of the Newfoundland Supreme Court in *Kennedy v. Canadian Saltfish Corporation* followed the *Dayco* decision in a non-unionized setting and awarded damages to the plaintiff whose retiree coverage had been reduced. It is noteworthy that in the *Kennedy* case, the employer did not eliminate benefits, but simply reduced them, following Mr. Kennedy's retirement. The Court held that the plaintiff was entitled to damages for an amount sufficient to allow him to acquire the additional benefits that had been taken away.

These decisions and others suggest that a company's ability to change retiree benefits is limited on the fundamental basis that the retiree benefit plan promise vests at the time of retirement unless the employer has explicitly and specifically reserved the right to make changes in the future. A number of decisions have also considered retiree benefits as earned throughout an employee's active career, forming part of his or her remuneration.

A plan sponsor should review all prior communication and obtain a legal opinion if changes to benefits for existing retirees are being considered. Offering existing retirees a choice between the current plan and the new flexible benefit plan can help ensure the plan sponsor is not subject to litigation.

FINANCIAL CONSIDERATIONS

The accounting treatment of postretirement benefits is governed by *Section 3461* of the *Canadian Institute of Chartered Accountants (CICA) Handbook*. The rules require that employers charge the cost of all postretirement benefits against income over the working lifetime of employees. The Canadian standard mirrors U.S. *FAS Statement 106*.

The expense calculation takes into account expected future medical costs, not just the cost of benefits payable today. It also includes an accrual for all active employees, reflecting the benefits they are expected to receive in retirement based on the likelihood that they will stay employed until they become eligible for postretirement benefits. The combination of projected medical cost increases and inclusion of the entire workforce produces a much larger expense than determined under the previous practice of expensing only the claims of current retirees as incurred.

Since the introduction of *Section 3461* on January 1, 2000, many Canadian employers have changed their postretirement benefit plans to limit, reduce, or even eliminate their liabilities. Changes have included:

1. Modifying plan provisions to:
    (i) Reduce coverage;
   (ii) Cap health care costs where feasible;
   (iii) Introduce cost management approaches; and
   (iv) Limit the risk of government offloading.
2. Limiting eligibility for retiree benefits. Many organizations automatically provide full benefits to any employee who retires — which, in some cases, could mean a 55-year-old employee with two years of service. A minimum of ten, fifteen, or even twenty years of service may be more appropriate.
3. Implementing or increasing retiree cost sharing. One approach is to vary the employer premium subsidy by age and service at retirement. For example, an employer may decide to provide full benefit coverage for someone retiring at age 62 with thirty years of service, but require employees who retire before age 62 or with less than thirty years of service to pay a percentage of the retiree premium.
4. Putting a cap on the employer financial commitment for retiree benefits. This cap could be set at a level that would not be reached for several years. Thus, it

would not affect benefits payable currently, but would limit the amount of medical inflation that needs to be reflected in calculating the liabilities and expenses.

5. Eliminating retiree benefits. This may apply to:
    (i) Future employees only. All current employees would be grandfathered.
    (ii) All employees not yet eligible to retiree, plus all future employees. Employees eligible to retire plus current retirees would be grandfathered.
    (iii) All employees who retire after a specified grandfathering period (frequently two years), plus all future employees. Employees retiring within the two-year window, plus all current retirees, would be grandfathered.

Because of the legal issues arising out of the *Dayco* and *Kennedy* decisions described earlier, very few Canadian employers eliminate retiree benefits for current retirees.

ENROLMENT ISSUES

Often, in order to help maintain the financial integrity of the retiree flexible benefit plan and to protect against adverse selection, the retiree plan is subject to different enrolment rules than those in the employee plan. Considerations include:

* Should retirees re-enrol every year? Every other year? Every five years? At age 65? Only on a change in family status? Or should elections be irrevocable? Sometimes these decisions are influenced more by communication and administrative considerations than by financial issues.
* When in the year should enrolment be scheduled? With many retirees travelling outside Canada for an extended period, a fall enrolment window, which is typical for employee plans, may not be appropriate for retirees.
* Under what circumstances, if any, should a retiree be allowed to increase coverage (e.g., at age 65, or in the event of a loss in spouse's coverage)?
* When a retiree dies, what, if any, coverage and/or company subsidy should be continued to a surviving spouse?
* Can a new family member, such as a new spouse, be added as a covered dependant?

Typically a retiree may elect any option at retirement. Many plans have an annual enrolment for retirees; however, other approaches are also common. In some plans, elections are irrevocable unless the retiree has a life event and makes a request to change coverage. For other plans, increases in coverage may only be allowed if the retiree turns age 65, since provincial coverage often changes at this age (e.g., prescription drug benefits). To further protect against adverse selection, as well as to simplify administration and communication, plans often permit only a reduction in coverage, even with a life event.

COMMUNICATION AND ADMINISTRATION CONSIDERATIONS

One of the significant challenges of a retiree flexible benefit plan is communicating with and seeking elections from retirees. There is generally less connection between the employer and retirees over time than there is with active employees. This is particularly true for employees who retire under defined contribution pension plans and do not receive a pension from their former employer. As a result, many retiree plans require employees to make their elections only at the time of their retirement.

The considerations discussed under "Enrolment Issues" on page 195 are also often driven by administrative considerations, due to the extra effort required to keep in contact with retirees.

While the Internet has made it feasible for retirees to keep in touch with their plan and to enrol online, enrolment for retirees still requires greater effort than for the active population, who can readily be reached by the employer through the employment arrangement. Combine this with potential comprehension issues as the retiree ages and the need to deal with third parties designated by the retiree (e.g., the retiree's children may need to be authorized to make elections, etc., on behalf of the aging parent). This causes many employers to keep the administrative requirements to a minimum, at the risk of reducing some of the plan's flexibility.

Another administrative consideration when designing a retiree flexible benefit plan is the administration of retiree contributions. This element may potentially be overcome through design features such as regular indexation of deductibles and or limits to offset the need for a contribution; however, this approach only captures the plan "users" and not all of the "members" who do not claim under the plan. Another approach may be to arrange with the insurance carrier/plan administrator to establish pre-authorized chequing arrangements through the bank accounts of individual retirees.

A final administrative consideration is managing the number of retiree plans provided by an employer. Many of the closed legacy retiree plans have dwindling membership and are becoming awkward and/or expensive to administer. Introducing a flexible benefit plan may allow an employer to shift retirees to the new plan and, therefore, streamline the number of plans under administration.

Finally, employers need to be clear in their communication with retirees around the employer's right to make changes to the plan design and funding arrangements in the future. It was a lack of clarity on this topic that has resulted in employers being unable to make changes to existing retiree plans at the risk of litigation. So any plan information needs to have wording that protects the employer's right to make changes.

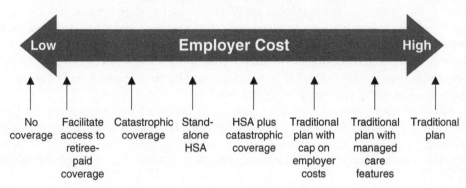

Figure 9.1
Range of Retiree Medical Plan Designs

| No coverage | Facilitate access to retiree-paid coverage | Catastrophic coverage | Stand-alone HSA | HSA plus catastrophic coverage | Traditional plan with cap on employer costs | Traditional plan with managed care features | Traditional plan |

§ 9.3 HEALTH CARE

SPECTRUM OF RETIREE HEALTH CARE BENEFITS

The range of potential options for a retiree flexible benefit plan is wider than the range found in a typical employee plan. The key reasons are the desire to limit the long-term costs of retiree health care and the prevalence of provincially sponsored prescription drug benefits for seniors. While cost containment is a factor in the design of many employee plans, it is a much more widespread and dramatic concern in retiree plans. Many employers believe they do not have any responsibility to offer extensive, open-ended coverage for their retirees.

Figure 9.1 shows the spectrum of medical plans provided today. At the left end of the spectrum are employers that provide no retiree coverage, or facilitate the retiree's ability to purchase private coverage through a third-party provider. In the middle are employers that offer health spending accounts and/or catastrophic plans with high deductibles and limited covered expenses. At the right end of the spectrum are employers that provide traditional medical and dental plans, in some cases with caps on their liability. Retiree flexible plans often include options from several points along this spectrum.

FULL FLEX

A full flexible retiree benefit plan has the same general attributes as a plan for active employees. It can help the employer manage health care costs while at the same time provide retirees access to choices in medical coverage that may appeal to a limited group of retirees — from nursing home coverage to out-of-Canada coverage.

Options

Due to the higher consumption of medical services among retiree groups than among employee groups, most retiree plans provide more restricted coverage than active employee plans. A flexible retiree plan may include several traditional indemnity options, frequently with some limitation on the services covered or the maximum benefits provided. These options could be employer-sponsored plans or plans sponsored by an outside organization.

Retiree plan features that are most often excluded or significantly limited through maximums or frequency limitations are hospital coverage, private-duty nursing, and out-of-Canada coverage. In addition, many retiree plan designs contain annual and/or overall lifetime limitations, while active employee plans do not.

A full flex retiree plan may also include a catastrophic option and a health spending account (HSA). The HSA can be particularly appealing to retirees who are eligible for coverage through one or more sources, such as a working or retired spouse's plan. A flexible retiree plan may allow a retiree to choose lower coverage and make use of a spending account during a period of time when access to other coverage is available.

Financial/Pricing

There are many ways to establish the pricing of a retiree flexible benefit program. As in employee plans, a retiree plan can utilize either a credit-based structure or a net pricing approach. Credit-based pricing readily allows the employer to vary the company subsidy based on years of service and/or age at retirement, much like the accrual of benefits under a defined benefit pension plan.

Approaches used to determine the health care credits for a retiree in a flexible plan include:

- An annual fixed credit for all eligible retirees (e.g., $1,000);
- An annual credit based on service (e.g., $50 per year of service), or age, and/or dependent status; and
- A lump sum credit (e.g., $25,000) intended to last the retiree's life. The retiree can use the credits as a "bank" and draw down the "account" each year, based on the options selected, until the account is exhausted.

The employer should have a defined strategy for the growth of the credits in the future (not unlike similar decisions required for an active employee flexible benefit plan).

SIMPLIFIED RETIREE FLEX

Stand-Alone Health Spending Account

Some employers have replaced their traditional retiree health care plans with a health spending account (HSA). The annual contribution to the HSA can be a flat amount for all retirees (e.g., $1,000), or can be based on service and/or age (e.g., $35 for every year of service, to a maximum of $1,200). The contribution may or may not change over the retiree's lifetime. Additional credits for dependants may be part of the allocation.

A stand-alone HSA is very effective at limiting the employer's current and future costs, as the credit is typically independent of health care inflation. From the retiree's perspective, an HSA is very effective at covering predictable, lower-cost services, such as dental and vision care. However, it does not protect the retiree from major expenses, such as large prescription drug costs and private-duty nursing. To overcome this deficiency, some employers provide a catastrophic medical plan in addition to an HSA.

Health Spending Account Plus Catastrophic Coverage

This structure provides retirees with a health spending account that can be used to purchase a catastrophic health care plan. The catastrophic plan can be provided by the employer, a third party selected by the employer, or from the open market, selected by the retiree.

The structure typically includes:

- An annual employer HSA contribution similar to that discussed for a stand-alone HSA.
- A catastrophic plan with a very high deductible, on the order of $2,500 or more, and restricted coverage for services such as hospital and out-of-country coverage and, in some cases, prescription drugs.
- An option or requirement for the retiree to pay the catastrophic premium from the HSA.

The appeal of this structure for employers is the opportunity to cap the accounting and funding liability to the amount contributed to the HSA.

Example

To illustrate the HSA-plus-catastrophic approach, consider the following design:

1. Annual HSA contribution: $2,000.

2. Catastrophic plan:
  (i) Deductible: $3,000 single; $4,000 family
  (ii) Co-insurance: 80 per cent; 100 per cent after out-of-pocket limit is reached
  (iii) Annual out-of-pocket limit: $6,000 single; $8,000 family.
3. Covered expenses: prescription drugs, private-duty nursing, medical appliances.
4. Annual premium for the catastrophic plan: $400 single; $800 family.

The relationship between the two plans is shown in Figures 9.2 and 9.3.
   The single retiree in Figure 9.2 is left with a net HSA balance of $1,600 after paying the $400 catastrophic premium. The retiree would, therefore, be fully re-imbursed for the first $1,600 of health care expenses in the year. After reaching $1,600, the retiree would be responsible for the next $1,400 of expenses, at which point the $3,000 catastrophic plan deductible would be met. The catastrophic plan would then pay 80 per cent of any covered expenses exceeding $3,000 in the year. Once the retiree had paid $6,000 out of pocket through a combination of the $3,000 deductible and the 20 per cent co-payment, the catastrophic plan would reimburse 100 per cent for the balance of the year.
   In HSA-plus-catastrophic arrangements, employers should monitor the design and pricing of the catastrophic plan. If the plan is not monitored, the premium for the catastrophic coverage will increase and eventually exceed the amount

Figure 9.2
Example of HSA Plus Catastrophic Plan — Single Coverage

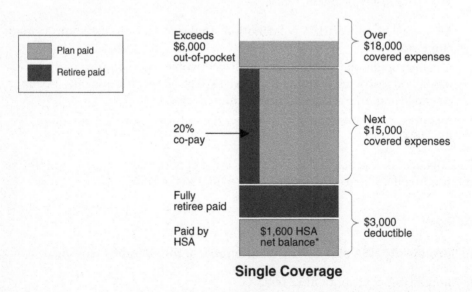

Single Coverage

* $2,000 HSA allocation less $400 catastrophic premium

Figure 9.3
Example of HSA Plus Catastrophic Plan — Family Coverage

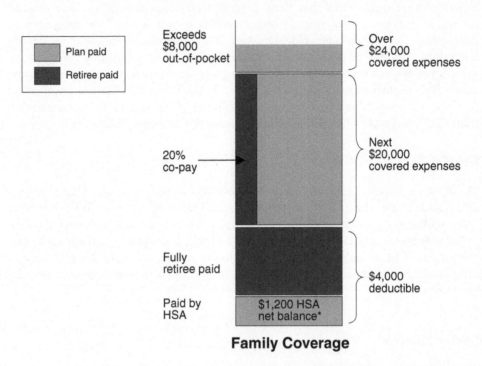

Family Coverage

* $2,000 HSA allocation less $800 catastrophic premium

credited to the HSA. This may occur earlier than the employer anticipates, be-cause more retirees reach the catastrophic deductible each year. This causes the rate of inflation in the plan to significantly exceed the general health care trend rate. Increasing the catastrophic deductible from time to time to keep pace with health care inflation should alleviate this concern. The risk of the premium over-taking the HSA allocation can also be mitigated by using a third-party plan, but such plans typically have greater restrictions (which can include medical evi-dence or pre-existing condition limitations) and are, therefore, of less value to retirees.

ISSUES

Regardless of the ultimate design of the flexible retiree plan, there are two issues that should be addressed: the co-ordination of the prescription benefit with provin-cial plans, and whether or not out-of-Canada health coverage should be provided.

Prescription Drugs

Employers should ensure that their prescription drug plan administrators are taking advantage of any and all opportunities to administer the programs in conjunction with provincial plan features. For example, Ontario's drug benefit formulary contains limited use restrictions, a feature that requires claimants to submit paperwork through their doctor to gain access to certain drugs. In many cases, the employer's drug plan adjudicator is not ensuring that the application process has been completed before providing reimbursement for a medication that might potentially have been eligible under the provincial plan.

Out-of-Canada Coverage

Many retiree benefit plans do not provide out-of-Canada coverage. There are several reasons: first, the cost of coverage is much higher for retirees since they have more opportunity for travel than active employees; second, the high cost of medical care outside Canada, combined with the higher exposure risk, means insurers are reluctant to provide insurance for retirees; and third, there are a variety of other sources for out-of-Canada coverage on the open market, such as association/affinity plans.

DENTAL BENEFITS

Dental plan coverage can be incorporated in a retiree flexible benefit plan, with the appropriate attention paid to plan design and pricing just like under an active employee flexible benefit plan. Orthodontia coverage, however, is typically not required and most of the plan utilization tends to occur in the major services. It is interesting to note that dental plan per capita costs tend to peak in the fifties and then decline.

§ 9.4 DEATH BENEFITS

Retiree life insurance is emerging as a benefit area where employers are offering more choices. There are several key reasons for this recent growth in popularity.

Under the *Income Tax Act*, all amounts of employer-provided life insurance coverage (with the exception of a $10,000 self-insured death benefit) create a taxable benefit to the retiree. When employers introduce flexible benefits for active employees, one of the pricing decisions tends to be a decoupling (or "unblending") of the active employee life insurance premium rate from the retiree premium rate. This change is often made to establish "realistic" pricing for active employees. As a result, the underlying retiree premium rate increases, without the subsidy from the active employee plan. Consequently, retirees see a substantial (two to four times) increase in their taxable benefit. As a result, many retirees question the value of coverage that they feel they no longer need and that creates a taxable benefit they may not be able to afford. This situation provides an opportunity for the employer to allow retirees to opt down or out of life insurance coverage completely. A side benefit to this practice is that it can be used to generate funds that the retiree can then use to pay for the cost of retiree health benefits, which continue to escalate dramatically in cost.

§ 9.5 PROVINCIAL ISSUES

In the past, retiree prescription drug plans had more options for plan design than those for active employees because of the extent of coverage provided by provincial drug plans for seniors, typically those over age 65. In the last decade, however, provincial governments have made a variety of changes to their seniors' drug plans, resulting in substantial cost-shifting to employer-sponsored retiree plans. The successful retiree flexible benefit plan design must contend with these requirements.

QUEBEC

As discussed in Chapter 5, Quebec requires all residents to have prescription drug coverage, either through an employer-sponsored plan or from the government program administered by the Regie de l'assurance-maladie du Quebec (RAMQ). Individuals under age 65 must elect employer coverage, if available. The employer coverage must provide benefits at the same or higher level than the RAMQ standard plan, currently 71 per cent co-insurance for drugs on the provincial formulary after an annual $145.20 deductible, with 100 per cent coverage after an $881 out-of-pocket maximum. As a result, employers with retiree drug coverage must offer at least one option meeting the RAMQ requirements for Quebec early retirees.

At age 65, the Quebec retiree is automatically covered by RAMQ, even if an employer-sponsored plan is available. Opting out is permitted if there is an alternate source of coverage. Since RAMQ requires a significant contribution from participants ($538 per adult per year), many retirees would opt for their prior employer's plan to avoid the premium. This would cause a dramatic cost shifting from RAMQ to the private sector. To prevent this, and keep retirees in RAMQ, many employers charge a substantial premium for post–age 65 RAMQ-equivalent coverage. These employers believe this approach is warranted because the RAMQ premium is subsidized by the Quebec government; the actual cost of providing post-65 prescription drug coverage is significantly higher than the RAMQ premium.

Employers can still provide retiree prescription drug benefits that supplement the RAMQ plan, at their discretion.

NOVA SCOTIA

Nova Scotia's PharmaCare plan provides prescription drug coverage to seniors over age 65, as long as they do not have coverage through a private plan. To prevent employers from cancelling their retiree drug coverage for Nova Scotia retirees, the legislation requires employers to offer drug coverage in Nova Scotia if they provide this coverage elsewhere in Canada. In other words, Nova Scotia has mandated that its plan has second-payer status. As a result, the cost of providing retiree benefits for Nova Scotia retirees is significantly higher than for retirees in most other provinces.

BRITISH COLUMBIA

British Columbia has also effectively become second payer for many retirees by introducing an income-based deductible. The deductible ranges from 0 per cent of income for families with net income under $15,000 to 3 per cent for families with net income exceeding $30,000. Once the deductible is reached, "Fair PharmaCare" pays 70 per cent of drug costs until the income-based out-of-pocket limit is reached, at which point the benefit increases to 100 per cent. Enhanced benefits are provided if at least one family member was born before 1940. Details of British Columbia's plan are shown in Table 9.1 and Table 9.2.

Table 9.1
British Columbia's Fair PharmaCare Plan

Net Annual Family Income	Family Deductible*	PharmaCare Pays	Family Maximum (after which PharmaCare Pays 100%)*
Less than $15,000	None	70%	2% of net income
$15,001 to $30,000	2% of net income	70%	3% of net income
Over $30,000	3% of net income	70%	4% of net income

*The deductible and family maximum are based on income bands.

Table 9.2
British Columbia's Enhanced Fair PharmaCare Plan
(if at least one family member was born before 1940)

Net Annual Family Income	Family Deductible*	PharmaCare Pays	Family Maximum (after which PharmaCare Pays 100%)*
Less than $33,000	None	75%	1.25% of net income
$33,001 to $50,000	1% of net income	75%	2% of net income
Over $50,000	2% of net income	75%	3% of net income

*The deductible and family maximum are based on income bands.

The introduction of the 1940 birth-year condition effectively eliminates the "age 65" definition common in other provinces, and shifts costs to individual retirees and private plans.

The Fair PharmaCare Plan only reimburses drugs listed in the PharmaCare formulary (which includes approximately 7,100 of the 11,400 prescription drugs approved for sale in Canada). This limited drug coverage, in combination with the introduction of Fair PharmaCare, has shifted significant costs onto employer-sponsored plans — in fact, as a result of the changes, the cost for employer-sponsored retiree drug benefits in British Columbia increased almost 55 per cent. Employers with British Columbia retirees must, therefore, decide whether prescription drugs should form a part of the retiree flexible benefit plan.

ONTARIO

Ontario introduced legislation in late 2006 to reform the Ontario Drug Benefit plan (ODB), which covers residents over age 65 as well as social assistance recipients. One of the reforms was designed to ensure that the ODB became the second payer for "working seniors with private insurance plans." At time of writing, it was unclear how and when the government will implement this change. Preliminary discussions with the government indicate that the criteria to be used to determine what constitutes a "working senior" will be an individual over age 65 who is working and has access to private drug coverage.

What is unclear is whether the private drug coverage must be from the current employer. If the "coverage" does not have to come from the same source as where the senior is working, a number of possible scenarios arise. Consider the following:

- **Example 1** — Individuals who continue employment past age 65 and have drug coverage through their employer. The employer-sponsored plan will be first payer for the senior's drugs, as opposed to the ODB. At this point it is clear that in this situation the government intends that the private plan will be the first payer.

- **Example 2** — Retirees with postretirement medical coverage who take a part-time job with an employer who does not offer benefits. Depending on the interpretation of the government's definition of "working senior," the retiree benefit plan from the former employer may now become first payer for drug coverage because of the retiree's new part-time job.

- **Example 3** — Individuals over age 65 who work part-time and have coverage available through their spouse's plan (either a working spouse or a retired spouse with postretirement benefits). Again, due to the lack of clarity in the definition of working senior, the spouse's benefit plan could become first payer in this situation.

These examples illustrate the potentially broad impact and significant additional cost to employers. It is clear that companies who have active employees with benefits over age 65 will see their drug costs increase as a result of this legislation. However, the potential impact on employers with postretirement benefit plans whose retirees supplement their income with part-time employment is much greater.

SUMMARY

The changes in retiree programs are only beginning. The prospect for more change, increasing financial concerns on the part of employers, and for more diverse retiree needs and options, should encourage more employers to consider flexible benefits as a vehicle for providing retiree benefits.

Ten

Retirement

§ 10.1 INTRODUCTION

Flexibility in retirement benefits is not a new concept. However, to date, relatively few employers have included retirement choices as specific options within flexible programs. For an employer to offer true choice-making in the retirement area, the goal would be to allow employees to reduce retirement benefits in exchange for cash or credits that could be used for other benefit purposes or to apply cash or credits from other areas to the purchase of additional retirement benefits. Structuring retirement plans in this manner raises a host of technical and practical issues that employers need to address if they wish to include retirement options in their flexible programs.

This chapter discusses how retirement options conceptually could be included within a flexible program. In general, defined contribution plans can be integrated into a flexible program more readily than defined benefit plans.

§ 10.2 OBJECTIVES FOR CHOICE-MAKING IN RETIREMENT

The reasons for wanting to include retirement choices in a flexible program generally parallel the motivations for offering choice in other benefit areas, with a few differences. As in the case of other benefits, one reason for offering choice is to meet individual employees' needs and preferences, particularly in cases where the employer is unwilling or unable to increase retirement benefits for all employees on a company-paid basis. Retirement benefit enhancements may also be an area that holds significant appeal for only a minority of the employee population, while the majority has greater interest in other benefit areas. Providing choices enables employees to meet their own special needs, such as permitting earlier retirement, making up for a short career with the current employer, or otherwise supplementing existing retirement benefits.

Another motivation for including retirement as a choice area is to provide an additional option for unused flexible credits (amounts remaining after the purchase of supplemental medical, dental, life insurance, and other coverage). Some employers are concerned about employees cashing out employer-provided benefit credits, yet they recognize that cash represents an attractive flexible program option to employees. In these cases, allowing unused credits to be deposited to a Registered Retirement Savings Plan (RRSP) or Deferred Profit Sharing Plan (DPSP) provides a tax-effective alternative to the receipt of cash.

A different motivation for reviewing the retirement area while designing a flexible program is to determine whether it could be a potential source of credits for the flexible program. This approach may have merit in creating additional credits in situations where the trimming back of a high-value pension plan would do little to diminish either employee retirement security or the employer's competitive position.

§ 10.3 LINKING DEFINED BENEFIT AND FLEXIBLE BENEFIT PLANS

The reasons that relatively few employers have included defined benefit retirement choices as specific options within choice-making programs include:

- The nature and structure of defined benefit plans, which typically provide benefits based on the employee's final average earnings and years of service at retirement. This makes it difficult to set an accurate price tag on increments of pension very far in advance of the employee's actual retirement date (or at least without knowledge of the intended retirement date).
- Volatility in stock markets and decreasing bond yields have generally resulted in large increases in pension costs, making the setting of fixed price tags more risky.
- The complexity of the various plans and pension benefit legislation has caused many employers to avoid further complicating their plans.
- By establishing group RRSPs, many employers have been able to meet employee needs for additional retirement income in a simpler way, as well as provide a tax-favoured vehicle for employee contributions.

Changes to the *Income Tax Act* over the past 10 to 15 years have encouraged some employers to offer flexible pension plans. These plans have been either multiple option pension plans (i.e., three different plans, each costing the employer the same amount) or variable employee contribution plans (one core benefit level provided by the employer with different ancillary benefits available — early retirement benefits, indexing, death benefits, etc. — depending on employee contributions).

DEFINED BENEFIT PLANS AS A SOURCE OF FLEXIBLE CREDITS

Conceptually, an employer with a defined benefit plan could allow employees to cut back their future service benefits and, in return, receive credits that may be used to purchase additional benefits in other areas or taken in cash. The cutback is limited to future service benefits, because a cutback in previously accrued benefits is generally prohibited by law.

All, or a portion, of the savings attributable to the reduction in future service benefits would be used as a credit generator within the flexible program. Employees would be able to use those funds inside the flexible program — possibly with an option to retain the retirement aspect of those funds through deposit in a companion DPSP or money purchase pension plan.

There are, however, difficulties in determining the appropriate credits and guarding against the possibility of adverse selection against the employer. Consider a final average earnings pension plan. Adverse selection can occur if the credits derived from future service benefits are based on assumed pay increases and the employee leaves in the next few years. In this case, employer costs will be higher than would otherwise be the case.

Although used infrequently in recent years, the approach of releasing credits as a funding source for the flexible program could have merit in certain situations. An employer may already be considering the consolidation of different pension plans having different benefit levels, such as after a merger or acquisition, or generally re-evaluating the structure of a pension plan that provides higher benefits than may be necessary for competitive reasons.

DEFINED BENEFIT PLANS AS AN OPTIONAL FLEXIBLE BENEFIT

In theory, a plan sponsor with a defined benefit pension plan could establish a core benefit and allow employees to buy higher benefits using credits from other benefit areas or payroll dollars. For example, the core benefit might be a future service benefit for each year of service equal to 1 per cent of pay with the option to buy an additional 0.5 or 1 per cent of pay using flexible credits or payroll deduction dollars. The employee could make a different election each year.

In practice, few employers structure pension options within choice-making plans in this manner. However, such options are more feasible outside of choice-making plans, where individual equity in price tags is not as important. The unpopularity of this approach within a flexible plan stems primarily from:

- Difficulty in determining price tags, especially for a final average earnings plan;
- Possible risk in terms of the potential for subsidization of employee choices;
- Difficulty in complying with regulatory requirements of federal and provincial authorities; and
- Additional plan administration.

Another problem is that the plan will incur extra costs if an employee buys additional benefits with today's dollars and receives higher pay increases than assumed in the calculation of price tags.

Because of this risk and the difficulty in setting price tags, an employer may wish to allow employees the option of only buying/selling units of pension based on current pay. For example, this could be 0.5 per cent of current pay or units of $10 per month.

§ 10.4 LINKING DEFINED CONTRIBUTION AND FLEXIBLE BENEFIT PLANS

A growing number of employers use their defined contribution plan as a funding source for their flexible program. As well, many employers allow employees to direct unused credits to an RRSP or DPSP.

DEFINED CONTRIBUTION PLANS AS A SOURCE OF FLEXIBLE CREDITS

For a defined contribution pension plan, a portion of employer monies can be made available for employee elections within the flexible program. A money purchase pension plan, for example, may require an employer contribution of 5 per cent of pay. The employer could introduce flexibility by allowing employees to elect some percentage of pay, say 2 per cent, which could be used as a source of credits for the flexible program, instead of having this money flow into the pension plan. While it is theoretically possible, very few employers have introduced this type of flexibility within pension plans.

This approach is much more common with non-pension defined contribution plans where all or a portion of a savings plan match or the annual allocation in a profit-sharing plan could be made available to employees for use in the flexible program.

This approach, referred to as the financial security structure in Chapter 4, is particularly attractive where the employer wishes to improve the tax effectiveness of the flexible plan by making additional pre-tax funds available for the employee. The structure also tends to have appeal in situations where an employer's objective is to focus employee attention on the total compensation aspect of pay and benefits. Finally, a savings or profit-sharing plan may be very rich and, conversely, employer credits in the flexible program may be insufficient for some employees to fully cover their benefit needs. Ultimately, however, whether savings or profit-sharing monies should be used as a funding source in the flexible program depends on employer objectives in the benefits and retirement area and the level of retirement income already provided through other retirement plans.

DEFINED CONTRIBUTION PLANS AS AN OPTIONAL FLEXIBLE BENEFIT

The option for employees to direct unused employer contributions to a defined contribution plan, such as an RRSP, DPSP, or registered pension plan, is simple to introduce, popular with employees, and as a result is very common in flexible plans.

A design consideration that needs to be addressed is the treatment of unused credits directed to a savings plan; specifically, will excess credits be eligible for employer matching funds? Although it is not common practice, an employer could decide to grant a matching contribution for unused credits as a way to promote saving for retirement. Alternatively, incentives might include matching on a profit- or performance-related basis, or purely discretionary matching.

It should be noted that any unused credits directed to a savings plans or additional matching contributions allocated to these credits does not create any additional tax room for the employee — these amounts are counted toward the aggregate tax limits allowed by the Canada Revenue Agency.

§ 10.5 ISSUES TO BE CONSIDERED

REGULATORY ISSUES

Care must be taken to ensure that the retirement options within a flexible plan conform to the requirements of pension benefit legislation across Canada.

TAX ISSUES

Similarly, retirement plans must recognize the *Income Tax Act* rules on maximum tax deductibility of retirement contributions. These rules set a uniform limit on tax-assisted savings of 18 per cent of earnings to specified dollar maximums. In the February 2005 federal budget, the dollar maximums were increased for future years, through 2009. After that, the limits will be indexed to the growth in the average national wage. The limits are shown in Table 10.1 on page 212. Different limits are provided for Registered Pension Plans (RPPs), also known as Money Purchase Pension Plans (MPPPs), Deferred Profit Sharing Plans (DPSPs), and Registered Retirement Savings Plans (RRSPs).

Employers who sponsor RPPs or DPSPs are required to report a Pension Adjustment (PA) for each employee who was a plan member during the year. The PA, which reflects the benefits a plan member has earned during the year under employer-sponsored plans, is subtracted from the member's comprehensive

Table 10.1
Contribution Limits for Registered Plans

Year	MPPP Limit	DPSP Limit	RRSP Limit
2006	$19,000	$9,500	$18,000
2007	20,000	10,000	19,000
2008	21,000	10,500	20,000
2009	22,000	11,000	21,000
2010	*	*	22,000
2011	*	*	**

* To be indexed to the growth in the average wage.
** The RRSP limit equals the preceding year's RPP limit.

contribution limit. This determines the maximum RRSP contribution the plan member may make in the following year.

- For DPSPs, the PA is the total of the employer's contributions in respect of the employee, plus any forfeited amounts and related investment earnings that are allocated to the employee.
- For MPPPs, the PA is the total of the employer's contributions in respect of the employee, plus any contributions by the employee, plus any forfeited amounts and related investment earnings allocated to the employee.
- For defined benefit plans, the PA is determined directly from the benefit formula and, where applicable, the employee's pensionable earnings in the year.

The defined benefit PA is not affected by the presence of ancillary benefits in the pension plan — for example, benefits such as indexing, unreduced early retirement pension, early retirement bridging benefits, and death benefits. In other words, two pension plans having an identical benefit formula — say, 1.5 per cent of final five-year average pay for each year of service — will have identical PAs for employees with the same pay, even if one plan is "loaded" with ancillary benefits and the second provides none. This tax simplification has led to the emergence of flexible defined benefit pension plans, as discussed later in this chapter.

It is also important to realize that the defined benefit PA does not depend on the age of the employee. The calculation is based on the assumption that $1 of pension at retirement costs $9 to provide (the factor of 9). The $9 cost is the same whether the employee is age 20, where the true cost is less than $1, or 64, where the true cost is likely much greater than $9. This age neutrality has led to the emergence of choice pension plans that allow an employee to elect whether to participate in a defined benefit plan (more attractive for older employees) or a defined contribution plan (more attractive for younger employees — especially those who wish to contribute the maximum to an RRSP).

When implemented, the "factor of 9" was intended to reflect the provisions of public sector plans, which typically have very rich ancillary benefits. Specifically, the factor of 9 assumes the following:

- Benefits are indexed from retirement to increases in the Consumer Price Index less 1 per cent.
- Full benefits are available at age 63.
- Benefits are payable for the lifetimes of both the member and the member's spouse, with benefits continuing at a reduced level (60 per cent) on the death of the member.

Very few private sector plans provide such rich ancillary benefits. Nevertheless, members in private sector plans are "charged" PAs, with a corresponding reduction in RRSP room, as if they did receive these benefits. As a result, those plan members are charged for benefits which they are never likely to receive.

Furthermore, the factor of 9 assumes that the member stays with the company for a full career of 35 years. For a member who leaves a company after a short period of service, the value of benefits a member actually receives may be far less than what the member was "charged" in terms of lost RRSP room.

This opportunity cost to participate in defined benefit plans has led to the emergence of flexible pension plans that give the member the opportunity to buy some of the ancillary benefits for which he or she has been charged with no corresponding increase in the member's PA.

Several years after the introduction of the tax rules for retirement savings, the Pension Adjustment Reversal (PAR) was introduced as a means to reinstate RRSP room that was "lost" when a plan member terminated from an RPP or DPSP and received a lower lump sum value than the aggregate PAs reported.

To the extent that flexible credits are released from retirement benefits as a funding source for non-retirement benefits, an employee gains tax room for retirement savings, subject to the above rules. On the other hand, to the extent that unused credits are applied to purchase additional pension benefits or allocated to the DPSP portion of a savings plan, available tax room is reduced.

ADMINISTRATIVE ISSUES

Special procedures are needed to administer the pension options within a flexible benefit plan. Any pension benefits purchased by employees using flexible credits must be fully vested. Therefore, it is necessary to keep track of these benefits separately from the benefits that are subject to the normal vesting requirements of the pension plan. Tracking of benefit amounts can be complex. For example, some benefits may be based on final average earnings, while other benefits may be of a fixed-dollar nature.

One consideration in including defined contribution plans as an option in a flexible plan may be the compatibility of the employer's payroll and record-keeping systems. Most defined contribution plans are designed to accept employee contributions in the form of a percentage of pay. Under a flexible program, un-used credits usually would be dispersed to employees as a specific dollar amount (paid out each pay period or on a one-time basis at the end of the year). The record-keeping system for the plan needs to be able to accept specific dollar amount — a modification to the system may not be worth the administrative effort involved if both the number and dollar amount of deposits are expected to be low. On the other hand, funds flowing out of the retirement plan to the flexible plan usually are easier to accommodate, since credit allocations to employees typically are based on a combination of a percentage of pay plus a flat-dollar amount.

OTHER ISSUES

For most employers, the level and structure of existing retirement plans will exert primary influence on any decisions relating to the flexible program. For example, an employer that already has a rich defined benefit pension plan may have little incentive to offer more under a flexible approach. Instead (and depending on other considerations), introduction of a flexible program may provide the impetus for a cutback in that plan — in this case, a substantial portion of the cost savings would flow through to employees in the form of higher credits or expanded benefit options under the flexible program.

However, the majority of employers may find themselves in other situations — for example, recognizing that employees would welcome an additional opportunity to supplement pension income, and (perhaps) to seek an additional source of credits for the flexible program. In these situations, the following checklist of considerations may prove helpful:

- Would enough employees — or enough key employees — elect retirement choices to justify any added administrative expense? For example, would it be worthwhile to develop pension options, or modify record-keeping systems to accept the flow of funds between the flexible benefit plan and the defined contribution plan — or both?
- Given the expected flexible program credit structure, what is the likely deposit to each arrangement?
- How much tax room exists in an RRSP or DPSP plan to accept an additional source of contributions?
- How important is a cash option to employees?
- Where does the pension plan rank relative to competitive norms?

- How well is the existing pension plan understood by employees?
- What parallelism (if any) in terms of matching, withdrawal, and so forth, will be accorded unused credits deposited in the DPSP versus regular amounts?
- How would pension options be funded? How much risk is the employer willing to bear in terms of the potential for future subsidization?

§ 10.6 RETIREMENT CHOICES OUTSIDE THE FLEXIBLE PROGRAM

To complete the discussion of retirement plans as an option, mention should be made of options that do not fall into the category of "pure" flexible options; that is, they are not of equivalent value and do not allow employees the opportunity to use credits in other benefit areas. They are optional retirement programs and can take several forms. The driving force behind most of these plans is the desire to maximize the tax effectiveness of defined benefit plans, which is restricted by the simplistic PA calculation methodology described earlier.

TAX EFFECTIVENESS OF DEFINED BENEFIT PENSION PLANS

One of the first reactions pension experts had to the Pension Adjustment (PA) calculation for a defined benefit plan was that it was inequitable. As mentioned previously, two identically paid employees working for different employers would have the same PA (and, therefore, the same RRSP room), merely because their pension formulas were the same. The fact that one employee might have a much richer pension plan because of the presence of ancillary benefits is not reflected in the PA calculation.

To overcome this inequity and to maximize an employee's ability to contribute to an RRSP, some employers redesigned their defined benefit pension plans. Four possible approaches were generally considered:

- Cut back the defined benefit formula and increase ancillary benefits.
- Give employees a choice of two or three equal cost-defined benefit plans.
- Allow employees to make optional contributions to purchase ancillary benefits.
- Give employees choice between a defined contribution plan and a defined benefit plan.

CUT BACK DEFINED BENEFITS AND INCREASE ANCILLARIES

The first approach was simple: cut back the benefit formula, increase the ancillary benefits, and maintain the same employer cost. For example, if the original pension plan had a 1.5 per cent final five-year average pay formula with low ancillary benefits, the new plan might have a 1 per cent formula, along with the richest ancillaries permitted (e.g., indexation, unreduced early retirement at age 60, etc.).

Under the redesigned plan, the new PA would be significantly less than the PA under the original plan, yet the new plan provides similar values and has a similar cost to the employer. The employee gains by having substantially more RRSP room.

Why didn't more employers go this route? There were two major problems. First, convincing employees that they were better off under a 1 per cent pension plan with richer ancillary benefits than under a 1.5 per cent plan with less rich ancillaries, was a major communication challenge. It was particularly hard to explain the change to an employee who did not intend to contribute to an RRSP. Second, although the old and new plans could be designed to have the same employer cost for the average employee, not all employees are average. If the new plan provided a full pension at age 60, the employee retiring at age 60 would benefit, but the employee staying to age 65 would receive a lower-value pension than he or she would have received under the old plan. Similarly, the new plan would likely provide a 60 per cent survivor pension to the spouse if the retiree died first — a valuable benefit for the married retiree, but not for the single retiree.

OFFER CHOICE OF DEFINED BENEFIT PENSION PLANS

The second redesign approach overcame these two problems by allowing employees to choose which plan suited them better — the current plan (high formula, low ancillary), or the new plan (low formula, high ancillary). A third option (medium formula, medium ancillary) might be added between the current and new plans.

This structure overcame the perceived cutback under the unilateral change described above, because the employee would choose the optimum plan based on personal circumstances and tax considerations. The program could allow employees to change options once a year, once every five years, or could have a maximum of one or two changes in a career. The administrative and communication challenges in this type of flexible pension program are obvious.

PROVIDE AN OPTIONAL ANCILLARY ACCOUNT WITHIN A DEFINED BENEFIT PENSION PLAN

The third approach is a form of flexible pension plan that also allows employees to tailor benefits and tax savings to their personal circumstances. In this program, the employer provides the basic pension plan — 1.5 per cent highest five-year average pay in the earlier examples. Employees do not contribute to this base plan, but they are permitted to make optional contributions to an ancillary account to purchase ancillary benefits. The employee contributions, subject to prescribed limits, are tax-deductible and do not reduce the individual's RRSP room.

The contributing employee chooses from a menu of ancillary benefits, such as indexing and survivor benefits. This choice could be made at the time the employee contributed, with the cost being based on the type of benefit and the employee's age. (Indexing for a 30-year-old might cost 3 per cent of pay, for example.) In most plans, the choice is made at retirement, with the accumulated contributions made over the employee's career used to purchase the specific ancillary benefits that the employee chooses. The latter approach is more attractive to the employee whose exact needs — and the price to satisfy those needs — will not be known until retirement.

Regardless of the approach used, the plan must satisfy the requirements of the *Income Tax Act* and Canada Revenue Agency's prescribed requirements regarding flexible defined benefit pension plans. These rules are published in *Newsletter 96-3* and plans complying with the rules are known as "newsletter plans." The major requirements set out in the newsletter are:

- Optional contributions must be characterized as optional ancillary contributions when they are made and cannot later be recharacterized.
- The 50 per cent employer funding rule (which requires that employee contributions plus accumulated interest must not provide more than 50 per cent of the value of the contributory benefit earned after the pension reform date in the pension jurisdiction) must be applied to the total employee contribution (regular plus optional) and to the total benefit (basic plus optional ancillary benefits).
- None of any excess funds remaining in the optional ancillary account, after all ancillary benefits have been purchased, may be paid to the employee. All excess amounts must be forfeited and remain in the pension fund.
- The maximum optional ancillary contribution equals:
  - The lesser of 9 per cent of the member's compensation and $1,000 plus 70 per cent of the member's pension credit (similar to pension adjustment) for the year, minus
  - Any regular contributions made by the member.
- Plan members who leave cannot take the ancillary account as a lump sum unless they also commute their basic pension.

OFFER CHOICE OF DEFINED BENEFIT OR DEFINED CONTRIBUTION PENSION PLAN

The fourth structure allows employees to choose the type of retirement plan that best meets their needs and to change the type of plan as their needs change. This approach is driven less by tax issues and more by the desire to address different employee situations.

Pension professionals have debated the merits of defined benefit and defined contribution plans for many years. Points debated include risk, benefit adequacy, nature of the pension promise, and employee comprehension. The tax rules just described have added tax-effectiveness to the debate. As mentioned earlier, the rules can dramatically overstate the PA for a young employee participating in a defined benefit plan.

Because there is no right answer for an entire employee group to the defined benefit versus defined contribution debate, some employers give employees the choice between these two types of plans. For example, employees could participate in either a 1.5 per cent highest average pay defined benefit plan or receive a defined contribution allocation of 5 per cent of pay. The difficulties of offering these choices can include:

- **Adverse selection.** Costs for a defined benefit plan rise with age, whereas they are level for the type of defined contribution plan outlined above. If employees are permitted to switch from the defined contribution plan to the defined benefit plan when the latter costs more (the "crossover point" — 5 per cent of pay, in the example), then company costs would rise overall. This adverse selection effect can be minimized by prohibiting or limiting switching from defined contribution to defined benefit, or by having a defined contribution amount that mirrors the costs of a defined benefit plan by increasing with service. For example, the plan could have an employer contribution of:

Service (Years)	Percentage of Pay
Under 5 years	3%
5–9 years	5%
10–19 years	7%
20+ years	9%

- **Employee comprehension.** If pension professionals can't agree on which type of plan is better, how can employees be expected to choose? The answer is a thorough, well-thought-out communication plan which typically includes a comprehensive workbook, employee meetings, an interactive computer program enabling employees to model their own situation, and a hotline for answering employee questions.
- **Cost.** Maintaining both a defined benefit plan and defined contribution plan is the best of all worlds for the employee. However, it may be the worst of all worlds for the employer, because of the increase in administrative costs.

§ 10.7 SUMMARY

To date, few employers have introduced choice-making within defined benefit and flexible benefit programs along the lines outlined in this chapter. In large part, employers have had concerns regarding the complexities involved in determining appropriate pricing strategy, and the issues involved in administering the pension options and complying with the requirements of the regulatory authorities. Many employers sponsor separate flexible pension arrangements, typically "newsletter plans" and flexible benefit plans. However, these plans are not integrated and employer funds or credits do not move between plans.

On the other hand, defined contribution plans, particularly non-pension plans such a savings programs, are readily integrated with flexible benefit plans. As plan sponsors increase their emphasis on total compensation and employee flexibility, this "financial security" approach is expected to become even more prevalent.

Eleven

Emerging Benefits

§ 11.1 INTRODUCTION

The growth of flexible benefits has been driven by a number of forces that will, for the most part, continue to influence employers and employees. As a result, in the coming years we will see more employers adopt flexible benefit plans and will see an expansion of the types of benefits offered under these plans.

This expansion of flexible benefits will be driven by a number of factors that have contributed to the popularity of flexible benefit plans — changes in the workforce, enhanced employee appreciation of benefits, and the need of employers to control benefit costs.

The pressures for new benefits — such as long-term care coverage, educational benefits for dependants, financial planning, and enhanced dependant daycare programs — will continue to grow. Flexible benefit programs will enable an employer to respond to these pressures without creating long-term and extensive financial commitments that may be beyond the employer's reach. Similarly, flexible benefit plans address employers' desires to introduce cost-saving programs (such as managed drug formularies) in a way that preserves employees' opportunities to keep more expensive indemnity options, but uses the pricing mechanism to reflect the relative cost of the different alternatives.

Flexible benefit programs usually allow employees to select the appropriate level of coverage within traditional benefit areas, such as supplemental medical, dental, life insurance, and disability. Options need not be limited to traditional programs, however. The flexible structure allows employers to add new benefits to the range of employee choices, and at the same time it allows the employer to decide whether or not to subsidize the cost of the benefits.

Although employees are very creative when asked what other options should be added to a flexible benefit program, not all of their suggestions are feasible or appropriate. Among the characteristics that make a benefit an attractive choice within a flexible benefit program are:

- **Group purchasing power.** Employees may be able to pool their resources and negotiate better rates than they could individually receive.

- **Risk sharing.** The basic principle of insurance applies where an individual may not be able to absorb the cost of a catastrophic event, such as a fire or an accident. In this case, each member of the group bears a small, acceptable portion of the risk.

- **Employer selection of provider.** Individuals are faced with an overwhelming array of providers for insurance (such as home and auto) and investments (such as RRSPs). By selecting a provider, the employer provides a valuable service to the employee.

    However, this factor works both ways. Many employers are reluctant to introduce certain benefits (such as home and auto insurance and critical illness insurance), because of the implied endorsement of the provider. Negative reaction from one employee, because of a disputed claim, could overwhelm the positive impact from introducing the plan.

- **Payroll deduction convenience.** Most benefits discussed in this chapter may be purchased using payroll deductions. Since most payroll systems can handle multiple payroll deductions, the administrative cost to the employer to introduce a new benefit is minimal.

- **Fill gaps in other company plans.** Traditional benefit plans provide coverage against the financial risk of many contingencies. However, there are some gaps in the coverage. A health spending account is an example of a benefit that fills such a gap so well that it has become mainstream. The account covers health care expenses not reimbursed under traditional benefit plans. (Chapter 7 covers expense and other accounts.)

- **Tax advantages.** Some benefits may be provided on a more tax-effective basis by an employer than the employee could receive by purchasing them outside the group plan. This occurs where part or all of the premium or cost paid by the employer does not generate a taxable benefit for the employee. Group critical illness plans are an example. Under a flexible program, the employee could direct flexible credits to pay for the coverage. As discussed later, this may not produce a taxable benefit for the employee.

- **Exchange for unwanted benefits.** A new benefit may be very attractive to the employee if it can be obtained in exchange for an unwanted benefit.

- **Saving time.** Some benefits can be provided through the employer in order to save time for employees. Time saving is a frequently cited need among employees. An example is financial planning, which if provided at lunchtime via "brown bag" seminars, could save employees the significant amounts of time ordinarily involved in locating a provider and attending a seminar. Other examples could be a dry-cleaning drop-off service, a banking machine on site, or an in-house cafeteria. These benefits may not always be tax-effective, and may be offered in tandem with a flexible program. Depending on the particular workforce, they may be appreciated by employees more than the more traditional benefits.

The balance of this chapter discusses emerging benefits in three general categories: work and family benefits, financial benefits, and other benefits.

§ 11.2 WORK AND FAMILY BENEFITS

SABBATICAL LEAVE PLANS

For many years, teachers have had the ability to take periodic paid sabbaticals. In 1986, employees in other occupations became eligible to defer a portion of their salary (and taxes) until they take a sabbatical. This occurred when Section 248(1) of the *Income Tax Act* was amended to restrict tax advantages enjoyed by many employees, who, in the past, elected to defer the receipt of a portion of their salaries. However, sabbatical plans were specifically exempted from these Section 248(1) salary deferral rules.

Under a sabbatical plan, an employee is entitled to defer a portion of salary for a limited period of time on a tax-neutral basis. The deferred salary is not taxable until the employee actually receives it. However, any investment income earned must be paid out to the employee each year. All earnings paid to the employee are taxable in the year.

Design Features

In order to be accorded favourable tax treatment, sabbatical plans must meet certain criteria. These are contained in Regulation 6801 to the *Income Tax Act* and are discussed below.

- **Eligibility and enrolment.** The regulations specify that a sabbatical plan must be "an arrangement in writing between an employer and the employee." Therefore, to enrol in the plan, each member must sign an agreement. The agreement may be quite brief — similar to an enrolment form that refers to the plan and sets out the employee's percentage of salary deferred, deferral period, and sabbatical period.
- **Amount of deferral.** An employee may defer up to one-third of salary each year. Employees may be given the option of deferring a range of percentages of salary, say, any multiple of 3 up to 33.3 per cent.
- **Election to defer.** The election to defer must be made prior to the beginning of each calendar year. The election should be made far enough in advance of the

next year to allow the payroll department enough time to make the necessary adjustments.

For administrative simplicity, employees should not be entitled to make more than one election per year. However, employers may find it prudent to allow an exception in cases of financial hardship.

- **Deferral period.** The maximum deferral period is six years. The deferred salary must be received in income no later than in the seventh year.

  An employer's staffing requirements will dictate the degree of flexibility permitted as to the selection of an employee's sabbatical deferral period. A cushion at the end of the deferral period may be used to avoid complications arising from unforeseen changes in staffing needs. For example, if an employee's deferral period is limited to five years, an employer may reserve the right to extend the employee's deferral by up to one year, in the case of internal staffing complications.

  A typical design allows for a deferral of 20 per cent of salary each year for five years, with the sixth year being the sabbatical period at 100 per cent of pay. Universities frequently have "four over five" programs. Four years of contributions are made, at 20 per cent of pay, with the applicant living on 80 per cent of normal salary in the fifth year.

- **Sabbatical period.** The length of the sabbatical period must be no less than six consecutive months, commencing immediately after the deferral period. The only other requirement is that the employee returns to employment after the sabbatical period for a period at least as long as the sabbatical period. For example, if an employee's sabbatical period is one year, the member must return to work with the employer for at least a year.

  A situation might arise where an employee decides not to return to the employer following the sabbatical. Canada Revenue Agency would likely reassess the individual's tax returns for the years the salary was deferred.

- **Pay during sabbatical period.** The Income Tax Regulations stipulate that no salary or wages be paid to an individual while on sabbatical leave, apart from the accumulated deferred earnings. However, reasonable fringe benefits, usually provided to employees, may continue to be offered.

- **Restitution.** Plans need to make provision for employees who are partway through the sabbatical plan and then terminate employment, become disabled, or die. The employee's accumulated deferred salary typically would be refunded to the employee or his or her estate.

- **Funding of the plan.** The plan may be either funded or unfunded. Under the funded approach, the employee's deferred salary would typically be contributed to a trust fund or other interest-bearing account. With the unfunded approach, a book reserve would be established to keep an accounting of employees' deferred salaries. Interest would not ordinarily be credited.

  The funded approach is normally preferable. It provides employees with greater security. Employees also get full value for their contributions, because investment earnings are credited. A slight disadvantage of the funded approach is administrative complexity. However, the financial institution (trust company or insurance company) holding the funds ordinarily would be responsible for administration.

- **Pension and benefit issues.** Employers must decide how to treat pension and group insurance benefits under a sabbatical program. The central issue concerning benefits is whether pension and group benefits are based upon an employee's actual earnings (salary less deferral) or upon nominal earning (full earnings, disregarding deferred salary).

  The employer can decide which earnings should be used to calculate employee benefits such as life and disability insurance. However, there is no such latitude for registered pension plans. Under a registered pension plan, Canada Revenue Agency requires that the pension benefit be based on actual earnings. Because of this, employers either advise employees not to reduce their salary in anticipation of a sabbatical if they intend to retire within a few years of returning from the sabbatical, or they agree to make up any pension shortfall through a supplemental, non-registered plan.

A Typical Sabbatical Plan

The key features of a typical sabbatical plan are summarized below.

- **Funding.** Employees are eligible to apply employer credits toward the sabbatical plan. In addition, they may elect to take a reduction in their current salary to fund their sabbatical leave.
- **Eligibility.** Typically, employees must have a minimum of two years of service. The arrangements must be in writing between the employee and the company.
- **Deferral maximum.** The usual maximum is 33 per cent of salary each year (in multiples of 3 per cent). The maximum deferral period is five years. The company reserves the right to delay an employee's sabbatical by up to one year because of internal staffing needs.
- **Sabbatical period.** Typically, plans specify a one-year maximum, with a six-month minimum.
- **Sabbatical period compensation.** Only the deferred money accumulated to date may be paid in compensation. An employee may not receive any other pay or compensation. If an employee leaves the employer, becomes disabled, or dies, the accumulated deferred salary is refunded to the employee or his or her estate.
- **Funding of the plan.** Deferred salaries are physically put aside into a trust. Any income the deferred funds earn must be taken as taxable income in the year it is earned.

LONG-TERM CARE

An attractive benefit that may become popular as provincial plans cut back coverage for nursing homes in Canada is long-term care coverage. This coverage provides financial support for elderly individuals who can no longer take care of themselves. Hospitalization and rehabilitation usually are not features of the coverage. The most obvious example of a long-term care facility is a nursing home.

All provinces have user fees for nursing homes, meaning that funding for accommodation is shared by the resident and the province.

Although provincial health insurance plans cover a portion of the cost, the individual may be left paying a significant amount. For example, the cost to an individual for a private room in a government-subsidized Ontario nursing home exceeds $2,000 per month. Residents' fees vary significantly from province to province, from a low of about $12,000 annually for a private room in Alberta to over $57,000 per year in Nova Scotia. However, where residents don't qualify for government funding, or where they want control over the level of care received and the type of accommodations, the total fees are borne entirely by the resident or the resident's family.

Over the last five years, costs have climbed annually by an average of 3.7 per cent in Canada's residential care facilities for the aged.

Nursing homes can provide different levels of care:

- **Skilled nursing.** For persons requiring constant supervision and treatment by a Registered Nurse under the direction of a doctor.
- **Intermediate care.** For persons requiring part-time services of skilled medical personnel.
- **Custodial care.** Involves the services of an individual who can assist in dressing, walking, eating, and other daily activities.

Other types of long-term care that may be available include:

- **Home care.** Can be skilled or unskilled care, provided in the individual's or a relative's home.
- **Adult day care.** Provides custodial care services given outside the individual's home.
- **Respite care.** Refers to temporary services provided to relieve the person who normally assumes primary care responsibility.

Long-term care may become a popular benefit, because of demographic changes, changes in family structures, and changes in work patterns.

- **Demographic changes.** The elderly population is the fastest-growing segment of our population. With better health care and medical technology, people are living longer. With increased longevity, the risk of needing long-term care increases as well. Life expectancy beyond age 65 today is comparable to what life expectancy beyond age 60 was thirty years ago, and is increasing rapidly. A 2003 report by Statistics Canada states that life expectancy at age 65 for males is 17.4 years, and for females is 20.8 years.

Due to increased life expectancy, people aged 85 and over have become the fastest-growing segment of our aging population. Meanwhile, the baby boom generation is becoming more interested in how to provide care for parents.

- **Changes in family structures.** Although families have historically been the main providers of long-term care for their elderly members, lifestyle patterns have increased the need for others to care for elderly parents.

- **Changes in work patterns.** Women have traditionally been the caregivers for parents and parents-in-law. As more women have entered the workforce, their ability to be providers of long-term care to their elderly relatives has diminished.

Inadequacy of Current Forms of Care

Because they are living longer, the elderly have become more susceptible to chronic health conditions, and, as a result, require more assistance over longer periods. Current safety nets are becoming inadequate to deal with such health and custodial needs. Residential living communities, while highly touted as a solution, are often too expensive and built in insufficient numbers to solve long-term care needs.

Provincial plans only cover a portion of nursing home costs and do not always cover other types of long-term custodial care services.

Insurance Product Features

Perhaps the most viable option for long-term care is in the form of group insurance policies. More than 135 U.S. insurers now offer long-term care products, with over 3 million policies currently in force. Of these, about ten insurers offer group policies.

To date, few Canadian policies are available, and at the end of 2004, according to the Canadian Life and Health Insurance Association (CLHIA), fewer than 50,000 Canadians were covered under long-term care insurance plans.

In the United States, basic plan design typically includes the following features:

- **Covered providers.** Expenses for nursing care, home care, adult care, and respite care are typically covered.

- **Benefits.** Two approaches are common: future purchase and automatic increase. The future purchase alternative provides a set dollar amount, such as $200 per day. The daily dollar benefit may vary, depending upon the facility (skilled nursing facility, custodial nursing home, and so forth). Any charges in excess of the daily benefit are paid by the insured or covered under an incremental policy added later. Under the automatic increase approach, the purchaser picks a starting coverage level and inflation assumption. The coverage level automatically increases to address inflation.

- **Contributions.** Most employers (98 per cent) require their group long-term care plan to be 100 per cent employee contributory through after-tax payroll deductions. (Canada Revenue Agency has not ruled on whether or not long-term care services are "qualified" medical expenses.)
- **Eligibility.** One, some, or all of the following group classifications may be covered in a given policy: employees, retirees, spouses, and parents.
- **Maximum benefit periods.** These typically range from three to ten years. The longer the benefit period, the higher the premium for the policy. Policies that do not have benefit periods will use overall dollar maximums.
- **Inflation protection.** This is an option that can increase the daily fixed benefit by a certain percentage (usually 3 to 5 per cent) for a specified number of years.
- **Portability.** If the employee terminates employment or the group plan is discontinued, the employee can continue with an individual policy.
- **Waiver of premium.** This feature eliminates premiums once the benefits received equal a specified number of days of nursing home benefits.
- **Age at entry-level premiums.** This refers to the "employee pay all" premium, which generally is fixed and based on age at the time of the initial purchase.

Along with these features, group long-term care policies are usually governed by the following benefit eligibility requirements:

- **Pre-existing conditions.** This requires that a specified period of time must pass after a policy is effective (usually six months) before benefits will be paid for any condition that the covered person had during a specified period before the coverage went into effect (usually six to twelve months before).
- **Elimination period.** This provision defines the number of days the covered person must be confined in a facility, or the number of home care service days the covered person must have received, before policy benefits begin. These periods usually range from fifteen to 120 days.
- **Prior hospitalization.** Long-term care plans require a minimum number of hospital days (usually three), before a beneficiary qualifies for coverage. They also may require the hospitalization not to occur within a limited number of days following the start of such coverage.
- **Exclusions.** Policies generally do not pay for services that are related to suicide, confinements outside of the country, war or an act of war, mental or nervous conditions, alcoholism, mental retardation, or certain other health conditions. However, Alzheimer's disease and other organic mental disorders generally are covered.

Design Considerations

If long-term care coverage becomes prevalent in Canada, employers will have to consider several issues in designing the program. Perhaps the most important is whether or not sufficient long-term services will be available in the community to provide the benefits that have been purchased. Another consideration is whether or not the coverage is necessary, in light of provincial health insurance programs. Other considerations include employee interest, possible government mandates, employee pressure for employer contributions, and tax regulations.

CHILD CARE

Child care would seem to be a natural benefit for inclusion in a flexible benefit program, because it would make the benefit program more attractive to many employees. Employers might also benefit from the introduction of child care, because it could reduce absenteeism and improve the hiring and retaining of employees. However, few, if any, flexible programs include child care for a simple reason: there are no tax advantages to including this benefit within a flexible benefit program. Therefore, the employee is no better off arranging child care through the employer's flexible program than outside it — unless, of course, the employer subsidizes the cost.

Contrast this to the situation in the United States, where an employee may have his or her salary reduced by up to $5,000 per year for reimbursement of child care (or other dependant care) expenses. No tax is payable on such reimbursements.

Although child care is not offered as a flexible benefit option, the changing demographics of the workplace, which have helped flexible plans flourish, have also encouraged some employers to address the child care needs of employees.

Types of Child Care Benefits

The child care benefits available outside a flexible plan cover a wide range, from on-site day care to referral services.

- **On-site care.** Some employers provide daycare facilities in their building. This could be a major advantage to the employer in recruiting and retaining valuable employees. Employers typically provide the facility for free, so employees only have to pay for the daycare staff. The employer subsidy for on-site care is not a taxable benefit to the employee. Reasons that more employers do not offer this benefit include cost, insurance, legal liability issues, difficulty in providing on-site day care in a multiple-location company, necessity of complying with local legislation (access to green space and so forth), and perceived inequity of subsidizing one group of employees.

- **Subsidized private day care.** Employers may subsidize the cost of private daycare facilities selected by employees. The subsidy is a taxable benefit to the employee.

- **Education and referral services.** A number of commercial and non-profit services are available to provide information to employees covering general issues on day care (types of day care available, for example) and specific information on providers. Some services provide telephone counselling to answer employees' questions. Others offer computerized databases that can be installed at the employer's offices. Employees who have questions can sign on and get a list of after-school daycare facilities within five kilometres of the office, for example.

- **Flexible work schedules.** Many employers have addressed the needs of working parents by introducing flexible work hours. Others grant employees a number of "personal days" each year that can be used for looking after a sick child, doctor's visits, and so forth.

- **Emergency and overnight care.** A few companies will pay for emergency child care to look after a sick child. Normally, there is a maximum of five days' payment per year. One company goes as far as paying the cost of overnight babysitting should the employee and spouse both need to travel out of town on the same night.

ELDER CARE

A growing concern of many employees is the need to look after elderly parents. As the population ages, baby boomers are being faced with the dual concerns of looking after their children and their parents. The term "sandwich generation" has been coined to describe this phenomenon. Successful employers will be those who find innovative ways of addressing the needs of the sandwich generation.

The programs adopted by employers to date are very similar to those used to address child care needs:

- **Information.** Seminars or a library can help educate employees on the needs and problems of the elderly and describe what services are available.

- **Referral.** A number of commercial and non-profit services are available to provide information to employees, covering types of elder care available and providing specific information on local resources. The services range from telephone counselling to computerized databases that can be installed at the employer's offices.

- **Flexible work schedules.** Employers can help address employee needs in this area by introducing flexible work hours.

CONCIERGE SERVICES

It is often stressful and distracting for employees who are working full-time to accomplish tasks required in their everyday lives. Some companies offer a concierge benefit for employees in an effort to help them improve their work/life balance. Concierge services can perform a variety of tasks, from grocery shopping and walking the dog to finding the best estimate from contractors or the most reputable auto mechanic. They can also be utilized for business purposes, such as gathering product information and finding the appropriate advertising firm. Concierge services may be offered year-round, or in some cases may be available to employees specifically for the holiday season. Some companies have included concierge services as an option in their flexible benefit plans, or have allowed employees to direct flexible credits to buy these services.

§ 11.3 FINANCIAL BENEFITS

REGISTERED EDUCATION SAVINGS PLAN

Other than Registered Retirement Savings Plans, Canadians have few tax-effective investment options available. One of the options is a Registered Education Savings Plan (RESP) which permits earnings on investments made for education to grow tax-free. Income earned in the RESP, plus any government grants paid into the RESP, are payable to the student beneficiary while attending a qualified education program. The student pays tax on the income when received, while the original capital is returned to the subscriber.

RESPs have been available for many years as individual arrangements. Recently, a number of RESP sponsors have designed group plans to be offered to employees through their employers. An RESP could be an attractive option in either a flexible or a traditional employee benefit program. It meets most of the criteria of a valuable option, as listed in Section 11.1 — it has tax advantages, is paid by payroll deduction, fills a gap in coverage, and makes the process easy for the employee because the employer selects the provider.

How Does an RESP Operate?

The rules governing RESPs are contained in Section 146.1 of the *Income Tax Act*. A typical group plan works as follows:

Structure

- **Types of plans.** There are two types of RESPs — individual plans and family plans:
  - Individual RESPs have one beneficiary. Contributions may be made for a maximum of 22 years.

- Family RESPs can have several beneficiaries, who must be related to the subscriber. The accumulated earnings may be paid to any of the beneficiaries and the Canada Education Savings Grant (CESG) payments may be shared among beneficiaries, to a maximum of $7,200 per beneficiary. Contributions may be made up to the year each beneficiary turns 21.

- **Deposits.** The subscriber (employee) contributes to a qualified RESP in the name of a beneficiary (child).

- **Beneficiary.** The beneficiary is normally the employee's child. However, the beneficiary could be a grandchild, niece, nephew, godchild or someone un-related in an individual RESP. In fact, the beneficiary of an individual RESP could be an adult. All RESPs allow the contributor to change the beneficiary.

Contributions

- **Contribution limits.** The deposit can be as a single lump sum or as periodic payments. The annual contribution limit for all RESPs for a beneficiary is $4,000, while the lifetime limit is $42,000. (The March 2007 Federal Budget proposed to eliminate the $4,000 annual limit and increase the lifetime limit to $50,000.)

- **Over-contributions.** Any payments in excess of the annual or lifetime limits incur a 1-per-cent-per-month penalty.

- **Payroll deductions.** Premiums are paid by after-tax payroll deductions. The contributor is not entitled to a tax deduction for the premium.

- **Government assistance.** Most contributors are eligible for government assis-tance in funding their RESPs. This assistance can come in three forms.
  - *Canada Education Savings Grant (CESG).* The federal government will match 20 per cent of the first $2,000 of annual contributions for beneficiaries age 17 and under (The March 2007 Federal Budget proposed to increase the maximum match from $400 (20% of $2,000) to $500.). Additional amounts may be paid for lower-income subscribers.
  - *Canada Learning Bonds* provide up to an additional $2,000 RESP grant for modest-income families.
  - *Alberta Centennial Savings Plan (ACES)* provides up to an additional $800 RESP grant for Alberta children born after December 31, 2004.

  CESG and ACES government assistance payments can be made in addition to the annual and lifetime RESP contribution limits.

Investments

- **Investments.** Some RESPs invest in balanced pooled funds. Others allow the contributor to select from a number of mutual funds or, in some cases, to have self-directed investments.

- **Investment earnings.** No tax is payable by the subscriber, the beneficiary, or the trust on any investment earnings in the trust. However, the beneficiary pays tax on investment earnings when they are paid out as Educational Assistance Payments (EAPs).

Payouts

- **Educational Assistance Payments (EAPs).** Income earned on the contributions, plus any government assistance paid into the plan, is paid to the beneficiary as an EAP. Typically, the beneficiary can receive a maximum of $5,000 in educational assistance payments before completion of thirteen weeks in a row of a qualifying education program. After this period, the beneficiary can receive any amount. Payments are taxable income to the student beneficiary in the year received.

- **Accumulated Income Payments (AIPs).** Normally investment earnings are payable to the beneficiary as EAPs. However, if the beneficiary cannot make use of the earnings, they may be paid to the subscriber if the plan has been in existence for ten years and the beneficiary has reached age 21. CRA has other criteria that also permit AIP.

  The AIP is taxable income to the recipient. In addition, there is a 20 per cent additional (penalty) tax. These taxes may be avoided by transferring up to $50,000 into the taxpayer's RRSP or spousal RRSP, assuming sufficient RRSP room is available.

- **Maturity.** The total deposits are refunded to the subscriber when the plan matures. Since the contributions were made with after-tax payroll deductions, refunds are tax-free. Trustee or administration charges are deducted either from the subscriber's capital or from the income the RESP earns. Investment earnings and any government assistance payments are retained in the plan for payment to the beneficiary.

General

- **Qualifying education programs.** A qualifying education program is a post-secondary course of study that lasts at least three weeks in a row with at least ten hours of instruction or work each week. If the program is at a foreign educational institution, it must last at least thirteen weeks. Qualifying programs include apprenticeships, programs offered by trade schools, CEGEPs, colleges, universities, and other institutions certified by the Ministry of Human Resources and Skills Development.

- **Postponement.** RESPs sometimes allow the student to skip a year or two of education. The EAPs could resume if the beneficiary returned to complete his or her studies.

- **Portability.** If the employee terminates, the RESP can be continued on an individual basis. Instead of payroll deductions, the premium would be paid directly to the issuer by the former employee.

- **Term.** There is a twenty-six-year limit on an RESP.

FINANCIAL PLANNING

Few flexible benefit programs offer financial planning options. However, some form of financial planning can complement the choices offered within the choice-making program. Like many other benefits described in this chapter, there are a wide range of financial planning services available. They include:

- **Group seminars or lectures.** These are frequently offered at lunch time and cover topics such as RRSPs, life insurance, investments, estate planning, and so forth. Topics related to the choices within the flexible plan (such as life insurance) can be scheduled to coincide with the annual flexible plan enrolment.
- **Individual counselling.** One-on-one sessions between an investment or financial counsellor and the employee can be scheduled. Typically, these sessions are limited to executives, because of the high cost.

There are two important considerations in setting up financial counselling sessions. First, the cost is generally a taxable benefit, if paid for by the employer. (There are some exceptions — pre-retirement counselling, mental and physical health counselling, and re-employment counselling are not taxable.)

Second, the employer should make sure that the counsellor is independent and not merely a representative of a financial institution looking for ways to sell commissionable products.

GROUP MORTGAGES

For many years, financial institutions have offered subsidized mortgages to their staff as an employee benefit. The benefit was usually tax-effective, because part or all of the subsidy was provided tax-free to the employee. In some cases, the employer could pay 3 per cent or more of the mortgage interest and not generate a taxable benefit to the employee. In recent years, the interest in this benefit has declined, because there has been little or no tax-free benefit due to low interest rates. (See "Tax Considerations" on the next page.)

The concept of tax-effective group mortgages was made available to all types of employers in the late 1980s, when several insurance companies developed group products. Under the group plans, the employee is free to negotiate the payment terms of the mortgage and the amortization period with the insurance company. The interest rate charged by the lender is usually a competitive current rate. If the employee leaves the company, the mortgage is converted to an individual mortgage.

Tax Considerations

As discussed in Chapter 12, the value of any benefit provided to an employee by an employer is taxable to the employee, unless there is a specific exemption in the *Income Tax Act*. One of the few exemptions is for an employer subsidy of an employee mortgage. The subsidy is only taxable to the employee to the extent that it reduces the effective interest rate below a government prescribed rate. For example, if an employee secures a mortgage at 7 per cent and the prescribed rate is 5 per cent, then the employer could pay 2 per cent, without this subsidy being taxable income to the employee. If the employer paid 3 per cent, then 1 per cent would be taxable income and 2 per cent would be tax-free. The prescribed rate is based on the 91-day Treasury Bill rate at the beginning of the preceding quarter. The prescribed rate is changed every three months and cannot exceed the prescribed rate on the date the mortgage is issued. If the rate decreases in the future, the employee receives a larger tax-free benefit.

To ensure that the employer subsidy is not taxable if it falls between the gross and prescribed rates, the employer must pay it directly to the lending institution.

Plan Design Features

The employer needs to decide upon several design features when installing a group mortgage benefit plan, including:

- **Eligibility.** The plan may be extended to all employees, or it may be limited to a group, such as all salaried employees.
- **Waiting period.** The plan might require a six- or twelve-month waiting period before the employee can make use of the plan.
- **Direct subsidy amount.** An employer must decide whether or not to subsidize the mortgage. Most employers, other than those in the financial sector, do not want the additional cost of paying part of an employee's mortgage.
- **Other sources of subsidy.** An alternative would be to allow the employee to direct credits from the flexible benefit program to subsidize the mortgage. Credits should be considered as a company-paid subsidy by Canada Revenue Agency and not generate a taxable benefit unless the net employee rate falls below the prescribed rate. Before adding this benefit to a flexible plan, the sponsor should review the available credits to determine if they would be sufficient to provide a meaningful subsidy.

  Another source of subsidy could be the employee's agreeing to forgo a future salary increase in exchange for an equivalent mortgage subsidy. Although Canada Revenue Agency has stated that it will not accept such an arrangement and will apply the doctrine of constructive receipt, many tax experts believe the approach is defensible as long as the irrevocable election is made before the employee becomes entitled to the salary increase.

§ 11.4 OTHER BENEFITS

HOME AND AUTO INSURANCE

Most employees have home and auto insurance through their broker or insurance agent. Does it make sense for an employer to offer group coverage as an option within a benefit plan? Many employers believe so and include these plans as part of a benefit program (flexible or otherwise). Group home and auto plans offer the convenience of payroll deductions, company selection of the insurer, and, in some cases, lower rates for employees.

Under these plans, employees are free to use the group insurance plan or to continue with their personal arrangements. Most eligible employees request a group quotation before the expiry of their own coverage to see if the group plan offers any savings. The following features should be considered in designing a plan and in selecting an insurance carrier:

- **Cost.** Employees may have high expectations that their premium for group home and auto insurance will be significantly lower than what they are currently paying. However, in many cases, the savings will be smaller than expected or nonexistent. In many provinces, insurers are prohibited from offering lower rates to employers than they do to the general public. As a result, the "household name" insurers do not offer group insurance, because they cannot undercut their individual premiums. Instead, insurance is offered through specialized insurers that only offer group coverage. For this reason, the name of the group carrier may be unknown to employees.

  (The reason for the prohibition on offering lower rates to groups is unclear; after all, there is no similar prohibition on group life insurance premiums. A cynic might suggest that the home and auto insurance agents were more effective lobbyists than were life insurance agents.)

- **Tax effectiveness.** There are no tax advantages to employees in buying home and auto insurance through their employers, either through payroll deductions or with flexible credits. If the benefit is purchased with credits, the cost will be a taxable benefit to the employee.

- **Enrolment date.** Home and auto insurance does not easily fit into an annual flexible benefit enrolment cycle. Since individuals' personal coverage comes up for renewal throughout the year, it is common for group coverage to continue this practice. So the enrolment is spread throughout the year, instead of being concentrated on one date like the rest of the flexible program. Therefore, it is very difficult to integrate the coverage fully with the rest of the flexible program, and, as a result, credits freed up from other benefits cannot easily be used to pay for home and auto coverage.

  To overcome this, some employers require that all home and auto policies for their employees mature on a common date. This makes it possible to co-ordinate the benefit with other plans. Insurance carriers generally resist a common anniversary date, because it makes it too easy for employers to compare insurance rates and potentially change carriers in the future.

- **Location of employees.** Most or all insurance companies offering group coverage will claim to provide services in all provinces, except where provincial auto insurance eliminates the need for private coverage. A national employer should ask for references from the insurer to determine how consistent the administration is across Canada and how well the insurer serves rural areas.

- **Policy provisions.** If home and auto insurance is offered in conjunction with a full flexible benefit program, it is imperative that the coverage be flexible. For example, in auto insurance, employees should be given a range of deductibles to choose from, a range of liability limits, and so forth. For home insurance, replacement cost coverage, coverage on seasonal residences, boats and motors, and so on, should be available.

- **Administration/claims payment.** Many employees elect not to introduce group home and auto insurance, because of the fear that poor administration will cause the plan to backfire. If claims are rejected by the insurer, or take a long time to be paid, employees will complain to the employer. The best advice is to ask other companies what their experience has been with the particular insurer.

CRITICAL ILLNESS INSURANCE

Critical illness insurance provides a lump-sum payment if an insured individual is diagnosed with an illness specified in the insurance policy and the individual survives for a specified period of time. Coverage is generally available on an individual, creditor, or group basis. Group coverage has not yet become popular, primarily because of the relatively high premium charged for the coverage and because many employers and advisors believe this coverage duplicates disability insurance and therefore does not meet a compelling need.

A Typical Group Critical Illness Plan

Group critical illness coverage is offered by all major insurance carriers. Typical features include:

- **Benefit amount.** Coverage is generally offered in units of $10,000 to $25,000, up to maximums of $250,000 to $500,000.

- **Underwriting rules.** Evidence of good health is normally required to purchase coverage; however, some group policies allow up to $25,000 or occasionally $50,000 of coverage without any medical evidence if certain participation levels are reached.

- **Illnesses covered.** A wide range of illness can be included in the group policy. Normally an insurer would offer three or four levels, covering some or all of the following conditions:
  - Alzheimer's disease
  - Aorta surgery
  - Benign brain tumour
  - Blindness
  - Cancer (life-threatening)
  - Coma
  - Deafness
  - Heart attack
  - Kidney failure
  - Loss of independent existence
  - Loss of speech
  - Major burns
  - Major head trauma
  - Major organ transplant
  - Motor neurone disease
  - Multiple sclerosis
  - Occupational HIV infection
  - Paralysis
  - Parkinson's disease
  - Stroke
- **Waiting period.** The individual must survive at least thirty days following the commencement of the illness.

Pricing

The cost of critical illness insurance depends on the amount of coverage and the age and health of the individual.

Taxation

Any lump sum benefit payments arising from a critical illness policy are tax-free to the covered individual. Some policies provide a refund of contributions if the individual does not contract one of the covered illnesses. The Canada Revenue Agency (CRA) is reviewing whether or not such a refund should be taxable income to the individual or estate.

The CRA has ruled that, in certain situations, employers can pay for coverage without triggering a taxable benefit to the employee equal to the premium. According to a 2002 ruling, CRA concluded that a critical illness policy may qualify as a "sickness and accident insurance" policy. As a result, any premiums paid by the employer (either directly or through flexible credits) would not result in a taxable benefit to the employee. Because sickness and accident insurance is not defined in the *Income Tax Act*, CRA referred to the Alberta provincial insurance legislation to reach its decision for the ruling. Therefore, employers who are considering adding critical illness as an employer-paid benefit should take care to confirm the tax status of the benefit in all provinces where they operate.

Any premiums paid by the employer would normally be tax-deductible.

GROUP LEGAL

The Canadian Auto Workers (CAW) negotiated a group legal services plan for its members in 1984. Despite much publicity, few organizations outside the auto industry have adopted legal plans.

Where plans are provided, the employee may have specified legal services — wills, home purchases, marriage contracts, and so forth — performed by a legal panel. Normally, the employee is not permitted to use the plan to sue the employer.

The structure of a group legal plan is similar to that of the capitation dental plan described in Chapter 5 — the employer pays a fixed fee per employee to the provider and the employee must use the services of specified provider (lawyer or dentist). The reaction of the legal profession to group legal plans has been similar to that of the dental association to capitation plans; it doesn't like the concept and argues that it removes an employee's freedom of choice. An obvious advantage of such plans, however, is the potential for lower-than-average fees, which larger employers are able to negotiate.

One reason legal plans have not become more popular is that the employer premium for the coverage is taxable to the employee — so any credits used to purchase group legal coverage would be taxable income to the employee. Therefore, unlike dental, there is no tax advantage to providing legal benefits through a flexible program. Another difficulty in including group legal in a flexible program is adverse selection — any employees who anticipate having legal expenses in the coming year will purchase the coverage. The cost of coverage would therefore escalate and could become prohibitive.

CAR LEASING

Firms offering fleet-leasing policies to employers claim they offer significant savings to employees due to group purchasing power. Typically, the employee decides on a car and options and then places an order with the fleet operator. Normally, there is a minimum number of months of instalments (six is common) that the employee must make before the balance can be paid off.

FITNESS CLUBS

These are usually restricted to specialized fitness centres and would exclude sports and social clubs, such as golf and curling clubs. Any employer subsidy of the cost (either a direct subsidy or through flexible credits) is taxable income to the employee, unless there is a business purpose for the membership.

WELLNESS

Wellness has become an important focus of the overall health care package offered by employers. Employers are increasingly embracing the philosophy that improving employee health makes good economic sense. Studies have shown that for every dollar spent on workplace health programs, savings to the organization ranged from $1.50 to $3 and more. These savings are realized through reductions in disability days and sick leave, as well as the cost of health care and worker's compensation. Besides cost savings, other desirable effects of wellness programs often include higher levels of productivity and enhanced worker retention and engagement.

Linking wellness plans to flexible benefit plans can take the form of specific flexible credit allocations for exhibiting desired behaviour (e.g., completing a health risk assessment, participating in regular exercise) or a more subtle linking of philosophies between a wellness plan and the flexible benefit plan.

Part Three

Legal and Regulatory Environment

Twelve

Taxation of Flexible Benefits

§ 12.1 INTRODUCTION: THE TAX FRAMEWORK

The unique features of flexible benefit plans raise some interesting and very important income tax issues that are key to the design of such plans. Although there are no specific provisions in the income tax legislation dealing with flexible benefit plans, there is a framework within which these plans operate.

Flexible benefit plans should be scrutinized from at least two perspectives: individual benefits and overall structure. The *Income Tax Act* contains specific provisions for the taxation of individual benefits, such as life insurance and supplemental medical insurance. These provisions apply to benefits provided under a flexible benefit plan. The *Income Tax Act* also defines certain vehicles or categories that, from a structural perspective, might apply to a flexible benefit plan, such as salary deferral arrangements, retirement compensation arrangements, employee benefit plans, employee trusts, and private health services plans.

The concept of choice with flexible benefit plans, the choices that are made available, and the manner in which choices are made, is an important determinant of how the benefits in a plan may be subject to income tax. Generally, choices between benefits must be made prospectively, namely, in advance of the plan year, and must be irrevocable for the duration of the plan year. And, if the choices in a flexible benefit plan are only among taxable benefits or only among non-taxable benefits, rather than between taxable and non-taxable benefits, the income tax treatment is more straightforward.

The information in this chapter has been obtained from many sources: the *Income Tax Act* and Regulations, Canada Revenue Agency Information Circulars and Interpretation Bulletins, advance tax rulings and technical interpretations of Canada Revenue Agency (published and unpublished), and private correspondence and meetings with senior Canada Revenue Agency officials over the course of the past twenty years. While much of the previous uncertainty with respect to the taxation of flexible benefit plans has been clarified, there remains some uncertainty, which we hope will be clarified in the coming years.

§ 12.2 *INCOME TAX ACT* AND POLICY

In order to determine the income tax treatment applicable to a flexible benefit plan, the following sources of information should be reviewed:

- The *Income Tax Act* and Regulations
- Canada Revenue Agency Information Circulars
- Canada Revenue Agency Interpretation Bulletins
- Canada Revenue Agency Advance Tax Rulings
- Canada Revenue Agency Technical Interpretations
- Court decisions.

INCOME TAX ACT AND REGULATIONS

As mentioned above, the *Income Tax Act* contains provisions that address the taxation of individual benefits and that provide an overall structure. A basic starting point is subsection 5(1):

> **Income from office or employment** — Subject to this Part, a taxpayer's income for a taxation year from an office or employment is the salary, wages and other remuneration, including gratuities, received by the taxpayer in the year.

Within the context of a flexible benefit plan, this provision raises certain issues, such as:

- What is the meaning of "salary, wages and other remuneration"? Is the value of a benefit a form of remuneration? If so, how may the value be determined? These questions are relevant if a benefit does not fit squarely within another provision in the *Income Tax Act*.
- What is the meaning of "received"? If an employee has a choice to receive a benefit but does not actually receive it, will the value of the benefit be deemed taxable under this subsection? Again, these questions become relevant if the entitlement to a benefit is not specifically dealt with in another provision in the *Income Tax Act*.

Section 6 of the *Income Tax Act* specifically addresses the taxation of benefits and enumerates certain benefits that are subject to income tax. Paragraph 6(1)(a) sets out the general rule that all benefits are subject to income tax, and then provides some exceptions:

> **Amounts to be included as income from office or employment** — There shall be included in computing the income of a taxpayer for a taxation year as income from an office or employment such of the following amounts as are applicable:
> **Value of benefits** — the value of board, lodging and other benefits of any kind whatever received or enjoyed by the taxpayer in the year in respect of, in the course of, or by virtue of an office or employment, except any benefit . . .

The general conclusion is, then, that all benefits are taxable unless exempted. Note the distinction between the reference in subsection 5(1) to amounts "received" and the reference in paragraph 6(1)(a) to benefits "received or enjoyed." Is this intended to create a broader tax net? Does this have any application to the existence of choice of benefits under a flexible benefit plan?

The exceptions listed under paragraph 6(1)(a), namely those benefits that are not subject to income tax, at least under subsection 6(1), are:

- Benefits derived from contributions to a registered pension plan, a group sickness or accident insurance plan, a private health services plan, a supplementary unemployment benefit plan, a deferred profit-sharing plan, or a group term life insurance policy
- Benefits under a retirement compensation arrangement, an employee benefit plan, or an employee trust
- A benefit in respect of the use of an automobile
- A benefit derived from counselling services in respect of mental or physical health, re-employment, or retirement of the taxpayer
- Benefits under a salary deferral arrangement.

Some of these benefits are subject to income tax under other provisions in the *Income Tax Act*. The taxation of specific benefits and arrangements is dealt with further on in this chapter.

This chapter does not examine the *Quebec Tax Act* in detail. Most of the provisions of the *Quebec Tax Act* relating to the taxation of benefits of Quebec residents are, in all material respects, identical to the provisions of the *Income Tax Act*. One notable exception is the taxation of medical and dental benefits. See Section 12.8 for details of the Quebec differences.

CANADA REVENUE AGENCY INFORMATION CIRCULARS AND INTERPRETATION BULLETINS

Information Circulars ("ICs") and Interpretation Bulletins ("ITs") set out Canada Revenue Agency's administrative policies regarding the interpretation and application of various provisions of the *Income Tax Act*. They have been published since 1970 and are an invaluable source to determine the manner in which Canada Revenue Agency is likely to administer the *Income Tax Act*.

Although ICs and ITs do not have the force of law, they can generally be relied upon as a reflection of Canada Revenue Agency's interpretation of the law. The ITs relevant to flexible benefit plans are included in the Appendix of this book.

CANADA REVENUE AGENCY ADVANCE TAX RULINGS

As described in *IC 70-6R5*, Canada Revenue Agency established a procedure whereby taxpayers can ask Canada Revenue Agency for advance tax rulings ("ATRs") on proposed transactions. Canada Revenue Agency adopts the administrative position that ATRs are binding on Canada Revenue Agency in respect of the particular taxpayer and transaction. A ruling request must be made in advance of the transaction being ruled on. An advance fee equal to five hours of work plus GST is prescribed in *IC 70-6R5*.

All ATRs are released to the general public in an edited form, thereby protecting any confidential information detailed in the ATR itself.

CANADA REVENUE AGENCY TECHNICAL INTERPRETATIONS

Canada Revenue Agency provides opinions or technical interpretations on various issues related to the interpretation and administration of the *Income Tax Act*. These are also provided for in *IC 70-6R5*. There is no fee for this service. These requests are typically made on a no-name basis, and Canada Revenue Agency does not consider itself bound by these opinions. They do, however, provide very helpful guidance on technical issues. There have been many technical interpretations on features of flexible benefit plans over the past several years. Some of these are referred to later in this chapter.

COURT DECISIONS

Court decisions are also a helpful source of guidance in interpreting the *Income Tax Act*. However, there have not been many court cases on the taxation of benefits.

§ 12.3 TAXATION OF SPECIFIC BENEFITS

The *Income Tax Act* is relatively clear regarding the income tax treatment of specific benefits. It is important to have a clear understanding of the taxation of each benefit in designing the choices available under a flexible benefit plan and in setting up the administration system.

SUPPLEMENTAL MEDICAL BENEFITS

Medical benefits may be provided to employees on a non-taxable basis. (However, in the province of Quebec, such benefits are subject to income tax under the *Quebec Tax Act*.) The premiums (if any) paid for the coverage and the benefits, when paid, are not subject to income tax. Medical benefits may be provided through a traditional insurance policy, on an administrative services only (ASO) or cost-plus basis, or as a straight reimbursement without any involvement of an insurance carrier. The most typical approach for larger employers is to provide the benefits under an ASO contract with an insurer. Under this approach, the insurance company acts as the claims adjudicator and payor, while the employer pays an administration fee and reimburses the insurer for claims payments.

In order for the benefits to be provided on a tax-free basis, the plan should qualify as a private health services plan (PHSP). A PHSP is one of the listed exceptions in subparagraph 6(1)(a)(i) of the *Income Tax Act* to the general principle that all benefits are taxable. If the medical benefit plan does not qualify as a PHSP, the only other possible category might be a "group sickness or accident insurance plan," also referred to in subparagraph 6(1)(a)(i). PHSPs are discussed in more detail in Section 12.4.

Briefly, a medical benefit plan will qualify as a PHSP if the benefits provided under the plan are medical expenses that would otherwise qualify toward a medical expense tax credit. Qualifying medical expenses are listed in subsection 118.2(2) of the *Income Tax Act*, together with some refinements in regulation 5700, and are described in some detail in *Interpretation Bulletin IT-519R2 (Consolidated)*. These are contained in the Appendix.

Paragraph (a) of subsection 118.2(2) specifically recognizes payments for services to the taxpayer (employee) or the employee's spouse or common-law partner or a dependant. "Common-law partner" is defined in subsection 248(1) to include persons (whether of the same or opposite sex) who have cohabited for at least a year or are the parents of a child.

Subsection 118(6) defines "dependant" as a person who is dependent upon the employee for support and who is either:

- the child or grandchild of the employee or the employee's spouse or common-law partner, or

- the parent, grandparent, brother, sister, uncle, aunt, niece, or nephew of the employee or the employee's spouse or common-law partner, if resident in Canada at any time in the year.

Subsection 118.2(2) specifies that payments to "medical practitioners" are eligible medical expenses. This includes more than just medical doctors. *IT-519R2* elaborates on the meaning of this term. Medical practitioners include "a broad range of individuals in the medical profession" who are authorized to practise under the laws of their local provincial jurisdiction. Examples given are osteopaths, chiropractors, naturopaths, physiotherapists, chiropodists, psychologists, acupuncturists, and dietitians. Not all provinces recognize these various practitioners. Provincial legislation must be canvassed to ensure that a practitioner will be considered a medical practitioner for purposes of subsection 118.2(2), and that payments to such persons will qualify as eligible medical expenses.

    Drugs and medicines are eligible medical expenses. Paragraph (n) of subsection 118.2(2), however, specifies that to be eligible, a drug must be prescribed by a medical practitioner and recorded by a pharmacist. Drugs that are purchased without a prescription, such as over-the-counter drugs and medications that are in the experimental stage, are therefore not eligible medical expenses.

DENTAL BENEFITS

Dental benefits may also be provided on an insured basis, under an ASO contract, or as a reimbursement. The premiums and benefits payable under a dental plan may be provided on a non-taxable basis in the same manner as medical benefits, under a PHSP. Paragraph (a) of subsection 118.2(2) of the *Income Tax Act* includes amounts paid to a dentist in respect of dental services as eligible medical expenses. Paragraph (n) includes drugs prescribed by a dentist and recorded by a pharmacist. Paragraph (p) includes certain services of a "dental mechanic," such as denture work.

VISION CARE BENEFITS

Vision care benefits may be provided on a non-taxable basis, through a traditional insurance contract, an ASO contract, or as a straight reimbursement. Vision care benefits are included in the definition of medical expenses in paragraph (j) of subsection 118.2(2) of the *Income Tax Act*. Amounts paid for "eye glasses or other devices for the treatment or correction of a defect of vision" are eligible if prescribed by a medical practitioner or optometrist. Seeing-eye dogs and related expenses are also included under paragraph (l) of subsection 118.2(2).

LIFE INSURANCE

Premiums paid toward life insurance for employees are taxable to the employees, by virtue of subsection 6(4) of the *Income Tax Act*. The benefits payable to the beneficiaries are not subject to income tax. Subsection 6(4) brings into income any premium amounts paid under a group term life insurance policy, which is defined in subsection 248(1) as a policy of life insurance or disability insurance for employees. This definition is important in determining how life insurance premiums will be taxed. If a life insurance policy does not fit within the definition of a group term life insurance policy, the premiums paid for the coverage will be taxed under paragraph 6(1)(a), rather than subsection 6(4).

The method used to calculate the taxable benefit under subsection 6(4) is set out in Regulations 2700–2704. The taxable benefit for an employee is defined as the average cost of the insurance under the policy for the "premium category" applicable to the employee. The regulations recognize the creation of premium categories in life insurance policies and the calculation of taxable benefits according to such categories. For example, a policy may have separate categories for smokers and non-smokers, retirees and active employees, or union and non-union employees. However, the regulations prohibit creating separate categories based on age or gender.

This potentially creates a mismatch within flexible benefit plans between the price tags and the taxable benefits. Frequently, the price tags for life insurance coverage under such plans are based on the actual cost of coverage for individuals and reflect age, gender, and smoker status. The taxable benefit, on the other hand, being based on average cost of coverage within premium categories that cannot distinguish by age or gender, will be quite different.

There are a couple of ways to overcome this mismatch:

- Create separate group term life insurance policies for distinct age and gender groups.
- Create a policy that falls outside the definition of group term life insurance policy.

The regulations do not prohibit an employer from creating several group term life insurance policies for an employee population. An employer could create separate policies for males and females, separate policies for defined age groups, or a combination of the two. In this manner, the taxable benefit would more closely approximate the price tags under the policies.

A life insurance policy that includes coverage for spouses or other dependants of employees will not meet the definition of group term life insurance policy. The taxable benefit in this case will be imposed under paragraph 6(1)(a) rather than subsection 6(4). Under paragraph 6(1)(a), the taxable benefit may be calculated using individual rates, rather than being required to use average rates. This eliminates any mismatch between the price tags under a flex plan and the taxable benefits.

One point worth noting is that in determining the life insurance premium for an employee, under Regulation 2700, if the life insurance plan is combined with accidental death and dismemberment (AD&D) insurance, the premium for the AD&D coverage must be excluded.

DEPENDANT LIFE INSURANCE

Premiums paid for life insurance for dependants are taxable under paragraph 6(1)(a) of the *Income Tax Act*. The taxable benefit may be calculated using the premium rate applicable to the individual (i.e., reflecting the age, gender, and smoker status of the dependant). Other methods may be used if they are actuarially justifiable and reasonably approximate the cost of providing the benefit to the employee.

ACCIDENTAL DEATH AND DISMEMBERMENT INSURANCE (AD&D)

Premiums paid for AD&D insurance are not taxable to employees. Premiums for this coverage are excluded from income tax under subparagraph 6(1)(a)(i), by virtue of the reference to "group sickness or accident insurance plans." The benefits payable under such policies are also not subject to income tax.

DEPENDANT ACCIDENTAL DEATH AND DISMEMBERMENT INSURANCE

Premiums paid for and benefits payable under AD&D insurance for spouses or other dependants of employees are also not taxable to employees and beneficiaries, for the same reasons described in the paragraph above.

SHORT-TERM DISABILITY (STD) BENEFITS

The most common manner of providing STD benefits is through salary continuation, with the benefit amount expressed as a percentage of regular pay. Such payments will be fully taxable to employees under either subsection 5(1) or paragraph 6(1)(a) of the *Income Tax Act* and subject to regular statutory deductions.

Any plan that provides sickness or accident insurance on a funded or insured basis, rather than as salary continuation, will be taxed as follows:

- By virtue of subparagraph 6(1)(a)(i) of the *Income Tax Act*, employer contributions made toward such a plan are not taxable to employees when they are made, as long as the plan is a group plan. If a plan is established for an individual, the employer contributions will be taxable to the employee.

- The benefits payable under such group plans will be taxable under paragraph 6(1)(f) if there has been any employer contribution toward the benefits.
- By virtue of subparagraph 6(1)(f)(v), the amount of employee contributions made toward the benefits will be deducted from the taxable benefit.
- If the plan is paid for entirely by employees, the benefits paid from the plan will not be taxable to the employees.

Canada Revenue Agency characterizes funded or insured plans as "wage loss replacement plans" and published *Interpretation Bulletin IT-428* on these plans to give guidance to taxpayers. There have also been a number of technical interpretations of these plans, particularly concerning the issue of whether or not a plan is employee-paid or employer-paid and the extent to which both types of plans can be connected. This is discussed in more detail in the next section, "Long-Term Disability Benefits."

LONG-TERM DISABILITY (LTD) BENEFITS

LTD benefits are covered by the same provisions in the *Income Tax Act* as STD benefits. Generally, contributions by an employer to an LTD plan will not be taxable to employees; however, benefits paid from such plans will be taxable. The largest distinction, from an income tax standpoint, is between employee-paid and employer-paid plans.

Often, flexible benefit plans offer a choice between employee-paid (non-taxable) and employer-paid (taxable) LTD benefits. Plan sponsors must be careful to design the LTD options so that the employee-paid LTD option could not be characterized as partly employer-paid. Otherwise, the benefits paid from the plan would become taxable. In particular, if the flexible plan uses a credit-based pricing structure, no credits should be used to pay for the employee-paid LTD option, since credits are considered company funding.

Canada Revenue Agency has given some guidance on this through technical interpretations. Canada Revenue Agency has taken the position for some time that it is possible to have employer-paid LTD benefits and employee-paid LTD benefits paid from one insurance policy. The benefits paid under the employee-paid portion of the policy can maintain their tax-free status if certain conditions are met.

In *Technical Interpretation #9417685*, dated October 20, 1994, Canada Revenue Agency stated that:

> It is a question of fact as to whether or not the benefits under a particular policy are derived from participation in an employer-provided plan. In order for two plans, which are covered by the same insurance policy, to be considered separate plans, the level of benefits, the premium rates, the qualifications for membership and other terms and conditions of each of the plans must not be dependent upon the existence of the other plan.

Where a single premium rate is established based on the experience of all the employees (in an employee-paid plan and an employer-paid plan), it is our view that all the employees are covered by the same plan notwithstanding that employer contributions are only required in respect of some employees.

Under a flexible benefit plan that offers employees a choice between one or more employee-paid (LTD) plans and one or more employer-paid (LTD) plans, the benefits may be provided under one policy, but the employee-paid plans cannot in any way depend upon the employer-paid plans. It is, however, possible to provide a basic employer-paid plan and a second-tier employee-paid plan if the employee-paid plan does not depend upon the employer-paid plan.

§ 12.4 TAXATION OF FLEXIBLE BENEFITS

Given the tax treatment applicable to individual benefits discussed in Section 12.3 above, there are provisions in the *Income Tax Act* and Canada Revenue Agency administrative policies that govern the structure of a flexible benefit plan. These principles will have an impact on how the entire plan is subject to tax.

INPUTS AND OPTIONS

Canada Revenue Agency regards flexible benefit plans as plans with *inputs* — sources of funds that employees can direct toward certain benefits — and *options* — the various avenues open to employees to allocate the funds. Examples of *inputs* are flexible benefit credits that the employer allocates to employees, or credits generated through opting down or out of certain coverages. The *options* in a flexible benefit plan will be the various benefit choices, which could include a health spending account, the purchase of vacation days, deposits to a group registered retirement savings plan, or cash.

According to paragraph 7 of *Interpretation Bulletin IT-529*, the granting of credits to an employee will not confer a taxable benefit on the employee, provided certain criteria are met in the manner in which the options are elected. The options selected by an employee using those credits will be subject to income tax in the same manner as if they were provided individually in a traditional benefit program.

BENEFIT ELECTIONS

The basic rule applicable to a flexible benefit plan, in order to avoid immediate recognition of taxable income, is that benefit elections must be made on a prospective basis, namely, in advance of the plan year to which they relate. Typically, under a flexible benefit plan, employees will receive enrolment materials well in advance of the plan year, with all the financial information, to enable them to make choices before the start of the plan year. If choices are made after the start of a plan year, retroactively to the beginning of the plan year, some amounts may be subject to taxation in the employee's hands.

Another principle is that elections must be irrevocable by the employee for the duration of the plan year. One exception to this is in the event of a change in family status of an employee, otherwise known as a "life event." A "life event" is discussed in paragraph 6 of *IT-529* and includes events such as the birth or death of a dependant, a change in marital status, or the loss of insurance coverage under a spouse's employer's plan. In such event, an employee may change elections, provided that the change applies only to the future. Another exception is a change in employment status. For example, a change from part-time status to full-time status may require an employee to make changes to the originally selected benefits to reflect the increase or decrease in the amount of flex credits available to the employee. Again, in such an event, the change must apply only to the future.

CONSTRUCTIVE RECEIPT

The doctrine of constructive receipt is often referred to, but not often applied, by Canada Revenue Agency in the taxation of flexible benefit plans. Canada Revenue Agency's role is to administer the *Income Tax Act*; it, therefore, prefers to rely on specific provisions of the *Income Tax Act*, rather than judicial doctrines.

It is beyond the scope of this book to examine the doctrine of constructive receipt in detail, but it is often misunderstood and misapplied. Please refer to *Canadian Tax Paper No. 71*, titled *Timing and Income Taxation: The Principles of Income Measurement for Tax Purposes*, by B.J. Arnold, published by the Canadian Tax Foundation. At page 91, Mr. Arnold defines the doctrine as follows:

> Generally, according to the doctrine of constructive receipt, where an amount of income is readily available to a cash basis taxpayer, it will be considered to have been received by him whether or not he chooses to take possession of it. An amount will be considered to be readily available to a taxpayer if it has been earned, it is a fixed amount, and the payer is both able and willing to pay.

Yet, according to a Tax Court of Canada case, *Markman v. R.*, [1989] 1 C.T.C. 2381, constructive receipt:

> ... applies only when a payment has been made by a payor to a party who is not the payee, but was made for the benefit of the payee or in satisfaction of an obligation contracted by him. As the expression "constructive receipt" implies there must have been a payment and that payment must have been received by someone before the doctrine may be invoked.

In the context of a flexible benefit plan, employers should be aware that the doctrine exists and that it may apply in some circumstances. In paragraph 8 of *IT-529*, Canada Revenue Agency states that if, after the beginning of the plan year, the flexible program allows an exchange of unallocated or newly allocated flexible credits for cash, a transfer of credits between benefit options, or a selection of benefits (other than a reselection following a "life event" or change in employment status or an initial selection by an employee now entering the flexible benefits program), then the employee will be considered by Canada Revenue Agency to be in constructive receipt of employment income equal to the value of the allocated flexible credits. The effect of such an interpretation would lead to an income inclusion for the employee equal to the value of all benefits received out of the flexible program, despite the fact that some of the benefits would not have been so included if they were instead offered separately from the flexible program. As a result, care must be taken in the design of the flexible program to ensure that unintended tax consequences do not occur.

STATUTORY ARRANGEMENTS AND PLANS

There are certain plans described in the *Income Tax Act* that sponsors of flexible benefit plans should know about and take into consideration. Certain features of flexible benefit plans may unwittingly fall within the definition of one or more of these plans, with income tax consequences to the plan sponsor and to the employees who participate in the plan. Each plan is defined in subsection 248(1) of the *Income Tax Act* and has distinct income tax characteristics, as described below. These plans are specifically addressed in paragraph 12 of *IT-529*. The benefits payable from these plans are exempt from income tax under paragraph 6(1)(a); however, they are subject to income tax under subsequent provisions within section 6 (with the exception of private health services plans).

Salary Deferral Arrangements

Salary deferral arrangements (SDAs) are defined as a sort of catch-all for any funded or unfunded arrangements under which a taxpayer is intending to defer payment of income tax to a subsequent calendar year. It is defined as:

> ... a plan or arrangement, whether funded or not, under which any person has a right in a taxation year to receive an amount after the year where it is reasonable to consider that one of the main purposes for the creation or existence of the right is to postpone tax payable under this *Act* . . . in respect of an amount that is on account or in lieu of, salary or wages of the taxpayer for services rendered by the taxpayer in the year or a preceding year...

Excluded from the SDA definition are disability insurance plans, group sickness or accident insurance plans, supplementary unemployment benefit plans, vacation pay trusts, certain education and training plans, and sabbatical plans.

Employers who sponsor flexible benefit plans will generally want to avoid having any aspect of a plan characterized as an SDA. If an amount payable to or credited to an employee is characterized as an SDA payment, it will be taxable to the employee under paragraph 6(1)(i) of the *Income Tax Act*. Due to the way flexible benefit plans are commonly designed, with prospective elections, twelve-month plan years, and limited rollovers into future years (see "Private Health Services Plans" on the next page), the SDA rules should not apply.

Retirement Compensation Arrangements

Retirement compensation arrangements (RCAs) are defined as funded plans to provide benefits for employees, generally on termination of employment or at retirement. Excluded from the definition are disability plans, group sickness or accident insurance plans, supplementary unemployment insurance plans, vacation pay trusts, and SDAs. Canada Revenue Agency publishes an *RCA Guide* to assist employers in understanding the mechanics of RCAs.

Most employers will want to avoid application of the RCA rules because of the unfavourable income tax treatment. Contributions made to an RCA are subject to a 50 per cent refundable tax, as are annual earnings in the RCA. The refundable tax is held by Canada Revenue Agency on an interest-free basis. As benefits are paid out, the tax is refunded to the RCA at the rate of $1 for every $2 of benefits paid out.

It would be unusual for any part of a flexible benefit plan to be characterized as an RCA, because typically the benefits in a plan are not funded for termination of employment or retirement. RCA treatment may, however, apply to a plan in which funds are accumulated toward the purchase of retiree benefits. Any funded plan in which funds are accumulated over time should be tested against the RCA rules.

Employee Benefit Plans

Employee benefit plans (EBPs) are funded plans under which contributions are made to a custodian for the benefit of employees. Unlike RCAs, under EBPs the benefits do not have to be reserved for an employee's termination of employment or retirement. For this reason, it is easier for a flexible benefit plan or part thereof to be characterized as an EBP. *Interpretation Bulletins IT-502* and *IT-502SR* provide details on EBPs.

The following plans are excluded from the definition of EBP in the *Income Tax Act*: group sickness or accident insurance plans, private health services plans, supplementary unemployment benefit plans, group term life insurance policies, disability insurance plans, vacation pay trusts, certain education and training plans, SDAs, and RCAs. Paragraph 4 of *IT-502* sets out these exclusions in more detail.

Employer contributions to EBPs are not tax-deductible until benefits are paid out and current income in the EBP is exhausted. Contributions to EBPs and annual earnings in the fund are not taxable to employees. Benefits, when paid out, are taxable. An example of an EBP might be a funded plan to provide coverage for medical expenses outside the definition of "medical expenses" in subsection 118.2(2) of the *Income Tax Act*. Such a plan would not qualify as a private health services plan and is, therefore, probably not exempted from the definition of an EBP. In these cases, it might be simpler to provide an unfunded reimbursement plan, rather than a funded plan that is characterized as an EBP.

Employee Trusts

Employee trusts are described as arrangements under which an employer contributes amounts to a trustee to provide benefits for employees. The benefits must vest when the payments are made and the amount of the payments on behalf of the employees may not differentiate based on an employee's position, performance, or pay.

The annual contributions to and earnings in the trust must be allocated to the employee's beneficiaries. The plan trustee must file an election to qualify the plan as an employee trust. The contributions and earnings are taxable to the employees.

This vehicle is not often used, because amounts vest immediately and are taxable. However, it can be a useful tool for after-tax accumulations, as an alternative to an employees profit-sharing plan. Paragraphs 34 to 46 of *IT-502* provide additional details about employee trusts.

Private Health Services Plans

A private health services plan (PHSP) is defined as an insurance plan for the coverage of hospital expenses or medical (and dental) expenses, or both, apart from provincial health care plans such as OHIP. Almost all flexible benefit plans contain what is variously called a health spending account, health care spending account, or health care expense account, which is intended to qualify as a PHSP. Health spending accounts are discussed in detail in Chapter 7.

Interpretation Bulletin IT-339R2 describes PHSPs in detail. Exercise caution in using *IT-339R2*, because it is out of date in certain respects. Because a PHSP is defined in the *Income Tax Act* as a contract of insurance or a plan in the nature of insurance, there are certain inherent characteristics that Canada Revenue Agency looks for in determining whether or not a particular plan qualifies as a PHSP. Paragraph 3 of *IT-339R2* states that a PHSP is:

- an undertaking by one person
- to indemnify another person
- for an agreed consideration
- from a loss or liability in respect of an event
- the happening of which is uncertain.

The insurance element and the associated risk of loss are key features of PHSPs. Canada Revenue Agency has formulated administrative policies regarding what it considers a sufficient degree of risk in order for a plan to qualify as a PHSP.

IT-339R2 clarifies that the eligible expenses under a PHSP can be in respect of dental care, but all expenses must be those that "normally would otherwise have qualified as a medical expense under the provisions of subsection 118.2(2) in the determination of the medical expense tax credit" (paragraph 4 of *IT-339R2*). Canada Revenue Agency disregards the qualifier "normally" — if an expense payable under a plan is not a medical expense under subsection 118.2(2), the plan will not qualify as a PHSP.

It is important for a plan to precisely define what expenses are covered in order to avoid the plan paying expenses that are not eligible under the *Income Tax Act*. Canada Revenue Agency *Technical Interpretation #9430065* elaborates on this issue. Although Canada Revenue Agency, so far, has not required employers to produce plan documents for flexible benefit plans, this may be appropriate in some cases, particularly where a third party claims adjudicator, such as an insurance company, is not being used.

A PHSP may be administered on a traditional insured basis, on a cost-plus or ASO basis with an insurance company, or strictly on a reimbursement basis by the employer. Typically, health spending accounts within flexible benefit plans are administered on either an ASO basis or as reimbursements by the employer. Canada Revenue Agency prefers the use of an independent third party, such as an insurance company, as a claims adjudicator to ensure that the expenses paid from the plan are eligible medical expenses.

HEALTH AND WELFARE TRUSTS

Canada Revenue Agency recognizes a vehicle that it has defined as a health and welfare trust (H&WT), which is sometimes used by employers as a means of funding certain employee benefits, either within flexible benefit plans or outside of such plans. *Interpretation Bulletin IT-85R2* (refer to the Appendix) describes H&WTs in detail. Basically, it is an arrangement through which one or more of the following insured benefits are funded through a trust:

- Group sickness or accident insurance benefits
- Private health services plan benefits
- Group term life insurance benefits.

Canada Revenue Agency recognizes that certain employers, particularly those with employees covered by collective bargaining agreements, establish trust arrangements into which the employers, and in some cases the employees, contribute specified amounts toward providing the above health and welfare benefits. To qualify as an H&WT, the funds cannot revert to the employer or be used for any purpose other than providing health and welfare benefits. The employer contributions must be obligatory and enforceable by the trustee.

If the plan qualifies as an H&WT, the employer contributions will be tax-deductible. The employees are not subject to income tax when the contributions are made. The benefits, when paid, are subject to tax in the same manner as they would be if they were paid outside the H&WT. Net income in the trust, after payment of benefits, is subject to payment of tax by the trust.

If a funded plan is established and it does not qualify as an H&WT, it could be a salary deferral arrangement, a retirement compensation arrangement, an employee benefit plan, or an employee trust. Canada Revenue Agency stated the following in *Technical Interpretation #9430065*:

> Where an employer contributes funds into a plan for the benefit of its employees, the plan will be considered an employee benefit plan or an employee trust as defined in subsection 248(1) of the *Act* unless the plan qualifies as a health and welfare trust as described in *Interpretation Bulletin IT-85R2, "Health and Welfare Trusts."* Where part of a single plan could be regarded as a health and welfare trust and another part as an employee benefit plan or employee trust, the plan will be treated as an employee benefit plan or employee trust, as the case may be, unless the portion of the plan which would otherwise qualify as a health and welfare trust is accounted for separately from the portion which qualifies as an employee benefit plan as stated in paragraph 4 of *IT-85R2*.

HEALTH SPENDING ACCOUNTS

Health spending accounts (HSAs) are typically provided as an option under flexible benefit plans. Please refer to Chapter 7 for more detail on HSAs. Because HSAs are intended to qualify as PHSPs, there are certain Canada Revenue Agency guidelines that should be followed carefully.

As discussed in Section 12.4, an employee's election to allocate funds to various options under a flexible benefit plan must be made in advance of the plan year and must be irrevocable. Therefore, if an employee allocates employer funds to his or her HSA, those amounts cannot later be withdrawn. They must be used within the HSA in respect of eligible expenses. Given that an employee's allocation is an estimate of an amount sufficient to cover anticipated claims in the following plan year, at the end of the plan year the employee will either have unused funds or an excess of claims.

Canada Revenue Agency has adopted the following rules with respect to roll-overs of credits and claims:

- Excess HSA balances may be rolled over for up to twelve months after the end of a plan year and be used to reimburse the following year's expenses (see paragraph 16 of *IT-529*).

- The one-year rollover period for unused balances does not have to expire on termination of employment or retirement. For example, if an employee terminates employment or retires in the middle of a plan year and has unused flexible benefit credits, the flexible benefit plan may permit the employee to submit claims that arise during the remainder of the plan year. Please refer to *Technical Interpretation #9311525*, dated August 9, 1993.

- Alternatively, unreimbursed expenses may be rolled over for up to twelve months after the end of a plan year and may be claimed from the following year's HSA (see paragraph 16 of *IT-529*).

- Note, however, that the participant must have allocated funds to the HSA in the prior year in order to be allowed to roll expenses forward. Otherwise, according to the Canada Revenue Agency, the HSA would not have the requisite element of insurance, as there would be little or no risk. Please refer to *Technical Interpretation 2005-0126211E5*, dated November 24, 2005.

- A plan that permits employees to roll over both excess claims and unused allocations will not qualify as a PHSP. Paragraph 16 of *IT-529* specifically states that a plan which permits the carry forward of either the unused allocation or eligible medical expenses (but not both) will not be disqualified as a private health services plan solely by reason of the carry forward provision in the plan. Therefore, any plan that allows both claims and unused credits to roll over would not qualify as a PHSP.

- Reasonable "grace periods" following the end of a plan year within which an employee can submit a claim are acceptable, according to an ATR (advance tax ruling). The flexible benefit plan in that case had a December 31 plan year-end. The plan permitted employees to submit claims by January 31 of the following year, for claims that arose prior to December 31.

- Unused flexible benefit credits may be rolled over on retirement to a retiree HSA. The same ATR referred to in the above point confirmed this.

- Although administratively complex, it is possible in some circumstances to offer employees the choice each plan year between rolling over excess expenses or unused flexible benefit credits. It may be advisable to obtain a ruling or opinion in advance of adopting this design.

- A portion of a bonus may, under appropriate circumstances, be allocated to an employee's HSA. Hewitt Associates obtained an ATR permitting employees to allocate a portion of a bonus to which they may become entitled to in the future to their HSA, to be used for eligible medical and dental expenses. For more details please refer to document number 2004-0091211R3, dated November 24, 2004.

VACATION TRADING

The trading of vacation days is a fairly common feature in flexible benefit plans. Thirty per cent of plans surveyed in the *2005 Hewitt Associates Survey of Employer Attitudes to Flexible Benefits* included vacation buying or selling.

Vacation Buying

Paragraph 23 of *IT-529* specifically addresses vacation buying. Essentially, a flexible program may include an option whereby an employee can obtain additional vacation time. If the additional vacation time is funded through the allocation of flexible credits, the design of the flexible plan typically requires the employee to use the purchased vacation within the plan year in which it was acquired. If the flexible plan allows the purchased vacation to be carried forward to a subsequent plan year, Canada Revenue Agency may consider the arrangement to be a salary deferral arrangement (SDA). Therefore, to remain on-side, any unused purchased vacation should be cashed out or forfeited before the end of the plan year.

Vacation Selling

Paragraph 22 of *IT-529* specifically addresses the selling of vacation time. In the event an employee forgoes or "sells" vacation or other amounts in exchange for additional flex credits under a flexible plan, the value of the amount so forgone is included in the employee's income at the time the additional flex credits are credited.

SALARY ADJUSTMENTS

There are many ways to generate funds for flexible benefit plans by way of salary adjustments that are appealing from an employee net cost perspective, but which may have unfavourable income tax consequences. There are many ways to adjust employees' salaries, either unilaterally by the employer or with some choice on the part of employees; for example, by reducing or eliminating a future pay increase, reducing or eliminating a future bonus, or simply reducing existing pay levels.

Plan sponsors must be cautious about using salary adjustments as part of a flexible benefit plan. Paragraph 9 of *IT-529* sets out Canada Revenue Agency's position with respect to such a strategy. The paragraph states that the conversion of any portion of the employee's salary to flex credits will result in an income inclusion of the amount of salary so converted. Accordingly, if an employee forgoes an amount to which he or she will become entitled, such as a negotiated salary increase or vacation, Canada Revenue Agency takes the position that the amount of remuneration that is forgone will be included in the income of the employee.

It remains a question of fact whether an employee has forgone an amount to which he or she would have become entitled. For example, the renegotiation of an employment contract upon the expiry of a prior contract which includes a reduced salary and additional flex credits will not result in an income inclusion for the employee. Please refer to paragraph 9 of *IT-529* for more details on salary adjustments.

Note: While explicit salary reduction in exchange for pre-tax flexible credits is not permitted, CRA has clarified that employees may allocate a portion of an upcoming bonus to their flexible credit pool in certain circumstances. This would provide significant tax advantages for employees with large health care expenses. Please refer to document number 2005-0139631R3, dated April 5, 2006.

FLEXIBLE BENEFITS FOR RETIREES

Flexible benefits for retirees are gaining in popularity. Thirty-six per cent of the employers surveyed in the *2005 Hewitt Associates Survey of Employer Attitudes toward Flexible Benefits* that have flexible benefit plans extend such plans to retirees.

Basically, such coverages and benefits under flexible benefit plans for retirees are subject to the same income tax provisions as plans for employees. Benefits for retirees are subject to income tax under paragraph 56(1)(a) of the *Income Tax Act*.

§ 12.5 FEDERAL GOODS AND SERVICES TAX

The 6 per cent federal goods and services tax (GST) is not applied to employee benefits, with some exceptions that are not relevant to this chapter.

Administration fees under administrative services only (ASO) arrangements are subject to GST. However, if the arrangement includes a stop-loss provision, it will be considered insurance rather than ASO, and the administrative services will not be subject to GST.

§ 12.6 PROVINCIAL SALES TAX

Group insurance premiums are subject to retail sales tax (RST) in Ontario and Quebec. The RST in Ontario is 8 per cent and in Quebec is generally 9 per cent.

There have been a lot of questions in both provinces about who remits the RST under different arrangements — the employer or the insurer — and whether or not the payment of the RST on behalf of an employee confers a taxable benefit on the employee. While most of the issues have been addressed by the authorities, the following summarizes the rules applicable in Ontario.

The Ontario Ministry of Finance has clarified that the RST on employer premiums should be remitted to the insurer, who then remits the RST to the government. Although the RST regulations state that employers are required to remit the RST on employee premiums to the government, employers may elect to remit the RST to the insurer, together with the RST on employer premiums in respect of other coverages.

Canada Revenue Agency has provided some guidance on whether the payment by an employer of RST on group benefit premiums confers a taxable benefit on employees. The basic rule is: if the underlying premium is taxable to the employee, for example, life insurance, the payment of the RST will also be a taxable benefit. If the underlying premium is not taxable, payment of the RST by the employer will not confer a taxable benefit on employees.

If an employer pays the RST on an employee-paid LTD plan, the payment of the RST will confer a taxable benefit. Fortunately, Canada Revenue Agency has confirmed that the payment of the RST by the employer will not jeopardize the status of the LTD plan. The benefits paid from the plan will continue to be paid on a tax-free basis.

§ 12.7 PREMIUM TAXES

All provinces levy a premium tax, ranging from 2 to 4 per cent of the insured premium. For example, Ontario charges 2 per cent on all insured premiums, and on all uninsured claims costs and administrative charges. The appropriate rate to charge depends on which province or territory the employee lives in. A summary of the various taxes applicable to group benefit plans is included in Table 2.1.

§ 12.8 PROVINCIAL ISSUES

The major difference between Quebec and the rest of Canada in the taxation of benefits is that in Quebec, AD&D, medical, and dental premiums are subject to Quebec income tax. This has administrative implications both for employers with only Quebec employees and for employers who have employees in other provinces.

Revenue Quebec has confirmed that in determining the taxable benefit in a traditional insured plan, an employer may use either the premium rate for all employees across Canada or the premium rate applicable to Quebec employees. Revenue Quebec recognizes that many national employers do not track premium rates by province — in this case, the national premium rate may be used to calculate the taxable benefit. The taxable benefit should also take into account whether an employee has single or family coverage, and what options the employee has elected.

In Quebec, insurance premiums are subject to 9 per cent retail sales tax and a premium tax of 2.35 per cent. These taxes are included in the taxable benefit to employees, with the result that employees pay tax on tax.

Revenue Quebec has confirmed that health spending accounts are taxable, as they are deemed to be insurance under the private health services plan definition. However, employees are not subject to Quebec income tax at the time funds are allocated to the account. Rather, employees are subject to tax as benefits are paid out. Revenue Quebec has also confirmed that employers are not required to withhold income tax on these payments during the year. Instead, the taxable amount is simply reported on the annual Relève 1. However, income tax is required to be withheld throughout the year on the taxable benefit amounts attributable to other benefits.

§ 12.9 SUMMARY

The taxation of group benefits, particularly from an *Income Tax Act* perspective, plays an important role in the design of any flexible plan, as well as in the individual choices employees make. In order to utilize flexible credits in the most tax-effective manner, employees must understand the income tax implications of the their choices.

In addition to income tax implications, flexible benefits are subject to a number of other taxes, both provincial and federal. Table 12.1 that follows on pages 264–266, summarizes the various taxes applicable to group benefits.

Table 12.1
Taxes Applicable to Group Benefit Plans

	Fully or Partially Insured Plans			Fully Uninsured Plans (ASO)[1]		
	Premium Tax	PST	GST/HST	Premium Tax	PST	GST/HST
British Columbia	2% of insured premium	N/A	N/A	N/A	N/A	6% of administrative charges
Alberta	2% of insured premium	N/A	N/A	N/A	N/A	6% of administrative charges
Saskatchewan	3% of insured premium	N/A	N/A	N/A	N/A	6% of administrative charges
Manitoba	2% of insured premium	N/A	N/A	N/A	N/A	6% of administrative charges
Ontario	2% of insured premium plus uninsured claims costs and administrative charges	8% of insured premium plus uninsured claims costs, administrative charges, and premium tax	N/A	Health, dental, and fully employee-paid disability plans: 2% of uninsured claims costs and administrative charges	Health, dental, and fully employee-paid disability plans: 8% of uninsured claims costs and administrative charges. Employer-paid disability plans: 8% of uninsured claims costs and administrative charges	6% of administrative charges and premium tax on administrative charges for health, dental, and fully employee-paid disability plans; 6% of administrative charges for employer-paid disability plans

Table 12.1

Taxes Applicable to Group Benefit Plans (*Continued*)

| | Fully or Partially Insured Plans | | | Fully Uninsured Plans (ASO)[1] | | |
	Premium Tax	PST	GST/HST	Premium Tax	PST	GST/HST
Quebec	2.35% of insured premium plus uninsured claims costs, and administrative charges	9% of insured premium plus uninsured claims costs and administrative charges and premium tax	N/A	2.35% of uninsured claims costs, and administrative charges	9% of uninsured claims costs plus 7.5% of administrative charges, plus premium tax and GST when administration performed in Quebec	6% of administrative charges and premium tax on administrative charges
New Brunswick	2% of insured premium	N/A	N/A	N/A	N/A	6% of administrative charges or 14% of administrative charges plus premium tax when administration performed in New Brunswick
Nova Scotia	3% of insured premium	N/A	N/A	N/A	N/A	6% of administrative charges or 14% of administrative charges, plus premium tax when administration performed in Nova Scotia

(Continued)

Table 12.1

Taxes Applicable to Group Benefit Plans (*Continued*)

	Fully or Partially Insured Plans			Fully Uninsured Plans (ASO)[1]		
	Premium Tax	PST	GST/HST	Premium Tax	PST	GST/HST
Prince Edward Island	3.5% of insured premium	N/A	N/A	N/A	N/A	6% of administrative charges
Newfoundland and Labrador	4% of insured premium plus all uninsured claims costs, and administrative charges	N/A	N/A	4% of all uninsured claims costs, and administrative charges	N/A	6% of administrative charges and premium tax on administrative charges or 14% of administrative charges, plus premium tax when administration performed in Newfoundland and Labrador
Northwest Territories	3% of insured premium	N/A	N/A	N/A	N/A	6% of administration charges
Yukon Territory	2% of insured premium	N/A	N/A	N/A	N/A	6% of administration charges
Nunavut	3% of insured premium	N/A	N/A	N/A	N/A	6% of administration charges

Note:
1. A pure ASO plan is defined as a plan where there is no element of insurance, i.e., no pooling arrangement. Administrative charges and expenses are subject to GST/HST. An ASO plan with a stop-loss provision is considered a financial service, and is therefore GST/HST exempt.

Thirteen

Discrimination Issues

§ 13.1 INTRODUCTION

Compensation and benefit plans have come under increased scrutiny by Canadian courts as individuals and interest groups have focused their attention on employment discrimination issues. This trend will no doubt continue well into the future.

Employers' obligations are governed by a maze of federal and provincial legislation, which can be challenging to navigate. The first question is whether a business is subject to federal or provincial employment law. This is a constitutional question, based on the *Constitution Act, 1867*, which differentiates between matters subject to federal jurisdiction and those subject to provincial jurisdiction. If federal law applies to the enterprise, its employees are considered to be "included employment," and the federal government has authority. Examples of federal businesses include banking, telecommunications, and interprovincial transportation.

However, the vast majority of businesses are subject to provincial law — even those with locations in several provinces. The employees of those businesses are considered to be engaged in "excluded employment," so federal employment laws do not apply. Instead, the employers are governed by the law of the province or territory where their employees work.

§ 13.2 *CANADIAN CHARTER OF RIGHTS AND FREEDOMS*

The *Canadian Charter of Rights and Freedoms* sets an overall policy of nondiscrimination and equality within Canadian society. It is entrenched as part of Canada's Constitution and can override federal and provincial government legislation that violates its provisions.

The Charter does not apply directly to the acts of private individuals; it applies only to the acts of government or institutions exercising governmental functions. With regard to traditional and flexible benefit plans, the Charter could be used in a court application to strike down specific laws that permit discrimination in some instances. Specific discrimination laws are discussed in more detail in Section 13.3. For example, if a provincial government were to be challenged on its employment standards discrimination provisions, and the discrimination were found to be unjustified, the legislation would be struck down. Employers in the province would then have to alter any existing benefit plans to eliminate such discrimination.

Section 15(1) of the Charter states that:

Every individual is equal before and under the law and has the right to the equal protection and equal benefit of the law without discrimination and, in particular, without discrimination based on race, national or ethnic origin, colour, religion, sex, age or mental or physical disability.

Section 15(1) is not limited to the grounds of discrimination listed above, but can also encompass related grounds, such as marital status.

The Charter does not provide absolute rights. All Charter rights are subject to the limits outlined in Section 1, which states that:

The Canadian Charter of Rights and Freedoms guarantees the rights and freedoms set out in it subject only to such reasonable limits prescribed by law as can be demonstrably justified in a free and democratic society.

In order to justify a Section 15 infringement under Section 1 of the Charter, the government must show a pressing and substantial reason for the infringement, and prove that the scope of the discrimination is proportional to that reason.

§ 13.3 SPECIFIC LEGISLATION

Each Canadian jurisdiction has enacted laws governing discrimination in employment. This includes the federal government, whose laws protect federal public sector employees and employees engaged in federal-jurisdiction occupations.

Generally, these laws are known as human rights and fair employment practices laws. They range in form from general "equal treatment" provisions to equal pay for equal work and equal pay for work of equal value (pay equity), to specific prohibitions against discrimination in benefit plans. (Equal pay for equal work and equal pay for work of equal value are discussed in Sections 13.4 and 13.6, respectively.) Each province has set its own standards by way of legislation. See Table 13.1 for a list of relevant legislation in each jurisdiction.

Table 13.1
Discrimination-Related Statutes

Jurisdiction	Statutes
Federal (Canada)	*Canadian Human Rights Act*, R.S.C. 1985, c. H-6, as amended
	Employment Equity Act, S.C. 1995, c. 44, as amended, and the Federal Contractors Program
Alberta	*Human Rights, Citizenship and Multiculturalism Act*, R.S.A. 2000, c. H-14, as amended
British Columbia	*Human Rights Code*, R.S.B.C. 1996, c. 210, as amended
Manitoba	*Human Rights Code*, C.C.S.M. c. H175, as amended
	Employment Standards Code, C.C.S.M. c. E110, as amended
	The Pay Equity Act, C.C.S.M. c. P13, as amended
New Brunswick	*Human Rights Act*, R.S.N.B. 1973, c. H-11, as amended
	Employment Standards Act, S.N.B. 1982, c. E-7.2, as amended
	Pay Equity Act, S.N.B. 1989, c. P-5.01, as amended
Newfoundland and Labrador	*The Human Rights Code*, R.S.N. 1990, c. H-14, as amended
Northwest Territories	*Human Rights Act*, S.N.W.T. 2002, c. 18, as amended
Nova Scotia	*Human Rights Act*, R.S.N.S. 1989, c. 214, as amended
	Labour Standards Code, R.S.N.S. 1989, c. 246, as amended
	Pay Equity Act, R.S.N.S. 1989, c. 337, as amended
Nunavut	*Human Rights Act*, S.Nu. 2003, c. 12, as amended
Ontario	*Human Rights Code*, R.S.O. 1990, c. H.19, as amended
	Employment Standards Act, 2000, S.O. 2000, c. 41, as amended
	Pay Equity Act, R.S.O. 1990, c. P.7, as amended
Prince Edward Island	*Human Rights Act*, R.S.P.E.I. 1988, c. H-12, as amended
	Pay Equity Act, R.S.P.E.I. 1989, c. P-2, as amended
Quebec	*Charter of Human Rights and Freedoms*, R.S.Q. c. C-12, as amended
	Pay Equity Act, S.Q. 1996, c. 43, as amended
	An Act Respecting Equal Access to Employment in Public Bodies and Amending the Charter of Human Rights and Freedoms, S.Q. 2000, c. 45, as amended
Saskatchewan	*The Saskatchewan Human Rights Code*, S.S. 1979, c. S-24.1, as amended
	The Labour Standards Act, R.S.S. 1978, c. L-1, as amended
Yukon	*Human Rights Act*, R.S.Y 2002, c. 116, as amended
	Employment Standards Act, R.S.Y. 2002, c. 72, as amended

EQUAL TREATMENT PROVISIONS

Most of the jurisdictions guarantee "equal treatment with respect to employment." For example, Section 5(1) of the Ontario *Human Rights Code* states that:

> Every person has a right to equal treatment with respect to employment without discrimination because of race, ancestry, place of origin, colour, ethnic origin, citizenship, creed, sex, sexual orientation, age, record of offences, marital status, family status, or disability.

"Equal treatment with respect to employment" may encompass many things, such as hiring, promotion, termination, retirement, compensation, benefits, and so on. Some jurisdictions deal specifically with compensation and benefits; many have formal or informal policies for administering their legislation in those areas.

Benefits for Same-Sex Spouses

The issue of benefits for same-sex spouses has focused attention on the relationship between human rights legislation and employment benefits in a number of jurisdictions. Courts have held that the denial of benefits to same-sex spouses is discriminatory on the basis of either sexual orientation or family status.

Generally, both courts and human rights tribunals have required employers to provide welfare benefits to same-sex spouses where they provide them to opposite-sex spouses. For example, see *Leshner v. Ontario* on the issue of spousal pension benefits, and *Clinton v. Ontario Blue Cross* on welfare benefits.

However, the issue is not entirely free from doubt. *Egan v. Canada*, a 1994 decision of the Supreme Court of Canada, ruled that the government could legally distinguish between opposite- and same-sex couples in granting spousal benefits under the *Old Age Security Act*. Benefits were denied to the same-sex spouse. But a more recent Supreme Court of Canada decision, *M. v. H.*, ruled that spousal support for common-law spouses under a provincial family law statute had to be extended to same-sex spouses as well as opposite-sex spouses. This would appear to indicate that the Court has backed away from the stance taken in *Egan*, and that it may be unlikely to support a distinction in spousal employment benefits for same-sex spouses.

Furthermore, since the *Egan* ruling, most jurisdictions have changed their human rights laws to specifically include sexual orientation as a protected ground of discrimination. Even where that has not been done — for instance, in Alberta — protection may be "read into" the law. In *Vriend v. Alberta*, Alberta's failure to include protection in its human rights statute on the ground of sexual orientation was found to be a breach of the Charter. It was held that protection on that ground must be "read into" the *Human Rights, Citizenship and Multiculturalism Act*.

NON-DISCRIMINATION IN BENEFITS

The regulators in most jurisdictions recognize circumstances where distinctions based on age, sex, marital status, and other protected grounds may be valid. For example, many provinces allow employers to contribute different amounts on behalf of different classes of employees for pensions and for benefits such as life, supplemental medical, and dental insurance, where there is an actuarial basis for making a distinction. The actuarial basis would typically be related to gender (women on average live longer than men and, therefore, have lower life insurance costs, but may have higher disability and medical costs) or age (costs of most group benefits increase with age). Most jurisdictions specifically exempt age distinctions in these situations, and some, including Ontario, Quebec, and British Columbia, also exempt gender distinctions.

Many jurisdictions (notably, Alberta, British Columbia, Ontario, Quebec, and the federal government and its agencies) permit exceptions on grounds of marital status. For example, an employer would be able to provide health insurance coverage to a married employee and extend coverage to the employee's spouse and children. A single employee would receive individual coverage, which would be less valuable than family coverage.

Figure 13.1 summarizes some of the key prohibited grounds of discrimination in each province and territory.

Ontario has the most extensive legislation governing non-discrimination in benefits. That legislation is examined in detail below.

Benefit Entitlement

Entitlement to benefits, as well as the terms of the benefits or contributions, can be an issue. Some jurisdictions have specific exemptions dealing with an employee's entitlement to benefits. However, the exemptions with regard to benefit plans are not consistent among jurisdictions. When structuring a benefit package, an employer must be aware of these differences.

For example, some human rights statutes define age for employment purposes as less than 65 years. This means, for example, that benefit programs that provide coverage only until age 65 do not contravene the Code. In many other provinces, however, this is not the case.

One situation that has been troublesome for employers is benefits coverage for pregnant employees or employees on maternity or parental leave — particularly the right to disability benefits. Generally, any differential treatment based on

Figure 13.1
Prohibited Grounds of Discrimination

	Federal	Alberta	British Columbia	Manitoba	New Brunswick	Newfoundland & Labrador	Northwest Territories	Nova Scotia	Nunavut	Ontario	Prince Edward Island	Quebec	Saskatchewan	Yukon
age	x	x	x	x	x	x	x	x	x	x	x		x	x
ancestry	x	x	x	x	x		x		x	x			x	x
citizenship	x								x	x				
colour	x	x	x	x	x	x	x	x	x	x	x	x	x	x
creed	x	x		x		x	x	x	x	x	x		x	x
dependence on alcohol/drugs	x													
disability	x	x	x	x	x	x	x	x	x	x	x	x	x	x
ethnic origin (background)	x	x		x		x	x	x	x	x				x
family status	x	x	x	x	x		x	x	x	x	x		x	x
marital or civil status	x	x	x	x	x	x	x	x	x	x	x	x	x	x
national origin/ nationality	x			x	x	x	x	x			x	x	x	x
pardoned conviction	x								x					
place of origin		x	x		x	x	x		x		x		x	
political belief			x	x	x	x	x			x	x	x		x
pregnancy	x	x	x		x	x	x		x		x	x		
race	x	x	x	x	x	x	x	x	x	x	x	x	x	x
religion	x	x	x	x	x	x	x	x	x	x	x	x	x	x
sex	x	x	x	x	x	x	x	x	x	x	x	x	x	x
sexual orientation	x	x	x	x	x	x	x	x	x	x	x	x	x	x
social condition					x		x		x			x		
social origin						x								
source of income		x		x				x			x		x	

pregnancy may be treated as sex discrimination. Illness during pregnancy should be treated like any other illness, even if it is a result of the pregnancy itself and not an unrelated medical condition. It is still a health-related absence, and should be treated the same as any other health-related absence.

Ontario Regulation 286/01, the *Benefit Plans Regulation* under the *Employment Standards Act*, requires employers to provide the same benefit entitlements to employees on pregnancy leave or parental leave as are provided to employees who are on other types of leave. This means that an employer may exclude coverage under a company's short- or long-term disability plan for a female employee who is on maternity or parental leave, provided coverage is not extended to other employees who are on other types of leaves. If the employer normally extends coverage to employees on other leaves of absence, then women on maternity or parental leave must also be given coverage. Women on maternity leave continue to be entitled to other benefits under employment-related benefit plans, including pension plans, life insurance plans, accidental death plans, extended health plans, and dental plans. Employers are also required to continue to make contributions to such plans.

Non-Discrimination in Benefits — Ontario

The general rule in Ontario is stated in Section 44(1) of the *Employment Standards Act*:

> Except as prescribed, no employer or person acting directly on behalf of an employer shall provide, offer or arrange for a benefit plan that treats any of the following persons differently because of the age, sex or marital status of employees.
>
> 1. Employees.
> 2. Beneficiaries.
> 3. Survivors.
> 4. Dependants.

On the basis of this section — as well as Section 25(2) of Ontario's *Human Rights Code*, which adds family status to the exempted grounds — Ontario employers are prohibited from discriminating on the basis of age, gender, marital status, or family status in providing benefits to employees, unless permitted by the regulations. While the *Employment Standards Act* refers to "benefit plan" in the broadest of terms, the *Human Rights Code* specifies that the non-discrimination rule applies to "an employee superannuation or pension plan or fund or a contract of group insurance between an insurer and an employer that complies with the *Employment Standards Act* and the regulations thereunder." The combined terminology includes all conventional individual and group insurance plans, pension plans, savings plans, and other fringe benefits.

Ontario Regulation 286/01 to the *Employment Standards Act* outlines the exceptions to the general rule contained in Section 44(1) of the act (Regulation 286/01 is reproduced in the Appendix). For some benefits, Regulation 286/01 differentiates between voluntary employee-pay-all plans and plans paid for in whole or in part by employer contributions. The rules for employee-pay-all plans are generally less restrictive than the employer-paid plan rules.

- **Group life — employee-pay-all plans.** Employee contributions for group life insurance may be lower for females than for males. Regulation 286/01 permits a differentiation in employees' contributions to a voluntary employee-pay-all life insurance plan where the differentiation is made on an actuarial basis because of sex (Section 5(a)).

  It is also permissible either to have higher premiums for older employees or to provide lower benefits for older employees. The regulation permits a differentiation in the benefits under, or the contributions to, a voluntary employee-pay-all life insurance plan where the differentiation is made on an actuarial basis because of age (Section 7(a)).

- **Group life — employer contributory plans.** Regulation 286/01 permits an employer to pay more for male employees where the differentiation is made on an actuarial basis in order to provide equal group life benefits (Section 5(b)).

  A contribution differential is also justified between older and younger employees where it is made on an actuarial basis in order to provide equal benefits (Section 7(b)).

- **Group life — all plans.** Differentiation in benefits on the basis of marital status is allowed where periodic benefits are paid to an employee's surviving spouse for the lifetime of the surviving spouse or until the spouse becomes the spouse of someone else. Benefits of less than $25 per month that have been commuted to a lump sum payment are also included (Sections 6(1)(a) and 6(2)).

  Differentiation in benefits is also allowed where a benefit is payable to an employee upon the death of the employee's spouse (Section 6(1)(b)).

  Differential contributions by an employee or an employer on the basis of marital status are permitted where the life insurance plan provides for periodic benefits to an employee's surviving spouse (Section 6(1)(c)).

  Note that "spouse" in this context includes common-law spouses as defined in the benefit plan itself (definition of "marital status"). While same-sex partnerships are no longer explicitly included in the regulation, there is still implicit protection for same-sex partners by virtue of the *Human Rights Code* and the case law, as discussed earlier.

- **Disability — employee-pay-all plans.** The employee premium for disability coverage can differ by the gender and age of the employee. Regulation 286/01 permits a differentiation in an employee's rate of contributions to a voluntary employee-pay-all short- or long-term disability insurance plan, where the differentiation is made upon an actuarial basis because of the employee's age or sex (Section 8(a)).

In practice, however, few employers reflect age in the employee premiums and very few employers, if any, use gender-distinct premiums.

- **Disability — employer contributory plans.** The rules for disability are similar to those for life insurance: the employer can pay higher premiums for certain categories of employees in order to equalize benefits. The regulation permits a differentiation in an employer's contributions to a short- or long-term disability insurance plan, where the differentiation is made upon an actuarial basis because of the employee's age or sex and in order to provide equal benefits under the plan (Section 8(b)).

- **Supplemental medical and dental — employee-pay-all plans.** Although it is rarely, if ever, done, it is permissible to base employee premium rates on the employee's gender. The regulation permits a differentiation in the rate of employee contributions to a voluntary employee-pay-all health benefit plan, where the differentiation is made upon an actuarial basis because of sex (Section 9(a)).

- **Supplemental medical and dental — employer contributory plans.** Employers can pay more for female employees in order to equalize medical and dental benefit levels. The regulation permits a differentiation in an employer's contributions to a health insurance plan, where the differentiation is made upon an actuarial basis because of the employee's sex and in order to provide equal benefits under the plan (Section 9(b)).

  Employers must pay the same proportional cost for single and family coverage. Section 9(d) permits a differentiation in an employer's contributions to a health insurance plan, where there are specified premium rates and where the differentiation for employees having or not having marital status is on the same proportional basis. This regulation was introduced to ensure that employers did not discriminate against single employees by paying, say, 100 per cent of family premiums and only 50 per cent of the single employee premiums. However, the wording may also prohibit the reverse; paying 100 per cent of single premiums and only 50 per cent of family premiums.

- **Supplemental medical and dental — all plans.** Section 9(c) of Regulation 286/01 also provides for additional dependant health insurance coverage by permitting a differentiation in benefits or employee contributions because of marital status. This differentiation can be made in order to provide benefits for an employee's spouse or dependent child, where the differentiation in benefits or employee contributions based on marital status is made in order to provide benefits for an employee's spouse or dependent child.

APPLICATION OF PROVINCIAL RULES TO FLEXIBLE BENEFIT PLANS

Most of the legislation governing equal treatment in employment and non-discrimination in benefits was created long before the first flexible benefit plan was introduced in Canada.

The legislation and regulations generally provide exemptions on a plan-by-plan basis and do not consider whether a benefit program as a whole is discriminatory. The plan exemptions may differ by factor: for example, marital status is a permitted exemption for an employer supplemental medical contribution but not for an employer long-term disability contribution. How are the exemptions to be applied to a flexible benefit plan, where the employee has control over employer funding and decides how it will be used?

A question also arises because of the distinction between employee-pay-all plans and plans to which the employer contributes. Technically, flexible credits are characterized as an employer contribution; therefore, any benefit purchased with credits is an employer-paid benefit, even though in most other respects the plans resemble employee-paid plans.

Example

Consider an employer who offers a competitive level of supplemental medical insurance as a standard option in a flexible benefit program using a credit-based pricing structure. In this example, employees would receive an employer contribution (flexible credits) equal to the cost of this option. Therefore, an employee with a family might receive $1,500 in credits (the cost of the competitive supplemental medical option for a family), while a single employee might receive, say, $600 in credits (the single employee cost). All employees would, therefore, have sufficient credits to purchase the competitive supplemental medical option. However, an employee could, instead, elect a higher or lower level of supplemental medical coverage or decide to opt out of medical altogether and use the credits to purchase other benefits such as life insurance. Some programs would permit the employee to take the credits in cash. If both the single employee and the married employee in this example buy life insurance or take cash, the married employee would receive more than twice as much as the single employee. Is this a permitted exception to the general non-discrimination rule in Section 44(1) of Ontario's *Employment Standards Act*?

Since the permitted exceptions differ by benefit area, an employer contribution that is permissible in one benefit area could technically violate the rules in another area, if the employee voluntarily elects to spend it in another area. The employer has no way of knowing how each employee intends to spend the credits, and no control over how they are spent, because of the concept of choice inherent in flexible benefits.

For instance, in our example, the single employee received $600 in credits, while the family employee received $1,500. This is permissible under Section 9(d) of Regulation 286/01, if the credits are spent to buy supplemental medical coverage. However, if the two employees elect to spend the employer contribution on disability coverage, the family employee could purchase more than the single employee. This may violate Section 8(b) because the disability benefits are not equal.

Would a flat contribution of, say, $1,100 per employee, regardless of family status, prevent this anomaly? Possibly not, because a younger employee could purchase more life insurance than an older employee, where the group life contribution depends on age. This appears to violate Section 7(b), because the resulting company-paid life insurance benefits are unequal.

Proposed Clarification for Flexible Plans

As the previous example shows, virtually any credit/pricing structure could be technically at odds with the rules, because it could violate at least one section of the regulation. This result is clearly illogical and arguably contrary to public policy. If one takes a narrow interpretation of the rules out of context, one can conclude that it is impossible to design a non-discriminatory flexible benefit plan.

How should this be clarified? The best solution would be for regulators to add a regulation specifically dealing with flexible plans.

To illustrate how such a proposed regulation could work, assume there is a standard set of benefit options that the employer wishes to pay for fully by allocating sufficient credits so each employee can provide for his or her own premium. Under a special flexible benefit regulation, this structure would be permitted, assuming the employer contribution was non-discriminatory, if every employee elected this standard set of benefits. The program would not become discriminatory merely because some employees voluntarily elected to spend the employer credits on a different set of options.

Minimizing the Risk of a Successful Challenge

In the absence of such a regulation, however, what can an employer do to minimize the risk? The first step is to discuss the situation with legal counsel. Although many of the provincial authorities have been adopting narrow interpretations of the legislation, many employers interpret the regulations more liberally. The regulations concerning employer-paid plans use the term "rate of contribution of an employer for a disability (or health or group life) plan." The employer contribution to a disability plan that is part of a flexible program could be interpreted as the number of flexible credits designed to allow the employee to purchase a specified level of disability benefit. If an employee spends the employer disability contribution elsewhere, this does not change the employer disability contribution, nor the fact that it was allocated in a non-discriminatory manner consistent with the regulations.

The report of Ontario's 1975 Task Force, which was used to develop the Ontario regulations, contains wording that would justify the pricing/credit structure described earlier. The report states:

> One approach to employee benefit plans which has attracted a great deal of discussion, but which has not yet been widely accepted, is the "cafeteria approach." Under this approach, an employer would provide each employee with a given benefit plan contribution, which the employee could allocate to the various types of benefits as he or she saw fit. The amount of each type of benefit which a given employee would receive would necessarily be determined on a money purchase basis; i.e., the amount of each benefit would be whatever could be purchased from the portion of the contribution allocated to that benefit by the employee, on the basis of actuarial cost factors corresponding to that employee's age and sex. The main advantage of this cafeteria approach is that each employee can tailor the benefit package to suit his or her own particular circumstances, taking into account such factors as state of health, nearness to retirement, number of dependants, and other financial considerations. However, this approach suffers from the same drawbacks as the employee-pay-all approach, since a contribution level that produces adequate benefits on the average will not necessarily produce adequate benefits for the high-cost employees.

The problem outlined in the last sentence — high-cost employees not having enough credits to buy adequate coverage where the contribution level buys adequate benefits on average — was also identified by employers as a shortcoming of flexible programs. Therefore, instead of calculating an average contribution level for all employees, flexible plans frequently grant more credits to higher-cost employees (families, for example), so that they will have enough to purchase an adequate level of benefits. Therefore, the Task Force encouraged the growth of flexible credit structures that recognize that the cost of providing adequate benefits differs by employee.

Employers may decide to prohibit the purchase of group life benefits with flexible credits, in order to minimize the risk of a discrimination challenge. A major concern of Ontario regulators is that older employees would not have sufficient credits to purchase company-paid life insurance. By making life insurance fully employee-paid, this concern is eliminated.

Summary

Unfortunately, there is no definitive answer to this question, for at least three reasons:

- Some jurisdictions permit some degree of age, gender, and marital discrimination in determining the employer contribution to traditional benefit plans. However, as described, their rules do not cover flexible plans.

- Other jurisdictions prohibit marital discrimination. Therefore, even traditional supplemental medical and dental plans may technically violate human rights legislation in these areas because the employer pays more for family coverage than for single coverage.
- National employers must deal with different jurisdictions, each having a different set of rules.

While this issue appears likely to remain unresolved for some time to come, we are unaware of any successful discrimination challenges to the pricing of flexible benefit options.

§ 13.4 EQUAL PAY FOR EQUAL WORK

Equal pay for equal work is commonly understood to refer to legislation that specifically redresses gender discrimination in pay practices. In actual fact, the more general "equal treatment provisions" described in Section 13.3 effectively disallow pay discrimination on all the listed prohibited grounds. For example, an employer would be prohibited from providing different amounts of pay solely based on an employee's race, marital status, age, and so forth.

Some jurisdictions have enacted specific provisions directed at gender discrimination within the framework of "equal treatment" legislation. For example, Section 42 of Ontario's *Employment Standards Act, 2000* states:

42. (1) No employer shall pay an employee of one sex at a rate of pay less than the rate paid to an employee of the other sex when,

(a) they perform substantially the same kind of work in the same establishment;
(b) their performance requires substantially the same skill, effort and responsibility; and
(c) their work is performed under similar working conditions.

(2) Subsection (1) does not apply when the difference in the rate of pay is made on the basis of,

(a) a seniority system;
(b) a merit system;
(c) a system that measures earnings by quantity or quality of production; or
(d) any other factor other than sex.

(3) No employer shall reduce the rate of pay of an employee in order to comply with subsection (1).
(4) No trade union or other organization shall cause or attempt to cause an employer to contravene subsection (1).

(5) If an employment standards officer finds that an employer has contravened subsection (1), the officer may determine the amount owing to an employee as a result of the contravention and that amount shall be deemed to be unpaid wages for that employee. (S.O. 2000, c. 41)

In other words, if two jobs in an establishment are substantially the same, an employer is not entitled to differentiate pay on the basis of sex. The jobs are to be evaluated on the basis of skill, effort, responsibility, and working conditions in deciding whether they are substantially the same.

Because benefits are considered part of "pay," the concept of equal pay for equal work will have an impact upon the provision of benefits and the design of flexible benefit plans. The value of benefits should be factored in to any equal-pay-for-equal-work analysis. This is, of course, subject to any recognized exemptions in providing benefits in a discriminatory manner.

§ 13.5 PAY EQUITY

Equal pay for equal work deals only with sex discrimination in substantially similar jobs. Pay equity goes one step further, to address discrimination by requiring equal pay for work of equal value, even where the jobs are not substantially similar. While many provinces have pay equity laws for public service employees, Ontario's pay equity legislation is the most extensive, covering all public and most private sector employees in Ontario.

Pay equity legislation is designed to bring the pay of women in traditionally undervalued female-dominated job classes to the same level as men in comparable male-dominated job classes. Comparable jobs can vary widely. When the jobs are compared, so too are the compensation levels of each job. For purposes of pay equity legislation, compensation includes benefits.

Employers should be aware of pay equity legislation when developing or evaluating their flexible benefit plans. Although it is unlikely that a flexible benefit plan on its own would violate pay equity legislation, the value of all benefits for which a value can be ascertained will be included in the compensation of employees when comparing jobs for pay equity purposes.

§ 13.6 EMPLOYMENT EQUITY

Employment equity legislation seeks to improve the workplace representation of four designated groups: women, visible minorities, aboriginal persons, and persons with disabilities. Employment equity programs require that employers remove barriers and adopt positive practices in order to achieve increased representation of the designated groups within their workplace.

Several jurisdictions have, or have had at times, programs that apply to their own public service. In addition, the federal jurisdiction has a law, the *Employment Equity Act*, that applies to any federal-jurisdiction employer that employs 100 or more employees.

Both the federal jurisdiction and Quebec also have contract compliance programs that apply to organizations seeking government contracts. The program requires that all employers with at least 100 employees adhere to employment equity principles voluntarily in order to be eligible to tender for government contracts.

As with pay equity, employers should be aware of employment equity requirements when developing or evaluating their flexible benefit plans. However, it is unlikely that a flexible benefit plan on its own would violate employment equity principles or be identified as a barrier to increased employment of the designated groups.

Part Four

Structure and Financing

Fourteen

Pricing

§ 14.1 INTRODUCTION

If flexible benefits were viewed as a car, the pricing structure would be recognized as the engine. It is the pricing structure that puts the program in motion — or brings it to a standstill. Employees choose from their menu of options by comparing the cost for the benefit choices and then matching the various alternatives to their individual needs. If the pricing is not well thought through, excessive employer costs or too many employees electing the same option could result. These types of results defeat the purpose of a flexible benefit program. Employer costs should be controlled, not unbridled. Employee selections should be those that best meet individual needs. The typical employee workforce has diverse needs and those needs should manifest themselves by employees selecting a wide variety of benefit options.

There are three interrelated components of any pricing structure — price tags for the options, credits or company subsidy available to employees, and the net cost to the employee.

CREDIT-BASED PRICING VERSUS NET PRICING

Pricing structures may be communicated by the explicit use of price tags and credits (credit-based pricing) or through the use of the net employee cost (net pricing).

There are several key advantages to both the credit-based and net pricing approaches:

	Credit-Based Pricing	Net Pricing
Advantages	Communicates the true value of the underlying plan options	Simpler to communicate
	Easier to manage and communicate cost increases going forward	Simpler to administer

In the case of net pricing, the employer should develop the implicit price tags and credits in order to fully understand the nature of the costs and subsidies involved.

STRUCTURE OF THIS CHAPTER

This chapter will focus on the development of price tags and flex credits, making regular reference to how the net pricing approach can be derived from these components. The chapter is organized as follows:

Section 14.2 examines setting objectives for the financial structure of a flexible program and demonstrates how objectives influence the pricing of options and the allocation of credits. Next, Section 14.3 explores the pricing of program options, focusing on pricing health care benefits (generally medical, dental, and vision) and on pricing insured benefits (life insurance and long-term disability). The discussion then moves on to the derivation and allocation of credits under a flexible program in Section 14.4, and the chapter concludes with suggestions of how to test the pricing structure.

See also the chapters in Part Two for a brief discussion of pricing for various benefits, including vacation and retirement.

It should be noted that although the focus of this chapter is on first-year pricing, the same processes and procedures apply for subsequent-year changes to the financial structure of a flexible program. (See Chapter 15, "Financial Analysis," for additional discussion of subsequent-year pricing.)

§ 14.2 SETTING OBJECTIVES

FOUR PRICING OBJECTIVES

After an organization has developed the basic design of a flexible benefit program, the next step is to price the options and decide on the sources, amount, and allocation of credits or employer subsidy. Neither of these steps can be accomplished, however, without examining employer objectives for the financial structure of a flexible program. Experience shows that employers frequently have four goals or objectives they want to accomplish through the pricing structure. These objectives may be summarized as follows:

Objective 1 — Realistic Pricing

Option price tags should be set realistically to reflect the value of the coverage. That is, the price tags for the benefit options should closely represent the value of each option. Using realistic price tags will enhance employee understanding and appreciation of program costs and allow benefit choices to be made freely without the influence of incentives or disincentives.

It is important to note that "realistic" price tags reflect the expected claims of the whole group and are set independently, as if only one option were being offered. Realistic price tags do not reflect the full impact of adverse selection and therefore will not match the pattern of claims expected for each option when several options are offered. Thus, even under the realistic pricing objective, there will be some inherent cross-subsidies between options, as illustrated in Table 14.1.

To illustrate the calculations used to develop Table 14.1, consider Option 2, which has a relative value of 50 per cent of Option 3. In other words, in the absence of adverse selection, an employee in Option 2 would be expected to receive 50 per cent of the claims reimbursement paid to an employee in Option 3. Since expected claims for employees in Option 3 are $1,000 per year, the Option 2 expected claims equal 50 per cent of $1,000, or $500. Therefore, the realistic price tag for Option 2 is set at $500. Because lower-claiming employees will have a tendency to elect Option 2, the expected claims for this option are actually only $300, not $500.

Relative values are usually calculated using insurance underwriting methodology. A value is determined for the base plan according to the characteristics — such as deductibles, out-of-pocket maximums, co-insurance percentages, and cost management features — of the plan. Values are then calculated for the options and a relative value is determined by dividing the option value by the base plan value. Relative values usually are most readily calculated by the employer's insurer or consultant.

Table 14.1
Derivation of Realistic Price Tags

	Relative Value	Claims Before Adverse Selection	Expected Claims Reflecting Anticipated Selection	"Realistic" Price Tags
Option 1	0%	$ 0	$ 0	$ 0
Option 2	50%	$ 500	$ 300	$ 500
Option 3	100%	$1,000	$ 900	$1,000
Option 4	150%	$1,500	$2,000	$1,500

Objective 2 — Equity

Each employee should receive an equal dollar amount or percentage of pay in flexible credits or in implicit employer subsidies. If benefit dollars are to be considered another form of compensation, allocating credits based on age, number of dependants, and so forth, represents an inappropriate allocation of employer dollars — akin to awarding pay increases on factors other than merit.

Objective 3 — No Losers

To prevent negative employee perceptions of a new program, each employee should be able to repurchase prior coverage (or, if unavailable, the most comparable coverage) with no increase in costs.

Objective 4 — No Additional Company Cost

Although cost objectives in implementing flexible benefit plans will differ, the most common financial objective is that there should be no additional employer cost. Cost neutrality in this perspective typically means that the new plan will cost the same as the old plan would have in the next plan year. This is an important clarification for employers in framing their objectives. For example:

- Current plan cost in 2007 = $1,000,000.
- Projected cost of current plan in 2008 = $1,100,000 (10 per cent inflation).
- Projected cost of new flex plan in 2008 = $1,100,000 (cost neutral).
- If the employer actually wishes to freeze the current cost at $1,000,000 in 2008, this will require a 9 per cent cutback in the design or company funding of the new plan.

This cost-neutral objective usually relates only to the program design components of the plan. Additional company resources are often allocated to the implementation, communication, and administration of the plan.

PRICING APPROACHES

As desirable as each of these four pricing objectives might be, it is generally impossible to achieve all four simultaneously under a flexible program. The primary reason is that most organizations currently do not allocate employer dollars for benefits equally to all employees, which makes it difficult to attain Objective 2 without violating one of the other three objectives.

One example is found in life insurance, where all employees may be charged a flat rate per $1,000 of insurance regardless of age, resulting in a subsidy of older employees by younger employees.

Example 14.1
Current Supplemental Medical Plan Claim Costs (per Employee)

	Employee Coverage Status	
	Single	Family
Annual supplemental medical claims cost	$700	$1,400
Employee contributions (10% of total)	(70)	(140)
Employer cost	$630	$1,260
Per cent of employees in status group	50%	50%
Average cost	$945	

Another example is supplemental medical and dental coverage, where employees with dependents may not pay the full cost of the dependant coverage, resulting in a larger employer subsidy for employees with families than for single employees. Consider the pressures created for a flexible program structure when medical benefits for dependants are heavily subsidized. In a typical situation, a plan might have medical claims costs that average $700 for single coverage and $1,400 for an employee covering dependants. As illustrated in Example 14.1 above, the employer might require a 10 per cent contribution from all employees, producing an employer cost of $630 for single coverage and $1,260 for family coverage, even though the average cost for the covered group is $945.

The employer wants to implement a flexible program offering options in supplemental medical. One option will be the current plan (Option A) and the two new options will be lesser-valued plans — Option B, which is valued at 80 per cent of the current plan, and Option C, which carries 60 per cent of the current plan's value. Expected claims cost under each of the options, ignoring the effects of adverse selection, is shown in Table 14.2.

The issue for the employer is how to structure the pricing of the options in a manner that achieves all four of the objectives cited earlier.

There are many different approaches or alternatives to choose from for the pricing structure, including:

1. Flat-credit structures

2. Buy-back structures

3. Election-based structures.

Table 14.2
Expected Supplemental Medical Claims under Flexible Program Options (per Employee)

	Single	Family
Option A (current plan)	$700	$1,400
Option B (valued at 80% of Option A)	560	1,120
Option C (valued at 60% of Option A)	420	840

But as is explained next, each approach will achieve only three of the four employer objectives — none will achieve all four objectives.

FLAT CREDITS

The first approach is a flat credit allocation (see Tables 14.3 to 14.5). This approach involves allocating an equal amount of credits to all employees. (In what follows, the credits referred to are either actual credits for credit-based pricing structures or implicit credits (i.e., company subsidy) in net pricing structures.)

Since all employees receive equal credits, Objective 2 (equity) is always achieved in a flat-credit structure. The amount of credit will determine which of the other three pricing objectives are not met. In order to illustrate this, three variations on the flat credit structure are discussed below. They are:

- Family credits. Each employee receives credits or subsidies equal to the current company cost for family coverage (i.e., $1,260 in Example 14.1)
- Average credits. Each employee receives credits or subsidies equal to the current average company cost for all members (i.e., $945 in Example 14.1)
- Single credits. Each employee receives credits or subsidies equal to the current company cost for single coverage (i.e., $630 in Example 14.1)

Family Credits

In this approach, the flat credit is set to the highest amount necessary to ensure that Objective 3 (no losers) is met. In other words, all employees receive a subsidy or credit equal to the current company cost for a family ($1,260) (see Table 14.3).

The employee covering a family under this approach must pay $140 for Option A — which is no change from the current plan. However, the single coverage employee experiences a windfall of $630 at the expense of the employer (receives

Table 14.3
The Family Credit Approach

		Credit-Based Pricing		Net Pricing
		Price Tag	Credit	Employee Cost
Option A	Single	$ 700	$1,260	$(560)
(current plan)	Family	1,400	1,260	140
Option B	Single	560	1,260	(700)
	Family	1,120	1,260	(140)
Option C	Single	420	1,260	(840)
	Family	840	1,260	(420)
Average employer cost per employee			$1,260	

net cash or credit of $560 compared to a $70 contribution under the prior plan), raising average company cost from $945 to $1,260 per employee. Therefore, Objective 4 is not achieved.

Objectives achieved:

Objective 1 — Realistic Prices	Objective 2 — Equity	Objective 3 — No Losers	Objective 4 — No Additional Company Cost
Yes	Yes	Yes	No

Because of the additional company cost, this approach is rarely, if ever, used to determine the employer subsidy.

Average Credits

The second approach calculates average cost of the current plan per covered employee ($945) and allocates that amount to each employee (see Table 14.4).

Again, prices are based on expected claims and the credit allocation is equal for all employees. By definition, this approach produces no additional employer cost — the credits equal the average cost of the prior plan. However, the approach produces both winners and losers. That is, there are employees who are better off (singles) and employees who are worse off (families), relative to the coverage they had under the prior plan. For instance, the employee covering a family under Option A will now pay $455, versus $140 under the prior plan. Objective 3 is, therefore, not reached.

Table 14.4
The Average Credit Approach

		Credit-Based Pricing		Net Pricing
		Price Tag	Credit	Employee Cost
Option A	Single	$ 700	$945	$(245)
(current plan)	Family	1,400	945	455
Option B	Single	560	945	(385)
	Family	1,120	945	175
Option C	Single	420	945	(525)
	Family	840	945	(105)
Average employer cost per employee			$945	

Objectives achieved:

Objective 1 — Realistic Prices	Objective 2 — Equity	Objective 3 — No Losers	Objective 4 — No Additional Company Cost
Yes	Yes	No	Yes

Single Coverage Credits

The third alternative is the single coverage credit approach (see Table 14.5). Credits are allocated to all employees at a level equal to the company cost of the employee-only coverage ($630).

Table 14.5
The Single Credit Approach

		Credit-Based Pricing		Net Pricing
		Price Tag	Credit	Employee Cost
Option A	Single	$700	$630	$ 70
(current plan)	Family	770	630	140
Option B	Single	$560	$630	$ (70)
	Family	490	630	(140)
Option C	Single	$420	$630	$(210)
	Family	210	630	(420)
Average employer cost per employee			$945	

In order to meet the objective of no losers, prices for family coverage in all options were reduced by $630. This was done in order to reduce the Option A price tag from $1,400 to $770, so the net cost to employees remains $140.

The average company cost for all employees remains at $945 — $630 in credits for everyone plus a $630 implicit subsidy of the price for the 50 per cent of employees with families. The result, of course, is in contradiction to Objective 1. Prices for family coverage now are unrealistically low. Also, the relationship between family status levels is inaccurate. Thus, it is more difficult for employees to make reasonable decisions when prices do not reflect true cost or value.

Objectives achieved:

Objective 1 — Realistic Prices	Objective 2 — Equity	Objective 3 — No Losers	Objective 4 — No Additional Company Cost
No	Yes	Yes	Yes

Net Pricing and Flat Credit Approaches

Flat credit approaches are unlikely to be communicated on a net pricing basis.

Generally, net pricing approaches are applied to pricing scenarios that can be easily described to employees using only the right-hand column in the tables. As can be seen from Tables 14.3 and 14.4, showing only the right-hand column would make it very difficult to communicate the pricing rationale to employees.

Table 14.5 could actually be described in terms of a net pricing approach, where both the incremental cost and the net credit are set at double the family amount for singles. While this approach could be used to describe a net pricing approach, the fact that families receive more net credits than singles electing Option B and C means that the company would probably not use this approach to actually communicate this variation on net pricing.

If the net credits may be taken as cash or the equivalent, the net pricing structure could possibly violate human rights legislation by discriminating based on family status.

BUY-BACK PRICING

A second approach is referred to as the buy-back approach (see Table 14.6). This method allocates credits based on the average cost of each employee to the employer prior to the flexible benefit program. The allocation takes into account the differing cost of employees based on whether or not they cover dependants.

There are no winners and losers because employees can choose Option A and receive the same coverage at the same cost as under the prior plan. However, some

Table 14.6
The Buy-Back Approach

		Credit-Based Pricing		Net Pricing
		Price Tag	Credit	Employee Cost
Option A	Single	$ 700	$ 630	$ 70
(current plan)	Family	1,400	1,260	140
Option B	Single	$ 560	$ 630	$ (70)
	Family	1,120	1,260	(140)
Option C	Single	$ 420	$ 630	$ (210)
	Family	840	1,260	(420)
Average employer cost per employee			$ 945	

employees — that is, those not covering dependants — may feel it is inappropriate that those covering dependants receive an additional $630 in benefit value from the employer. Benefit value equity (Objective 2) is not achieved.

This inequity is especially apparent in Option B and Option C, where employees with dependents actually receive more money to elect lower coverage than do single employees. Even though the price tag in these options is higher for families than for singles, the excess credits to families are also higher.

Objectives achieved:

Objective 1 — Realistic Prices	Objective 2 — Equity	Objective 3 — No Losers	Objective 4 — No Additional Company Cost
Yes	No	Yes	Yes

Net Pricing and the Buy-Back Approach

The buy-back approach can be used in a net pricing scenario, in that the net employee cost column can be communicated logically to employees without the need to describe the underlying price tags and credits.

The rationale communicated to employees around this approach is as follows:

- The company provides funding at a level between the cost of Option A and Option B.
- When employees elect Option A, the additional cost they pay is determined based on their family status, with families paying twice as much as single employees.
- Similarly, when employees elect Option B or Option C, the excess company funding is allocated in the same proportion, with families receiving twice as much funding as singles.

Caution

If employees can take the excess credits or net savings in cash or the equivalent, this approach may violate human rights legislation concerning discrimination based on family status.

ELECTION-BASED PRICING

A variation on the buy-back approach moves one step closer to achieving all four of our objectives (see Table 14.7). This approach uses the same price tags and

Table 14.7
The Election-Based Approach

		Credit-Based Pricing		Net Pricing
		Price Tag	Credit	Employee Cost
Option A	Single	$ 700	$ 630	$ 70
(current plan)	Family	1,400	1,260	140
Option B	Single	$ 560	$ 630	$ (70)
	Family	1,120	1,190	(70)
Option C	Single	$ 420	$ 630	$ (210)
	Family	840	1,050	(210)
Average employer cost per employee			less than $945	

credits as the buy-back structure for Option A. However, for Options B and C, the approach gives families fewer credits than they receive in Option A. The "election-based" credits for families are determined so that all employees who elect Option B and all who elect Option C have the same net cost, regardless of their family status.

The pricing in Table 14.7 was determined as follows:

- **Step 1:** The single price tags/credits/employee cost for Options A, B, and C were determined as shown in Table 14.6.
- **Step 2:** The family price tags/credits/employee cost for Option A were also determined as in Table 14.6.
- **Step 3:** The family price tags for Options B and C were set equal to those in Table 14.6.
- **Step 4:** The family net cost for Options B and C was set equal to the net cost for single coverage as determined in Step 1 (i.e., $(70) for Option B; $(210) for Option C).
- **Step 5:** The family credit for Options B and C was calculated to produce the net cost as determined in Step 4.

By giving fewer credits to families who opt down, the employer is effectively treating family and single employees equally from a cash basis. Every employee who receives net credits from the employer (i.e., has a net cost less than $0) will be treated the same (compensation equity). Complete equity (Objective 2) is still not achieved, but much of the inequity has been eliminated.

Objectives achieved:

Objective 1 — Realistic Prices	Objective 2 — Equity	Objective 3 — No Losers	Objective 4 — No Additional Company Cost
Yes	Equity in net employee cost in some options	Yes	Yes

Because this approach comes closest to meeting all four objectives, it is frequently used for both credit-based and net pricing plans. However, since the family credit is dependent on the actual employee election, it is the most complex approach to administer and communicate for credit-based plans.

Net Pricing and the Election-Based Approach

This structure is relatively easy to communicate to employees under a net pricing approach. The rationale can be communicated as follows:

- The company provides funding at a level between the costs of Option A and Option B.
- When employees elect Option A, the additional cost they pay is determined based on their family status, with families paying twice as much as single employees.
- When employees elect Option B or Option C, they are given a flat amount of additional company funding — the amount is independent of their family status.

ADOPTING A STRATEGY

The pricing structure for a flexible program creates the potential for a dilemma, although it is one that can be remedied by setting priorities. Addressing key issues, such as those that follow, can help an organization establish a strategy for the structure of a flexible benefit program.

- What broad organizational goals should be reflected in the pricing structure?

    Addressing the question of organizational pricing goals will bring to the surface attitudes toward equity (Objective 2) and its appropriateness within an organization's culture.

    Does the company view benefits primarily as protection for employees and their families? If so, this may indicate that differing credits may be appropriate for employees with greater need for protection (i.e., buy-back approach).

Or are benefits viewed as another element of compensation? This may argue against differentiation by family status or age (i.e., flat credits).

- What are the objectives for the flexible benefit program?

    If future cost management is a goal, the employer may insist on experienced-based prices (Objective 1) where the cost is effectively severed from the form of benefits. The use of realistic prices effectively forces the employer's cost to be equal to the credits allocated to employees. Thus the employer cost is more easily identified and managed.

    If immediate cost containment is a goal, no additional cost (Objective 4) at the program's genesis would also likely be a requirement. If immediate cost reduction is a goal, some employees will be losers (Objective 3), either through reduced coverage or increased employee contributions.

    The employer may also want to enhance the employee's appreciation of benefit value, which would incline the organization toward a realistic pricing structure (Objective 1) to clearly communicate plan value.

    The preceding discussion focuses on only a few of the possible program objectives and their implications for pricing. The point is that these objectives should be considered when adopting a strategy for the structure of a flexible program.

- What are employee expectations of the new plan?

    The success of a flexible benefit program will vary, depending on employee reaction to the organization's pricing strategy. For example, the idea of benefit losers (Objective 3) may or may not be acceptable, depending upon the organization's financial situation and the benefit programs of competitors. On the other hand, benefit value equity (Objective 2) may not be an issue. The current employee mood should be taken into account when the organization develops its price/credit strategy.

After considering questions such as these and setting priorities, an organization's strategy will begin to form. The strategy may include all of the basic approaches discussed earlier, a combination of several, or some variation, as will be discussed later in this chapter. What the objective-setting process will certainly do, though, is crystallize a pricing strategy that is consistent with the organization's desires and set the stage for making decisions on pricing.

§ 14.3 PRICING PLAN OPTIONS

When pricing the options in a flexible program, it is helpful to separate benefits into two categories: health care benefits and insured benefits. Health care benefits have high claim frequency and the per claim amount is relatively low. Benefits in this category include supplemental medical, prescription drugs, dental, and vision. Because of the nature of these plans, the insurance risk is often held by the company, involving the insurer on an administrative services only (ASO) basis. In the case of an ASO underwriting arrangement, the company has far greater latitude in setting the pricing of the flexible benefits plan.

Insured benefits are those where claim frequency is low and per claim amount is high. Benefits in this category include life insurance, long-term disability, and AD&D. Most employees will never incur a claim for these benefits, but if they do, the claim is large. Claim costs can fluctuate dramatically from year to year. Costs are not evaluated in terms of annual claims, but in terms of premiums set by an insurance carrier. These premiums are based on a combination of the probabilities of claims and the expected annual costs, based largely on actuarial data and the experience of the company. Since these plans generally have premium rates that are set by an insurance carrier, the nature of the pricing structure is more rigid and leaves the company less ability to set its own pricing.

Many of the basic components of pricing health care and insured benefits are the same. The following discussion covers the pricing of flexible benefits in general, with specific reference to health care or insured benefits where the approach differs. For the purpose of illustration, the section will focus on supplemental medical benefits as an example of health care benefits, and long-term disability (LTD) as an example of insured benefits.

PRICING STEPS

The pricing of benefit options can vary dramatically, depending on the organization's objectives for pricing and the program in general. No matter what the objectives are and what pricing scheme is desired, actual or realistic prices for the benefit options should be determined first. Basically, the pricing process can be divided into eight steps:

1. Data collection and analysis;
2. Preliminary option pricing;
3. Preliminary subgroup pricing;
4. Anticipation of changes;
5. Taxes and administration fees;
6. Adjustments to realistic price tags;
7. No coverage option pricing; and
8. Pricing by business unit or location.

The first five steps are used to determine the realistic prices.

In the case of insured benefits, these steps are often performed by the insurance carrier that will be insuring the benefits. Since the insurance carrier is the ultimate determiner of the underlying option cost, it will determine the underlying premium rates (i.e., realistic price tags).

In contrast, for health care benefits, while the insurer may recommend budget rates based on its analysis, companies are generally free to set their deposit rates as they deem appropriate. Therefore, the company will need to be able to go through steps 1 through 4 in order to derive the underlying realistic pricing.

Step 1 — Data Collection and Analysis

The first step in pricing involves collecting data on the current plan over the past few years. This includes claims data for the covered group, administration fees, premium costs for an insured plan, and participation data by dependant coverage category. The number of years of data needed for credible analysis depends largely on the size of the covered group, as well as the benefit area being priced.

The collection of data serves two purposes. One is that the data will serve as the basis for pricing all of the options in a benefit category. The other is that the data should provide some indication of past cost trends and which factors to use to anticipate cost increases for the coming year.

During this process, the organization should review the data already available and determine what additional data should be collected in the future. Data requirements to properly track a flexible benefit plan are more detailed than for a traditional benefits plan and will need to be planned for in advance. The employer will want to set up data-tracking mechanisms now, as data will be crucial to future-year pricing, to determining the program's financial position, and to managing the program's costs.

Organizations should recognize that the reflection of a plan's claims experience in prices for future years might very well lag by one year. New prices will often need to be developed three to five months prior to the beginning of the next plan year. Data will be available for only six to eight months of the current year when the pricing analysis for the next year needs to be performed. Employers will be forced either to allow the reflection of experience in pricing to lag by a year or to attempt to project the experience based on partial-year data.

Collecting data for retiree benefits presents additional difficulties. Because the coverage provided by provincial health plans is different before and after age 65, companies should attempt to track experience data separately for these two groups. Employers may also wish to track experience by province, due to the differences in provincial PharmaCare programs. Because of the small size of some retiree groups, many employers estimate retiree claims based on the experience of their active employees. This projection involves "aging" the active experience and adjusting for differences in provincial plan design, mix of pre- and post-65 retirees, and the different family mix for retirees (e.g., fewer dependants).

Step 2 — Preliminary Option Pricing

After claims data has been gathered and a per-covered-employee cost determined, the next step is option pricing. Option pricing consists of determining a fair price

Table 14.8
Preliminary Option Pricing Example — Medical

Option	Relative Value	Base Plan Claims per Employee	Preliminary Price
A (current plan)	100%	$1,400	$1,400
B	80%	1,400	1,120
C	60%	1,400	840

for each benefit option, based on covered employee claims experience in the current plan.

Option pricing requires that a relative value for each option be determined, usually based on the current plan. Relative values represent the expected claims patterns of the options, ignoring the effect of adverse selection. The value of one plan (typically the current or pre-flex plan) is set at 100 per cent and the value of the other plans are set relative to this plan.

Using these relative values and current claims data, preliminary option prices can be calculated. For example, if the employer calculates that the current plan (Option A) is worth $1,400 per employee and two new options, B and C, are worth 80 per cent and 60 per cent of the current plan respectively, the preliminary prices would be set as shown in Table 14.8.

So far, the prices are preliminary, because they are based on claims data that is one or possibly two years old and adjustments have not yet been made for plan changes, adverse selection, or different employee utilization patterns. A later step will involve adjusting the preliminary prices for these and other factors.

Step 3 — Preliminary Subgroup Pricing

Subgroup pricing is a method of dividing the pricing structure into smaller groups with similar characteristics. Subgroup pricing helps minimize adverse selection by creating more equitable prices for different groups of employees.

For benefits such as medical and dental coverage, the most common category is dependant coverage. The range of alternative dependant categories includes:

- Employee-only, family;
- Employee-only, employee-plus-one, employee-plus-two-or-more-dependants;
- Employee-only, employee-plus-spouse, employee-plus-children, family; and
- Employee-only, employee-plus-one, employee-plus-two, employee-plus-three dependants, family, and so forth.

Some insured benefits, such as life insurance or LTD, may have more subgroup categories than health care benefits. Possible categories include age, gender, and smoker status, as these risks are significantly age- and gender-related. In addition, the life insurance risk also depends on whether or not the insured person is a smoker.

Because of the close relationship between age and need in benefits such as life insurance, age-graded rates tend to be considered equitable. Rates graded by age, gender, and smoker status also decrease the potential for adverse selection by being more competitive with market rates for life insurance. For example, if a flat rate per $1,000 of coverage were charged for life insurance, younger employees, females, and non-smokers could probably buy it cheaper on the open market. Older employees, especially males and smokers, however, would recognize the low price and purchase the coverage. The true cost of the benefit would then be much more than the flat rate being charged. Age-graded rates help eliminate this potential problem.

In order to use age-graded rates and yet allow employees to buy back their previous coverage, many employers use a combination of flat rates and age-graded rates. A typical plan might use flat rates to determine the price tags up to the employer-paid coverage provided by the previous plan (e.g., two times salary). Then, for coverage levels above two times salary, age-graded rates would be used. Since employer credits would be provided for two times salary, there are no losers under the plan and age-graded rates would be used at least for a portion of the plan. For life insurance, many pricing structures also reflect gender and smoker status.

Although the true cost of both medical and LTD coverage is also highly age- and gender-related, the majority of companies do not vary medical or LTD prices by these categories at this time.

The more pricing subgroups an organization introduces, the more "equitable" the pricing structure becomes as prices better reflect the specific employee group costs. However, using multiple subgroups complicates employee communication and administration.

Step 4 — Anticipation of Changes

After the preliminary prices have been derived, some adjustments will be required. The preliminary prices are based on claims data a year or two old. Annual claim costs, especially supplemental medical claims, cannot be expected to remain static. There are many reasons why claims experience will likely change:

- **Medical/dental inflation.** General increases in the cost of health care services are to be expected. In recent years, annual cost increases for medical and prescription drug claims have been between 8 and 15 per cent for many Canadian employers — versus less than 3 per cent for general inflation. Similarly, dental costs have been increasing between 5 and 7 per cent per annum recently, even though provincial dental fee guides have been increasing 4 per cent or less over the past few years. Costs are rising faster due to increasing utilization of services.

- **Technological improvements.** The cost of medical care may increase at a faster rate than medical inflation alone, because of the expense of new technology to improve diagnosis and treatment.

- **Plan changes.** Claims data from earlier periods require adjusting for any recent plan changes that affect benefit levels.

- **Adverse selection.** In a flexible benefit program, employees are given a financial incentive to choose the plan that best fits their needs. However, if the probability of their needs is too predictable, adverse selection will result. In order to minimize or eliminate the cost of adverse selection, adjustments to the preliminary pricing may be required. (See also Chapter 16, "Adverse Selection.")

- **Shift in government benefits.** Cost shifting from the provincial health insurance plans to the private sector has become a reality for employers today. Many provinces have ceased to cover services such as routine eye exams and paramedical practitioners such as chiropractors and physiotherapists. The expectation is that this cost shifting will continue, further increasing the cost of private medical plans.

- **Smarter consumers.** While this is not usually factored into the pricing in the first year, there is mounting experience that price increases under flexible benefit programs are lower than under traditional benefit plans. A large part of this decrease has been attributed to employees becoming "smarter consumers of services" (e.g., individuals deciding they don't need to visit the dentist every six months for proper dental care). In communicating a flexible benefit program, many employees learn for the first time how much their benefit programs cost. With this knowledge, many employees see how their spending directly affects the cost of the plan. As a result, first-year price tags are often overstated by some amount. Since this overstatement is difficult to identify in advance, it is not generally anticipated in the first-year pricing.

If plan design changes were made, the cost impact can be reasonably estimated through the relative-value pricing methodology. As for utilization changes and adverse selection, their expected impact is difficult to estimate until subsequent years, when the actual results of the program can be measured.

Changes in utilization after introducing a flexible program may produce reductions in cost (because employees are often moving to medical plans with greater cost sharing through deductibles and co-insurance levels) and the exact amount of this change will depend on many aspects of plan pricing, communication, and corporate culture. Estimating expected adverse selection is also very speculative, and reflecting an inaccurate estimate in the pricing could actually exacerbate the adverse selection problem.

Since utilization and adverse selection estimates can have a significant impact on a flexible benefit program over time, an attempt should be made to estimate these factors in advance. However, poor estimates can lead to inappropriate decisions with regard to a flexible benefit program due to a misunderstanding of the costs involved. In order to better facilitate these decisions, some experts have developed databases to estimate the impact of utilization and adverse selection.

Unlike health care benefit prices, which are adjusted for a variety of anticipated changes, insured benefits are susceptible to only one primary influence — adverse selection. However, pricing for adverse selection in insured benefits is extremely difficult. Adverse selection is better addressed by age-grading prices, limiting maximum benefits, limiting benefit increases from year to year, or including underwriting restrictions. Typically, prices are not adjusted for anticipated changes.

Step 5 — Taxes and Administration Fees

In addition to the claims costs, the total cost to the plan will also include insurance carrier administrative costs, premium taxes, and, in some provinces, provincial sales taxes. Employers implementing a flexible benefit program will need to decide whether or not to reflect these additional plan costs in the employee pricing. There are two schools of thought on this issue.

The first viewpoint maintains that if the employer's objective is to communicate the true value of the plan with realistic pricing (Objective 1), then taxes and administrative fees should be included.

The second argument is that if employee price tags are increased for these items and employee credits are also increased, then employees who elect lower-valued options will receive credits reflecting taxes and administrative expenses that will not be incurred. Some employers view this as giving employees more than they deserve to opt down, in which case either the credits would need to be adjusted or the price tags would be set to exclude taxes and administration fees. Others view this as the proper way to recognize that the employee is reducing the plan's cost. They also feel including these amounts increases the incentive for electing lower options.

Step 6 — Adjustments to Realistic Price Tags

The preceding steps describe how realistic prices are developed. Approaches that involve adjusting these prices using implicit subsidies are discussed in this section.

- **Subsidized pricing.** Subsidized pricing represents an indirect form of credit allocation. Realistic price tags are determined using the single risk pool approach. Price tags that differ substantially from realistic prices are another form of employer funding being allocated to employees on a subsidized basis.

The subsidies can take the form of across-the-board percentage subsidies (for example, prices are 80 per cent of realistic prices); constant flat-dollar subsidies (for example, the price for covering dependants is $100 less than the actual cost); or simple price reductions. Whether subsidized prices reflect an added company cost will depend upon the interrelationship between prices and credits.

There are several reasons why an employer may opt for price subsidies. The employer may want to encourage the selection of a particular option because of cost savings expected from that option. In other words, the employer may want to provide an incentive for employees to choose one option over another. Conversely, the employer may want to limit the potential for adverse selection in an option by encouraging more employees to select it (e.g., dental coverage).

Many employers try to avoid extensive price subsidies. One reason is that subsidies tend to skew employee selection decisions by masking the value of the benefit options. Subsidies also can restrict the ability of a flexible program to serve as a cost-management tool, because some of the costs are hidden and thus more difficult to control. In addition, it can be difficult to re-price consistently in future years, if prices are artificially derived from the start.

When pricing subsidies are used, determining the employer cost of a flexible benefit program also becomes more difficult. For each option, the employer cost is determined as follows:

Employer cost = expected claims + expenses + credits − price tags
(for plans using credit-based pricing); or

Employer cost = expected claims + expenses − prices
(for plans using net pricing)

- **Carve-out pricing.** The extreme example of subsidized pricing is carve-out pricing. This scheme is essentially a different way to communicate realistic prices. For instance, if the program is designed with a core or required minimum option, the employer may prefer to have employees see a price of $0 for this option. In addition, the employer may want to use this structure to minimize the visible difference in credits (or prices) by coverage category (family versus single). For example, assume the realistic prices for supplemental medical options in a flexible benefit program are as follows:

	Price	
Option	Single	Family
A (enhanced)	$700	$1,400
B (current)	560	1,120
C (core)	420	840

If the employer believes a core option should be priced at $0, the carve-out pricing scheme subtracts the price of Option C from Options A and B to produce the following prices:

Option	Price	
	Single	Family
A (enhanced)	$280	$560
B (current)	140	280
C (core)	0	0

The single carve-out prices include an implicit subsidy of $420 per employee (the cost of the core plan), while the family prices include an $840 subsidy.

All forms of subsidized pricing have their drawbacks. The employee will not have as full an appreciation of the total cost of the different options, and it is often difficult to explain to employees what the prices represent. Future price increases may also be more difficult to explain, because they will be larger relative to the price shown.

For LTD, when all options must be purchased with flex credits, pricing subsidies can be applied, with similar issues and drawbacks as discussed above in the case of medical pricing. However, if some LTD options are employee-paid (and therefore the benefits received are non-taxable), subsidized or carve-out pricing is not feasible, as this would jeopardize the non-taxable status of the plan benefit.

Step 7 — No-Coverage Option Pricing

The issue of whether to allow employees to waive coverage entirely in health care benefits is sometimes an area for considerable debate within an organization. One area of concern is philosophical. What is the employer's responsibility to ensure that employees are protected? Does it go beyond the protection provided by provincial medicare plans? Another concern is adverse selection — the fear that only the healthiest (lowest-cost) employees will choose no coverage and, therefore, receive significantly more in credits than the program would have paid in claims. This result would increase total employer costs. As discussed in Chapter 16, adverse selection concerns can usually be managed through design and pricing decisions. Employees who choose no coverage often have coverage available under another plan (for example, that of the spouse's employer) and there is no evidence that these employees are healthier than other covered employees.

In theory, the issue is a straightforward cost question. Knowing what the average employer-paid cost would have been for these no-coverage employees (assuming they had remained in the plan) would indicate what the opt-out credits should be. In this context, the cost would be the actual claims paid plus any administrative expenses and taxes associated with those claims.

Another issue relates to the generosity of the rebate for opting out of coverage. The claims cost of these employees is no longer left to chance occurrence during the year; it is fixed by the opt-out credits given to these employees. Moreover, the dollars are hard dollars, not the soft-dollar exchange of prices and credits evident for employees who remain in the plan. Employers take many different approaches, but because of the lack of margin for error, the opt-out credits are often conservatively estimated at less than the expected value.

Step 8 — Pricing by Business Unit or Location

The preceding steps are generally applied as a whole to the population eligible for the flexible program. However, there may be instances when an employer wants to price different business units or locations separately:

- The company has locations in both high-cost and low-cost provinces and wants to reflect these differences.
- The employer operates in different business markets, each with its own set of competitive practices (e.g., a company may have an engineering division and a distribution division, each with its own set of competitors).
- The organization wants to give local managers greater control over their overhead expenses. In this case the employer may elect to have price tags common to the entire company, but have credits set differently in each location.

Any of the above situations could incline an employer toward business unit or location pricing. However, consideration should be given to some of the special circumstances that arise:

- If the company varies the net employee cost of coverage between business units or locations, there may be issues of internal equity.
- Similarly, differences in net employee cost can hinder the ability to transfer employees internally.
- If the goal is to give local managers more control over benefit costs, then the internal accounting for benefits must be designed so that each location or business unit is only charged for its own experience. In general, the approach taken in pricing the flexible benefit program should be carried through in the benefit accounting system. This will ensure that managers see similar sets of numbers in the flexible benefit program pricing and in their internal charge-backs.
- Business unit pricing is generally advocated by those units who will come out with lower costs, but consideration needs to be given to the impact on other business units where costs may be higher.

- Some business units may not be large enough to be priced on their own because the claims data would not be credible. As a result, companies who use business unit or location pricing often use an internal pooling for large claims and internal credibility weighting when determining budgets for individual units based on recent claims experience.

Many of these obstacles have prevented employers from adopting business unit pricing. However, with more and more companies giving local managers greater responsibility for profits, more managers are likely to be interested in separate pricing structures by location or business unit.

§ 14.4 FLEXIBLE CREDITS

In one sense, credits are simply one half of the pricing equation, since prices and credits can be adjusted to net out to the desired result for each employee. For this reason, price tags and credits are discussed together in the previous section.

In addition to the credits specifically generated from an individual benefit area, there are often additional sources of credits available to employees. Three key elements must be developed to form a credit structure for a flexible benefit program. These include the sources, the amount, and the allocation of credits. When developing credits, the points discussed next apply to the second and later years, as well as the first year of program operation.

SOURCES OF CREDITS

Where does the money come from? Conceptually, the sources of funds for a flexible program originate with either the employer or the employee. Practically, how those funds are derived is somewhat more complicated. The employer usually is not making an arbitrary decision about the flexible credits and their origin. Rather, funds are generated from a combination of identified sources.

Current Benefits

Current benefits that will become part of a new flexible benefit program all have employer costs associated with them, net of any employee contributions. The fact that a benefit is included under the new flexible program can create a credit pool equal to the cost of those current benefits. This cost can be cut back, added to, or held constant, depending on the cost strategy of the organization. In any event, current plan funding represents a major source of credits.

Benefit Reductions

Another potential source of credits is benefit reductions — not necessarily reduction of the benefits included in the flexible program, but reductions in other benefit areas. For example, an organization may conclude that vacation entitlement is too high and that a reduction is in order. Some portion of the future savings may be passed on to employees in the form of credits.

On the other hand, a benefit plan may be eliminated for one reason or another (for example, a minimal vision plan may be dropped), and the resulting cost savings may flow into the credit pool.

Additional Employer Money

A third source is additional employer money. The employer may want to add to the credit pool to provide dollars for a new benefit plan, to make the overall program more attractive, to reward employees for an especially profitable year, and so forth. Of course, this avenue only applies to those employers not wishing to reduce benefit costs.

This additional employer money can be allocated in a number of different ways, including:

- Flat dollar amount per employee (e.g., $200 per employee).
- Flat dollar amounts based on family status (e.g., $100 per single employee and $200 per family). This scenario might be appropriate when a benefit is eliminated in exchange for flex credits calculated to provide additional value to families; for example, the elimination of a vision care program that covered employees and their dependents.
- Percentage of pay (e.g., 1.5 per cent of pay to each employee). In this case, the credit might replace a pay-based benefit program that is being eliminated. For example, if the company moved from a company-paid LTD plan to an employee-paid LTD plan, this type of pay-based credit might be appropriate.

Wellness Credits

As an alternative to simply giving employees an allocation of credits, some companies make employees "earn" their credits through health- or wellness-related initiatives.

Examples of wellness credits include:

- $100 for committing to exercising at least three times a week
- $100 for pledging not to smoke in the coming year

- $50 for having a physical in the previous year
- $25 for participating in the company's online health risk assessment
- $25 for attending an internal wellness seminar.

In general, the amount of funds involved in these kinds of wellness pledges is quite nominal (e.g., $25 to $100 per pledge) but is used to reinforce a wellness message by the company. Employers normally accept the employee's pledge to comply with the particular initiative and do not attempt to monitor compliance.

Renegotiation of Compensation

As discussed in Chapter 12, "Taxation of Flexible Benefits," the Canada Revenue Agency (CRA) has recently ruled that employees can redirect a portion of their bonus into flex credits on a tax-effective basis as long as certain conditions are met.

Variations on this approach include companies who take a holistic total compensation view and may allocate a portion of an employee's annual pay increase into flex credits (e.g., instead of giving an employee a 3 per cent increase in base pay, the employee instead receives a 2 per cent increase in base pay and 1 per cent of pay in additional flex credits). Employers intending to use this approach should ensure that it complies with CRA requirements.

Employee Payroll Deductions

Depending on the benefit levels that employees select, their credit allocation may not be sufficient to cover all benefit needs. To make up the shortfall, employees use payroll deductions to supplement the credit pool. The opportunity for employees to use payroll deductions to supplement credits is common practice. In fact, it is rare in today's environment to have a flexible program that is fully employer-paid. As discussed in Chapter 2 of this book, there are significant differences between credits (employer pre-tax dollars) and deductions (employee after-tax dollars).

AMOUNT OF CREDITS

Defining the sources does not necessarily define the size of the credit pool, although identifying the sources helps set parameters for the amount. For example, one source will be the cost of the current plans, such as supplemental medical. The employer, however, may not want to incur the same cost as at present for medical coverage. As the employer examines each of the benefit plans to be included in the flexible program, the company will want to evaluate current cost levels to see how much should be used to generate credits. Using this component approach, the employer can identify how many dollars from current benefits will be available for credits.

The employer will also be identifying the amount of additional dollars from possible reductions in other benefit areas or simply how much additional benefit cost the organization is willing to support.

After the amount of credits generated from different sources has been identified, the employer needs to view the result in terms of what the credit pool actually represents: the employer cost of the benefit program. Ultimately, equating the total credit pool to benefit costs is the concept that makes flexible benefits an efficient benefit cost-management tool.

Future Flex Credit Amounts

The decision on the amount of available employer credits should be considered for future years as well as the current year, at least in a strategic sense. Conceptually, a strategy should be developed for how the credit pool is intended to increase in future years. The decision may be a totally discretionary decision every year or it may be as structured as the amount necessary to support a specified level of benefits. The strategy may tie credit-pool increases to salary increases, company profitability, or even some outside index. The point is to bring future strategy into focus so that the flexible benefit program has some direction for managing benefit costs.

ALLOCATION OF CREDITS

The third and final task in developing the credit structure is to determine how to allocate credits to employees. There are almost as many variations in credit allocation structures as there are flexible benefit programs. However, these structures generally flow directly from only a few key considerations: the concept of equity in benefit value, the employee's ability to repurchase current (or equivalent) benefits, and organizational objectives.

Equity in Benefit Value

From the outset, if an employer wants to achieve equity in benefit value (Objective 2 from the earlier discussion), price tags for benefit options will be set realistically and credits allocated on a per capita basis. Some organizations have adopted this structure in the first year. However, they have also accepted the consequences of this structure. Employees will be either better or worse off compared to their prior program. Many employers who agree with the concept of benefit value equity cannot accept these consequences, at least not all in one year. Instead, many prefer to phase in the approach over a number of years.

Some organizations also have attempted to achieve apparent benefit value equity by allocating equal credits and changing the price tags to achieve the desired net result. However, a limitation of this approach is that it merely disguises in the price tag subsidy the portion of the credit allocation that is not equal for all employees.

Repurchase of Current Program

Ensuring each employee's ability to repurchase the current program or some other stated level of benefits was also discussed earlier as Objective 3 — no losers under a flexible program. If this objective is a high priority, it will be a major factor in the design of the credit allocation structure. The most straightforward method of guaranteeing that each employee will be able to purchase a given level of benefits is through a component allocation structure, as discussed on the next page.

Organizational Objectives

Because of their significance, employee benefit costs cannot be considered in a vacuum and neither should the credit allocation formula for a flexible program. The organization's allocation of credits, be it an explicit allocation or implicit in a net pricing structure, is really an allocation of employer benefit dollars. Organizational objectives, then, will have an impact on the method of allocating those benefit dollars. An examination of organizational objectives will help to illustrate this concept.

- **Cost management.** An organization may feel that management of benefit costs is a top priority. This objective would lead the organization to a very explicit credit allocation structure in which credits are equivalent to employer costs, and no costs are hidden in the price tags.
- **Profit sharing.** Some organizations feel strongly that there should be a link between business results and all aspects of the employee's relationship with the company, including benefits. This can be accomplished in the flexible benefit program by allocating more or less credits based on the profitability of a division or the company as a whole.
- **Service recognition.** Employers may want to recognize and reward employees who are loyal to the organization. Credits may then vary by years of service.
- **Social responsibility.** Some employers consider it a social responsibility to provide benefits to employees, independent of other benefit-related objectives. This responsibility may lead the employer to: (1) support a selected level of benefits, (2) require employees to select a minimum level of coverage, (3) limit the employee's ability to cash out credits, (4) subsidize certain benefits that the employer believes should be encouraged, (5) not vary credits by profitability or service, or (6) limit aggressiveness in managing costs.

- **Benefit value equity.** Employers who believe equity in benefits is an aspect of total compensation may eventually want to allocate credits on a per capita basis.
- **Employee performance.** Employers may wish to link a portion of the credits to employee performance. For example, an above-average performer could receive a bonus, such as an extra $100 in credits or 25 per cent additional credits.
- **Health awareness or other corporate initiatives.** The credit allocation system can reinforce a health awareness campaign or other initiative by the employer.

The objectives an organization has for the allocation of credits will almost always have some internal inconsistencies. Identifying the priorities and finding the right mix of objectives can be a difficult step within the design of a flexible program.

Component Credit Allocation

Component allocation is a structure whereby credits are allocated to employees for each type of benefit and the sum of the components is the employee's total credit allocation. A certain number of credits are provided for supplemental medical, dental, life insurance, vision, LTD, and so forth. In so doing, it becomes readily apparent where the credit shortfalls or excesses exist for each type of benefit. Component allocation is also consistent with credit source determination, because the cost of the current benefit program is determined on a component basis. A component allocation method also lends itself better to a financial analysis of each of the types of benefits individually. Expected employer cost (credits) and expected total cost (price tags) are available for each benefit to compare to actual employer cost and actual total cost.

Component credit allocation can be refined beyond benefit type to subgroups of employees in much the same manner as subgroup pricing. Credits can be allocated based on dependant status, either actual number of dependants or by coverage chosen. In addition, the credit allocation may vary by province and possibly age. An age- or geography-based structure may be appropriate if price tags are calculated on that basis. It is highly unlikely that employers would vary credits by gender or smoker status. The component credit structure with a subgroup allocation does not necessarily mean employees will be able to purchase a given level of coverage, but it will be easier to measure and ensure the desired result for each employee.

Component credit allocation often leads to a formula type of allocation. Because of the different nature of benefits (some being pay-related and some not), the ultimate allocation may be based on a formula with a flat-dollar component and a percentage-of-pay component. For example, assume that the credits allocated

Example 14.2
Component Credit Allocation

Benefit	Credits
Medical	$630
Dental	$500
Vision	$50
Death	1% of pay
LTD	0.5% of pay

for each type of benefit are as shown in Example 14.2 for a 45-year-old employee earning $40,000 per year. The credits are calculated using the following formula:

$$\$1,180 + 1.5\% \text{ of pay} = \$1,180 + (0.015 \times \$40,000) = \$1,780$$

§ 14.5 TESTING THE PRICING STRUCTURE

To determine the feasibility of the total structure, price tags and credits must be viewed in combination or through the use of the net employee cost as a key indicator. A key determinant of how the components fit together is the way employees are affected. In this regard, a winners and losers analysis can be extremely valuable.

In addition, an analysis of employer cost should be performed. The analysis will entail accumulating the credits explicitly allocated to employees, the expected value of the implicit credits (price subsidies), and the changes in costs due to employee selection patterns. These elements can be captured together, using our earlier cost formula (Cost = Expected claims + Expenses and Taxes + Credits − Price tags).

Finally, the structure should be reviewed from a broader perspective. Getting too close to all the "numbers" can obscure a primary purpose for a flexible program — meeting the needs of employees. Reviewing the structure for reasonableness can bring the program back into focus.

WINNERS AND LOSERS ANALYSIS

A winners and losers analysis is simply a comparison of an employee's situation before and after implementation of the flexible benefit program.

- What were the benefits each employee was receiving prior to the new program?
- What was the employee's cost?

- How does this compare to the employee's cost for similar benefits purchased under the flexible approach?
- How many dollars are available for other uses if the employee chooses a different combination of benefits?
- What will the result be if the organization follows a different pricing strategy in the future?

To illustrate, a very simple first-year winners and losers analysis of a supplemental medical plan is provided in Example 14.3, using the pricing example used in Table 14.4 (Average Credits) which is reprinted here as Table 14.9.

The winners and losers analysis is an attempt to outline, in dollars, the employee's perspective of choices compared to the prior year. The analysis may bring

Table 14.9
The Average Credit Approach

		Credit-Based Pricing		Net Pricing
		Price Tag	Credit	Employee Cost
Option A	Single	$ 700	$945	$(245)
(current plan)	Family	1,400	945	455
Option B	Single	560	945	(385)
	Family	1,120	945	175
Option C	Single	420	945	(525)
	Family	840	945	(105)

Example 14.3
Winners/Losers Analysis

Option	Price Tags	Employee Credits	Net Employee Cost	Analysis
A Single	$700	$945	$(245)	Lower cost/Same benefit — Winner
Family	1,400	945	455	Higher cost/Same benefit — Loser
B Single	560	945	(385)	Lower cost/Lower benefit — Trade-off
Family	1,120	945	175	Higher cost/Lower benefit — Loser
C Single	420	945	(525)	Lower cost/Lower benefit — Trade-off
Family	840	945	(105)	Lower cost/Lower benefit — Trade-off

to the surface flaws in the pricing structure in terms of unintended effects on employees.

The out-of-pocket cost to the employee under the prior plan and the flexible plan can be compared to determine who wins and who loses under the flexible pricing structure.

EMPLOYER COST ANALYSIS

Some analysis should be performed to determine expected employer cost, especially if cost management is a goal of the flexible program. This analysis involves identifying the obvious employer costs, credits plus price subsidies, and also the not-so-obvious costs. These not-so-obvious costs include:

- **Adverse selection.** Will the plan costs rise if employees are allowed to choose their own benefits? If so, how much?
- **Dependant coverage.** Will the program likely cause employees to change their decisions on where to cover their dependants? If so, what is the likely cost impact?
- **Benefit utilization.** If employees change their benefit elections, will that change likely affect their propensity to use the services the benefits cover? If so, what might be the impact?

Since these areas of cost are somewhat nebulous, in the early days of flexible benefit programs they were very difficult to identify prior to implementation of the program. With increasing experience in flexible benefit programs, some experts now have databases of enrolment and claims experience that can be used in estimating these costs in advance. Identifying and calculating an expected employer cost of the plan is an important exercise in determining the appropriateness of the pricing structure and the ultimate success of the program. (See also Chapter 15 for a broader discussion of employer financial analysis.)

REASONABLENESS

It is difficult to define exactly what this final step may include for each employer. The employer should be asking the same kinds of questions a typical employee will ask, such as:

- Do I understand the options?
- Do the price tags make sense?
- How does the price for one option compare to the price for another?
- Are the choices clear, or are the options and their price tags so similar as to be indistinguishable?

- Is one option an obvious choice over all others, no matter what my situation?
- Are the credits adequate for my needs?
- Is the employer paying a fair share of the cost?

At times, the employer may become too close to the plan to remain fully aware of the employee's perspective. An alternative is to test the flexible benefit program with a sample group of employees. Pre-testing the plan with employees could bring to light subtle problems with the pricing structure that otherwise may be difficult to identify. After pre-testing, it is often the case that pricing and pricing objectives will be revisited to reflect the employee's perspective. Pre-testing may also provide a necessary measure of confidence in the program prior to implementation.

Fifteen

Financial Analysis

§ 15.1 THE CHALLENGE OF PREPARING A FINANCIAL ANALYSIS

Conceptually, a financial analysis of a flexible program involves little more than calculating the cost (either historical or projected) of the benefit program. In practice, however, preparing a cost analysis is considerably more complex, in many ways resembling art as much as science. This is true in three situations where a financial analysis is necessary:

- Prior to implementing a flexible plan.
- Analysing the historical cost of an existing flexible plan.
- Predicting the future cost of an existing flexible plan.

All three of these situations will be discussed in this chapter.

The purpose of this chapter is to outline the various types of financial analyses applicable to a flexible program, to discuss the uses of these analyses, and to provide a conceptual framework in which the financial analyses can be performed.

§ 15.2 CALCULATING THE COST OF FLEXIBLE OPTIONS

The first step in any financial analysis is to determine the claims generated by the plan. In a flexible plan, the claims for each option are separately calculated and analysed. They are then adjusted for anticipated design, experience or utilization changes and summed to produce the total plan claims cost.

CALCULATING THE INDIVIDUAL OPTION COSTS

Although introducing a flexible program may create a number of advantages for an organization and its employees, there may also be significant costs involved. Senior management will often require a "dollars-and-cents" analysis of the impact of a new flexible benefit program before approving plans for implementation.

Employer Costs

Under a traditional benefit plan, the employer's cost equals the premiums paid to the insurance carrier, less any employee payroll deductions. If the plan is not insured, the total cost of the program equals the claims paid, plus any expenses associated with administering the program. The employer cost of a non-insured benefit program is, therefore, the claims plus expenses less any payroll deductions.

Determining the employer cost under a flexible benefit program is more complicated, particularly for plans using a credit-based pricing structure. The total plan costs remain the same — claims plus expenses. However, the employer cost calculation must reflect not only the claims and expenses paid to the carrier, but also the credits paid to employees and price tags charged back to employees.

When net pricing is used, the employer cost is determined using the following formula:

$$\text{Employer Cost} = \text{Claims} + \text{Expenses} - \text{Employee Cost}$$

When credit-based pricing is used, the employer cost is calculated as follows:

$$\text{Employer Cost} = \text{Claims} + \text{Expenses} + \text{Credits} - \text{Price Tags}$$

The calculation of the employer cost is illustrated in Table 15.1 using four scenarios:

- A traditional pre-flexible plan.
- A flexible plan using the net pricing approach.
- A flexible plan using credit-based pricing with realistic price tags.
- A flexible plan using credit-based pricing. In this example the price tags incorporate a significant employer subsidy.

As illustrated in Table 15.1, the same employer cost can be derived through a number of different pricing approaches.

Employee Costs

Employees are charged a price tag that depends on which option they choose. Employers may provide credits to employees to help pay the price tag. The net

Table 15.1
Calculating Employer Cost

	(1) Claims + Expenses	(2) Price Tags	(3) Credits	(4) Net Employee Cost (2) − (3)	(5) Employer Cost (1) − (4)
Pre-Flex	$1,000,000	$2,000,000	0	$200,000	$800,000
Flexible Example A (Net Pricing)	$1,100,000	$3,000,000	0	$300,000	$800,000
Flexible Example B (Realistic Price Tags)	$1,100,000	$1,100,000	$800,000	$300,000	$800,000
Flexible Example C (Subsidized Price Tags)	$1,100,000	$600,000	$300,000	$300,000	$800,000

employee share of the benefit program cost is calculated as follows:

$$\text{Employee Cost} = \text{Employee Net Cost} = \text{Price Tags} - \text{Credits}$$

This calculation may produce a positive or negative number. If employees choose enhanced options with higher price tags than company-provided credits, employees will make up the difference through payroll deductions (i.e., positive employee cost). If employees elect less valuable options with lower price tags than company-provided credits, employees receive the net difference in the form of excess credits; in other words, there is a negative employee cost.

CALCULATING THE TOTAL PLAN COSTS

These calculations for a single option hold true for financial analysis at various levels:

- In each option — to determine the cost of an option and to allocate the cost between the employer and employees participating in that option.
- In aggregate — to determine overall program cost and to allocate that cost between the employer and employees.
- For individuals — to determine the cost for an individual employee and to allocate the cost between the individual and the employer.

The first step in analysing the overall cost of a new or existing flexible program is to determine the potential areas of significant cost changes from one year to the next (increases or decreases). Although certainly not a complete list, the following provides an indication of the types of items that might be considered for a broad flexible program:

Cost Savings Areas

- Specific benefit reductions, such as an increase in the medical deductible, a reduction in co-insurance, implementation of caps on services, and so forth;
- Increases in employee contributions;
- Decreases in medical utilization due to higher deductibles and co-payment amounts;
- Savings arising out of specific cost management features;
- Decreases in dental utilization due to higher deductibles and co-insurance amounts;
- Decreases in claims arising from employees dropping out of the program in dual-coverage situations;
- Forfeitures from health spending accounts;
- "Float" within health spending accounts (resulting from later payment by the company); and
- Potential savings in ongoing administration (due to consolidation of multiple benefit programs or computerizing previously manual processes).

Cost Increase Areas

- Implementation costs (communication, administration, legal documentation, consulting fees, staffing requirements);
- Ongoing operational costs (communication, administration, and so forth);
- Increased participation in optional, partially subsidized benefits (due to the increased communication effort or pricing approaches);
- Credits provided on waiver of coverage (if non-participating employees previously resulted in no company costs);
- Election experience (adverse selection);
- Improvements in specific benefits (for example, updating plan maximums) made in conjunction with the introduction of or improvements to the flexible program; and
- Increases in Canada/Quebec Pension Plan taxes and employer payroll taxes (if benefits can be converted into cash).

Not all of these items will apply in each situation, and other items that are specific only to that employer may arise. The point is that any cost factor that is significant in magnitude and can be reasonably evaluated should be included in a cost

Table 15.2
Projecting Total Employer Costs

	(1) Expected Claims + Expenses	(2) Price Tags	(3) Credits	(4) Net Employee Cost (2) − (3)	(5) Employer Cost (1) − (4)
Dental Option 1	$ 200,000	$ 200,000	$ 400,000	$(200,000)	$ 400,000
Dental Option 2	$ 800,000	$ 800,000	$ 600,000	$ 200,000	$ 600,000
Medical Option 1	$ 500,000	$ 500,000	$1,000,000	$(500,000)	$1,000,000
Medical Option 2	$1,250,000	$1,250,000	$1,000,000	$ 250,000	$1,000,000
Health Spending Account	$ 250,000	N/A	N/A	$ 0	$ 0

analysis. Any cost factor that is likely to be significant, but cannot be evaluated with reliability, should be included as a "best guess" or with a range of results.

The example shown in Table 15.2 illustrates the projected company cost for a plan with two medical options, two dental options, and an HSA.

Note that in Table 15.2, employees allocate a total of $250,000 to the health spending account. This analysis assumes that all employees will fully utilize their HSAs, resulting in claims equal to the allocations. However, because of the forfeiture rules under health spending accounts (see Chapter 7 for details), the $250,000 in fact represents the maximum possible claims. When the actual experience for this plan is reviewed, the amount of forfeitures from employees will revert to the company, reducing the company's cost for the flexible plan. This HSA forfeiture saving is very difficult to predict in advance and, therefore, is not usually factored into initial program cost projections. However, in subsequent years, if this figure is found to be material, it should be included as part of the ongoing experience analysis.

§ 15.3 PRE-IMPLEMENTATION FINANCIAL ANALYSIS

Financial analysis is useful in helping an organization design a new flexible program or revitalize an existing plan. This includes deciding which benefit areas to incorporate in the program, the design of the options within a benefit area, the prices to charge for each option, and the amount of credits, if any, to allocate to each participant. The objective is to design the program to meet the company's financial objectives and to ensure that the financial impact on employees is reasonable and appropriate. (Financial considerations that are key to these design decisions are covered in earlier chapters on specific benefit areas and plan pricing.)

In the early days of flexible programs, developing an initial design was relatively simple. Option designs were similar and few benefit areas were included. However, recent designs have become more robust as employers include new types of plan provisions (e.g., drug formularies) and new sources of employer funding, and add more benefit areas for choice. Financial analysis has grown in importance in the initial design because it enables employers to focus efforts on those benefit areas where choice is financially worthwhile. In addition, analysis of pre-flexible experience contributes to effective design and pricing structures in critical cost areas (e.g., supplemental medical and dental).

BENEFIT AREAS INCLUDED

As a general rule, it is appropriate to offer choices in benefit areas where employee needs vary, costs are significant, selection costs can be managed, and management supports the concept. Problems with any one of these factors may be sufficient reason to exclude a benefit area from the program. Financial analysis helps employers determine the degree to which employee needs vary and the cost consequences of choice.

For example, in deciding which benefit areas to incorporate in the program, an employer with a very young and healthy workforce might decide that less generous choices in the basic life and long-term disability area are inappropriate, because the financial analysis of current plan costs demonstrates that few dollars could be released for use in other benefit areas.

In contrast, an enrolment analysis of the prior plan might demonstrate the need for less costly supplemental medical or long-term disability options. Simple retirement income projections may demonstrate that an existing savings plan provides adequate flexibility for retirement benefits, encouraging a design that allows employees to allocate savings plan amounts into the flexible benefit plan.

Analysis of vacation forfeitures or carry-over patterns provides an indication of potential employee interest in vacation buying and selling, as well as potential hard-dollar costs of including time off in the flexible program.

INITIAL OPTION DESIGN

Analysis of employee demographics, prior benefit enrolment patterns, and benefit payments will contribute to effective option design.

Some examples include:

- Analysis of prior enrolment in optional life benefits may demonstrate the appeal of a reduced core coverage, if a high proportion of employees (e.g., over 50 per cent) waive optional coverage. Conversely, high enrolment in the maximum prior coverage might indicate the appeal of still higher life insurance options.

- Analysis of claim distribution patterns helps employers focus on medical option designs that result in meaningful value differences for employees (e.g., identifying that 90 per cent of employees claiming paramedical services claim the per visit maximum may indicate a desire for an option with a higher maximum).

- Projections of vacation buying and selling costs under several alternative design scenarios will help employers focus on appropriate limits on number of days available for choice.

INITIAL OPTION PRICING

Since pricing structures for life insurance, disability, and time-off options are usually quite simple, little analysis is required to establish prices. Realistic pricing is the most common approach in all these areas (i.e., price tags that reflect the full value of the option).

However, medical and dental option pricing requires much more extensive analysis. To develop option prices that reflect real differences in value for a given employee workforce, it is helpful to conduct a detailed analysis of claims by amount and by type of service. Then, the impact of option features (such as deductibles, internal limits on services, and co-insurance limits) on the relative value of the new plan options can be accurately determined. Projecting the impact of alternative pricing scenarios on enrolment patterns, claim patterns, and resulting costs will help employers focus on the most appropriate approach. Pricing of medical options is discussed in detail in Chapter 14.

IMPLEMENTATION COSTS

Perhaps the most important type of financial analysis conducted surrounding the design and implementation of a flexible program is that aimed at determining whether an organization should adopt such a program. In effect, is a flexible program worth the implementation effort and cost? The answer to this question will be easy to arrive at in some situations (clearly yes or clearly no), but arriving at an answer will be quite complex in other situations. Even after a financial analysis is complete, the degree to which non-financial objectives are being accomplished must be considered before a final "go/no go" decision is made.

In the following discussion it is assumed that the plan design and pricing have been finalized and the review of the financial impact on individual employees (evaluating winners and losers) has yielded satisfactory results.

For some employers, the financial analysis will show an increase in costs in the first year of a program (particularly if implementation costs are simply treated as a first-year expense rather than being amortized), reaching a break-even point in the third or fourth year.

Most employers, however, absorb the implementation costs and do not try to recover them in future years. In these cases, the financial analysis would typically show a break-even situation in the first year.

Future cost savings would be projected if the employer subsidy were assumed to increase at a slower rate than claims. Otherwise, the anticipated costs of the flexible plan would equal those of the prior, non-flexible benefit program.

CASH FLOW PATTERNS

Quite apart from the issue of whether costs will increase or decrease by introducing a flexible program, an organization's cash flow patterns are likely to be altered. Although this is often overlooked (and may not be important in some organizations), a brief financial analysis of the impact on cash flow may prove useful.

If employees are able to take cash in lieu of certain benefits, the timing of cash payments may be accelerated. If added vacation days may be purchased but unused days must be cashed out at year-end, a significant drain on cash flow could occur in December. If supplemental medical or dental benefits are reduced as an element of a flexible program, claims costs may rise dramatically between the announcement and the effective dates.

Three factors affect cash flow in any benefit area where employees may elect lower coverage than the pre-flexible level — claim payments (plus expenses), credit allocations, and price tags.

For example, in the supplemental medical area, claim lags from the prior plan year typically result in relatively high claim payments under administrative services only (ASO) arrangements in the first few months of the flexible program, when run-off from the prior plan is still being processed and paid. Then, cash flow for claim payments drops off, typically reflecting lower numbers of covered individuals as well as larger deductibles and co-payments. After about eight or nine months, as more employees in the low-cost options meet their deductibles and out-of-pocket limits, cash flow for claim payments starts to stabilize and more closely track the pattern seen in the prior plan.

This unusual pattern of "paid claims" makes it difficult for carriers to project medical trend factors as employers attempt to do subsequent-year pricing in July and August. Later in the year, as more experience unfolds, the trend factors may be refined.

Cash flow projections also should reflect the impact of credits and price tags that are typically distributed uniformly throughout the year. For example, if employees can opt down, fewer premiums will be collected than under the prior plan. Excess credits will be paid out, resulting in higher cash outflow to employees in their paycheques. Of course, over the course of a plan year, claim payments should be lower on average for those employees who opt down, balancing out the annual effect of decreased employee contributions.

Table 15.3
Impact of Employee Contributions on Company Cost

Year	(1) Claims	(2) Employee Contributions	(3) Company Cost (1) − (2)
Conventional Plan	$1,000,000	$ 0	$1,000,000
Flexible Plan	$1,300,000	$300,000	$1,000,000

CLAIMS PROJECTIONS

Most cost projections for flexible programs focus on the impact of changes on incurred claims, while the controller, for instance, is likely to be focusing on cash outlay for the year (i.e., paid claims). Therefore, comparisons of budgeted expense versus actual cash flow can look peculiar unless the user knows what to expect.

Another often overlooked element of projecting costs under a flexible plan is the impact on the total claims. Sometimes within organizations, claims (e.g., ASO claims under a medical plan) are incorrectly taken to represent the entire cost of the benefit plan. This can be especially true in organizations where employee contributions have been small or nonexistent in the past. In these organizations, accurate claims estimates should be prepared prior to implementing a flexible plan. Table 15.3 illustrates the confusion that can occur in a company that introduces richer medical options under their flexible benefit plan, with corresponding higher employee contributions.

The company cost of the flexible plan, $1,000,000 in this case, is the same as the cost of the conventional plan. However, when viewed in isolation, the 30 per cent increase in claims would appear to indicate that the company cost has increased substantially with the introduction of flexible benefits.

Much time can be spent in explaining how flexible benefits financial analysis works when results like the 30 per cent claims increase in Table 15.3 are not anticipated.

§ 15.4 EVALUATING EXPERIENCE OF A FLEXIBLE PLAN

Despite its importance, actually conducting this form of financial analysis can be very difficult. Often, the most significant problem is the lack of reliable and timely experience data. The design and pricing decisions resulting from this process need to be communicated to employees and their elections need to be recorded prior to the beginning of the next plan year. Therefore, this analysis normally needs to occur at least three or four months prior to year-end. However, the claims experience available in a self-insured situation will, at best, cover only the first half of the year (especially in the medical and dental areas, where there is typically a one- to two-month lag between the time claims are incurred and the time they are paid by the insurance company or third-party administrator). As a result, pricing decisions usually must be made on the basis of limited data for the prior year, extrapolated to a full-year basis.

Extrapolating half-year data to a full-year basis, although necessary, can be complicated by a number of factors, which may make simply doubling the half-year results inappropriate. Among these complicating factors are the claims lag mentioned earlier, the continuing monthly increase in costs due to inflation, and the tendency for claims to be higher in the second half of the year than in the first half, after more participants have exceeded their deductible.

Employers can minimize the potential for frustration by anticipating upcoming data needs and taking steps to facilitate the early collection and categorization of results, particularly for medical and dental experience. Steps in the data collection process include:

- Advise insurers, third-party administrators, or internal systems staff of the need and deadline for detailed analysis of elections and claims experience.
- Provide parameters for reporting actual experience — by employee group (such as active versus retired, hourly versus salaried), location, or division.
- Request itemization of employee data by type of coverage (Medical Plan A, Medical Plan B, and so forth) and coverage category (employee-only, employee-plus-one-dependant, and so forth).
- In a managed care environment, make sure enough information will be provided to measure how well the approach is working and how it is being used by employees.
- Establish tracking systems to identify and isolate specific large claims that could potentially distort the results, particularly for options elected by a small number of employees.

It is typical to see medical experience by option as being quite different from what would be produced if employees made their selections with no knowledge of their anticipated usage (see Chapter 16, "Adverse Selection"). For example, the pattern of actual versus expected claims experience might be on the order of that shown in Example 15.1. The expected claims column shows the claims that would occur if employees did not base their choices on their anticipated medical usage in the coming year.

If the actual experience is substantially different in the aggregate from what was expected, the data should be reviewed to determine whether the experience is likely to be reliable as a predictor for the future. Perhaps an unusually high or low number of major claims occurred during the experience period, but this pattern is unlikely to reoccur. In a small group, for example, the average claims experience under a low option might actually exceed the average claims experience under a

Example 15.1
Variation in Actual versus Expected Claims Experience

Option	(1) Number of Employees	(2) Option Price Tag	(3) Expected Claims* $(1) \times (2)$	(4) Actual Claims	(5) Actual as Per Cent of Expected $(4) \div (3)$
High	1,000	$2,000	$2,000,000	$2,200,000	110%
Intermediate	500	$1,500	$ 750,000	$ 670,000	89%
Low	1,000	$ 500	$ 500,000	$ 380,000	76%
Total	2,500		$3,250,000	$3,250,000	100%

*Assumes no adjustment for anticipated adverse selection or utilization changes.

high option, due to one or two very large unexpected claims of employees who selected the low option. This experience should be identified in the analysis, but it is probably inappropriate to fully reflect it in the development of future prices.

§ 15.5 FINANCIAL ANALYSIS AND FUTURE PRICING DECISIONS

One of the more important reasons for preparing a financial analysis is to assist organizations in making option pricing and design decisions for future years. This is especially important for medical and dental coverages, but is relevant in other benefit areas as well.

For example, when medical options are included in a flexible program, prices need to be assigned for each option and for each coverage category (employee-only, employee-plus-spouse, and so forth) within the options. In developing these prices, it is important to ensure that the selection process is not biased toward specific choices, that employees are not overcharged as a group, that contributions are set appropriately, and so forth. Although the experience of each option may not be the only factor incorporated in a pricing decision, clearly it will be a major determinant of the next year's pricing. Even employers who are fully insured need to monitor the financial experience of each option because their insurer will be comparing the program with others it underwrites to evaluate prices for coverage in subsequent years.

MULTI-YEAR COST PROJECTIONS

Multi-year projections are useful in illustrating the potential impact of various inflation and health care trend scenarios on employee and employer costs under alternative pricing strategies. For example, the three-year projections in Example 15.2

Example 15.2
Three-Year Projection of Employee Costs

Year	(1) Price Tag	(2) Credit	(3) Net Employee Cost (1) − (2)
Year 1	$1,000	$900	$100
Year 2	$1,100	$945	$155
Year 3	$1,210	$992	$218

clearly demonstrate that it is easier to justify a given "dollar" level of increase in employee costs from year to year if price tags are large (closer to realistic) than if they are heavily subsidized, or if a net pricing approach is used (i.e., no credits).

In Example 15.2, price tags increase by 10 per cent each year and employer credits increase by 5 per cent. This concept is much easier to communicate than the same approach under a net pricing scenario. If net pricing is used, net employee cost increases by 55 per cent in Year 2 and 41 per cent in Year 3. While both the credit-based and net pricing approaches produce the same cost to the employee and employer, the leveraging effect of the hidden employer subsidy may make the same dollar increase seem unreasonable in the net pricing case. Multi-year projections under alternative scenarios help bring out the significance of pricing structure decisions.

Three- or five-year projections also help employers focus on realistic goals for future cost savings. In some situations, employers start out with unrealistic expectations for future cost savings simply because they do not know the degree to which they would have to shift costs to employees to realize long-term goals for cost savings. Continuing with the previous example, an employer might have an initial objective of holding health care costs steady for the first year of a flexible program. However, once management realizes that the net effect could mean a first-year increase of 50 per cent in employee contributions over the pre-flexible program level, it might reassess cost savings goals (or at least restate the objective to allow greater flexibility in responding to unanticipated experience, such as an exceptional number of large claims).

PRICING FOR FUTURE YEARS

After the employer has accumulated, reviewed, and adjusted the historical experience, it must decide on the future year's option prices. Again, this subject is discussed mainly from a medical and dental perspective, since these benefits are more often self-insured and differences in option experience can be great. (Also, setting prices for the next year based on the current year's experience will require

some estimate of the expected increase in medical or dental claims due to inflation. Estimates of the expected trend factor for the next year are typically available
from insurance companies and other sources.)

Once a flexible program is in operation, an employer must re-address option
design and option pricing issues for the upcoming year. An important part of this
annual process is financial analysis of the experience for the current year (and
possibly past years). This analysis will often form the backdrop for the option
pricing portion of the process and sometimes will also influence option design
issues.

The purpose of this financial analysis is to help answer the following kinds of
questions:

- Are the actual aggregate program costs consistent with those projected for the
  year?
- Were the individual options fairly priced? If not, what changes may be necessary?
- Does the experience under the program or under any specific option suggest
  particular design changes?
- What level of company credits (or subsidy in a net pricing plan) in conjunction
  with the option prices will produce the appropriate level of company cost?
  What level will seem fair/reasonable to employees?

Assuming the medical experience shown in Example 15.1 (110 per cent of expected
claims for the high option and 89 per cent and 76 per cent for the other options),
the issue arises as to how much weight (if any) the individual option experience
should be given in considering next year's option prices.

One alternative is to ignore the variations from the expected, as long as overall
medical program experience is in line with what was expected (as is the case in
Example 15.1). Under this approach, the option prices will maintain the same
approximate relationships from year to year, offering a sense of stability from the
employee's perspective.

At the other extreme is a full reflection of the difference actually experienced
between the options. In Example 15.1, such an approach would increase the spread
between the high-option and the low-option prices by nearly 50 per cent in a single
year. This would quickly drive many employees away from the highest option. In
some situations, this form of "option self-destruction" may, in fact, be an objective
— a way to eliminate an unduly rich medical plan through the mechanism of
pricing. In other cases, this may be inappropriately disturbing to those participants
who are inclined to select the highest-level medical option.

An intermediate approach is often used that reflects only a portion of
the experience-based differences in option costs. This might result in nudging

employees away from the high option (or at least encouraging them to consider other options), rather than driving them away.

As part of this decision, one important (and often overlooked) step should be undertaken. The prices presented to employees need to make sense relative to the coverage levels being provided. This is particularly true if the full experience difference is to be used and, therefore, the pricing spread between the options is to be dramatically increased. The price differentials between the options should be compared with the differences in benefits payable under the options to ensure that employees are being presented with reasonable choices.

For example, if the difference in deductibles under two medical options (high and intermediate) would produce no more than a $100 gain to employees in coverage, the difference in prices between the options should not exceed $100. Employees should not be asked to pay more for an option than they could receive in coverage, regardless of the actual experience (which could have been unusual in a given year). Likewise, the contributions required by employees between options and coverage categories should make economic sense. Single coverage in a particular option should cost no more than family coverage. Cash back to employees in the low option plan should not exceed the credits given for taking no coverage. In effect, the option choices and price tags need to be reviewed for logic in the eyes of employees, as well as for how well they reflect actual experience.

COMPARING THE COSTS OF THE FLEXIBLE PLAN TO THE PRIOR PLAN

The following question is often asked several years after implementation of the flexible plan — "Did the plan save us money?" In order to effectively answer this question, we need to look at both the cost of the flexible plan and the probable cost of the prior plan had it continued.

Examples 15.3, 15.4, and 15.5 illustrate the components of such an analysis. These examples illustrate the costs for an organization that had a traditional plan in Year 0, and then introduced a flexible plan in Year 1. Example 15.3 presents the actual cost of the traditional plan in Year 0 and the expected costs in Years 1 and 2 had the traditional plan continued. Example 15.4 shows the actual costs of the flexible plan in Year 1 — these costs are calculated in Year 2, once the Year 1 experience is known. Finally, Example 15.5 presents the estimated costs of the flexible plan in Year 2 based on the actual Year 1 results.

Example 15.3 projects the pre-flexible plan costs to Years 1 and 2 using the following assumptions:

- No change in employee headcount.
- Medical inflation of 10 per cent per annum.
- Dental inflation of 5 per cent per annum.
- No increase in employee contributions.

Example 15.3
Projecting Employer Costs of Prior (Pre-Flexible) Plan

	Prior Plan (Actual Costs — Year 0)	Prior Plan (Projected Costs — Year 1)	Prior Plan (Projected Costs — Year 2)
Medical per Employee			
1 Cost per Employee	$ 1,600	$ 1,760	$ 1,936
2 Employee Premium	400	400	400
3 Employer Cost (1 − 2)	1,200	1,360	1,536
Total Medical			
4 Number of Employees	2,500	2,500	2,500
5 Claims plus Expenses (1 × 4)	$4,000,000	$4,400,000	$4,840,000
6 Total Employee Cost (2 × 4)	1,000,000	1,000,000	1,000,000
7 Total Employer Medical Cost (5 − 6)	3,000,000	3,400,000	3,840,000
Total Dental			
8 Total Employer Dental Cost (similar calculation to above)	$3,000,000	$3,150,000	$3,307,500
Total			
9 Total Employer Cost (7 + 8)	$6,000,000	$6,550,000	$7,147,500

Example 15.4
Actual Costs of Flexible Plan — Year 1

	Option 1	Option 2	Option 3	Total
Medical per Employee				
1 Cost per Employee	$ 400	$ 1,300	$ 2,700	N/A
2 Price Tags	800	1,360	2,260	N/A
3 Flex Credits	1,000	1,360	1,360	N/A
4 Employee Cost (2 − 3)	(200)	0	900	N/A
5 Employer Cost (1 − 4)	600	1,300	1,800	N/A
Total Medical				
6 Number of Employees	500	1,000	1,000	2,500
7 Claims plus Expenses (1 × 6)	$200,000	$1,300,000	$2,700,000	$4,200,000
8 Price Tags (2 × 6)	400,000	1,360,000	2,260,000	4,020,000
9 Flexible Credits (3 × 6)	500,000	1,360,000	1,360,000	3,220,000
10 Total Employee Cost (8 − 9)	(100,000)	0	900,000	800,000
11 Total Employer Medical Cost (7 − 10)	300,000	1,300,000	1,800,000	3,400,000
Total Dental				
12 Total Employer Dental Cost (similar calculation to above)	$630,000	$945,000	$1,575,000	$3,150,000
Total				
13 Total Employer Cost (11 + 12)	$930,000	$2,245,000	$3,375,000	$6,550,000

Example 15.5
Projected Costs of Flexible Plan — Year 2

	Option 1	Option 2	Option 3	Total
Medical per Employee				
Medical Inflation	8%	10%	12%	
1 Cost per Employee	$ 432	$ 1,430	$ 3,024	N/A
2 Price Tags (Increased in line with medical inflation)	864	1,496	2,531	N/A
3 Flex Credits (Increased 5%)	1,050	1,428	1,428	N/A
4 Employee Cost (2 − 3)	(186)	68	1,103	N/A
5 Employer Cost (1 − 4)	618	1,362	1,921	N/A
Total Medical				
6 Number of Employees	500	1,000	1,000	2,500
7 Claims plus Expenses (1 × 6)	$216,000	$1,430,000	$3,024,000	$4,670,000
8 Price Tags (2 × 6)	432,000	1,496,000	2,531,200	4,459,200
9 Flexible Credits (3 × 6)	525,000	1,428,000	1,428,000	3,381,000
10 Total Employee Cost (8 − 9)	(93,000)	68,000	1,103,200	1,078,200
11 Total Employer Medical Cost (7 − 10)	309,000	1,362,000	1,920,800	3,591,800
Total Dental				
12 Total Employer Dental Cost (similar calculation to above)	$661,500	$992,250	$1,653,750	$3,307,500
Total				
13 Total Employer Cost (11 + 12)	$970,500	$2,354,250	$3,574,550	$6,899,300

The two-year projection of the prior plan costs shown in Example 15.3 is then compared to the actual costs in Year 1 and projected costs in Year 2 of the flexible benefit plan developed in Examples 15.4 and 15.5.

Example 15.4 reveals that the cost of the flexible benefit plan, excluding implementation, is the same as what the prior plan would have cost in Year 1 ($6,550,000). However, once implementation costs are reflected, the flexible plan would cost more than the prior plan in the first year. As discussed earlier in this chapter, this is a typical result, since many employers are willing to incur the implementation costs as an investment to produce long-term cost savings.

The projected costs in Year 2 shown in Example 15.5 assume medical inflation ranges from 8 per cent in the lowest option to 12 per cent in the highest option. Price tags are assumed to increase at the same rate as inflation, namely 8 to 12 per cent, depending on the option. The increase in flex credits is limited to 5 per cent. The combined effect of employee prices increasing faster than credits (8 to 12 per cent versus 5 per cent) means that employees absorb a larger and larger share of costs each year. This reduces the employer cost relative to what it would have been in the absence of flexible benefits. This is evident in Example 15.5, where the total employer cost is projected to be $6,899,300 in Year 2 versus $7,147,500 had the prior plan continued. The estimated saving of $248,200 must be reduced by any increased administrative and communication costs attributable to flexible benefits.

In order to prepare such an analysis, the employer must make certain decisions and assumptions, including:

- What is the appropriate time period for the evaluation?
- Should one-time implementation expenses be treated as first-year expenses spread over multiple years or excluded from the analysis?
- What assumption should be made regarding employee election patterns?
- What experience is likely to occur under self-insured options?
- What strategy will be used for future increases in option prices and credits?
- What levels of future inflation and pay increases are appropriate?

§ 15.6 DATA REQUIREMENTS

The data requirements for the financial analysis of a flexible plan are not much more extensive than those needed for the tracking of a traditional program. Most of the data can be readily obtained from standard insurance carrier reports. From the start, employers should agree with carriers and third-party administrators on the data needed for effective analysis and repricing. Important data elements include:

- **Claim lag reports.** These reports lay out "claims paid by month incurred" (i.e., the dollar amount of claims incurred in January and paid in (a) January, (b) February, (c) March, etc.). Claim lag reports for each medical option are valuable for tracking and projecting cash flow. This is most significant to a company requiring reasonably accurate projections for accounting and budgeting purposes, because high deductibles or out-of-pocket limits in some options can trigger radically different cash flow patterns when compared with a single pre-flexible plan.
- **Aggregate claims experience.** Most employers receive periodic reports from their carriers or claim administrators that compare claims incurred and paid (plus expenses) with budgeted monthly amounts (i.e., actual experience versus expected experience). These are typically referred to as "loss ratio reports." These reports are valuable in tracking the degree of selection and for setting increases to budgeted rates or premiums for the next plan year. It is important to clarify with the carriers or plan administrators that this data should be

collected *by option and coverage category*. Since option enrolment patterns change from year to year, it is rarely sufficient to report only total results.

- **Enrolment pattern.** In order to properly analyse the claims data, it is essential to know how many employees elected each option as well as what coverage category they chose (employee only, employee plus one dependant, etc.). The enrolment patterns can fluctuate monthly due to changes in family status, terminations, or new hires. Therefore, a monthly tracking of enrolments will facilitate a more accurate claims analysis.

- **Incurred charges by amount of claim.** This data has not traditionally been reported to employers by their carriers or claims administrators. However, it is very valuable in evaluating the differences in value to employees of various medical and dental options. In addition, if the data is sorted by option, employers can gain more insight into the patterns and degree of adverse selection that occur in flexible programs. A typical distribution of incurred charges by amount clearly demonstrates that most insured individuals submit only small claims in any given year. Most of the dollars spent on covered charges are attributable to a very small number of individuals.

- **Incurred claims by type of service.** Most claims administrators maintain standard reports that summarize the number and dollar amount of charges incurred by type of service (hospital, vision, prescription drugs, and so on). Isolating the most costly procedures helps in analysing adverse selection and in determining future price tags. For flexible benefit plans, it is very useful to have this information both by each option and in aggregate.

- **Prescription drugs by type.** In addition to tracking incurred claims by service, many organizations find it useful to track prescription drugs by type, particularly those organizations that have implemented managed care features. Tracking prescriptions by type can give an organization an indication of the overall health of employees. For organizations considering implementing a managed drug formulary, it can indicate whether or not such a formulary would be appropriate and, if so, what drugs should be covered.

The above data elements are most valuable if sorted by category (e.g., employee, spouse, children; active; retired under age 65, retired over age 65). It is also important to isolate the effect of disabled participants.

Sixteen

Adverse Selection

§ 16.1 INTRODUCTION

Few concepts are more feared — or misunderstood — in the field of flexible benefits than adverse selection. The concern is that any offering of choice, whether inside a flexible program or otherwise, ensures that "bad risks" will be drawn to certain options, automatically driving up the cost of the coverage and producing negative financial results. This misunderstanding occurs for various reasons.

Until they embark on a flexible benefit project, few employers might anticipate the leverage that exists for controlling experience through plan design and option pricing. In effect, design and pricing operate as levers within a flexible program to contain the potential for adverse selection.

Another reason is that adverse selection within flexible programs is often confused with higher claims costs. In practice, the risk of higher claims resulting from a move to choice-making is often nonexistent, due to the structure of most flexible programs. In supplemental medical, for example, the pre-flexible plan is frequently offered as the highest-valued option in the program. Some proportion of employees will opt down in coverage from that level, thereby lowering aggregate claims costs. As a result, the adverse selection issue in flexible programs relates more to the level of reward or incentive provided to employees through credits or lower prices to elect lower-valued coverages or to opt out of the program altogether.

Finally, the adverse selection issue presumes that employees are able to predict benefit plan utilization — both for themselves and their families — with a high degree of accuracy. Except in unusual situations (such as an employee anticipating orthodontic expenses for a child), experience shows that the types of calamities covered by most benefit plans are "unknowable" in advance, particularly in family-coverage situations. Further, emotion often clouds what otherwise might be strictly economic decisions in the benefit area. In effect, security and budgeting often are more powerful influences on employee benefit plan elections than the profit motive.

The purpose of this chapter is to discuss the concept of adverse selection as it relates to flexible programs, and to explain the types of approaches used to minimize the potential for unfavourable financial experience. Note that most of the discussion concentrates on the potential for adverse selection to occur in medical and dental plans, paying limited attention to other benefit areas.

§ 16.2 ABOUT ADVERSE SELECTION

To understand adverse selection, it may be helpful to review the general principles underlying the concept of insurance. True insurance occurs when the likelihood of a claim is completely unknown or random, but the potential consequences are so great that few people would forgo paying a modest amount to gain the coverage. Consider an illustration.

Table 16.1 shows a hypothetical distribution of claims in a given year for a supplemental medical plan covering a group of 100 employees. The price of the coverage equals $1,800 — or the same amount as the average employee's claims. In order to simplify the illustration, retention, reserves, administrative fees, sales taxes, and other costs have been excluded.

The majority of the members in the group incur claims that are lower than the price of the coverage. In effect, these employees are "losers" under the plan (shown in italics) in that their cost exceeded what they received in terms of benefits. A few employees are "winners" under the plan (shown in bold typeface) in that their claims exceeded the price of the coverage. Still, all of the members of the group are willing to pay the average price to protect against the risk of incurring a large medical claim. This is the principle of insurance — the risk of an event occurring is spread over a group of people with none of the members able to predict individual or family unit experience.

Table 16.1
Illustration of Winners and Losers in Medical

Annual Claim Range	Number of Employees	Average Claim	Total Claims	Total Premiums	Claims Less Premiums
$0–$249	*20*	*$ 125*	*$ 2,500*	*$ 36,000*	*$(33,500)*
$250–$999	*30*	*650*	*19,500*	*54,000*	*(34,500)*
$1,000–$2,499	*30*	*1,600*	*48,000*	*54,000*	*(6,000)*
$2,500 and over	**20**	**5,500**	**110,000**	**36,000**	**74,000**
	100	$1,800	$180,000	$180,000	$ 0

Adverse selection is created when employees know or can reasonably predict the probability of an occurrence. For example, based on the previous illustration, if all the participants could predict their medical claims, only employees with claims in excess of $1,800 would purchase the insurance. Those with claims below that amount would be better off without the coverage. So the provider of the insurance would experience a shortfall in revenue to pay the cost of the claims. In the jargon of the insurance industry, employees would have "selected against" the plan.

Another way to illustrate the concern over adverse selection is in the area of vision coverage. Assume that an employer wants to cover vision expenses on an insured basis. Further, assume that the price of the insurance is $75, and the cost of frames and lenses, for example, is $300. As the need for vision care is very predictable, only those employees who expect to use the benefit will elect the coverage. In time, the plan will be covering only the bad risks (i.e., those who need glasses), so eventually the price of the insurance will equal the cost of the frames and lenses — $300. The principles of insurance will fail to operate.

Vision represents one of the most extreme examples of the potential for adverse selection to occur. The other area with significant potential is dental. The chief reason is that the risk the insurance is intended to cover is almost totally predictable. If the event the insurance protects against is less predictable, the potential for adverse selection diminishes proportionately. For example, at the opposite end of the spectrum in terms of predictability is AD&D coverage. The incidence of an accident occurring is considerably more difficult to predict, so the potential for adverse selection to arise to such an extent as to influence plan costs is relatively minimal.

In the middle of the spectrum in terms of the potential for adverse selection are supplemental medical, long-term disability, and group life. One of the reasons medical represents a medium, rather than extreme, possibility for adverse selection is the relative unpredictability of most claims, particularly for a family. Few employees know with certainty what their level of medical plan utilization will be in a given year. Further, decisions on medical as well as other benefit areas often are clouded by emotion. Many employees want the best medical protection for themselves and their families, whether or not the coverage represents a good deal financially. Finally, medical plan elections often are based on factors unrelated to the specific options offered — namely, the availability of coverage through a spouse's employer. For these kinds of reasons, adverse selection often turns out not to be the nemesis it first appears, simply because employees cannot make fully rational economic decisions in every case.

Another reason that the impact of adverse selection can be reasonably contained is that proper program design and option pricing further shrink its potential for occurring. For example, offering coverage for the most predictable types of expenses — such as vision, hearing, and sometimes dental — through health spending accounts — rather than on an insured-plan basis — effectively avoids any potential for adverse selection. But this type of "easy" solution is not always available or practical. Instead, adverse selection needs to be controlled through other means. The purpose of the next section is to explore the range of solutions available to employers for controlling adverse selection through restricting choice (design) and varying costs (pricing).

§ 16.3 CONTROLLING ADVERSE SELECTION

Adverse selection is dependent on two variables. One is the availability of choice, and the other is the predictability of the occurrence. For example, if a benefit is predictable, but choice is unavailable, no adverse selection will occur because of the absence of choice. On the other hand, if a benefit is available for selection in numerous forms and amounts, but occurrence of the benefit need is completely unpredictable, again, no adverse selection will result because of the absence of predictability. Therefore, the freer employees are to choose and the more accurate their ability to predict, the greater will be the concern over adverse selection.

If an employer's goal is to eradicate any potential for adverse selection, that objective can be achieved. However, the means would involve radically restricting the choices available to employees or prohibitively inflating the prices of the options. Instead, most employers elect to tolerate some amount of adverse selection, essentially as a necessary evil in flexible benefit programs. That is, they will use the levers of design and pricing to control the magnitude of the potential for adverse selection, but they will otherwise accept the risk of some modest increase in costs, because of the advantages to be gained from choice-making and the potential for savings in other aspects of the program. In medical and dental, for example, reduced utilization by employees electing options with higher deductibles and co-payment amounts may offset all or most of any cost increases resulting purely from unfavourable experience.

The following material examines the control that can be exerted over adverse selection through the design and pricing of specific benefit options.

DESIGN APPROACHES

As discussed previously, restricting choice reduces the effect of predictability and therefore limits the potential for adverse selection to arise. Numerous design approaches can be used to contain the potential for unfavourable experience, some of which are used more frequently in certain benefit areas than others. In general, however, these types of design approaches include the following:

- **Limit the frequency of choice.** Some employers limit the frequency with which employees may move in or out of specific benefit options (for example, every two or three years instead of annually). This type of design restriction is particularly effective in the more predictable benefit areas, such as vision or dental. In effect, the longer the period of coverage (or no coverage), the more difficult it is for the employee to predict expenses or specifically influence the timing of incurring those expenses.

- **Limit the degree of change.** Many plans restrict changes to one level of coverage per year. For example, an employee electing medical Option 2 in the first year would be permitted to increase to Option 3, decrease to Option 1 or make no change for the second year. Choices above Option 3 would be off limits for the second year.

  This staircase rule is very common in dental plans, to prevent employees from manipulating the system — without the rule, employees could elect the richest option in the first year and submit large claims, opt out in the second year and receive flexible credits, elect the rich option in the third year, and so on.

  A variation of the staircase rule is the "up staircase rule" that permits one increase per year but has no restrictions on decreases.

  These staircase rules make it difficult for an employee to make major changes in benefit levels based on knowledge of upcoming expenses.

  A number of flexible benefit programs combine the two approaches just described. They use the staircase rule and add the restriction that employees electing the richest option must remain in it for at least two or three years. This combined approach might be appropriate in supplemental medical, for example, if the richest option contains vision coverage with a two-year maximum benefit, while the other options have no vision care.

- **Level the spread between options.** In some coverage areas, such as dental or long-term disability, it may be appropriate to minimize the difference between high and low options to avoid extremes in employee elections. Many employers offer a core coverage specifically for this reason. Core coverage promotes a larger covered employee group, thereby spreading the financial risk over a wider population. Another variation, used most frequently in life insurance, is including maximum benefit limitations, such as fixed-dollar amounts or percentage-of-pay multiples. These types of restrictions serve to moderate the impact of adverse selection.

- **Require proof of insurability.** Many programs require proof of insurability before employees may increase coverage in long-term disability or life insurance.

- **Group certain coverages together.** Some flexible programs package certain options; for example, dental or vision coverage with supplemental medical. This has the effect of reducing the employee's ability to predict specific benefit plan utilization, and it also causes elections to be based on factors in addition to the employee's expectation of incurring a claim. The extreme example of this approach is the modular structure for a flexible benefit plan whereby all benefits are grouped together. This type of restriction has never been particularly popular, because the trade-off for minimizing adverse selection is reduced flexibility to employees.

- **Delay full payment.** Another approach is to delay or restrict full payment of benefits. In dental, for example, lower benefits might be paid in the first six months (or one year) following a period of no coverage. In the disability area, delayed enrolment might make benefits effective only one year after the date of the election or subject to a shorter maximum duration for a disability that occurs in the first year of coverage. These types of design restrictions help prevent the possibility of a "windfall" accruing to employees inclined to move in and out of coverage — and also discourage such patterns of election.

- **Offer a health spending account.** As mentioned earlier, some employers cover certain health-related expenses — such as vision and occasionally dental — only through a health spending account. This strategy reduces the insurance element from these types of benefits, thereby fixing the benefit cost and eliminating any potential for adverse selection.

- **Maintain parallel design.** Consistency in option design helps avoid differences in coverage that employees may be able to manipulate. For example, orthodontia coverage might be offered with each dental option and at the same level of plan payment. Similarly, vision, prescription drug coverage, and so forth, might be attached to each supplemental medical plan option. If the specific coverage pertains to a predictable benefit, it typically makes sense to include it consistently throughout all like options.

- **Test the program with employees.** Although not a design restriction, many employers test preliminary program design with employees. Testing may bring to light any potential weaknesses in the design that later could produce adverse selection. Any shortcomings in the proposed program then can be corrected before implementation. Separately, testing also can provide a firmer basis for the actual pricing of flexible program options.

Restrictions on choice are often waived when an employee experiences a life event, such as marriage or the birth of a child. In these cases, employees are often allowed to change coverage without proof of insurability or other restrictions. Since there is a clear reason for changing coverage, the risk of employees selecting against the plan in these cases is minimal.

Well-designed plan restrictions can be tremendously effective in controlling the potential for adverse selection. Since adverse selection is predicated on the choice and predictability of benefits, employers can selectively restrict choice and thereby reduce the potential for additional costs. However, design restrictions need to be used judiciously so as not to reduce excessively the flexibility and, therefore, the usefulness of choice-making programs to employees.

Unfortunately, there are many times when design restrictions are either inappropriate or insufficient as a defence against adverse selection. The other available lever is pricing.

PRICING ALTERNATIVES

As a general rule, anticipating adverse selection in the pricing of plan options is difficult to accomplish. In many respects, pricing, employee elections, and experience are interconnected to such an extent as to form almost a circular chain. That is, pricing decisions influence selection patterns, which in turn affect experience. Using experience to set prices influences employee elections so that prices are affected yet again. The circular flow — almost like a dog chasing its tail — is almost impossible to interrupt. However, some measure of relief can be achieved through a number of pricing strategies designed to limit the magnitude of the cost impact that may be produced by adverse selection.

Risk-Based Pricing

One approach is to price options in a way that reflects the expected risk or cost of the benefit. Consider, for example, age-related pricing in life insurance. Life insurance coverage is often charged to employees at the same flat rate regardless of age. However, the value of life insurance is distinctly age-related because the risk of death increases with age. If a flat rate is charged to everyone, older employees will recognize that the price for the coverage represents a bargain, while younger employees will find the rates inflated. As a result, a disproportionate number of older employees will select higher levels of coverage, which will increase the plan costs and eventually increase the price the company needs to charge employees. Younger employees will seek coverage outside the benefit program, because better deals exist elsewhere. Age grading the prices can help minimize the potential for adverse selection costs. It could also minimize adverse selection in long-term disability options, since the probability of disability also increases with age. However, almost all employers use the same percentage of pay for all ages under LTD plans.

Many employers reduce the risk even further by recognizing the employee's gender and smoker status in setting group life rates. These two factors can have a dramatic impact on costs — the rate for a male smoker might be three or four times that of a female non-smoker the same age. Employers who use age, gender, and smoker status are trying to duplicate the risk categories established for individual life insurance.

Why don't all group life plans recognize age, gender, and smoker status?

- Administering different premium schedules could increase the cost and complexity of the program.

- The employer may currently be using the same rate for all employees. Introducing risk-related rates would significantly increase the cost for some employees — often the employees who have the ultimate say in approving such a change.

- The risk to the employee of misrepresenting smoker status, whether deliberately or inadvertently, may be too high a price for the employer to pay. If a declared non-smoker, generally someone who has not smoked a cigarette in the past twelve months, dies and was actually a smoker, the insurance company may decide not to pay the benefit. In Quebec, the Superior Court ruled that Industrial Life Insurance Company did not have to pay $100,000 life insurance and $50,000 accidental death benefits to the beneficiary of Gilles Perron, who died in a 1985 car accident. Although the cause of death was unrelated to smoking, Perron knowingly misrepresented his status when applying for insurance. The Quebec Superior Court ruled that this voided his coverage.

- Group life premiums that are different for males and females may be prohibited at some future date on the grounds of discrimination. This happened in the United States in the early 1980s.

- Some employers feel "an employee is an employee" and the entire group should be treated equally and should be charged the same rate.

A similar risk-related pricing structure can be adopted in supplemental medical and dental through tiered pricing of the coverage. For example, employees covering several dependants typically would be inclined to select the richer plan options because of the greater probability of claims being incurred for a full family. To draw a cross-section of lower risks, for example, employee-only or employee-plus-spouse will require some differential in the pricing of the options. This is the reason many organizations use three or four coverage tiers based on family status for option pricing, rather than only one or two. Tiered pricing causes the relationships between options to be more realistic and, therefore, it reduces the potential for employees to select against a particular plan based on family size.

Employer Subsidization

Another relatively straightforward strategy for mitigating the effects of adverse selection is employer subsidization of the option prices. For example, an employer with two dental options may want to encourage broad participation in the plan. Subsidized pricing can make the coverage a "better deal" for more employees, thus encouraging participation. Higher participation will help spread the risk, thereby diminishing the potential for adverse selection.

Anticipating Adverse Selection in Pricing

However, even with age- or risk-related pricing or employer subsidies, an underlying difficulty with adverse selection is anticipating actual experience. Only rarely does expected experience precisely match actual utilization, especially in medical and dental. This problem is not unique to flexible programs, but it is heightened by the ability of the employee to choose levels of coverage.

Consider an example. Assume the employer offers three dental plan options: the current plan (now costing $100 per month) plus two lesser-valued coverages worth 80 per cent and 50 per cent, respectively, of the current plan. Pure actuarial pricing might suggest that the option price tags be set at $100, $80, and $50. One decision the employer will face is whether to anticipate the potential variance in claims experience and adjust the price tags accordingly or to operate the flexible program in the first year using these unadjusted price tags.

Adjustment of the price tags for anticipated experience can be accomplished in several ways. One approach is to reduce the reward to employees for opting down by loading the prices of the lesser-valued options. That is, instead of charging $80 and $50 for the lower coverages, the prices might be set at $100, $90 and $70. This solution would diminish the potential for over-rewarding the presumably good risks who elect lesser coverage, although at the expense of reduced flexibility to employees. Moreover, in practice, what is likely to happen under this approach is that more employees will remain clustered in the rich current plan because the incentive to consider the other options is diminished, rather than moving to plans with more cost-efficient designs, thereby thwarting cost-management objectives for the program.

A second alternative would be to push all of the cost of expected adverse selection (say, 2 per cent of dental cost) into the highest-valued option, but keep the prices for the other options at the same level. If half the employees are expected to remain in the high option, this might require about a 4 per cent increase in the high-option prices to recoup a 2 per cent total dental program cost. Prices under this strategy would be set at $104 for the current plan, and $80 and $50 for the other options. All of the cost of adverse selection has been added to the price of the highest-valued option — so employees effectively cannot buy back their prior coverage without paying more.

Further, to avoid paying more for the prior plan, a greater-than-expected number of employees will likely be driven to the lower-valued options, thereby escalating the price for those options. However, the net effect, most likely, will be positive,

Table 16.2
Adverse Selection

Option	Per Cent of Employees Electing	Actuarial Value	Actual Experience	Effect of Adverse Selection
High	45	$91	$108	+19%
Intermediate	49	78	63	−19
Low	6	25	22	−12
Average monthly cost		$80.67	$80.79	+0.1%

in that these are the options with higher deductibles and co-payment amounts and other cost management features. Ironically, some added cost savings are likely to have been achieved as an unintended result of the concern over adverse selection — but at the risk of employee dissatisfaction over the increased cost to purchase the prior plan.

A variation on this strategy would be to spread the cost of the anticipated adverse selection over the price of all the options; for example, increasing the price of each option by 2 per cent. Here the original relative relationships between the plans have been maintained and greater equity has been achieved by spreading the cost of adverse selection produced by offering choice to all employees, but a similar problem exists with the ability of employees to buy back the former coverage.

The practical difficulties with anticipating adverse selection incline some employers to use unadjusted pricing — at least in the first year of a flexible program's operation. The prices are set at the pure actuarial level and adjusted only after the combined effect of adverse selection costs and utilization savings are better known. Under this type of scenario, it would not be unusual to see expected versus actual experience on the order of magnitude shown in Table 16.2.

This example is based on the actual experience of one organization. It illustrates an important issue that arises with adverse selection. That is, the effect of adverse selection will be felt disproportionately across the options, producing both positive and negative results. The actual claims experience under any one option, particularly in medical and dental, will likely vary from what would be expected under a completely random election process. But claims experience that is greater than expected in one option will usually be offset in full or in part by claims experience that is lower than expected in other options, so the impact on the aggregate experience of the program is likely to be modest. In Example 16.2, the total impact of adverse selection is an increase in the average plan cost of 12 cents per month, or about 0.1 per cent.

Table 16.3 illustrates another organization's experience. While the effect of adverse selection is more pronounced for each option than shown in Example 16.2,

Table 16.3
Adverse Selection

Option	Per Cent of Employees Electing	Actuarial Value	Actual Experience	Effect of Adverse Selection
High	26	$107	$190	+78%
Intermediate	70	100	72	−28
Low	4	60	12	−80
Average monthly cost		$100.22	$100.28	+0.1%

the overall cost of adverse selection produced only a similar 0.1 per cent increase in claims.

It should be noted also that higher-than-expected claims experience may not always be negative. That is, on occasion, an employer may want to encourage adverse selection to occur naturally as a means of phasing out an option. This might be the case in situations where the highest-valued option is considered too rich, but the employer is concerned about the employee relations impact of eliminating the option by decree. Instead, the employer might keep the pricing of each option on a self-supporting basis. Over time, migration of the heaviest users to the option will cause the price to rise prohibitively, in which case the option will have priced itself out of the market.

SUMMARY

To summarize, adverse selection in choice-making programs does not represent a benign influence on plan costs. It is an issue that requires careful attention and consideration. The point is, however, that numerous strategies and techniques can be employed to limit its potentially damaging effects. In combination, the levers of program design and option pricing can be activated in such a manner as to shrink most of the potential for adverse selection to a manageable level.

Seventeen

Insurance Considerations

A typical flexible benefit program contains many benefit options that require involvement by an insurance carrier. Life insurance, short-term disability, long-term disability, medical, and dental options often will be underwritten for smaller employers or administered by a carrier for larger organizations.

§ 17.1 INSURANCE PROVIDERS

The Canadian insurance marketplace has changed considerably over the last two decades, primarily as a result of mergers and acquisitions. Figure 17.1 illustrates the consolidation of group insurance carriers, resulting in the domination of the marketplace by three major group insurers.

All three of these large insurance carriers (along with many of the firms they have acquired) have many years of experience underwriting benefits and adjudicating claims for flexible benefit plans.

In addition, there are several other carriers in the Canadian marketplace that provide insurance services for traditional group benefit plans, but in many cases have chosen not to underwrite or provide claims administration for larger or more complex flexible benefit plan designs. These insurers include:

- Blue Cross organizations: Atlantic Blue Cross, Medavie, Alberta Blue Cross, Pacific Blue Cross;
- Desjardins;
- Green Shield;

Figure 17.1
Consolidation of Group Insurance Carriers

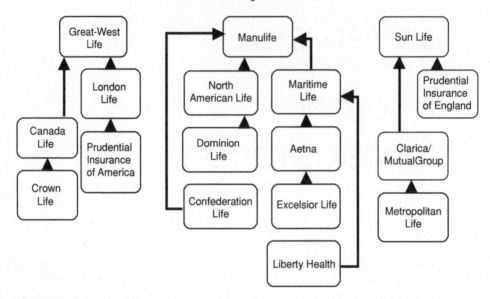

- Industrial Alliance;
- SSQ; and
- Standard Life.

It is likely that some of these insurers will enhance their claims payment systems in the coming years to accommodate flexible benefit plan designs so they can compete more directly with the three largest carriers.

The major implications of insurance carrier marketplace consolidation for plan sponsors include:

- The need to develop a strong working relationship with their current insurer because of the limited number of alternative carriers from which to choose;
- The reluctance of some carriers to accommodate unique plan designs;
- The impact on insurer fees and other charges arising from only a few insurers competing for plan sponsors' business; and
- The advantages of using carriers other than the big three in some circumstances.

The major implications for the remaining insurance carriers are:

- The challenges to continued growth;
- Market/product differentiation;
- Use of technology to generate efficiencies; and
- More creative plan design and adjudication capabilities.

In addition, the smaller group carriers will need to decide whether to competitively challenge the three largest carriers in the area of supporting flexible benefit plans.

It is interesting to note that most of the major U.S. and/or global insurers have left the Canadian market to Canadian-based insurers. This is a reflection of the maturity and competitiveness of the Canadian group insurance market. This situation has implications for U.S.-based employers that would like to leverage their insurer arrangements to obtain cost advantages for their Canadian operations: most U.S.-based carriers are either not licensed to underwrite in Canada and/or do not have reciprocal arrangements in place with a Canadian insurer. An alternative approach to leverage a U.S. and/or global insurance carrier affiliation is to utilize a feature known as multi-national pooling. Most of the Canadian insurers are aligned with one of several multi-national pools that exist to underwrite insurance across many countries on behalf of a single employer.

§ 17.2 THE INSURER'S PERSPECTIVE

INSURANCE RISK CONCERNS

Some appreciation of the carrier's financial risk will help in understanding the insurer's perspective on flexible benefit programs. To a carrier, an employer who designs a benefit program (whether flexible or otherwise) and then tells someone else to insure it is attempting to play poker with a stranger's money. The "player" organization risks little, while the stakes are high for the "stranger." Although this may not be an issue for large employers (who typically self-fund many of their benefits), it is a concern for smaller employers who insure most or all benefits.

As background, it may be useful to discuss the three universal methods of insuring group benefit programs, whether they are traditional designs or flexible benefit designs: pooled, experience-rated, and partial insurance (including self-insurance).

Pooled insurance is the most familiar concept. Auto insurance is pooled. A driver is placed in a pool with others sharing similar characteristics. The experience of the pool influences the rates the individual is charged. At year-end, no premium is returned, even if a particular driver avoided having an accident, and neither is any deficit applied to the policy of a driver who had an accident. So the slate is wiped clean each year. In the next year, however, rates might increase if the driver who had the accident is reassigned to the pool with the one-accident drivers. Pooled group insurance of this kind is typically used for organizations that have 200 or fewer employees. In this situation, the employer purchasing the insurance is required to pay only the annual premium, whether there are any claims or not. Each year the insurer resets the premium, depending upon how the overall pool of premiums received versus claims and expenses performed. Competitive pressures from the marketplace also have a bearing on the premium rate the insurer chooses to set for the next year.

Experience-rated insurance requires a full financial accounting at the end of each plan year. If any premium is left after the insurer deducts all claims, allocates reserves, and recovers all expenses, the employer receives that difference. Conversely, if a deficit occurs, that amount is charged interest, carried forward, and recovered by the insurer either as a lump sum or, more commonly, through premium increases in future years. Although all deficits potentially can be recovered, an insurer will have two incentives to avoid deficit situations: (1) initial loss of cash flow, and (2) possible termination by the employer of the policy prior to full deficit recovery. This kind of insurance is the most common group benefit financing method.

Partial insurance is a generic term for any arrangement by which the employer self-insures the coverage up to a predetermined limit; above the limit, the carrier's liability begins. The limit might be by claim, by individual, by total-claims-expected-per-year, or some other variation. Partial insurance is quite common in long-term disability, for example, where the employer pays the claims for, say, the first two or three years of an employee's disability. For claims that extend beyond that time period, the benefit is paid by the insurer. Another example would include a stop-loss arrangement where the employer would self-insure all claims up to a predetermined limit (called the stop-loss or pooling limit), say $10,000, after which any further claims for the year would be paid by the insurer. The insurer would charge a premium rate for accepting the risk that claims may exceed the stop-loss limit. This approach is commonly used for medical plans where there is a risk of unexpected large drug claims that a company may wish to insure against. The risk to an insurance carrier under a partial insurance arrangement is very similar to the risk under any other insurance arrangement. Large or excessive claims will trigger deficits. Partial insurance arrangements may be experience-rated or pooled, so any deficits may or may not be recoverable in future years.

In each case involving insurance, then, the carrier is at risk to some degree and will seek to protect itself by influencing plan design, requiring evidence of insurability for especially risky benefits, or increasing rates to avoid deficit positions.

The four primary influences on risk are:

- **Volume,** or number of participants in the benefit plan;
- **Liability,** or size of potential claim reimbursement;
- **Probability,** or predictability of a claim occurrence; and
- **Selection patterns,** namely, the availability of choice when compared to the predictability of the occurrence — high users will tend to select the richest plan.

For example, a $200,000 life insurance benefit is not a high risk for a carrier insuring a 5,000-employee organization, if only 100 employees are eligible for this benefit based on pay. The total annual life insurance premium from this organization will easily absorb the one or two large claims that might occur in a year. The same benefit for a fifty-employee organization with a much smaller annual premium would be considered risky.

To explain the effect of selection patterns, consider the 5,000-employee organization with a flexible benefit program under which all employees are eligible to purchase a $200,000 benefit. If only ten people do so — who are all 64 years old and perhaps not in the best of health — and the other employees take little or no coverage, the total annual premium is far less than $200,000. This is an extreme example, but it serves to illustrate what a carrier will recognize as adverse selection and, therefore, potential risk. These and other more subtle variations are types of risk potential that appear in various aspects of flexible programs. (See also Chapter 16 for ways to minimize this type of risk.)

INSURER ADMINISTRATIVE CONCERNS

Insurance carriers provide most employers with a substantial number of administrative services:

- Participant eligibility maintenance and benefit verification;
- Life, disability, and health claims processing;
- Premium/fee statement preparation; and
- Conversion policy maintenance.

Administrative concerns that might result from flexible benefit programs typically would arise from the eligibility maintenance and claims processing functions.

Not all carriers have participant eligibility maintenance and benefit verification systems designed to handle flexible benefit plans; however, most carriers have sophisticated computerized systems in place that can readily process almost any medical or dental claims that may be generated by a flexible benefit program. The function of processing claims for multiple-option medical programs, for example, should not even require a systems change. Carriers simply use the same procedures required to process different plans for different divisions of the same company — a capability built into all systems years ago.

The carrier's systems specialists are generally co-operative when it comes to making some changes to adapt to unusual plan features and/or creating file formats to accept participant eligibility information. Of course, the size of an organization will influence the carrier's interest in customizing systems and procedures. The 100-employee organization, for example, probably will have to accept the limitations of its carrier, simplify the plan, or attempt to select an alternate carrier with a more flexible system.

Inflexibility of a computer system, however, does not in itself void a carrier's ability to administer a particular program. Since manual intervention may be required for any client's unusual program features, this approach is available, at least as a backup measure, to the carrier. However, manual intervention tends to slow down claims payment, increase administration costs, and increase the risk of inaccurate reimbursements or incorrect tracking of plan limits.

A good flexible benefit program should be designed to meet an employer's specific needs and objectives and should not be unduly restricted by systems limitations. However, some preliminary planning regarding possible administrative snags could reduce the amount of time-consuming carrier negotiations or the number of manual intervention situations that might be required of a carrier with a less sophisticated claims payment system.

§ 17.3 AVOIDING POSSIBLE INSURER ADMINISTRATIVE STUMBLING BLOCKS

Although an employer designs a flexible benefit program to meet organizational objectives, designing around the major carrier concerns can often be accomplished without significant compromises. Creativity in plan design can ameliorate insurance carrier concerns in a number of areas. The following design discussion is organized by major benefit area.

SUPPLEMENTAL MEDICAL

Adverse Selection

In an insured or partially insured situation, the insurance carrier's objective in underwriting supplemental medical coverage is to rate the benefit plan options to anticipate any adverse selection that might occur. That is, the high users may tend to pick the highest coverage possible, and the low users may tend to opt out or choose the least coverage possible. If this occurs, it results in less spreading of the risk and a higher cost per employee in the richest option than in a situation where all employees participate in a single plan. The carrier will typically reflect some expectation of adverse selection in the rates charged to the employer.

Methods available to the plan sponsor to minimize adverse selection are outlined in Chapter 16. In addition, that chapter discusses alternative ways of developing the option prices that are communicated to employees — which may differ from those developed by the carrier.

Core versus Opt-Out Provision

Insurers typically will be much more comfortable underwriting risk when employees are provided a minimum level of coverage. Core coverage promotes a larger covered employee population, thereby allowing the insurer to spread the risk over a larger financial base. Allowing an opt-out provision in a plan could increase an underwriter's concern over adverse selection. However, if an employer's current non-flexible program requires employees to pay for coverage and therefore allows opt-outs, inclusion of an opt-out provision will probably not substantially change employee participation under the flexible benefit program.

The core versus opt-out concern also arises in other benefit areas, but it is most pronounced in health care (supplemental medical, dental, and vision).

Evidence of Insurability

Occasionally, insurers will require evidence of insurability in the form of a health statement before covering someone who previously opted out of coverage. In these cases, coverage can be denied or restricted by lower limits to employees or dependants based on their health statement responses, or a physical may be required before coverage is approved. Although this approach is an effective safeguard against adverse selection, it also restricts employee choice-making and results in some administrative difficulties. This approach is rare in Canada, because the financial risk to the insurer is much lower than in the United States, where requiring evidence of insurability is more common.

Claims Administration

Stumbling blocks might arise in claims administration if the employer designs an unusual option that cannot be easily programmed into the insurer's claims-processing computer system. These snags are not directly related to the introduction of medical choices, but they might occur because specific medical plan provisions were changed in the course of the flexible program design process. Simple changes made to an employer's plan in order to create options (in terms of deductibles and co-insurance, for example), and some of the more common flex design innovations, typically do not affect the insurer's ability to process claims electronically. For example, most carriers can handle multiple co-insurance levels within the same plan (say, 80 per cent drugs, 100 per cent other charges, or 80 per cent for drugs on a formulary and 60 per cent for all other drugs) without manual intervention. Most of the group insurance carriers offer automated administration systems for health spending accounts.

However, other less typical changes that might require manual intervention include:

- Non-standard benefits or benefit limits: for example, co-ordination of benefits provisions that limit reimbursement to the plan co-insurance level, such as 80 per cent, and not the more typical 100 per cent reimbursement level.

- Certain cost-containment features, such as unique drug formularies or deductibles. These features tend to be administered by pharmacy benefit managers (PBMs) contracted or operated by the carrier and must be incorporated in conjunction with a direct-pay drug card, although some carriers can also administer them on a reimbursement basis (with PBM assistance).

- Combined supplemental medical and drug deductibles and maximums where a PBM adjudicates drug claims on a direct-pay basis and an insurer adjudicates all other medical claims. Some carriers require manual intervention to administer combined medical and drug maximums/deductibles, as two systems are being used (e.g., if the plan includes a $50 deductible for all expenses, manual runs are done daily to ensure that the deductible is not exceeded). Other carriers cannot administer them at all. This problem can be avoided by designing the plan without common deductibles/maximums for drugs and other medical expenses.

- Out-of-pocket limits in the plan. These features limit the individual's total exposure through deductibles and co-insurance to a predetermined amount, say $500. Some carriers can administer these maximums without manual intervention, but the problems described above can occur where there is PBM involvement.

- Three or more coverage categories instead of two: for example, employee, single parent, couple, and family. Carriers can adjudicate claims by category, but some have difficulty tracking and reporting claims by category. Instead, standard claim reports tend to split out claims by employee, spouse, and other dependants. Claim reporting by category is required when repricing the plan.

- Different benefits for dependants (e.g., 90 per cent co-insurance for employees, 80 per cent co-insurance for dependants).

These administrative difficulties should not discourage employers from adopting these provisions, but employers should be aware that some slight changes in design might enable insurers to avoid manual intervention. Audits of insurance carrier claim payments show that errors and average claims turnaround time are greater in situations where manual intervention is used.

DENTAL

Adverse Selection

The financial effect of adverse selection on dental plans is typically greater than on supplemental medical plans, because dental expenses are much more predictable than medical expenses.

Claims Administration

As with flexible medical options, the mere offering of choices in dental creates few inherent claims administration problems. However, there are certain plan provisions that might create stumbling blocks.

One provision that might cause administrative concern to a carrier is providing different benefits for dependants (e.g., 90 per cent co-insurance for employees, 80 per cent co-insurance for dependants).

Employers might find alternative approaches to cost containment that will be as effective (or more effective) than this type of limitation, without the administrative difficulties.

Carriers continue to expand their automated claims-processing capabilities with the growth and expansion of flexible benefit plans. For example, it used to be difficult for carriers to administer different claim frequencies within plans, such as different recall periods for adults and children. However, now most can automatically adjudicate this type of plan design provision.

Orthodontia

Because orthodontic expenses are probably the most predictable and discretionary of all dental expenses, the risk of adverse selection is greater than for other dental procedures. As a result, most plans provide employees with orthodontia reimbursement only when combined with one or more of the other dental choices and occasionally through health spending accounts.

It is even more rare to see a stand-alone orthodontia option than a stand-alone vision care benefit (see the next page for a discussion on vision care options), in part because the coverage maxima are higher: for example, $2,500 lifetime for orthodontia versus $200 per twenty-four months for vision care.

Network Dental Plans

Network dental plans have gained acceptance in the U.S. over the last decade, but not in Canada. They are provided by organizations that have negotiated reduced fees with selected panels of dentists. Expenses are usually reimbursed in full, except for small co-payments.

A network dental plan could be an attractive addition to choices in dental, especially in a situation where the employer has chosen to offer only one standard dental option. The dental plan could result in substantially higher benefits to employees.

Despite these advantages, however, network plans have not gained any acceptance among practitioners or patients in Canada. This situation may change, however, as dental cost containment becomes a more urgent priority for Canadian employers.

In the meantime, carriers are not in a position to administer a network arrangement if a company wants to incorporate one in its flexible benefit plan unless the plan design follows a common approach.

VISION

Adverse Selection

Because vision care expenses are even more predictable and discretionary than dental expenses, the risk of adverse selection is greater. However, the greater risk is offset, to some extent, by relatively low benefits payments for vision care. As a result of the risk, some employers choose to provide employees with vision care reimbursement only through health spending accounts.

Alternatively, employers who prefer to offer a vision care benefit may create a core vision plan or include a vision benefit in all of the supplemental medical options. Another alternative would be to include vision under several, but not all, of the medical options. The prices of these plans should reflect the adverse selection cost. This cost is reduced by restricting movement in or out of the options. A two- or three-year enrolment or restricting movement to one level up or down per year will accomplish this. Or, the vision options could be packaged with dental options to reduce such movement, although this is not a common design.

LIFE INSURANCE

Adverse Selection

Insurers are not typically as concerned about adverse selection in life insurance as they are in health care benefits. The total costs are usually less, the predictability of claims much smaller, and the experience they have in dealing with choice-making plans in life insurance is much greater.

Evidence of Insurability

Insurance carrier underwriters will have some concerns, although modest, in the area of life benefit selection at the initial enrolment. Under many flexible benefit plans, the employee is no longer provided with employer-paid basic life and given the opportunity to buy additional coverage. Instead, credits are allotted by the employer, and the employee is permitted to select as much coverage as he or she needs, often including the opportunity to take very low levels of coverage. This potential volatility and/or reduction in total coverage may promote conservative underwriting practices, unless the program is properly presented and priced.

In particular, a carrier usually will wish to impose evidence-of-insurability requirements for benefits exceeding a certain level. This level is typically based on employer size or total anticipated life volume. In a 1,000-employee company with a maximum $1 million lifetime benefit, employees might be required to submit evidence of insurability for amounts exceeding $600,000, or a specific multiple of annual pay, say two times pay.

If possible, it is often preferable to avoid such an evidence-of-insurability approach. A denial of benefits may result in a reselection of choices by the employee. The final denial might not be communicated by the carrier until after the program has gone into effect, resulting in a reprocessing of that employee's election form and possibly retroactive adjustment to payroll deductions. Where an employee is waiting for approval past the program's effective date, care should be taken when communicating choices on the confirmation statements. If the statement shows the higher elected amount, a comment should be included stating that the full coverage will be effective after carrier approval of the evidence. If the statement shows the lower amount until the higher amount is approved, an employee will not see the full level of payroll deductions that will ultimately be in force. The number of instances where evidence has not been approved by the plan-effective date can be reduced by negotiating performance guarantees with the carrier, starting the evidence process early, having a medical underwriter on site, and/or using a short-form medical questionnaire.

When transitioning to a flexible benefit plan, carriers are usually willing to "grandfather" any large benefits being carried by employees under the current program without evidence of insurability. If that specific large amount is not exactly available under the new plan design, with some discussion, carriers are usually willing to "grandfather" up to the next higher option level.

Another item of concern for some carriers is the issue of open enrolment — employees being allowed to choose any level of coverage in the first year of the plan, with no evidence requirement. Open enrolment can make first-year administration much easier for the employer, particularly when moving to a new carrier, because it eliminates the need to collect medical evidence forms from every employee who increases coverage. If a carrier will not allow an open enrolment, a compromise, such as allowing open enrolment except where increases have previously been declined, allowing coverage up to, say, three times pay without evidence, or allowing a one-level increase over the current coverage, can frequently be reached.

Dependant Life

Some insurance carriers restrict the maximum spouse's life insurance benefit to a certain percentage — for example, 50 or 100 per cent — of the employee's life benefit. Most carriers, however, no longer have such a requirement. Instead, they impose evidence of insurability requirements similar to those summarized above.

Care should be taken if using a U.S. insurer to underwrite the life insurance portion of a flexible benefit plan. Considerations include whether or not the U.S. carrier is licensed to underwrite in Canada, and the fact that some U.S. states have maximum dependant life benefit amounts (e.g., $5,000), while others restrict dependant benefits to a percentage of the employee's benefit.

LONG-TERM DISABILITY

As in other benefit areas, insurers will want to spread the risk associated with long-term disability benefits across as large a population as possible. A typical stumbling block that occurs with disability is the misunderstanding of a flexible program's funding for plans using a credit-based structure. Without a full understanding of the overall flexible program structure, a carrier's underwriter might see a completely voluntary long-term disability plan and rate it using large adverse selection margins, assuming the high risks will be more likely to choose the coverage. In reality, the program may be designed to provide each employee with enough credits to purchase at least a minimum level of long-term disability coverage. This mechanism does not guarantee that all employees will opt for the coverage, but participation in the option will be substantially greater than enrolment in a purely voluntary plan, where the employee pays the full cost of the coverage.

Some insurers are concerned about their risk in plans offering taxable and tax-free long-term disability benefits. As discussed in Chapter 6, the taxable plan is funded by the employer, while the tax-free plan is funded by the employee using payroll deductions.

To maintain the tax-free status of the payroll deduction plan, it is important that no employer money be used to fund it. This causes a problem where the experience in this tax-free plan is poor and the insurer wants to increase the premium. If the experience in the taxable plan is favourable, the resulting taxable plan premiums would be lower, and this could drive many employees away from the tax-free plan and into the taxable plan. This would make it impossible for the insurer to recover the deficiency in the tax-free plan. To prevent this, the insurer may be tempted to use any surplus in the employer-paid taxable plan to offset a deficit in the employee-paid tax-free plan. Such a transfer would jeopardize the tax-free status of the employee-paid plan, since this employer-paid plan surplus would be considered an employer contribution. The concern of the insurer is mitigated when a high proportion of employees elect the tax-free plan.

One additional possible administrative and/or adverse selection problem concerns the status of employees already receiving LTD benefits when a new plan is introduced. These employees would continue to receive the disability benefits they had already qualified for, but employers should decide in advance which other benefit coverages apply (e.g., medical, dental) to these employees until they return to active work. Allowing them to elect new coverage creates a potential adverse selection issue, as well as enrolment and communication challenges. Another approach is to keep them covered under the old pre-flexible plan or automatically "map" them into the new plan options that are closest to their pre-flexible benefit plan. In either case, this should be built into the administration system and communicated to the carrier and employees.

§ 17.4 WORKING WITH THE INSURER

In order to work effectively with an insurance carrier on installation of a flexible benefit program, the employer needs to consider issues related to communication, negotiation, and implementation. Many insurance carriers have implemented flexible benefits for their own staff, and a number insure and administer flexible benefit plans for a large number of their clients. While this experience has increased carrier understanding of how flexible plans work, there are still varying capabilities and interpretations on design, pricing, administration, and reporting.

COMMUNICATING WITH THE INSURER

Early notification to an insurer that a flexible benefit plan is being considered could help avoid future complications. Carriers who have experience with flexible benefit programs will have insights to offer regarding the interaction of flexible options with their own systems, procedures, and underwriting guidelines. During this initial notification and discussion, an employer might recognize the need to solicit proposals from other carriers, if the existing carrier's capabilities are insufficient.

Another objective of early notification is to create an atmosphere of openness, where carrier input is sought and fostered. The carrier representatives — underwriters, systems analysts, claims supervisors, contract specialists — will begin to share in the team approach to flexible benefits, enhancing the chances for a smooth implementation.

In some situations, the line between the insurer's constructive input and inflexibility may be unclear. Employers should design flexible benefit programs to meet their own needs, while recognizing that some concessions to insurance carrier underwriting or administration limitations might be necessary, particularly for the smaller employer.

NEGOTIATING WITH THE CARRIER

Carrier negotiations on flexible benefit programs typically involve one or more of the following issues:

- Insurance rates
- Benefit limitations
- Administrative procedures.

As discussed earlier, insurers might view the flexible benefit program as a risk, re-sulting in conservative underwriting — that is, high rates. To temper the risk, the carrier might wish to limit the maximum benefits available or require evidence of insurability for some benefits. Also, carrier systems limitations or standard proce-dures might inhibit the flexible benefit program design or administration.

All of these issues are negotiable, to some degree. Prior to negotiating any issue, the employer should estimate the size of the "bargaining chips" involved. That is, how motivated is the carrier to accommodate the employer and retain the account? Any or all of the following factors can influence the insurer's perspective:

- **Size of organization.** A large client represents lower risks and higher prof-itability to an insurer. However, the employer's size might be viewed in more than one way, based on the company's geographic location and on the carrier's current book of business in the office that would be handling the account.
- **Presence of a traditional benefit program.** A company with a small number of employees in a flexible plan might be very attractive to an insurer, if the company also sponsors a large traditional benefit program for a different group of employees, for example, a union group.
- **Life insurance volume.** Life insurance continues to be a profit leader for insurance companies, so substantial life benefits make any package extremely attractive to a carrier.
- **Employer prestige.** An insurance carrier may enhance its image in a commu-nity by including the most respected local organizations on its list of clients.

With this understanding of the carrier's perspective, the employer can discuss issues openly and honestly, recognizing that some concessions might be necessary.

SELECTING A NEW CARRIER

Many employers can maintain their existing insurers when a flexible benefit pro-gram is adopted. However, sometimes, "irreconcilable differences" require that an employer's existing carrier be replaced. These circumstances can arise in the following kinds of situations:

- The insurer's services or rates have been uncompetitive, and a change in car-riers would have been considered regardless of the proposed program design.
- The employer learns the insurer is not committed to underwriting flexible benefit plans. Examples of a lack of commitment include unreasonable pricing of flexible options, strict adverse selection controls, and high fees to administer the program. One measure of capability and commitment is whether or not the insurer provides a flexible benefit plan for its own employees.

- After some preliminary discussions with the insurer, the employer finds that the insurer's systems or services are unable to adapt to flexible benefits.

- The employer uses two or more insurers to underwrite the current benefit package and determines that consolidation of all benefits under one carrier will simplify flexible benefit administration.

- The insurer displays a lack of understanding of flexible plans. It is important that the entire insurance company team understands how flexible benefit plans operate, from the service representative to the administrative and underwriting staff. Problems can occur when underwriters apply traditional methods to analyse flexible plan experience. For example, an insurance company analysed the first-year enrolment patterns under three long-term disability options (minimum coverage of 50 per cent) and proposed the following rates:

Option	Benefit	Rate
1	50%	$0.75 per $100 of pay
2	60%	$0.53 per $100 of pay
3	70%	$0.61 per $100 of pay

- The underwriter reviewed the characteristics of employees enrolling in each plan separately and, since older employees tended to take the 50 per cent option, proposed a rate that was higher than under the other two options. The results did not make sense when the plan was viewed as a whole, and if implemented, would actually increase the insurer's risk. Anyone in the 50 per cent option would re-enroll in the 60 per cent option for the lower premium. Thus, the older employees would be covered for a larger benefit at a lower cost. The proposed pricing structure would cause, not prevent, adverse selection.

- The flaw in logic that generated these rates was the failure to recognize that everyone has a 50 per cent benefit — the employees in the 60 per cent option have 50 per cent, plus 10 per cent additional, while those electing 70 per cent have 50 per cent, plus 20 per cent additional. The premium for the 50 per cent plan should reflect the characteristics for all employees, while the premium for the higher options should be the cost of the 50 per cent option, plus the cost for the additional 10 per cent or 20 per cent. The cost for the additional amounts should reflect the demographics of those electing the 60 and 70 per cent options.

Definitions and assumptions change from carrier to carrier. The employer must ensure that the carrier representatives have a clear understanding of the program as designed by the employer. Searching for a replacement in conjunction with implementing a flexible program may not be the best timing for the employer, but in certain situations may be warranted.

IMPLEMENTING THE PROGRAM

Insurers have had considerable experience implementing new benefit plans under traditional benefit programs, for both existing and new clients. Except for any unusual flexible program details created by the addition of choice, the administrative work will be handled by the insurer just like any other new program. Assuming that the employer and the carrier have planned the implementation process well and assigned project completion dates, the implementation will proceed smoothly.

However, to increase the likelihood of a smooth transition, the following is a short checklist of carrier administrative responsibilities that need to be addressed:

Systems

- Adapt and/or capture employee eligibility data to include new benefit choices, as well as how that data is reported on the electronic file from the client, third-party administrator, or the carrier's own flexible benefit administration systems.
- Program claims payment system with new benefit options and plan provisions.
- Establish the appropriate categories for maintaining and reporting enrolment and claims experience.

Employee Communication

- Prepare any required explanatory and enrolment materials and new cards (e.g., identification, direct-pay drug, emergency medical).
- Enhance the Web site to provide access to information on the various options and claims histories (particularly health spending account balances), as well as access to appropriate claim forms.

Contracts

- Amend policies to reflect new benefits.

Final rates must be established by the insurer before the employer begins communicating the program to employees. This timing is sometimes an issue. Because of communication, enrolment, and systems requirements, an employer might need final rates between three and six months before the effective date. This issue of rate delivery timing should be addressed in preliminary discussions with the insurer. Rates for self-funded coverages, of course, can be developed at any time, since insurer involvement is not an issue, other than for administrative fees, if they are to be incorporated in the plan pricing.

REPRICING/RENEWALS

Renewal rates for flexible benefit plans are also required earlier than for a traditional plan, often four to six months before the plan anniversary date. The timing of the renewal process should be negotiated in advance and the carrier should be clear on the appropriate categories required for repricing.

In the first year of a flexible benefit plan, this advance rate renewal requirement can be an issue for insured benefits, since very little claims experience under the new plan is available to assist in setting the renewal rates. In some cases, it might be better to negotiate a two- or three-year rate guarantee when establishing the initial pricing, so that when the renewal occurs, there is sufficient claims experience available to appropriately determine any rate adjustments. It must be recognized that a rate guarantee may raise the rate slightly, so this should be taken into consideration, along with the specific funding arrangements, when deciding whether to negotiate any guarantees.

In an insured plan, price tags often (but not always) match the premium charged by the carrier for medical and dental plans. Where they are the same, care must be taken to ensure that the carrier has set the premium rates correctly. The plan's experience must be viewed as a whole rather than by individual option, so that employees are not driven away from the highest options.

THE CARRIER AS FULL-SERVICE ADMINISTRATOR

Insurance carriers' primary focus has traditionally been to provide claims administration and insurance. With the growth in flexible benefit plans, a number of insurers now offer ongoing administrative support for their clients' flexible benefit plans — election tracking, payroll reporting, taxable benefit calculation and reporting, eligibility reporting, and so forth (see Chapter 21 for a complete discussion of flexible benefits administration). This additional level of service now offers plan sponsors a choice besides using internal systems or a third-party/outsourcing provider to administer the plan.

In most cases, the insurers have added this administrative capability more to meet client demands than as a specific business or growth opportunity. As a result, many of the operational elements tend to be standardized rather than being able to accommodate a variety of unique, client-specific plan design requirements. When deciding whether to use an insurer as the administrator, employers must consider:

- How unique the plan needs to be versus accommodating the insurer's administrative requirements;
- The potential loss of any negotiating power when the insurer establishing the premium rates and operating costs is also the administrator — if a change

in insurer later becomes necessary, a change in administrator will also be required;

- The insurer's experience or systems — most have just entered the administrative arena and/or have newly updated systems; and

- How many similar clients they provide administrative support to and what the level of service/satisfaction has been for those clients.

Part Five

Communication

Eighteen

Communicating with Employees

§ 18.1 INTRODUCTION

Even with the most carefully crafted design and the most efficient administration system, the level of success of a flexible benefit program depends on one uncontrollable element: people. Benefits, after all, are for employees.

Whether it's the launch of a new flexible program, the introduction of changes to an existing program, or an annual re-enrolment, employee reaction will determine how well the flexible program meets its objectives, and that reaction will be shaped during the implementation process.

Today, most employees are aware of the concept of benefit choice-making and in some environments have even lobbied employers for a flexible program. Still, when actually faced with making decisions in areas they may never even have thought about before, the mere fact of the change can trigger all the emotions associated with protecting the status quo: fear, uncertainty, suspicion, anxiety. If such potential employee concerns are not dealt with adequately, then all the time, money, and effort spent designing the program might just as well never have been spent.

Flexible programs work best when employees use them well—when they make benefit choices that suit their families' needs, make changes as their life situations change, focus on wellness and prevention to help manage costs, and make wise consumer decisions as users of the plan. Communication in a variety of forms can be used effectively to motivate this type of behaviour, and at the same time raise awareness about the plan, build employee knowledge and understanding about their benefits and available choices, and manage the expectations and perceptions associated with cost-sharing.

While communication is just one aspect of the overall implementation, it can represent the single largest hard-dollar cost, particularly for employers with few internal design or production resources. Therefore, communicating a flexible program requires a strategy — a strategy designed to achieve the best results for the time and dollars spent, recognizing that employees have a significant role to play in the final success or failure of the program.

A TARGETED COMMUNICATION STRATEGY

Increasingly, employers are using flexible benefit programs to ask their employees to take on additional cost sharing or become wiser health care consumers. They are asking employees to accept and appreciate their benefits, and change their attitudes and behaviour.

This shift towards managing perceptions and attitudes requires a "marketing" approach not traditionally seen in benefits communication. More and more employers are applying marketing techniques to assess their internal audiences and to target their communications in a way that will resonate with employees.

"Know your audience" is perhaps one of the most important marketing principles that can be applied in the development of the targeted communication strategy. To be effective, the communication strategy should look at the employees' current communication environment, the corporate culture, the perceived impact of introducing the flexible benefits program (i.e., positive, neutral or negative), and any other factors that may influence how employees will perceive the program. Gathering employee feedback early on in the process is a great way to ensure that the communication strategy is on target.

"Know your product" is also critical when setting a communication strategy. In this situation, the product is the flexible benefits program, including the plan design features and administrative functionality. For this reason, it is important to always involve members of the design team and administrators during the initial communication planning. These team members "know the product," and can help to identify communication opportunities or potential issues that should be addressed when setting the initial communication approach.

While each flexible benefit program is unique, and each communication strategy is different, experience shows that there is a logical order to the planning and information flow:

- **Step One: Gather employee feedback.** Focus groups or other methods of gathering feedback can be used. Results should be summarized for use in Step Two.
- **Step Two: Develop a plan.** The company should identify an overall communication approach and work plan consistent with the organizational environment and program goals. Set measurable goals and determine how you will measure results.

- **Step Three: Announce the program.** Begin the rollout to employees with announcements that properly position the program while managing employee expectations and perceptions.
- **Step Four: Educate employees.** This step focuses on education to help employees understand the program and make their personal benefit choices.
- **Step Five: Enrol employees.** At this stage, employees will need to make their decisions and submit their enrolment choices.
- **Step Six: Measure and follow up.** Communication doesn't end with enrolment. Measure results. Did you achieve your goals? An effective communication strategy addresses ongoing opportunities to educate employees as they use the plan throughout the year.

The remainder of this chapter examines these steps in more detail.

§ 18.2 GATHERING EMPLOYEE FEEDBACK

"Employee listening" offers a great opportunity to discover employees' communication preferences, test the plan design and enrolment patterns, and identify any potential issues that may affect the way employees will perceive the flexible program. Employee feedback can also be extremely useful for planning and targeting communications for annual re-enrolments.

Gathering feedback during an initial implementation is typically done by way of employee focus groups, while feedback for re-enrolment planning is typically done by way of an online employee survey.

Employee focus groups should involve a random but representative selection of the company's population base. It is important to hear from a variety of demographic groups, since perceptions of the flexible program may vary significantly depending on an employee's family status and benefit needs.

Often, companies make assumptions about how employees will react to the benefit changes or the choices they will make. However, experience shows that the actual results can be quite different from what companies expect.

Example 1: A company that needed to introduce benefit reductions held a series of focus groups to gather feedback on the proposed changes. The company told participants what result they needed to achieve and proposed a design, but said they were willing to consider other designs to reach their goal. The company found that the participants were more understanding of the situation than expected, and appreciated the opportunity to have input into the process.

Example 2: A company was concerned that if cash was an option for unused flex dollars, employees would make poor choices in order to get additional cash. Instead, test enrolments showed that employees elected appropriate levels of coverage, and selected the Group RRSP over cash for unused flex dollars.

Clearly, the importance of involving employees in the process goes much deeper than just the feedback they can provide. The listening process demonstrates to employees that their input is valued and helps them feel a stronger connection with the company. This, in turn, creates stronger buy-in and can lead to these employees becoming advocates for the flexible program.

§ 18.3 DEVELOPING A PLAN

Flexible benefit communication is almost always more extensive, more technical, and broader in scope than other employee benefit communication undertakings. However, this communication effort is also an excellent opportunity to stimulate employee interest in benefits, to strengthen awareness and appreciation of employer expenditures for benefits, and to promote greater understanding and "ownership" of benefit coverages.

Planning the process carefully helps save time, money, and considerable effort down the road. The result of a careful, co-ordinated planning effort is a written document — a blueprint that can be followed as the benefit communication campaign unfolds. While such a document is often changed and updated as implementation proceeds, its purpose is to keep the campaign on track.

To get the planning started, assemble a small team that will be responsible for the communication effort. This team should include communicators, production co-ordinators, and technical resources, such as a member of the plan design team and an administrator. You may also consider including field representatives in your planning team as a way to bring in a different perspective.

The technical resource people on the team bring a strong understanding of the product and delivery system. Their input is particularly important during planning to ensure that all potential opportunities or issues are raised up front, rather than facing last-minute "discoveries" that can be costly and can affect the team's ability to deliver on time.

Once the team is assembled, invest some time in reviewing the task ahead and analysing the communication environment at the company. In short, make sure all team members are starting from the same place.

ANALYSING THE ENVIRONMENT

The first thing for the planning team to consider is the overall company environment in which the flexible benefits communication will be delivered. The team should consider such issues as:

- Current business environment, both inside the company and among competitors — how the company is faring economically and how employees have seen the results (e.g., layoffs, bonuses); how the new flexible program or the program changes reflect the company's business strategy; and any good news or bad news that may be delivered around the same time as the implementation or enrolment.

- Employee relations climate — how employees are feeling about the company before the changes or updates are announced; morale in the field versus morale at company headquarters; relations with unions or groups seeking unionization; recent history of benefit or compensation increases or cutbacks.

- Scope of the program — how flexible benefits fit within the company's total rewards structure; which benefits are included; what the level of employee risk would be if a "wrong" decision is made; which parts of the program will change the most and require more explanation; which benefit areas have been historically sensitive for employees.

- Existing communication channels — technology; employee perceptions of the current enrolment process, communication channels and capabilities; benefit communications that worked well and not so well in the past; other communication opportunities.

Once the planning team has a shared understanding of the communication environment, the focus can narrow to the communication campaign.

ANALYSING THE AUDIENCE

Next, the team needs to do a detailed analysis of the audiences for this flexible benefit communication. The goal here is to identify the various audiences, review their communication preferences and capabilities, and create a plan to address their specific needs.

In most instances, the general employee population is the primary audience to consider. If focus groups or a post-enrolment survey were conducted, it is helpful at this point for the communication team to review the employee feedback. This information will help the team understand how employees view the program and any impending change, what they like or dislike about the program, and where there may be areas of confusion.

Keep in mind that each employee is not only an employee, but also a potential consumer of flexible benefits. As employees, their openness to the company's message will reflect their past experiences and history with the company. As consumers, they have personal preferences and opinions that will impact their perception of the flexible benefits program.

In addition to the broad employee base, most companies have other audiences to consider. These may include senior staff, who may need advance notice; human resource staff, who may require additional training to support the program; field staff, who may or may not have the technical capabilities to access online or electronic communication; new hires, who are learning about the company's benefit program for the first time; employees on different types of leaves, who may or may not be participating in the program; retirees, who may be confused if they hear about changes to the active employee program; and other potential audiences within the company.

To manage costs, most companies strive to deliver one generic communication to employees and then address the unique needs of each individual audience separately. Identifying these audiences up front in the communication plan makes it easier for the communication team to determine areas where messaging may vary for different audiences; keep track of any unique or one-off communication requirements; and prevent any last-minute discoveries that may impact the team's ability to deliver.

SETTING OBJECTIVES AND CHOOSING MESSAGES

One of the most important tasks in the planning process is for the team to decide just what they want to tell employees and how they want the message told. This is done by setting objectives and establishing parameters that will guide the communication effort.

Broad objectives, such as emphasizing the value and competitiveness of the flexible program, or improving employee understanding of benefit costs, will be useful for defining the key messages to be conveyed to employees. However, objectives also serve as success measures for the communication initiative. So, be sure to identify some specific, measurable objectives, such as defining the target percentage of active enrolments. The planning team's study of the company's background and climate should tie into this objective-setting process.

Once the overall objectives have been agreed to, the planning team should list the most important messages — the central issues or ideas to convey to employees through the communication effort. For example, if the objective is to educate employees about flexible benefits, the messages may include "Flexible benefits let you tailor your coverage to meet your own needs," or "You can take advantage of important tax benefits." If, on the other hand, the objective is to explain cost sharing, the message may be "Flexible benefits let you spend company dollars on the benefits that are most important to you."

The unique character and environment of the organization should lead naturally to the right objectives and specific messages for the communication campaign.

As the team is planning the messages, consideration should be given to linking the flexible program to a broader concept, such as total compensation, human resource programs, or an internal employee brand. Experience has shown that when flexible benefits are positioned within a broader context, employees are less likely to judge each individual benefit against their current benefits, and are more likely to see the value of the program in its entirety.

DEFINING MEDIA AND APPROACH

Once the planning team has identified what they want to say, they need to turn their attention to how they want the message delivered — the media for getting the message from the company to the employee. The task of the planning team is to determine which vehicles make the most sense, given what they know about the company's audiences, technology, environment, objectives, and budget.

In today's hectic world, choosing media is more than just getting the message out. The media choices need to catch employees' attention and cut through the clutter and clamour of the daily routine. If the communication goal is to attract attention and motivate a new set of employee behaviours, is e-mail the best choice of medium? It may be, or it may not be. The communication team would need to look carefully at the company and its current communication environment before making this decision.

Despite the vast array of possible media choices available, most flexible programs are communicated using multiple combinations of generally available types of media — print and online communications, face-to-face meetings, multi-media shows, video, and other electronic communications.

Deciding which media to use, however, is only half the battle for grabbing attention. The theme and graphic design also create impact and build recognition for the communication campaign. Remember, linking the communication visually to a broader total compensation or human resources identity can improve employees' perceptions of value.

The team will need to make sure the media and the approach reflect the objectives and are appropriate for the environment. It is probably unwise to create an expensive-looking campaign if the flexible program is accompanied by cost containment messages.

Finally, consideration should be given to creating a style guide that captures the defined vocabulary for the campaign. This guide can be shared with team members, reviewers, translators, and proofreaders to ensure consistency in terminology. In a complex flexible program, inconsistent terminology can be a source of significant confusion for the employees, so it is important that all parties "speak the same language."

ESTABLISHING SCHEDULES, RESPONSIBILITIES, AND BUDGETS

To complete the planning process, a schedule for implementation must be established, responsibilities assigned, and budgets approved. Typically, an employer will need more time, more people, and more money to communicate flexible benefits in the first year than in later years.

Communication planning needs to occur well in advance of the targeted implementation date. Interestingly, the lead time for getting a campaign under way tends to vary little by the size of the organization. In general, the planning process involves about the same magnitude of effort regardless of the number of employees eligible for the program.

To assign responsibilities, the planning team must first consider any internal resources the organization can bring to bear, including the corporate communication staff, training department, Web programmers, print shop and mail room, and even graphic designers from the marketing department, if appropriate. The ability of those individuals to meet the demands of writing and producing the information and enrolment materials must also be considered. For example, the challenge of writing about flexible benefits is different from most corporate communication. The writer must thoroughly understand the program design, choice-making process, and enrolment process. The importance of these materials to the overall success of the flexible benefit program should not be underestimated. Careful attention must also be paid to translation. For example, in-house translators, who specialize in your business, will need to take time to familiarize themselves with the terminology of a flexible benefit program.

It is difficult to generalize about budgets for flexible benefit communication. So many elements will vary from company to company and campaign to campaign. Are you introducing a new flexible program or program changes? How much education is needed? How many audiences do you need to communicate to? What media have the team chosen? While communications will likely be one of the most expensive parts of the overall project, many companies, in hindsight, say that they would do more communication.

One way to manage costs is to take an "evergreen" approach to developing the materials. This simply means separating transitional or launch-specific information from the core information that needs to be available on an ongoing basis. The transitional information will only apply during the launch for existing employees. The core, or "evergreen," material can be used during the launch and for future new hires joining the program.

When budgeting, the planning team must consider these issues:

- The internal resources (soft dollars) available and the external support (hard dollars) that will be needed;
- The complexity of the flexible program and the scope of the communication plan (as may be expected, more complicated plans and more elaborate rollouts require more communication);
- The company environment (some companies simply have more information to send or more audiences to deal with);
- The media included in the plan (print, electronic, video, etc.), including any design elements that will affect costs (colours, programming requirements, illustrations or photographs, etc.);
- The need to produce materials in English and French; and
- If print media are used, the quantity of the materials needed, and method of distribution.

It may be helpful to include a representative from the company's marketing or corporate communications group in this process to get a better understanding of the costs. These representatives may also be able to arrange discounted prices by negotiating with their regular suppliers.

There's no question that flex communications represent significant dollars. But when compared to the cost employers pay every year to provide benefits to employees, and considering the value to be gained when employees understand and appreciate a flexible program (or even their benefits for the very first time), the numbers begin to appear less overwhelming. When setting communication budgets for a flexible program communication, therefore, it is helpful to remember that with proper planning, costs can be controlled and managed.

Once the communication plan has been completed and approved, the campaign development can begin.

§ 18.4 ANNOUNCING THE PROGRAM

A successful announcement phase needs to recognize that the company will seldom have the first word. The grapevine has often taken care of that, particularly if the new plan design or changes have been tested in focus groups. In hallways, break rooms, and plant floors, the news about flexible benefits may be out, and possibly inaccurately so. By the time the employer is ready with the big announcement, employees may have already formed opinions about the program based on the bits of information that they have heard. Announcing a new flexible benefit program or changes to an existing plan in this environment can be seen as a marketing challenge.

Clearly, the nature of the program will impact employee opinions. Cost containment initiatives may raise concerns; other designs may have employees anxious to participate. The company needs to think carefully about how to position the announcement, given the anticipated employee climate. If staff reductions have employees up in arms, a straightforward, low-key announcement may demonstrate sensitivity to employee concerns. Similarly, a year five re-enrolment does not likely require a high-profile launch, but rather a straightforward "business as usual" approach. However, if the program is highly anticipated, kicking off the campaign with a splashy announcement may help the company leverage this positive mood.

One thing is certain. The announcement is not the place to load up on details. It is an introduction to the program, with more information to come as employee understanding of the program builds.

The announcement should focus on the big picture — why the change is happening and how it links to broader business or company strategies. It also needs to be catchy enough to get employees' attention and motivate them to keep reading or listening. To the extent possible, announcement communication should be short, simple, straightforward, and honest.

Before the announcement is released, it is a good idea to get managers and human resources staff up to speed so they can support employees during the rest of the communication effort.

§ 18.5 EDUCATING EMPLOYEES

Educating employees about the program is perhaps the most important step in the communication process. It is during this step that employees see the personal impact of the changes. They learn how the program works and what is changing, and look at their own personal situations to consider their choices. During this time, employees need reassurance, support, and access to information.

The question is: how much information is enough? Experience has shown that too much information too soon can cause confusion and negative perceptions of the program. Initially, communications should focus on the key concepts that all employees need to understand, such as what's changing and how to make their choices and complete their enrolment. Other more detailed information also needs to be readily available as reference, but may not be essential for the initial communication. Remember, there will be lots of time for employees to continue learning.

From a legal perspective, disclosure of all the important details is essential. However, it is just as important that employees actually read the material, and this may not happen if they get too bogged down in details. The key is to balance both of these needs by making detailed reference materials available, while ensuring that the actionable communications are clear and simple.

When planning the educational aspect of the launch, the team should consider the following points:

- Provide summary level and detailed information. Employees are inundated with information every day. Some people diligently read through it all, while others just skim the headings. The communication team can help their readers by providing materials that allow the "skimmers" to quickly and easily find the key information, while also giving the "detailers" the additional background they need.

- Communicate simply and often. Experience indicates that for a typical full-flexible program, employees will need to devote several hours to their decision process. The volume of information alone, not to mention the importance of the decisions being required, indicates that reinforcement of the messages is critical.

- Offer diversity. Different people are attracted by different media. Some read newsletters; others do not. Different company locations may have very different media needs. Communicate in different ways, at different times, and remember to provide a forum for getting questions answered.

- Throughout your communication, remember that education is a linear learning process. One concept builds on another as employees expand their understanding. This brings up an interesting consideration about using a Web site as the primary communication vehicle for the launch. By their very nature, Web sites are modular. Users can jump from section to section and back again, without reading the pages in between. This is great for fast and easy access to specific reference information, but it can be confusing for someone learning about flexible benefits for the first time. That's why many companies still include print materials and/or face-to-face communications for education purposes.

To launch a new flexible program or introduce program changes, employees consistently give high marks to face-to-face communications. Employee presentations provide an excellent opportunity to explain the changes and market the program. However, meeting face-to-face with all employees is not always feasible. Fortunately, there are many alternatives available to meet the company's objectives, budgets, and facilities, including Web meetings, video or teleconferencing, CDs, and DVDs, to name a few.

If internal resources are used to run employee meetings, it may be worth taking the time and spending the money needed to thoroughly train the meeting leaders and human resources staff. Experience has shown that providing a "train-the-trainer" program makes a significant difference in the confidence of the meeting leaders and their ability to influence the implementation in a positive way.

Online or printed newsletters or regular articles posted on the company intranet can also be very effective vehicles for time-releasing details about the program in specific environments. The key is to take the audience into account when choosing the media for the education phase. If an electronic newsletter will not work, maybe a simple brochure sent to the employees' homes will.

If it is in line with the overall objectives, reinforce the program with other attention-grabbing communications. Create a campaign for the company's video bulletin boards, run contests on the intranet, broadcast voicemails, consider promotional material for coffee rooms, or schedule demonstration days in the cafeteria to teach employees how to use the tools available to them.

Finally, whatever media elements are chosen, find the hot buttons for the audience — the appeals — and sell them with creativity, simplicity, and directness. Keep in mind that what appeals to the various audience segments may not necessarily be the same thing as the company's "most important issue." Once the planning team identifies what will sell the message, design the communication materials around those ideas.

§ 18.6 ENROLLING EMPLOYEES

By the time employees reach the enrolment stage, they should have received enough information to have a basic understanding of any changes, and the concepts and important details of the program. They should feel satisfied that they understand "how this affects me" and the company's rationale for this communication.

Enrolment communication can make or break an implementation. The primary goal is to have employees complete their enrolments accurately and on time. To do this, the communications must be clear, simple, and direct, and the process must be relatively easy and non-threatening.

While this may sound straightforward enough, creating simple and unified enrolment communications is very challenging. Just think, enrolment is where past communications, Web sites, computer systems, administration, and communication all come together in one unified voice to the employees.

To be effective, the enrolment communication must build on the foundation laid during the education process and take into account the needs of other disciplines. It needs to be:

- **Personalized.** Enrolment is where employees see the actual personal and financial impact of their choices. Whether they enrol online or on paper, they will need to know the amount of their personal flex credits in credit-based flexible plans, and the costs of the different benefit options, based on their own personal situation.

- **Clear and easy to follow.** Provide examples and simple instructions, directing employees through the process. If enrolment is to be done online, include screen-by-screen instructions and explanations. If enrolment is paper-based, be sure to cross-reference materials and provide pre-filled-in examples to follow.

- **Consistent.** Keep the anxiety level low by using terms and phrases made familiar by earlier communication. These should be the same words and phrases used by administrators or phone support staff. There should be no surprises and no last-minute changes in terminology to confuse employees.

- **Complete.** Tell employees what they need to think about and what they can ignore for now.

- **Positive.** This is the chance to revisit the big picture, to look at the overall goals of the program, and to define a future direction for benefits and compensation at the company. After concentrating on the details for a period of time, employees will welcome the opportunity to put the pieces together.

Enrolment communications are directly impacted by the program administrative capabilities. In today's world, Web-based solutions offer employees flexibility and direct access to their benefits at any time, night or day. Online enrolment offers several advantages:

- Built-in controls can ensure that the employee completes the enrolment thoroughly and accurately (e.g., pre-loading personal information, automating the calculations, requiring that key input fields be completed, correction boxes that provide immediate guidance and direction, defaults, etc.);

- The capability for employees to run "what if" scenarios to see how their benefit choices may impact their flex credits, price tags, and payroll deductions; and,

- Online instructions so the supporting communications do not need to be as extensive.

Although Web-based solutions are the norm, there are some situations where paper enrolment may be required, particularly when employees have limited computer access. In these situations, paper enrolment must be completely synchronized with the administration system, which is why the administrators should be involved early on in the development of the materials.

All the goodwill earned through the announcement and education stages can reap rewards for the employer now. If enrolment materials are personalized, simple to use, and easy to understand, employee confidence and appreciation for the program will grow, and the enrolment process will meet with fewer errors overall.

§ 18.7 MEASURING AND FOLLOWING UP

Are employees satisfied with flexible benefits? Did the team achieve their overall objectives? At the time of enrolment, the final answer to that question is still probably nine to twelve months away. However, it is still critical to gather initial feedback and reactions in order to measure the success of the implementation. This doesn't have to be a cumbersome project. It can be done quite effectively by simply posting a brief online survey on the enrolment Web site.

If the enrolment process has gone well, most employees will be fairly satisfied with the idea of choice-making. However, the true test will come over time as they continue to use the program and see how their choices work out. That is when follow-up communication can make a major difference.

Unfortunately, the implementation team usually disbands after enrolment. Each discipline goes its own way, usually on to other concerns or new projects. This feeling of closure at enrolment time is natural. However, a concerted effort is necessary to keep up the flow of information. Ultimately, employees will judge the program by how well they remember the elections they made, how easily they can get a question answered, how efficiently claims are processed, and how the company manages re-enrolments. These are all terrific opportunities for the company to provide ongoing guidance and education about the program, to continue encouraging positive reactions.

The follow-up communication stage is really never over, but it is probably most critical in the first twelve months after implementation. To be effective, follow-up communication should be confirming, consistent, and complete.

For communication to be *confirming*, employees should be able to view their benefit choices online at any time. They should also be able to print a confirmation of their benefit choices once they have completed their online enrolment. This confirmation tells employees that their elections were understood and recorded accurately. It will also serve as a reminder of what coverage they have when they need to use their plans, months down the road.

To be *consistent*, simply keep up the good work. If the communication approach used for implementation worked (graphics, theme, terminology, etc.), do not abandon it now. As other communication materials are developed, build on what has gone before. To be *complete*, think about filling in the gaps. Stay connected with the program administrators to monitor the ongoing questions and concerns that employees have, and view these as potential communication opportunities. Also, now is the time for expanding intranets and providing benefit handbooks that lay out all the details. Take some time to review the program reference material and repackage or reorganize as needed.

Perhaps the most important job in the follow-up phase is the communication leading up to and surrounding annual enrolments. Re-enrolment provides an opportunity for the company to make things better, to learn from any mistakes made during implementation, and to broaden the base of employee satisfaction. Taking time to evaluate the previous year's communication efforts can help immeasurably planning the next year's communications.

Evaluation is the key. Remember setting communication objectives? Before planning future communication efforts, it is essential to evaluate the success of the initial campaign. If the planning team set measurable objectives, the company has built-in yardsticks for measuring the relative success of the implementation. Follow-up research or listening to employees also can help in this evaluation process.

§ 18.8 SPECIAL CONSIDERATIONS

Ideally, this six-step approach to communication will lead to a successful implementation. Particularly if the company is offering a good news benefit package, the communication effort, although extensive, can be fairly straightforward.

However, not all companies will be serving up good news. In some situations, the communications are accompanied by cost containment messages. In others, employers must approach a workforce mindful of past economic or organizational problems. Even at companies where almost everything lines up in the good news column, pockets of employees may react differently from the population as a whole. For these companies, communication can be seen as the most unpredictable factor in a flexible benefits implementation. Many of the particular communication problems such companies will face are emotional in nature, while others are simply related to getting the job done. Either way, successfully solving these communication problems is essential, because it can have a major positive effect on employee acceptance of the flexible program.

EMPLOYEE UNCERTAINTY

Whether they are hearing about flexible benefits for the first time, or are just learning about changes for re-enrolment, a common employee reaction is uncertainty. Employees know that they'll need to make decisions in an area that could have a significant effect on their financial security, but this may be an area that they know little about.

Disarming employee uncertainty is a gradual process. It starts with the confidence projected by company representatives as they communicate the changes, and it usually ends once employees have successfully made their decisions and enrolled. The communication campaign can encourage this process by including some basic strategies:

- **Focus on personalized communication.** Provide materials that will help employees understand how their decisions affect their personal situation. Find ways to demonstrate the balance between benefit cost and risk in a personal way. Any opportunity employees have to try different scenarios with real numbers will help them make decisions they can feel good about.

- **Provide real-life examples.** The flexible program is designed for people to use, so provide employees with examples of how real people might elect and use their benefits.

- **Emphasize the implications.** To be comfortable with choice-making, employees need to know more than the facts and figures. They also need to understand the implications of what they are doing, the reasons why one employee might choose differently from another. Although a line must be drawn between informing and giving employees advice, just offering employees a list of considerations can help.

- **Provide an effective question-and-answer network.** Employees should know about and feel comfortable approaching a designated person for answers to their questions. An effective network of this type can be crucial in resolving misunderstandings, clearing up complaints, and facilitating decision making.

EMPLOYEE SUSPICION

In some environments, employees may view a flexible program as management attempting to "sneak something past them." An unstable business or employee relations environment is the best breeding ground for employee suspicions. This type of negative organizational background will affect any changes the employer makes. And when a flexible benefit plan is being used as an opportunity for increased cost sharing or other perceived cutbacks, negative employee perceptions can develop very quickly.

In these situations, it is best to deal with the issues as quickly as possible and not let this type of negative environment fester. The more turmoil employees get into about an issue — real or perceived — the harder it will be to get them back on side.

The good news is that, of all possible communication problems, employee suspicion succumbs most easily to the right communication strategy. Success depends, in part, on having realistic goals. It may be impossible to get all employees to embrace the program completely, but it will be possible to help many of them understand the reasons behind the changes and to accept the business decisions as necessary, no matter how unpleasant.

The best policy is to be straightforward. For employees to support the program, they must know the whole story. Companies should have confidence in their benefit design and address any trade-offs openly. Tell both sides of the story and give employees the reasons behind the decisions. A high degree of management and supervisory support for the program can help here. Although employers should not market the program beyond its merits, experience shows that a substantial number of employees will see cost sharing as a fair trade for the benefit of flexibility.

§ 18.9 SUMMING UP

Communication is one of the most important aspects of the implementation process. The employer simply has no other choice but to communicate and communicate well. Therefore, companies need to realize that a flexible benefit program will take a major commitment of money and people. It will require that they think differently about communications. Look at new media possibilities. Identify new strategies. And, most important, plan the communication effort in detail so both time and money can be used wisely.

Experience shows that all the resources it takes to communicate a flexible program are worth it in the end. When the communication job is done well, when employees are comfortable with the program and trust the process, the company's other objectives for flexible benefits—even cost management—are more easily attained.

Nineteen

Training the Implementation Staff

§ 19.1 INTRODUCTION

While often seen as two separate disciplines, employee communication and training are inextricably linked when either introducing or overhauling a flexible benefits plan. Without the enthusiasm, understanding, and support of human resources staff, meeting leaders, and other implementers, it is unlikely that employees will receive the kind of education and personal attention they need to appreciate the full value of the flexible program.

The implementation staff are a critical part of the communication strategy. Their potential for influencing employee behaviour (positively or negatively) is far greater than for any other vehicle in the communication campaign. These are the people who will be involved in the implementing the new or modified flexible plan — hosting employee meetings, running Webcasts, or holding question-and-answer sessions. The implementation staff should also include the administrators who will be staffing benefit hotlines and otherwise answering questions employees might have about enrolment or their specific coverages under the flexible program.

The level of success of the new or modified flexible benefit program depends on the ability of the implementation team to communicate and educate. Still, most employers spend more time, money, and effort preparing the launch materials than they do preparing their front-line people.

Meeting leaders and human resources representatives need more information than do employees. They must have more in-depth knowledge of the program. They must have specific skills in leadership, counselling, and administration. They also must have positive, realistic attitudes. And they must have it all sooner, so that they are equipped and ready to support the employees.

For this reason, organizations implementing a new flexible benefit plan or changing an existing plan are really facing two communication campaigns: one for employees and an additional one, less elaborate but nevertheless complete, for the implementation staff. The campaigns must be integrated and compatible, although unfolding along separate timelines and using different media plans.

§ 19.2 DETERMINING/ANALYSING THE TRAINING AUDIENCES

As with communication, the first step in designing training is to determine the audiences and analyse their needs and preferences. One way to approach this task is to list all the roles that must be filled during implementation and then determine appropriate resources to fill them. Below are some of the roles that should be considered when implementing or changing a flexible benefit plan, along with typical information needs:

- **Meeting leaders** need enough technical knowledge about flexible benefits to answer most employee questions. They also need presentation skills and positive attitudes about flexible benefits.
- **Benefit administrators** need a comprehensive understanding of the program: how it works, how the options and pricing work, and how the program is administered.
- **Meeting co-ordinators** need strong organizational skills to schedule and co-ordinate logistics for employee meetings, including make-up sessions.
- **Telephone/hotline helpers** need strong technical knowledge and good telephone and interpersonal skills.
- **Enrolment helpers** need a solid understanding of the enrolment process, flexible benefits, how the pricing works, and the issues involved in making wise benefit decisions. They need the ability to deal well with employees on a one-on-one or small-group basis.
- **Co-ordinators** need to know the steps involved in implementing the program, including all communication and training tasks. They also need to understand and support critical dates for steps such as distribution of materials and return of completed enrolment forms.
- **Technical experts** need a thorough understanding of all technical aspects of the program in order to answer difficult questions from employees and from human resources staff members.

In fact, the same group of people may be asked to play several roles. Generally, though, the scope of implementation and training is too broad to be handled by human resources alone. For that reason, many organizations implementing a flexible benefit program or introducing significant flexible benefit changes solicit help from departments outside human resources.

SELECTING MEETING LEADERS

In selecting meeting leaders, it is helpful to consider the roles they will play. For instance, will meeting leaders simply conduct a series of employee meetings or Webcasts? Or will they be asked to provide follow-up help, such as one-on-one enrolment counselling?

Once the scope of leaders' responsibilities is defined, an organization can determine how many leaders will be needed. The number of leaders needed will depend on the number of employees to be reached, and the format for reaching them. For example, hosting face-to-face employee meetings will require more meeting leaders than holding Webcasts or conference calls, and full educational sessions will require more time (and more meeting leaders) than simple question-and-answer sessions.

Other factors to consider include staffing needs for multiple shifts, whether training can be held for random groups or must be department-based, and whether key employee subgroups (such as union/non-union) must be trained separately.

Departments that could be called on to supply meeting leaders include corporate communications, training, and sales. Employees in these groups often meet several of the criteria; what they lack (such as technical knowledge of the program) can be supplied through training.

OTHER AUDIENCES

In most implementations, the following audiences will also need some form of training, even if they are not assigned meeting leader roles:

- **Managers/supervisors** — in management briefings or similar presentations that provide an overview of the program and the business reasons behind it.
- **Human resources administrators** — in department briefings and through hands-on skills training, as appropriate.

In some organizations, other groups also may need training, depending on the communication and training objectives and on certain special situations or needs. One company with an extremely diverse population determined that it needed to train a number of rank-and-file employees, along with meeting leaders. The employees were needed to attend meetings so they could assist leaders with translation and help build credibility with their peers. They also were asked to serve as enrolment helpers after meetings were held.

ANALYSING THE TRAINING AUDIENCES

Once the various training audiences are defined, the next step is to analyse them. These considerations are important:

- What do they already know about flexible benefits and about any program changes?
- What knowledge and skills will they need to perform their roles successfully?
- What will motivate them to communicate the program in a positive manner?
- What experience have they had conducting training? If they are experienced, how will this training effort differ from those in the past?
- Besides a formal training session, what tools do they need to fulfill their roles?

Once the analysis is complete, the training team is ready to design training. It is important to consider the different types of training that may be required, based on the needs of the audiences.

§ 19.3 DESIGNING THE TRAINING

The effectiveness of any training program will be judged by how successfully the meeting leaders and human resources staff do their implementation jobs. Success usually depends on the mastery of certain knowledge and skills used to carry out various roles. When designing a training program, the organization should spend some time identifying the specific knowledge, skills, and attitudes needed, based on the current environment, company objectives, and training roles identified.

TRAINING FOR KNOWLEDGE

Knowledge includes the facts and figures: plan provisions, election processes, and role definitions. But while technical details need to be mastered, training for knowledge should also focus on the big picture: how the program works in the context of the organization's compensation philosophy and objectives.

Two approaches are commonly utilized to build up leaders' knowledge. The most common approach is to conduct a large training session where participants can ask questions, get the most up-to-date information, and build on the knowledge they already have. A variety of educational tools can be utilized, including presentations, small group break-outs, and quizzes.

Another approach is to time-release information, which gives the organization an opportunity to communicate knowledge in a variety of formats. Newsletter articles, videos, online tools, summaries, reviews, and opportunities for self-testing or peer discussion — all can be effective in helping participants acquire the knowledge they need in a more self-directed manner.

A key goal or outcome is that all leaders will be able to present in a common, consistent way.

TRAINING FOR SKILLS

In addition to acquiring a new base of knowledge about flexible benefits, meeting leaders and human resources staff will need to learn or improve certain soft skills — such as probing to ensure understanding, or dealing with difficult questions.

Unlike training for knowledge, training for soft skills requires practice. The training should start by providing models, demonstrations, or case studies, and then move on to application — feedback sessions with small groups, or role-playing exercises. This type of training typically requires an interactive, in-person, group training session.

People acquire new skills at different rates. Be sure to allow enough time for the majority of participants to become confident in their abilities to use the new skill or behaviour. If they feel unsure or unprepared, that uncertainty will be the primary message transmitted to the employee group.

TRAINING FOR ATTITUDES

An area that often is overlooked is that of attitudes. The attitudes of meeting leaders, human resources staff, and others involved in a flexible benefit program are critical to the program's success. In developing training, consider the organization's needs as well as the backgrounds of those being trained.

For instance, does the organization need people who can "sell" the new or changed program? Or is it sufficient for those trained to present the facts in a fairly neutral manner? Are there negative messages that will require significant skill to communicate? Are the training participants excited about the program and/or any changes that are being implemented? Or are they uncertain about the need for change?

The training team will need to set clear objectives to address participant attitudes, because whatever attitudes exist will be contagious. It is useful to reference the communication plan at this point and build on it when designing training.

TRAINING SESSIONS

The approach to training varies widely among organizations. It depends on several factors:

- The scope of the communication and implementation support required (i.e., a flexible benefits implementation will require more extensive training than introducing simple program changes).

- The role of the meeting leaders and human resource staff and their experience as trainers. Are they professional trainers from the internal training area? Are they benefits staff members? A combination of both? Or are they members of the implementation team?
- The type of training required. Do they need knowledge-based training only? Or do they need soft skills training?
- The environment. Are there issues outside of benefits that may come up during training? Will trainers need to know how to handle difficult training situations? Are flexible benefits seen as a positive change, or are they viewed as necessary to control costs or change employee behaviour?

Depending on these factors, the training approach may simply be a Web meeting with a walk-through of the employee materials and online tools, or it may be a face-to-face multi-day training session that provides enough time for skill building and application of knowledge.

Regardless of what training approach is used, a pre-defined agenda for the training session is a must. Attendees should have a clear understanding of the expectations for them and what their role will be in the implementation.

Training is always more effective when the participants are involved in the process — learning and doing rather than just listening. A great exercise to help the participants understand the personal impact of the program launch or changes is to have them complete a mock enrolment so that the participants go through the thinking process and discuss the considerations.

Time on the agenda should also be allowed for some form of activity and group interaction. An excellent opportunity for this is when the group addresses how they will handle tough questions. Half the group can make up the questions, and the other half can formulate the response through group discussion. Or participants could pass a hat full of tough questions and try their hands at individual responses. There are lots of options for this form of group involvement.

For many initiatives, informal training continues even after the formal training is completed. This may be facilitated by establishing a centralized feedback mechanism that allows the training participants to share their experience and to hear how others handled issues or difficult situations. This allows the participants to fine-tune as they go.

§ 19.4 FOLLOW-UP

Once the training is complete and all the elections are entered and confirmed, the real everyday work begins. While the administrative process will continue to be fine-tuned over a period of time, three specific types of follow-up are extremely valuable but often overlooked:

- **Debrief trainers/meeting leaders.** They are in the best position to describe what went right and what went wrong with the process. They can explain how the employee communication materials should be improved and describe how smoothly the enrolment process went.
- **Say thank you.** People have stretched beyond their usual limits to support the flexible benefits program. A simple thank you — unassociated with any other task-related communication — will speak volumes.
- **Keep the team informed of what is ahead.** Implementation-related issues will continue to be important following the effective date of the new or changed program. Keep human resource representatives and others up to date on enrolment patterns, status changes, and other information that could have an effect on how they do their jobs.

§ 19.5 SUMMING UP

Experience proves that taking the time, making the effort, and spending the money necessary to thoroughly train meeting leaders and human resources staff makes a significant difference in the implementation process — whether this is a first-year flexible benefits program launch, or changes to the plan in year five. When the support team is well-trained, enrolments are bound to go more smoothly — during this enrolment and in future years. When people feel confident about their implementation roles, that confidence will infuse their normal daily tasks and continue to influence other employees, as well as the entire organization, in a positive way.

Twenty

The Role of Employee Listening

Whatever the design of a flexible benefit program may be, building employee understanding and support will be a critical factor in achieving the program's objectives. Gathering employee opinions about flexible benefit needs can help an organization focus on the design features and communication messages that will create or add to positive employee perceptions, reduce employee concerns or resistance, and ultimately align employees' perceptions and behaviours with flexible benefit program objectives.

The reasons for seeking employee input on flexible benefit issues have changed in recent years. Employee input has long been valued by benefits managers in building or restructuring benefit programs, but increasing cost pressures have changed the manner and purpose of obtaining much of that input. Emerging purposes for listening to employee opinions about flexible benefits include:

- Involving employees in determining benefit plan features and options that will maximize the value of benefit expenditures within a limited budget;
- Identifying the most effective approaches to educating employees about flexible benefits and related cost management issues; and
- Learning ways to create empathy for the employer in its efforts to manage costs and change behaviour.

§ 20.1 WHEN TO LISTEN TO EMPLOYEES ABOUT FLEXIBLE BENEFITS

A first step to finding whether there is a need to listen to employees' views on flexible benefits is to target the research focus. There are four stages at which gathering employee input can be of value for studying employee reactions to flexible benefits:

- Before program design, to identify current levels of benefit understanding, perceptions of quality, and employees' benefit-related needs, concerns, and goals;
- After program design, to test-market the proposed flexible benefit program, and learn what messages are key to employee understanding, appreciation, and comfort with choice-making;
- After communication development, to test the appeal and impact of graphics, media, and key messages and assumptions; and
- After implementation, to learn whether targeted levels of employee understanding and satisfaction have been met, to measure the impact on behaviour, and to determine whether additional communication or design changes are needed to address issues arising in ongoing flexible program administration.

BEFORE PROGRAM DESIGN

Employee listening can serve several purposes prior to program design.

First, listening can provide a perspective or context for task force decision making. As any organization that has worked on a flexible program can attest, there are times when the development process comes to a standstill because agreement cannot be reached on design issues. Often the deadlocks are based on conflicting hypotheses about employee needs, concerns, and goals. For example, one person states that employees will not care about more life insurance; another argues that the organization should not communicate the flexible program as being a "big deal" because all that is happening is that employees are being given choices, with no additional company dollars; another holds that only one dental option is needed, because all employees will buy the most dental coverage possible. Employee listening provides definitive information to prove or disprove such hypotheses and keep the design process moving.

A second reason for conducting employee listening prior to program development is related to the basic nature of flexible programs — the emphasis is on meeting individual employees' benefit needs. Preliminary employee listening identifies individual benefit preferences and priorities and defines what needs to be done by the organization and the employee to meet those needs.

AFTER PROGRAM DESIGN

After a preliminary design has been developed, employee listening can be used to test reactions to the proposed program and to identify employee information needs. Specifically, listening can answer five important questions about the implementation of a proposed program.

First, listening can assess how employees react to the philosophy underlying the proposed program design. Listening can probe how employees react to key design considerations, such as the equity of the option pricing, the need for improved cost control, and so forth. Insights into these overall reactions provide a valuable framework for understanding employee attitudes toward and perceptions of individual program components.

Second, listening for design purposes can determine how employees will react to the particular option features proposed and answer such questions as how well the design meets employee needs, whether it offers the right number of choices, and what changes employees would make to the program if given the chance. This information illuminates the perceived value of each of the various options and helps the employer see whether the design specifics are right from the employees' perspective. Research after program design typically examines employee reactions to:

- The range of benefit options across types of benefits and within benefit types (supplemental medical, dental, life, disability, time off);
- Specific design features of the benefit options (co-payments, deductibles, fee schedules, drug formularies, maximum benefits, pay replacements); and
- Pricing of benefit options (by family status, age, income, gender, health status, or smoker status).

Third, through a mock enrolment exercise, listening can be used to develop projections of choices that the entire employee population might make under the proposed program. Such information on likely elections can also help assure the employer that assumptions made regarding option pricing and adverse selection are appropriate for the particular organization.

Fourth, listening can probe whether the planned content and approach of flexible benefit communication materials are appropriate. Under the flexible approach, decision-making responsibility rests with the employee, so there is little room for misunderstanding or omissions. Listening can assess the appropriate approach and quantity of communication. For example, the research can answer the following questions: What flexible benefit information is best delivered by the benefits department? Is the use of a DVD or employee meeting important to assure consistency in explaining program rationale? What do employees recall about the most recent benefits communications they've been sent? Research focusing on these issues will pinpoint the effectiveness of communication media, prioritize the allocation of media dollars, and help decide whether media changes are needed.

Fifth, listening can uncover whether there are differences in understanding and appeal of a flexible program among employee subgroups and help in fine-tuning final program design and communication.

AFTER COMMUNICATION DEVELOPMENT

Listening after plan design will provide a comprehensive view of employees' assessment of the proposed program and the planned communication approach. To ensure that the program's targeted changes in employee attitudes and behaviours are met, an organization may want to consider an additional step — small-group testing of communication at critical points, such as:

- The appeal and motivational impact of graphics, themes, and key messages;
- The ability of the media plan to meet the media preferences of different demographic and attitudinal subgroups;
- The clarity of descriptions and presentations.

Small groups might be called together three times during the course of implementation: to test graphics/themes and the media approach; to test manuscript copy announcing the flexible benefit program and describing its key philosophies and components; and to "pilot" an employee meeting. In each case, a few groups of twelve to fifteen employees each would help identify the key communication issues and materials to achieve the program's objectives for employee enrolment, understanding, and appreciation.

AFTER PROGRAM IMPLEMENTATION

After the program's introduction, employees must prepare for second, third, and subsequent enrolments. They will read and study the communication materials, discuss the various benefit options, review last year's expenses to estimate upcoming health spending account deposits, assess whether they should increase their coverage, and so forth. In subsequent years, listening can be useful in probing such issues as:

- How smoothly did the enrolment process go? Many benefit managers say they hear only about the problems and feel the need for a more realistic and well-rounded picture of how the process worked.
- Are communication pieces effective? Are employees reading them? Should some materials be added or dropped? What questions or confusions still exist? Have new issues arisen?
- Are employees paying as careful attention to the process in subsequent years? Are they actively rethinking their choices each year, or do they become content to stay with their prior elections? Probing the reasons for employee elections can become important, particularly in situations where the employer was counting on employees opting for certain coverages in subsequent years.

- Are the enhanced levels of benefit appreciation and understanding initially associated with a flexible approach being maintained? Do employees understand and appreciate benefits more once they have experience with choice-making? Or are employees settling back to pre-flexible levels of awareness?

§ 20.2 WHEN NOT TO LISTEN TO EMPLOYEES ABOUT FLEXIBLE BENEFITS

There are two situations in which employee input on flexible benefits should not be gathered. The first situation involves dangerous questions. The second involves dangerous answers.

A dangerous question is one in which the flexible benefit education presented to employees would reveal a controversial message before the business case and top management support for the change is obtained. This might be the case, for example, in the event of a freeze on the company's subsidy for benefits or a significant increase in out-of-pocket costs. All interested groups need to be informed of the messages to be shared and the likely employee relations impact.

A dangerous answer is one to which the organization is unwilling to respond. For instance, do not ask employees their opinion of a new benefit pricing approach if the intent is to proceed with the change regardless of employees' reactions. Instead, focus the research on determining the best strategy for communicating the new approach.

§ 20.3 USES AND PURPOSES OF EMPLOYEE LISTENING

Organizations study employees' attitudes toward flexible benefits in order to:

- Assess the current environment;
- Build employee awareness/agreement with objectives;
- Determine key perceived advantages and disadvantages;
- Uncover benefit-related needs, concerns, and goals;
- Learn how much planning/preparation employees have done to meet their needs;
- Simulate the enrolment process;
- Identify enrolment patterns;
- Measure/monitor flexible benefits impact; and
- Evaluate the effectiveness of communication media.

ASSESS THE CURRENT ENVIRONMENT

Employee reactions to flexible benefits can both affect and be affected by an organization's overall environment. The value of assessing these situations is to gain a sense of whether reactions to benefits can be attributed to the benefits themselves or to other work-related factors. This insight can help guide the appropriate tone, perspective, and approach for communication about benefits.

As employers plan for the introduction of a flexible benefit program, there are environmental factors to consider that may impact perceptions of flexible benefits. It is important to learn whether employees enthusiastically support the change as visible proof that the organization is concerned for the individual. Or, will employees resist the change, because recent downsizing and cost reduction efforts have raised suspicion and anxiety that this is simply a way of reducing benefits? Clearly, studying the environmental "filters" employees will use in evaluating flexible benefits will help determine the appropriate strategy for the program's introductory and ongoing communication. The research can help ensure that the communication builds on, supports, and reinforces positive employee perceptions of the environment, and addresses and lessens any negative perceptions.

BUILD EMPLOYEE AWARENESS/AGREEMENT WITH OBJECTIVES

These days, many organizations are making changes to their benefit programs to control costs, as well as to meet diverse employee needs. Employees' reactions to the efforts are often mixed. Some employees eagerly accept the need for change and see the connection between managing benefit costs and meeting business goals. Others directly resist the need for change and may view new cost-sharing features as unreasonable, perhaps due to concern about a lack of commitment by the company to support benefits in the future. Learning which attitudes exist among employees before presenting the program objectives can identify what design and communication approaches will best build employee ownership and support.

DETERMINE KEY PERCEIVED ADVANTAGES AND DISADVANTAGES

Another reason for studying reactions to flexible benefits is to determine a program's key appeals and issues. Employees base impressions of a benefits program on many different considerations — the level of benefit coverage, the cost of those benefits, expectations for future cost increases, internal (across work groups) and external (across similar organizations) competitiveness, and the consistency of messages about benefits and other aspects of the business. Employee research can identify the most significant or valued aspects of the program which deserve particular communication emphasis, and which need change or further explanation.

Uncovering concerns and anxieties blocking acceptance of a flexible benefit program is another potential value of employee research. The design of the program may be sound and may allow employees to buy back current coverage at no additional cost, but employees may still not support its introduction. In this case, employees may focus their attention on the employer's commitment to subsidizing benefits in the future. Advance warning of this concern can give the information needed to be sure the organization sets expectations appropriately for the company's and employees' respective responsibilities for paying for benefits in the future. Uncovering issues early in the planning process will allow employers to respond to employee concerns proactively and avoid misunderstanding or confusion later in the process.

UNCOVER BENEFIT-RELATED NEEDS, CONCERNS, AND GOALS

Benefit preferences vary considerably by demographic subgroups, such as family situation, age, and income. Employee needs, concerns, and goals are also impacted by situational issues — an employee relations issue at a particular location, differences in business goals or results by division, or a widely dispersed employee population. Research targeted to these employee subgroups and situations can probe how best to structure the communication of flexible benefits for each.

A large Canadian organization with employees spread over 1,000 locations faced many challenges in introducing flexible benefits to its workforce. Health-related needs and concerns were the first priority for the employees, according to results of a survey. However, lifestyle issues like balancing work/personal life, dealing with stress, and having fun were also important. This led to different expectations for flexible benefits among these employees than among employees at many other organizations. Focus group reactions to the proposed flexible benefit design showed significant shifts away from current options to best accommodate individual situations and lifestyles. Choice and responsibility for making benefit decisions were welcomed by these employees.

LEARN HOW MUCH PLANNING/PREPARATION EMPLOYEES HAVE DONE TO MEET THEIR NEEDS

Employers and employees share the responsibility for meeting employee needs, concerns, and goals. In order to understand how much responsibility employees are taking for getting their needs met, questions are often asked about the relative importance of needs and how much planning an employee has done to meet those needs. These findings direct employer activities in providing resources, tools, and communication, in addition to the benefit coverage, to meet their needs. Posing these questions also reinforces the idea that employees have some responsibility for meeting their own needs.

SIMULATE THE ENROLMENT PROCESS; IDENTIFY ENROLMENT PATTERNS

A valuable outcome of a focus group process is to determine the questions and concerns that would be likely to arise during the actual enrolment process. While a great deal of information is compressed into a relatively short time-frame, focus group participants provide many suggestions about making the enrolment process easier.

In some cases, an overnight enrolment exercise is used to give employees time to review their personal situation as they consider their enrolment choices. Employees are asked to select the options and coverage categories they would likely choose in an actual enrolment. This data allows potential adjustments to be made to the projected enrolments during the design phase.

MEASURE/MONITOR FLEXIBLE BENEFIT DESIGN IMPACT

The flexible benefit program should encourage certain employee attitudes and behaviours. Many employers hope that employees will judge the program to be fair, adequate, competitive, and easy to understand. In addition to enrolment and usage statistics, employee research can measure and monitor the degree to which a design achieves the desired impact, and identify areas that need additional attention.

EVALUATE THE EFFECTIVENESS OF COMMUNICATION MEDIA

Flexible benefit information is communicated in many ways — some formal and intended (a statement of benefit objectives), some informal (the grapevine), some unintended (the perceived inconsistency of benefit cutbacks despite record profits). It is important to evaluate the impact and effectiveness of each communication source. It is also critical to evaluate the interaction and consistency of the various communication sources — employee handbook, enrolment materials, human resources' responses to benefit questions, and so on. Analysing both the separate and combined impact of these varied sources will allow development of strategic and tactical media plans to best deliver desired flexible benefit messages and avoid inconsistency between messages.

§ 20.4 LISTENING AS COMMUNICATION

The listening process is itself a form of employee communication — an important and visible message that management cares about employee opinions. However, the listening process will raise employee questions. Why is the company asking about benefits? What will be done with the information gathered? How will things change as a result of the study?

CREATING APPROPRIATE EXPECTATIONS

Listening to employees to gather reactions to a proposed flexible benefit program is itself an act of communication. It says to employees that benefits are being studied with the intent to make changes. Listening will raise expectations that results of the research will be acted upon.

Concerns about raising employee expectations causes some organizations to shy away from conducting employee research. Raising expectations is not really a problem, though. The only problem is raising inappropriate expectations.

To create appropriate expectations, an announcement or cover memo can be distributed to explain the reasons for studying flexible benefits, and carefully set out the parameters of the study. It is also important to identify the other considerations — financial and administrative, for instance — that will impact final decisions about flexible benefits.

CAPITALIZING ON GOODWILL CREATED

The listening process can capitalize on the employee relations value of seeking input. Even if only a small number of focus group interviews are to be conducted, an announcement of a study can be sent to all employees. After any type of listening, follow-up communication should identify ways employee suggestions were addressed or explain why they were not addressed, if that is the case. This turns the process into a two-way communication channel and provides an opportunity to explain both employees' and management's points of view.

An additional communication opportunity presents itself for employee listening on flexible benefits. A key communication message for any flexible benefit program is that a flexible approach responds to individual employee needs. The listening process can help reinforce the broader message of flexible benefits by stressing that employees are being asked to identify their needs to be sure the program suits them as well as possible within the benefit budget available.

§ 20.5 RESEARCH TECHNIQUES

There are two distinct approaches that can be used to gather employee input: quantitative and qualitative. Quantitative listening involves some sort of questionnaire or survey, administered by paper and pencil or electronic forms. Qualitative listening involves in-person interviewing, either one-on-one or in small group meetings. In addition, several combinations or hybrid approaches have been developed to gather both quantitative and qualitative data.

An analogy may help clarify the differences between the two approaches. Quantitative surveys are similar to a telescope. They provide a broad picture of what is on the horizon. Qualitative interviewing is more like a microscope. It studies the way individual components work together to form a whole. Attitudes toward any issue are the result of a number of factors. Certainly, facts play a part, but only a part. Expectations, rumours, trust, misunderstanding, interest, apathy, and personal situations all affect employee attitudes. Quantitative listening identifies the key factors present in a particular environment; qualitative interviewing identifies how the factors work together to shape attitudes.

QUANTITATIVE LISTENING

The purpose of quantitative listening is to determine statistically how many employees feel a certain way, to measure how strongly people feel on particular issues, and whether various employee subgroups have similar or different points of view. The challenge is to develop a survey questionnaire that is comprehensive and clear. The questionnaire must address all the relevant issues, and employees must understand and be capable of responding to the questions asked. The questionnaire must also be appropriately designed to allow effective interpretation of results by avoiding leading or ambiguous questions. In some cases, a survey pre-test is done on a small cross-section of employees to determine the appropriateness, interpretation, and base of understanding of the survey.

The primary advantage of a quantitative survey is that it provides definitive statistics. The results quantify precisely how many employees agree and how many disagree with whatever questions have been asked. For example, the results can quantify how many employees are comfortable with benefit choice-making, how many are not, how many express interest in various options, and so forth.

The second advantage is that detailed analyses can be performed to determine whether different groups of employees have different opinions. For example, subgroup analysis can pinpoint whether employees in different family situations have different reactions toward the way a flexible credit allowance is allocated, whether special communication needs exist at different locations, and so on.

If a standardized survey is used, a third advantage is that the results allow valuable database comparisons to be made in order to determine if an organization's employee reactions are typical or atypical. This information can then be used to identify issues unique to that employer's environment that may call for special attention.

The fourth advantage is that an electronic or written survey is a more efficient, less time-consuming way to reach a large number of employees than face-to-face meetings with the same number of employees. This is of particular benefit for organizations with a widely scattered workforce. In such circumstances, a questionnaire is perhaps the only practical way to involve employees in outlying locations and to reach such locations with a positive message of management's interest in their opinions.

There are also some disadvantages inherent in quantitative surveys, however. Most significant is the limited opportunity provided for employee education. While this is a minor issue when testing general employee benefit preferences, it is a critical drawback when testing reactions to a specific flexible program design, especially one with substantial cost management changes. For employees to provide well-informed reactions and opinions, in-person education with the opportunity for questions and answers is needed. If the goal is to change employee attitudes and behaviour patterns in the use of costly benefits such as medical and retirement, this education component is crucial.

A second limitation of a quantitative survey is that the reasons for and feelings behind the opinions identified cannot be probed very well. The data will clearly determine whether employees think their new flexible benefit program is "average," "above average," or "below average," but it will fail to explain *why* employees hold those opinions. What program are employees comparing this one to when they judge benefit quality? Are some of the benefits more prominent in their minds than others when they make that judgment? Are they less concerned about life insurance because medical is their top priority? Inability to track such thought patterns is one of the limitations of a quantitative survey.

Finally, there is an issue that can be an advantage or a disadvantage, depending upon the objectives of the employee listening exercise. A quantitative survey is very high profile; the questionnaire makes it evident that a particular issue or benefit area is being explored. If a benefit improvement is going to be introduced or additional flexibility is to be offered with no benefit cutback, the advance notice can be a plus. The survey can be the early signal that something is coming and a visible sign that the employee perspective is being taken under advisement. Feedback of the survey results can also serve as a first step in the communication campaign to build excitement about the change.

On the other hand, if there is a cutback under study, the high profile can work to the employer's disadvantage. If management is not prepared to communicate the details and answer employee questions and concerns, a qualitative listening approach is more appropriate.

QUALITATIVE LISTENING

The purpose of qualitative listening is to discover why particular employee attitudes exist. Opinions are formed as a result of many considerations, including facts, misinterpretations, rumours, expectations, past experiences, and emotions. How key factors work together to create opinions about flexible benefit programs can be sorted out through in-person discussions. With this knowledge, ways to maintain the positive attitudes you want to reinforce or strengthen, and ways to correct or overcome any negative attitudes can be identified.

For testing interest in choice-making, qualitative listening typically takes the form of focus group interviews. This involves gathering together a cross-section of employees in groups of twelve to fifteen at a time. A trained focus group facilitator leads the discussion, making sure that the discussion stays on track, that all employees participate, and that no one dominates the discussion. The goal is to tap into or replicate the type of employee discussion that takes place in the hallways, cafeterias, and lounge areas of an organization.

Generally, focus groups are most effective with a diverse mix of participants — employees with different lengths of service, different family situations, and a mix of men and women. Such diversity tends to generate a more lively discussion. As a fringe benefit, a mixed group also helps participants to see that different needs and opinions exist and that management is facing the challenge of satisfying a variety of needs.

One point to consider, however, is that mixing focus group participants in terms of grade or pay level may create problems. Benefit discussions often generate comments about family budgets, such as the affordability of an option involving higher medical co-payments. In such situations, lower-income employees could feel uncomfortable with others earning more and refrain from speaking freely. On the other hand, those at a higher income level may feel reluctant to hurt the feelings of others who are more concerned than they are about increased costs. Separating group participants by income or position avoids these problems.

What are the advantages and disadvantages of qualitative listening? The primary advantage is that face-to-face interaction provides the opportunity to track how attitudes are formed, indicating how to target communication to reinforce positive attitudes, as well as how to change or overcome negative attitudes or employee misperceptions.

Another advantage of qualitative interviewing is that the focus group meeting format provides an opportunity for employee education. Employees can be provided with a presentation on a proposed flexible benefit program and have a chance to ask questions. Meeting leaders have a chance for follow-up questioning to be sure employees truly have a good understanding of the information presented and to ensure that employee feedback is based on informed opinion.

In terms of disadvantages, the main drawback is that the results are not quantifiable. The emphasis is on what and why, not how many.

A second possible disadvantage is the potential for group dynamics to affect results. Someone with a very negative attitude, for example, may repeatedly voice complaints and try to dominate the group, or participants may voice only polite agreement to avoid confrontation or repercussions. The meeting leader must be well trained to respond to and balance both kinds of participation.

Finally, as is true for quantitative listening, the approach itself can offer either an advantage or disadvantage. Qualitative interviewing is relatively low profile. Only small numbers of employees are involved, relatively little is in print, and the discussion is open-ended. Qualitative listening is less likely to produce negative repercussions within the environment, but it is also less likely to generate significant employee interest.

COMBINATION APPROACHES

Quantitative and qualitative listening are often combined in order to reap the advantages of both. For example, preliminary qualitative focus groups might be used to identify specific issues with the current benefit structure, and a follow-up survey might then be used to quantify employee attitudes about those issues. Or, a questionnaire that determines employee needs and attitudes may be followed up with qualitative focus groups that probe the reasons behind the attitudes of importance, interest, or concern.

Since the initial explanation of flexible benefits can be complex, a special "hybrid" focus group called an employee study group is often used. This involves gathering employees together for a group discussion, beginning the session with an educational presentation, and concluding the session with each participant completing a questionnaire giving his or her informed opinion on the subject. In some cases, employees also complete an enrolment form based on a personal report of their benefit options and price tags to simulate the enrolment process. This comprehensive process typically requires a three- to four-hour meeting.

SELECTING THE BEST APPROACH

No single approach works best for everyone. Whether a quantitative, qualitative, or a combination approach should be used depends on:

- What information is to be collected;
- What kinds of data are needed in order to make decisions;
- Whether the employer expects to find significant variations in relevant attitudes among different groups of employees;
- How important it is to understand employees' reasons for their answers;
- The intended use of the information;
- How much attention management wants to draw to the study; and
- The time-frame and budget for collecting the information.

§ 20.6 THE RESEARCH PROCESS

PERSPECTIVE

Before deciding to proceed with any employee listening, consideration should be given to environmental issues, such as:

- The usual means of communicating with employees, and how employees are likely to react to a listening study given that prior experience;

- The prevailing employee relations climate; and
- Management's willingness to share the study purpose with employees and to respond to the listening results with either actions or communications.

Such issues can affect both the validity of the listening results and the impact of the listening exercise on overall employer/employee relations.

SETTING OBJECTIVES

To ensure that listening produces the information needed, it is important to consider the way the results are to be used. In defining objectives, consider these issues:

- Is information needed to help decide the appropriateness and value of a flexible program?
- Are the results to be used for a go/no-go decision?
- Is there already a commitment to introducing a flexible benefit program, with employee input being sought only to fine-tune program design?
- Is plan design set and is the goal to assess communication issues and needs?
- Will the research study be the first step in alerting employees to possible flexible benefit changes?
- What expectations should be created or avoided regarding the role employee input will play in flexible benefit design or communication decisions?

Answers to these questions will dictate when the listening should be conducted and whether quantitative or qualitative listening is more appropriate.

In setting objectives, it is important to also step back to consider the bigger picture: to define the issues to be explored, to pin down the specific information needed. At the same time, there is a need to hypothesize a bit about the end results of the research, to ask a series of "what if" questions — what if it is learned that employees feel flexible benefits are only being introduced to control costs? What if employees are expecting significantly more flexibility? Hypothesizing a range of possible results will allow anticipation of issues that might be explored in planning the initial research.

SELECTING PARTICIPANTS

Which employees should participate, how many should participate, and how the participants should be selected depends on several issues:

- The size and nature of the employee population;
- Whether there are subgroups of special interest;

- Statistical precision and certainty about findings required for the types of decisions to be made; and
- "Face validity" or "believability" of results for the people who will review them.

To determine the proper sample, sampling technique and sample size must be considered.

Sampling Techniques

Which sampling technique will best suit the organization's needs depends upon the listening objectives. If the interest is in very precise statistical results to infer information about the total population, a larger random, stratified, or cluster sample would be used. If the interest is in testing the waters, where only general reactions are needed, a smaller random sample or a purposive sample would be appropriate.

The following describes these various sampling methods in more detail:

- A random sample could be used if the intention is for everyone in the population to have an equal possibility of being selected. (A simple example would be selecting every twentieth name from an employee roster arranged in a non-ordered fashion, with the starting name chosen randomly.)
- A stratified random sample is more appropriate, however, if there are many subgroups of interest within the population, such as specific job categories, work locations, or demographic subgroups. This involves separating the population into these key subgroups (or "strata"), and then selecting participants from within each subgroup. Selection from within each subgroup would be made randomly.
- A disadvantage of a stratified random sample may exist, however, if there are widely dispersed work locations and the employer wants to conduct in-person listening meetings. In that case, selecting a stratified random sample would include some employees from all locations, resulting in complex logistics and significant travel expenses.

   To avoid such a scattered sample, while maintaining statistical projectability, a cluster stratified sample could be used. This involves selecting a limited number of locations typical of overall employee population, and then randomly selecting employees from just those locations.
- A purposive sample is appropriate if the interest is in learning the opinions of targeted employee segments, such as new hires, bonus-eligible managers, employees nearing retirement, or perhaps high-performers with "superior" performance evaluations. Selection from within the targeted segment can then be done randomly if the number of possible participants is large.

Sample Size

If listening participants are chosen properly, the reaction of a sample of employees can be used to predict the reactions of the total population. To accomplish this, consider what degree of precision and certainty about the results is required for the types of decisions to be made.

Typically, if statistical validity is required, the use of an electronic or mail survey is preferred. Response rates on electronic benefits surveys typically range from 50 to 70 per cent, while the response rates for paper surveys are somewhat lower, ranging from 40 to 60 per cent. Response rates are influenced by a number of factors — well-communicated surveys on important topics tend to experience the highest response rates.

For example, for large populations, say over 5,000 employees, a total sample size of 400 (assuming a random sampling process is used) would provide a confidence level of 95 per cent, with a confidence interval of 5 per cent. This means there is 95 per cent certainty that results gathered are within 5 per cent of the results that would have been obtained by surveying all employees. In order to attain a sample size of 400, 800 employees would have to be surveyed electronically, based on an expected response rate of 50 to 70 per cent.

Focus groups or study groups are designed to gather a representative cross-section of opinions rather than a high level of statistical validity. Typically 100 to 150 employees are invited to participate in groups of twelve to fifteen employees.

ADMINISTRATIVE PROCEDURES

Study procedures must be carefully defined and monitored to ensure the success of the listening effort. Timing and responsibilities should be set for:

- Scheduling: Managing the listening process (survey administration, focus group logistics), co-ordination of development, and review of materials.
- Administration: How participants in qualitative interviews should be assigned to groups; whether questionnaires should be administered by mail, electronically, by telephone, or in group meetings.
- Logistics of the listening process: Setting up meeting space for focus groups, inviting and confirming participants, following up to encourage a good focus group or survey participation rate.

ANALYSIS

Employee responses must be considered in relationship to one another to find the proper perspective and interpretation. An analysis should:

- Review the overall results, and look for significant trends — the most positive and most negative results, the most surprising or unexpected results.

- Identify areas of deviation from the overall trends among employee demographics or work subgroups.
- Tie together results that have a meaningful correlation, such as perceptions of current versus proposed benefits, or the impact of agreement with flexible benefit objectives on appreciation of the plan. Survey results should be able to be tied to other important metrics used by the organization over time, such as claims experience, health care cost inflation, or benefit costs per employee.

The key to meaningful analysis, and to a successful listening study, is to compile the results in a way that identifies potential actions that increase the chances of designing a successful flexible program.

§ 20.7 ETHICS IN LISTENING RESEARCH

Conducting research places important responsibilities on those responsible for gathering, analysing, reporting, and storing participant information. More specifically, it requires that the research be performed according to standards established to protect the rights of research participants.

The following key phrases describe ethical protections that have been established within the social research community to help protect the rights of research participants:

- Voluntary participation
- Informed consent
- Privacy — confidentiality, anonymity, and data storage

Each of these is discussed in detail below.

VOLUNTARY PARTICIPATION

The principle of voluntary participation means that employees under consideration for involvement in listening research must have the option to decline participation, either before the research begins or while it is underway. Ideally, participants should be informed at the time they are invited that participation is encouraged but is voluntary, and that declining to participate will have no adverse effect on them.

Consequently, when using a research approach involving participant sampling, additional "back-up" participants should be selected. These "back-ups" can then be used as substitutions should any invited participants decline.

In addition to meeting ethical standards, conducting listening research using voluntary participation can help in collecting valid data by avoiding input from individuals who feel coerced into participating and who may not, therefore, provide their genuine viewpoints.

INFORMED CONSENT

Closely related to the principle of voluntary participation is informed consent. Informed consent in the context of employee listening means that the individuals involved have agreed to participate in the research based on a factual understanding of:

- The purpose of the research;
- The information they will be asked to provide;
- How the information will be collected;
- How the collected information will be used and/or reported; and
- Commitments regarding data privacy.

While it is unusual to ask participating employees to sign a consent form, it is incumbent on those conducting listening research to provide participants with full disclosure of the information in the points listed above. Those who choose to participate based on an understanding of this information are deemed to have given their consent.

This underscores the need for careful planning in advance of the listening research to ensure that all pertinent information about the research has been defined and can be communicated to invited participants.

PRIVACY— CONFIDENTIALITY AND ANONYMITY

Employee listening can be a worthwhile and important part of the flexible benefits design process and implementation. It can, however, bring to the surface employee attitudes, beliefs, opinions, behaviours, and background information that are personal and/or controversial. Therefore, it is the responsibility of all those involved in conducting the research, and in using the research results, to ensure that information provided by participants is not shared in a form that can negatively affect those providing it.

Confidentiality

Almost all research guarantees confidentiality, meaning that personally identifying information will only be made available to persons directly involved in the research. However, confidentiality is open to wide interpretations and it is therefore important to clarify just what information will be made available to whom. Personally identifying information should be strictly limited to only those individuals with a legitimate need to access it. The following serve as general guidelines:

- **Quantitative research** — Access to individual survey responses should be limited to the individual(s) performing data input of the responses, and to the individual(s) responsible for analysing, compiling, and storing the raw survey data. Reporting of survey results should adhere to the *principle of ten* — results should only be reported for demographic groups (e.g., gender, organization group, age category, etc.) with ten or more responses. This is a recognized data reporting standard for assuring confidentiality of individual survey responses.

- **Qualitative research** — Access to individual responses will be available to the facilitator/interviewer, as well as a note-taker, if one is used. Findings from this research can report information such as themes, benefit program selections, and direct quotes from participants, provided the identity of any participant cannot be reasonably derived from what is presented.

Anonymity

Related to confidentiality is anonymity, but there is a very important distinction between the two. Committing to participant anonymity basically means participants will remain anonymous to anyone involved in the research, including the researchers themselves. To make this assurance, the use of a third party for data collection — either quantitative or qualitative — is required, as is a guarantee that the third party will not make available any individual data to the employer.

While the anonymity standard is clearly a stronger assurance of privacy, it is also a more difficult one to accomplish.

PRIVACY — DATA STORAGE

Confidential records (e.g., survey questionnaires, focus group notes) should be stored in an area with restricted access, with consideration given to stripping documents of any personal identifiers. Electronic files should be password protected. Individuals having access to this data should be clearly identified, as should their responsibility for maintaining data privacy.

The importance of commitments to the privacy of participants' information, along with the means required to honour these commitments, underscores the importance of thorough planning and communication before listening research is conducted.

Part Six

Administration

Twenty-One

Managing Administration

§ 21.1 GETTING STARTED

INVOLVING THE ADMINISTRATORS

Administering a flexible benefit program is more complicated than administering a traditional benefit program. Administration is a major consideration from the standpoint of both implementation and ongoing processing. It makes sense, therefore, to involve key administrators as early as possible in the plan design process. The plan design and plan objectives are major factors in determining the cost and feasibility of flexible program administration.

Departments with administrative procedures and systems that typically are affected most by a flexible program include benefit administration, payroll, finance, and data processing. The individuals who can provide the best input on the impact of a proposed program on these areas are the ones most familiar with the current procedures and systems. These procedures and systems include the administration of current benefit programs, payroll processing, financial reporting, and payroll and human resource information systems. Without the involvement of these individuals, what may seem like a minor issue to the program designers could make the administrative tasks considerably more costly or, in the worst case, impossible.

If, for some reason, it is not possible to involve representatives from each administrative area in the initial plan design, it may be appropriate to refrain from finalizing the plan design until an administrative evaluation can determine the program's full effect on administration.

DEVELOPING A DETAILED PROGRAM DESIGN

Once the basic plan design is complete and approved by management, there likely will be many open design issues remaining that affect administration. To determine which open issues need to be addressed, first look at policies, procedures, and systems associated with the current benefit program. Which existing requirements also must be met by the flexible program? Second, study each aspect of the proposed flexible program and determine its effect on each employee category (full-time, part-time, etc.) and employee status (retired, temporary, leave of absence, etc.). Third, identify new benefit administration requirements created by the flexible program (such as health spending account processing, annual re-enrolment, and so on).

Here are some examples of the kinds of questions that may be resolved in the detailed design process:

- What data items are required (for example, date of birth, hire date, number of dependants)?
- What information is necessary to administer the co-ordination of health care benefits features (dependants' names, dates of birth, spousal coverage)?
- What are the eligibility requirements for each employment category covered under the flexible program?
- How will flexible credits elected as cash be allocated to employees? What will be the frequency of allocation (for example, lump sum at the end of the year, equal instalments each pay period)?
- How will changes in compensation during the plan year affect pay-based coverage amounts and employee costs?
- What coverage, if any, will be given to employees who fail to turn in enrolment elections?
- How will employee coverages and costs change due to changes in employment status? Family status?
- How are status changes handled? What changes are permitted?
- What are the reporting requirements of the flexible program to insurance carriers? Third-party administrators? Accounting? Employees?
- How is the life insurance benefit rounded? To the nearest $1,000? Higher than $1,000? What about long-term disability?
- What coverage will newly eligible employees receive? When do they become eligible?
- What are the components of pay (i.e., base earnings, bonuses, commissions, etc.) for pay-related plans? What is the timing of pay changes vis-à-vis the enrolment period?

Finalize specifications for the administrative system(s) only after the detailed program design is complete. Otherwise, either the system may end up driving the plan design, instead of supporting the program, or it may become impossible to define the system because there are too many open issues.

ADMINISTRATIVE FUNCTIONS

Whether the flexible program is limited in scope, including only health care choices, or broad in offering choices in many benefit areas, the same basic administrative activities need to be performed. The administrative functions of most flexible programs include enrolment in the program, ongoing coverage administration, health spending account record-keeping, payroll processing, and insurance carrier reporting.

§ 21.2 ENROLMENT PROCESSING

TYPES OF ENROLMENT

Flexible program enrolments can be classified as annual enrolment of all participants and enrolment of newly eligible employees. The difference in the administrative activities involved in each enrolment type is principally one of scale. Annual enrolments usually involve all eligible participants, whereas newly eligible enrolments may involve only a small number of employees.

The first annual enrolment involves all eligible employees. Administering the initial annual enrolment usually begins three or more months before the program effective date. In subsequent plan years, all eligible employees may be required to re-enrol, as options, option prices, and flexible credit allocations, if any, change from year to year. Even though all eligible employees are involved in an annual re-enrolment, employee understanding of the flexible program is greater than in the first program year. Therefore, the annual re-enrolment effort may not require as much time to plan or execute. If no changes occur in either options or prices, annual re-enrolment may be limited to employees wishing to change their elections.

For many employees in an organization introducing a flexible benefit plan, the concept of flexible benefits will be new. Therefore, many employers try to allow enough time for employees to understand the program, including discussing options with other family members. Interim coverage in critical benefit areas may be provided to new employees until the employee is eligible for enrolment in the flexible program. This approach provides employees with basic coverage while they are considering their flexible program elections. Interim coverages or longer waiting periods are used frequently by organizations with high employee turnover in the first months following employment.

DATA COLLECTION AND VERIFICATION

For a new plan, the first step in the enrolment process is the collection and verification of participant data required by the plan design and administrative requirements for the program. Flexible programs typically require data that is similar to that required by non-flexible programs, including name, unique employee identification number, work location or home address, date of birth, date of hire, pay, and employment category.

Dependant data is not usually required in advance for a new plan unless the data is readily available to be converted from another system. Where dependant data is not available, the participant will enter the information as part of the enrolment process. Spouse's date of birth is especially important if a spousal life insurance plan is included in the program and the premium rates are based on a spouse's age.

Beneficiary data may also be converted from a prior system, provided the paper forms with original signatures are available. If the beneficiary data is not available or is unreliable, employees can elect new beneficiaries as part of the enrolment process. Since an original form is required for a valid beneficiary designation, the form must be printed, signed, and returned before the designation can take effect. Employees in Quebec may not be able to change their beneficiary designation if the original was made irrevocable.

Collection of the required data involves identification of the data source and/or consolidation of data to a central source. This depends on the degree to which data is already centralized, and the accessibility of the data to the enrolment system.

Verification of data is very important, especially when accuracy can affect an individual's eligibility for the program or the options and option prices available. Such data may include pay, age, length of service, employment category, employment status, and work location.

Clearly, if required data resides in one place and is reasonably accurate, this initial step of the enrolment process for a new flexible plan requires less time and effort than if data must be collected from several sources, or if the accuracy of the data is unreliable.

For a re-enrolment, the collection of data is not necessary if the enrolment system has been updated on a regular basis throughout the year. Where the enrolment system is only used once a year for annual enrolment, data must be updated as described above.

It is critical to ensure that data collection, storage, and related administration functions are compliant with Canadian privacy legislation, which was recently strengthened with the passage of the *Personal Information Protection and Electronic Documents Act (PIPEDA)*. Here are some suggestions for complying:

- Limit the use of data to only those elements needed for administration. For example, administrators should use a unique employee identification number instead of the social insurance number as an identifier.

- Create an environment where a password is required to access information on confidential data.
- Ensure that access to the administration system, databases, and facilities is secure to ensure that the privacy of data is maintained.

PERFORMING CALCULATIONS

After required data has been collected and verified, the next step in the enrolment process is to determine which options are available for each eligible participant and to compute the corresponding price tags. If a credit-based pricing approach is being used, then the flexible credits must also be calculated. Eligibility is based on factors such as service, employment status, employment category, location, and possibly age. For a limited program offering the same options and pricing for everyone, no individual calculations are necessary. On the other hand, under a broad flexible program, price tags for some options, such as life insurance, may be based on pay, age, and gender. Similarly, supplemental medical and dental price tags may vary based on factors such as an employee's work location, province of residence, coverage category, or employment status. And in credit-based pricing structures, the employer may allocate flexible credits based on individual participant characteristics, such as pay or length of service.

Depending on the plan rules, it may be necessary to lay out which options are available to each participant for the year. For example, the plan may require that participants remain in the same medical or dental plan for a minimum number of years. In the case of life insurance or long-term disability, an increase in coverage over the current level may require evidence of insurability. The system must be able to monitor these requirements.

For programs with variable elements, as described above, each employee's available options and corresponding price tags and flexible credit allowance, if any, will have to be individually calculated.

ENROLMENT MATERIAL

The scope of the program and the sophistication of the enrolment system will affect the type of enrolment materials used. The enrolment process for a flexible program is usually conducted online through a Web-based enrolment application with little or no printed personalized information. In most cases, the only personalized information participants receive is a notification that includes their unique identification number and a temporary password enabling them to access the system. The non-personalized materials provided to support the enrolment could include printed or online electronic enrolment guides. Chapter 18 discusses the communication of a flexible plan in more detail.

COLLECTING PARTICIPANT ELECTIONS

There are several common approaches to processing election decisions:

- Automated Web-based enrolment applications
- Voice response systems
- Paper enrolment forms.

Automated Web-Based Enrolment

Online or Web-based enrolment is the most common approach for collecting and processing enrolment information. Historically, the availability of computers with Internet access has been a consideration in deciding whether or not to adopt Web-based enrolment. Today, access to computers at work or home is not an issue for most participants. Where participants don't have computer access at work or at home, kiosk terminals in the workplace are an alternative. A printer is also typically required to produce beneficiary forms, evidence of insurability forms, and personal confirmation statements.

Web-based enrolment normally involves the following steps:

- **Logging on.** Participants access the Web-based enrolment application and log on using their identification number and password. Where the password is temporary, the participant is prompted to select a new, permanent password.
- **Enrolling.** The participant is guided through a number of steps, including verification of personal data and updating or adding dependant information. In credit-based pricing structures, the individual credits must also be determined and presented. Option prices, and benefits eligibility are calculated and displayed. The participant then selects the appropriate options for his or her situation.
- **Reviewing.** Participants can review their elections and change them, if desired, at any time up to the enrolment deadline.
- **Printing forms.** After making the benefit elections, participants will have an opportunity to review and update their beneficiary information and complete any evidence of insurability forms. Typically, these forms can be printed out directly from the Web-based enrolment application.
- **Confirming.** The final step is to review the personal confirmation statement that shows the participant's elections, payroll deductions, dependants, and their coverage. Beneficiary information may also be included on the statement. Confirmation statements may be printed by the participant. Printing is unnecessary in cases where the administration system allows the confirmation statement to be viewed online at any time throughout the year.

Interactive Voice Response (IVR)

Interactive voice response (IVR) systems allow employees to enter their enrolment elections using the telephone. By following instructions from a pre-recorded script, employees enter their election decisions by pressing the appropriate numbers on the telephone key pad. Most IVR systems immediately verify the validity of the elections and notify the participant of any incorrect choices.

IVR systems are no longer commonly used in the enrolment process. The set-up costs to establish an IVR system can be quite high and, therefore, IVR is not cost-effective for most employers. In addition, Web-based solutions provide enhanced functionality and an improved enrolment experience for employees.

Paper Forms

Paper forms are also no longer commonly used for collecting election decisions. The forms require participants to enter their election choices and price tags, and may require employees to indicate whether they will pay for their benefit choices with pre-tax company dollars (flexible credits) or post-tax payroll deductions. Since this approach is manual, it is the most prone to errors. The administration system must identify enrolment errors as elections are entered by administrative staff.

ENROLMENT MONITORING

A status monitoring program is an essential part of the enrolment system where large numbers of participants are involved or where the enrolment process involves multiple locations. Status monitoring allows the administrator to determine which participants have not yet enrolled or have incomplete enrolments on the system. More sophisticated systems can automatically send an e-mail reminder to these participants.

POST-ELECTION REPORTING AND ANALYSIS

After the annual enrolment is completed, statistical and analytical reports may be produced for use in analysing the impact of the program. The election analysis reports can be used to determine such matters as:

- Is the program meeting the needs of employees?
- Is the program meeting management objectives? (For example, if health care cost containment is an objective, are employees electing the managed care options?)

- What changes in the benefit program should be considered for next year? (For example, should some options be replaced if few participants are electing them?)

Election analysis reports have the most value when reports from one year are compared to reports from another year. Election analysis reports typically include summary information on elections in each of the benefit areas, as well as on the overall use of employer contributions (flexible credits in many plans) and payroll deductions. Information may be broken down by age, service, pay level, family status, location, and so forth.

§ 21.3 ONGOING ADMINISTRATION OF COVERAGE

Another area of flexible benefit administration is the ongoing administration of benefits for both participants enrolled in the program and new employees prior to their eligibility for the flexible program.

Ongoing coverage administration under a flexible program differs somewhat, although not greatly, from ongoing administration under a traditional benefit program. In most cases, as an organization moves from traditional benefits to flexible benefits, existing ongoing administration procedures need only be modified. In some broad flexible programs, new procedures or systems need to be developed.

One requirement of ongoing administration may be to process interim coverage for new employees. This requirement depends on the design of the program. If the program provides employees with some basic levels of coverage prior to eligibility for the flexible program, new employees need to complete enrolment forms to authorize payroll deductions, if any. Interim coverage enrolment processing is included as a function of some flexible program enrolment systems. However, interim coverage enrolment often is administered outside the flexible program enrolment system, for simplicity.

Coverage change processing occurs throughout the year. In general, an employee may change coverage if the employee has a family status change, such as marriage, divorce, or birth/adoption of a child. If an employee terminates or transfers to an employment status that is not eligible for full benefits under the flexible program — for example, from full-time to part-time — the employee's coverage may change. A change in pay may mean that an employee's pay-related coverages, such as life or disability insurance, are increased or decreased. If this occurs, the employee's cost of coverage may or may not change. Flexible credit allowances based solely or partially on pay or family status also may change.

Enrolment change procedures are established to process these coverage changes. Typically, these enrolment changes are performed by the participant through the Web-based enrolment application. Where the enrolment system is not available year-round, paper forms may be used.

The resulting new elections and deduction rates are then updated in the payroll and insurance carrier systems. This is typically handled through a periodic electronic file submission, but can also be done with a manual or paper-based update where the volume of activity is low. In larger plans, with over 500 participants, electronic file transmission is the most common approach.

§ 21.4 FLEXIBLE ACCOUNT ADMINISTRATION

FLEXIBLE ACCOUNT ENROLMENT

Almost all flexible benefit programs include a flexible account (health spending or personal) as part of their design. Many organizations also provide perquisite accounts for their executives. The administration of perquisite accounts is typically handled by the employer and practices vary considerably from company to company. This section, therefore, only deals with the administration of health spending and personal accounts.

If the flexible program offers choice-making in a variety of benefit areas, enrolment in the flexible account is part of the annual enrolment in the program. If the flexible program consists solely of a health spending account, annual enrolment in the program still is required.

Chapter 7 discusses the design of flexible accounts. In particular, it is important to recall that for flexible spending accounts only employer contributions can be used to fund the account. According to Canada Revenue Agency, employees cannot use payroll deductions, salary reduction, or vacation selling to fund a health spending account. While employee payroll deductions could theoretically be used to fund personal accounts, virtually all such accounts are funded solely by company money.

Each year, the employee allocates a number of employer dollars to the account. The funds may be posted to the employee's account monthly, quarterly, or once a year. Throughout the year, the employee requests reimbursement for any eligible expenses, up to the current balance in the account. At the end of the year, any remaining health spending account balance may be either rolled over to next year's account, or forfeited. The plan design will determine which of these applies. Unused personal account balances are normally rolled over from one year to the next.

RECORDING EMPLOYER CONTRIBUTIONS

Employer contributions are periodically posted to each participant's account maintained by the record-keeping system. The record-keeping system is typically designed to update employee accounts automatically with elected employer amounts on a periodic basis, such as monthly, quarterly, or annually (the most common approach). Updating generally occurs at the beginning of the period. The administrator then must verify that the correct amount was allocated to each employee's account and make adjustments to account balances if necessary. For example, an adjustment may be required if an employee was on an unpaid leave of absence, but was still showing an allocation on the record-keeping system.

Amounts deposited to a health spending account are non-taxable, while amounts to the personal accounts are generally taxable on deposit, not when reimbursed. Therefore, amounts deposited to the personal accounts must be recorded to payroll as a taxable benefit to the employee.

PROCESSING REQUESTS FOR REIMBURSEMENT

To begin the payment processing cycle, the employee must complete a request-for-reimbursement claim form and attach the required supporting documents. For health spending and personal accounts, a bill, receipt, or cancelled cheque may provide the required documentation for eligible expenses. Note that most insurance companies allow participants to have the unreimbursed portion of a health or dental claim automatically paid from the health spending account. Where this is not the case, employees must first submit covered health care expenses to the insurance carrier or claims processor. Once the claim is paid, the explanation of benefits form from the claims processor is submitted to the health spending account administrator for reimbursement of the unpaid portion of the expense. Claim submission procedures and a list of eligible expenses should be communicated to employees during enrolment in the health spending or personal account, along with sample claim forms.

Personal account claims approval may be done externally by an insurance company or other third-party administrator, or internally by program administrators. Health spending account claims approval is typically outsourced due to the complexity of administration and to privacy issues.

The claims approval process includes the following steps:

- Checking the employee's program eligibility. This step may be aided by an automated record-keeping system.
- Checking that expenses were incurred during the appropriate program year.
- Checking for supporting documentation.
- Determining whether expenses qualify as eligible expenses. Canada Revenue Agency publishes a list of eligible health care expenses for income tax purposes. This list is frequently used by organizations to define the expenses eligible for payment from a health spending account. However, some employers use a more restrictive list in order to simplify plan administration and communication. The list of expenses that may be paid from a personal account is developed by the employer.
- Checking that the form is signed by the participant.

The request for reimbursement form should be designed for easy data entry into the claims payment system. Benefit categories may be coded to allow the system to track account usage. This information is helpful in analysing the types of expenses submitted against the accounts. Other information may include the dates expenses were incurred, the amounts requested for reimbursement, and the names of the providers of services. A claims form normally includes space for several expenses and benefit types in order to streamline claims processing administration.

Other ways to control the administrative effort are to limit the frequency of submissions (to once a month, for example) and to set minimum submission and claim payment amounts (such as $50). Usually, these limits are waived during the final processing month of the plan year to accommodate year-end employee submissions.

Once the request for reimbursement is approved by the claims processor, it is processed for payment. Usually, requests for reimbursement are authorized for payment to the extent of the employee's account balance. Payments typically are made to the participant, not to the provider of services.

The frequency of reimbursement generally depends on the plan design and the insurance company's (or third-party processor's) capabilities. Payment timetables are communicated to employees during enrolment.

If the account is based on monthly or quarterly posting of employer contributions, some claims will exceed the current account balance and may have to be resubmitted following the next updating of the account. To avoid this administrative complexity, many claims payment systems have a pending feature. This eliminates the need to resubmit claims because the record-keeping system pays the claim to the extent of the account balance and automatically holds the remaining claim amount for future payment, once funds become available.

The claims payment system should produce an explanation of payment for each participant receiving a reimbursement during the processing period. The statement typically includes paid and pending amounts and the ending account balance. Year-to-date employer contribution and payment information also may be included.

TERMINATED EMPLOYEES

An important issue to address in the detailed plan design phase of implementation is how to handle the health spending account balances for terminating employees. The initial reaction of benefit administrators is to stop an employee's participation on or shortly after termination of employment. Some qualify the decision to stop participation based on the reason for termination (voluntary termination versus layoff, etc.). Most cite administrative costs as the primary reason for wanting to terminate accounts prior to the end of the plan year.

Nonetheless, the majority of employers ultimately decide, for a combination of administrative and design reasons, to leave terminated employee accounts open until the accounts for active employees are closed following the plan year end.

In deciding how to treat terminated employees, consider the following questions:

- How will employee terminations be communicated to and recorded on the health spending account record-keeping system?
- If accounts remain open beyond termination, but are closed prior to the end of the plan year, how will the record-keeping system know when to close the accounts?
- If exceptions to the rule are made, how will these be determined? How will the accounts be reopened?
- If the accounts are left open, how will payments to terminated employees be distributed?

YEAR-END PROCESSING

Because employees may not receive all of their year-end bills or explanations of benefits until after the plan year ends, most organizations keep accounts open for a period of time after the end of the plan year. During this period, the record-keeping system will need to maintain two sets of accounts for each participant: the current year accounts and the prior year accounts. In most cases, the grace period is from one to three months after the plan year ends. During this period, only claims for expenses incurred during the prior year may be submitted against the prior year's account balance.

After the completion of the grace period, the remaining balance from the prior year will either be rolled over to the current year or forfeited, depending on the plan design.

Health spending accounts where the balance is forwarded from the prior year to the current year have an additional provision whereby the rolled-over amount must be used in the current plan year. Any remaining funds from the rolled-over amount will be forfeited at the end of the current plan year (i.e., funds can be carried forward for only one plan year). Once the rollover occurs (i.e., the end of the grace period), prior year claims can no longer be processed.

Health spending accounts where the remaining balance is forfeited at the end of each year normally allow prior year claims to be paid out of the current year account (i.e., instead of rolling over money, the claims are rolled over).

These are the two approaches currently acceptable to Canada Revenue Agency. They are described in detail in Chapter 7.

REPORTING ACCOUNT ACTIVITY TO PARTICIPANTS

Most flexible account record-keeping systems produce an explanation with each payment. This statement usually includes a breakdown of all payment activity for the reporting period, including pending amounts as well as paid reimbursements. In addition, periodic activity statements are typically produced for each participant. These statements provide a beginning and ending balance, and a summary of employer contributions and claims activity.

Even if periodic account statements are provided, there will be occasions when participants will have questions about their accounts. These questions may concern overall account balances or specific contribution or claim activity. Administrators need access to up-to-date account information in order to respond to employee questions.

RECONCILING THE FLEXIBLE ACCOUNT AND THE GENERAL LEDGER

The final flexible account requirement is reconciliation to the general ledger. Typically, the reconciliation process occurs with a frequency consistent with an organization's standard accounting cycle.

The funding of a flexible account involves the creation of an accrued liability. This liability represents an amount of money set aside by the employer to pay for eligible expenses that will be reimbursed in the future. The liability account is increased each time the rolled-over balances are deposited in the following year's account. The administrator, however, must be able to distinguish between the rolled-over amount and the current year funds in order to reimburse expenses properly. For this reason, maintaining the current year account separate from the prior year account may ease administration and accounting requirements.

Basic journal entries are made to the general ledger accounts to correspond to each step in the administrative process. Employer funds directed to the account are accounted for as a benefit expense (the debit), which is offset by an entry to an accrued liability account (the credit). This liability account is a control account, which ties to the sum of the account balances for all participating employees. (Note that the employee is an unsecured creditor with respect to the employer for his or her account balance, until a reimbursement request has been submitted.)

At the end of the reimbursement processing cycle, when payments are issued to participants, the reimbursement amount becomes payable to the employee, and another entry is made. This entry takes the total of all payable amounts, and then debits the accrued liability account and credits accounts payable. Alternatively, the payment can be charged directly to the accrued liability account.

Once reimbursement cheques are created and issued to employees, a final payment entry is made. This entry is a debit to accounts payable and an offsetting credit to cash.

The final transaction to consider is the account closure transaction. When unused health spending account funds are forfeited by employees on termination or at year end, the total forfeiture amount is a debit to the liability account and a credit to the company's benefit expense account. The health spending account record-keeping system, therefore, can aid the accounting process by providing total contributions, total reimbursements, and closing account balances for the accounting period.

§ 21.5 CHANGES TO PAYROLL PROCESSING

Whether the flexible program is broad or limited in scope, implementation of the program almost always involves some changes to the payroll system.

If a new flexible benefit enrolment system is implemented to accommodate the flexible benefit program, or if the existing benefit plan enrolment system is modified significantly, the payroll system will need to be modified to interface with the enrolment system. This is because payroll deductions and applicable taxes for the program are reported to payroll by the enrolment system each year following annual enrolment. The enrolment system also reports deductions and taxes throughout the year for new employees and for employees who are changing their coverages.

If the plan allows employees to purchase vacation days through payroll deductions, the net pay computation will need to be adjusted, because taxes are not applicable to these amounts. Unlike after-tax payroll deductions used to purchase benefits such as optional group life and dependant life, the deduction to buy vacation days is pre-tax. This is because employees who purchase vacation days with payroll deductions are, in effect, taking time off without pay. Naturally, they don't pay tax on earnings they don't receive.

Other questions that should be asked about changes to the payroll system are:

- Are new deduction fields required? Is room available?
- What should be shown on the pay stub? Is there space for new information?
- What changes will have to be made to the calculation routines?
- Will current benefit calculation tables have to be modified or removed?
- Will any changes be required to taxation procedures?
- How does the payroll system handle retroactive deductions when coverage is back-dated?

§ 21.6 INSURANCE CARRIER REPORTING

Another function of ongoing administration is the production of group insurance reports. Periodically, the total coverage costs for each benefit option should be computed and reported. For insured plans, this entails the calculation and payment of required premiums to the insurance carriers. For self-insured benefits, it involves the calculation of adequate funding levels to cover expenses and to maintain reserves. Any appropriate administration fees, premium taxes, and provincial sales taxes also need to be reported to carriers.

Periodic health care eligibility files are produced for the health care claims processor(s), typically on a weekly, bi-weekly, or monthly basis. This information includes each participant's health care benefit election, enabling the claims processor to certify coverage. The administrative system (or, in some cases, the payroll system) produces the eligibility file for the claims processor both at the end of the annual enrolment process and periodically throughout the year.

§ 21.7 ADMINISTRATIVE STAFFING REQUIREMENTS

ELECTION ENTRY

While it is uncommon for an employer to handle election entry in house, this function could have a large impact on staffing requirements if it is not outsourced.

If paper enrolment is used, on the average, five or ten minutes' time is required to enter one election form into an online enrolment system. Given that the typical enrolment volume is about 80 to 90 per cent of employees for a new plan, and an average of 70 per cent of employees for a re-enrolment, the volume of forms to process can be significant.

Paper enrolment is no longer common, as participants most often enter elections directly to a Web-based enrolment application.

OTHER STAFFING CONSIDERATIONS

Other functions to be considered when assessing the impact of the flexible program on staffing include:

- Administrator and employee education
- Production and distribution of enrolment communications
- New employee enrolments
- Enrolment change processing
- Employee coverage and spending account status inquiries
- System changes as a result of changes to premiums, pricing, legislation, design, mergers, new populations, and other factors.

Twenty-Two

Administration Solutions

§ 22.1 EVALUATING ADMINISTRATIVE ALTERNATIVES

While there are many good alternatives available for administering a flexible benefit plan, implementing the plan is a lengthy and detailed process. The key to the success of the implementation effort is carefully evaluating the range of administrative solutions and selecting the alternative that best matches the organization's human resources and business objectives, plan design, and administrative needs.

EVALUATION PROCESS

The evaluation of administration alternatives typically begins immediately following development of the preliminary plan design. The first decision to be made is whether to administer the flexible plan in house or to outsource the activities to a third party. Although plan design is an important factor, other issues affecting the decision include:

- The number of eligible participants
- The organization's human resource and business objectives and strategies
- The degree to which human resource activities are centralized or decentralized
- The extent to which other human resource activities are outsourced
- The timing of plan implementation
- The availability, cost, and expertise of internal technology and administration resources

- The organization's long-term plans for plan enhancements or modifications
- The organization's merger, acquisition, and divestiture history and future strategy
- The implementation and ongoing administration budgets for the project
- The organization's strategic direction in terms of computer technology.

Ideally, an evaluation committee should be formed to discuss each of these factors and use them in an evaluation process. The evaluation process may take weeks or months to complete, depending on the number of alternatives under consideration and the selection techniques used.

EVALUATION COMMITTEE

As with any decision-making process, the number of people on the evaluation committee likely will have a direct relationship to the length of time needed to make a decision. However, in order to make the right decision, the right people need to participate in the evaluation process. In general, it is usually more efficient in the long run to sacrifice time, rather than short-cut the process by eliminating an area that could have significant input into the evaluation process.

A committee to evaluate flexible benefit administration alternatives ideally consists of individuals from all of the following areas:

- Benefit administration
- Human resource management
- Human resource information systems (or benefit systems)
- Management information systems
- Finance.

Each of these areas needs to be represented, usually by people who have both decision-making authority and a working knowledge of day-to-day activities in the area. Again, both functional levels need to be represented, whether in the form of one person or more.

ADMINISTRATIVE ALTERNATIVES

There are a broad range of in-house administration and outsourcing alternatives, ranging from internally developed spreadsheets to full multi-process outsourcing. Within each of these alternatives a number of further options are available. Specifically the alternatives include:

- In-house administration:
  - Spreadsheet software
  - Installed flexible benefit administration system

- Shared administration responsibility:
  - Co-sourcing
- Outsourcing:
  - Plan administration outsourcing
  - Plan and participant administration outsourcing (full outsourcing)
  - Multi-process outsourcing.

In-House Administration Using Spreadsheet Software

Smaller organizations can use commercial spreadsheet software to semi-automate flexible plan administration. In some cases, spreadsheet software has been used successfully to administer even a broad flexible plan for a small number of participants.

Word processing is used to produce personalized statements for participants.

In-House Administration Using Installed Software

Flexible plan administration systems may be developed or purchased for installation on an organization's internal computer network.

The system may be installed on a single PC accessed centrally, on computer servers within a local area network (LAN), or in the organization's mainframe environment. A LAN or mainframe installation gives multiple administrators simultaneous access to the system and database from decentralized locations.

Most administration systems provide employees with Internet access to enrolment tools and information about their benefits, using their own unique identifier and password. To accommodate this through an in-house solution, organizations must ensure that the installation environment is capable of providing this access.

In addition, administration modules are available within some broader human resources information systems (HRIS). This solution provides the advantage of a shared database with HRIS, eliminating the need for internal file transfers.

Network or mainframe-based systems are especially advantageous to larger organizations with centralized data processing. In this kind of environment, additional hardware seldom is required to support the flexible plan. Existing data communication networks may be used to support decentralized administration. Systems maintenance is performed by the technology department, along with the ongoing maintenance performed for other administration systems, such as payroll and accounting.

Personal computer and mainframe systems are available from a variety of benefit consulting firms and software vendors. Caution is advised in selecting a system, as there is a wide variance in the number and type of administration features offered.

Purchasers should also be cautious of systems developed in the United States, as the tax issues in Canada are very different from those in the United States. In addition, the requirement for French language support is not easily accommodated within systems developed in the United States. If purchasing U.S.-developed software, make sure that the system has already been modified for use in Canada.

Co-Sourcing — A Shared Administrative Responsibility

Co-sourcing refers to the transferring of some day-to-day benefit administration activities to a third party. This typically includes the annual enrolment process, system and data maintenance, file processing, and some report generation.

An administrator gains access to the system through an Internet or data communication link to the host computer. To the administrator, a co-sourcing service will provide the same functional capabilities as a system installed on the employer's own computer.

The co-sourcing vendor would typically provide the organization's employees with Internet access to benefits information. The organization's administration department maintains all direct contact with employees and acts as a liaison between employees and the outsourcing provider. In a co-sourcing environment, administrators have online access to software located on a vendor's computer.

Like installed personal computer systems and mainframe-based systems, a co-sourcing service must interface with the organization's payroll and other administration systems, whether they are internal or provided by external providers. Reports generated in a co-sourcing environment are typically available for access online for local printing.

Co-sourcing offers many advantages over installed systems for certain organizations. The pros and cons of each type of administrative approach are explored further under the heading "Decision Criteria" on page 434.

Co-sourcing services for flexible plans are offered primarily by benefit consulting firms and insurance companies.

Plan Administration Outsourcing

The outsourcing approach to administration takes much of the work out of the hands of the organization's administrators. This approach is in widespread use for many flexible plans in the United States and Canada.

Plan administration outsourcing refers to the transferring of day-to-day benefit administration activities to a third party. This includes the annual enrolment processing and the processing of new plan entries and terminations. The plan administration outsourcing provider would typically provide the organization's employees with Internet access to enrolment tools plus information concerning their benefits. The organization's administration department maintains all direct contact with employees and acts as a liaison between employees and the outsourcing provider.

Full Outsourcing (Plan and Participant Administration)

In addition to outsourcing the plan administration activities, many organizations also outsource participant administration. In these cases, the outsourcing provider deals directly with the plan participants, leaving the employer with responsibility for strategic activities such as plan design and pricing. When participant administration is outsourced, employees have access to enrolment tools and benefits information through the Internet. They can also contact the outsourcing provider through a 1-800 telephone number and, in some cases, through an interactive voice response (IVR) system. Employees can change plan coverage levels, inquire about account balances, process a claim, enrol, and get general information about the plan through the provider.

Outsourcing operates similarly to co-sourcing in terms of interfaces between the provider of the service, the user's systems, and the insurance carrier. Interfaces are typically accomplished via electronic file transfer.

Outsourcing services for flexible plans are offered primarily by benefit consulting firms and insurance companies.

Multi-Process Outsourcing

The broadest approach to the outsourcing of administration is referred to as multi-process outsourcing. Under multi-process outsourcing, an organization transfers most, if not all, of its transactional and administrative human resources activities to a third party.

Organizations adopting a multi-process approach are typically outsourcing activities such as:

- Flexible and traditional benefits administration
- Pension administration
- Payroll processing
- HRIS management
- Recruiting
- Compensation administration
- Disability management
- Participant interaction.

Multi-process outsourcing services are offered primarily by human resource and technology outsourcing providers.

DECISION CRITERIA

Human Resources and Business Strategies

To ensure that an effective administrative solution is selected, the overall objectives and strategies of the business must be considered. This is particularly important in deciding between in-house administration and outsourcing. Many businesses today are deciding to focus their people resources on activities that are related to the strategic direction of the business. Human resource strategic activities typically include establishing policies and practices relative to the delivery of pay and benefit plans, and the design of those plans. Plan administration may not be seen as a strategic activity and, therefore, may be outsourced in order to free up resources to focus on strategic activities.

Figure 22.1 illustrates an organization's ongoing involvement for various flexible benefits administration solutions.

Figure 22.1
Ongoing Involvement of Human Resources and Information Systems in Flexible Benefits Administration

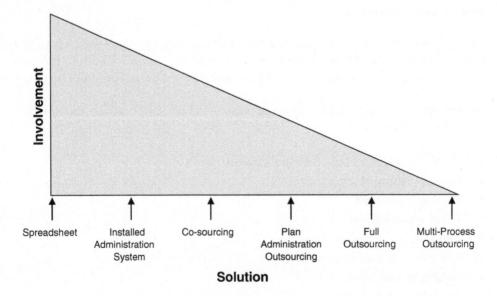

Many larger organizations are taking outsourcing to a broader multi-process level by viewing all non-strategic human resource activities as transferable to a third party. Multi-process outsourcing is becoming more and more common in the United States. In Canada this approach has so far been adopted by only a few of the largest organizations.

Plan Design

The design of the flexible plan is an important factor in selecting an administrative approach. For instance, if the plan calls for minimal choice-making and no employee-specific calculations, the plan may be administered internally by the payroll/personnel system with minor enhancements. However, if the plan is broader in scope, with many employee-specific components, either outsourcing or a new administrative system may be required. For example, if the plan offers employees choice in most benefit areas, annual enrolment, and the opportunity to allocate excess flex credits among several accounts, a robust administrative solution is needed.

All plan details need not be determined prior to the selection of the administrative approach. However, the approach selected needs to have the flexibility to handle unforeseen changes as the plan design is finalized.

Number of Participants

In-house administration using spreadsheet software may be a good alternative for organizations with fewer than 500 plan participants. Larger groups typically require more sophisticated solutions if in-house administration of the plan is desired.

Size is not a limiting factor when evaluating co-sourcing and outsourcing alternatives. These solutions are feasible for organizations of any size, even those with as few as 500 employees. The strategic direction of human resources and the business, the cost of the solution, the desire to decentralize administration, and the availability of internal information systems and administration resources often are more important issues to consider.

Centralized versus Decentralized Administration

For in-house administration, some approaches lend themselves better to decentralized processing than others. In either co-sourcing, LAN, or mainframe environments, an organization can support decentralized administration with multiple administrators accessing the system, and still retain central control and produce summary-level reports. In a stand-alone personal computing environment, decentralized processing is more difficult.

Outsourcing of flexible plan administration is well suited to organizations that have decentralized operations. In this environment, the outsourcing of administration generally frees up time for more human resources employees than it does in a centralized environment where there may only be one or two employees handling administration.

Implementation Timetable

The timing of plan implementation has an impact on an organization's decision to build, buy, or outsource, as well as on the type of system to implement. In almost all cases, building a system internally, either as a module within HRIS or from scratch, will take more time than buying a comparable system or outsourcing to a vendor.

Once a decision has been made to buy or outsource, the type of approach chosen will be a factor in the amount of time required for implementation. All other factors being equal, a co-sourcing or outsourcing approach will have the least impact on an organization's internal resources and therefore may be implemented faster than other administrative alternatives.

Information Systems and Administrative Resources and Expertise

The availability, expertise, and cost of internal information systems (IS) resources is an important factor to consider when evaluating administrative alternatives. Not only is IS support a key issue during implementation, but it also remains a major factor in ongoing support of the system. The amount of IS resources required through implementation and ongoing support is greater with an in-house solution than with outsourcing.

The availability, expertise, and cost of benefit administration resources also is a factor to consider in selecting the best approach, particularly when choosing between in-house and outsourced administration.

Plans for Program Expansion

Just as the initial plan design is a consideration in selecting an administrative solution, planning for future expansion is also important. For example, an in-house personal computer–based system may be adequate to support a small organization's plan with minimal choice-making. However, if the plan is expanded in a subsequent year to include broad choice-making, the revised plan may exceed the capacity of the system and internal administration and IS resources. The same problem may occur if the plan is expanded to include new employee groups or additional business units, either through a change in eligibility rules or through a merger or acquisition.

Budgets

Implementation and ongoing administration budgets are almost always factors in the selection of an administrative solution. Building an administrative system is in most cases more expensive than licensing a software package. However, given the time and internal IS resources, some organizations prefer the soft-dollar expense of in-house development to the hard-dollar cost of buying a system, using a co-sourcing service, or outsourcing.

When the decision is made to buy a system or outsource, budget constraints may be a factor in deciding what type of approach to implement. When reviewing the cost of each alternative, both implementation and ongoing costs are taken into consideration.

The costs to consider under each alternative include:

- One-time planning and software set-up charges
- Hardware purchases (if necessary)
- Compensation and benefits for administration and information systems personnel
- Cost of turnover — severance, recruitment, and training
- Developmental training
- Office space
- Hardware and network maintenance
- System licence or maintenance fees
- Future system modifications.

When comparing the cost of administration alternatives, it is important to look at the overall costs for each approach in relation to the services provided by each vendor. Some vendors include administration and payroll consulting services, training, administration manuals, and other consulting services in their product fees. Other vendors' product fees include only the software or service.

Strategic Direction

It is also important to consider the strategic direction of the organization in terms of advancing computer technology. A common strategy today is to promote employee self-service in all aspects of human resources administration, removing paper forms and an organization's administration staff from the process. Some software vendors and internally developed solutions may not be in a position to comply with these objectives.

Widespread availability of access to the Internet, either in employees' homes or in the workplace, has changed the way organizations administer their benefit plans. The provision of an Internet Web site as a way for employees to access their benefits is now a standard component of almost all administration solutions. Many organizations are also using scanning and imaging of forms as an alternative to manual data input and paper files.

This advancement of computer technology has made it increasingly difficult for organizations to manage their benefits administration internally. This is a key component in the growth of outsourcing over in-house administration.

VENDOR ASSESSMENT

Many different approaches may be used to evaluate administrative alternatives, ranging from very informal to very formal. One of the most common approaches involves issuing a request for proposal (RFP), selecting finalists based on responses to the RFP, and allowing each finalist to demonstrate capabilities in a subsequent meeting with the evaluation committee. Whether or not an RFP is issued, the committee will want to meet with each of the vendors to ensure a mutual understanding of the needs and constraints of the organization. Actually seeing a demonstration of a system or participant administration capabilities also will help in assuring the committee of the vendor's ability to deliver a suitable solution within the required time-frame and budget.

Once the type of administrative solution is decided upon and the range of acceptable providers narrowed, how does an organization assess each vendor's ability to deliver as promised?

One of the best ways to assess a vendor's qualifications is to ask for and check references. Ask for references from organizations:

- In the same industry
- With a similar plan design
- Of comparable size
- In the same geographical area
- With the same administration alternative
- Who have used the vendor or system for more than one year.

When checking references, talk to both administrative and systems personnel. Find out about both the implementation process and ongoing service delivery provided by the vendor. Also meet with the people who will be implementing the system or service. How much experience do they have in similar implementations?

Another factor to consider is the range of services provided by the vendor. During implementation of the flexible plan, the design, communication, and administration project teams will be working closely together to ensure that the administrative solution supports both the plan design and the communication approach. For organizations using consultants for design and/or communication, many implementation difficulties can be reduced if the same consultant is helping with plan administration. For instance, the administrative system must support the detailed plan design, both during annual enrolment and throughout the plan year.

§ 22.2 IMPLEMENTING THE ADMINISTRATIVE SOLUTION

DEFINING SPECIFICATIONS

Regardless of whether the flexible plan administration is to be handled internally or outsourced, the first step in implementation involves defining system specifications. During this step, the implementation project team will work to:

- Develop an implementation workplan
- Design the functional and technical specifications for the system, based on the plan design and administrative rules
- Identify updates to existing administrative support systems and procedures such as payroll, personnel, and accounting systems
- Define the interface requirements between each applicable system, including:
  - Frequency
  - Mode (electronic transfer, file, etc.)
  - Data requirements.

PROGRAMMING AND TESTING

This step is the most difficult and time-consuming phase of implementation. Who takes responsibility for this step depends on whether the system is being developed in house, licensed from a vendor, or outsourced. For systems developed in house, the responsibility lies with internal resources, while an outsourced solution is typically set up and tested by the vendor. A licensed system may require a combination of internal and vendor resources.

To support the initial annual enrolment in a broad flexible plan, the system typically is fully tested and ready to begin enrolment processing at least three to four months before the plan effective date.

TRAINING ADMINISTRATORS

With an outsourced solution there is little involvement from an organization's administration resources, so training is minimal. The focus of training in this environment is on understanding the flow of information and data between the organization and the outsourcing vendor. The outsourcing vendor is responsible for training its administration resources.

With an in-house system approach, administrator training is an important part of the implementation process. Enrolment training takes place prior to the initial enrolment. Ongoing administration training may be deferred until just prior to the plan effective date.

The approach to training is tailored to meet the needs of the organization. If administration is going to be decentralized, training may be done at each administrative location. Alternatively, administrators may be assembled at one company location or trained at a neutral site.

Part Seven

Experience

Twenty-Three

Case Studies

§ 23.1 INTRODUCTION

The first twenty-two chapters of this book present the theory and technical considerations surrounding flexible benefits. This chapter focuses on seven employers who have applied the theory and solved the technical issues to introduce flexible benefits for their employees.

The primary focus of each of the case studies is summarized below.

LAYING THE GROUNDWORK FOR FLEXIBLE BENEFITS

The Business Development Bank of Canada (BDC) was faced with a challenge — some employees were so satisfied with their traditional benefit plan that they opposed moving to flexible benefits. BDC's successful flexible benefits launch required two prerequisites: a firm conviction on the part of senior leadership that this was the right direction for the organization and a thorough, two-way communication strategy.

FLEXIBLE BENEFITS AND TOTAL REWARDS

AstraZeneca positioned flexible benefits as a key element of an integrated total rewards program to provide customized benefit coverage as well as to encourage retirement savings.

FLEXIBLE BENEFITS FOR SMALLER ORGANIZATIONS

Gibson Energy's experience illustrates that a flexible benefits plan is a very viable option for small employers and can even help with an organization's growth strategy. One of the keys for Gibson was a robust, online administrative solution.

USING FLEXIBLE BENEFITS TO FACILITATE A MERGER

Following its merger with Compaq, Hewlett-Packard (HP) wanted to rapidly introduce a benefit plan for the new organization. HP elected to use the Compaq flex plan as its foundation and add certain unique features from the former HP plan. The resulting program meets the organization's needs as well as those of a very diverse workforce.

THE FLEXIBILITY TO MANAGE COSTS

IBM Canada used its flexible benefits program to help make employees more aware of health care costs, resulting in workers who are not only wiser consumers, but motivated to adopt a healthier lifestyle.

FLEXIBLE BENEFITS IN A UNIONIZED ENVIRONMENT

PotashCorp's experience shows that introducing a flexible plan is feasible in a unionized environment. Unionized workers at this Saskatchewan-based resource company were eager to have the same choices as were available to the non-unionized workforce. To accomplish this, the union was willing to leave the overall plan structure intact and negotiate specific coverage levels within each benefit.

FIXING A BROKEN FLEXIBLE BENEFITS PLAN

GlaxoSmithKline's recovery from a false start illustrates that if flexible benefits are not meeting the needs of employees, the problem may well lie with the design of the program, rather than the concept of flex itself.

§ 23.2 BUSINESS DEVELOPMENT BANK OF CANADA — LAYING THE GROUNDWORK FOR FLEXIBLE BENEFITS

The Business Development Bank of Canada (BDC) is a financial institution wholly owned by the government of Canada. BDC plays a leadership role in delivering financial, investment, and consulting services to Canadian small businesses, with a particular focus on the technology and export sectors of the economy. It currently has a workforce of approximately 1,600 employees in Canada.

BACKGROUND

BDC introduced its flex plan, "Your Benefits Program," on January 1, 2003. However, preparations to launch the plan, including employee communication, began well over a year in advance.

CHALLENGE

BDC had a number of objectives for its flex plan:

- Maintain the already excellent competitive position with its comparator group so as to continue to attract and retain top talent;
- Add flexibility to all of its human resources programs, including benefits and later pensions, in order to better meet employee needs; and
- Raise knowledge and understanding of benefits amongst employees.

These are all good reasons to introduce flexible benefits. However, this course of action was not without risk for BDC. Employee satisfaction with regard to benefits, measured by means of an annual engagement survey, was very high at the time flex was introduced — about 80 per cent. Making radical changes to the traditional benefits program ran the risk of decreasing employee satisfaction.

In addition, many of BDC's employees had come from other banking institutions, where flex had been introduced with some negative reaction. When the concept of flex was first mentioned at BDC, the news was greeted with various levels of skepticism across the employee population. In some parts of the country, there was considerable employee push-back to making the switch to flex. While BDC's goal was not to use flex to reduce benefit costs, some employees believed that they would pay more for the same coverage if flexible benefits were provided.

SOLUTION

BDC's Robert Yuzwa, Director, Human Resources Policy and Programmes, and Maryse Corbella, Senior Manager Total Rewards, highlighted the key factors behind the successful launch of the organization's flex plan:

1. **Getting buy-in from senior management.** BDC's leaders were fully behind the implementation of the flex plan. Their support trickled down to management and from there to employees. The HR team responsible for implementing flex spent a considerable amount of time with senior management, ensuring that they understood and endorsed the plan. This backing was important for the plan to be seen as a corporate initiative, made for sound business reasons, rather than merely an HR one.

2. **Listening to employees.** "Invest the time in focus groups to design a plan that is meaningful to your demographics," recommends Corbella. During the design phase, BDC conducted focus groups with representative samples of employees at all levels from across the country, as well as a special employee design group consisting of HR and other representatives of the major demographic groups. This latter group in particular served as a reality check for the design of the plan. For instance, while vacation selling was initially included as an option — senior management expected it to be a popular choice — feedback from employees indicated that vacation buying was what they wanted. Today, 30 per cent of employees buy up to an extra week of vacation a year, while very few sell their time off.

3. **Making communication a priority.** BDC ensured that it gave itself enough time — and resources — to fully communicate its flex plan to employees, before, during, and after the launch. During the initial design phase, BDC made no secret about its plans to introduce flex, sharing information with employees by means of a series of newsletters. The first one provided a definition of flexible benefits, while subsequent issues shared more details as the launch of the plan drew closer. BDC also went on a cross-country tour, spending around two hours in each of its locations to discuss the plan with groups of employees just prior to implementation. On enrolment, BDC provided employees with a comprehensive, fully bilingual, hard-copy enrolment guide that walked them through all their choices and also sent them a letter with their password to enrol online. This well-thought-out and thorough communication strategy unrolled over the course of a year so that by the time the plan was finally introduced employees were ready for it.

4. **Ensuring administration is robust.** "Unless you've tested your flex administration system and know it operates flawlessly, all the time and energy that you've invested in design and communication will be for nothing," says Yuzwa. "If enrolment and record-keeping aren't reliable, the success of your flex plan is at risk."

5. **Getting necessary help.** "Launching a flex plan is not a do-it-yourself project for your HR team," points out Corbella. "Consult with professionals who have done this before."

RESULTS

The BDC flex plan has been a resounding success. Concerns about a negative impact on employee engagement have proved unfounded. Scores have increased steadily since the plan was implemented, reaching 91 per cent in 2006 when employees were asked if the plan met their needs. In the first year, active online enrolment was 98 per cent — a successful result that was shared with employees. In the following years active enrolment remained very high.

GOING FORWARD

BDC's flexible benefits program is clearly meeting its employees' needs, as indicated by its employee engagement scores. While not an immediate priority, the organization does plan to take a "pulse check" of the plan regularly. However, Yuzwa doesn't feel that major changes will be required, even in the face of the changing Canadian workforce: "Our employees were a diverse group when the plan was first designed, so it already appeals to a variety of employees." However, he acknowledges that BDC must be at least "mindful" of benefit cost increases going forward. "Reducing costs was not on the agenda when we designed the plan. But if future increases became unpalatable for BDC, then we would re-work the plan," explains Yuzwa. "We don't anticipate any changes at this point, however. In fact, since we introduced flex, our benefit cost increases have gone down slightly."

§ 23.3 ASTRAZENECA — FLEXIBLE BENEFITS AND TOTAL REWARDS

AstraZeneca is one of Canada's and the world's leading research-based pharmaceutical companies. The company is dedicated to the discovery, development, manufacturing, and marketing of innovative prescription medicines that both improve and save lives.

AstraZeneca has over 65,000 employees worldwide in 100 countries and invests roughly US$3.5 billion in research and development (R&D) annually.

Across Canada, there are approximately 1,450 employees at AstraZeneca Canada Inc. (AZC). Of that number, more than 125 highly skilled scientists are employed at a state-of-the-art AstraZeneca R&D Montreal (AZRDM) basic research facility. Scientists at AZRDM are focused on finding new and innovative therapeutic solutions to treat acute and chronic pain.

BACKGROUND

When pharmaceutical companies Astra and Zeneca merged in 1999, the newly formed organization, AstraZeneca Canada Inc., seized the opportunity to redesign prior existing benefits programs as one enabling part of its new business strategy. Within the context of its strategic framework, organizational values, and culture, it decided to adopt a "total rewards" approach to programming that would support the company's goal of becoming an employer of choice in Canada and enhance the value delivered to employees. In an increasingly competitive environment, the company recognized how such an approach could help it attract and retain top talent and drive employee engagement to ensure its future success.

CHALLENGE

The concepts supporting the new business strategy and human resources focus were designed to create a new employee benefit plan that was distinctive and competitive within a pharmaceutical industry known for offering comprehensive benefit programs. AstraZeneca Canada also wanted the plan to be consistent with its philosophy of treating employees like its customers, ensuring employee wellness was part of its cornerstone and addressing the comprehensive needs of a highly educated, diverse workforce.

Beyond that, however, AstraZeneca Canada wanted to ensure that the design was aligned with and reinforced its total rewards philosophy, with its message to employees that they shared the accountability when it came to accessing the available benefits that were just right for them. Its desire to add even more choice than is traditionally offered in a flexible benefits plan required increased emphasis on clear and continuing company communication, not only when the plan was launched, but also on an ongoing basis.

SOLUTION

The result was a "Lifestyle Solutions" program that enables employees to thoughtfully consider and then choose their health care coverage, retirement savings, and other benefits as elements of a complete "total rewards" package that caters to their evolving lifestyle needs. In effect, the program and other ancillary features, such as a comprehensive Wellness & Fitness program, address the "total employee" and his or her family needs at work or at play.

AstraZeneca members receive "lifestyle dollars" to purchase benefit coverage. This branding emphasizes the notion of choice — of employees having the opportunity to make quality benefit selections that are appropriate for them, their families, and their way of life.

The design of the plan extends beyond customized health care coverage, offering a range of options for spending excess lifestyle dollars. There are four levels of coverage for medical and dental programs. Employees are provided with enough lifestyle dollars to purchase the highest level of medical and dental coverage in the program. Since the plan was implemented, AZC has absorbed thus far the full cost of price escalation, so that employees have been fully insulated from rising costs. This has been a conscious company decision congruent with its desire to be a caring and responsible employer.

By contributing to the retirement savings plan as part of the Lifestyle Solutions program, employees can increase the amount of lifestyle dollars they have to spend, since a portion of the employer's matching contribution is added to the pool of lifestyle dollars.

Excess lifestyle dollars, accumulated through employees' choosing to reduce their levels of coverage when appropriate, as well as by taking advantage of company matching retirement savings plan contributions indicated above, can be deposited into a variety of accounts:

1. A health spending account for reimbursement of medical, prescription drug, and dental expenses not covered by the company or provincial plan.
2. A personal account to cover a wide variety of eligible health, wellness, and lifestyle expenses. Unlike deposits to the health spending account, however, lifestyle dollars diverted to a personal account are taxed as income at the time of deposit.
3. An optional savings plan with three components:
   a. employee RRSP
   b. spousal RRSP
   c. a non-registered savings plan.

KEEPING EMPLOYEES INFORMED

Offering additional choices requires additional effort when it comes to communication, notes Bev Haines, Manager, Lifestyle Solutions, at AstraZeneca: "While many of our employees were familiar with 'cafeteria style' benefits before the launch of our plan, it was essential that we took the time to ensure they understood the unique design features of our benefits program on plan roll-out."

AstraZeneca utilized a communication strategy that also offered the opportunity to link key business objectives, according to Toni Garro, Vice-President, Human Resources: "By reinforcing our key corporate messages, such as striving to be an employer of choice, it not only made it easier for employees to understand the design objectives of the new plan; it allowed us to build on and reinforce why we chose our 'total rewards' philosophy. Employees at AstraZeneca are proud of the work they do and the difference they make with patients and within the Canadian health care system. And the company believes that highly engaged employees deliver a better customer experience, which translates to better business results. As such, providing employees and their families with a comprehensive plan that allows for the ability to customize their benefits and income security from a wide range of options sends a clear message that our employees are valued. This range of options complements other salary and bonus plans that, in total, deliver a sound competitive package. Engaged and committed employees make the difference to our company's success, our competitiveness in the marketplace, and the value we deliver to our doctors, patients, and the communities we serve across Canada."

RESULTS

AstraZeneca Canada has consistently been selected by *The Globe and Mail Report on Business* as one of the Top 50 Best Employers in Canada. "Though benefits are not the primary reason why employees stay or join our organization," says Garro, "the fact that the Lifestyle Solutions program has been created with diverse needs in mind sends a message to employees and their families that their needs are important to the company and that we recognize the individual and varied needs of our workforce."

Since the launch of the plan, AstraZeneca's employee communication and Web-based re-enrolment facilities have continued to emphasize the responsibility employees have for creating a benefits package for themselves and their families. "For employees to truly 'flex' their coverage to meet their current needs, they need to make choices annually," points out Haines. "As well, life events, such as the addition of a new family member, necessitate the need to adapt their benefits to changing circumstances."

GOING FORWARD

"Annual re-enrolment also presents an opportunity for the company to review the benefit plan every year," says Haines. "We want to ensure that it remains competitive and continues to meet employee needs." Employee feedback is solicited regularly by survey and the company continues to assess the value of total rewards programs.

"Organizations shouldn't switch from a traditional benefits plan to a flex plan just because their competitors are doing so," states Garro. "It takes time and sustained quality effort to make such a program work well. Our employees deserve no less. We see our program as part of our employment value proposition and we leverage our Lifestyle Solutions program to attract and retain top-notch employees, as well as enhance our reputation as an employer of choice in Canada."

§ 23.4 GIBSON ENERGY — FLEXIBLE BENEFITS FOR SMALLER ORGANIZATIONS

Gibson Energy Ltd. is an independent midstream oil and gas service provider. Since 1953, it has played a significant role in the country's oil and gas industry by linking upstream producers with downstream refiners, using its transportation, distribution, and other capabilities.

The company has approximately 600 employees in Western Canada, 525 of whom are eligible members of its flexible benefits plan. Plan members are a mix of full-time salaried and hourly workers, as well as part-time employees.

BACKGROUND

When Gibson introduced its flex plan in 2001, it had 360 benefit-eligible employees. At that time, flex was still unusual for smaller organizations. However, the company's motives for implementing flex were clearly linked to its business plan: it wanted to grow and it needed to keep benefit costs down.

Gibson was convinced that flex would help with attraction and retention by enabling it to offer the same benefit choices available to employees of some larger organizations in the industry. It also realized that new employees would likely represent an increasingly diverse group, with different needs. Gibson wanted to be able to meet those needs.

Before making the decision to go flex, Gibson benchmarked its benefits against those of its competitors and determined that its program was very generous — definitely in the upper quartile for medical and dental coverage. With the ever-increasing cost of health care benefits and the prospect of a growing employee population, Gibson opted to switch to a flexible benefits plan in order to contain costs and to give employees a better understanding and appreciation of the benefits the company provided.

CHALLENGE

Gibson readily acknowledges that operating a flexible benefits plan for a company of its size presented a challenge, due to the number of geographical locations of its operations across Western Canada (more than twenty-five), the size of these locations (from as small as three to as large as fifty employees), and the diverse nature of its workforce, including unionized employees.

Gibson also did not want to "take away" any benefits, but wanted to control costs through opting-down options and increase employee understanding of the value of the benefits and how they could help control costs. In other words, employees could change their behaviour by becoming informed consumers of benefits.

SOLUTION

Gibson attributes the success of its plan to the input from initial employee focus groups, as well as its extensive communication efforts at both the launch of the plan and ongoing — especially at re-enrolment time. In addition, making good use of available technology helped to streamline administrative efforts.

Smaller organizations have the distinct advantage of being able to meet more easily with employees when a new flex plan is launched. In Gibson's case, following a series of town hall meetings, human resources representatives visited most locations and worked with individuals to help them make their benefit choices. Association hourly employees (Alberta Bargaining Unit) were eligible to join the flex plan and were included in focus groups when the plan was in the design phase, so that they were part of the development and communication of the program.

These in-person communication and assistance efforts were complemented by publishing an *Enrolment Guide* that provided employees with step-by-step instructions for choosing their benefits and enrolling, along with timely e-mail circulars called "Benefiting You" that provided more details of the flex plan and other employee benefits.

HR resources are still available to explain any changes to the plan. The need for one-on-one communication has diminished as employees have become familiar with flex, but is still offered, especially for new employees.

Following the launch of the plan, Gibson completed an acquisition, which brought a new union into the picture. This new group needed to be convinced of the merits of the flex plan, so there was much discussion over a period of a few months. Gibson shared what employees — both bargaining and non-bargaining — had said about the plan. At the end of the day, the new union voted 82 per cent in favour of the flex plan.

Gibson also utilized technology to ease the flex administrative burden. Right from the start, Gibson modified its in-house system to capture employee enrolment information. It also offered a "benefits hotline" at enrolment, particularly geared towards employees in outlying areas, with a commitment to answer any questions within 24 hours. More recently, Gibson introduced online enrolment to streamline the enrolment process for both the participant employees and for human resources.

RESULTS

Gibson's annual enrolment numbers are impressive: 84 per cent of eligible employees enrolled in the first year it offered flex, with those numbers increasing to 88 per cent and, most recently, after implementation of the online enrolment technology, to 92 per cent.

"There is no doubt that the online flex enrolment tool has made administration much easier and has really made flex a viable option for organizations of our size," says Rick Luciani, General Manager, Human Resources & Administration, at Gibson. "It's also likely saved us half a year's salary for a data entry person."

Luciani doesn't want to downplay the administrative challenge flex presents for smaller organizations, however. He explains: "We are spending more time on our benefits plan but in a different way. Instead of transactional activities, the efforts of the HR team are geared towards ensuring that our employees understand the plan and make the choices that are right for them. As a result, our employees have a better understanding and appreciation for Gibson's benefit plan. That's rewarding from both an HR and a corporate perspective." In addition, Luciani points out that this need for communication decreases over time, as employees become more familiar with the plan.

As far as costs go, Gibson was paying out around 7.5 per cent of payroll for benefits prior to the flex plan. Over the first three years of the plan, expenses dropped to between 6.25 and 6.75 per cent of payroll. Gibson tracked the movement of employee choices over this period and saw that half were opting for lower medical coverage and 40 per cent were choosing lower dental coverage than had previously been given to them under the traditional benefits program.

Luciani points out, however, that because the business objective was not necessary to lower benefits costs, but to contain them, the company has enhanced its flexible benefits plan, driving expenses back up to around 7.25 per cent of payroll. "We've added critical illness coverage as well as a wellness account that's funded on a matching basis," says Luciani.

In fact, having a flexible benefits plan has made it very easy for Gibson to include new benefits that enhance strategic HR objectives. "A new focus for us has been on wellness," says Luciani. "Our new wellness account has a two-tier structure. The company pays for a medical assessment. In addition, we match employee contributions, to a maximum of $200 annually. Employees can pay for their share either through payroll deductions or by using flex credits. The money in the wellness account can be used for something like a fitness membership. Around 100 employees are taking advantage of this offer, now in its third year."

GOING FORWARD

Luciani sees Gibson's flexible benefits program as one component of a total rewards program that provides a real competitive advantage. "Our flex plan has been very positively received by our employees," he states. "Flex is not yet common amongst organizations of our size and it has been extremely useful in attracting people to our company." And the flex plan is also helping with retention: employee satisfaction scores with respect to benefits have never been higher.

The other real plus is the relative ease that a flex plan affords when it comes to making design changes that are of real value to employees. "A flex plan has definitely made it easier for us to be more nimble when it comes to providing new benefits," says Luciani. "We're looking into several possible future enhancements, like sabbaticals and the ability to redirect a company bonus into a health spending account or RRSP. If it makes sense to offer these choices, we'll do so as part of our flex plan."

§ 23.5 HEWLETT-PACKARD — USING FLEXIBLE BENEFITS TO FACILITATE A MERGER

Hewlett-Packard (Canada) Co., established in Montreal in 1961, is a wholly owned subsidiary of California-based Hewlett-Packard Co. — a technology solutions provider to consumers, businesses, and institutions around the world. HP Canada delivers solutions that span IT infrastructure; personal computing and access devices; global services; and imaging and printing to Canadian consumers, enterprises, and small and medium businesses.

BACKGROUND

Hewlett-Packard merged with Compaq in 2002. Each company previously had a flexible benefits plan. There was no question that the newly merged company would also offer a full flexible benefits program to employees.

CHALLENGE

The global mandate in each country where HP had operations was not to "reinvent the wheel." The benefits program for the merged company was not to be a brand new plan. Rather, the goal was to look at the plans offered by the two original companies and choose one. The key factor was speed: HP had developed an "adopt and go" strategy for the merger to ensure that it was accomplished quickly. In making the choice, management was to assess the two plans against cost and choose the more cost-effective one, as long as HP maintained a competitive position in the marketplace and employees' needs were met. In the end, the Compaq plan was selected in Canada, with some minor variations borrowed from the original Hewlett-Packard plan.

SOLUTION

One of the key features of the former Hewlett-Packard plan that survived the merger and became part of the plan for the merged organization was a funding mechanism designed to control costs and maximize tax effectiveness. Employee base pay is reduced to 98 per cent, with the other 2 per cent given as flex credits on top of what HP funds. If employees opt not to use all their flex credits to purchase benefits, the excess may be deposited into a health spending account or group RRSP, or taken as taxable cash. This arrangement allows employees to channel their money and use it tax-effectively, if they choose to do so.

The result is a plan that is cost-neutral to the company, despite rising health care costs. "Flex credits increase with salary increases," points out Rick Schwartz, Director of Compensation and Benefits for HP Canada. "However, if employees find that they have insufficient credits to purchase everything they want, they have the option of cutting back or paying for additional coverage. The choice is theirs — something our employees appreciate."

While the merger offered the opportunity for some redesign advantages, it definitely produced some administrative challenges. While Hewlett-Packard previously only had two grandfathered retiree groups receiving benefits under former plans, following the merger there were at least half a dozen such groups. According to Schwartz, there was only one solution: "We outsourced administration."

RESULTS

Because HP Canada places considerable emphasis on cost containment, it is vigilant about analysing costs every year and "fine tuning" as needed. "We're tweaking the plan, rather than redesigning it," says Schwartz. "It's much easier to do so with a flex plan than a traditional one."

Because they are paying for part of their benefit coverage, HP Canada employees are more aware of the cost of benefits. "It's obvious whenever we adjust coverage or price tags," states Schwartz. "We are very upfront when it comes to explaining the rationale for any changes and employees understand and appreciate the information."

During the first annual enrolment in the merged plan in the fall of 2002, HP Canada provided employees with an enrolment package, including a booklet. Since that time, the organization has done away with paper and provides online information. In addition, HP Canada employees enrol online by means of its outsourcing provider's user-friendly technology.

GOING FORWARD

Since HP Canada employees have a vested interest in the cost of their benefit plan, they also merit input into the coverage provided. "Our workforce is aging," says Schwartz. "Only a few years ago, the average age was 38 and now it's 41. This means that we're considering expanding the benefits under our flex plan to cover such things as eldercare, critical illness insurance, and funding for future nursing home care."

Beyond appropriate benefit coverage, however, Schwartz encourages organizations that are thinking of implementing flex to consider tax-effectiveness during the design phase. "If you can incorporate elements that allow employees to be compensated more tax-effectively and take the time to communicate it properly, employees will really appreciate it, particularly if they are high income earners."

HP Canada knew going into the merger that it would end up with a flexible benefit plan. "Because both predecessor organizations had flex plans and it was easier for us to continue with flex on integration," says Schwartz. "However, the merger presented us with the opportunity to take one plan and modify it to better meet both employer and employee needs."

§ 23.6 IBM CANADA — THE FLEXIBILITY TO MANAGE COSTS

IBM is the world's largest information technology company and one of Canada's leading providers of advanced information technology products and services, including computer systems, software, networking systems, storage devices, and microelectronics.

In Canada, IBM has approximately 19,000 employees enrolled in the company's flexible benefit plan.

BACKGROUND

IBM Canada has offered a flexible benefit plan since 1994. The plan has proven to be popular with employees. Nevertheless, as health care costs continued to escalate, IBM became concerned with finding a way to deal with rising benefit expenditures.

From its inception, IBM's flex plan was grounded in the philosophy of cost sharing: as health care costs increased, those increases would be shared between the company and the employees. Part of IBM's rationale for this approach was that cost sharing would encourage employees to keep the cost of the plan down — by shopping around for lower prescription costs and asking about lower-priced drugs, for example.

However, certain factors beyond IBM's control were making cost containment a more pressing issue, including provincial de-listing of certain products and services that had previously been covered under government health care plans; increased usage of health care services, especially with the high cost of some new drugs; and an aging workforce that would likely have increased health care needs.

CHALLENGE

Even with a history of cost sharing in place, IBM was concerned that asking employees to contribute more might erode employee engagement and impact the market-competitiveness of the benefit plan. The human resources team was given the mandate of finding ways to contain benefit costs without sacrificing employee satisfaction.

SOLUTION

Wendy Howe, Manager, Employee Benefits and Well-Being Services at IBM Canada, describes the means used to meet this mandate. "Our efforts were focused on two primary channels: changing behaviour by educating our employees about costs so that they became better consumers of health care products and services, as well as using technology to provide convenience, self-service, and cost control through operational efficiency."

Measures implemented by IBM in the mid-2000s include the following:

1. **Employee responsibility for pharmacy dispensing fees.** This fee is the deductible, so if employees want to reduce their own expenses, they are encouraged to go to pharmacies with lower dispensing fees. The fact that there is such a variation in fees was an eye-opener to many employees.

2. **A drug card with a formulary.** While employees no longer have to pay for prescriptions up front, the formulary provides a two-tier reimbursement system, encouraging them to use drugs on the formulary. The electronic drug card system also provides IBM with valuable data on drug plan utilization.

3. **Electronic claims.** Claims are submitted electronically, rather than on paper, to provide convenience to employees and reduce plan operating costs. Employees also receive their explanation of benefits (EOB) statements online, which saves mailing costs.

4. **Direct deposit.** Claim cheques are deposited directly into employee bank accounts. No more paper cheques or postage — better for employees and IBM.

5. **Paper drug card.** If employees lose their card or it is destroyed, they simply print another copy right away. IBM saves the expense of plastic drug cards.

6. **Online benefits information/online benefits enrolment.** Employees get the information they need about their benefits when they need it, including on annual enrolment. IBM doesn't have to print booklets or updates to the plan.

RESULTS

"Our employees have become partners with IBM to control health care costs," says Howe. "They are able to make their own choices about health care — and the associated costs — without the company forcing its own preferences."

While IBM has been successful in its efforts to contain costs without sacrificing employee engagement, Howe does want to manage expectations.

"Implementing cost sharing requires a shift in employees' way of thinking," she says. "They have to adapt from an entitlement mentality. That isn't going to happen overnight."

In addition, Howe cautions against being overly zealous in implementing cost-sharing measures, for fear of loss of competitive position. IBM revisited a couple of its earlier cost-management efforts, such as a modified co-ordination of benefits (COB) restriction, since the insurance carriers found them complex to administer, other organizations hadn't followed suit, and employees found them confusing, which hindered IBM's cost-management objectives. Later, however, instead of re-ducing COB, the company implemented a 20 per cent top-up plan, with 100 per cent reimbursement available as an option.

GOING FORWARD

To complement its benefit cost containment strategy, IBM has also introduced wellness initiatives designed to encourage employees to lead a healthy lifestyle. Employees record their physical activity using an online tracking tool and earn flex credits. The Employee Assistance Program offers nutritional counselling and online health risk assessment tools. In addition, there is a difference in life insur-ance rates for smokers and non-smokers after only $10,000 of coverage.

"IBM will continue its efforts to educate employees about both health care costs and healthy living," says Howe. "At the same time, employees will have the flexibility to make their own choices."

§ 23.7 POTASHCORP — FLEXIBLE BENEFITS IN A UNIONIZED ENVIRONMENT

PotashCorp is the world's largest fertilizer enterprise by capacity, producing the three primary plant nutrients (potash, phosphate, and nitrogen). Its products are used by fertilizer, feed, and industrial customers on six continents. PotashCorp has corporate offices in Saskatoon, Saskatchewan, and Northbrook, Illinois, as well as production facilities in five countries. In total, it employs approximately 5,000 people, including about 1,800 in Canada.

BACKGROUND

PotashCorp was the first Canadian organization to introduce flexible benefits in a unionized environment, launching its program on July 1, 1990, for employees at its Rocanville, Saskatchewan, potash mine.

CHALLENGE

PotashCorp introduced flex benefits for its salaried workforce in 1989. While flex was not then common in its industry, especially amongst smaller employers, PotashCorp had been looking for a relatively low-cost way to do something for employees following a downsizing and at a time when salary increases were relatively low. Offering flexible benefits proved to be a real morale-booster — so much so that, a year later, the union representing around 350 hourly employees at Rocanville asked for flex for its members as well.

PotashCorp had seen a number of positive results following the launch of the flex plan for salaried employees. Providing flexible benefit choices enabled it to meet the needs of its wide range of employees — from old to young, from office employees to those working in the plant, and from those living in rural areas to those resident in urban locations. In addition, flex had raised employee awareness of the benefits they had — something that had previously been overlooked or taken for granted.

Accordingly, PotashCorp believed that extending its flexible benefits program to the Rocanville unionized employees would be a win–win for both the employees and the company. The challenge was finding a way to do so that wouldn't require PotashCorp to design, communicate, and administer two different plans.

SOLUTION

The solution, according to Darryl Barclay, Senior Director, Human Resources, for PotashCorp, was "to keep the plan design for the hourly group as close as possible to the plan already in place for the company's staff employees."

"In our case," states Barclay, "because the unionized workers were interested in having flexible benefits, the union representing them was motivated to accept the same plan design that was provided to salaried employees."

PotashCorp used the same communication strategy when it introduced flex credits for unionized employees that it had developed for the salaried employee plan roll-out. "Not only had our communication efforts clearly been successful with the staff group, they were also particularly well-suited for a unionized environment," says Barclay. "We emphasized what employees would gain by having flexible benefits. We proved to them that they could have exactly the same coverage under the flex plan by using a modelling exercise, and then showed them their alternatives if they wanted to exercise their options."

RESULTS

The options for both unionized and non-unionized employees at PotashCorp remain virtually the same even now. "We started with a good plan," points out Jane

Thomas, PotashCorp's Manager, Pension and Benefits. "We make any adjustments on January 1st each year and, because we want to keep the same plan for both employee groups, unionized employees often receive increases even when they're not negotiated." PotashCorp's flex plan also includes some features that are extremely well-regarded and used by unionized employees, including the ability to buy extra vacation with excess flex credits.

PotashCorp continues to be pleased with its flex plan. "Because we were relatively early adopters of flex, even for salaried employees, in Canada, we had some trepidation when we launched the plan," says Barclay. "We certainly feared that flex would mean a lot of extra work for our HR team. While that was definitely the case on the launch of the plan and when we redesigned it in 2002, both administration and communication is now easier than we had anticipated. Annual enrolment now goes very smoothly."

Thomas is convinced that flexible benefits have helped with attraction and retention. "Our staff and the Rocanville unionized workers have a better understanding of their benefits and appreciate having the ability to choose options that are meaningful to them," says Thomas. "Even now, our competitors still offer primarily traditional benefit programs for unionized employees, so our flex plan is a differentiator in the marketplace."

GOING FORWARD

PotashCorp is keen to have its plan keep pace with changing times. While there are no immediate plans to make drastic changes, it reviews its plan annually and keeps current with what is "new and exciting," according to Thomas, with respect to both flex and employee benefits in general.

"PotashCorp has learned that its employees — unionized and salaried — appreciate choice. Wherever we can, we offer them options," says Barclay. "For example, when we introduced a matching gift program, we designed it so employees could choose the cause to support. Our employees are diverse individuals and providing them with flexibility — in benefits and otherwise — is important."

§ 23.8 GLAXOSMITHKLINE — FIXING A BROKEN FLEXIBLE BENEFITS PLAN

GlaxoSmithKline Inc. (GSK) is one of the world's leading research-based pharmaceutical and consumer health care companies. The Canadian operation employs approximately 1,800 employees.

BACKGROUND

What prompts an organization to revamp its flexible benefits plan only two years after it was introduced?

GSK introduced its flex plan in May 2002 when Glaxo Wellcome, which provided a traditional benefits plan, merged with SmithKline Beecham, which provided a fully flexible plan. The fact that flex plans were becoming more common in the pharmaceutical industry, given their employee appeal was a key consideration in adopting a flexible plan for the new organization.

Before the plan was introduced at GSK, the company sought feedback, and discovered that its employees did not understand what flex meant, or the responsibility that they would have under such a plan. To prepare for launch, GSK held ongoing employee information sessions designed to increase employees' understanding and comfort level with the new plan.

CHALLENGE

By the end of 2003, employees made it clear that the flex plan was not meeting their needs. Employee focus groups indicated only a 20 per cent satisfaction rate with the plan's content and its coverage levels.

This point was driven home even more convincingly when GSK took part in the *Best Employers in Canada* study. While GSK was named as one of the year's 50 best employers, employees gave very low marks to the benefits program. (Only 58 per cent of employees agreed with the statement "My benefits meet my family's and my needs well.") Even though research establishes that benefits have little impact on employee engagement as long as they are at least competitive, GSK decided that fixing its flex program had to become a priority if it was going to remain an employer of choice.

SOLUTION

GSK persevered with the idea of offering flexible benefits rather than reverting to a traditional plan. The first step in improving the plan was to understand in more detail why employees were dissatisfied. To that end, GSK engaged a third party to conduct focus groups with employees, and found that the plan was failing in the following respects:

1. Certain aspects of the plan were not supportive of the pharmaceutical industry or even of GSK's own business philosophy (e.g., there was no reimbursement for vaccines; there was 100 per cent reimbursement for generic prescriptions, but not brand name pharmaceuticals).
2. Administrative support — whether via the Web site or through the call centre — was not effective.
3. Communication materials were neither sufficiently comprehensive nor timely.

GSK's *Best Employers in Canada* results, the findings of an independent bench-marking analysis plus the focus group feedback, were shared with GSK's Canadian executive team. The team readily authorized changes, with two caveats: the changes had to be cost-neutral overall and all third parties with responsibility for the plan had to work together as partners, even if they were competitors. These third parties included a consulting firm that was handling the redesign of the flex plan as well as communications, another that managed administration, and the health insurance provider.

RESULTS

GSK, working with the third parties, redesigned its flex plan to be more aligned with the company's business philosophy and improved both administrative support and communication. Throughout this process and afterwards, GSK held more focus groups with its "Early Eyes" Group — a cross-section of employees representing all divisions and all levels. Not only did these employees add much value to the process by providing input and reviewing communication pieces prior to finalization and publication, they had an overwhelmingly positive reaction to the revamped plan and became ambassadors for its acceptance among the rest of the employee population.

In mid-2004, GSK again asked employees to weigh in on the benefits program by means of an online survey. This time, the satisfaction level was rated at 82 per cent. In addition, 78 per cent of employees responded positively to the statement around whether the company's benefits program was meeting their needs and those of their family well — a 20 per cent increase in just one year. GSK has retained its status as one of the country's 50 best employers, moving steadily up the ranks.

GOING FORWARD

Heide Scicluna, GSK's Director, HR, is a strong advocate of flexible benefits, even after having gone through the "re-flex" process. "All the concerns typically expressed about flex programs — that employees won't understand the program well enough to make the right choices to meet their needs, that flex is impossible to administer, and that all employees will elect the highest level of coverage — are not necessarily accurate provided the education, communication, and implementation plans are well managed."

So what steps does Scicluna recommend other organizations take in order to avoid the false start with flexible benefits that GSK experienced? "Recognize that employees must own the flex plan in order for it to be effective," she advises. "That means that it is essential that they have a good understanding and appreciation of the plan. Involve them in the design process, go 'above and beyond' when it comes to employee communication, and check in with your own 'Early Eyes' Group frequently to ensure the plan continues to meet employee needs."

Employee feedback has helped the GSK flex plan to evolve, with the latest addition being a personal spending account. While it's a taxable benefit, employees can use the account for virtually any expense — a family vacation, a home theatre, or even to cover the cost of gasoline, for example.

If GSK decides to introduce changes into its plan in the future, Scicluna is convinced that involving employees in the process and transparent, complete communication will ease the transition: "GSK's employees know that we're serious when it comes to ensuring that our flexible benefits program provides them with the coverage they need."

Part Eight

Global Trends

Twenty-Four

International Flexible Benefits

§ 24.1 INTRODUCTION

In this chapter, we will describe the global trend toward flexible benefits.

Flexible benefits means different things in different countries, but broadly it is intended to enable employees to choose the way some of their compensation package is delivered. Different countries have different "menu" items and different tax, legislative, and cultural environments, which in turn dictate different structures. However, the rationale for introducing flexible benefits is broadly the same — to help manage employers' compensation costs and deliver better value to employees.

Flexible benefit plans can be considered from two perspectives — where the money comes from (employer or employee) and how the money may be spent (core plans or choices). Funding is one of the main reasons that flexible benefit design varies from country to country.

We will consider first the forces that shape flexible benefits in each country, some of the advantages that companies see a flexible approach providing, and finally some of the issues that seem to block flexible benefits. We will then examine the approaches to flexible compensation, flexible rewards, or flexible benefits in several countries around the world, including Australia, Brazil, China, Hungary, the Netherlands, the United Kingdom, and the United States.

NATIONAL ENVIRONMENTS FOR FLEXIBLE BENEFITS DIFFER

Changes in employee benefit programs do not occur in a vacuum. The concept of flexible benefits has taken hold in varying degrees in many countries, depending on the tax, health care, legislative/regulatory, and national cultural environments. These common pressures seem to play a role around the globe, either to encourage or discourage the prevalence of employee choice-making.

Tax Treatment

Tax laws in most countries long ago recognized the difficulty of allowing employee choices among compensation elements that are subject to different tax rules. If a company car is not a taxable benefit, for example, and if choice-making does not trigger a taxable event, companies may allow employees to choose whether to take a car in lieu of cash — a choice between (taxable) cash and a (non-taxable) car, taking advantage of provisions in the tax code.

As in Canada, most tax jurisdictions have a notion of constructive receipt. If the employee has a choice of cash instead of some benefit, the benefit is treated like cash for tax purposes. Tax laws may not offer any particular advantage to employee choices, but if the tax laws are neutral, there are other reasons than tax efficiency to introduce flexible benefit programs.

On the other hand, the opportunity for an employee or executive to convert taxable cash into a non-taxable benefit is a way for the company to deliver more value at the same cost. The higher the tax rates, the more motivated employees, executives, and employers may be to find ways to deliver compensation in the most tax-efficient way. If the tax laws are favourable in a country, they can help make flexible benefits more attractive.

In some jurisdictions, legislation (as in the U.S.) or regulatory guidance (as here in Canada) has been enacted that enables employee choices.

National Health Care Systems

Flexible benefits arose historically in the U.S. primarily in response to medical care provided by employers. There is no broad-based national health care in the U.S.; health care coverage for most Americans is provided through employers. In the 1970s and 1980s, employers realized that they could save money by not offering coverage (and not paying premiums) for someone who already had adequate coverage through a working spouse.

The growth of flexible benefits outside the U.S. may be somewhat limited by the existence of national health care systems, which relegate company-sponsored health care programs to relatively small cost supplements and remove one of the primary inducements for flexible programs. However, in countries where employers play a role in providing medical benefits, such as in Brazil, there is room for employee choices and growing interest in offering such choices.

There is currently a global crisis in health care. New technology has a high price, and technological improvements combined with an older population have put stresses on all health care systems. In government-sponsored systems, there is the added strain of changing demographics (fewer working people contributing to the system relative to the number of retirees receiving benefits, and for a longer period of time). One obvious short-term remedy that government programs take is to push costs off to employers, so the growing importance of employer-sponsored medical plans is an expected future trend, even in countries with a strong socialized medical system. And, with employer-sponsored medical plans comes a more favourable environment for flexible benefits.

Legislative/Regulatory Environment

The regulatory infrastructure rarely keeps up with a changing or innovative environment, regardless of whether the market is sophisticated or not. Thus, the legal framework may not yet be in place.

In Canada and the U.S., the regulatory framework to support flexible benefit plans is in place, thus enhancing the viability and prevalence of flexible benefit programs.

In Australia and a few other countries, there is legislation that is friendly to flexible benefits. Australian flexible benefits are subject to a fringe benefit tax as well as a goods and services tax, so the most common areas for flexible approaches are additional contributions to the retirement plan, company cars, and business equipment, such as home computers. Flexible benefit programs are a prevalent practice in Australia and in countries with a similarly favourable legal setting.

In the U.K. and a few other countries, the legislation is basically neutral to flexible benefits, neither encouraging nor discouraging it. U.K. plans tend to focus on company cars, vacation/holiday, child care, additional insurance, club memberships, and similar services. Flexible benefits are often a "hot issue" in countries with this type of neutral legislation.

In some countries, legislation is very restrictive of flexible benefits. Flexible benefit programs are, therefore, less prevalent, although there is often interest in learning more about what flexible approaches are and what they can do.

National Culture

The national culture in some countries puts more emphasis on the individual than on the group/family/team. In most studies, the U.S. comes out as very heavily focused on the individual rather than the group. It is, therefore, not surprising that flexible benefits would have originated in the U.S. and would now be prevalent practice, even among smaller companies.

The countries that tend to rank highest in individualism after the U.S. are Australia, Great Britain, Canada, the Netherlands, and New Zealand. There is little surprise that most of these countries are where flexible benefit programs have had the most growth and appeal.

Flexible benefits put the emphasis on the individual employee making choices, rather than the company (group) making the decisions. This may not be immediately well received in countries that put more emphasis on the societal obligations of the employer than on the responsibility of the individual, and stronger communication efforts may be necessary.

ADVANTAGES OF FLEXIBLE BENEFITS FOR COMPANIES

Whether the external conditions are encouraging or discouraging, many companies feel that flexible benefits may offer some business advantages. The national environment will influence the significance of these flexible benefit drivers.

More Cost-Effective Delivery

A flexible approach can help the employer set in place a mechanism for reducing or controlling costs over the long term. Under a traditional program, cost savings can only be achieved through increasing administrative efficiency, cutting back coverages (not possible in some jurisdictions, except for future hires), or passing along higher costs to employees. A flexible approach allows an additional option — allowing employees to trade off among coverages and to structure their own flexible package efficiently, based on each individual's needs.

This is often described as allowing the employer to separate decisions about the cost of compensation from decisions on the form of compensation. The growing popularity of defined contribution retirement plans is an example of this, where the company costs are set and the amount of ultimate benefit received by the employee varies based on investment performance. Another example is the Australian system (discussed in detail later), where a total compensation package is set (so that company costs are fixed) and the employee can arrange the package to best suit his or her individual tax and personal situation.

Competitive Edge

The problem of attracting and retaining talent is now being felt in many countries and in many industry sectors. In some environments, organizations implementing flexible programs tend to be regarded as innovative, responsive, or leading-edge companies. Following "best practices" that "empower" employees to make their own choices can be seen as a significant competitive advantage in the labour market. For example, in the U.K., flexible benefit plans are seen in the technology and banking industries as effective ways for companies to differentiate themselves, especially in attracting younger employees.

Harmonizing Benefit Programs Following Merger/Acquisition

Flexible benefits can be used as a mechanism for combining the benefit programs of merged or acquired organizations within a country. Merging programs often leads to "cherry picking" the richest elements (or plans) from each operation, so that the total package is very expensive and very generous. On the other hand, continuing separate programs may not be the ultimate business goal. The flexible approach allows the employer to offer benefit options that may resemble but not duplicate prior coverages. Employees can reconstruct their earlier coverages within the flexible framework.

This must be done with caution, as there may be legal restrictions. For example, the European Union has directives on the transfer of undertakings that can restrict the ability of a company to alter benefit programs. Conceptually, a flexible benefit plan can allow employees in both operations to construct their own prior coverage.

Another legal restriction in many countries in continental Europe and Latin America is that of "acquired rights." "Acquired rights" is the legal principle that any repeated, regular payment (or procedure) on the part of the employer towards the employee becomes a term and condition of employment (part of the employment contract) and cannot be reduced or taken away. Conversion to a flexible plan must be able to be justified in court as not being a reduction in benefits.

Encouraging a Total Compensation Perspective

Flexible plans require more communication and explanation to the employees. One advantage of a flexible plan is the increased understanding of "what the company is spending on me," leading to better appreciation of the employer and improved employee perceptions of their total compensation package.

Company expenditures for benefits can be translated into direct pay equivalents (at least in the minds of the employees, if not in actuality) and thus become more "real" to the employees. By putting a currency value on the employer's total compensation costs and allowing the employee to decide how to direct those expenditures, the line separating direct pay, benefits, and perquisites becomes less distinct.

One effect of the total compensation viewpoint is to reinforce the thought that benefit costs, like the costs of direct pay, can and should be controlled. Some multinational companies look to flexible compensation or flexible benefit programs in many national locations to support their global HR total compensation strategies.

OBSTACLES TO FLEXIBLE BENEFITS

Companies also perceive common drawbacks when considering flexible benefits in most environments. The national environment will influence the significance of these obstacles.

Administrative Cost and Difficulties

In countries like Canada and the U.S., where flexible plans have been around for some time, companies take the administration of such plans in stride. However, in environments where flexible benefits are fairly new, there may not be administrative systems in place that can adequately handle employee choice-making. Traditional vendors (such as insurance companies and third-party administrators) may not be equipped to handle such programs; the software may not exist and the vendors may not be familiar with (or comfortable with) the administrative processes required for flexible benefits.

Communication to Employees

Some managers feel that flexible benefit plans are complicated and too difficult to communicate to employees. In some cases, the complexity runs deeper than managers may want to admit — for example, the employees may not understand their current benefit programs. Employee communication/education around the world has a long way to go. Certainly, any program that involves employees making choices must also involve more complicated communication than a program with no employee choice. The degree of complexity depends largely on the specific program being communicated. In the United States, the complexities of communicating "full flex" have helped lead to what are now called "choice plans" or "net pricing plans" that are easier to communicate.

Corporate Culture

The underlying framework of flexible benefits is that the individual employees must choose for themselves and make decisions for themselves. One common source of resistance is the company being fearful of the consequences if employees make inappropriate choices.

Some decisions, of course, have almost always been left to the individual employee; for example, naming a beneficiary for a company-provided life insurance policy.

But there are some areas — such as selection of investments for retirement funds — where the typical blue-collar employee may not have the education or knowledge for making sound choices. There are some purchasing decisions that are better made by experts within the company than by each employee. On the other hand, the employee nearing retirement age may have different investment needs than the younger employee.

Another example of inappropriate choice might be the employee who does not purchase life insurance — a decision that a surviving spouse may greatly regret. Companies sometimes offer a "core" of required benefits so that employees cannot opt out of life insurance altogether. However, young, single employees with no family attachments may consider that they have less need for life insurance, while the sole wage-earner in a large family may have considerable need for protection against loss of income through death or disability.

The evidence from companies that have had flexible benefits for a long time is that employees are able to make wise decisions, suited to their situation, so long as they are given adequate information.

Vendor Reluctance

All voluntary benefit programs contain an element of what insurance companies call adverse selection. Employees choose one benefit over another because they know they will use the benefit, or because they know they will need the benefit if an unforeseen event occurs.

Adverse selection occurs when employees can accurately anticipate their use of benefits and choose the option that provides the most coverage at the least cost. Refer to Chapter 16 for more information on adverse selection.

The insurance companies are wary of adverse selection. Insurance rates are usually based on average (expected) claims for an average group of employees and premiums could be inadequate if the group being covered is no longer average, but has a higher proportion of employees more likely to make claims that are greater than expected.

The fact is that the insurance companies can and do eventually adjust to the new environment and find that insuring flexible benefit programs can be a lucrative business. The design of the flexible program can help control the potential for adverse selection.

The other reason for vendor reluctance is the administrative cost. In a country where flexible benefits are just gaining popularity, or have been adopted by only a handful of companies, vendors may not be equipped to handle employee choice — they lack the software, the forms, and the administrative expertise.

One way to cope with reluctance on the part of the insurance vendors is for the employer to take on some of the risk through self-insurance, assuming the employee population is large enough to make this feasible.

§ 24.2 FLEXIBLE BENEFITS IN VARIOUS COUNTRIES

Flexible benefit plans outside Canada look different due to the national environment and the importance of perceived advantages and drawbacks in each country. However, while international flexible benefit plans may look different from their Canadian counterparts, the attractions of employee choice-making will ensure that these international variations will find local supporters.

The following sections examine the approaches to flexible compensation, flexible reward, or flexible benefits in several countries around the world, including Australia, Brazil, China, Hungary, the Netherlands, the United Kingdom, and the United States.

AUSTRALIA

In Australia, flexible benefit programs have been firmly established and are in place at a large number of employers.

Australia and New Zealand have for some time imposed tax on the company giving the fringe benefits rather than on the employee receiving them. As a result, fringe benefits often delivered a much more tax-effective outcome than did taxable salary. Arguably, this produced the most extensive flexible programs in the world, with the widest range of employee choices, since companies were generally open to offering as many benefits as possible within a total compensation framework.

The story has changed much over the years and both the Australian and New Zealand governments have made several amendments to the governing legislation. The value of benefits in both countries has been greatly eroded by these changes. Following the reform of the fringe benefits tax (FBT) and the introduction of the goods and services tax (GST) in 2000, many of the benefits formerly offered under flexible packages have been dropped, since they provide no tax advantage to the employee compared to cash and no cost savings to the company.

Tax-free benefits such as laptop computers, or benefits that are taxed at a reduced rate such as company cars and car parking costs, can still provide great value to both employers and employees within the flexible package.

The tax effectiveness of pension plans varies significantly among employees, depending on their individual circumstance. As a consequence, employees can tailor their pension to their needs, with many employers requiring only that legislative minimum levels of pension contributions be made. Employees are then allowed to "salary sacrifice" additional amounts into their pension plan from their total compensation package.

In addition, recent federal budget proposals would increase the tax effectiveness of pension contributions, especially for high earners. Pension plans are likely to be an extremely attractive benefit for the older workforce, especially for those at a high marginal tax rate.

In general, while tax advantages in some areas may be dwindling, the "employment cost" — the total value of providing benefits, including all related taxes and gross-up for non-deductibility — has continued to be accepted as the common approach in compensation and benefit communication. Those companies that have not used this total compensation packaging to communicate the full value of the compensation package are being seen as left behind in the quest to attract employees. Despite the tax changes, the total package approach, with some flexibility in how it is delivered, still makes strong sense in the Australian context.

BRAZIL

The interest in flexible benefits in Brazil is fairly new. Approximately fifteen companies had implemented plans by the end of 2006, although many additional companies are in the planning stages. Flexible benefits are seen as innovative and dynamic and a way to distinguish "leading-edge" employers in the highly competitive job market.

The primary factors underlying this growing interest include:

- **Cost containment.** Prior to 1994, Brazil's hyperinflation meant that human resource managers needed to focus on trying to establish competitive salary increases; benefits were almost an afterthought. In 1994, the hyperinflation was brought under control and attention began to shift to controlling benefit costs.

- **Private medical system.** Brazil has a national medical program with all clinical, surgical, maternity, and dental services provided for all citizens from government-approved centres. Because the program is not sufficient to meet all health care needs, most companies in Brazil offer medical plans for all employees and dependants through the private health care system. Now that rising health care costs have captured attention, some cost-containment approaches in the private system (such as managed care or networks that provide medical services) are being employed.

  Several health care trends are helping create an environment favourable to flexible benefits. Employers have begun shifting health care costs to employees through co-payments and maximums. Employers are also employing alternative funding arrangements, including self-insurance, stop-loss insurance, and other protections against catastrophic or "shock" claims. Companies are investing in wellness and prevention programs, health education, and improved employee communications about health care. Finally, retiree health care and associated costs are a growing concern.

- **Demographics.** In Brazil, as in Canada, traditional benefit programs were established decades ago, but the workplace of the 1950s and 1960s was very different from the workplace today. Today, a significant percentage of the workforce is female; there are many non-traditional families, more single employees, as all the same demographic changes felt around the world are manifested in Brazil.

- **Legislation.** There is no particular legislation in Brazil to enable flexible benefit plans but, broadly speaking, benefits are not taxable to employees, while salary is. This lays the groundwork for the interest in flexible benefits.

Because benefits are not taxed, it is very attractive to set up a spending account under which employees are given a fixed amount (or a percentage of pay) that can be used to purchase a range of benefits. There is usually a core benefit program provided, including life insurance, health care, luncheon vouchers, and sometimes a defined contribution retirement plan. Typical choices in addition to the core program include education costs, enhancement of company-provided health care benefits, increasing life insurance, additional contributions to defined contribution retirement plan, supermarket vouchers, and transportation vouchers (for gas, for instance).

Some companies offer loans as a choice, repaid by the employee within a twelve-month period with no interest charge. But cash cannot be an option. If cash is included as a choice, the tax authorities would likely view the whole account as "salary" rather than "benefits" and, therefore, it would be taxable.

The major obstacle in Brazil is the perceived lack of competent administration. This is changing rapidly, as companies begin to adopt flexible plans and service providers and third-party administrators become more adept.

CHINA

In China, the prevalence of flexible benefits is still low in the general market, while the level of interest in flexible benefits has been rising over the past few years. Organizations participating in Hewitt Associates' *2005 Flexible Benefits Survey* in China indicate that:

- 8 per cent have implemented a flexible benefit plan;
- 6 per cent are currently implementing a flexible plan;
- 18 per cent will implement a flexible plan within the next two years;
- 52 per cent will implement a flexible plan but are not sure when;
- 1 per cent once had a flexible plan but reverted back to a traditional plan; and
- 15 per cent never had a flexible plan and are not interested in developing one.

Advantages and Obstacles

The main factor driving flexible benefits in China is to provide a diverse workforce with benefits that suits their needs. Offering flexible choice in benefits also enhances awareness of and perceived value of employee benefits. Some regard flexible benefits as an innovative benefits delivery model that differentiates the employer in the market. Employees also regard themselves as empowered and trusted by the employer to make responsible choices for themselves.

Tax treatment is not a driver of flexible benefits in China. Benefits that would be included in a flexible plan are taxable to an employee — employer contributions are deemed as employee salary income and are subject to individual income tax, and employee contributions are made on an after-tax basis.

As in Canada, survey results show that employers perceive the administrative complexity, difficulty in communications, and possible increases to overall benefit costs as obstacles to implementing flexible benefits. Unlike in Canada, those who have implemented flexible benefits found their real challenges included the administrative complexity as well as tax issues and a lack of knowledge or experience.

Flexible Options

In China, employers are attracted by the fact that they could add a "flexible element" to their traditional benefit plan design. Some examples of flexible options are:

- **Flexible savings plan.** The plan sets up two funds with different purposes: housing and pension. The employees are given the choice to direct a certain percentage of employer contribution into both funds, although the employer often sets up a minimum percentage for the pension fund to ensure that employee retirement benefit is appropriately secured.
- **Flexible spending account.** The total budget is fixed, while the employees are given the choice to use the fund in certain designated usage, for example, education assistance, personal car assistance, or top-up employee/dependant medical coverage.

According to Hewitt Associates' *2005 Flexible Benefits Survey*, flexible benefits options that are either widely available (for companies that have a flexible benefits plan) or considered as widely available (for companies that plan to implement flexible benefits in the future) include:

- Medical
- Group insurance
- Financial security
- Time off with pay
- Lifestyle spending account.

Summary

The use of flexible benefits has remained a hot topic in China for the past few years and the interest level has been high. Although the expertise and experience with flexible benefits for employers in China is still developing, the idea of flex has evolved from a new concept to a viable approach that some of the leading companies are exploring.

The drivers behind flexible benefits are different from those in Canada, where controlling benefit costs is typically one of the top priorities. In China, employers are more concerned with offering tailored benefits to suit employees in different phases of their life cycle. This is regarded as a strong attraction and retention tool — the perceived value of benefits is increased.

HUNGARY

Flexible benefit plans, or "cafeteria plans" as they are called in Hungary, are of growing interest. Flexible plans offer choice in a "menu" of benefits that are separate and distinct from salary. A typical plan may allow choice among six to eight benefit items, within a certain cost limit. According to Hewitt Associates' recent survey of Hungarian employers with best human resource practices, 44 per cent of participants have implemented a flexible benefit plan, and another 30 per cent are considering introducing a flexible benefit program.

Advantages and Obstacles

The main reasons to implement flexible benefits are the tax treatment and social security contribution allowance, effectively managing the organization's spending on benefits, and improving employee satisfaction.

In general, the corporate culture is open to operating flexible benefit programs, which are increasingly widely used. Vendor companies provide the various benefits included in the menu and it is possible to outsource the complete flexible benefits administration.

Flexible Options

Employees choose benefit items from the menu for the year (or at the start of employment). Choices are illustrated below, based on their tax implications:

- **Benefits with individual tax allowance limits.** Maybe the most important benefits from this group are the voluntary pension fund contribution (which is tax-free to 50 per cent of the monthly minimum wage) and meal tickets.
- **Benefits with common (umbrella) tax allowances limit.** This group consists of voluntary health and aid fund contributions, local travel, season tickets, computer and Internet subsidies, vacation vouchers, cultural event vouchers, and school subsidies.
- **Benefits supplementing obligatory benefits.** In addition to legally prescribed benefits, such as occupational health care or commuting support for those living outside of a city, employers can offer higher than the prescribed level of support or supplementary services, such as on-site health clinics, first-aid courses, dental care, and medical screening for management.

- **Taxable benefits.** There are some additional benefits that are offered despite being taxable. The most popular of these include cellular phones, home fund deposits, and company cars.

THE NETHERLANDS

The labour market is looking for more flexibility in work arrangements, and employers and the government are responding by introducing flexibility with regard to the way employees are paid.

The most common variety of flexible benefits currently found in the Netherlands provides a core set of benefits with some individual choice available to the employee. Many of the choices in these plans involve trade-offs between time and money. For example, employees can trade wages for sabbatical leave, vacation buying, and parental leave for child care.

These trade-offs, along with choices within the retirement plan, are fairly common in Dutch organizations, even in traditional industry sectors.

Effective January 1, 2006, the government introduced a tax-deductible savings program, called the Lifespan Leave plan, in an attempt to increase the flexibility of the labour market. Under the Lifespan Leave plan, an employee can save up to 12 per cent of annual pay (with some restrictions) to use for sabbaticals, part-time work, and also early retirement. Employers use the incentive to provide flexible benefits.

Full flex is less common, but it is of growing interest. Technology and larger financial services companies are early adopters of flexible benefits, with executives and younger workers tending to embrace the concept more readily than other employees.

The primary factors influencing the interest in flexible benefits include:

- **Tax treatment.** The tax treatment of a benefit in the Netherlands does not depend on whether it is delivered through a flexible benefit plan or directly. In principle, all benefits are taxable when granted. However, retirement benefits and other annuity-type benefits are not taxable until the benefit payment is received (drawdowns from the Lifespan Leave plan are considered in this category) and contributions to such plans are tax-deductible. Thus, there is no particular tax advantage to exchanging taxable gross salary for taxable benefits.

- **Cost containment.** Health care costs are increasing at a greater rate than general inflation. Before January 1, 2006, most employers paid part of the health care premium. This is becoming less prevalent following the introduction of a mandatory national health care system based on the *Health Care Insurance Act* on January 1, 2006. Employers pay a mandatory contribution toward the new health care system, but to avoid cost increases, most employers no longer contribute toward health insurance policies.

UNITED KINGDOM

In the U.K., flexible plans are rapidly becoming the market norm rather than a differentiating factor. In a recent survey, about two-thirds of U.K. companies expressed interest in considering or developing a flexible benefit plan.

National Environment

Generally speaking, only a few benefits enjoy tax advantages, whether through a flexible plan or not. Employee contributions to a pension plan, premiums for long-term disability, life insurance benefits, and health screenings for employees are not taxable. Financial counselling relating to a company-sponsored pension plan can be provided by the employer and is not taxable to the employee. Training or education assistance that is job-related can be provided tax-free by the company. There are a few others.

However, other than this small list, there is no particular tax advantage to having, say, a sports club membership paid by the company, compared to having the company give the employee cash to buy the membership. Thus, flexible benefit plans do not offer any particular income tax advantage.

The one arena where there is some tax advantage is National Insurance contributions (social security contributions). Basically, any elements provided as benefits through a flexible plan rather than cash are immune from National Insurance contributions by the employee. There are two exceptions — retail vouchers and transportation costs, such as rail passes for commuting. Interestingly, since there is a ceiling for National Insurance contributions, savings on these contributions are effectively limited to the lower-paid employees. Unlike in many countries, where use of flexible benefits is a method for the higher-paid employees to reduce their tax burden, these plans provide more tax relief for the lower-paid employees in the United Kingdom.

Objectives

Basically, there are two drivers behind the focus on flexible benefits:

- The prevalent motivation for companies is to meet the diverse needs of employees in order to better attract and retain them. When companies consult with employees about a flexible benefits plan, the results are overwhelmingly favourable.
- Following a merger or acquisition, a flexible approach is considered a way of harmonizing the different benefit plans without always giving the "better" feature. Under the EU regulations on transfer of undertakings, existing benefits may not be reduced (not even voluntarily). However, the position taken by most companies is that putting both operations in the same flexible benefits plan is not a reduction in benefits since employees could "buy" their old benefit

package. This has not, to date, been tested in the courts; however, companies are proceeding on the assumption that, at worst, the pre-merger employees would be compelled to buy back their old benefit package.

One of the advantages of the flexible plan is the ability to provide employees with group purchasing rates. A plan may provide theatre tickets, travel or property insurance, professional advice, laundry services, home computers, or similar features. The advantage to the employee is the ability to purchase such goods and services at lower group pricing rates. This can be extremely attractive, especially for low- or middle-income levels.

Approach

Generally, the approach in the U.K. towards flexible benefits is in the form of allowing employees to "trade" salary or other benefits through a process of contractual negotiations as a source of funding for flexible benefits. This reflects a growing acceptance that the opportunities for flexible benefits in the U.K. are driven by the total package and not just by the expenditure for benefits.

There are two general approaches. The most common describes each employee's package as having a base salary and "flex fund value" (flexible credits) that can be "spent" on benefits. Of growing interest, however, is flexible rewards (rather than flexible benefits), where there is no separation into different programs. The employer determines the overall package value and the employees elect their preferred mix of pay and benefits within that value. The delivery of the package, however, is ultimately at the discretion of the employer.

The most common options for flexible benefits are time off with pay (vacation), medical, and dental insurance. Other areas commonly include pension, life insurance, child care, medical exams, and critical illness insurance.

Another trend has been towards expanding eligibility. Many companies began flexible benefits focused on a select subgroup of employees (for example, executives). However, there is now a significant shift towards covering all employee groups.

Unions in the U.K. are not opposed to flexible benefits. In fact, overwhelmingly, unions have responded favourably when there has been advance consultation.

Obstacles

Insurance companies in the U.K., as recently as a few years ago, were very concerned about adverse selection and administration under flexible benefit plans. That tension has relaxed as the insurers become more comfortable with flexible plans.

The greatest obstacle to flexible benefits is seen as coping with administrative issues. However, as these plans become more popular and as technology adapts, employers are seeing that the administration is not as large a problem as they first thought. The second obstacle is seen as the cost of implementation.

UNITED STATES

Flexible benefits originated in the U.S. with the *Revenue Act of 1978*: Section 401(k) of the Internal Revenue Code permits employees to make trade-offs between taking cash or deferring compensation into a retirement income plan. Section 125 permits cafeteria plans, where employees can choose between taxable cash and non-taxable benefits without incurring tax. Both sections are linked, to permit choice-making among three forms of compensation:

- Cash;
- Welfare benefits (health, life insurance, etc.); and
- Deferred compensation/retirement income.

There were a number of forces behind the initial legislation, such as changing demographics, the increasing cost of employer-paid medical benefits, and a national culture that favours individual responsibility.

U.S. companies continue to reinvent benefits, consistent with emerging business strategies and new attitudes towards the employment relationships. Over time, employers have offered either full credit-based or net pricing flexible benefit plans.

Leading-edge employers are making changes, creating programs that meet non-traditional needs. These include financial education, general education, dependant care, legal services, and time/convenience. Alternative working arrangements (such as flexible hours, a compressed workweek, job sharing, and telecommuting) are by far the most popular of these non-traditional benefits. Long-term care insurance, group auto insurance, group prepaid legal services, and group financial planning services are now often found as choices.

Overall the largest evolution in flexible benefits in the United States is in the area of health care.

Over the last twenty-five years, high medical inflation has fuelled changes to health care offerings. Employer-sponsored health care answers have migrated over time from managed care to reductions in plan design and increases in employee contributions, and on to the current focus on consumer-driven health plans (CDHPs). The overall private health insurance drivers have remained the same over time:

- Meet diverse employee needs;
- Limit company costs, especially in health care;
- Enhance benefit value; and
- Add benefit choice.

Health Care Delivery

Flexible private health insurance plans generally fall into three distinct categories: traditional indemnity (fee for service) insurance, managed care, and consumer-driven models. The later two are defined below. Over the past twenty-five years, the focus has shifted from traditional indemnity insurance to managed care and more recently to CDHPs.

Managed Care

Managed care involves the provision of health care by a third party that, for a prepaid, fixed premium (rather than fee for service), contracts to deliver a whole spectrum of medical care. By integrating the payment for and delivery of health care, managed care systems attempt to keep costs down by managing the behaviour of both health care providers and health care consumers.

There are five primary managed care models in the United States; three of the five are health maintenance organizations (HMOs):

- **Staff model HMO** — salaried HMO staff, either in one facility or through hospitals owned by or under contract with the HMO, provide patient, laboratory, and diagnostic services.

- **Network or group model HMO** — independent, multi-specialty groups provide a specified range of benefits at an agreed rate through a contract with the HMO.

- **Independent practice association (IPA)** — an HMO network of individual physicians and health care professionals provides services. The physicians work in their own offices and bill the IPA at a discounted fee-for-service or fixed rate for treating enrolled patients.

- **Preferred provider organizations (PPOs)** — a number of otherwise unconnected doctors and hospitals offer discounted services to an insurance company. Consumers choose their doctors from a list and pay extra for providers who are not on the list.

- **Point-of-service plan (POS)** — members can choose either a managed care program or network, or "out-of-plan" services. Members pay more for out-of-plan services.

Enrolment in these plans has shifted from the once-dominant staff model HMO to PPO plans.

Consumer-Driven Models

Due to the steady erosion in the cost differences among the various managed care models, the next generation of employee health plans is based on consumer-driven models. These are health care designs that use more aggressive cost-sharing techniques to influence health care usage.

Table 24.1
Comparison of Health Reimbursement Arrangements (HRAs) and Health Savings Accounts (HSAs)

Factor	HRA	HSA
Legislation	Introduced in 2002 by the IRS	Introduced in 2003 by the *Medicare Prescription Drug, Improvement and Modernization Act*
Contribution Source	Employer only	Employer and employee contributions
Taxability of Contribution	Non-taxable	Pre-tax employee contributions. Employer contributions non-taxable
Carry Over Account Balance Year-to-Year	Yes	Yes
Contribution Level	Established by employer	IRS defines contribution levels

One of the models is the health reimbursement arrangement (HRA), which typically has a relatively low premium for catastrophic health insurance coverage and an employer-funded health reimbursement account to be used for routine health costs. For serious illnesses or higher, unforeseen medical expenses, the plan requires high deductibles to be met (US$1,000–US$2,000, or more) before paying 100 per cent of expenses.

Another model is the health savings account (HSA). While health care flexible spending accounts similar to the health spending accounts in Canada have existed for quite some time in the U.S., federal legislation passed in 2003 introduced the HSA. As in Canada, an HSA is a trust or custodial account established exclusively to receive tax-favoured contributions on behalf of eligible individuals. Amounts contributed to an HSA accumulate on a tax-free basis and are not subject to tax if they are used to pay for eligible medical expenses for the employee and dependants. Unlike in Canada, in the U.S., contributions made in one year and not used to pay expenses in that year may be used to pay eligible medical expenses in later years. Money in an HSA can be used tax-free for eligible medical expenses at any age, including into retirement. Also, HSAs can only be used if the individual enrols in a high-deductible health plan alongside the HSA. A comparison between HRAs and HSAs is shown in Table 24.1.

Other consumer-driven models include:

- **Customized design** — provides employees with a basic plan and the option to choose different levels of coverage based on their needs. This is similar to "build your own benefits" as outlined in Chapter 5.

- **Multi-tier networks** — participants are given the opportunity to make cost and quality choices each time they need care, based on their choice of facilities.
- **Defined contribution** — an employer provides a set subsidy as well as multiple options for health coverage.

Summary

Flexible benefits began in the United States in the late 1970s and now constitute a common method of delivering benefits. Both full flexible credit-based models and net pricing models are currently used. Over time, health care inflation has continued to drive the evolution of flexible benefit plans, from traditional indemnity insurance to managed care and now to consumer-driven health care. Legislation in 2002 and 2003 promoting tax effective savings for health care in the form of health reimbursement accounts and health spending accounts encouraged a shift towards defined contribution-style health savings plans.

SUMMARY

Our world tour of flexible benefit plans serves to highlight the differences between countries in the prevalence and design of flexible benefit plans. From Brazil, China, and Hungary, where the concepts are fairly new but interest is growing, to Australia and the United Kingdom, where use of flexible benefits is more common and a broad range of benefits and compensation are included, to the United States, where, for almost three decades, flexible benefit plans have evolved to better control employers' cost of benefits and influence plan usage.

Whatever the country, the main drivers are similar but to varying degrees — the tax and legislative environments, national health systems, and national culture all play a part in shaping flexible benefit plans.

So too are the advantages and the obstacles similar. Organizations across the world look to flexible benefit plans to control costs, provide them with a competitive edge, help harmonize benefits following a merger or acquisition, and support a total compensation message. However, they also recognize that implementing a flexible benefit program to some degree may lead to more challenges in administering and communicating the plan, possible difficulty in securing vendors, and a shift in corporate culture as employees are asked to make choices in the way their benefit package is delivered.

We see the forces shaping flexible benefit plans growing stronger and continue to witness an ever-growing global interest in flexible benefits.

Appendix — Government Publications

The following publications are contained in this Appendix:

REVENUE CANADA TAXATION

INTERPRETATION BULLETIN

NUMBER: IT-339R2

DATE: August 8, 1989

SUBJECT: Income Tax Act
Meaning of "Private Health Services Plan"

REFERENCE: Subsection 248(1) (also paragraphs 6(1)(a), 18(1)(a), 118.2(2)(q)
and 118.2(3)(b))

Application

The provisions discussed below are effective for the 1988 and subsequent
taxation years. For taxation years prior to 1988, refer to Interpretation
Bulletin IT-339R dated June 1, 1983.

Summary

This bulletin discusses the meaning of a "private health services plan" and
describes some of the arrangements for covering the cost of medical and
hospital care under such a plan. It also discusses the tax status of
contributions made to such a plan by an employer on behalf of an employee and
the circumstances under which the premium costs incurred by an employee
qualify as medical expenses for purposes of the medical expense tax credit.

Discussion and Interpretation

1. Contributions made by an employer to or under a private health services
plan on behalf of an employee are excluded from the employee's income from an
office or employment by virtue of subparagraph 6(1)(a)(i). On the other hand,
an amount paid by an employee as a premium, contribution or other
consideration to a private health services plan qualifies as a medical
expense for purposes of the medical expense tax credit by virtue of paragraph
118.2(2)(q). The amounts so paid must be for one or more of

(a) the employee
(b) the employee's spouse and
(c) any member of the employee's household with whom the employee is
connected by blood relationship, marriage or adoption.

For further comments on the medical expense tax credit see the current
version of IT-519.

For purposes of the Act, a "private health services plan" is defined in
subsection 248(1).

2. The contracts of insurance and medical or hospital care insurance plans
referred to in paragraphs (a) and (b) of the definition in subsection 248(1)
of "private health services plan" include contracts or plans that are either
in whole or in part in respect of dental care and expenses.

3. A private health services plan qualifying under paragraphs (a) or (b) of the definition in subsection 248(1) is a plan in the nature of insurance. In this respect the plan must contain the following basic elements:

(a) an undertaking by one person,
(b) to indemnify another person,
(c) for an agreed consideration,
(d) from a loss or liability in respect of an event,
(e) the happening of which is uncertain.

4. Coverage under a plan must be in respect of hospital care or expense or medical care or expense which normally would otherwise have qualified as a medical expense under the provisions of subsection 118.2(2) in the determination of the medical expense tax credit (see IT-519).

5. If the agreed consideration is in the form of cash premiums, they usually relate closely to the coverage provided by the plan and are based on computations involving actuarial or similar studies. Plans involving contracts of insurance in an arm's length situation normally contain the basic elements outlined in 3 above.

6. In a "cost plus" plan an employer contracts with a trusteed plan or insurance company for the provision of indemnification of employees' claims on defined risks under the plan. The employer promises to reimburse the cost of such claims plus an administration fee to the plan or insurance company. The employee's contract of employment requires the employer to reimburse the plan or insurance company for proper claims (filed by the employee) paid, and a contract exists between the employee and the trusteed plan or insurance company in which the latter agrees to indemnify the employee for claims on the defined risks so long as the employment contract is in good standing. Provided that the risks to be indemnified are those described in paragraphs (a) and (b) of the definition of "private health services plan" in subsection 248(1), such a plan qualifies as a private health services plan.

7. An arrangement where an employer reimburses its employees for the cost of medical or hospital care may come within the definition of private health services plan. This occurs where the employer is obligated under the employment contract to reimburse such expenses incurred by the employees or their dependants. The consideration given by the employee is considered to be the employee's covenants as found in the collective agreement or in the contract of service.

8. Medical and hospital insurance plans offered by Blue Cross and various life insurers, for example, are considered private health services plans within the meaning of subsection 248(1). In addition, the Group Surgical Medical Insurance Plan covering federal government employees qualifies as a private health services plan within the meaning of subsection 248(1). Therefore, payments made by an individual under any such plan qualify as medical expenses by virtue of paragraph 118.2(2)(q).

9. Private health services plan premiums, contributions or other consideration paid for by the employer are not included as medical expenses of the employee under paragraph 118.2(2)(q) by virtue of paragraph 118.2(3)(b) and are not employee benefits (see 1 above). They are however, business outlays or expenses of the employer for purposes of paragraph

18(1)(a). On the other hand, contributions or premiums qualify as medical expenses under paragraph 118.2(2)(q) where they are paid directly by the employee, or are paid by the employer out of deductions from the employee's pay. The amounts so paid must be for one or more of

(a) the employee,
(b) the employee's spouse and
(c) any member of the employee's household with whom the employee is connected by blood relationship, marriage or adoption.

REVENUE CANADA TAXATION

INTERPRETATION BULLETIN NUMBER: IT-428

DATE: April 30, 1979

SUBJECT: INCOME TAX ACT
Wage Loss Replacement Plans

REFERENCE: Paragraph 6(1)(f) (also paragraph 6(1)(a) and
section 19 of the Income Tax Application Rules, 1971)

1. Paragraph 6(1)(f) provides that, for 1972 and subsequent
taxation years, amounts received on a periodic basis by an
employee or an ex-employee as compensation for loss of
income from an office or employment, that were payable
under a sickness, accident, disability or income
maintenance insurance plan (in this bulletin referred to as
a "wage loss replacement plan") to which the employer made
a contribution, are to be included in income, but subject
to a reduction as specified in that paragraph for
contributions made by the employee to the plan after 1967.
Before 1972, such amounts received by a taxpayer were not
included in income.

2. Paragraph 6(1)(f) does not apply to a self-employed
person inasmuch as any amount received by such person in
the way of an income maintenance payment would not be
compensation for loss of income from an office or
employment. With regard to "overhead expense insurance" and
"income insurance" of a self-employed person, see
Interpretation Bulletin IT-223.

Exemption for Plans Established before June 19, 1971

3. Transitional provisions in section 19 of the Income Tax
Application Rules, 1971 stipulate that amounts that would
otherwise be included in income under paragraph 6(1)(f) are
to be excluded if they were received pursuant to a plan
that existed on June 18, 1971 and were in consequence of an
event that occurred prior to 1974. Comments on these
transitional provisions, particularly with regard to
admissible and non-admissible changes in pre-June 19, 1971
plans, appear in IT-54. It is to be noted that, for 1974
and subsequent taxation years, the exemption in section 19
of the ITAR is applicable only if amounts received by a
taxpayer are attributable to an event occurring before
1974. In this context, the word "event" has reference to
the thing that caused the disability. In the case of an
accident, for example, although the effect on the
taxpayer's health may not have become noticeable or serious
until 1974 or a later year, the "event" would have occurred
before 1974 if the accident took place before 1974 and the
later disability was directly attributable to the accident.
Similarly, in the case of a degenerative disease such as

muscular dystrophy, the "event" is the onset of the disease however much later the incapacity occurs. On the other hand, a recurring disease, such as a seasonal allergy or chronic tonsillitis, would qualify as an "event" only for the particular period of one attack.

4. For an illustration of the calculations involved where both paragraph 6(1)(f) of the Act and section 19 of the ITAR apply to a particular taxpayer, in different taxation years, see 25 below.

Meaning of a "Wage Loss Replacement Plan"

5. In the Department's view, a plan to which paragraph 6(1)(f) applies is any arrangement, however it is styled, between an employer and employees, or between an employer and a group or association of employees, under which provision is made for indemnification of an employee, by means of benefits payable on a periodic basis, if an employee suffers a loss of employment income as a consequence of sickness, maternity or accident. This arrangement may be formal in nature, as evidenced by a contract negotiated between an employer and employees, or it may be informal, arising from an understanding on the part of the employees, that wage loss replacement benefits would be made available to them by the employer. Where the arrangement involves a contract of insurance with an insurance company, the insurance contract becomes part of the plan but does not constitute the plan itself.

6. Where it is apparent that a plan was instituted with the intention or for the purpose of providing wage loss replacement benefits, the assumption will be that it is a plan to which paragraph 6(1)(f) applies unless the contrary can be established. Such a plan will be considered to exist where, for example, payments under the plan are to commence only when sick leave credits are exhausted or where benefits are subject to reduction by the amount of any wages or wage loss replacement benefits payable under other plans. A supplementary unemployment benefit plan, as defined in subsection 145(1), is not considered to be a plan to which paragraph 6(1)(f) applies.

7. A plan for purposes of paragraph 6(1)(f) of the Act and section 19 of the ITAR must be an "insurance" plan. Those provisions are not applicable, therefore, to uninsured employee benefits such as continuing wage or salary payments based on sick leave debits, which payments are included in income under paragraph 6(1)(a). It is to be noted that, while a plan must involve insurance, it is not necessary that there be a contract of insurance with an insurance company. If, however, insurance is not provided by an insurance company, the plan must be one that is based on insurance principles, i.e., funds must be accumulated, normally in the hands of trustees or in a trust account,

that are calculated to be sufficient to meet anticipated claims. If the arrangement merely consists of an unfunded contingency reserve on the part of the employer, it would not be an insurance plan.

8. An employer may contribute to separate plans for different classes or groups of employees. For example, there may be one plan for clerical staff and another plan for administrative staff. Each plan will be recognized as a separate plan. In other circumstances, an employer may have one plan that provides for short-term sickness benefits and another plan that provides for long-term disability benefits. Each such plan normally would be considered a separate plan for all purposes but, if desired, they may be treated as one plan provided they comply with the following conditions:

(a) the same classes of employees are entitled to participate in both plans, and
(b) the premiums or other cost of each plan is shared in the same ratio by the employer and the employees.

9. An association of employers, or a health and welfare trust that is organized and managed by or on behalf of both employers and employees in a certain industry, may establish a plan with an insurer that is available to all employer-members. In these circumstances, if there is one insurance contract between the insurer and the association of employers or the health and welfare trust and the contract was entered into after June 19, 1971, there is considered to be one plan. Where employees contribute to the cost of benefits provided by a health and welfare trust, see paragraph 6 of IT-85R regarding the amount that may qualify as an employee's contribution for purposes of subparagraph 6(1)(f)(v). For plans that existed prior to June 19, 1971 see paragraph 7 of IT-54.

10. Where the nature of employment in a particular industry is such that it is usual for employees to change employers frequently (e.g. the construction industry) and the continuity of wage loss replacement benefits can be assured only if such benefits are provided under a plan administered by a union or a similar association of employees rather than directly by the various employers, the arrangement between the participating employers and the organization representing the employees is viewed as a single wage loss replacement plan.

Lump-sum Payments

11. If a lump-sum payment is made in lieu of periodic payments, that amount will be considered to be income under paragraph 6(1)(f).

12. Some contracts of employment may provide for payment of

periodic benefits to employees in respect of loss of income
due to disability and may also provide that employees will
receive a lump-sum payment on retirement, resignation or
death based on the value of unused sick leave credits
accumulated under that plan. Even though these separate
arrangements may be jointly funded by employer-employee
contributions, it is the position of the Department that
such lump-sum payments are not a periodic payment under a
wage loss replacement plan to which paragraph 6(1)(f)
applies but are taxable in the employee's hands by
subsections 5(1) and 6(3) as remuneration received by them
pursuant to their contract of employment. To the extent
that a part of the lump sum payment has been funded by
employee contributions not deducted by the employee under
subparagraph 6(1)(f)(v) in computing the portion of amounts
taxable under paragraph 6(1)(f), the accumulated employee
contributions in respect thereof (but not any interest
credited thereon) would represent a return of capital to
employees and need not be included as part of the taxable
lump sum payment.

Employee's Contribution

13. Employee contributions that are deductible under
subparagraph 6(1)(f)(v), are restricted to those that were
made to the particular plan from which the benefits were
received. Thus, if an employee changes employment and
becomes a beneficiary under the plans of the new employer,
the employee may not deduct the contributions made during
the previous employment from benefits received from the new
employer's plan. For this purpose, a change in employment
is not considered to take place where an unincorporated
business is incorporated or where there has been a merger
or amalgamation. Also, the continuity of an existing plan
is generally not affected by internal alterations in the
plan, such as a change in the insurer or an improvement in
benefits. However, for purposes of section 19 of ITAR, an
increase in benefits after June 18, 1971, in a pre-June 19,
1971 plan may be viewed as the creation of a new plan as
indicated in paragraph 4 of IT-54. On the other hand, where
an employee, because of a promotion or job
reclassification, is moved from one of his employer's plans
to another, such as a move from the "general" plan to the
"executive" plan, contributions to the former plan would
not be deductible in respect of benefits received from the
latter plan.

Employer's Contributions

14. For benefits received by an employee under a wage loss
replacement plan to be subject to tax in his hands under
paragraph 6(1)(f), the plan must be one to which the
employer has made a contribution out of his own funds. An
employer does not make such a contribution to a plan if he
merely deducts an amount from an employee's gross salary or

wages and remits the amount on the employee's behalf to an insurer. In these circumstances, the employee's remuneration for tax purposes is not reduced by the amount withheld and remitted by the employer to the insurer. Where the employer has made an actual contribution to a plan, paragraph 6(1)(a) provides that it is not to be included in the income of the employees if the plan is a "group sickness or accident insurance plan". It is considered that this exemption in paragraph 6(1)(a) applies to any of the three types of plans mentioned in paragraph 6(1)(f), provided that they are group plans.

15. If an employer should have a plan that is in part a wage loss replacement plan and in part a plan that provides for other types of benefits, the employer must be prepared to identify that part of any premiums paid by him, or other contribution by him to the plan, that relates to the other types of benefits included in the plan and, similarly, the part of the employees' contributions, if any, that relate to the wage loss replacement part of the plan. This information is required to determine whether the wage loss replacement plan is one to which the employer has contributed and the relevant amount of an employee's contribution for purposes of subparagraph 6(1)(f)(v).

Employee Pay-All Plans

16. An employee-pay-all plan is a plan the entire premium cost of which is paid by one or more employees. Except as indicated under 21 below, benefits out of such a plan are not taxable even if they are paid in consequence of an event occurring after 1973, because an employee-pay-all plan is not a plan within the meaning of paragraph 6(1)(f).

17. It is a question of fact whether or not an employee-pay-all plan exists and the onus is generally on the employer to prove the existence of such a plan. It should be emphasized that the Department will not accept a retroactive change to the tax status of a plan. For example, an employer cannot change the tax status of a plan by adding at year-end to employees' income the employer contributions to a wage loss replacement plan that would normally be considered to be non-taxable benefits. On the other hand, where an employee-pay-all plan does, in fact, exist and it provides for the employer to pay the employee's premiums to the plan and to account for them in the manner of wages or salary, the result is as though the premiums had been withheld from the employee's wages or salary. That is, the plan maintains its status as an employee-pay-all plan if the plan provided for such an arrangement at the time the payment was made.

18. If, under a wage loss replacement plan, the employer makes contributions for some employees, but not all, the plan will not be considered to be an employee-pay-all plan

even for those employees who must make all contributions themselves. It is the Department's view that all payments out of a wage loss replacement plan to which the employer has contributed are subject to the provisions of paragraph 6(1)(f) regardless of the fact that the employer's contributions may be on account of specific employees only.

19. Where the terms of a plan clearly establish that it is intended to be an employee-pay-all plan, the plan will be recognized as such even though the employer makes a contribution to it on behalf of an employee during an elimination period (i.e. the period after the disability but before the first payment from the plan becomes due). During this period normally there would be no salary or wages from which the contribution could be deducted. Any amount so contributed by an employer should be reported as remuneration of the employee on whose behalf it was contributed in order to maintain the employee-pay-all character of the plan.

20. Where an employer pays, on behalf of an employee, the premium under a non-group plan that is

(a) a sickness or accident insurance plan,
(b) a disability insurance plan, or
(c) an income maintenance insurance plan,
the payment of the premium is regarded as a taxable benefit to the employee. The payment by the employer is not viewed as a "contribution" by the employer under the plan, and paragraph 6(1)(f) does not apply to subject to tax in the employee's hands any benefits received by him pursuant to the plan.

21. Whether or not the benefits an employee receives under a plan are required to be included in his income is governed both by the type of plan in effect at the time of the event that gave rise to them and any changes in the plan subsequent to that time. When a pre-June 19, 1971 plan, or an employee-pay-all plan, is changed and becomes a new taxable plan, an employee who was receiving benefits at the time of the change may continue to receive them tax-free thereafter but only in the amount and for the period specified in the plan as it was before the change. Where the new taxable plan provides any increase in benefits, whether by increases in amounts or through extension of the benefit period, the additional benefits must be included in income since they flow from the new taxable plan. Where an employee is receiving benefits under a taxable plan at a time when it is converted to a new employee-pay-all plan, the benefits he continues to receive subsequent to the date of conversion, to the extent that they were provided for in the old plan, will remain of an income nature because they continue to flow from the old taxable plan.

Claimant's Survivors

22. If the payment of wage loss replacement benefits should continue after the death of an employee who was receiving such benefits, paragraph 6(1)(f) is not applicable to such benefits paid to the widow or other dependent for the reason that the amounts received do not relate to a loss of income from an office or employment of the recipient. Such payments, however, may be viewed as being received in recognition of the deceased employee's service in an office or employment and be included in income as a death benefit if they exceed the exemption provided in subsection 248(1).

Information Returns

23. Paragraph 200(2)(f) of the Income Tax Regulations stipulates that every person who makes payments pursuant to a wage loss replacement plan is required to file Form T4A information return. The law does not require that income tax be deducted from such payments.

U.I.C. Employee Premium Rebate

24. A wage loss replacement plan may qualify the employer for a reduction in unemployment insurance premiums under subsection 64(4) of the Unemployment Insurance Act, 1971. This subsection also provides that five-twelfths of any such reduction must be used by the employer for the benefit of his employees. The benefit may be conferred directly by the employer, indirectly through an employees health and welfare trust or in any other manner, but it will only be tax-free in an employee's hands if it is conferred in the form of a benefit specifically exempt from taxation by paragraph 6(1)(a).

Computation of Benefit

25. The following is an example of the computation of the amount of payments received under a wage loss replacement plan that is included in income pursuant to paragraph 6(1)(f):

Assume:

(a) Employee's contributions (in addition to employer's contributions)

*** The following table (a and b) is represented in three columns in print. Column 1 is the year; column 2 is the amounts; column 3 is Cumulative Balance. ***

Year: 1968-71; Amounts: $110 per annum; Cumulative Balance: $440
Year: 1972; Amounts: 120; Cumulative Balance: 560
Year: 1973; Amounts: 140; Cumulative Balance: 700
Year: 1974; Amounts: 140; Cumulative Balance: 840

Year: 1975; Amounts: 140; Cumulative Balance: 980
Year: 1976; Amounts: 140; Cumulative Balance: 1120
Year: 1977; Amounts: 160; Cumulative Balance: 1280

(b) Payments received

Year: 1972; Amounts: $200; Cumulative Balance: $200
Year: 1973; Amounts: 300; Cumulative Balance: 500
Year: 1974; Amounts: 240; Cumulative Balance: 740
Year: 1975; Amounts: 1000; Cumulative Balance: 1740
Year: 1976; Amounts: 100; Cumulative Balance: 1840
Year: 1977; Amounts: 1000; Cumulative Balance: 2840

(c) The plan was in existence prior to June 19, 1971 and
remains unchanged.

(d) The payments received out of the plan in 1974, 1975,
1976 and 1977 are as a result of events occurring after
1973.
Amount Included in Income:

1972 and 1973 - none of the payments received are income
because of section 19 of the ITAR

1974 - lesser of:
a) payments received in 1974 $240
b) aggregate of payments received after 1971 $740
less:
aggregate of contributions made after 1967 840
NIL
amount to be included under paragraph 6(1)(f) NIL

1975 - lesser of:
a) payments received in 1975 $1000
b) aggregate of payments received after 1971 $1740
less:
aggregate of contributions made after 1967 980
($1740 minus 980) = 760
amount to be included under paragraph 6(1)(f) $760

1976 - lesser of:
a) payments received in 1976 $100
b) payments received in 1976 $100
less:
contributions made in 1976 140
NIL
amount to be included under paragraph 6(1)(f) NIL

1977 - lesser of:
a) payments received in 1977 $1000
b) payments received since the most recent year during
which a benefit was taxable under this provision (1975)
$1100
less:
contributions made since 1975 300

```
($1100 minus 300) = 800
amount to be included under paragraph 6(1)(f) $800
```

NO.:   **IT-470R (Consolidated)**   DATE: See *Bulletin Revisions* section

SUBJECT: INCOME TAX ACT
            Employees' Fringe Benefits

REFERENCE: Paragraph 6(1)(*a*) (also sections 118.8 and 118.9; subsections 5(1), 6(3), 6(6), 6(19) to (22), and 118.5(1); paragraph 18(1)(*l*) and subparagraph 6(1)(*b*)(ix)).

Latest Revisions – ¶s 6, 7, 9, 18, 19, 37, 46 & 47

Revenue Canada's income tax interpretation bulletins (ITs) provide technical interpretations and positions regarding certain provisions contained in income tax law. Due to their technical nature, ITs are used primarily by departmental staff, tax specialists, and other individuals who have an interest in tax matters. For those readers who prefer a less technical explanation of the law, the Department offers other publications, such as tax guides and pamphlets.

While the comments in a particular paragraph in an IT may relate to provisions of the law in force at the time they were made, such comments are not a substitute for the law. The reader should, therefore, consider such comments in light of the relevant provisions of the law in force for the particular taxation year being considered, taking into account the effect of any relevant amendments to those provisions or relevant court decisions occurring after the date on which the comments were made.

Subject to the above, an interpretation or position contained in an IT generally applies as of the date on which it was publicized, unless otherwise specified. If there is a subsequent change in that interpretation or position and the change is beneficial to taxpayers, it is usually effective for future assessments and reassessments. If, on the other hand, the change is not favourable to taxpayers, it will normally be effective for the current and subsequent taxation years or for transactions entered into after the date on which the change is publicized.

If you have any comments regarding matters discussed in an IT, please send them to:

Director, Business and Publications Division
Income Tax Rulings and Interpretations Directorate
Policy and Legislation Branch
Revenue Canada
Ottawa ON K1A 0L5

This electronic version of this document is the official version.

On November 1, 1999, Revenue Canada will begin operations as the Canada Customs and Revenue Agency.

Contents

Application

This bulletin is a consolidation of the following:

- IT-470R dated April 8, 1988, as revised by Special Release dated December 11, 1989; and
- subsequent amendments thereto.

For further particulars, see the "Bulletin Revisions" section near the end of this bulletin.

Summary

This bulletin discusses various common types of "fringe benefits" and indicates whether or not their values should be included in income. Part A of the bulletin deals with amounts to be included in income while Part B deals with amounts not to be included in income.

Discussion and Interpretation

INTRODUCTION

¶ 1. The information herein refers to cases where there is an employee-employer relationship but does not necessarily apply if the employee is also a shareholder or relative of the owner of the business.

¶ 2. Except where the Act provides otherwise, taxpayers are generally taxable on the value of all benefits they receive by virtue of their employment. The more common "fringe benefits" are discussed below and have been classified generally as taxable benefits or as non-taxable privileges. In the second group there may well be a point beyond which the "privilege" concept is no longer valid, i.e., the advantage to the employee is, in fact, a form of extra remuneration. Then the "fringe benefit" is viewed as a taxable benefit.

¶ 3. Where an amount in respect of a taxable benefit should be included in income, the employer must determine its value or make a reasonable estimate of it and include that value in the box provided on form T4 Supplementary under the heading "Employment Income Before Deductions" and also in the appropriate box in the area entitled "Taxable Allowances and Benefits".

PART A – AMOUNTS TO BE INCLUDED IN INCOME

Board and Lodging

¶ 4. The *Income Tax Act* refers specifically to board and lodging as a benefit derived from employment. This includes board and lodging regularly furnished as a perquisite of the employment, as is common for hotel employees and domestic and farm help. The value placed on this benefit should approximate its fair market value. Where subsidized board and lodging is provided to an employee the value of the benefit for "board" is determined on the basis described for subsidized meals (See ¶ 28 below); the "lodging" benefit will be valued at the fair market value of the accommodation less the amount charged to the employee.

¶ 5. However, by virtue of subsection 6(6), an exception to the above rules is made in respect of board and lodging received by an employee whose duties are performed at a remote location or, in some circumstances, at a special work site. This exception is discussed in IT-91R3, "Employment at Special or Remote Work Sites".

Rent-Free and Low-Rent Housing

¶ 6. When an employer provides a house, apartment, or similar accommodation to an employee rent-free or for a lower rent than the employee would have to pay someone else for such accommodation, the employee receives a taxable benefit. The employer is responsible for reasonably estimating the amount of such a benefit, which would normally be considered to be the fair market rent for equivalent accommodation had the employee rented from a third party, less any rent paid. However, section 110.7 provides a deduction for living accommodation for an individual who resides in an area that is either a "prescribed northern zone" or a "prescribed intermediate zone". See the current version of Interpretation Bulletin IT-91, *Employment at Special Work Sites or Remote Work Locations*, for information on the northern residents deductions.

Travel Benefits

¶ 7. An amount received, or the value of a benefit received or enjoyed, by virtue of employment in respect of travelling expenses incurred by an employee, the employee's family or both is a taxable benefit, unless the amount is an allowance which falls within the exceptions in paragraph 6(1)(*b*) or is an amount described in subsection 81(3.1) or otherwise excluded from income under subsection 6(6). However, an individual may be eligible for the northern residents deduction in subsection 110.7 in respect of certain travel benefits received by the individual or the individual's family from an employer who deals at arm's length with the individual, to the extent the value of the benefits is included in the individual's income for the taxation year from employment and not otherwise deducted. See the current version of Interpretation Bulletin IT-91, *Employment at Special Work Sites or Remote Work Locations*, for information on the northern residents deductions.

Personal Use of Employer's Motor Vehicle

¶ 8. The current version of IT-63 should be consulted.

Gifts (Including Christmas Gifts)

¶ 9. A gift (either in cash or in kind) from an employer to an employee is a benefit derived during or because of the individual's employment. When the value of a gift commemorating a wedding, Christmas or similar occasion does not exceed $100 and when the employer does not claim its cost as an expense in computing taxable income, the gift is not required to be reported as income of an employee. This practice will only apply to one gift to an employee in a year, except in the year an employee marries in which case it will apply to two gifts.

When an employee is rewarded by an employer with merchandise or other non-cash items, the fair market value of the award must be included in the employee's income. If an item is personalized with a corporate logo or engraved with the employee's name or a message, the fair market value of the item may be negatively affected. In such cases, the amount to be included in the employee's income may be reduced by a reasonable amount, having regard to all the circumstances. Depending on the value of a particular award, the existence of a logo may have little, if any, impact on the fair market value of the item. When the award given is a plaque, trophy or other memento of nominal value for which there is no market, it is not necessary to include any amount in an employee's income as a taxable benefit. See ¶s 10 to 13 for information on holiday trips, other prizes and incentive awards.

An employer-provided party or other social event, which is generally available to all employees, will be accepted as a non-taxable privilege if the cost per employee is reasonable in the circumstances. As a guideline, those events costing up to $100 per person will be considered to be non-taxable. Ancillary costs, such as transportation home, would increase that amount. Parties costing more than that are generally considered to be beyond the privilege point and may result in a taxable benefit.

Holiday Trips, Other Prizes and Incentive Awards

¶ 10. Where an employer pays for a vacation for an employee, the employee's family or both, the cost thereof to the employer constitutes a taxable benefit to the employee under paragraph 6(1)(a). Similarly, where a vacation property owned by an employer is used for vacation purposes by an employee, the employee's family or both, there is a taxable benefit conferred on the employee under paragraph 6(1)(a) the value of which is equivalent to the fair market value of the accommodation less any amount which the employee paid therefor to the employer. In any case, the taxable benefit may be reduced if there is conclusive evidence to show that the employee was involved in business activities for the employer during the vacation.

¶ 11. In a situation where an employee's presence is required for business purposes and this function is the main purpose of the trip, no benefit will be associated with the employee's travelling expenses necessary to accomplish the business objectives of the trip if the expenditures are reasonable in relation to the business function. Where a business trip is extended to provide for a paid holiday or vacation, the employee is in receipt of a taxable benefit equal to the costs borne by the employer with respect to that extension.

¶ 12. There may be instances where an employee acts as a host or hostess for an incentive award trip arranged for employees, suppliers or customers of the employer. Such a trip will be viewed as a business trip provided the employee is engaged directly in business activities during a substantial part of each day (e.g., as organizer of activities); otherwise it will be viewed as a vacation and a taxable benefit, subject, of course, to a reduction for any actual business activity.

¶ 13. Where an employee receives a prize or other award related to sales or other work performance from his or her employer, the fair market value of such an incentive is regarded as remuneration to be included in income under section 5 of the Act. Similarly, the fair market value of any award not regarded as remuneration that is received by an employee

(a) in respect of,

(b) in the course of, or

(c) by virtue of

the employee's office or employment is also included in income from an office or employment by virtue of paragraph 6(1)(a). (See also IT-75R2, "Scholarships, Fellowships, Bursaries, Prizes and Research Grants".)

Frequent Flyer Program

¶ 14. Under this program, which is usually sponsored by an airline, a frequent air traveller can accumulate credits which may be exchanged for additional air travel or other benefits. Where an employee accumulates such credits while travelling on employer-paid business trips and uses them to obtain air travel or other benefits for the personal use of the employee or the employee's family, the fair market value of such air travel or other benefits must be included in the employee's income. Where an employer does not control the credits accumulated in a frequent flyer program by an employee while travelling on employer-paid business trips, the comments in ¶ 3 above will not apply and it will be the responsibility of the employee to determine and include in income the fair market value of any benefits received or enjoyed.

Travelling Expenses of Employee's Spouse

¶ 15. Where a spouse accompanies an employee on a business trip the payment or reimbursement by the employer of the spouse's travelling expenses is a taxable benefit to the employee unless the spouse was, in fact, engaged primarily in business activities on behalf of the employer during the trip.

Premiums under Provincial Hospitalization and Medical Care Insurance Plans

¶ 16. Where an employer pays all or a part of the premiums or contributions that an employee is otherwise required to pay to a provincial authority administering a provincial hospital insurance plan, a provincial medical care insurance plan, or both, the amount paid is a taxable benefit to the employee.

¶ **17.** Where an employer pays an amount to an employee in respect of the employee's premium under a provincial hospital or provincial medical care insurance plan, the amount paid is a taxable benefit to the employee.

Employer-Paid Educational Costs

¶ **18.** When training is taken primarily for the benefit of the employer, there is no taxable benefit whether or not this training leads to a degree, diploma or certificate. A taxable benefit arises when the training is primarily for the benefit of the employee.

The following guidelines assist in the determination of whether there is a taxable benefit; however, they do not necessarily apply in non-arm's length relationships or in specific examples in which there is evidence that the benefit was in fact primarily for the employee. This will be the case, for example, if the employee and the employer have entered into an arrangement under which the remuneration ordinarily paid to the employee is reduced in recognition of training costs incurred by the employer.

There are three broad categories of training:

Specific Employer-Related Training: Courses which are taken for maintenance or upgrading of employer-related skills, when it is reasonable to assume that the employee will resume his or her employment for a reasonable period of time after completion of the courses, will generally be considered to primarily benefit the employer and therefore be non-taxable. For example, fees and other associated costs such as meals, travel and accommodation which are paid for courses leading to a degree, diploma or certificate, in a field related to the employee's current or potential future responsibilities in the employer's business, will not result in a taxable benefit.

General Employment-Related Training: Other business-related courses, although not directly related to the employer's business, will generally be considered non-taxable. Examples of non-taxable training would include stress management, employment equity, first-aid and language skills. Normally, in-house training will not be considered a taxable benefit.

Personal Interest Training: Employer-paid courses for personal interest or technical skills that are not related to the employer's business are considered of primary benefit to the employee and thus taxable. For example, fees paid for a self-interest carpentry course would result in a taxable benefit.

¶ **19.** Employees who have their eligible tuition fees paid for or reimbursed by their employer and have not received a taxable benefit are not entitled to claim the tuition tax credit. In addition, the education amount is not available, in any case, when employees have their eligible tuition fees paid for or reimbursed by their employer or when they receive remuneration while taking training in connection with their duties of employment.

¶ **20.** Where an educational institution which charges tuition fees provides tuition free of charge or at a reduced amount to an employee of the institution, or to the spouse or children of the employee, the fair market value of the benefit will be included in the employee's income.

¶ **21.** For 1984 and subsequent taxation years, any reasonable allowance (including tuition fees) received by an employee from the employer to cover the away-from-home education of a child will not be included in the employee's income by virtue of subparagraph 6(1)(*b*)(ix), so long as the child is in full-time attendance at a school which primarily uses for instruction the official language of Canada primarily used by the employee and the school is in a community not farther from the place where the employee is required to live than the nearest community in which there is a school having suitable boarding facilities and providing instruction in that language. To the extent that tuition fees paid by the employer for the employee's child are, by virtue of subparagraph 6(1)(*b*)(ix) not included in the employee's income, they may not be used in determining a tax credit for tuition fees (see the current version of IT-516). Before 1984 the allowance was excluded from income only if the school was the closest available providing instruction in that language without regard to the suitability of accommodation.

¶ **22.** In computing tax payable, a student may be eligible for a non-refundable federal tax credit under subsection 118.5(1) in respect of tuition fees paid by or on behalf of the student (or the fair market value of free tuition provided to the student to the extent that it is reported as a taxable benefit). Any unused portion of such a credit (to a maximum of $600) may be transferred to, and claimed as a tax credit by, the student's spouse under section 118.8, or the student's parent or grandparent under subsection 118.9(1) (see the current version of IT-516). For the tax implications of scholarships, fellowships, bursaries, prizes and research grants, see the current version of IT-75.

Cost of Tools – Reimbursement

¶ **23.** Where an employer makes payments to its employees to offset the cost of tools that the employees are required to have in order to perform their work, the amount of the payment must be included in the employees' incomes.

Wage Loss Replacement Plans

¶ **24.** Refer to IT-428, "Wage Loss Replacement Plans".

Interest-Free and Low-Interest Loans

¶ **25.** Refer to IT-421R, "Benefits to Individuals, Corporations and Shareholders from Loans or Debt".

Financial Counselling and Income Tax Return Preparation

¶ **26.** Financial counselling services or income tax return preparation provided directly (for 1990 and subsequent taxation years) or indirectly by an employer normally produce a taxable benefit to the employee who receives the benefit. However, financial counselling services in respect of the re-employment or the retirement of an employee will not result in a taxable benefit to the employee (see ¶ 46 below).

PART B – AMOUNTS NOT TO BE INCLUDED IN INCOME

Discounts on Merchandise and Commissions on Sales

¶ 27.   Where it is the practice of an employer to sell merchandise to employees at a discount, the benefits that an employee may derive from exercising such a privilege are not normally regarded as taxable benefits. However, this does not extend to an extraordinary arrangement with a particular employee or a select group of employees nor to an arrangement by which an employee is permitted to purchase merchandise (other than old or soiled merchandise) for less than the employer's cost. Furthermore, this treatment does not extend to a reciprocal arrangement between two or more employers whereby the employees of one can exercise such a privilege with another by whom the employees are not employed. A commission received by a sales employee on merchandise acquired for that employee's personal use is not taxable. Similarly, where a life insurance salesperson acquires a life insurance policy, a commission received by that salesperson on that policy is not taxable provided the salesperson owns that policy and is obligated to make the required premium payments thereon.

Subsidized Meals

¶ 28.   Subsidized meals provided to employees will not be considered to confer a taxable benefit provided the employee is required to pay a reasonable charge. A reasonable charge is generally defined as one that covers the cost of food, its preparation and service. Where less than a reasonable charge is paid, the value of the benefit is that cost less the amount paid by the employee.

Uniforms and Special Clothing

¶ 29.   An employee who is supplied with a distinctive uniform which is required to be worn while carrying out the duties of employment or who is provided with special clothing (including safety footwear) designed for protection from the particular hazards of the employment, is not regarded as receiving a taxable benefit.

¶ 30.   Payments made by an employer to a laundry or dry cleaning establishment for laundry or dry cleaning expenses of uniforms and special clothing, or directly to the employee in reimbursement of such expenses, do not constitute a taxable benefit to the employee.

Subsidized School Services

¶ 31.   In remote or unorganized areas employers frequently assume, initially at least, responsibility for essential community services of a kind normally borne by a municipal organization. Where the employer provides free or subsidized school services for children of the employees, a taxable benefit is not considered to accrue to the employees. This does not extend to a payment of an educational allowance directly to the employee by the employer, which is a taxable benefit unless excepted by subparagraph 6(1)(b)(ix) as described in ¶ 21 above.

Transportation to the Job

¶ 32.   Employers sometimes find it expedient to provide vehicles for transporting their employees from pick-up points to the location of the employment at which, for security or other reasons, public and private vehicles are not welcome or not practical. In these circumstances the employees are not regarded as in receipt of a taxable benefit. However, a reimbursement or allowance paid to the employee for transportation to and from the location of employment must be included in income. Subsection 6(6) provides an exception to this latter rule. See also IT-91R3, "Employment at Special or Remote Work Sites".

Recreational Facilities

¶ 33.   Where employees generally are permitted to use their employer's recreational facilities (e.g., exercise rooms, swimming pools, gymnasiums, tennis, squash or raquetball courts, golf courses, shuffle boards) free of charge or upon payment of a nominal fee, the value of the benefit derived by an employee through such use is not normally taxable. The taxable benefit received by an employee who is provided with board, lodging and accommodation is discussed in ¶s 4 to 6 and 10 above.

¶ 34.   Similarly, where the employer pays the fees required for an employee to be a member of a social or athletic club the employee is not deemed to have received a taxable benefit where the membership was principally for the employer's advantage rather than the employee's. See also IT-148R2, "Recreational Properties and Club Dues".

Removal Expenses

¶ 35.   Where an employer reimburses an employee for the expenses incurred by the latter in moving the employee and the employee's family and household effects either because the employee has been transferred from one establishment of the employer to another or because of having accepted employment at a place other than where the former home was located, this reimbursement is not considered as conferring a taxable benefit on the employee.

¶ 36.   In addition, where the employer pays the expense of moving an employee and the employee's family and household effects out of a remote place at the termination of the employment there, no taxable benefit is imputed.

¶ 37.   In ordinary circumstances, if an employer reimburses an employee for a loss suffered by the latter in selling the family home upon being required by the employer to move to another locality or upon retirement from employment in a remote area, the amount so reimbursed is not income of the employee if it is not greater than the actual loss calculated as the amount by which the cost of the home to the employee exceeds the net selling price received for it. Similarly, where an employer guarantees to give to an employee an amount equal to the amount by which the fair market value of the home (as independently appraised) exceeds the actual selling price obtained, the amount so given is not income in the hands of the employee. Should the employer buy the home from the employee, no taxable benefit is included in the employee's income if the price paid by the employer does not exceed the greater of the cost of the home to the employee and the current fair market value of comparable homes in the same area.

Note, however, that the following rules apply after February 23, 1998—except in respect of an "eligible relocation" of an individual in connection with which the individual began employment at a new work location before October 1998, in which case they apply to the 2001 and subsequent taxation years.

A taxable benefit must be included in a taxpayer's income for an amount paid at any time, in respect of a housing loss (other than an "eligible housing loss"), to or on behalf of the taxpayer or a person who does not deal at arm's length with the taxpayer, in respect of an office or employment.

A "housing loss" at a particular time is basically the greater of

(a) the adjusted cost base of a taxpayer's residence at that time; and

(b) the highest fair market value of the residence within the six-month period that ends at that time;

minus

(c) if the residence is disposed of before the end of the first taxation year that begins after that time, the lesser of the proceeds for the residence and the fair market value of the residence at that time; or

(d) in any other case, the fair market value of the residence at that time.

A taxpayer is also required to include in income as a taxable benefit all amounts paid, in respect of an "eligible housing loss", to or on behalf of the taxpayer or a person who does not deal at arm's length with the taxpayer, in respect of an office or employment, to the extent of the amount (if any) by which one-half of the amounts so paid in the year or a prior year exceed $15,000, minus any amounts for this taxable benefit already included in the taxpayer's income for preceding years. An "eligible housing loss" is a housing loss in respect of an eligible relocation of a taxpayer or a person who does not deal at arm's length with the taxpayer. An "eligible relocation" is basically a relocation to enable the taxpayer to carry on a business or to be employed at a new work location in Canada or to be a student in full-time attendance enrolled in a program at a post-secondary level at a university, college or other educational institution (the location of which is also referred to as the "new work

location"), and both the taxpayer's old residence and new residence are located in Canada, and the new residence is located at least 40 kilometres closer to the new work location than the old residence. The taxpayer can designate only one residence for purposes of the eligible housing loss (e.g., the taxpayer could not designate both a house and a cottage).

¶ **38.** An employee who is not reimbursed, or is only partly reimbursed, for removal expenses may be able to claim certain of the expenses incurred as a deduction from income under section 62 of the Act. See also IT-178R2, "Moving Expenses".

Premiums under Private Health Services Plans

¶ **39.** Where an employer makes a contribution to a private health services plan in respect of an employee, no taxable benefit arises to the employee.

¶ **40.** Benefits provided to an employee under a private health services plan are not subject to tax in the employee's hands. "Private health services plan" is defined in subsection 248(1). (See also the current version of IT-339, "Meaning of Private Health Services Plan" and IT-85, "Health and Welfare Trusts for Employees".)

Employer's Contribution under Provincial Hospitalization and Medical Care Insurance Plans

¶ **41.** Where an employer is required, under a provincial hospital insurance plan, a provincial medical care insurance plan, or both, to pay amounts to the provincial authority administering such plan or plans (other than with respect to the contributions or premiums that an employee is required to make under the plan), the payment of such amounts does not give rise to a taxable benefit to employees.

Transportation Passes

¶ **42.** Airline passes available to airline employees will become taxable only if the employee travels on a space-confirmed basis and is paying less than 50 per cent of the economy fare available on that carrier for that trip on the day of travel. The value of the benefit will be the difference between 50 per cent of the economy fare and any amount reimbursed to the carrier for that trip.

¶ **43.** Employees of bus and rail companies will not be taxed on the use of passes.

¶ **44.** Retired employees of transportation companies will not be taxed on pass benefits under any circumstances.

Public Office Holders

¶ **45.** A public office holder may be required to incur the costs of establishing, maintaining or dismantling a blind trust set up to enable that person to comply with the Conflict of

Interest and Post-Employment Code for Public Office Holders. Where such costs are reimbursed to that person by the Government of Canada in accordance with that Code, no taxable benefit is considered to arise for income tax purposes, since the person is obliged to incur the expenses only by reason of his or her office or employment. The above comments will also apply to such costs incurred, and any reimbursement thereof, under any substantially similar arrangements affecting public office holders at the provincial or municipal level.

Employee Counselling Services

¶ 46.   There is no inclusion in income for any benefit derived by an employee from counselling services provided or paid for by the employer in respect of:

(a)   the mental or physical health of the employee or an individual related to the employee, but not including a benefit attributable to an outlay or expense to which paragraph 18(1)(*l*) applies, or

(b)   the re-employment or retirement of the employee.

This applies to such services as tobacco, drug or alcohol counselling, stress management counselling, and job placement and retirement counselling.

Professional Membership Fees

¶ 47.   The payment of professional membership fees by an employer on behalf of employees is not a taxable benefit if the employer is the primary beneficiary of the payment. Whether the employer is the primary beneficiary is a question of fact. When the professional association is related to an employee's duties, and membership is a requirement of employment, the fact that the employer is the primary beneficiary will be accepted, and consequently, there is no taxable benefit resulting from the payment. However, when membership is not a condition of employment, the question of primary beneficiary must still be resolved. The employer will be responsible for making this determination; however, the employer must be able to justify its decision should the Department request this.

Bulletin Revisions

Since the issuance of IT-470R on April 8, 1988, there have been no revisions to ¶ 1, 2, 3, 4, 5, 10, 11, 12, 13, 15, 16, 17, 20, 24, 25, 27, 28, 29, 30, 31, 32, 33, 34, 35, 36, 38, 39, 41, 42, 43, 44 or 45.

¶s 6 and 7 were revised to delete comments regarding the northern residents deductions that are out of date and to refer to the current version of Interpretation Bulletin IT-91, *Employment at Special Work Sites or Remote Work Locations*, for information on the northern residents deductions. [August 11, 1999]

¶ 8 and the heading preceding it were last revised by Special Release dated December 11, 1989.

¶ 9 was expanded to include coverage on Christmas parties and performance and merit awards given by an employer to employees. [August 11, 1999]

The last sentence of ¶ 14 was added by Special Release dated December 11, 1989.

¶s 18 and 19 and their heading were revised to reflect a change in interpretation concerning benefits from educational costs. [August 11, 1999]

The second last sentence of ¶ 21 was revised by Special Release dated December 11, 1989.

¶ 22 was last revised by Special Release dated December 11, 1989.

At the end of ¶ 23, there was previously a sentence which read as follows: "However, where an employee is reimbursed by the Government of Canada for the cost of tools under the Government's Assistance Program – Workers Metric Tools, that reimbursement is not included in income." That sentence was removed by Special Release dated December 11, 1989 because reimbursements were no longer made under the Government's Assistance Program – Workers Metric Tools.

¶ 26 and its heading were last revised by Special Release dated December 11, 1989.

¶ 37 was expanded to provide comments on new provisions that took effect after February 23, 1998 and others that apply to the 2001 and subsequent taxation years. [August 11, 1999]

¶ 40 was last revised by Special Release dated December 11, 1989.

¶ 46 was added to the bulletin, by Special Release dated December 11, 1989, to discuss proposed legislative changes regarding employee counselling services. ¶ 46 was then revised to reflect the fact that these proposed changes have been enacted as law. [August 11, 1999]

¶ 47 was added to explain the Department's position on an employer's payment of professional dues. [August 11, 1999]

CANADA CUSTOMS AND REVENUE AGENCY

INTERPRETATION BULLETIN NUMBER IT-502

DATE: March 28, 1985

SUBJECT: INCOME TAX ACT
Employee Benefit Plans and Employee Trusts

REFERENCE: Paragraphs 6(1)(g) and 6(1)(h) (also sections 32.1, 104 and 107.1;
subsections 6(10), 18(10), 70(2) and 212(17); paragraphs 6(1)(a), 12(1)(n),
(n.1), 18(1)(k), (o), 87(2)(j.3), 88(1)(e.2), 108(1)(j) and 110.2(4)(g); and
the definitions of employee benefit plan and employee trust in subsection
248(1))

At the Canada Customs and Revenue Agency (CCRA), we issue income tax
interpretation bulletins (ITs) in order to provide technical interpretations
and positions regarding certain provisions contained in income tax law. Due
to their technical nature, ITs are used primarily by our staff, tax
specialists, and other individuals who have an interest in tax matters. For
those readers who prefer a less technical explanation of the law, we offer
other publications, such as tax guides and pamphlets.

While the comments in a particular paragraph in an IT may relate to
provisions of the law in force at the time they were made, such comments are
not a substitute for the law. The reader should, therefore, consider such
comments in light of the relevant provisions of the law in force for the
particular taxation year being considered, taking into account the effect of
any relevant amendments to those provisions or relevant court decisions
occurring after the date on which the comments were made.

Subject to the above, an interpretation or position contained in an IT
generally applies as of the date on which it was published, unless otherwise
specified. If there is a subsequent change in that interpretation or position
and the change is beneficial to taxpayers, it is usually effective for future
assessments and reassessments. If, on the other hand, the change is not
favourable to taxpayers, it will normally be effective for the current and
subsequent taxation years or for transactions entered into after the date on
which the change is published.

Most of our publications are available on our Web site at: www.ccra.gc.ca

If you have any comments regarding matters discussed in an IT, please send
them to:

Manager, Technical Publications and Projects Section
Income Tax Rulings Directorate
Policy and Legislation Branch
Canada Customs and Revenue Agency
Ottawa ON K1A 0L5

or by email at the following address: bulletins@ccra.gc.ca

Contents

Summary

Discussion and Interpretation

Employee Benefit Plans

Employee Trusts

Summary

1. Prior to 1980, certain plans existed in which an employee and an employer would arrange to defer payment of part or all of the employee's compensation by placing the compensation in the custody of a third party. Provided the employee had no immediate right to the compensation, the tax on the compensation would be deferred until it was eventually paid to the employee by the third party, whereas the employer would receive an income deduction in the year it was paid to the third party. These plans (commonly referred to as deferred compensation plans) were not subject to the provisions of Division G of the Act which regulates deferred and other special income arrangements.

2. This bulletin discusses the provisions which were introduced, effective for taxation years after 1979, to match the timing of the deduction from the employer's income with the inclusion of deferred compensation in the employee's income.

Discussion and Interpretation

Employee Benefit Plans

Definition

3. Subject to the exclusions in 4 below, an employee benefit plan is any arrangement under which the employer or someone not dealing at arm's length with the employer makes contributions to another person (called a custodian) and under which one or more payments will be made to or for the benefit of employees, former employees or persons with whom the employees and former employees do not deal at arm's length (hereinafter collectively referred to as "EBP beneficiary or EBP beneficiaries"). An arrangement which provides only for payment or payments to be made in respect of benefits which are expressly excluded from income by reason of subparagraph 6(1)(a)(i) of the Act is not an employee benefit plan.

4. Exclusions from the definition of employee benefit plan in subsection 248(1) include the following:

(a) Registered Pension Funds or Plans as defined in subsection 248(1),

(b) Group Sickness or Accident Insurance Plans, discussed in the current version of IT-85 (Modified by Correction Sheet CS 24 dated April 20, 2001)

(c) Private Health Services Plans as defined in paragraph 110(8)(a) and discussed in the current version of IT-339 (Modified by Correction Sheet CS 24 dated April 20, 2001)

(d) Supplementary Unemployment Benefit Plans as defined in subsection 145(1),

(e) Deferred Profit Sharing Plans as defined in subsection 147(1),

(f) Group Term Life Insurance Policies as defined in subsection 248(1) (Reference to IT-227R has been deleted since IT-227R and its Special Release were cancelled by the Index to Interpretation Bulletins and Technical News dated December 31, 2001)

(g) Employees Profit Sharing Plans as defined in subsection 144(1),

(h) Wage Loss Replacement Plans of the type described in paragraph 6(1)(f) and discussed in the current version of IT-428 (Modified by Correction Sheet CS 24 dated April 20, 2001)

(i) Vacation-with-pay Trusts as described in paragraph 149(1)(y) and discussed in the current version of IT-389 (Modified by Correction Sheet CS 24 dated April 20, 2001)

(j) Employee Trusts as defined in subsection 248(1) (see 34 below),

(k) Plans the sole purpose of which is to educate or to train employees to improve their work or work related skills and, abilities, and

(1) Prescribed funds or plans under Regulation 6800.

Where an employer makes contributions to a custodian which are then used to fund several types of benefit plans, some of which are excluded from the definition of an employee benefit plan, it is necessary for the employer to identify the portion of each contribution that relates to each separate plan. If the custodian of such an omnibus arrangement does not account separately for the income and disbursement of the component plans, it may be necessary to regard the total arrangement as an employee benefit plan and treat it accordingly in respect of the timing and amounts of both the employer's expense deductions and the EBP beneficiaries' receipt of benefits or income under the arrangement.

5. The Department considers the reference to "another person" in the definition of an employee benefit plan as a reference to an entity other than the employer but would include a trust for which the employer is trustee. However, the employee benefit plan provisions would not apply to the situation where the employer merely sets up an unfunded provision or reserve within the employer's accounts to cover future commitments to employees.

Tax Result to Employee

6. As a result of subparagraph 6(1)(a)(ii), no amount is required to be included in an employee's income in respect of any benefit received or enjoyed by the employee by reason of an employee benefit plan. Under paragraph 6(1)(g), however, all amounts received out of or under the plan or from the disposition of an interest in the plan constitute income from an office or employment to the recipient in the year received except to the extent that they represent one or more of the following amounts:

(a) a death benefit received upon or after the death of an employee in recognition of the employee's service in an office or employment before the deduction described in the definition of death benefit in subsection 248(1) (a death benefit however, is taxable under subparagraph 56(1)(a)(iii)),

(b) amounts which represent a return of the EBP beneficiary's own contributions, or in the case of a deceased EBP beneficiary, the refund of the deceased's contributions to an heir or a legal representative thereof (a return of contributions is discussed further in 15 below), or

(c) a superannuation or pension benefit which is attributable to services rendered by the person while not resident in Canada (payments of this type are taxable by virtue of subparagraph 56(1)(a)(i) in the hands of a resident).

7. All amounts received by the EBP beneficiaries out of the plan, except those described in 6(a), (b) and (c) above, constitute income from an office or employment to the EBP beneficiaries regardless of the nature (e.g. capital gains, dividends) of the amounts when received by the plan and regardless of the fact that such income may have previously been taxed in the custodian's hands.

8. Where property other than cash is distributed in satisfaction of all or part of a beneficiary's interest in a trust governed by an employee benefit plan, it is the fair market value of the property which is taken into account in determining the amount to be included in income from an office or employment pursuant to paragraph 6(1)(g). The beneficiary is deemed, by subparagraph 107.1(b)(ii), to have acquired the property at a cost equal to the greater of its fair market value at that time and the adjusted cost base to the beneficiary of the relevant interest in the trust disposed of (immediately before that time). Since the beneficiary is also deemed to have disposed of the interest in the trust for proceeds of disposition equal to the adjusted cost base of the interest (immediately before that time) by virtue of paragraph 107.1(c), no gain or loss is recognized on its disposition. Thus, where the fair market value of the property distributed is less than the adjusted cost base of the interest in the trust disposed of, the cost base of the property is increased over its fair market value by the amount of the difference.

9. If property distributed is depreciable property of a prescribed class and the capital cost to the trust exceeds the deemed cost to the beneficiary, the capital cost to the beneficiary is deemed by paragraph 107.1(d) to be the amount which was the capital cost to the trust. The difference is deemed to have been allowed to the beneficiary as capital cost allowance. In a subsequent disposition of the property by the beneficiary there is a potential for recapture of capital cost allowance deducted by the trust.

10. The Department considers an amount to have been received by an EBP beneficiary out of the plan upon the earlier of the date upon which payment is made and the date upon which the EBP beneficiary has constructively received a payment. Constructive receipt is considered to apply in situations where an amount is credited to an EBP beneficiary's debt or account, set apart for the EBP beneficiary or otherwise made available to the EBP beneficiary without being subject to any restriction concerning its use. Consideration will be given to the application of subsection 56(2) (indirect payments) where payments are made to persons other than the employee or former employee while living.

11. Where the terms of an employee benefit plan provide that an employee entitled to benefits thereunder may elect to defer the receipt of a lump-sum amount payable on death, retirement or other termination of employment, it is the Department's view that the amount so deferred would normally be taxed in the year of actual receipt provided the election to defer is made prior to the termination of employment. Where, for instance, the plan specifies that an amount becomes payable 30 days after a particular event, the election must be made prior to the 30th day after such event. If, however, the plan specifies that the amount becomes payable on the happening of a particular event and the amount is to be paid within 30 days thereafter, the election must be made prior to the particular event.

12. Subsection 70(2) may be applicable on the death of an EBP beneficiary in respect of an entitlement by reason of membership in an employee benefit plan. However, such a determination depends upon the nature of the deceased's interest in the plan and is unaffected by the plan's qualification as an employee benefit plan. Factors taken into account in determining whether or not an amount is a "right or thing" are discussed in the current version of IT-212 (Modified by Correction Sheet CS 24 dated April 20, 2001), but

subsection 70(2) will generally be applicable to a funded deferred compensation arrangement whereas it will not generally be applicable to a lump-sum payment out of an unregistered pension plan.

13. Paragraph 110.2(4)(g) denies the pension income deduction for employee benefit plan payments whether reported under paragraphs 6(1)(g) or 56(1)(a).

14. Since payments out of an employee benefit plan represent income from an office or employment, subsection 212(17) specifically excludes these payments from Part XIII tax when paid to a non-resident of Canada. Such payments attributable to services rendered in Canada will be taxed under Part I as income from employment as provided by subsection 2(3), paragraph 6(1)(g) and subparagraph 115(1)(a)(i) unless exempted by a tax convention.

15. EBP beneficiary contributions to the plan are not deductible for tax purposes in any circumstances. As discussed in 6 above, a return of EBP beneficiary contributions by the plan is not included in income. Furthermore, the following amounts are not taxable in the year received from the plan because subsection 6(10) deems them to be a return of amounts contributed to the plan by the individual:

(a) an amount included in the income of an individual in a year previous to the year in which it was received from the plan, and

(b) where an employee trust subsequently becomes an employee benefit plan, a defined portion of amounts previously allocated and taxed when the plan was an employee trust.

The defined portion in (b) above is calculated as the lesser of

(c) the unpaid amounts which were allocated to the individual or a deceased person of whom the individual is an heir or legal representative when the plan was an employee trust, and

(d) the individual's share of the cost amount of the employee trust's assets less its liabilities immediately before ceasing to be an employee trust

minus

(e) amounts previously received out of a plan by the individual or a deceased person of whom the individual is an heir or legal representative when the plan was an employee benefit plan and which were deemed to be a return of contributions under (b) above.

Tax Result to Employer

16. After the 1979 taxation year, paragraph 18(1)(o) denies a deduction for employer contributions to an employee benefit plan. However, by virtue of subsection 18(10), the denial of a deduction does not apply

(a) to the portion of contributions with respect to non-residents, who are regularly employed abroad, for services rendered while non-residents, or

(b) where the plan custodian is a non-resident, to the portion of contributions with respect to employees who were not resident in Canada, or who were resident for a period (excluded period) of not more than 36 of the 72 months prior to the contributions and were beneficiaries under the plan before becoming resident, for services performed or to be performed while they are non-residents or during the excluded period.

17. Commencing with the 1980 taxation year, an employer's deduction is conditional upon contributions to the plan being included in the income of employees. Section 32.1 provides specific rules to achieve this result and to ensure that the deduction available to an employer is limited to contributions in respect of the employer's own employees or former employees.

18. By virtue of paragraph 32.1(1)(a), the employer's deduction for a taxation year is the amount allocated under subsection 32.1(2) to the employer for that year by the plan custodian to the extent it does not exceed the aggregate of the employer's contributions for the year or a preceding year to the plan that were neither previously claimed as a deduction nor refunded. Paragraph 32.1(1)(b) provides a final deduction to the employer once the plan's obligations to EBP beneficiaries have been satisfied and none of the property of the plan will thereafter be available to the employer. This final deduction is also limited to the portion of amounts previously contributed to the plan that has neither been deducted by nor refunded to the employer.

19. Pursuant to subsection 32.1(2), the plan custodian determines the amounts to be allocated to the employer. This allocation represents the payments out of the plan during the year (other than a return of contributions - see 6(b) above) to the employer's employees or former employees or their estates or heirs that exceed the income of the plan for the year. Consequently, payments from the plan are considered to be first a return of EBP beneficiary contributions, secondly a distribution of the plan's income for the year, thirdly a distribution of employer contributions and finally a distribution of the plan's prior years' income, if any.

20. Pursuant to subsection 32.1(3), the income of the plan for a year excluded from the allocation to the employer as noted above is determined as follows:

(a) where the plan is a trust, its income for the year determined without reference to subsections 104(4) to (26), and

(b) in any other case, the aggregate of the non-capital portion of all payments made under the plan in the year by the custodian.

21. Paragraph 12(1)(n.1) requires an employer to include in income for a taxation year the amounts received in that year from an employee benefit plan (other than amounts required by paragraph 104(13)(a) to be included in income under paragraph 12(1)(m)) to the extent they exceed the amount by which the aggregate of

(a) contributions to the plan for the year or a preceding year, and

(b) prior inclusions in income under paragraph 12(1)(n.1)

exceeds the aggregate of

(c) deductions with respect to contributions to the plan in computing income for that year and any preceding year, and

(d) amounts received from the plan in prior years (other than amounts included in income by virtue of paragraph 12(1)(m)).

22. In general, the amount required to be included by an employer in income under paragraph 12(1)(n.1) is the excess of amounts received to date over the undeducted portion of the employer's contributions made.

Example

Employer Contributions Year 1 $3,000 Year 2 $1,000 Total $4,000

Plan Earnings Year 1 $300 Year 2 $200 Total $500

Payments to Employee Year 1 $2,000 Year 2 $100 Total $2,100

Return of Contributions to Employer Year 1 $300 Year 2 $2,100 Total $2,400

Deduction to Employer (Section 32.1) Year 1 $1,700 Year 2 NIL Total $1,700

Computation of 12(1)(n.1) inclusion

Amounts received to date Year 1 $300 Year 2 $2,400

Less: Amounts contributed to date Year 1 $3,000 Year 2 $4,000

 Less: Amounts deducted to date Year 1 $1,700 Year 2 $1,700

Undeducted portion of contributions Year 1 $1,300 Year 2 $2,300

Paragraph 12(1)(n.1) inclusion Year 1 NIL Year 2 $100

23. For the purposes of section 32.1, the Department considers that if an amount has been constructively received by an employee (see 10 above), the plan has made a constructive payment to the employee.

24. In multi-employer plans, if one of the corporate members were to be liquidated before the termination of the employee benefit plan, the benefit of the deduction discussed in 17 above would be lost unless the liquidation is one to which subsection 88(1) applies, in which case the parent corporation would be deemed to be a continuation of the liquidated subsidiary company by virtue of paragraphs 87(2)(j.3) and 88(1)(e.2). Paragraph 87(2)(j.3) also provides a similar "rollover" upon amalgamation of a predecessor corporation's entitlement to the deduction under section 32.1.

Transition Period

25. For plans in existence prior to 1980 which meet the definition of an
employee benefit plan, the Department accepted for the 1980 taxation year a
claim for an expense deduction in respect of the employer's contributions
provided the EBP beneficiaries reported such amounts as income so that the
matching concept was present. When such amounts (as well as amounts which
were taxed in years prior to 1980 and allowed as a deduction to the employer)
are subsequently paid out of the plan in 1980 and subsequent years, clause
32.1(1)(a)(ii) will preclude a further deduction by the employer and
paragraph 6(10)(a) will provide the EBP beneficiaries with treatment of the
amounts as returns of EBP beneficiary contributions.

Tax Result to Custodian

26. Where the plan is not a trust, the custodian is taxable on the plan's
income which has not been paid out in the year at the custodian's applicable
tax rate. Contributions are not included in gross income nor are payments out
of those contributions or prior years' accumulated income deductible by the
custodian.

27. Where the plan is a trust, the trust is taxable on its income determined
under Part I. Contributions are not included in gross income and payments out
of those contributions or prior years' accumulated income are not deductible
by the trust.

28. The trust includes in its gross income the amount of its income from the
investment of trust property and other income incidental to the operation of
the trust. Where gross income (i.e., the aggregate of its income from all
sources) exceeds $500 in the taxation year (and in certain other
circumstances indicated on the form) the trustee must file form T3, Trust
Information Return and Income Tax Return.

29. In determining the income of the trust for a taxation year there may be
deducted, in the following order:

(a) expenses incurred in earning the investment or other income of the trust,

(b) expenses related to the normal operation of the trust (including those
incurred in the collection of and accounting for contributions to the trust)
except to the extent that such expenses are expressly not allowed under the
Act, and

(c) pursuant to paragraph 104(6)(a.1) amounts paid to beneficiaries
(including an employer where the trust so provides) out of current year's
trust income including amounts to which they have an unrestricted right (see
10 above).

The remainder of the income of the trust is subject to income tax under
section 122 of the Act. As an inter vivos trust, the taxation year of the

trust coincides with the calendar year. Amounts which have been taxed in the trust will also be included in beneficiaries' income when received in a later year. That is, additional tax becomes exigible if the income of the trust is not paid annually to beneficiaries.

30. Where the trust distributes property other than cash to beneficiaries in satisfaction of all or part of their interest in the trust, the trust is deemed by paragraph 107.1(b) to have disposed of the property for proceeds equal to its cost amount to the trust immediately before that time. Cost amount is defined in subsection 248(1). That is, if the trust held property and distributed it to beneficiaries after its value had appreciated, there would be no tax consequences to the trust. On the other hand, if the trust sells the property at a gain and fails to distribute the gain to the beneficiaries within the taxation year, the trust will be taxed upon the gain and the beneficiaries will be taxed upon the amount distributed to them in a subsequent year.

31. If the trust is a non-resident its income from trust property would not be subject to Part I tax except possibly under section 94. (See the current version of IT-447.) (Modified by Correction Sheet CS 24 dated April 20, 2001) However, such income from Canadian sources may be subject to withholding tax under Part XIII.

Employee Savings Plans

32. Typically the terms of an employee savings or thrift plan provide that the employer's contributions will be a percentage of employee contributions. There may be a vesting period and withdrawal restrictions. Where such a plan is administered by a custodian, it will normally fall within the definition of an employee benefit plan and be subject to the employee benefit plan rules outlined above. However, an employee savings or thrift plan will not be an employee benefit plan provided that the plan is structured in such a way that the employer's contribution is a payment of salary and paid to the plan custodian at the direction of the employee. Consequently, there are four tax treatments possible with regard to the employer contributions:

Situation 1. Employer makes payments to plan at employee direction
Status of Plan Not an EBP
Employee Taxed under 5(1)
Employer Immediate deduction from income

Situation 2. Employer's contribution to plan constructively received by employee at time of contributions
Status of Plan EBP
Employee Taxed under 6(1)(g) at time of contribution
Employer Deduction under 32.1 at time of contribution

Situation 3. Vesting of employer's contributions to the plan is delayed and constructive receipt is present on vesting
Status of Plan EBP
Employee Taxed under 6(1)(g) at time of constructive receipt
Employer Deduction under 32.1 at time of constructive payment

Situation 4. Constructive receipt of employer contributions not present
Status of Plan EBP
Employee Taxed under 6(1)(g) at time of actual receipt
Employer Deduction under 32.1 at time of actual payment

Profit Sharing Plans (Other than Employees and Deferred Profit Sharing Plans)

33. A profit sharing plan that is neither an employees profit sharing plan as defined in subsection 144(1) nor a deferred profit sharing plan as defined in subsection 147(1) generally falls within the definition of an employee benefit plan and therefore is subject to employee benefit plan rules outlined above. Paragraphs 18(1)(k) and 18(1)(o) prohibit a deduction for an employer's contribution to a profit sharing plan or an employee benefit plan respectively. If a profit sharing plan that falls within the definition of an employee benefit plan could receive the exemption in some given circumstances under subsection 18(10) (see 16 above), paragraph 18(1)(k) would still prohibit a deduction to the employer at the time of contribution. However, section 32.1 allows the employer a deduction for employer contributions when they are paid out to the employees regardless of the fact that the plan is a profit sharing plan.

Employee Trusts

Definition

34. Subject to the exclusions in 36 below, an employee trust is an arrangement established after 1979 which meets all of the following conditions:

(a) payments are made by an employer to a trustee in trust for the sole benefit of employees or former employees of the employer or employees or former employees of a person who does not deal at arm's length with the employer (the term "employee(s)" in the following paragraphs on employee trusts includes "former employee(s)");

(b) the right to the benefits vests in the beneficiaries at the time of each payment;

(c) the amount of a benefit does not depend on the beneficiary's position, performance or compensation as an employee;

(d) the trustee allocates annually to beneficiaries the amount as set out in 37 below; and

(e) the trustee elects in the return of income filed within 90 days from the end of the first taxation year of the trust to be an employee trust.

35. A qualifying arrangement that subsequently fails to meet any of the above conditions ceases to be an employee trust and thereby becomes an employee benefit plan trust subject to the employee benefit plan provisions. However, as discussed in 15 above, subsection 6(10) provides relief from double

taxation in respect of previously taxed allocations.

36. By virtue of the definition in subsection 248(1) of the Act, an employee trust does not include

(a) an employees profit sharing plan defined by subsection 144(1),

(b) a deferred profit sharing plan defined by subsection 147(1),

(c) a deferred profit sharing plan which has been revoked, or

(d) any trust established before 1980.

37. Pursuant to paragraph (b) of the definition of employee trust in subsection 248(1), the amount to be allocated annually to beneficiaries by the trustee, in a reasonable manner, consists of the aggregate of

(a) employer contributions for the year including contributions from a person who does not deal at arm's length with the employer,

(b) income of the trust for the year computed without reference to subsection 104(6) (other than a taxable capital gain) from a property or other source other than a business, and

(c) a capital gain of the trust for the year from the disposition of property,

less the aggregate of

(d) the loss of the trust for the year (other than an allowable capital loss) from a property or other source other than a business, and

(e) a capital loss of the trust for the year from the disposition of property.

This annual allocation does not provide for the allocation of negative amounts to beneficiaries, and such amounts may not be applied against the trust's income of other years. For example, if capital losses exceed capital gains, non-business income and employer contributions in a year, the capital losses are not deductible by beneficiaries because no amount can be allocated to beneficiaries. While a capital loss in a year reduces the amount to be allocated to beneficiaries in that year, it may not be applied to reduce future capital gains or allocations.

Tax Result to Employee

38. No amount is required to be included in employees' incomes under paragraph 6(1)(a) in respect of any benefit actually received or enjoyed by reason of participation in an employee trust. However, under paragraph 6(1)(h) beneficiaries must include in their income from an office of employment amounts allocated to them by the trustee (see 37 above) for the year regardless of the nature (e.g. capital gains, dividends) of the amounts when received by the trustee. Consequently, the beneficiaries are taxed only

on amounts allocated each year which may differ from amounts paid into or distributed by the employee trust during that year.

39. Where a beneficiary is in receipt of a distribution in kind from an employee trust in settlement of all or part of the beneficiary's interest in the trust, the beneficiary is deemed, pursuant to paragraph 107.1(a), to have acquired the property at a cost equal to its fair market value at that time. If the property is depreciable property of a prescribed class and the deemed cost is less than the capital cost to the trust, paragraph 107.1(d) provides that the capital cost to the beneficiary is deemed to be the amount that was the capital cost to the trust. The difference is deemed to have been allowed to the beneficiary as capital cost allowances. Thus, in a subsequent disposition of the property by the beneficiary, there is a potential for recapture of capital cost allowance deducted by the trust. Paragraph 107.1(c) provides that the beneficiary is deemed to have disposed of the interest or part interest in the trust at its adjusted cost base.

40. The provisions of paragraph 110.2(4)(g) (denial of pension income deduction) and subsection 212(17) (exclusion from Part XIII tax) discussed in 13 and 14 above also apply to payments out of an employee trust.

41. Contributions to an employee trust by employees are neither deductible for income tax purposes nor taxed on distribution. See also 15(b) above concerning an employee trust which subsequently becomes an employee benefit plan.

Tax Result to Employer

42. In the absence of a specific provision in the Act to deny employers a deduction for their contributions to an employee trust, the provisions of subsection 9(1) and paragraph 18(1)(a), subject to the general limitation of reasonableness under section 67, apply to permit a deduction to employers. However, if an employee trust is also a profit sharing plan, other than an employee's profit sharing plan as defined in subsection 144(1) or a deferred profit sharing plan as defined in subsection 147(1), paragraph 18(1)(k) denies a deduction to the employer for contributions to such a trust. This is in contrast to an employee benefit plan that is also a profit sharing plan where, as outlined in 33 above, a deduction would be available to the employer.

43. All amounts received by an employer or by a person with whom the employer does not deal at arm's length, out of or under an employee trust, are income to the recipient in the year received pursuant to paragraph 12(1)(n).

Tax Result to Employee Trust

44. Qualification as an employee trust requires the annual allocation of all non-business income of the trust to its beneficiaries. The allocation of business income if any, is precluded by subsection 104(6). Net business income is taxed in the trust at the rates specified in section 122. The trustee must file form T3, Trust Information Return and Income Tax Return

where gross business income exceeds $500 in the taxation year and in certain other circumstances indicated on the form.

45. Where an employee trust distributes property other than cash to beneficiaries, the trust is deemed by paragraph 107.1(a) to have disposed of the property for proceeds equal to its fair market value at that time, creating the possibility of recapture of capital cost allowances and capital gains or losses in the trust.

46. The comments in 31 above also apply to an employee trust which is a non-resident trust.

General Comments Applicable to Employee Benefit Plans and Employee Trusts

47. By virtue of the definition of "trust" in paragraph 108(1)(j), the following provisions of subdivision k (sections 104 to 108) do not apply to a trust governed by an employee benefit plan or an employee trust:

(a) subsections 104(4) and (5) dealing with deemed periodic realizations,

(b) subsections 104(12), (14) and (15) dealing with preferred beneficiary elections, and

(c) sections 105 to 107 dealing with benefits under trusts and transactions involving interest in trusts.

48. Amounts to be included in income of recipients or beneficiaries as outlined in 6 and 38 above, which for taxation purposes will be regarded as salary or wages derived from an office or employment, whether derived from an employee benefit plan or an employee trust, will not be subject to either Canada Pension Plan contributions or unemployment insurance premiums. In the case of payments out of or under an employee benefit plan, a requirement to withhold income tax will arise at the earlier of the date payment is made to the recipients or the date on which they acquire an unrestricted right to receive payment. No liability for withholding is incurred by a trustee in respect of allocations or payments made to beneficiaries out of or under an employee trust. The trustee or custodian, as the case may be, is required to make an information return to report both the amounts allocated under an employee trust and payments out of or under an employee benefit plan. Form T4A is the prescribed form.

49. The Act does not restrict the investments which an employee benefit plan or an employee trust may acquire. However, refer to 10 above concerning use of plan funds by an EBP beneficiary.

CANADA CUSTOMS AND REVENUE AGENCY

INTERPRETATION BULLETIN NUMBER IT-502

DATE: May 31, 1991

SUBJECT: SPECIAL RELEASE
Employee Benefit Plans and Employee Trusts

Application

This Special Release updates Interpretation Bulletin IT-502, dated March 28, 1985. The application of the comments in this bulletin has been substantially limited by amendments to the law enacted in 1986 and 1987.

Depending upon their terms and characteristics, certain plans or arrangements that formerly would have been "employee benefit plans," subject to the treatment outlined in paragraphs 3 to 33 of the bulletin, will not so qualify if they fall within the definition of a "salary deferral arrangement" or a "retirement compensation arrangement," set out in subsection 248(1). Reference should be made to the Act in determining the tax treatment of contributions to and benefits received out of the latter two arrangements. A plan or arrangement that qualifies as an "employee trust" is expressly excluded from both the salary deferral arrangement and retirement compensation arrangement definitions in subsection 248(1) and, accordingly, can continue to receive the tax treatment outlined in paragraphs 34 to 49 of the bulletin.

Bulletin Revisions

1. Paragraph 4 is amended by removing the word "and" at the end of item 4(k) and adding the following immediately after item 4(l):

"(m) Salary Deferral Arrangements, in respect of a taxpayer, under which Deferred Amounts are required to be included as benefits under paragraph 6(1)(a) in computing the taxpayer's income (the terms "salary deferral arrangement" and "deferred amount" are defined in subsection 248(1)), and

(n) Retirement Compensation Arrangements, as defined in subsection 248(1) (see also the current version of the Department's Retirement Compensation Arrangement Guide).

2. Paragraph 13 of the bulletin is cancelled and replaced by the following:

"13. For 1987 and earlier taxation years, paragraph 110.2(4)(g) denied the pension income deduction for employee benefit plan payments whether reported under paragraphs 6(1)(g) or 56(1)(a). For 1988 and subsequent taxation years, paragraph 118(8)(e) similarly denies the pension tax credit."

3. In paragraph 21 of the bulletin, the reference to paragraph 104(13)(a) is

replaced by a reference to paragraph 104(13)(b).

4. Paragraph 35 is cancelled and replaced by the following:

"35. A qualifying arrangement that subsequently fails to meet any of the above conditions ceases to be an employee trust. If it does not then meet the definition of either a salary deferral arrangement or a retirement compensation arrangement in subsection 248(1), the arrangement will become an employee benefit plan trust subject to the employee benefit plan provisions. However, as discussed in 15 above, subsection 6(10) provides relief from double taxation in respect of previously taxed allocations."

5. Paragraph 40 of the bulletin is cancelled and replaced by the following:

"40. The provisions of paragraph 118(8)(e) (denial of the pension tax credit after 1987) and subsection 212(17) (exclusion from Part XIII tax) discussed in 13 and 14 above also apply to payments out of an employee trust. For 1987 and earlier taxation years, paragraph 110.2(4)(g) denied the pension income deduction."

6. Paragraph 47 is amended by adding the following after item (c) thereof:

"For taxation years of trusts commencing after 1987, the following provisions of subdivision k are also inapplicable to a trust governed by an employee benefit plan or to an employee trust:

(d) subsection 104(5.2) relating to resource properties, and

(e) subsections 104(13.1) and 104(13.2) dealing with rules for designating certain distributions that will not be taxable in the hand of beneficiaries."

NO.:   **IT-519R2 (Consolidated)**   DATE: See *Bulletin Revisions* section

SUBJECT: INCOME TAX ACT
Medical Expense and Disability Tax Credits and Attendant Care Expense Deduction

REFERENCE: Sections 64, 118.2, 118.3 and 118.4 (also sections 64.1, 118, 118.7 and 118.8; subsections 6(16) and 117(2) and paragraph 117.1(1)*(b)* of the *Income Tax Act* and section 5700 of the *Income Tax Regulations*)

Latest Revisions – ¶s 11, 34, 53 and 67

At the Canada Customs and Revenue Agency (CCRA), we issue income tax interpretation bulletins (ITs) in order to provide technical interpretations and positions regarding certain provisions contained in income tax law. Due to their technical nature, ITs are used primarily by our staff, tax specialists, and other individuals who have an interest in tax matters. For those readers who prefer a less technical explanation of the law, we offer other publications, such as tax guides and pamphlets.

While the comments in a particular paragraph in an IT may relate to provisions of the law in force at the time they were made, such comments are not a substitute for the law. The reader should, therefore, consider such comments in light of the relevant provisions of the law in force for the particular taxation year being considered, taking into account the effect of any relevant amendments to those provisions or relevant court decisions occurring after the date on which the comments were made.

Subject to the above, an interpretation or position contained in an IT generally applies as of the date on which it was published, unless otherwise specified. If there is a subsequent change in that interpretation or position and the change is beneficial to taxpayers, it is usually effective for future assessments and reassessments. If, on the other hand, the change is not favourable to taxpayers, it will normally be effective for the current and subsequent taxation years or for transactions entered into after the date on which the change is published.

If you have any comments regarding matters discussed in an IT, please send them to:

Manager, Technical Publications and Projects Section
Income Tax Rulings Directorate
Policy and Legislation Branch
Canada Customs and Revenue Agency
Ottawa ON K1A 0L5

This electronic version of this document is the official version

Contents

Attendant Care Expense Deduction in Computing
Income (¶s 68-71)
Proposed Refundable Medical Expense Tax Credit (¶ 72)
Proposed Medical Expense Tax Credit for Training (¶ 73)
Appendix
Bulletin Revisions

Application

This bulletin is a consolidation of the following:

- IT-519R dated April 6, 1998; and
- subsequent amendments thereto.

For further particulars, see the "Bulletins Revisions" section
near the end of this bulletin.

Summary

The medical expense tax credit, the disability tax credit and
the attendant care expense deduction all provide tax relief for
individuals. The medical expense tax credit applies to
individuals who have sustained significant medical expenses
for themselves or certain of their dependants. The disability
tax credit applies to individuals who have a "severe and
prolonged mental or physical impairment" or for individuals
who support certain dependants with such an impairment.
The attendant care expense deduction is available to
individuals who are entitled to claim the disability tax credit
and who have incurred expenses for personal care that are
necessary to enable them to work.

An individual may claim a non-refundable tax credit for
medical expenses (referred to in this bulletin as the "medical
expense tax credit") when calculating Part I tax payable. The
amount of the medical expense tax credit is determined by
multiplying the lowest personal tax rate percentage (17% in
1997) by the amount of qualifying medical expenses in
excess of certain minimum amounts. An individual may be
entitled to receive a refundable medical expense tax credit in
respect of the same medical expenses for which a medical
expense tax credit was claimed.

An individual who has a severe and prolonged mental or
physical impairment as certified by an appropriate medical
practitioner may claim a non-refundable "disability tax
credit" when calculating Part I tax payable. The amount of
the disability tax credit is determined by multiplying the
lowest personal tax rate percentage by $4,233 (for 1997). In
addition, any unused portion of the individual's disability tax
credit may be transferred to the individual's spouse or to a
"supporting individual."

A person entitled to a disability pension under the Canada or
Quebec Pension Plan or under an insurance policy is not
necessarily entitled to a disability tax credit under the *Income
Tax Act*.

Individuals with a disability entitling them to the disability
tax credit may also claim, under certain conditions, a
deduction in computing net income for amounts paid for
attendant care enabling them to earn certain types of income.
The maximum amount that may be claimed as a deduction is
$5,000; however, see the note following ¶ 69 below.

When a medical expense or disability tax credit relates to a
non-resident or a part-year resident, please refer to the
current versions of IT-171, *Non-Resident Individuals –
Computation of Taxable Income Earned in Canada and
Non-Refundable Tax Credits*, or IT-193, *Part-Year Residents
– Computation of Taxable Income and Non-Refundable Tax
Credits*.

Discussion and Interpretation

Severe and Prolonged Impairment

¶ 1.   Subsection 118.4(1) contains a set of rules that define
certain terms for purposes of the section 118.3 disability tax
credit and section 118.2 medical expense tax credit. There
will be subsequent references back to this paragraph when
applicable. Subsection 118.4(1) provides the following rules:

(a) An impairment is prolonged when it has lasted, or may
     reasonably be expected to last, for a continuous period
     of at least 12 months.

(b) An individual's ability to perform a basic activity of
     daily living is markedly restricted only when the
     individual is blind or is unable (or requires an inordinate
     amount of time) to perform such an activity, all or
     substantially all of the time, even with therapy and the
     use of appropriate devices and medication.

(c) A basic activity of daily living in relation to an
     individual means:

     (i) perceiving, thinking and remembering;

     (ii) feeding or dressing oneself;

     (iii) speaking so as to be understood, in a quiet setting,
            by another person familiar with the individual;

     (iv) hearing so as to understand, in a quiet setting,
            another person familiar with the individual;

     (v) eliminating (bowel or bladder functions); or

     (vi) walking.

(d) No other activity including working, housekeeping or a
     social or recreational activity is considered a basic
     activity of daily living.

(a) above describes an impairment as being prolonged if it is
expected to last for at least 12 months. This "expectation"
test is applied at the time the disability begins. However, a
claim will not be denied solely because the person dies
within the 12 month period.

In (b) above, an individual is viewed as being "markedly restricted" in performing a basic activity of daily living when the individual is restricted for at least 90% of the time. When the individual's ability to perform such an activity is not restricted for at least 90% of the time, the individual **may** be viewed as not being "markedly restricted."

In (b) above, it is a question of fact as to what is "an inordinate amount of time" for performing an activity; however, to meet the requirement that the activity takes an inordinate amount of time, the activity must take significantly more time than would be taken by an average person not afflicted with the impairment.

In addition to blindness, examples of other disabling conditions that could satisfy the rules discussed above are severe cardio-respiratory failure, severe mental impairment, profound bilateral deafness, and functional impairment of the neuro- or musculo-skeletal systems. Disabling ailments and conditions must generally be considered on a case-by-case basis, since it is the effect of the impairment on the ability to perform the activities of daily living, which effect differs between individuals, rather than the ailment or condition itself, which determines whether an individual is eligible for the disability tax credit.

References to Medical Professionals

¶ 2.   This bulletin uses the terms "medical doctor," "medical practitioner," as well as various other terms to describe individuals involved in the medical profession, in a way that is consistent with the terms found in the *Income Tax Act*. The term "medical doctor" is used in section 118.3 for purposes of the disability tax credit. Section 118.2, on the other hand, uses the term "medical practitioner" for purposes of the medical expense tax credit. "Medical practitioner" encompasses a broad range of individuals in the medical profession (see ¶ 3 below).

¶ 3.   For purposes of the medical expense and disability tax credits under sections 118.2 and 118.3, subsection 118.4(2) provides that a reference to a medical practitioner, dentist, pharmacist, nurse or optometrist means a person who is authorized to practice as such according to the following laws:

(a) for a service rendered to an individual, the laws of the jurisdiction in which the service is rendered;

(b) for a certificate issued for an individual, the laws of the jurisdiction in which the individual resides or of a province; and

(c) for a prescription issued to an individual, the laws of the jurisdiction in which the individual resides, of a province or of the jurisdiction in which the prescription is filled.

Medical practitioners authorized to practice in accordance with the above laws can include (depending on the applicable province or jurisdiction, as the case may be) the following:

(i) an osteopath;

(ii) a chiropractor;

(iii) a naturopath;

(iv) a therapeutist (or therapist);

(v) a physiotherapist;

(vi) a chiropodist (or podiatrist);

(vii) a Christian Science practitioner;

(viii) a psychoanalyst who is a member of the Canadian Institute of Psychoanalysis or a member of the Quebec Association of Jungian Psychoanalysts;

(ix) a psychologist;

(x) a qualified speech-language pathologist or audiologist such as, for example, a person who is certified as such by The Canadian Association of Speech-Language Pathologists and Audiologists (CASLPA) or a provincial affiliate of that organization;

(xi) an occupational therapist who is a member of the Canadian Association of Occupational Therapists;

(xii) an acupuncturist;

(xiii) a dietician; and

(xiv) a dental hygienist.

Additionally, a "nurse" includes a practical nurse whose full-time occupation is nursing as well as a Christian Science nurse authorized to practice according to the relevant laws referred to in subsection 118.4(2).

Note: Bill C-28 was given First reading in the House of Commons on December 10, 1997. Bill C-28, if enacted as proposed, will amend subsection 118.4(2) to include audiologists, after February 18, 1997, and medical doctors, for taxation years that end after November 1991.

Disability Tax Credit

¶ 4.   Subsection 118.3(1) provides the formula for determining the disability tax credit for an individual who has a severe and prolonged mental or physical impairment (referred to in this bulletin as the "person with a disability"). Under the formula, the disability tax credit for a particular year is determined by taking a fixed amount (which will increase from one taxation year to the next each time there is an annual indexation adjustment) and multiplying that amount by the lowest tax rate percentage referred to in subsection 117(2). For 1997, the disability tax credit is 17% of $4,233 = $720. For a taxation year other than 1997, the fixed amount and the lowest tax rate percentage can be found in the *General Income Tax Guide* for that year.

¶ 5. Subsection 118.3(1) also requires that the effects of the severe and prolonged mental or physical impairment of the person with a disability be such that his or her ability to perform a basic activity of daily living is markedly restricted. This must be certified in prescribed form by a medical doctor, or if the impairment is an impairment of sight, a medical doctor or an optometrist. (See the proposed amendment described below.) Form T2201, *Disability Tax Credit Certificate*, must be used for this purpose and filed with the income tax return of the person who is claiming the credit. The form will be reviewed to determine if the person with a disability is eligible for the disability tax credit before the income tax return is assessed. For this reason, the income tax return should not be electronically filed for the first year in which the disability tax credit is claimed. If the impairment is permanent, it is not necessary to file another Form T2201 in later years unless the circumstances change or unless the form is requested. If the impairment is temporary, a new form must be submitted if the period stated on the certificate has ended. See ¶ 1 above regarding the meanings of "prolonged," "basic activity of daily living" and "markedly restricted."

A person may be entitled to a disability pension under the Canada or Quebec Pension Plan, under workers' compensation legislation or under a private insurance arrangement but may not be entitled to claim the disability tax credit. For example, under the Canada Pension Plan a disability is severe if the person "is incapable regularly of pursuing any substantially gainful occupation." By contrast, for purposes of the disability tax credit, an impairment is severe if the person's ability to perform a basic activity of daily living is markedly restricted.

Note 1: Bill C-28 was given First reading in the House of Commons on December 10, 1997. Bill C-28, if enacted as proposed, will amend paragraph 118.3(1)(a.2) to permit a person authorized to practice as an audiologist to certify, after February 18, 1997, the existence of a severe and prolonged hearing impairment for the purpose of the disability tax credit.

Note 2: As part of the Federal Budget of February 24, 1998 a Notice of Ways and Means Motion to Amend the Income Tax Act was tabled in the House of Commons. One of the proposed amendments provides that after February 24, 1998 for the purposes of the disability tax credit, persons authorized to practice as

(a) occupational therapists be allowed to certify the existence of a severe and prolonged impairment with respect to an individual's ability to walk or to feed and dress himself or herself, and

(b) psychologists be allowed to certify the existence of a severe and prolonged impairment with respect to an individual's ability to perceive, think and remember.

¶ 6. Neither the disability tax credit outlined in ¶ 4 above nor the transfer of the disability tax credit outlined in ¶s 7 to 9 below may be claimed if the cost of **nursing home** care or remuneration for an **attendant** (subject to one exception, mentioned in ¶ 26 below) for the person with a disability is included as a qualifying medical expense under section 118.2 in calculating a medical expense tax credit of the person with a disability or of any other person.

¶ 7. Under certain circumstances, the unused portion of the disability tax credit of a person with a disability who is resident in Canada at any time in the year may be transferred under subsection 118.3(2) to another individual (the "supporting individual") who supports the person with a disability. Such a transfer may be made if one of the following conditions apply:

(a) The supporting individual has claimed in respect of the person with a disability

    (i) an equivalent-to-spouse tax credit or

    (ii) a dependant tax credit, if the person with a disability is the supporting individual's child or grandchild.

(b) The supporting individual could have claimed a personal tax credit described in (a) above (where the person with a disability is the supporting individual's parent, grandparent, child or grandchild) if the supporting individual were not married and the person with a disability had no income for the year and was 18 or more years old before the end of the year.

For a discussion of the equivalent-to-spouse tax credit and dependant tax credit, see the current version of IT-513, *Personal Tax Credits*.

¶ 8. The amount of disability tax credit that may be transferred to and claimed by the supporting individual under subsection 118.3(2) is

• the amount that the person with a disability may claim for the year as a disability tax credit under subsection 118.3(1) in excess of

• the person's Part I tax payable determined before deducting any tax credits except the personal, age and pension tax credits under section 118 and the tax credit under section 118.7 for employment insurance premiums and for Canada and Quebec Pension Plans contributions.

When more than one individual is entitled under subsection 118.3(2) to deduct a tax credit transferred from the same person with a disability for a taxation year, subsection 118.3(3) limits the total of all such deductions for that year to the maximum amount that could be claimed by one individual for that year if that individual were the only one entitled to use subsection 118.3(2) to claim a tax credit transferred from that person with a disability. If the individuals fail to agree on the portions to be claimed, the Minister may fix the portions.

If a spouse of a person with a disability claims any non-refundable tax credit in the year for the person with a disability under section 118 or 118.8 (that is, any personal tax credit for the person with a disability or any tax credit transferred from the person with a disability), a third person will not be entitled to a subsection 118.3(2) transfer of a disability tax credit from the person with a disability for the same year, even if that third person qualifies as a "supporting individual" of the person with a disability.

¶ 9.   Section 118.8 allows one spouse to transfer to the other spouse certain unused tax credits, including the unused portion of the transferring spouse's disability tax credit (if any). The amount that may be claimed as a tax credit under section 118.8 is determined by the following formula:

$A + B - C$

where

A   is the total of the amounts that the transferring spouse may claim for the year as tuition and education tax credits (up to a combined maximum of $680 for 1995 and $850 thereafter).

B   is the total of the amounts that the transferring spouse may claim for the year as age, pension and disability tax credits.

C   is the transferring spouse's Part I tax payable determined before deducting any tax credits other than the basic personal tax credit and the tax credits under section 118.7 for premiums for employment insurance and contributions under the Canada and Quebec Pension Plans.

For purposes of the *Income Tax Act*, the "spouse" of a taxpayer includes a person of the opposite sex who is cohabiting with the taxpayer at the time in a conjugal relationship if relevant conditions in subsection 252(4) are met.

A claim under section 118.8 cannot be made by an individual for a spouse if he or she were living separate and apart from that spouse at the end of the year and for a period of 90 days commencing in the year because of a breakdown of their marriage.

Medical Expense Tax Credit

¶ 10.   An individual may deduct a medical expense tax credit determined by the formula under subsection 118.2(1). Under the formula, assuming there is no adjustment as described in ¶ 16 below, the allowable portion of the qualifying medical expenses claimed is the portion of those expenses that exceeds the lesser of the following two amounts: a fixed amount ($1,614 for 1997—this will increase in subsequent years each time there is an annual

indexation adjustment), or 3% of the individual's net income for the year. The allowable portion of the expenses is multiplied by the lowest tax rate percentage for the year (17% for 1997) to determine the medical expense tax credit. For example, assume that an individual, whose net income for 1997 is $50,000, incurs $5,000 of qualifying medical expenses. Since 3% of $50,000 = $1,500 is less than the 1997 fixed amount of $1,614, the individual's medical expense tax credit is 17% of ($5,000 – $1,500) = $595. For a taxation year other than 1997, the fixed amount and lowest tax rate percentage can be obtained from the *General Income Tax Guide* for that year. Forward averaged amounts included in taxable income under subsection 110.4(2) do not form part of an individual's net income upon which the 3% calculation is based. However, 1997 is the last taxation year for which the forward averaging calculations are relevant.

¶ 11.   To qualify for the medical expense tax credit, the medical expenses must have been paid or deemed to have been paid (see ¶ 65 below) by either the individual or his or her legal representative for qualifying medical expenses as provided for in subsection 118.2(2) (see ¶ 18 below). Furthermore, the medical expenses used in calculating a medical expense tax credit for a particular taxation year:

(a)   must have been paid within any 12-month period ending in the calendar year, unless the individual died in the year; in which case, the medical expenses must have been paid within any 24-month period that includes the date of death (see ¶ 17 below);

(b)   must be proven by filing supporting receipts (except for certain vehicle and meal expenses discussed in ¶ 34) (see ¶ 67);

(c)   must not have been used in calculating a previous year's medical expense tax credit; and

(d)   must not have been reimbursed or be reimbursable (see ¶ 66 below).

¶ 12.   An individual's qualifying medical expenses are not restricted to those incurred or paid in Canada but they must have been paid on behalf of the **individual**, the individual's **spouse** or a **dependant** (see ¶ 13 below) of the individual. The word **"patient"** is used in the law **and throughout this bulletin** to refer to the individual or to the individual's spouse or dependant, as the case may be, on whose behalf the individual's qualifying medical expenses are paid.

¶ 13.   For purposes of the medical expense tax credit, a person qualifies as a "dependant" of the individual for a particular taxation year if all the following conditions are met:

(a)   The person is the child, grandchild, parent, grandparent, brother, sister, uncle, aunt, niece or nephew of the individual or of the individual's spouse.

(b)   The person is dependent on the individual for support at some time in the year.

(c)   The person is a resident of Canada at some time in the year. This residence requirement does not apply if the person is the child or grandchild of the individual or of the individual's spouse.

¶ 14.   If a medical expense was incurred in one year on behalf of a spouse or dependant but is not paid until the following year at a time when such person is no longer a spouse or a dependant, the expense can nevertheless qualify in the year of payment since the person referred to is only required to have been a spouse or a dependant at the time the expense was incurred.

¶ 15.   An individual may claim the medical expenses of a spouse or a separated spouse regardless of that spouse's income in the taxation year. A receipt in the name of either spouse is considered acceptable for a medical expense of either, and the amount of that expense may be used by either, as agreed between them.

¶ 16.   An **adjustment** must be made to the individual's medical expense tax credit if the medical expenses claimed include those paid on behalf of a "dependant" (the term "dependant" is explained in ¶ 13 above and does not include the individual's spouse) and the dependant has net income for the year which exceeds the "basic personal amount." (The basic personal amount is the base for calculating paragraph (c) of the description of B in subsection 118(1)— the individual tax credit. It is $6,456 for 1997 and will increase in subsequent years each time there is an annual indexation adjustment.) In the situation described above, there are two ways of calculating the adjustment. The first way is to follow the formula as described in **D** of subsection 118.2(1), which provides that the medical expense tax credit, as calculated in the manner described in ¶ 10 above, must be reduced by 68% of the excess of the dependant's net income over the basic personal amount. In the example in ¶ 10 above, in which the individual has net income for 1997 of $50,000 and claims qualifying medical expenses for that year of $5,000, the individual's medical expense tax credit would generally be 17% of ($5,000 – $1,500) = $595. Assume also, however, that the $5,000 in medical expenses claimed by the individual includes $4,000 paid on behalf of a dependant whose net income is $7,000. The formula in subsection 118.2(1) requires that the $595 tax credit be reduced by 68% of ($7,000 – $6,456) = $370. The reduced medical expense tax credit would therefore be $595 – $370 = $225. The second way of calculating the adjustment is to reduce the qualifying medical expenses claimed by four times the excess of the dependant's net income over the basic personal amount. In the above example, the reduction to the qualifying medical expenses claimed would be 4   ($7,000 – $6,456) = $2,176. The individual's medical expense tax credit would

therefore be calculated as 17% of ($5,000 – $1,500 – $2,176) = $225. Using the latter method makes it easier to determine whether it is to the individual's benefit to claim the medical expenses paid on behalf of the dependant. In the above example, if the dependant's net income was $8,000 instead of $7,000, the reduction to the medical expenses claimed would be 4   ($8,000 – $6,456) = $6,176. Since this reduction would be more than the $4,000 expenses paid on behalf of the dependant, it would not be to the individual's benefit to claim those expenses.

Medical Expenses Paid Subsequent to the Death of an Individual

¶ 17.   If the legal representative of a deceased individual has filed a return for the year of death and has subsequently (but within the time period specified for a deceased individual in ¶ 11(a) above) paid additional medical expenses, an adjustment in qualifying medical expenses and in the medical expense tax credit will be made, if requested, to reflect such payments.

Qualifying Medical Expenses

¶ 18.   Subsection 118.2(2) describes in detail the types of medical expenses that may qualify for the medical expense tax credit. Some of these expenses are described in the following paragraphs.

Payments to medical practitioners, hospitals, etc.

¶ 19.   Paragraph 118.2(2)*(a)* allows an individual to include, as a qualifying medical expense, an amount paid to a medical practitioner (see ¶ 3 above), dentist or nurse or a public or licensed private hospital for medical or dental services provided to the patient (for the meaning of "patient," see ¶ 12 above). The rules for determining whether a person is a medical practitioner, dentist or nurse for purposes of the medical expense tax credit are discussed in ¶ 3(a) to (c) above. Also shown in ¶ 3 above is a list of certain types of medical practitioners that (depending on the applicable province or jurisdiction) may meet these rules. Although some of the medical practitioners in that list are not doctors, their fees can qualify as being "for medical services," for purposes of a claim under paragraph 118.2(2)*(a)*, to the extent that the fees are for diagnostic, therapeutic or rehabilitative services.

¶ 20.   Payments made to partnerships, societies and associations for medical services rendered by their employees or partners are qualifying medical expenses as long as the person who provided the service is a medical practitioner, dentist or nurse authorized to practice in accordance with the laws discussed in ¶ 3(a) to (c) above. For example, the Arthritis Society employs physiotherapists to provide medical services to persons suffering from arthritis and rheumatism. Payments made to that society for the services of such employees are qualifying medical expenses. Other similar organizations are the Victorian Order of Nurses and The Canadian Red Cross Society Home Maker Services. Payments qualify only to the extent that they are for the period when the patient is at home. Payments for a period when the nurse is simply looking after a home and children when the patient is in hospital or otherwise away from home do not qualify since these would be personal or living expenses. In some instances, such as that of the Canadian Mothercraft Society, the visiting worker instead of the society may give the receipts but, if the worker can be regarded as a practical nurse, those receipts will be accepted.

¶ **21.**   If there is doubt as to whether an institution is a licensed private hospital (see ¶ 19 above), a Revenue Canada tax services office should be contacted for an opinion on the matter. Individuals should not rely on the name of the institution, since some hospitals do not have the word ì hospitalî in their official title. Possession of a municipal licence to carry on business does not necessarily qualify the institution. However, if the institution possesses a provincial licence designating it as a ì hospital,î subject to its meeting and maintaining standards set by local health, building and fire authorities, the institution may qualify as a hospital for income tax purposes.

¶ **22.**   When an institution is situated in another country and there is doubt as to whether it qualifies for purposes of the Act, the individual should obtain full particulars of the state or other licence under which it operates. The individual should also obtain details of the professional qualifications of the medical staff in attendance and of the medical or remedial care given to the patient to whom the expense relates. Doubtful cases may be referred, with full particulars, to any Revenue Canada tax services offi

Care of individual with mental or physical impairment

¶ **23.**   Paragraph 118.2(2)*(b)* allows an individual to include, as a qualifying medical expense, remuneration paid for one **full-time** attendant for a patient who has a severe and prolonged mental or physical impairment (see ¶ 1 above), or the cost of **full-time** care in a nursing home (see ¶ 30 below) for such a patient. The patient on whose behalf these medical expenses are paid must be a person with a disability for whom a disability tax credit could be claimed (that is, either by the person with a disability or by some other person, in accordance with the rules outlined earlier in this bulletin) for the taxation year in which these medical expenses were incurred if it were not for the rule described in ¶ 26 below. Also, for purposes of the medical expense tax credit, paragraph 118.2(2)*(b)* provides that, at the time the

remuneration is paid, the full-time attendant cannot be under 18 years of age or be the individualís spouse.

The expression ì one full-time attendantî is not intended to mean one attendant only looking after the patient on a continuous basis but rather several attendants could be utilized over a specific period of time so long as there is only one attendant for any given period of time.

The use of the expression ì full-time care in a nursing homeî is not intended to place a requirement of a minimum time spent caring for the patient but rather it implies the constant care and attendance required by an individual by reason of the injury, illness or affliction of the individual. To provide such care there must be appropriately qualified medical personnel in attendance in sufficient numbers on a 24-hour basis.

¶ **24.**   Paragraph 118.2(2)*(b.1)* allows an individual to include, as a qualifying medical expense, remuneration paid for attendant care in Canada of a patient who has a severe and prolonged mental or physical impairment (see ¶ 1 above). The claim for these expenses cannot be more than $5,000 ($10,000 if the patient died in the year). At the time the remuneration is paid, the attendant must not be under 18 years of age or be the individualís spouse. The patient must be a person with a disability for whom a disability tax credit can be claimed (that is, either by the person with a disability or by another person) for the taxation year in which the attendant care is given. The individual must file receipts (see ¶ 67 below), issued by the payee, for payment of remuneration for the attendant care. If the payee is an individual, such receipts should include that individualís social insurance number. It should be noted that remuneration paid for the attendant care of the patient cannot be claimed under paragraph 118.2(2)*(b.1)* if, for the taxation year in which that remuneration is paid, a section 63 child care expense deduction or a section 64 attendant care expense deduction (see ¶s 68 to 71 below) is claimed for the patient or if medical expenses paid on behalf of the patient are claimed (for purposes of calculating a medical expense tax credit) under paragraph 118.2(2)*(b)* as described above or under paragraphs 118.2(2)*(c)*, *(d)* or *(e)* as described in ¶s 27 to 30 below. While most claims under paragraph 118.2(2)*(b.1)* will be for a part-time attendant, a full-time attendant could also be claimed under that provision (as long as the above-mentioned dollar limit is observed) in order not to prevent a claim for the disability tax credit (see ¶ 26 below).

ì Attendant careî is care provided by an attendant who performs those personal tasks which the person with a disability is unable to do for himself or herself. Depending on the situation, such tasks could include meal preparation, maid and cleaning services, transportation, and personal services, such as banking and shopping. ì Attendant careî would also include providing companionship to the person with a disability. However, if a person is employed to do a specific task, for example, provide maid and cleaning services or transportation services, the provision of such a service would not be viewed as "attendant care."

Note: Bill C-28 was given First reading in the House of Commons on December 10, 1997. Bill C-28, if enacted as proposed, will amend paragraph 118.2(2)(b.1) to increase, for 1997 and later years, the maximum amount of paid remuneration for part-time attendant care eligible for the medical expense tax credit to $10,000 (from $5,000) and to $20,000 (from $10,000) if the individual dies in the year.

¶ **25.** Amounts that are actually paid to an attendant for salary or remuneration as well as the employer's portion of Employment Insurance premiums and Canada or Quebec Pension Plan contributions will qualify as medical expenses under paragraph 118.2(2)(b), (b.1) or (c). Imputed salary or remuneration will not qualify since no actual payment is made.

¶ **26.** As noted in ¶ 6 above, when an individual includes, as a qualifying medical expense, remuneration for an **attendant** or the cost of **nursing home** care for a patient (as described in paragraphs 118.2(2)(b), (c), (d), and (e)—¶ 23 above and ¶s 27 to 30 below) neither that individual nor any other person may claim the disability tax credit or its transfer referred to in ¶s 4 and 7 to 9 above for that patient. As an exception to this rule, the disability tax credit can still be claimed if remuneration for an attendant is claimed under paragraph 118.2(2)(b.1), which is subject to a dollar limit (see ¶ 24 above). Also, when attendant care expenses are included as qualifying medical expenses under any provision in subsection 118.2(2) for purposes of the medical expense tax credit, the same expenses cannot be deducted under section 64 (see ¶s 68 to 71 below) when determining the patient's income.

Care in a self-contained domestic establishment

¶ **27.** An individual may include, as a qualifying medical expense, remuneration paid for a **full-time** attendant for a patient in a self-contained domestic establishment in which the patient lives, provided that the following conditions in paragraph 118.2(2)(c) are met:

(a) A medical practitioner (see ¶ 3 above) certifies that, because of mental or physical infirmity, the patient is, and will likely continue for a prolonged period of indefinite duration to be, dependent on others for personal needs and care and, as a result, requires a full-time attendant.

(b) At the time the remuneration is paid, the attendant is neither the individual's spouse nor under 18 years of age.

(c) Receipts for payments to the attendant must be issued by the payee and include, if the payee is an individual, his or her social insurance number.

The medical practitioner may certify the patient's mental or physical infirmity in either a letter or by completing Form T2201, *Disability Tax Credit Certificate.*

Care due to lack of normal mental capacity

¶ **28.** Amounts that the individual has paid for the cost of **full-time** care in a nursing home (see ¶ 30 below) for a patient qualify under paragraph 118.2(2)(d) as medical expenses if the patient, due to lack of normal mental capacity, is and apparently will continue to be dependent upon others for personal needs and care. Receipts from the nursing home and a certificate from a medical practitioner (see ¶ 3 above) are required to support a claim for an expenditure of this nature (see ¶ 67 below). The medical practitioner may certify the patient's mental capacity in either a letter or by completing Form T2201, *Disability Tax Credit Certificate.*

Care in an institution and care and training in a school

¶ **29.** The costs paid for the care, or the care and training, of a patient at a school, institution or other place will qualify under paragraph 118.2(2)(e) as a medical expense when an appropriately qualified person has certified that patient to be a person who, by reason of a physical or mental impairment, requires the equipment, facilities or personnel specially provided by that place. The certification of the individual's need for specialized equipment, facilities or personnel must either be specific as to the school, institution or other place which provides the specialized equipment, facilities or personnel or be specific as to the type of equipment, facilities or personnel which is needed to provide care and training of a person with that type of physical or mental impairment. For example, if a medical doctor certifies that a person requires supervision by reason of Alzheimer's disease and the institution has personnel specifically trained to supervise people suffering from that disease, the fees paid to the institution would qualify as a medical expense; however, if the person requires general supervision for which no specific training is available, then the fees paid would not qualify as a medical expense. For purposes of paragraph 118.2(2)(e), "other place" may include an out-patient clinic or a nursing home (see ¶ 30 below). An "appropriately qualified person" includes a medical practitioner (see ¶ 3 above) as well as any other person who has been given the required certification powers under provincial or federal law. A patient (for example, a dependant) suffering from a behavioral problem arising out of a mental or physical impairment or suffering from a learning disability, including dyslexia, who attends a school that specializes in the care and training of persons who have the same type of problem or disability is considered to qualify under paragraph 118.2(2)*(e)*, and the expenses paid for the patient are qualifying medical expenses even though some part of the expenses could be construed as being tuition fees (see Rannelli v. MNR, 91 DTC 816, [1991] 2 CTC 2040, (TCC)). The school need not limit its enrolment to persons who require specialized care and training. A patient suffering from an addiction to drugs or alcohol can also qualify under paragraph 118.2(2)*(e)*. Consequently, when all the conditions of that paragraph, as discussed above, are met, the expenses paid for the care of the patient in a detoxification clinic qualify as medical expenses. Fees paid for a stop-smoking course or program are not considered to qualify as medical expenses under paragraph 118.2(2)*(e)* unless, in an exceptional case, such a course or program is part of a patient's medical treatment that is required because of a serious health deterioration problem and that is both prescribed and monitored by a medical practitioner.

¶ 30.   There is no requirement that a nursing home or a detoxification clinic be a public or licensed private hospital. The name of the institution will not affect the determination of whether it qualifies as a nursing home. While the care need not be full time, it must be stressed that equipment, facilities or personnel specially provided by the nursing home (or other place described in ¶ 29 above) must be specifically tailored for the care of persons suffering from the physical or mental impairment in question and that the other conditions set out in ¶ 29 above must be met, for the fees to qualify as medical expenses under paragraph 118.2(2)*(e)*.

Transportation and travel expenses of patient and accompanying individual

¶ 31.   An amount paid for transportation of a patient by ambulance to or from a public or licensed private hospital qualifies as a medical expense under paragraph 118.2(2)*(f)*.

¶ 32.   Under paragraph 118.2(2)*(g)*, an amount paid to a person engaged in the business of providing transportation services can qualify as a medical expense to the extent that the amount relates to transporting a patient between the locality where the patient lives and a location which is at least 40 kilometres away in order for the patient to receive medical services at that location. In order for such an amount to qualify under paragraph 118.2(2)*(g)*, it must be paid under the following circumstances:

(a)   Substantially equivalent medical services are unavailable within the patient's locality.

(b)   The patient takes a reasonably direct travel route.

(c)   It is reasonable, in the circumstances, for the patient to travel to that place for the medical services.

If a person engaged in the business of providing transportation services is not readily available, subsection 118.2(4) instead allows as a qualifying medical expense under paragraph 118.2(2)*(g)* reasonable expenses incurred for operating a vehicle (see ¶ 34 below) for transporting the patient provided that the above rules and circumstances are otherwise fulfilled. For this purpose, the term "vehicle" means any type of conveyance used to transport the patient by land, water or air including a vehicle owned by the individual claiming the expenses, the patient or a family member.

Whether a person engaged in the business of providing transportation services is "readily available" is a question of fact. However, where there is some urgency to a situation such that immediate or at least prompt transportation to the location providing the requisite medical service is necessary, and a person engaged in the business of providing transportation services cannot be located quickly or the service is available only after an unacceptable delay of time, it is accepted that the service is not "readily available." If the urgency does not exist or a person engaged in the business of providing transportation services is "readily available," an individual may not claim expenses under paragraph 118.2(2)*(g)* in respect of a vehicle owned by the individual, the patient or a family member.

If expenses for transporting the patient are being claimed under paragraph 118.2(2)*(g)* as described above, that provision also allows the same kind of expenses for transporting one individual who accompanies the patient provided that a medical practitioner (see ¶ 3 above) has certified that the patient is incapable of travelling without an attendant.

¶ 33.   Paragraph 118.2(2)*(h)* refers to travel expenses other than those referred to in paragraph 118.2(2)*(g)* (discussed in ¶ 32 above). Paragraph 118.2(2)*(h)* provides that an individual may include, as qualifying medical expenses, such other reasonable travel expenses (see ¶ 34 below) for a patient to obtain medical services if the patient travels to a place that is at least 80 kilometres away from the locality where he or she dwells to get the medical services, and provided the following other conditions are met:

(a)   Substantially equivalent medical services are unavailable within the patient's locality.

(b)   The patient takes a reasonably direct travel route.

(c)   It is reasonable, in the circumstances, for the patient to travel to that place for the medical services.

The individual claiming travel expenses for the patient under paragraph 118.2(2)*(h)* may also claim, under the same paragraph, the same kinds of travel expenses (that is, reasonable travel expenses other than those referred to in paragraph 118.2(2)*(g)*) for one individual to accompany the patient as long as the patient has been certified by a medical practitioner as being incapable of travelling without an attendant.

¶ 34. "Other reasonable travel expenses" in ¶ 33 refers to amounts expended for meals and accommodation for a patient and, where applicable, for an accompanying individual, while transportation costs in ¶ 32 include vehicle expenses. Vehicle expenses include both operating and ownership expenses. Operating expenses consist of fuel, oil, tires, licence fees, insurance, maintenance and repairs. On the other hand, ownership expenses refer to depreciation, provincial tax and finance charges. An individual has the option for 1999 and subsequent years of choosing either a **detailed** or **simplified method** of determining reasonable meal and vehicle expenses.

If the **detailed method** is chosen, receipts and records for those expenses incurred during the 12-month period chosen for medical expenses must be kept. The claim for vehicle expenses is calculated as follows: the kilometres travelled to obtain medical services divided by the total kilometres driven during that 12-month period, multiplied by the total vehicle expenses incurred during that period. Consequently, it is also necessary for a taxpayer to keep a record of the total number of kilometres driven during that 12-month period, as well as those travelled to obtain medical services. For example, if an individual drove 10,000 kilometres during the 12-month period chosen, 1,000 kilometres of which arose while travelling to obtain medical services, then 10% of the total vehicle expenses for that period may be claimed as a qualifying medical expense.

Alternatively, if the **simplified method** of calculating meal and vehicle expenses is used, supporting receipts are not required. In the case of meals, a flat rate per meal is claimed. For vehicle expenses, a record must be kept for the 12-month period chosen of the number of kilometres travelled to obtain medical services. The amount that may be claimed for vehicle expenses is determined by multiplying the number of kilometres travelled to obtain medical services by a flat per kilometre rate. Information on the current rate per meal and per kilometre is available from our Tax Information Phone Service (T.I.P.S.) at **1-800-267-6999**, or on our Web page at: **www.ccra.gc.ca/travelcosts**

As for accommodation expenses, they must be substantiated by receipts (see ¶ 67). Furthermore, the onus is on the individual claiming the medical expense tax credit to demonstrate that the amounts qualify as medical expenses. For example, the individual may have to show that an amount paid for lodging is necessary as a result of the distance travelled, or the condition of the patient for travel, and not solely for the sake of convenience.

Artificial limbs, aids and other devices and equipment

¶ 35. By virtue of paragraph 118.2(2)*(i)*, qualifying medical expenses include the purchase price or, where applicable, the rental charge or other expenses (for example, maintenance, repairs, supplies) related to the following:

(a) an artificial limb;

(b) an iron lung (see ¶ 36 below);

(c) a rocking bed for poliomyelitis victims;

(d) a wheelchair (see ¶ 37 below);

(e) crutches;

(f) a spinal brace (see ¶ 38 below);

(g) a brace for a limb (see ¶ 39 below);

(h) an ileostomy or a colostomy pad (see ¶ 40 below);

(i) a truss for a hernia;

(j) an artificial eye;

(k) a laryngeal speaking aid (see ¶ 41 below);

(l) an aid to hearing (see ¶s 42 and 43 below); and

(m) an artificial kidney machine (see ¶s 44 to 48 below).

¶ 36. The term "iron lung" (see ¶ 35 above) includes a portable chest respirator that performs the same function in substantially the same manner as the appliance ordinarily thought of as an iron lung. That term is also accepted as including a machine for supplying air (possibly in combination with oxygen or medication) to the lungs under pressure, for therapeutic use.

¶ 37. The term "wheelchair" (see ¶ 35 above) is not restricted to the conventional arm-powered or battery-powered wheelchairs but also includes scooters and wheel-mounted geriatric chairs.

¶ 38. The term "spinal brace" (see ¶ 35 above) includes a spinal support.

¶ 39. A "brace for a limb" (see ¶ 35 above) does not necessarily have to be something of a rigid nature, although at least one of the functions of the brace must be to impart some degree of rigidity to the limb which is being braced. Accordingly, that phrase is considered to include woven or elasticized stockings where these are of a kind that are carefully fitted to measurement or are made to measure. When a brace for a limb is necessarily built into a boot or shoe in order to permit a person to walk, the brace will be considered to include the boot or shoe.

¶ 40. "Ileostomy or colostomy pads" (see ¶ 35 above) include pouches and adhesives used for the same purpose. (See ¶ 49 below for products required because of incontinence.)

IT-519R2 (Consolidated)

¶ **41.** A "laryngeal speaking aid" (see ¶ 35 above) is an electronic type of instrument that assists a person to produce speech sounds. An artificial larynx or a similar type of speaking aid for a person who would otherwise be deprived of an effective speech capability may also qualify for purposes of the medical expense tax credit. Qualifying expenses related to these devices may include the cost of batteries, maintenance, repairs or replacements.

¶ **42.** In addition to the more usual hearing aid devices, an "aid to hearing" (see ¶ 35 above) includes:

(a) a device that produces extra-loud audible signals such as a bell, horn or buzzer;

(b) a device to permit the volume adjustment of telephone equipment above normal levels;

(c) a bone-conduction telephone receiver; and

(d) a "Cochlear" implant, which consists of a series of electrodes surgically placed in the sensory organ of a person who is profoundly deaf and for whom traditional hearing aids are not feasible.

¶ **43.** When a hearing aid is incorporated into the frame of a pair of eyeglasses, both the hearing aid and the eyeglass frame qualify under paragraph 118.2(2)*(i)*. The phrase "an aid to hearing" includes the batteries that are required for that purpose, and repairs. A listening device that is acquired to alleviate a hearing impairment by eliminating or reducing sound distortions for the purpose of listening to television programs, movies, concerts, business conferences or similar events, is also considered to qualify as an "aid to hearing" under paragraph 118.2(2)*(i)*.

¶ **44.** Qualifying medical expenses relating to an "artificial kidney machine" (see ¶ 35 above) include the costs of alterations to a home or the upgrading of the home's existing electrical or plumbing systems, provided that these costs are reasonable in the circumstances and are necessary for the installation of the machine. In addition to providing receipts to substantiate such costs, the individual should provide a certificate from the official at the hospital who authorized the installation of the artificial kidney machine stating that such expenditures were required to enable the hospital to install the equipment (see ¶ 67 below).

¶ **45.** When an artificial kidney machine is installed at the individual's residence, the following costs, to the extent that they are reasonable, may also be included as qualifying medical expenses under paragraph 118.2(2)*(i)*:

(a) repairs, maintenance, and supplies for the machine;

(b) water and electricity to operate the machine (see ¶ 46 below); and

(c) the costs of housing the machine (that is, municipal taxes, insurance, heating, lighting, and maintenance and repairs, but not including capital cost allowance or mortgage interest) or the portion of rent that is attributable to the room where the machine is kept (see ¶s 46 and 47 below).

¶ **46.** If it is not possible to determine the actual amount of one of the costs of operating or housing an artificial kidney machine, as referred to in ¶ 45(b) or (c) above, it will be necessary to allocate a reasonable proportion of the total amount of that particular cost for the whole home (for example, the total insurance or the total heating cost) in order to determine the portion that qualifies as a medical expense pertaining to the artificial kidney machine. However, no portion of a cost should be claimed if that cost cannot reasonably be considered to relate to the operation or housing of the machine. Thus, for example, a repair expense for another part of the home would not qualify. When an actual cost of operating or housing the machine can be determined, this actual cost must be used when determining the total which qualifies as a medical expense (for example, the amount of municipal taxes attributable to an addition to the home that houses the machine when such an amount can be ascertained from the property tax bill, or the cost of lighting repairs in the room where the machine is kept).

¶ **47.** In determining the portion of rent that qualifies as a medical expense for purposes of ¶ 45(c) above, the amount must be based on actual rent paid and not on the rental value of the room in a home that is owned.

¶ **48.** Necessary and unavoidable costs of transporting supplies for the artificial kidney machine may be included as qualifying medical expenses when the supplier will not deliver, as long as all of these conditions are met:

(a) The distance from the patient's residence to the nearest supply depot is at least 40 kilometres.

(b) The means of transportation is the least expensive available that is suitable in the circumstances.

(c) The quantity of supplies obtained is adequate for a reasonable period of time.

Products required because of incontinence

¶ **49.** The cost of diapers, disposable briefs, catheters, catheter trays, tubing or other products required by the patient because of incontinence caused by illness, injury or affliction are qualified medical expenses under paragraph 118.2(2)*(i.1)*.

Eyeglasses

¶ **50.** The cost of eyeglasses that qualifies as a medical expense under paragraph 118.2(2)*(j)* includes the cost of both the frames and lenses. The phrase "other devices for the treatment or correction of a defect of vision" in paragraph

118.2(2)*(j)* includes contact lenses. In all cases, a medical practitioner (see ¶ 3 above) (oculist or ophthalmologist) or an optometrist must prescribe the item. Laser eye surgery qualifies under paragraph 118.2(2)*(a)*.

Oxygen tents

¶ 51. The cost of buying or renting an oxygen tent or other equipment necessary to administer oxygen for medical purposes (including, for example, oxygen face masks, tanks containing oxygen under pressure) qualifies as a medical expense under paragraph 118.2(2)*(k)*.

Guide and hearing-ear dogs and other animals

¶ 52. The costs of acquiring and the care and maintenance (including food and veterinary care) of an animal qualify as medical expenses under paragraph 118.2(2)*(l)* as long as certain conditions are met. These costs must be paid on behalf of a patient who is blind, profoundly deaf or who has a severe and prolonged impairment (see ¶ 1 above) that markedly restricts the use of the patient's arms or legs. The animal must be specially trained to assist a patient in coping with his or her impairment and the animal must be provided by a person or organization one of whose main purposes is the training of animals for this purpose. The patient's reasonable travel expenses incurred for the purpose of attendance at, and reasonable board and lodging expenses incurred for the purpose of **full-time** attendance at, a school, institution or other facility that trains persons with the same kind of impairment in the handling of such animals will also qualify as medical expenses.

Bone marrow or organ transplants

¶ 53. Reasonable expenses, including legal fees and insurance premiums, paid to locate a compatible bone marrow or organ transplant donor for a patient and to arrange for the transplant, qualify as medical expenses under paragraph 118.2(2)*(l.1)*. Reasonable travel, board and lodging expenses (other than expenses described in paragraphs 118.2(2)*(g)* and *(h)* as discussed in ¶s 32 to 34 above) paid for the donor and the patient, in respect of the transplant, also qualify under paragraph 118.2(2)*(l.1)* as do any such expenses in respect of the transplant that are paid for one other person who accompanies the donor and for one other person who accompanies the patient. For these purposes, the option of using either the **detailed** or **simplified method** (described in ¶ 34) is available for calculating meal and vehicle expenses for 1999 and subsequent years.

Renovations and alterations to a dwelling

¶ 54. In the case of an individual who lacks normal physical development or who has a severe and prolonged

(see ¶ 1(a) above) mobility impairment, reasonable expenses relating to renovations or alterations to the individual's dwelling can be claimed as medical expenses under paragraph 118.2(2)*(l.2)*. To qualify, these expenses must be paid to enable the individual to gain access to the dwelling or be mobile or functional within it. Included in this category are reasonable expenses for necessary structural changes, such as:

(a) the purchase and installation of outdoor or indoor ramps where stairways impede the individual's mobility;

(b) the enlarging of halls and doorways to allow the individual access to the various rooms of the dwelling; and

(c) the lowering of kitchen or bathroom cabinets to allow the individual access to them.

The types of structural changes that could be eligible are not restricted to the above examples. "Reasonable expenses" pertaining to a particular structural change may include payments to an architect or a contractor.

Rehabilitative therapy

¶ 55. Amounts paid for reasonable expenses relating to rehabilitative therapy, including training in lip reading or sign language, incurred to adjust for the patient's hearing or speech loss qualify as medical expenses under paragraph 118.2(2)*(l.3)*.

Note: Bill C-28 was given First reading in the House of Commons on December 10, 1997. Bill C-28, if enacted as proposed, will add paragraphs 118.2(2)(l.4) to (l.7) for the 1997 and later taxation years. The paragraphs will add the following as medical expenses:

- *fees for sign language interpretation services paid on behalf of a patient with a speech or hearing impairment to a person who is in the business of providing such services—paragraph 118.2(2)(l.4);*

- *reasonable moving expenses (within the meaning of subsection 62(3), but not including any expense deducted under section 62 for any taxation year) in respect of a patient who lacks normal physical development or who has a severe and prolonged mobility impairment to move to housing that is more accessible by the patient or in which the patient is more mobile or functional, to a maximum of $2,000—paragraph 118.2(2)(l.5);*

- *reasonable expenses relating to the alterations to the driveway of the principal place of residence of a patient who has a severe and prolonged mobility impairment if the alterations are made to facilitate the patient's access to a bus—paragraph 118.2(2)(l.6); and*

- *the lesser of $5,000 and 20% of the amount by which*

  (a) the amount paid for the acquisition of a van exceeds

IT-519R2 (Consolidated)

(b) any amount referred to in (a) that is included because of paragraph 118.2(2)(m) in calculating a patient's medical expense tax credit for any taxation year

where the van, at the time of its acquisition or within 6 months thereafter, has been adapted for the transportation of the patient who requires the use of a wheelchair—paragraph 118.2(2)(l.7).

If the paragraphs are enacted as proposed, it is the Department's view that fees paid to an oralist interpreter would qualify under paragraph 118.2(2)(*l*.4) and reasonable expenses relating to the alteration of a driveway may be claimed under paragraph 118.2(2)(*l*.6) even if the patient uses a van for transportation rather than a bus.

Devices and equipment prescribed by regulation

¶ **56.** By virtue of paragraph 118.2(2)*(m)*, the list of devices and equipment which qualify for purposes of the medical expense tax credit has been expanded by means of the *Income Tax Regulations* (the Regulations), which are amended from time to time by order-in-council. An amount paid for a device or equipment cannot be claimed under paragraph 118.2(2)*(m)* unless the device or equipment:

(a) is prescribed by the Regulations;

(b) is for the patient's use as prescribed by a medical practitioner (see ¶ 3 above);

(c) is not described in any of the other paragraphs of subsection 118.2(2); and

(d) meets such conditions as are applicable to its use or as to the reason for its acquisition.

Part LVII (section 5700) of the Regulations, *Medical Devices and Equipment*, contains the list of prescribed devices and equipment for purposes of paragraph 118.2(2)*(m)* and sets out the conditions as to their use and reasons for their acquisition (see the Appendix to this bulletin).

Note: Bill C-28 was given First reading in the House of Commons on December 10, 1997. Bill C-28, if enacted as proposed, will amend, for 1997 and later taxation years, subsection 118.2(2)(m) to permit the setting of a maximum amount on the claim for a device or of equipment that qualify as a medical expense by virtue of Part LVII of the Regulations.

Preventive, diagnostic and other treatments

¶ **57.** Paragraph 118.2(2)*(n)* permits as a qualifying medical expense amounts paid for drugs, medicaments or other preparations or substances (other than those described in paragraph 118.2(2)*(k)*—see ¶ 61(a) below) that are prescribed by a medical practitioner or dentist and recorded by a pharmacist where the items that have been prescribed are to be used in the diagnosis, treatment or prevention of a

disease, disorder, abnormal physical state, or symptoms thereof, or in restoring, correcting or modifying an organic function.

A person suffering from diabetes is allowed to include as a qualifying medical expense the cost of insulin, under paragraph 118.2(2)*(k)*, or substitutes, under paragraph 118.2(2)*(n)*, as prescribed by a medical practitioner (see ¶ 3 above). When such a person has to take sugar-content tests using test-tapes or test tablets and a medical practitioner has prescribed this diagnostic procedure, the tapes or tablets qualify as devices or equipment under paragraph 118.2(2)*(m)* and Part LVII of the Regulations (see ¶ 56 above and item *(s)* of the Appendix). On the other hand, the cost of various kinds of scales, which diabetics frequently use for weighing themselves or their food, is not a qualifying medical expense.

¶ **58.** If a medical practitioner prescribes treatments in, for example, a hot tub or a whirlpool bath the cost of the treatment qualifies as a medical expense under paragraph 118.2(2)*(a)* if paid, for example to a public or licensed private hospital. However, if a hot tub or whirlpool bath is purchased, the cost does not qualify as a medical expense since it is not prescribed in Part LVII of the Regulations.

¶ **59.** Qualifying medical expenses under paragraph 118.2(2)*(o)* include the cost of laboratory, radiological and other diagnostic procedures or services, with necessary interpretations, for maintaining health, preventing disease or assisting in the diagnosis or treatment of any injury, illness or disability of the patient, as prescribed by a medical practitioner or dentist. An example of such expenses, which may not be covered by provincial health insurance, are the following expenses involved with artificial insemination:

(a) the in-vitro fertilization procedure;

(b) daily ultrasound and blood tests once the in-vitro procedure has begun;

(c) anaesthetist fees; and

(d) cycle monitoring fees.

¶ **60.** Payments made for acupuncture treatments are a qualified medical expense under paragraph 118.2(2)*(a)* only when the payments are made to a medical practitioner.

Drugs, medicaments and other preparations or substances

¶ **61.** For purposes of calculating the medical expense tax credit, there are two categories of drugs, medicaments or other preparations or substances (other than those included in the account of a medical practitioner (see ¶ 3 above) or hospital) the cost of which may qualify as medical expenses:

(a) the substances, mentioned in paragraph 118.2(2)*(k)* (insulin, oxygen and, for pernicious anaemia, liver extract and vitamin B12) which, for purposes of this paragraph, a medical practitioner must have prescribed, but which a pharmacy or any other type of store may sell without a written prescription; and

(b) the drugs (and other items), referred to in paragraph 118.2(2)*(n)*, which a medical practitioner or dentist must have prescribed, and which must be purchased from a pharmacist who has recorded the prescription in a prescription record.

¶ 62. Birth control pills which a medical practitioner has prescribed are considered to qualify under paragraph 118.2(2)*(n)* if a pharmacist has recorded the prescription.

Dentures

¶ 63. Frequently, a denture is prescribed and fitted by a dentist, even though it may have been made in a dental laboratory, and the payment qualifies under paragraph 118.2(2)*(a)* as an amount paid to a dentist. However, paragraph 118.2(2)*(p)* specifically provides that amounts paid for the patient to a dental mechanic or denturologist, who is authorized under the laws of a province to make or repair dentures or to otherwise carry on the business of a dental mechanic or denturologist, also qualify as medical expenses.

Premiums to private health services plan

¶ 64. Paragraph 118.2(2)*(q)* provides that any premium that the individual or his or her legal representative has paid to a private health services plan for that individual, the individual's spouse or a member of the household with whom the individual is connected by blood relationship, marriage or adoption (see the current version of IT-339, *Meaning of "Private Health Services Plan"*) may be included as a qualifying medical expense. However, premiums paid to provincial medical or hospitalization insurance plans cannot be included.

Medical expenses paid or deemed to have been paid

¶ 65. As indicated in ¶ 11 above, a medical expense cannot qualify for the medical expense tax credit unless it has actually been paid or is deemed to have been paid by the individual claiming the credit or by the individual's legal representative. Any reference throughout this bulletin to the "cost" of a particular medical expense is subject to this rule. Medical expenses paid or provided for by an employer but included in the employee's income are deemed by paragraph 118.2(3)*(a)* to have been paid by the employee and, therefore, can be claimed by the employee (assuming they otherwise qualify) for purposes of the medical expense tax credit under subsection 118.2(1). The employee is deemed to have paid such expenses at the time the employer paid or provided them.

Expenses That Do Not Qualify

¶ 66. Paragraph 118.2(3)*(b)* provides that qualifying medical expenses of an individual do not include any expense for which the individual, the patient or the legal representative of either such person has been, or is entitled to be, reimbursed except to the extent that the amount is required to be included in income and cannot be deducted in computing taxable income. Thus, for example, an amount reimbursed under a public or private medical, dental or hospitalization plan would not qualify for purposes of the medical expense tax credit. However, an amount reimbursed by an employer that is included in the employee's income would qualify provided the employee is not able to deduct the amount in computing taxable income.

Receipts

¶ 67. As indicated in ¶ 34, if the **simplified method** of calculating meal and vehicle expenses is chosen, receipts are not required for those amounts. However, all other expenses claimed as qualifying medical expenses must be supported by proper receipts. A receipt should indicate the purpose of the payment, the date of the payment, the patient for whom the payment was made and, if applicable, the medical practitioner (see ¶ 3 above), dentist, pharmacist, nurse, or optometrist who prescribed the purchase or gave the service. A cancelled cheque is not acceptable as a substitute for a proper receipt. If required forms, receipts or other supporting documents are not filed with the income tax return, such as when the return is electronically filed (E-filed), they should nevertheless be retained and readily available as they may subsequently be requested as proof of the claims being made or in support of the information being reported.

Note: Bill C-28 was given First reading in the House of Commons on December 10, 1997. Bill C-28, if enacted as proposed, will add audiologists, after February 18, 1997, and medical doctors, for taxation years that end after November 1991, to the list of individuals who can prescribe the purchase of or provide services that qualify as medical expenses.

Attendant Care Expense Deduction in Computing Income

¶ 68. Section 64 provides for a deduction, **in computing income** for the year, for attendant care expenses. "Attendant care" is considered to refer to the personal care that is necessary to enable the person with a disability to carry out one of the activities described in ¶ 69(b) below. "Personal care" is more than, for example, providing transportation to work. The deduction under section 64 can be claimed only by a person with a disability who qualifies for the disability tax credit for the year in accordance with the rules discussed in ¶s 4 and 5 above. Even if the disability tax credit is claimed under the rules discussed in ¶s 7 to 9 above by a supporting person or spouse rather than by the person with a disability, only the person with a disability may claim the section 64 attendant care expense deduction. Under section 64, the person with a disability can deduct the amounts he or she has paid in the year for attendant care provided in Canada to enable him or her to earn any of the types of income mentioned in ¶ 69(b) below. An amount cannot qualify for the deduction if it was paid to an attendant who, at the time of the payment, was under 18 years of age or was the spouse of the person with a disability. The total amount of the deduction allowed for the year is subject to the limitation described in ¶ 69 below. An attendant care payment cannot be deducted under section 64 when calculating income if it was claimed (for any taxation year) by the person with a disability or another person as a medical expense for purposes of the section 118.2 medical expense tax credit (see ¶ 26 above). A person with a disability claiming a section 64 attendant care expense deduction should prepare prescribed Form T929, *Attendant Care Expenses*, and retain it for examination. Note, however, that a section 64 attendant care expense deduction may not be made in a return filed under subsections 70(2), 104(23) or 150(4) (these are separate returns filed for a deceased taxpayer in respect of certain types of income) or with a return filed under paragraph 128(2)*(e)* (this is a return filed for a bankrupt person). Attendant care payments claimed under section 64 must be supported by receipts (see ¶ 67 above). Each receipt must be issued by the payee and, if the payee is an individual, must show his or her social insurance number.

¶ **69.** The attendant care expense deduction that a taxpayer who is a person with a disability may claim for the year under section 64 is limited to the least of these three amounts:

(a) the total of all attendant care payments that meet all the rules described in ¶ 68 above, paid by the taxpayer in the year to enable him or her to be employed, carry on a business (alone or as an active partner in a partnership), take a training course for which a training allowance was received under the *National Training Act* or carry on research or similar work for which a grant was received, less any reimbursements or other assistance (other than prescribed assistance or amounts included in income and not deductible in calculating taxable income) which the taxpayer received or is entitled to receive for the amounts paid;

(b) two thirds of the total of all amounts included in calculating the taxpayer's income from employment (including stock options and other employment benefits), carrying on a business (alone or as an active partner in a partnership), taxable training allowances (received under the *National Training Act*),

scholarships, fellowships, bursaries, prizes and research grants; and

(c) $5,000.

The *National Training Act* was repealed effective January 1, 1998.

Note: Bill C-28 was given First reading in the House of Commons on December 10, 1997. Bill C-28, if enacted as proposed, will amend section 64, for 1997 and later years, to eliminate the $5,000 limitation in (c) above.

¶ **70.** Section 64.1 provides a special rule for an individual who is absent from Canada for all or part of the year but is nevertheless a resident of Canada for tax purposes while absent (either because of residential ties with Canada or because he or she is deemed to be resident in Canada under section 250). For the period of the individual's absence, section 64.1 removes two of the requirements that would otherwise have to be met under section 64 for purposes of the attendant care expense deduction:

(a) the requirement that the attendant care be provided "in Canada"; and

(b) the requirement that the attendant payee's social insurance number appear on the receipt (this requirement remains, of course, if the attendant is a resident of Canada for tax purposes).

Therefore, if the individual is a person with a disability, he or she can claim the attendant care expense deduction for attendant care provided **outside** Canada, assuming all the other requirements of section 64 (as discussed in ¶s 68 and 69 above) are met.

¶ **71.** When determining income from employment in ¶ 69(b) above, subsection 6(16) should be kept in mind. Because of that subsection, benefits or allowances (not in excess of a reasonable amount) provided by an employer that relate to either of the following are not to be included when determining employment income:

(a) transportation to and from work, including parking near the work location, for an employee who is blind or who has a severe and prolonged mobility impairment that markedly restricts the employee's ability to perform a basic activity of daily living (for example, walking); or

(b) an attendant to assist the employee in performing the duties assigned if the employee has a severe and prolonged mental or physical impairment which markedly restricts his or her ability to perform a basic activity of daily living.

An amount will be accepted as reasonable if it is designed to cover the related costs incurred by an employee.

The rules contained in subsection 118.4(1) regarding the meanings of "prolonged," "markedly restricted" and "basic activity of daily living," which are described in ¶ 1 above, apply for purposes of the rules in subsection 6(16).

Proposed Refundable Medical Expense Tax Credit

¶ 72. *Note: Bill C-28 was given First reading in the House of Commons on December 10, 1997. Bill C-28, if enacted as proposed, will add section 122.51 to provide for a refundable medical expense tax credit for the 1997 and later years. This refundable credit will be available to an individual (other than a trust) and who has a net income of at least $2,500 in the year from all offices and employments as well as from businesses. Net income from offices and employment is the excess of salary, wages, employment related benefits and other remuneration including gratuities over the allowable deductions. The allowable deductions include registered pension plan contributions, annual union and professional dues, and other expenses as described in the guide Employment Expenses. Amounts received under wage-loss replacement plans are not included in this calculation of net income. The credit will be limited to the lesser of*

- *$500, and*
- *25% of the portion of expenses allowed for the purpose of claiming the medical expense tax credit.*

The credit will be reduced by 5% of the

- *total net incomes for the year of the individual who claims the credit and the individual's spouse in excess of*
- *$16,069.*

To qualify for the credit, an individual must be at least 18 years old before the end of the year and be resident in Canada throughout the year (or, where the individual dies in the year, throughout the portion of the year before the individual's death).

This credit can be claimed in respect of the same expenses as the medical expense tax credit and in addition to it.

The credit cannot be claimed on an income tax return filed under subsection 70(2) or 150(4) or paragraph 104(23)(d) or 128(2)(e).

Please see the example after ¶ 73.

Proposed Medical Expense Tax Credit for Training

¶ 73. *Note: As part of the Federal Budget of February 24, 1998, a Notice of Ways and Means Motion to Amend the Income Tax Act was tabled in the House of Commons. One of the proposed amendments would expand the list of expenses eligible for the medical expense tax credit for the 1998 and later taxation years to permit reasonable expenses for the training of an individual in connection with the care to be provided to a person who*

(a) is related to the individual,

(b) has a mental or physical infirmity, and

(c) is a member of the individual's household or is dependent on the individual for support.

Example of Refundable Medical Expense Tax Credit

Terry and Willy are married. Terry's net income from employment is $5,000 in example A and $10,000 in example B while Willy's business income is $15,000. Their combined medical expenses are $2,400 which Willy claims in example A and Terry claims in example B.

	Example A	Example B	Line
Willy's Income	$15,000	$15,000	(1)
Terry's Income	5,000	10,000	(2)
Family Income	$20,000	$25,000	(3)
Subtract	16,069	16,069	
Family Income in excess of $16,069	$3,931	$8,931	(4)
Medical Expenses	$2,400	$2,400	(5)
3% of the individual's income	450	300	(6)
Expenses allowed for medical expenses tax credit	$1,950	$2,100	(7)
Lesser of $500 and 25% of line 7	$487.50	$500.00	(8)
Subtract: 5% of line 4	196.55	446.55	(9)
Refundable Medical Expense Tax Credit	$290.95	$53.45	

Appendix
(see ¶ 56 above)

Part LVII of the Regulations
Prescribed Medical Devices and Equipment

For the purpose of paragraph 118.2(2)*(m)*, the following devices and equipment are prescribed under section 5700 of the *Income Tax Regulations* and, therefore, an amount paid for any such device or equipment that is prescribed for the patient's use by a medical practitioner (see ¶ 3 above) qualifies as a medical expense, subject to the conditions described below:

(a) A wig made to order for an individual who has suffered abnormal hair loss because of disease, medical treatment or accident.

(b) A needle or syringe designed to be used for the purpose of giving an injection.

(c) A device or equipment, including a replacement part, designed exclusively for use by an individual suffering from a severe chronic respiratory ailment or a severe chronic immune system disregulation, but not including an air conditioner, humidifier, dehumidifier, heat pump or heat or air exchanger.

(c.1) An air or water filter or purifier for use by an individual who is suffering from a severe chronic respiratory ailment or a severe chronic immune system disregulation to cope with or overcome that ailment or disregulation.

(c.2) An electric or sealed combustion furnace acquired to replace a furnace that is neither an electric furnace nor a sealed combustion furnace, when the replacement is necessary solely because of an individual's severe chronic respiratory ailment or a severe chronic immune system disregulation.

(d) A device or equipment designed to pace or monitor the heart of an individual who suffers from heart disease.

(e) An orthopaedic shoe or boot or an insert for a shoe or boot made to order for an individual, in accordance with a prescription, to overcome a physical disability.

(f) A power-operated guided chair installation, for an individual, that is designed to be used solely in a stairway.

(g) A mechanical device or equipment designed to assist an individual to enter or leave a bathtub or shower or to get on or off a toilet.

(h) A hospital bed, including any attachments to the bed prescribed for the patient.

(i) A device designed to assist an individual in walking, when the individual has a mobility impairment.

(j) An external breast prosthesis that is required because of a mastectomy.

(k) A teletypewriter or similar device, including a telephone ringing indicator, that enables an individual who is deaf or mute to make and receive telephone calls. (This will include visual ringing indicators such as flashing lights, as well as acoustic couplers, and teletypewriters providing either printed or visual display screen communications. The individual may be required to provide a certificate from a medical practitioner to establish that such equipment was obtained to mitigate the effects of a hearing or speech disability. Additional equipment and accessories provided to others in order to make telephone communications possible between those other persons and the individual who is deaf or mute may also qualify.)

(l) An optical scanner or similar device designed to enable an individual who is blind to read print.

(m) A power-operated lift or transportation equipment designed exclusively for use by, or for, an individual who is disabled to allow the individual access to different areas of a building or to assist the individual in gaining access to a vehicle or to place the individual's wheelchair in or on a vehicle.

(n) A device designed exclusively to enable an individual who has a mobility impairment to operate a vehicle.

(o) A device or equipment, including a synthetic speech system, braille printer and large print-on-screen device, designed exclusively for use by an individual who is blind, in operating a computer.

(p) An electronic speech synthesizer that enables an individual who is mute to communicate by using a portable keyboard.

(q) A device to decode special television signals to permit the script of a program to be visually displayed.

(q.1) A visual or vibratory signalling device, including a visual fire alarm indicator, for an individual who has a hearing impairment.

(r) A device designed to be attached to an infant diagnosed as being prone to sudden infant death syndrome in order to sound an alarm if the infant ceases to breathe.

(s) An infusion pump, including disposable peripherals, used to treat diabetes or a device designed to enable an individual with diabetes to measure blood sugar level.

IT-519R2 (Consolidated)

(t)   An electronic or computerized environmental control system designed exclusively for the use of an individual who has a severe and prolonged mobility restriction.

(u)   An extremity pump or elastic support hose designed exclusively to relieve swelling caused by chronic lymphedema.

(v)   An inductive coupling osteogenesis stimulator for treating non-union of fractures or aiding in bone fusion.

Note: The Minister of Finance published Explanatory Notes Relating to Income Tax *in connection with Bill C-28. The Explanatory Notes describe that, for 1997 and later taxation years, the list of expenses contained in Part LVII of the Regulations will be expanded to include the cost (up to $1,000) of an air conditioner prescribed by a medical practitioner as being necessary to assist an individual in coping with the individual's severe chronic ailment, disease or disorder.*

IT-519R2 (Consolidated)

Bulletin Revisions

¶ 1 of IT-519R2 dated April 6, 1998 was moved to the *Contents* section at the beginning of the consolidated bulletin.

¶s 2 to 74 of IT-519R2 have been renumbered as ¶s 1 to 73, respectively. Cross-referencing has been revised to reflect the above re-numbering. No other changes were made to those paragraphs of the bulletin, except as noted below.

¶ 11(b) (formerly ¶ 12(b)) has been changed to indicate that receipts are no longer required for certain meal and vehicle expenses as indicated in revised ¶ 34. [February 28, 2001]

¶ 34 (formerly ¶ 35) has been revised to reflect information concerning an alternative method of calculating certain

medical expenses which was announced by the CCRA in the News Release dated December 14, 1999 entitled *Two options now available for calculating travel expenses for moving and medical expenses, and for northern residents deductions* and the corresponding Fact Sheet dated December 1999 entitled *Travel expenses for northern residents deductions, medical and moving expenses.* [February 28, 2001]

¶ 53 (formerly ¶ 54) has been revised to include the two options for calculating meal and vehicle expenses referred to in revised ¶ 34. [February 28, 2001]

¶ 67 (formerly ¶ 68) has been modified as a consequence of the revision to ¶ 34 to indicate that receipts are not required if the simplified method is used. [February 28, 2001]

Think recycling!

Printed in Canada

NO.:   **IT-529**   DATE: February 20, 1998

SUBJECT: INCOME TAX ACT
           Flexible Employee Benefit Programs

REFERENCE: Paragraph 6(1)(*a*) (also subsections 6(3), 6(4), 15(1); the definitions of "salary deferral arrangement,"
            "retirement compensation arrangement," "group term life insurance policy" and "private health services plan"
            in subsection 248(1); paragraphs 6(1)(*f*), 6(1)(*g*), 6(1)(*h*), 6(1)(*i*), subparagraphs 56(1)(*a*)(i) and (iii))

Interpretation bulletins (ITs) provide Revenue Canada's technical interpretations of income tax law. Due to their technical nature, ITs are used primarily by departmental staff, tax specialists, and other individuals who have an interest in tax matters. For those readers who prefer a less technical explanation of the law, the Department offers other publications, such as tax guides and pamphlets.

While the ITs do not have the force of law, they can generally be relied upon as reflecting the Department's interpretation of the law to be applied on a consistent basis by departmental staff. In cases where an IT has not yet been revised to reflect legislative changes, readers should refer to the amended legislation and its effective date. Similarly, court decisions subsequent to the date of the IT should be considered when determining the relevancy of the comments in the IT.

An interpretation described in an IT applies as of the date the IT is published, unless otherwise specified. When there is a change in a previous interpretation and the change is beneficial to taxpayers, it is usually effective for all future assessments and reassessments. If the change is not favourable to taxpayers, it will normally be effective for the current and subsequent taxation years or for transactions entered into after the date of the IT.

A change in a departmental interpretation may also be announced in the *Income Tax Technical News*.

If you have any comments regarding matters discussed in this IT, please send them to:

Director, Business and Publications Division
Income Tax Rulings Directorate
Policy and Legislation Branch
Revenue Canada
Ottawa ON K1A 0L5

Interpretation bulletins can be found on the Revenue Canada Internet site at: www.rc.gc.ca

Contents

Application

This bulletin discusses various tax consequences that may apply to flexible employee benefit programs.

Summary

This bulletin discusses the tax treatment of flexible employee benefit programs. These programs, which are sometimes referred to as "flexible benefit plans" or "cafeteria plans," are not defined in the *Income Tax Act* but can generally be described as a program of delivering company benefits where the employees are able to select the type and level of coverage from among a menu of available benefits. These programs are generally implemented to permit employees to build an individualized benefit program that most closely meets their coverage needs and budget requirements and to change their benefit elections over time as their life circumstances change.

Income tax considerations are an integral part of the design of flexible employee benefit programs and an important aspect of the selection of benefits by the employee. The design of such programs would, for example, include the choices to be made by the employee between taxable and non-taxable benefits, the conditions attached to these choices and the method of purchasing the chosen benefits. Although the Act does not contain provisions that specifically apply to these programs as a whole, the design of the program must satisfy certain conditions in order to avoid adverse tax consequences for all benefits provided under the program. These conditions are discussed in the bulletin. Provided these conditions are satisfied, the various benefit components under the program are subject to specific provisions of the Act in the same manner as if they were offered on their own outside of the program. Therefore, depending on the particular benefit and how it is paid for, it may result in a taxable benefit to the employee or a non-taxable benefit.

The bulletin discusses these tax consequences in the context of a typical flexible employee benefit program, hereafter referred to in this bulletin as a **Flex Program**. However, since the purpose of such a program is to provide flexibility in the delivery of employee benefits, a particular flexible employee benefit program will not necessarily contain all the features described below, or it may be structured in a different format.

Discussion and Interpretation

Description of a Flex Program

¶ 1. Under one type of Flex Program, the employer allocates a notional amount (commonly called flex credits) to each eligible employee. Prior to the beginning of the plan year (see ¶ 4 below), the employees participating in the Flex Program allocate their flex credits to various benefits available under the Flex Program, some of which may result in a taxable benefit to the employee and some of which may not. The employer is then obligated under the terms of the Flex Program to provide the employee with the benefits so chosen. Typically, each employee will get a booklet from the employer explaining the details of the particular Flex Program and a worksheet to assist the employee in making choices. However, regardless of the manner in which the details of the Flex Program are communicated to the employees, the tax consequences described in this bulletin will not necessarily apply unless all eligible employees are informed of their rights under the Flex Program.

¶ 2. Another type of Flex Program permits employees to select a level of coverage for each benefit available under the Flex Program, ranging from no coverage to a premium level of coverage. A standard level of coverage is established by the employer for each benefit and a dollar value is assigned to each level of coverage above or below that standard. When an employee selects a level of coverage other than the standard established by the employer, the assigned dollar value for that level of coverage is either credited or debited to the employee's account. If an employee's selection of benefits results in a net deficiency, the additional amount

required to pay for the benefits so chosen is withheld from the employee's salary. Since the tax treatment of each benefit is determined separately, a Flex Program will normally permit an employee to choose which benefit is considered to have been purchased by that employee through the use of payroll deductions. The terms and conditions of the Flex Program will determine whether any surplus can be paid to the employee as additional remuneration.

¶ 3. The allocation of flex credits annually by an employer to its employees represents the employer's contribution to benefits. In the second type of Flex Program, all benefits which are not attributable to a payment by the employee are considered to be funded by means of a contribution by the employer. A Flex Program may also allow an employee to increase the level of benefits provided under the Flex Program or acquire additional benefits by means of payroll deductions or by forfeiting some other right, such as vacation leave. In the same manner as for other payroll deductions, an employee who uses payroll deductions to purchase benefit coverage is taxed on the gross amount of salary received and not the net amount of the employee's pay cheque.

Plan Year

¶ 4. A plan year is normally defined as a twelve-month period. However, in the case of the first year of a Flex Program, the plan year may be greater or less than twelve months so that the plan year will coincide with the year end designated in the Flex Program documentation. The plan year does not have to be the calendar year and does not have to be the same for all employees. For example, in order to ease the administration of a Flex Program, employers may require employees to make their annual selections prior to the month of their birth, in which case the selection would be valid for the plan year commencing with the month of their birth. In any event, the plan year should be explained in the Flex Program documentation available to all employees.

Tax Considerations in the Design of the Overall Flex Program

¶ 5. The concept of the plan year is important to a Flex Program if the program offers employees the choice of both taxable and non-taxable benefits. As a general rule, where one part of a Flex Program could be regarded as a health and welfare trust or similar arrangement and another part could be regarded as a salary deferral arrangement, a retirement compensation arrangement, an employee benefit plan or an employee trust, the statutory rules applicable to salary deferral arrangements, retirement compensation arrangements, employee benefit plans or employee trusts, as the case may be, will apply to the entire Flex Program. However, if the employees covered by the Flex Program are required to choose which benefits will be provided under the Flex Program and how the benefit will be funded prior to the beginning of the plan year (and, subject to ¶ 6 below, the selection is irrevocable), the Flex Program can be segregated

IT-529

into multiple parts and the taxation of the benefits offered under the Flex Program is not altered by the fact that it is provided under the umbrella of a Flex Program. While the discussion in this bulletin concerning the tax consequences of benefits provided through a Flex Program centres on whether or not a Flex Program is an employee benefit plan, the comments are applicable with the appropriate modifications, if the Flex Program is a salary deferral arrangement, a retirement compensation arrangement or an employee trust.

¶ 6.   Two exceptions to the requirement (described in ¶ 5 above) that the employee's selection of benefits be irrevocable for the duration of the plan year is the occurrence of a "life event" or a change in employment status. The term "life event" should be defined in the plan documentation if the Flex Program permits changes in the selection of benefits when such a life event occurs. A life event is typically defined to include events such as the birth or death of a dependant, a change in marital status or the loss of insurance coverage under a spouse's employer's plan. A change in an employee's place of residence which does not result in a change to the amount of flex credits allocated to the employee would not be an acceptable life event which would warrant a change to the employee's allocation of flex credits during the plan year. In certain circumstances, a Flex Program may permit an employee to make certain changes to accommodate a life event (i.e. decrease coverage in one area to provide additional coverage in another) without adversely affecting the tax treatment of benefits under the plan. This is only possible if the changes do not require a withdrawal of funds credited to that benefit option contrary to the terms of that policy or plan and the Flex Program's definition of life event is confined to events such as those described in this paragraph. Also, if the amount of flex credits allocated to an employee is altered by reason of a change in employment status (for example, a part-time employee may be entitled to less credits than a full-time employee), an employee may be required to make changes to the original selection of benefits to accommodate the increase or decrease in the amount of flex credits available. However, any such change cannot be made on a retroactive basis. For example, if an employee had selected a certain type of insurance coverage, any change to that coverage would only be effective from the date of that life event or change in employment status.

¶ 7.   Assuming that flex credits have no redemptive value and that nothing of value is forfeited by the employee to acquire such credits, flex credits are considered to be notional amounts in that a flex credit has no intrinsic value by itself. A Flex Program will not be considered to be an employee benefit plan if, under the terms of such a Flex Program, flex credits are notional and the employee is required to make an irrevocable selection of benefits to be provided with the flex credits before the beginning of the plan year (subject to the exceptions described in ¶ 6 above). The allocation of flex credits by an employer does not, in and by itself, normally give rise to a taxable benefit in the hands of the employee.

¶ 8.   If, after the beginning of the plan year, a Flex Program permits:

- an exchange of unallocated or newly allocated flex credits for cash (although the actual payment of cash, according to the employee's allocation of flex credits prior to the beginning of the year, may occur after the beginning of the plan year);

- a transfer of credits between benefit options; or

- a selection of benefits (other than a reselection of benefits described in ¶ 6 above or an initial selection by an employee who enters the Flex Program at any time during the plan year);

the employee will be considered to have constructively received employment income equal to the value of the allocated credits (unless the entire Flex Program is considered to be an employee benefit plan). This would result in the inclusion in the employee's income of the value of all benefits received out of the Flex Program even though some of the benefits would not have been so included if offered separately from the Flex Program. This is because a flex credit which can be saved and negotiated for cash at any time has a redemption value and is thus not considered to be a notional credit as described in the previous paragraph.

¶ 9.   While a portion of the flex credits allocated to an employee may be computed as a percentage of the employee's salary, the conversion of any portion of the employee's salary to flex credits will result in an income inclusion of the amount of salary so converted. Thus, if an employee forgoes an amount to which the employee is or will become entitled, such as a negotiated salary increase, vacation or bonus, the amount of remuneration forgone is included in income in the year in which the amount is converted to flex credits as explained in ¶ 22 below. On the other hand, when a contract of employment is renegotiated upon the expiry of a former employment contract to incorporate a decrease in the level of salary or wages to be paid to an employee over the term of the new contract and the new contract also provides for additional flex credits, the additional credits will not be required to be included in the employee's income as part of salary and wages. However, if an employment contract is renegotiated during the term of an employment contract to decrease salary and increase the allocation of flex credits, the additional credits so allocated will be included in the employee's income as salary. Also, the benefits acquired by means of the additional credits will be considered to have been provided through employee contributions.

Setting up a Flex Program

¶ 10.   All employees covered by the Flex Program must have legal access to the rights granted under the Flex Program. Generally, this means that the employees must have access to some document which outlines their entitlement under the Flex Program. As with health and welfare trusts, there is no formal registration procedure for a Flex Program and no requirement that the plan documents be submitted to Revenue Canada for approval prior to the implementation of the Flex Program. However, the advice of the local tax services office may be requested where there is any doubt as to whether the Flex Program could be considered to be an employee benefit plan, an employee trust, a retirement compensation arrangement or a salary deferral arrangement. Alternatively, an advance income tax ruling as described in the current version of Information Circular 70-6 may be requested. Full particulars of the Flex Program including a copy of all pertinent documents should accompany such a request.

Statutory Considerations

¶ 11.   In determining the tax consequences arising from a Flex Program, consideration must be given to whether the Flex Program falls within the definition in subsection 248(1) of a salary deferral arrangement, a retirement compensation arrangement, an employee benefit plan or an employee trust. Flex Programs are usually designed so that both taxable and non-taxable benefits can be provided through the same plan. However, failure to be excluded from the statutory rules governing an employee benefit plan, an employee trust, a retirement compensation arrangement or a salary deferral arrangement can result in adverse tax consequences where the intention is to provide non-taxable benefits to employees. The following is a brief explanation of these terms.

¶ 12.   Employee trust – This term is described in the current version of IT-502, *Employee Benefit Plans and Employee Trusts.*

Employee benefit plan – This term is described in the current version of IT-502. Virtually, all funded plans other than salary deferral arrangements and retirement compensation arrangements which provide employees with benefits (including payments by an employer under an insurance policy) could meet the definition of an employee benefit plan unless the plan fits within one of the statutory exclusions. The statutory exclusions which are common to Flex Programs are:

- private health services plans, including health care spending accounts as described in ¶ 14 below;
- group term life insurance policies; and
- group sickness or accident insurance plans.

Retirement compensation arrangement – This term is described in the *Retirement Compensation Guide*. The rules relating to retirement compensation arrangements are intended to prevent tax deferral on unregistered retirement savings plans that escape the salary deferral arrangement rules. Note that a Flex Program which permits an employee to allocate flex credits to a benefit option which is not expected to be provided until after a substantial change in services rendered by that employee (such as retirement), or the portion of the plan which relates to that choice, may be considered to be a retirement compensation arrangement.

Salary deferral arrangement – Briefly stated, a salary deferral arrangement is:

- a plan or arrangement (whether it is funded or not);
- between an employer and an employee who has a right to receive an amount under the arrangement; and
- one of the main purposes for the creation or existence of the right is to postpone the tax payable under the Act by the employee in respect of salary or wages for services rendered in the year or a preceding year.

It is important to note that the "right" mentioned in the definition includes any right that is subject to one or more conditions, unless there is a substantial risk that any one of those conditions will not be satisfied. As a result, the salary deferral arrangement rules cannot be avoided by making the employee's right to the funds subject to some condition which will likely be met anyway. For example, it is not relevant for the purpose of determining whether a Flex Program is a salary deferral arrangement whether or not the receipt of the deferred amount is contingent on:

- the employee remaining an employee for a minimum period of time;
- the employee not being dismissed for the cause or commission of a crime;
- the employee refraining from transferring or encumbering the employee's interest in the deferred amount; or
- the employee abstaining from competition or being available for consultation after retirement or termination of employment.

When all or part of a Flex Program meets the general definition of a salary deferral arrangement, the list of statutory exceptions must be examined. Those which are the most relevant to a Flex Program include:

- disability or income maintenance insurance plans;
- group sickness or accident insurance plans; and
- certain employer education and training plans.

Amounts deferred under a salary deferral arrangement are included in the employee's income in the year they are earned under paragraph 6(1)(*a*) by virtue of subsection 6(11). A deferred amount means an amount at the end of the year that the employee has a right to receive in the future.

Taxation of Individual Benefits

¶ 13.   Except for certain statutory exclusions, employees are taxed on the value of any benefit received or enjoyed because of their employment under paragraph 6(1)(*a*). The tax consequences relating to some of the various benefits which may be provided under a Flex Program are described below.

Health Care

¶ 14.   One option that may be found in a Flex Program is a secondary health care plan (sometimes called a "health care spending account" or a variation of that term). These plans are comprised of individual employee accounts that provide for the reimbursement of eligible medical and dental expenses as defined by the terms of the plan. A health care spending account may qualify as a private health services plan provided that it meets the criteria set out in the current version of IT-339, *Meaning of "Private Health Services Plan."* If it does not qualify as a private health services plan, the amount of any benefit received out of the plan will be taxable to the employee.

¶ 15.   While some health care spending accounts are only funded to the extent of claims actually made against the account (on a pay-as-you-go basis), an employer is obligated to reimburse employees for eligible costs incurred by the employee to the extent of the balance of credits remaining in the account. A credit in a health care spending account should not be confused with a flex credit. Since a health care spending account is designed to be a plan of insurance, the amount of credits in a health care spending account (as determined by the amount of flex credits applied to this benefit option as a result of an employee allocation) sets a ceiling on the amount that can be claimed under the plan of insurance. For this purpose, there may be a distinction under the terms of the Flex Program between when the amount is allocated by the employee (prior to the beginning of the plan year) and when that allocation is applied to the health care spending account so that the employee is able to claim expenses to the extent of the limit of health care insurance in force at the time the expense is incurred. Under some Flex Programs, the full amount of the allocation is applied to the health care spending account at the beginning of the year and under others, a proportionate amount is applied each pay period. As with other plans of insurance, an employee has no inherent right to the balance of credits applied to a health care spending account.

¶ 16.   One of the criteria for a private health services plan is that the plan must be a plan of insurance. In order for a health care spending account to qualify as a plan of insurance, there must be a reasonable element of risk. For example, if the plan or arrangement is such that there is little risk that the employee will not eventually be reimbursed for the full amount allocated to that employee annually, then the arrangement is not a plan of insurance and therefore, not a private health services plan. While a plan which includes a carry forward provision undoubtedly reduces the risk of loss to the employee, a plan which permits the carry forward of either the unused allocation or eligible medical expenses (but not both) up to a maximum of 12 months will not be disqualified as a private health services plan solely by reason of the carry forward provision in the plan.

¶ 17.   If an employee is able to withdraw or transfer an amount from a health care spending account (other than as a premium payable in respect of another private health services plan), the health care spending account will not be a private health services plan and all amounts received out of the account, including reimbursements of eligible medical expenses, will be included in the employee's income under paragraph 6(1)(*a*). For example, if an employee is able to

reallocate an amount which was previously applied to a health care spending account to another benefit option such as a group RRSP, the health care spending account will not qualify as a private health services plan because a contribution to an RRSP is not a qualified medical expense. However, the ability to reallocate credits to another private health services plan, such as a vision or dental plan will not affect the status of the health care spending account as a private health services plan.

¶ 18.   There will generally be no advantage to an employee in using payroll deductions to contribute to a health care spending account. Since the flex credits allocated to a health care spending account will typically set a limit on the maximum reimbursement payable under the plan and the employee is taxed on the gross amount of salary paid, including the amount withheld through payroll deductions to pay for benefits under the plan, a contribution of salary may result in the taxation of more income than the employee actually receives. While any contributions that are made by the employee to a health care spending account that is a private health services plan would qualify as a medical expense for the purpose of the medical expense tax credit, the medical expense tax credit may not fully offset the income inclusion and there is no mechanism by which an amount forfeited at the end of the year can be refunded to the employee.

Survivor Benefits

¶ 19.   Flex Programs may offer choices relating to benefits to be provided to an employee's spouse or dependants after the death of the employee. The taxation of the benefit depends, to a large part, on how the benefit is funded by the employer.

¶ 20.   Life insurance coverage for employees or former employees is taxable under subsection 6(4) if it is provided through a group term life insurance policy as defined in subsection 248(1). Since the definition of group term life insurance policy excludes a policy which provides coverage for anyone other than an employee or former employee, an employee's taxable benefit derived from an employer's contribution to a policy which provides coverage for a dependant or spouse is included in income under paragraph 6(1)(*a*). Thus, the benefit from a policy which covers both employees and their dependants is determined under paragraph 6(1)(*a*) but the benefit from a policy which otherwise qualifies as a group term life insurance policy which only covers employees and former employees is determined under subsection 6(4). The value of the benefit derived from life insurance coverage under a policy which is not a group term life insurance policy would ordinarily be the amount of premium paid by the employer in respect of such coverage. The rules for calculating the benefit to be included in income under subsection 6(4) are found in section 2700 of the *Income Tax Regulations*. Further information can be found in the Departmental publication T4130, *Employers' Guide to Payroll Deductions – Taxable Benefits.*

A payment of an uninsured amount by the employer to the surviving spouse or named beneficiary of an employee upon his or her death will ordinarily qualify as a death benefit as defined in subsection 248(1) even though the employee has allocated flex credits to ensure the payment of such amount. However, if the employer creates a fund, including an administrative services contract with an insurer, to provide for death benefits, the fund will likely be an employee benefit plan with the effect that the employer would not be entitled to a deduction for contributions to the fund until such time as the death benefit was paid. Since an administrative services contract with an insurer is not a policy of insurance, it is not a group term life insurance policy as defined in subsection 248(1).

Short-Term and Long-Term Disability Insurance

¶ 21.   Even though an employee may choose to use payroll deductions to acquire coverage under a disability insurance plan, any resulting benefit received out of the plan will be taxable under paragraph 6(1)(*f*) unless the entire plan is funded solely with payroll deductions. Since flex credits allocated to an employee represent the employer's obligation to provide benefits to the employee, a disability insurance plan will be considered a plan to which the employer has contributed when flex credits have been allocated by any employee to ensure coverage under that particular plan. If, however, an employer has two separate disability plans (one which is funded solely by the employees through payroll deductions and one that is funded by the employer) and the funds of the two plans are not cross-subsidized, benefits received out of the plan funded solely through payroll deductions will not be included in the employee's income and benefits derived from coverage acquired by means of an allocation of flex credits will be taxable to the extent provided by paragraph 6(1)(*f*). Employee-pay-all plans are discussed in the current version of IT-428, *Wage Loss Replacement Plans*.

Vacation Selling

¶ 22.   Where an employee forgoes vacation or other amounts to which the employee is otherwise entitled in order to obtain or increase the amount of flex credits available under the plan, the value of the amount forgone is included in the employee's income at the time the additional flex credits are so credited. For example, assuming that an employee is entitled to a $52,000 annual salary for working 49 weeks with 3 weeks of vacation leave, the employee will be taxed on $53,000, if the employee works an extra week in exchange for additional flex credits (whether or not the flex credits are applied to benefits which would have been taxable if funded by the employer's contribution). In this situation, the employee is considered to have paid for the additional benefits by way of additional services rendered. It is the trading of vacation entitlement by the employee that triggers a taxable event and not the use of the flex credits obtained. Even when the conversion of taxable employee

entitlements to flex credits is required under the terms of the Flex Program, an employee has a degree of control over the amount of salary or other entitlement forfeited by means of the choices available to the employee under the Flex Program.

Vacation Buying

¶ 23.   A Flex Program may include an option under which an employee may obtain additional vacation leave. If the additional leave is funded by way of payroll deductions, the leave is effectively unpaid leave. If it is funded through an allocation of flex credits, the terms of the plan will typically require the employee to use the purchased vacation within the plan year in which it is acquired. When a Flex Program permits vacation leave so purchased to be carried forward to a subsequent plan year, the arrangement may be considered to be a salary deferral arrangement. While vacation pay trusts are excluded from the definition of a salary deferral arrangement, an arrangement to pay for the vacation leave so purchased out of a trust would not qualify as a vacation pay trust as defined in paragraph 149(1)(*y*). The criteria for establishing a vacation pay trust are explained in the current version of IT-389, *Vacation Pay Trusts Established under Collective Agreements*.

Cash Payments, Transfers, Diversions

¶ 24.   When an employee chooses, prior to the beginning of the plan year, to receive a portion of his or her flex credits in cash or deposited into an RRSP, the amount so received or deposited is included in the employee's income as salary or wages when it is received or deposited. If the amount is placed into a registered plan such as an RRSP or an RESP, the terms of which require contributions to be made by the planholder or subscriber, the employee is considered to have received the amount of flex credits allocated to that benefit option and must include that amount in income. In the case of a contribution to an RRSP, the employee is entitled to a deduction to the extent permitted under the rules governing RRSPs. Other benefits available under a Flex Program will be included in an employee's income in the same way as they would if offered separately from the plan. For example, if one of the choices is a low interest loan from the employer, an interest benefit is calculated under section 80.4 and is included in income under subsection 6(9) of the Act.

Tax Implications to the Employer

¶ 25.   For greater certainty, no deduction is available to the employer solely by reason of the allocation of flex credits to an employee. In the case of benefits which are provided through a plan of insurance, subsections 18(9) and (9.01) impose restrictions on the amount that can be deducted in the year by the employer on account of contributions to fund a plan of insurance or on account of premiums paid in respect of a policy.

Benefits to Shareholders

¶ 26.   The comments in this bulletin apply only in respect of a Flex Program which is offered to a group of employees or former employees, as opposed to a group of shareholders and persons related to shareholders. When flex credits are allocated to an individual who is both an employee and a shareholder (or an employee who is related to a shareholder of the employer), the Flex Program benefits will be presumed to have been conferred upon the shareholder by reason of his or her shareholdings unless the participant is a member of a group of employees who participate in the Flex Program and the rules applicable to that Flex Program, including the allocation of flex credits and availability of benefit choices, are applied equally to all participants in the Flex Program. For comments concerning benefits provided to shareholders in their capacity as shareholders, see the current version of IT-432, *Benefits Conferred on Shareholders*. If a benefit is granted "qua shareholder," it will be taxed under subsection 15(1) without regard to any of the exceptions found in section 6. In addition, the corporation will not be entitled to a deduction for any amount paid on behalf of the shareholder.

Benefits to Former Employees

¶ 27.   Where a former employee is required to include an amount in income on account of the benefits described in this bulletin, the authority for taxing the benefit is found in either subsection 6(3) or paragraph 56(1)(*a*) depending on whether the obligation to provide the benefit arose immediately prior to, during or immediately after the former period of employment or at some other time. However, the amount to be included in the former employee's income will not exceed the amount that would otherwise have been included in income had the former employee been an employee at the time the benefit was conferred. For example, no amount will be included in the former employee's income on account of coverage under a private health services plan.

Related Bulletins and Guides

¶ 28.   The current versions of the following bulletins and guides contain information which may be applicable to a Flex Program.

Bulletins

IT-85	*Health and Welfare Trusts for Employees*
IT-227	*Group Term Life Insurance Premiums*
IT-247	*Employer's Contribution to Pensioners' Premiums Under Provincial Medical and Hospital Services Plans*
IT-339	*Meaning of "Private Health Services Plan"*
IT-389	*Vacation Pay Trusts Established under Collective Agreements*
IT-428	*Wage Loss Replacement Plans*
IT-432	*Benefits Conferred on Shareholders*
IT-470	*Employees' Fringe Benefits*
IT-502	*Employee Benefit Plans and Employee Trusts*
IT-508	*Death Benefits*
IT-519	*Medical Expense and Disability Tax Credits and Attendant Care Expense Deduction*

Guides

T4130	*Employers' Guide to Payroll Deductions – Taxable Benefits*

CANADA REVENUE AGENCY

INTERPRETATION BULLETIN

No: IT-85R2

DATE: July 31, 1986

SUBJECT: INCOME TAX ACT
Health and Welfare Trusts for Employees

REFERENCE: Paragraph 6(1)(a) and section 104 (also subsections 6(4), 12.2(3), (4), and (7), paragraphs 6(1)(f), 56(1)(d), and (d.1), 60(a), 110(8)(a) and subparagraphs 148(9)(c)(vii) and (ix); also section 19 of the Income Tax Application Rules, 1971 (ITAR)).

This bulletin replaces and cancels IT-85R, dated January 20, 1975. Proposals contained in the Notice of Ways and Means Motion of June 11, 1986 are not considered in this release.

1. The general thrust of paragraph 6(1)(a) is to include in employment income the value of all benefits received or enjoyed in respect of an employee's employment. However, there are a number of specific exceptions many of which can be described as benefits relating to the health and welfare of the employee. In some cases, the scope of the excepted benefits and applicable tax treatment are well established by other provisions of the Act, (, registered pension funds or plans, deferred profit sharing plans, supplementary unemployment benefit plans, the standby charge for the use of an employer's automobile, employee benefit plans and employee trusts). The treatment to be accorded to the other exceptions can be less clear, particularly when the benefits form part of an omnibus health and welfare program administered by an employer. The purpose of this bulletin is to describe the tax treatment accorded to an employee health and welfare benefit program that is administered by an employer through a trust arrangement and that is restricted to
(a) a group sickness or accident insurance plan (see 2 below),
(b) a private health services plan,
(c) a group term life insurance policy, or
(d) any combination of (a) to (c).

2. Paragraph 6(1)(f) sets out the treatment of periodic receipts related to loss of income from employment under three types of insurance plans to which the employer had made a contribution. These types of plans are sickness or accident, disability and income maintenance (also known as salary continuation). In the absence of any statutory definition, the Department generally accepts that an employer's contribution to any of the three types of
plans will be a contribution to a "group sickness or accident insurance plan" as described in subparagraph 6(1)(a)(i), provided that the particular plan is a "group" plan and an insured plan. This is based on the assumption that a "disability" resulting in loss of employment income would almost invariably arise from sickness or an accident and that an "income maintenance" payment would likely arise from loss of employment income due to sickness or an accident if not lay off (the latter reason justifying an exception under subparagraph 6(1)(a)(i) as a supplementary unemployment benefit plan). There

may be situations where these assumptions will prove invalid but, subject to this caveat, 1(a) above may also be read as a "group disability insurance plan" or "a group income maintenance insurance plan that is not a supplementary unemployment benefit plan".

Employee Benefit Plans and Employee Trusts

3. Employee benefit plans are broadly defined in subsection 248(1) and can encompass health and welfare arrangements. However, funds or plans described in 1(a) to (d) above are specifically excluded in the definition and are thus accorded the tax treatment outlined in this bulletin. Health and welfare arrangements not described in 1(a) to (d) above (for example, those not based on insurance) may be employee benefit plans or, less likely, employee trusts subject to the tax consequences outlined in IT-502.

4. Where part of a single plan could be regarded as a plan described in 1(a) to (d) above and another part as an employee benefit plan or an employee trust, the combined plan will be given employee benefit plan or employee trust treatment in respect of the timing and amounts of both the employer's expense deductions and the employees' receipt of benefits under the plan. However, if contributions, income and disbursements of the part of the plan that is described in 1(a) to (d) above are separately identified and accounted for, the tax treatment outlined in this bulletin will apply to that part of the plan.

Meaning of Health and Welfare Trust

5. Health and welfare benefits for employees are sometimes provided through a trust arrangement under which the trustees (usually with equal representation from the employer or employers' group and the employees or their union) receive the contributions from the employer(s), and in some cases from employees, to provide such health and welfare benefits as have been agreed to between the employer and the employees. If the benefit programs adopted are limited to those described in 1(a) to (d) above and the arrangement meets the conditions set out in 6 and 7 below, the trust arrangement is referred to in this bulletin as a health and welfare trust.

6. To qualify for treatment, as a health and welfare trust the funds of the trust cannot revert to the employer or be used for any purpose other than providing health and welfare benefits for which the contributions are made. In addition, the employer's contributions to the fund must not exceed the amounts required to provide these benefits. Furthermore, the payments by the employer cannot be made on a voluntary or gratuitous basis. They must be enforceable by the trustees should the employer decide not to make the payments required. The type of trust arrangement envisaged is one where the trustee or trustees act independently of the employer as opposed to the type of arrangement initiated unilaterally by an employer who has control over the use of the funds whether or not there are employee contributions. Employer control over the use of funds of a trust (with or without an external trustee) would occur where the beneficiaries of the trust have no claim against the trustees or the fund except by or through the employer.

7. With the exception of a private health services plan, two or more employees must be covered by the plan. Where a partnership seeks to provide health and welfare benefits for both the employees and the partners by means

of a trust, two distinctly separate health and welfare trusts (one for the partners and one for the employees) must be set up to ensure that the funds of each are at all times identifiable and that cross-subsidization between the plans will not occur. The exception in subparagraph 6(1)(a)(i) will of course not apply to such a trust established for the partners.

Tax Implications to Employer

8. To the extent that they are reasonable and laid out to earn income from business or property, contributions to a health and welfare trust by an employer using the accrual method of computing income are deductible in the taxation year in which the legal obligation to make the contributions arose.

Tax Implications to Employee

9. An employee does not receive or enjoy a benefit at the time the employer makes a contribution to a health and welfare trust. However, subject to 10 below, the tax consequences to an employee arising from benefits provided under such a trust are as follows:

Group Sickness or Accident Insurance Plans

(a) Where a group sickness or accident insurance plan provides that benefits are to be paid by the insurer directly to the employee, the premium paid by the trustees to the insurer for the employee's coverage will not result in a benefit to be included in the employee's income.

(b) Where this type of group sickness or accident insurance plan existed before June 19, 1971 and the requirements of section 19 of the ITAR are met (see IT-54, "Wage Loss Replacement Plans"), the benefits paid to an employee by the trustees or the insurers under such a plan in consequence of an event happening before 1974 will not result in a taxable benefit to the employee. Where these requirements are not met and in all cases of payments for events happening after 1973, the wage loss replacement benefits will be taxable under
paragraph 6(1)(f) (see IT-428, "Wage Loss Replacement Plans").

Private Health Services Plans (defined in paragraph 110(8)(a))

(c) Payment by the trustees of all or part of the employee's premium to a private health services plan does not give rise to a taxable benefit to the employee. Benefits provided to an employee under a private health services plan are also not subject to tax.

Group Term Life Insurance

(d) Payment by the trustees of a premium under a group term life insurance policy will not result in a taxable benefit to the employee unless the aggregate amount of the employee's coverage under one or more group term life insurance policies exceeds $25,000. (See IT-227R, "Group Term Life Insurance Premiums"). The provisions of section 12.2 which tax accrued amounts under a life insurance policy do not apply since a group term life insurance policy will be an exempt policy for that purpose.

(e) Where a group term life insurance policy provides for a lump sum payment to the employee's estate or a named beneficiary, the receipt of the payment directly from the insurer is not included in the recipient's income.

(f) Certain group term life insurance policies provide beneficiaries hereunder
with an option to take periodic payments in lieu of the lump sum payment and others provide only for periodic payments to beneficiaries. Prior to the introduction of the accrual rules in section 12.2 for 1983 and subsequent taxation years, benefits thus paid by the insurer to a beneficiary, whether as
a result of exercising the option or by the terms of the policy, were annuity payments that were income of the recipient (paragraph 56(1)(d)) who deducted the capital element of the annuity payment (paragraph 60(a) of the Act and Part III of the Regulations).

(g) For the 1983 and subsequent taxation years, paragraphs 56(1)(d) and 60(a) continue to apply to a beneficiary who is a holder and annuitant under an annuity contract if subsection 12.2(3) does not apply because of the exceptions in paragraphs 12.2(3)(c) to (e) or the application of subsection 12.2(7). Generally speaking, this will occur where the annuity contract
(i) is a prescribed annuity contract as defined in Regulation 304,
(ii) was acquired before December 2, 1982 under which annuity payments commenced before December 2, 1982,
(iii) is an annuity contract that was received as proceeds of a group term life insurance policy which was itself neither an annuity contract nor acquired after December 1, 1982, or
(iv) was acquired before December 2, 1982, can never be surrendered and in respect of which the terms and conditions have not been changed and is not the
subject of an election under subsection 12.2(4).

(h) For annuity contracts other than ones described in (g) above, the annuitant is required by subsection 12.2(3) for the 1983 and subsequent taxation years to include in income accrued amounts on every "third anniversary" of the contract. In addition, in any year that does not include a
"third anniversary", paragraph 56(1)(d.1) requires the inclusion of amounts in
respect of annuity payments received during the year under the contract. As an
alternative to the application of subsection 12.2(3) and paragraph 56(1)(d.1),
the annuitant may elect under subsection 12.2(4) (before annuity payments commence) to include accrued amounts on an annual basis. In each instance, the
issuer will provide the annuitant with a T-5 information slip indicating the amount of income to be reported in respect of the annuity contract.

Shared Contributions

10. In 9 above the trustees are assumed to be receiving contributions only from the employer to pay for the cost of benefits under the trust plan. However, the trustees may also receive employee contributions to pay a part of
the cost of the benefits being provided under the plan. If the plan does not

clearly establish that the trustee must use the employee contributions to pay all or some part of the cost of a specific benefit, then it will be assumed that each benefit under the plan is being paid out of both the employer and the employee contributions. If the benefit in question is otherwise taxable to
the employee, then in these circumstances a part of it is non-taxable. The non-taxable part is that proportion of the benefit received by the employee for the year that the total of employee contributions received by the trustees in the year is of the aggregate of the employer and employee contributions received by the trustees in the year. The above treatment will not apply if the benefit must be reported as income according to paragraph 6(1)(f) (see 9(b) above). However, the employee's contributions to plans referred to in 9(b) may be deductible for tax purposes from benefits received from the plan. See IT-428 for details.

Taxation of Trust

11. A trust which invests some of the contributions received and earns investment income, or has incidental income (other than contributions from employers and employees which are not included in computing income of the trust), is subject to tax under section 104 on the amount of such "trust income" remaining after the deductions discussed in 12 below. Where gross income (meaning, the aggregate of its income from all sources) exceeds $500 in the taxation year (and in certain other circumstances indicated on the form), the trustee is required to file form T3 (Trust Information Return and Income Tax Return).

12. In computing trust income subject to tax, the trust is allowed to deduct, to the extent of the gross trust income, the following expenses, premiums and benefits it paid, and in the following order:
(a) expenses incurred in earning the investment or other income of the trust,
(b) expenses related to the normal operation of the trust including those incurred in the collection of and accounting for contributions to the trust, in reviewing and acquiring insurance plans and other benefits and for fees paid to a management company to administer the trust, except to the extent that such expenses are expressly not allowed under the Act,
(c) premiums and benefits payable out of trust income of the current year pursuant to paragraph 104(6)(b). Benefits that are paid out of proceeds of an insurance policy do not qualify. Other benefits paid are normally regarded as having been paid first out of trust income of the year. However, premiums and benefits that would not otherwise be taxable in the hands of the employee by virtue of paragraph 6(1)(a) may be treated at the trustee's discretion as having been paid out of prior year's funds or current year's employer's contributions, to the extent that they are available, to avoid the application of subsection 104(13).

The remainder of the income of the trust is subject to income tax under section 122 of the Act. As an inter vivos trust, the taxation year of the trust coincides with the calendar year.

13. For administrative simplicity, payments of taxable benefits by the trustee to or on behalf of employees are to be reported on Form T4A by the trustee and not on the T3 Supplementary. Information on the completion of Form T4A is contained in the "Employer's and Trustee's Guide". Although the trustee is required to withhold income tax from taxable benefits paid to

employees, these amounts will not be subject to either Canada Pension Plan contributions or unemployment insurance premiums when paid by the trustee.

14. Although actuarial studies of the trust may recommend the establishment of "contingency reserves" to meet its future obligations, transfers to such reserves are not deductible for tax purposes by the trust.

Setting up a Plan

15. There is no formal registration procedure for a health and welfare trust and no requirement that the trust agreement be submitted to the Department for approval prior to the implementation of the plan. However, the advice of the District Taxation Office may be requested where there is any doubt as to the acceptability of the trust agreement as a health and welfare trust. Full particulars of the arrangement including a copy of all pertinent documents should accompany the request.

Registered Plans Directorate Newsletter, no. 96-3

November 25, 1996

Flexible Pension Plans

In this newsletter, we outline conditions that we are applying to flexible pension plans under the authority of subsection 147.1(5) of the Income Tax Act (the Act). The conditions are in addition to those imposed by the Act and the Income Tax Regulations (the Regulations) that have to be satisfied for a pension plan to qualify for registration under the Act.

In general terms, a flexible pension plan is a pension plan that allows members to make voluntary defined benefit contributions to acquire or improve ancillary benefits provided in connection with basic pension benefits accruing under the plan. A flexible pension plan allows members to improve their pension benefits to address their individual needs. Since ancillary benefits are disregarded in computing pension adjustments (PAs) and past service pension adjustments (PSPAs), members can improve their benefits without reducing the amount of deduction room available for registered retirement savings plan contributions.

Some examples of ways in which benefits might be improved under a flexible pension plan are as follows:

- lowering the age at which an unreduced pension can be paid or decreasing the early retirement reduction factor;

- indexing pensionable earnings, reducing the number of years used to calculate average earnings or replacing career average earnings with best or final average earnings;

- providing bridging benefits;

- indexing lifetime retirement benefits; and

- improving survivor benefits.

We define a flexible pension plan in the following section. A pension plan may provide for voluntary defined benefit contributions, without being a flexible pension plan. Only plans that fit the definition are subject to the additional conditions imposed in this newsletter.

Definitions

In this section, we define some terms we use in this newsletter. The appendix to this newsletter lists terms defined under the Act or Regulations.

Flexible pension plan - This means a pension plan the terms of which provide for optional ancillary benefits.

Optional ancillary benefit - This means any benefit (other than an exempt benefit) provided in respect of a pension plan member under a defined benefit provision of the plan as a consequence of the member having made optional contributions under the provision.

Exempt benefit - This means any of the following benefits provided under a defined benefit provision of a pension plan as a consequence of a member having made optional contributions under the provision:

a) lifetime retirement benefits provided to the member for a post-1989 period, to the extent that:

- the lifetime retirement benefits give rise to a pension credit or a provisional PSPA of the member that is greater than nil; or

- the lifetime retirement benefits increase the amount of a pension credit or a provisional PSPA of the member,

- or the lifetime retirement benefits would so give rise to or increase a pension credit or a provisional PSPA of the member if:

    o the amount determined under paragraph 8301(6)(b) of the Regulations and amount C in the formula in subsection 8303(3) of the Regulations were nil; and

    o paragraph 8301(7)(b) and subsection 8304(5) of the Regulations were disregarded;

b) lifetime retirement benefits provided to the member for a pre-1990 period that was not pensionable service of the member under the provision immediately before the benefits became provided;

c) additional lifetime retirement benefits provided to the member for a pre-1990 period that was pensionable service of the member under the provision immediately before the benefits became provided, to the extent that:

- the benefits are provided by increasing the effective benefit accrual rate under the provision; or

- at the request of the plan administrator, we have accepted in writing the benefits as exempt benefits;

d) benefits (such as indexing and survivor benefits) that are associated with exempt lifetime retirement benefits described in any of paragraphs a) to c), when the optional contributions as a consequence of which the benefits are provided are made together with the optional contributions as a consequence of which the associated lifetime retirement benefits are provided.

Optional contribution - This means the part, if any, of a contribution that a member of a pension plan makes under a defined benefit provision of the plan that, by exercising (or not exercising) a right in connection with the plan, the member could have prevented from being made under the provision.

Example

At the beginning of each year, members of a non-contributory plan are given the option of contributing 3% of earnings to the plan in that year. In return, the pension accrued to the member for the year is indexed. Such contributions are optional contributions since members can choose not to contribute to the plan in the year.

However, under certain circumstances, contributions that a member could have prevented from being made will not be considered to be optional contributions. This will be the case when the following conditions are satisfied:

- a member enters into a commitment to make regularly-scheduled contributions under a defined benefit provision of a pension plan;

- the contributions are to be made at a fixed rate determined no later than the time the commitment is entered into;

- the contributions are to be made for at least as long as the member accrues benefits on a current service basis under a defined benefit provision of the plan (or for a shorter time that we accept in writing);

- the benefits to be provided as a consequence of the member having made the contributions are established on a once-and-for-all basis at the time the commitment is entered into; and

- the employer does not participate in any other registered pension plan under which benefits could be provided to the member under a defined benefit provision (except to the extent that, at the request of the plan administrator, we have waived in writing this condition).

Example

New members of a pension plan are given the option, on a once-and-for-all basis, of contributing 3% of earnings to the plan each and every year in return for which the pension payable to the member is adjusted for increases in the cost-of-living. Members who choose not to contribute receive non-indexed pension benefits. Contributions made by a member as a result of this decision are not optional contributions.

Optional ancillary contribution - This means an optional contribution that a pension plan member makes under a defined benefit provision of the plan as a consequence of which optional ancillary benefits are provided under the provision in respect of the member.

Imposed conditions

In this section, we set out the additional conditions that we are imposing on flexible pension plans under the authority of subsection 147.1(5) of the Act.

Coming-into-force

Except as noted below, these conditions apply to all contributions made, and benefits provided, under a flexible pension plan after 1989.

These conditions do not apply to contributions made, or benefits provided, under a flexible pension plan before 1998 to the extent that they are made or provided under plan terms accepted by us before November 25, 1996. We would usually indicate our acceptance by registering the plan with the terms in it, or accepting a plan amendment with the terms in it.

These conditions also do not apply to contributions made, or benefits provided, under a flexible pension plan before 1998 to the extent that we have waived their application in writing.

Conditions

1. The terms of a flexible pension plan have to establish, on a once-and-for-all basis each time an optional contribution is made to the plan, whether or not the contribution is an optional ancillary contribution. This means that optional ancillary benefits can be provided as a consequence of a member having made an optional contribution only if the contribution is established as being for such benefits at the time it is made (although the specific benefits to be provided need not be established at that time). It also means that, when a contribution is established as being for optional ancillary benefits, it cannot subsequently be used to provide exempt benefits.

2. A flexible pension plan must not apply the 50% employer funding rule in subsection 21(2) of the Pension Benefits Standards Act, 19851, or any similar rule in provincial legislation, on a stand-alone basis to optional ancillary contributions and optional ancillary benefits.

Example

It is not acceptable for a flexible pension plan to provide additional benefits to a member simply on the basis that the member's optional ancillary contributions plus interest exceed 50% of the value of the member's optional ancillary benefits. However, it is acceptable to provide additional benefits when a member's total contributions (including optional ancillary contributions) plus interest exceed 50% of the value of the member's total benefits (including optional ancillary benefits).

3. The terms of a flexible pension plan have to clearly establish that, if the amount of optional ancillary contributions that a member makes under a defined benefit provision of the plan, plus the earnings on those contributions, exceeds the value of optional ancillary benefits that are provided under the provision in respect of the member, neither the member nor any beneficiary of the member has any entitlement in respect of the excess. For example, the excess could not be paid as a lump sum or in the form of additional lifetime retirement benefits.

However, this condition does not apply when such an excess arises only as a result of applying the 50% employer funding rule referred to in Condition 2. Also, it does not apply to prevent a refund of contributions under a defined benefit provision of a pension plan, as permitted under subparagraph 8502(d)(iv) or paragraph 8503(2)(h) or (j) of the Regulations.

4. If the terms of a flexible pension plan allow members to make optional ancillary contributions that are not current service contributions, i.e., not subject to the requirements of subparagraphs 8503(4)(a)(i) or (ii) of the Regulations, the plan must restrict the total optional ancillary contributions that a member is allowed to make in a calendar year (including those for current service) to the amount, if any, by which

a) the lesser of:

- 9% of the member's compensation for the year from employers participating in the plan; and

- $1,000 + 70% of the member's defined benefit pension credits for the year under the plan,

exceeds

b) the amount of current service contributions (other than optional ancillary contributions) that the member makes in the year under defined benefit provisions of the plan.

5. The terms of a flexible pension plan have to clearly set out the manner in which specific optional ancillary benefits provided in respect of a member are to be established for purposes of determining amounts payable on retirement, death, termination of membership, and full or partial wind-up of the plan.

Note

A plan could satisfy this condition in any number of ways. For example, it could indicate the specific optional ancillary benefits that are to be provided or it could require or grant authority to one or more individuals (such as the plan administrator, the member or the member's beneficiary) to make the optional ancillary benefit selection.

6. A flexible pension plan must not allow a member to commute optional ancillary benefits, except to the extent that the lifetime retirement benefits with which the benefits are associated are also being commuted.

7. A flexible pension plan must not allow optional ancillary benefits to be provided for pre-1990 periods unless the optional ancillary contributions as a consequence of which the benefits are provided are established, on a once-and-for-all basis at the time they are made, as being for benefits for pre-1990 periods (although the specific benefits to be provided do not have to be established at that time). This condition ensures the proper application of the deduction provisions in subsection 147.2(4) of the Act.

8. A flexible pension plan has to prohibit optional ancillary contributions from being made in any year that the plan is a designated plan. It must also prohibit optional ancillary benefits from being provided for any period in a year in which the plan is a designated plan.

9. Any information (such as employee booklets) made available to members of a flexible pension plan explaining how the plan works must also be provided to us. It must be submitted to us by the time it is made available to members or, if later, when the plan (or an amendment making the plan a flexible pension plan) is submitted to us for approval. However, if the information was made available to members, and the plan (or amendment) was submitted to us, before November 25, 1996, the deadline for submitting the information to us is extended to February 3, 1997.

We do not intend to review this material for approval. However, we wish to be able to assure ourselves that members are not inadvertently left with the impression that they may have an entitlement to the part (if any) of their optional ancillary contributions plus earnings that exceeds the present value of their optional ancillary benefits (see Condition 3 above).

Regulatory limits

As well as satisfying the conditions that are imposed in this newsletter, a flexible pension plan has to satisfy all requirements of the Act and Regulations that apply. Since optional ancillary contributions are made to a defined benefit provision, they must comply with all of the conditions that apply to defined benefit contributions. Similarly, optional ancillary benefits have to comply with all of the conditions that apply to defined benefits. The following examples illustrate this point.

Example 1

A flexible pension plan provides that, when a member retires before age 60, the member's benefits are reduced by 0.5% for each month between the month of retirement and the month in which the member attains age 60. As an optional ancillary benefit, the plan allows the member to elect a decrease in the early retirement reduction factor. To qualify for registration, the plan must ensure that the benefits are reduced at least by the amount required by paragraph 8503(3)(c) of the Regulations.

Example 2

A flexible pension plan provides for a terminating member who is vested to receive a lump sum payment equal to the greater of:

- the present value of the member's benefits (including optional ancillary benefits); and

- the amount of the member's contributions (including optional ancillary contributions) plus earnings.

Since the payment of either of these amounts is a permissible benefit under the Regulations——the former under paragraph 8503(2)(m), the latter under paragraph 8503(2)(h)——this benefit is an acceptable benefit and does not disqualify the plan from registration.

Example 3

A flexible pension plan provides non-contributory basic benefits. Deferred pensions are adjusted to reflect increases in the average wage. Pensions-in-pay are adjusted to reflect increases in the Consumer Price Index. A terminating member who is vested can elect to receive, instead of a deferred pension, a lump sum payment equal to the total of:

- the present value of the member's basic benefits, i.e., excluding optional ancillary benefits; and

- the greater of the present value of the member's optional ancillary benefits and the amount of the member's optional ancillary contributions plus earnings.

There may be circumstances when a member's optional ancillary contributions plus earnings will be greater than the present value of the member's optional ancillary benefits. If so, the resulting termination benefit payable under this plan would not be a permissible benefit under paragraph 8503(2)(h) because it is greater than the member's total contributions under the plan (assuming that subparagraph 8503(2)(h)(iii) does not apply). It is also not a permissible benefit under paragraph 8503(2)(m) because it is greater than the present value of the member's total benefits under the plan. Since there is no other provision in the Regulations that would support the payment of the benefit, it is not a permissible benefit and the plan does not qualify for registration.

Valuations and funding

Since flexible pension plan members can have no entitlement to any portion of their optional ancillary contributions that exceeds the present value of their optional ancillary benefits (see Condition 3), such excesses have to be considered to be available to fund other defined benefits provided under the plan. This must be reflected in any valuation of a flexible pension plan under which such excesses may arise.

If specific optional ancillary benefits to be provided under a flexible pension plan are not known when a valuation is prepared, the actuary must make assumptions as to what the benefits will be. Paragraph 8502(j) of the Regulations requires that the assumptions be reasonable and acceptable to the Minister of National Revenue. We will accept any assumptions that we consider to be reasonable. In order for us to make this assessment, the assumptions have to be clearly described in the valuation report, and the actuary has to be prepared to justify their suitability when asked to do so.

Where to get help

If you need more information or have questions, please write to:
Registered Plans Division
Revenue Canada
700 Industrial Avenue
Ottawa ON K1A 0L8
You can also call: (613) 954-0419 (service in English)

Appendix

In this appendix we identify the provisions in the Income Tax Act (ITA) and Income Tax Regulations (ITR) which contain definitions of terms we use in this newsletter.

- Administrator, ITA 147.1(1)
- Average wage, ITA 147.1(1)
- Bridging benefits, ITR 8500(1)
- Compensation, ITA 147.1(1)
- Consumer Price Index, ITR 8500(1)
- Defined benefit provision, ITA 147.1(1)
- Designated plan, ITR 8515
- Lifetime retirement benefits, ITR 8500(1)
- Member, ITA 147.1(1)

- Participating employer, ITA 147.1(1)
- Past service pension adjustment (PSPA), ITR 8303
- Pension adjustment (PA), ITR 8301
- Pension credit, ITR 8301
- Pensionable service, ITR 8500(1)

In general terms, this rule requires that, when a member's contributions plus interest under a defined benefit pension plan exceed 50% of the value of the benefits provided to the member under the plan, the member's benefits have to be increased by the amount that can be provided with the excess.

Income Tax Act
  PART I INCOME TAX
    DIVISION B COMPUTATION OF INCOME
      SUBDIVISION A INCOME OR LOSS FROM AN OFFICE OR EMPLOYMENT
        Inclusions

Amounts to be included as income from office or employment

6. (1) There shall be included in computing the income of a taxpayer for a taxation year as income from an office or employment such of the following amounts as are applicable

Value of benefits

(*a*) the value of board, lodging and other benefits of any kind whatever received or enjoyed by the taxpayer in the year in respect of, in the course of, or by virtue of an office or employment, except any benefit

(i) derived from the contributions of the taxpayer's employer to or under a registered pension plan, group sickness or accident insurance plan, private health services plan, supplementary unemployment benefit plan, deferred profit sharing plan or group term life insurance policy,

(ii) under a retirement compensation arrangement, an employee benefit plan or an employee trust,

(iii) that was a benefit in respect of the use of an automobile,

(iv) derived from counselling services in respect of

(A) the mental or physical health of the taxpayer or an individual related to the taxpayer, other than a benefit attributable to an outlay or expense to which paragraph 18(1)(l) applies, or

(B) the re-employment or retirement of the taxpayer, or

(v) under a salary deferral arrangement, except to the extent that the benefit is included under this paragraph because of subsection 6(11);

Income Tax Act
PART I INCOME TAX
DIVISION B COMPUTATION OF INCOME
SUBDIVISION A INCOME OR LOSS FROM AN OFFICE OR EMPLOYMENT
Inclusions

Group term life
insurance

6. (4) Where at any time in a taxation year a taxpayer's life is insured under a group term life insurance policy, there shall be included in computing the taxpayer's income for the year from an office or employment the amount, if any, prescribed for the year in respect of the insurance.

Income Tax Regulations
>   **PART XXVII GROUP TERM LIFE INSURANCE BENEFITS**
>   **Definitions & Interpretation**
>   **Definitions**

2700. (1) The definitions in this subsection apply in this Part.

"lump-sum premium" in relation to a group term life insurance policy means a premium for insurance under the policy on the life of an individual where all or part of the premium is for insurance that is (or would be if the individual survived) in respect of a period that ends more than 13 months after the earlier of the day on which the premium becomes payable and the day on which it is paid. (*prime globale*)

"paid-up premium" in relation to a group term life insurance policy means a premium for insurance under the policy on the life of an individual where the insurance is for the remainder of the lifetime of the individual and no further premiums will be payable for the insurance. (*prime d'assurance libérée*)

"premium category" in relation to term insurance provided under a group term life insurance policy means,

> (*a*) where the premium rate applicable in respect of term insurance on the life of an individual depends on the group to which the individual belongs, any of the groups for which a premium rate is established, and

> (*b*) in any other case, all individuals on whose lives term insurance is in effect under the policy,

and, for the purpose of this definition, a single premium rate is deemed to apply for all term insurance under a policy in respect of periods in 1994, and where individuals are divided into separate groups solely on the basis of their age, sex, or both, the groups are deemed to be a single group for which a premium rate is established. (*catégorie de primes*)

"term insurance" in relation to an individual and a group term life insurance policy means insurance under the policy on the life of the individual, other than insurance in respect of which a lump-sum premium has become payable or been paid. (*assurance temporaire*)

Accidental Death Insurance

(2) For greater certainty, a premium for insurance on the life of an individual does not include an amount for accidental death insurance. SOR/97-494, s. 1.

[RELATED PROVISION: SOR/97-494:

2. (1) Section 2700 of the Regulations, as enacted by section 1, applies to the 1994 and subsequent taxation years.]

2701. (1) Subject to subsection (2), for the purpose of subsection 6(4) of the Act, the amount prescribed for a taxation year in respect of insurance under a group term life insurance policy on the life of a taxpayer is the total of

(*a*) the taxpayer's term insurance benefit under the policy for the calendar year in which the taxation year ends,

(*b*) the taxpayer's prepaid insurance benefit under the policy for that calendar year, and

(*c*) the total of all sales and excise taxes payable in respect of premiums paid under the policy in that calendar year for insurance on the life of the taxpayer, other than

(i) taxes paid, directly or by way of reimbursement, by the taxpayer, and

(ii) taxes in respect of premiums for term insurance that, if the taxpayer were to die, would be paid otherwise than

(A) to the taxpayer,

(B) for the benefit of the taxpayer,

(C) as a benefit that the taxpayer desired to have conferred on any person.

_____

Bankrupt Individual

(2) Where a taxpayer who has become a bankrupt has two taxation years ending in a calendar year, for the purpose of subsection 6(4) of the Act, the amount prescribed for the first taxation year in respect of insurance under a group term life insurance policy on the life of the taxpayer is nil. SOR/97-494, s. 1.

[RELATED PROVISION: SOR/97-494:

2. (2) Sections 2701 to 2704 of the Regulations, as enacted by section 1, apply with respect to insurance provided in respect of periods that are after June 1994 except that, in their application with respect to insurance provided in respect of periods that are in 1994 and after June 1994,

(*a*) the portion of paragraph 2701(1)(*c*) of the Regulations before subparagraph (i), as enacted by section 1, shall be read as follows:

(*c*) the total of all sales and excise taxes payable in respect of premiums paid under the policy in 1994 and after June 1994 for insurance on the life of the taxpayer, other than]

2702. (1) Subject to section 2704, for the purpose of paragraph 2701(1)(*a*), a taxpayer's term insurance benefit under a group term life insurance policy for a calendar year is

(*a*) where

(i) the policyholder elects to determine, under this paragraph, the term insurance benefit for the year of each individual whose life is insured under the policy,

(ii) no premium rate that applies for term insurance provided under the policy on the life of an individual in respect of the year depends on the age or sex of the individual,

(iii) no amounts are payable under the policy for term insurance on the lives of individuals in respect of the year other than premiums payable on a regular basis that are based on the amount of term insurance in force in the year for each individual, and

(iv) the year is after 1995,

the amount determined by the formula

$$A - B$$

where

A is the total of the premiums payable for term insurance provided under the policy on the taxpayer's life in respect of periods in the year, to the extent that each such premium is in respect of term insurance that, if the taxpayer died in the year, would be paid to or for the benefit of the taxpayer or as a benefit that the taxpayer desired to have conferred on any person, and

B is the total amount paid by the taxpayer in respect of term insurance under the policy on the taxpayer's life in respect of the year; and

(*b*) in any other case, the amount, if any, by which

(i) the total of all amounts each of which is, for a day in the year on which term insurance is in effect under the policy on the taxpayer's life, the amount determined by the formula

$A \times B$

where

A is the amount of term insurance in effect on that day under the policy on the taxpayer's life, except the portion, if any, of the amount that, if the taxpayer were to die on that day, would be paid otherwise than

(A) to the taxpayer,

(B) to benefit of the taxpayer, or

(C) as a benefit that the taxpayer desired to have conferred on any person, and

B is the average daily cost of insurance for the year for the premium category in which the taxpayer is included on that day

exceeds

(ii) the total amount paid by the taxpayer in respect of term insurance under the policy on the taxpayer's life in respect of the year.

Average Daily Cost of Insurance

(2) The average daily cost of insurance under a group term life insurance policy for a calendar year for a premium category is

(a) subject to paragraph (b), the amount determined by the formula

$$(A + B - C) / D$$

where

A is the total of the premiums payable for term insurance provided under the policy on the lives of individuals in respect of periods in the year while they are in the premium category,

B is the total of the amounts paid in the year under the policy for term insurance in respect of periods in preceding years (other than amounts that have otherwise been taken into account for the purpose of subsection 6(4) of the Act), to the extent that the total can reasonably be considered to relate to term insurance provided on the lives of individuals in the premium category,

C is the total amount of policy dividends and experience rating refunds paid in the year under the policy and not distributed to individuals whose lives are insured under the policy, to the extent that the total can reasonably be considered to relate to term insurance provided on the lives of individuals in the premium category, and

D is the total of all amounts each of which is the amount of term insurance in force on a day in the year on the lives of individuals in the premium category on that day; or

(*b*) the amount that the policyholder determines using a reasonable method that is substantially similar to the method set out in paragraph (*a*).

Survivor Income Benefits

(3) For the purposes of this section, where the proceeds of term insurance on the life of an individual are payable in the form of periodic payments, and the periodic payments are not an optional form of settlement of a lump-sum amount, the amount of term insurance in effect on the individual's life on any day is the present value, on that day, of the periodic payments that would be made if the individual were to die on that day.

Determination of Present Value

(4) For the purpose of subsection (3), the present value on a day in a calendar year

(*a*) shall be determined using assumptions that are reasonable at some time in the year; and

(*b*) may be determined assuming that an individual on whose life the present value depends is the same age on that day as on another day in the year. SOR/97-494, s. 1.

[RELATED PROVISION: SOR/97-494:

2. (2) Sections 2701 to 2704 of the Regulations, as enacted by section 1, apply with respect to insurance provided in respect of periods that are after June 1994 except that, in their application with respect to insurance provided in respect of periods that are in 1994 and after June 1994,

(*b*) the portion of subparagraph 2702(1)(*b*)(i) of the Regulations before the formula in that subparagraph, as enacted by section 1, shall be read as follows:

(i) the total of all amounts each of which is, for a day in the year 1994 that is after June 1994 on which term insurance is in effect under the policy on the taxpayer's life, the amount determined by the formula

and

(*c*) subparagraph 2702(1)(*b*)(ii) of the Regulations, as enacted by section 1, shall be read as follows:

(ii) the total amount paid by the taxpayer in respect of term insurance under the policy on the taxpayer's life in respect of the period in the year 1994 that is after June 1994.]

2703. (1) Subject to section 2704, for the purpose of paragraph 2701(1)(*b*), a taxpayer's prepaid insurance benefit under a group term life insurance policy for a calendar year is

(*a*) where the taxpayer is alive at the end of the year, the total of all amounts each of which is

(i) a lump-sum premium (other than the taxpayer portion) paid in the year and after February 1994 in respect of insurance under the policy on the life of the taxpayer, other than a paid-up premium paid before 1997, or

(ii) 1/3 of a paid-up premium (other than the taxpayer portion) in respect of insurance under the policy on the life of the taxpayer that was paid

(A) after February 1994 and before 1997, and

(B) in the year or one of the two preceding years; and

(*b*) where the taxpayer died after June 1994 and in the year, the amount, if any, by which

(i) the total of all amounts each of which is a lump-sum premium (other than the taxpayer portion) paid under the policy after February 1994 in respect of insurance on the life of the taxpayer

exceeds

(ii) the portion of that total that was included in computing the taxpayer's prepaid insurance benefit under the policy for preceding years.

Taxpayer Portion of Premiums

(2) For the purpose of subsection (1), the taxpayer portion of a premium is the portion, if any, of the premium that the taxpayer paid, either directly or by way of reimbursement. SOR/97-494, s. 1.

[RELATED PROVISION: SOR/97-494:

2. (2) Sections 2701 to 2704 of the Regulations, as enacted by section 1, apply with respect to insurance provided in respect of periods that are after June 1994.]

2704. (1) For the purpose of subsection 2701(1), where the full cost of insurance under a group term life insurance policy in a calendar year is borne by the individuals whose lives are insured under the policy, each individual's term insurance benefit and prepaid insurance benefit under the policy for the year is deemed to be nil.

(2) Where the premiums for part of the life insurance (in this subsection referred to as the "additional insurance") under a group term life insurance policy are determined separately from the premiums for the rest of the life insurance under the policy, and it is reasonable to consider that the individuals on whose lives the additional insurance is provided bear the full cost of the additional insurance, the additional insurance, the premiums, policy dividends and experience rating refunds in respect of that insurance, and the amounts paid in respect of that insurance by the individuals whose lives are insured, shall not be taken into account for the purposes of this Part. SOR/97-494, s. 1.

[RELATED PROVISION: SOR/97-494:

2. (2) Sections 2701 to 2704 of the Regulations, as enacted by section 1, apply with respect to insurance provided in respect of periods that are after June 1994.]

2705. For the purpose of subsection 6(4) of the Act, as it applies to insurance provided in respect of periods that are in 1994 and before July 1994,

(*a*) a lump-sum premium paid under a group term life insurance policy after February 1994 in respect of an individual who is alive at the end of June 1994 is a prescribed premium; and

(*b*) insurance in respect of which a premium referred to in paragraph (*a*) is paid is prescribed insurance. SOR/97-494, s. 1.

[RELATED PROVISION: SOR/97-494:

2. (3) Section 2705 of the Regulations, as enacted by section 1, applies with respect to insurance that is provided in respect of periods that are in 1994 and before July 1994.]

Income Tax Regulations
PART LVII MEDICAL DEVICES AND EQUIPMENT

5700. For the purposes of paragraph 118.2(2)(*m*) of the Act, a device or equipment is prescribed if it is a

(*a*) wig made to order for an individual who has suffered abnormal hair loss owing to disease, medical treatment or accident;

(*b*) needle or syringe designed to be used for the purpose of giving an injection;

(*c*) device or equipment, including a replacement part, designed exclusively for use by an individual suffering from a severe chronic respiratory ailment or a severe chronic immune system disregulation, but not including an air conditioner, humidifier, dehumidifier, heat pump or heat or air exchanger;

(*c*.1) air or water filter or purifier for use by an individual who is suffering from a severe chronic respiratory ailment or a severe chronic immune system disregulation to cope with or overcome that ailment or disregulation;

(*c*.2) electric or sealed combustion furnace acquired to replace a furnace that is neither an electric furnace nor a sealed combustion furnace, where the replacement is necessary solely because of a severe chronic respiratory ailment or a severe chronic immune system disregulation;

(*c*.3) air conditioner acquired for use by an individual to cope with the individual's severe chronic ailment, disease or disorder, to the extent of the lesser of $1,000 and 50% of the amount paid for the air conditioner;

(*d*) device or equipment designed to pace or monitor the heart of an individual who suffers from heart disease;

(*e*) orthopaedic shoe or boot or an insert for a shoe or boot made to order for an individual in accordance with a prescription to overcome a physical disability of the individual;

(*f*) power-operated guided chair installation, for an individual, that is designed to be used solely in a stairway;

(*g*) mechanical device or equipment designed to be used to assist an individual to enter or leave a bathtub or shower or to get on or off a toilet;

(*h*) hospital bed including such attachments thereto as may have been included in a prescription therefor;

(*i*) device that is designed to assist an individual in walking where the individual has a mobility impairment;

(*j*) external breast prosthesis that is required because of a mastectomy;

(*k*) teletypewriter or similar device, including a telephone ringing indicator, that enables a deaf or mute individual to make and receive telephone calls;

(*l*) optical scanner or similar device designed to be used by a blind individual to enable him to read print;

(*m*) power-operated lift or transportation equipment designed exclusively for use by, or for, a disabled individual to allow the individual access to different areas of a building or to assist the individual to gain access to a vehicle or to place the individual's wheelchair in or on a vehicle;

(*n*) device designed exclusively to enable an individual with a mobility impairment to operate a vehicle;

(*o*) device or equipment, including a synthetic speech system, braille printer and large print-on-screen device, designed exclusively to be used by a blind individual in the operation of a computer;

(*p*) electronic speech synthesizer that enables a mute individual to communicate by use of a portable keyboard;

(*q*) device to decode special television signals to permit the script of a program to be visually displayed;

(*q*.1) a visual or vibratory signalling device, including a visual fire alarm indicator, for an individual with a hearing impairment;

(*r*) device designed to be attached to infants diagnosed as being prone to sudden infant death syndrome in order to sound an alarm if the infant ceases to breathe;

(*s*) infusion pump, including disposable peripherals, used in the treatment of diabetes or a device designed to enable a diabetic to measure the diabetic's blood sugar level;

(*t*) electronic or computerized environmental control system designed exclusively for the use of an individual with a severe and prolonged mobility restriction;

(*u*) extremity pump or elastic support hose designed exclusively to relieve swelling caused by chronic lymphedema;

(*v*) inductive coupling osteogenesis stimulator for treating non-union of fractures or aiding in bone fusion; and

(*w*) talking textbook prescribed by a medical practitioner for use by an individual with a perceptual disability, in connection with the individual's enrolment at an educational institution in Canada. SOR/80-948, s. 1; SOR/85-696, s. 17; SOR/87-716, s. 1; SOR/90-809, s. 1; SOR/94-189, s. 1; SOR/99-387, s. 1; SOR/2001-4, s. 1.

Employment Standards Act, 2000

ONTARIO REGULATION 286/01

Amended to O. Reg. 526/05

BENEFIT PLANS

Definitions

1. For the purposes of Part XIII of the Act and this Regulation,

"actuarial basis" means the assumptions and methods generally accepted and used by fellows of the Canadian Institute of Actuaries to establish, in relation to the contingencies of human life such as death, accident, sickness and disease, the costs of pension benefits, life insurance, disability insurance, health insurance and other similar benefits, including their actuarial equivalents; ("méthode actuarielle")

"age" means any age of 18 years or more and less than 65 years; ("âge")

"benefits" includes,

(a) an aggregate, annual, monthly or other periodic amount or the accrual of such an amount to which an employee, or the employee's beneficiaries, survivors or dependants is, are or will become entitled under a benefit plan provided on superannuation, retirement, disability, accident or sickness,

(b) any medical, hospital, nursing, drug or dental expenses or other similar amounts or expenses paid under a benefit plan, and

(c) any amounts under a benefit plan to which an employee is entitled on termination of employment or to which any person is entitled upon the death of an employee; ("prestations")

"dependant" means a dependant as defined in the relevant benefit plan, and "dependent child" and "dependent spouse" have corresponding meanings; ("personne à charge")

"disability benefit plan" means a benefit plan that provides benefits to an employee for loss of income because of sickness, accident or disability; ("régime de prestations d'invalidité")

"former Act" means the *Employment Standards Act*, R.S.O. 1990, c. E.14; ("ancienne loi")

"health benefit plan" means a benefit plan that provides benefits to an employee, a spouse or a dependant of an employee or deceased employee for medical, hospital, nursing, drug or dental expenses or other similar expenses; ("régime de prestations de maladie")

"life insurance plan" means a benefit plan that, on the employee's death, provides a lump sum or periodic payments to the employee's beneficiary, survivor or dependant, and includes accidental death and dismemberment insurance; ("régime d'assurance-vie")

"long-term disability benefit plan" means a disability benefit plan under which the payments or benefits to an employee are payable for a period of not less than 52 weeks or until recovery, retirement or death, whichever period is shorter; ("régime de prestations d'invalidité de longue durée")

"marital status" includes,

(a) the condition of being an unmarried person who is supporting, in whole or in part, a dependent child or children, and

(b) common law status as defined in the relevant benefit plan; ("état matrimonial")

"normal pensionable date" means the date specified in a pension plan at which an employee can retire from his or her employment and receive the regular pension benefit provided by the pension plan, whether the date is the day on which the employee attains a given age or the day on which he or she has completed a given period of employment; ("date normale de retraite")

"pension plan" means a benefit plan that provides benefits to a participating employee or to his or her spouse or dependant, on the employee's retirement or termination of employment, out of contributions made by the employer or the employee or both and the investment income, gains, losses and expenses on or from those contributions, and includes,

(a) a unit-benefit pension plan, under which the benefits are determined with reference to a percentage of salary or wages and length of employment or a specified period of employment,

(b) a defined benefit pension plan, under which the benefits are determined as a fixed amount and with reference to length of employment or a specified period of employment,

(c) a money purchase pension plan, under which the benefits are determined with reference to the accumulated amount of the contributions paid by or for the credit of an employee, and the investment income, gains, losses and expenses on or from those contributions,

(d) a profit sharing pension plan, under which payments or contributions by an employer are determined by reference to profits or out of profits from the employer's business, and the benefits are determined with reference to the accumulated amount of contributions paid by or for the credit of an employee and the investment income, gains, losses and expenses on or from those contributions, and

(e) a composite pension plan, which is any combination of the pension plans described in clauses (a) to (d); ("régime de retraite")

"sex" includes,

(a) a distinction between employees that excludes an employee from a benefit under a benefit plan or gives an employee a preference to a benefit under a benefit plan because the employee is or is not a head of household, principal or primary wage earner or other similar condition, and

(b) a distinction between employees in a benefit plan because of the pregnancy of a female employee; ("sexe")

"short-term disability benefit plan" means a disability benefit plan other than a long-term disability benefit plan; ("régime de prestations d'invalidité de courte durée")

"spouse" means a spouse as defined in the relevant benefit plan; ("conjoint")

"voluntary additional contribution" means an additional contribution by an employee under a pension plan, except a contribution whose payment, under the terms of the plan, obliges the employer to make a concurrent additional contribution. ("cotisation facultative supplémentaire") O. Reg. 286/01, s. 1; O. Reg. 335/05, s. 1.

Pension plans, permitted differentiation re employee's sex

2. (1) The prohibition in subsection 44 (1) of the Act does not apply in respect of a differentiation in the rates of contribution by an employer to a pension plan if the differentiation is made on an actuarial basis because of an employee's sex and in order to provide equal benefits under the plan. O. Reg. 286/01, s. 2 (1).

(2) The prohibition in subsection 44 (1) of the Act does not apply in respect of a differentiation made under a pension plan if,

(a) the *Pension Benefits Act* applies to the pension plan; and

(b) the differentiation is made,

(i) because of an employee's sex, and

(ii) in respect of employment before January 1, 1987, other than employment that is described in clause 52 (3) (b) or (c) of the *Pension Benefits Act.* O. Reg. 286/01, s. 2 (2).

(3) The prohibition in subsection 44 (1) of the Act does not apply in respect of a differentiation made under a pension plan if,

(a) the *Pension Benefits Act* does not apply to the pension plan; and

(b) the differentiation is made,

(i) because of an employee's sex, and

(ii) in respect of employment before July 12, 1988. O. Reg. 286/01, s. 2 (3).

(4) In subsections (2) and (3),

"differentiation" means a type of differentiation to which the prohibition in the predecessor of subsection 33 (2) of the former Act did not apply on December 31, 1987. O. Reg. 286/01, s. 2 (4).

Pension plans, permitted differentiation re marital status

3. (1) The prohibition in subsection 44 (1) of the Act does not apply to,

(a) an increase in benefits payable to an employee under a pension plan that provides for the increased benefits because the employee has a dependent spouse;

(b) a differentiation under a pension plan because of marital status, if the differentiation is made for the purpose of providing benefits that are payable periodically during the joint lives of an employee who is entitled to the pension and the employee's spouse, and thereafter during the life of the survivor of them, as provided in the pension plan; and

(c) a differentiation in the rates of contribution of an employer to a defined benefit or a unit-benefit pension plan that provides an increase in benefits to an employee because of marital status, if the rates of contribution of the employer differentiate between employees because of marital status. O. Reg. 335/05, s. 2.

(2) For the purposes of clause (1) (b), benefits are deemed to be payable periodically despite the fact that they are commuted, if the amount of the annual benefit payable to the employee at the normal pensionable date is not more than 2 per cent of the Year's Maximum Pensionable Earnings, as defined in the *Canada Pension Plan* in the year that the employee terminated the employment. O. Reg. 286/01, s. 3 (2).

(3) Clause (1) (b) does not apply if the *Pension Benefits Act* applies to the pension plan and the plan contravenes the provisions of that Act respecting joint and survivor pensions. O. Reg. 286/01, s. 3 (3).

Pension plans, permitted differentiation re employee's age

4. (1) The prohibition in subsection 44 (1) of the Act does not apply in respect of a differentiation that is made on an actuarial basis because of an employee's age and that relates to,

(a) the rates of voluntary additional contributions to a pension plan;

(b) the rates of contributions that an employee is required to make to a money purchase or profit sharing pension plan;

(c) the rates of contributions by an employer to a unit-benefit or defined benefit pension plan, unless the *Pension Benefits Act* applies to the plan and the plan contravenes the provisions of that Act respecting age differentiation;

(d) the rates of contributions by an employer to a money purchase or profit sharing pension plan,

   (i) when the employer transfers the assets from a unit-benefit or defined benefit pension plan to the money purchase or profit sharing pension plan, and

   (ii) if the differentiation is made in order to protect employees' pension benefits from being adversely affected by the transfer; or

(e) benefits payable to employees, if the *Pension Benefits Act*,

   (i) permits the differentiation, or

   (ii) does not apply to the pension plan. O. Reg. 286/01, s. 4 (1).

(2) Despite subsection (1), the requirement that a differentiation be determined on an actuarial basis does not apply to a differentiation described in clause (1) (a), (b) or (e) that is made in respect of the employment of a person before July 12, 1988. O. Reg. 286/01, s. 4 (2).

(3) The prohibition in subsection 44 (1) of the Act does not apply with respect to a provision in a pension plan that makes a differentiation because of age in establishing a normal pensionable date for voluntary retirees or an early voluntary retirement date or age, unless,

(a) the *Pension Benefits Act* applies to the plan; and

(b) the plan contravenes the provisions of that Act respecting normal retirement dates and early retirement pensions. O. Reg. 286/01, s. 4 (3).

Life insurance plans, permitted differentiation re employee's sex

5. The prohibition in subsection 44 (1) of the Act does not apply to,

(a) a differentiation in the contributions of an employee to a voluntary employee-pay-all life insurance plan that is made on an actuarial basis because of sex; and

(b) a differentiation in the contributions of an employer to a life insurance plan that is made on an actuarial basis because of an employee's sex and in order to provide equal benefits under the plan. O. Reg. 286/01, s. 5.

Life insurance plans, permitted differentiation re marital status

6. (1) The prohibition in subsection 44 (1) of the Act does not apply to,

(a) benefits under a life insurance plan that are payable periodically to the surviving spouse of a deceased employee for the life of the surviving spouse or until the surviving spouse becomes a spouse of another person;

(b) a benefit under a life insurance plan that is payable to an employee on the death of his or her spouse; and

(c) a differentiation in the contributions of an employee or an employer to a life insurance plan, if,

   (i) the differentiation is made because of marital status, and

   (ii) the life insurance plan provides benefits that are payable periodically to an employee's surviving spouse. O. Reg. 335/05, s. 3.

(2) Clause (1) (a) also applies to benefits of less than $25 a month that have been commuted to a lump sum payment. O. Reg. 286/01, s. 6 (2).

Life insurance plans, permitted differentiation re age

7. The prohibition in subsection 44 (1) of the Act does not apply to,

(a) a differentiation, made on an actuarial basis because of an employee's age, in benefits or contributions under a voluntary employee-pay-all life insurance plan; and

(b) a differentiation, made on an actuarial basis because of an employee's age and in order to provide equal benefits under the plan, in an employer's contributions to a life insurance plan. O. Reg. 286/01, s. 7.

Disability benefit plans, permitted differentiation re age, sex or leave of absence

8. The prohibition in subsection 44 (1) of the Act does not apply to,

(a) a differentiation, made on an actuarial basis because of an employee's age or sex, in the rate of contributions of an employee to a voluntary employee-pay-all short or long-term disability benefit plan; and

(b) a differentiation, made on an actuarial basis because of an employee's age or sex and in order to provide equal benefits under the plan, in the rate of contributions of an employer to a short or long-term disability benefit plan. O. Reg. 286/01, s. 8.

Health benefit plans, permitted differentiation re sex or marital status

9. The prohibition in subsection 44 (1) of the Act does not apply to,

(a) a differentiation, made on an actuarial basis because of sex, in the rate of contributions of an employee to a voluntary employee-pay-all health benefit plan;

(b) a differentiation, made on an actuarial basis because of an employee's sex and in order to provide equal benefits under the plan, in the rate of contributions of an employer to a health benefit plan;

(c) a differentiation in an employee's benefits or contributions under a health benefit plan because of marital status, if the differentiation is made in order to provide benefits for the employee's spouse or dependent child; and

(d) a differentiation in the rate of contributions of an employer to a health benefit plan, where there are specified premium rates and where that differentiation for employees having marital status and for employees without marital status is on the same proportional basis. O. Reg. 335/05, s. 4.

Participation in benefit plan during leave of absence

10. (1) A benefit plan to which Part XIII of the Act applies shall not disentitle an employee who is on a leave of absence described in subsection (2) from continuing to participate in the benefit plan during the leave of absence, if the benefit plan entitles an employee who is on a leave of absence other than one described in subsection (2) to continue to participate. O. Reg. 286/01, s. 10 (1).

(2) This subsection applies to,

(a) a leave of absence under Part XIV of the Act; and

(b) any longer leave of absence that the employee has applied for under a provision in the contract of employment that prevails under subsection 5 (2) of the Act. O. Reg. 286/01, s. 10 (2).

Former exclusion from certain benefit plans

11. If an employee was excluded from participating in a benefit plan or in a benefit under a benefit plan before November 1, 1975 and ceased to be so excluded on that date, the employee is entitled to participate as of that date. O. Reg. 286/01, s. 11.

Compliance not to be achieved by reductions

12. No employer shall reduce the employer's contributions to or the benefits under a health benefit plan in causing the plan to comply with Part XIII of the Act and this Regulation, or with Part X of the former Act or a predecessor of that Part and the related regulations. O. Reg. 286/01, s. 12.

Change to normal pensionable date under certain plans

13. Despite the application of Part X of the former Act or a predecessor of that Part to a pension plan that was in existence on November 1, 1975, if the normal pensionable date of a class of employees was increased in order to have the plan comply with that Part, an employee who is a member of that class is entitled to pension benefits on the normal pensionable date as provided by the pension plan before it was increased. O. Reg. 286/01, s. 13.

14. OMITTED (REVOKES OTHER REGULATIONS). O. Reg. 286/01, s. 14.

15. OMITTED (PROVIDES FOR COMING INTO FORCE OF PROVISIONS OF THIS REGULATION). O. Reg. 286/01, s. 15.

Glossary

Accidental Death and Dismemberment A form of insurance that provides a lump-sum payment in the event of accidental death or injury. The payment due in case of injury is a percentage of the death benefit, with the percentage based on the severity of the injury.

Administrative Services Only (ASO) An arrangement where plans are not underwritten (insured) by an insurer. The employer sets aside a fund from which the administrator (usually an insurance company) pays claims. No premiums are paid; the employer simply provides funds to pay the claims incurred under the plan and pays a fee to the administrator.

Advance Tax Ruling A binding ruling by the Canada Revenue Agency on a proposed income tax transaction.

Adverse Selection (Anti-Selection) Created when plan members elect certain insurance coverages because of a high likelihood of a claim. A terminally ill individual selecting additional life insurance is an extreme example of adverse selection.

Adverse Selection Controls Elements of a plan design that are intended to minimize the chance that a member will elect coverage because of the high likelihood of a claim. Examples include:
- Before members increase their life insurance coverage, they must provide evidence of good health;
- Members must remain in a dental coverage option for two years before being allowed to change to another option.

Benchmarking Measuring how a benefits program compares to its competitive target. The target is frequently expressed as a percentile. For example, the target competitive position may be the 50th percentile (meaning 50 per cent of plans in the comparator group should rank the same as or below the sponsor's plan).

Beneficiary A person who will receive benefits from an insurance plan or pension plan if the plan member dies.

Benefit Booklet Communication material designed to explain a benefit program to members. Generally, this material is intended to be less technical than the plan contract yet thorough enough to communicate all significant conditions and specifications. Can be printed or provided online.

Build Your Own Plans This U.S. design approach allows members to select various levels of coverage for a variety of services. Plan members select amongst various vendors and choose the level of deductible, co-insurance, and maximum.

Buy Back The ability of a participant in a flexible benefit program to repurchase the level of benefit coverage he or she had in the previous benefit program.

Cafeteria Plan *See* Full Flex.

Canada Health Act Sets out the principles of the health care system, including universality, portability, outlawing extra billing and user fees, and administration by provincial public authorities. Provinces control the health care system, and receive federal subsidies as long as they comply with the conditions of the act. Replaced the *Hospital Insurance and Diagnostic Services Act* of 1957 and the *Medical Care Act* of 1966.

Canada Pension Plan (CPP) Provides a retirement benefit of 25 per cent of adjusted average earnings to those who contribute to the plan during their working lives. This plan also provides disability pensions, survivor's pensions, orphan's benefits, and death benefits.

Canada Revenue Agency (CRA) Federal government department responsible for administering the *Income Tax Act (ITA)*.

Canadian Charter of Rights and Freedoms The Charter defines the fundamental constitutional rights of all Canadians.

Carve-Out Pricing A pricing system that sets a base price of $0 for the core option and sets prices of other options according to their incremental value.

Cash Value The amount an individual is entitled to receive on termination of a whole life or universal life insurance policy. Essentially, the cash value equals the premiums paid by the individual, plus interest, and less expenses, such as commission and insurance costs.

Catastrophic Plan A medical option whereby an individual has virtually no protection from higher-frequency, low-cost claims. But in the event of a major unexpected medical expense, such as a large prescription drug or an out-of-Canada claim, this option would reimburse the individual.

Change in Family Status Participants are generally permitted to change their flexible benefit choices between enrolment periods (e.g., mid-year), if they have a change in family status. Examples include marriage, divorce, birth or adoption of a child, loss of a spouse's coverage through death or loss of employment, and change in a child's full-time student status.

Chaoulli v. Quebec A 2005 Supreme Court decision that may change how some health services are delivered under provincial plans. Dr. Chaoulli argued that a one-year wait for a hip replacement for one of his patients violated the Quebec Charter. The Supreme Court agreed that the lack of timely health care violates an individual's right to life and security as guaranteed by the Charter.

Child Care Refers to a benefit plan whereby employers subsidize childcare services. These may include:
- On-site daycare centres;
- Payments to participants to subsidize private childcare arrangements; or
- Provision of childcare referral services, either in-house or through an outside provider.

Children's Life Insurance A group life insurance policy covering a member's children, generally those under age 19, or 25 if full-time students. Typically, children's life insurance options are for a flat amount (unrelated to employee pay) and are priced independent of age, gender, or number of children.

Choice-Making A benefit program that allows participants to choose among a number of options.

Claim A request to the insurance carrier by the insured person for payment of benefits under a policy.

Claims Incurred Claims for services performed during the plan year. The liability for a given plan year equals the claims incurred, even if they are not paid until the following year.

Claims Paid Claims for which the participant receives reimbursement within the plan year, even if the claims were incurred in the previous plan year.

Cluster Stratified Sample A method of randomly choosing participants for a survey or a focus group. A limited number of locations expected to represent many others are randomly selected and employees are then randomly chosen from each selected location.

Co-insurance The sharing of medical and dental expenses between the plan and the member. Co-insurance is typically the percentage paid by the plan. For example, 80 per cent co-insurance means 80 per cent is reimbursed by the plan and 20 per cent is paid by the member.

Component Credit Allocation Flexible credits are given to members for each type of benefit, and the sum of the components is the member's total credit allocation.

Concierge Services Perform a variety of tasks for employees, from grocery shopping and walking the dog to finding the best estimate from contractors or the most reputable auto mechanic.

Confirmation Statement A personalized statement showing a participant's flexible benefit elections as recorded on the enrolment system.

Constitution Act This legislation is the successor to the *British North America Act*. It sets out the constitutional division of powers between the federal and provincial governments.

Constructive Receipt A legal concept referring to a situation where a taxpayer is taxed on amounts he or she did not actually receive because the taxpayer had the right to take the payment in cash. The income is taxed whether or not the taxpayer actually receives this income.

Consumer-Driven Health Care A U.S. term for medical coverage that combines a high deductible plan with a flexible spending, health savings, or health reimbursement account.

Consumer Price Index (CPI) An index published monthly by Statistics Canada that measures the relative cost of a selected group of goods and services over time.

Conversion A provision in a group life insurance policy that allows an employee to change from group coverage to an individual policy upon termination of employment. Generally, conversion does not require evidence of insurability.

Co-ordination of Benefits A provision in a group insurance policy describing which insurer pays a claim first when two policies cover the same claim. The total payment is no more than 100 per cent of the claim.

Core Level of Benefits A basic level of benefits required by the employer. This benefit level is frequently fully employer-paid.

Core Plus Credits (Core Plus Options Plus Credits) *See* Full Flex.

Co-sourcing Refers to transferring some benefit administration activities to a third party. This typically includes annual enrolment processing, system and data maintenance, file processing, and some report generation. The organization's administration department gains access to the third-party system through an Internet or data communication link to the host computer and processes new plan entrants and terminations. The organization also retains all direct contact with participants.

Cost-of-Living Adjustment (COLA) An increase in wages, pension benefits, or disability benefits that follows the rise in the cost of living. This adjustment is usually calculated using a percentage of the annual increase in the Consumer Price Index, often with a maximum. In flexible benefit programs, this is frequently a provision in optional long-term disability plans.

Credit-Based Pricing A pool of credits is created from which participants can use to purchase benefits tailored to meet their own needs. The benefits come with a "price tag" and each participant spends credits to purchase benefits. If there is a shortfall, the employee pays the difference through payroll deductions. Any leftover credits are generally allocated to the participant in the form of taxable cash, a contribution to a Registered Retirement Savings Plan, a health spending account, or a taxable personal account.

Credit Formula A formula that defines the amount of credits to be provided under a flexible benefit plan. A credit formula may be a flat amount or based on a percentage of the employee's pay, years of service, or other such variables.

Credits (Flexible Credits, Flexible Dollars) The annual allowance of employer money received by each participant to spend on benefits in a credit-based pricing structure. One flexible credit is generally equal to one dollar.

Critical Illness Insurance Provides a lump-sum payment if an insured individual is diagnosed with an illness listed in the insurance policy and the individual survives for a specified period of time.

Deductible The amount an individual must pay out of pocket for medical and dental expenses before any benefits are available from the plan.

Default Coverages A set of coverages assigned to participants who do not return enrolment forms.

Deferred Profit Sharing Plan (DPSP) A type of defined contribution plan in which employer contributions are based on profits. The contributions and investment earnings are tax-protected while in the plan.

Defined Benefit (DB) Pension Plan A retirement plan that provides a specified benefit defined by a formula. Employees may or may not contribute to the plan. The employer's contribution is calculated to be sufficient to provide the promised benefit.

Defined Contribution (DC) Pension Plan A retirement plan that provides an individual account for each participant. Some defined contribution plans provide for both employee and employer contributions, while others allow contributions by one or the other. The ultimate benefit depends on the amount contributed to the account and the associated investment earnings.

Dental Capitation Plans (DMOs, Managed Dental Care, Network Dental Plans) An organization providing a broad range of dental care services for a fixed prepaid monthly fee (per capita). These services are provided by a specified group of dentists.

Dental Fee Guide Each year, the dental association publishes a list of reasonable and customary charges for dental services in the province. Dentists are free to charge more, less, or the same as the fee guide.

Dental Plan A plan that provides benefits for dental care. Typically, dental plans include coverage for preventive and basic work (examination, cleaning, fillings, X-rays), major restorative work (crowns, inlays, bridges) and may also cover orthodontia.

Dependant Generally a member's spouse and children, as defined in a contract. Under some contracts, parents or other members of the family may also be dependants.

Dependant Life Insurance A group life insurance policy covering a member's spouse and/or children. Typically, flat coverage amounts are provided for the spouse and children.

Direct Delivery (Mail Order) Pharmacy A preferred provider arrangement designed to be a low-cost alternative to traditional retail pharmacies. In Canada, the participant contacts the provider, who sends the prescription to the individual by courier, usually within 24 hours.

Dispensing Fee A charge added on to the cost of a prescription drug for the service provided by the pharmacist for filling the prescription. Dispensing fees vary from pharmacy to pharmacy and can range from about $3 to about $13.

Drug Card *See* Prescription Drug Card.

Drug Utilization Review (DUR) The process that determines the appropriateness of specific drug use for an individual with respect to patient history, diagnosis, and other drugs being used at the same time. Typically, this is an electronically driven program that assists the pharmacist by evaluating and screening each claim entered for elements such as the following: Are the refills requested too soon? Is the participant taking two drugs that may cause a reaction? Are duplicate therapies being prescribed for the patient? As a result, a prescription may be questioned or denied at the point of purchase.

Dynamically Frozen Formulary A variation of a frozen formulary. The only new drugs added after the freeze date are line extensions (e.g., new dosages) and generics. Another form of dynamically frozen formulary also adds new breakthrough drugs that are shown to be cost-effective and have no equivalent already on the formulary.

Elder Care A benefit program that provides a variety of care services for a participant's elderly relatives. Elder care programs can provide health services, day care, home support, educational programs, and other services to elderly people. An elder care plan may include:
- Direct subsidies to elder care facilities;
- Payment to participants to subsidize private elder care arrangements; or
- Provision of elder care referral services, either in house or through an outside provider.

Election Analysis Report A report that summarizes election patterns across all options and benefit areas.

Electronic Data Interchange (EDI) An arrangement by which information (e.g., a drug claim) is transmitted electronically to the adjudicator (e.g., prescription drug benefit manager), usually while the individual is waiting at the point of sale.

Eligibility Maintenance An ongoing administrative process to ensure that only those individuals who meet the plan's eligibility requirements are covered under the plan.

Eligibility Requirements The provisions of a group policy that state certain requirements that members of the group must satisfy in order to secure coverage for themselves or their dependants.

Employee Life Insurance A life insurance policy covering an employee under which the benefits are to be paid to a designated beneficiary upon the death of the employee. Benefit amounts are typically defined as multiples of pay (e.g., one times pay, two times pay, etc.) but may also be provided as a flat dollar amount.

Employee Listening The process of collecting information on employee attitudes and perceptions concerning a proposed company initiative. Often used to test the appeal of flexible benefits with a random sample of employees.

Employee Trust An arrangement under which an employer contributes amounts to a trustee to provide benefits for employees. Benefits must vest when payments are made and the amount of the payments on behalf of the employees may not differentiate based on an employee's position, performance, or pay.

Employment Equity Legislation that seeks to improve the workplace representation of four designated groups: women, visible minorities, aboriginal persons, and persons with disabilities. Employment equity programs require employers to remove barriers and adopt positive practices in order to achieve increased representation of the designated groups within their workplace.

Employment Standards Code Each province and the federal government establish minimum employment standards. These standards cover such issues as minimum wage, hours of work, and vacation.

Enrolment (Re-enrolment) The process by which participants choose options under the flexible benefit program. This is almost always an annual process for employee plans. It may be less frequent for retiree plans.

Equal Pay for Equal Work Legislation that redresses gender discrimination in pay practices.

Evidence of Insurability A health statement required by insurers before covering an individual. Typically required when increasing the level of coverage in life insurance or long-term disability, for example.

Exception Processes May allow a member to bypass a drug formulary because of a unique situation. Alternatively, exceptions may be allowed when the individual is currently taking a prescription drug on which he or she has been stabilized and going off the drug would cause a life- or limb-threatening condition.

Exclusions-by-Class Formulary Classes of drugs such as those used to treat obesity, erectile dysfunction (ED), male pattern baldness, infertility, smoking cessation, or cosmetic problems (e.g., Botox) are not considered medically necessary by some employers. These classes of drugs are sometimes referred to as "lifestyle" drugs and, when categorized as such, may be excluded from the list of drugs covered by a formulary.

Experience-Rated Insurance A way of financing insurance with a carrier that requires a full accounting at the end of each plan year. The employer receives any surplus or pays any deficit based on the difference between premiums charged and claims and expenses paid out.

Family Allowances Act An act that provided flat-rate payments on a per-child basis to families with children under 18. This benefit was wholly or partially taxed back above certain income levels ($50,000 in 1989). The *Family Allowances Act* was repealed in 1993 with the introduction of the child tax benefit.

Financial Security Approach Combines a full flex plan and a pension or group savings plan. The most common financial security plan allows employees to exchange part or all of their savings plan company match for additional credits in a flexible benefit plan. Alternatively, the funds could be deposited into their health spending account.

Flat-Dollar Allocation An employer contributes a specified dollar amount towards the funding of a flexible benefit plan.

Flexible Benefit Program (Flexible Compensation, Cafeteria Benefits) A benefit program that allows choice-making and gives the plan member control over how some of the company benefit premiums are to be spent.

Flexible Credits *See* Credits.

Flexible Dollars *See* Credits.

Flexible Expense Account (Flexible Account) A special fund set up by an employer that a participant can draw on to pay certain expenses. Typically, these accounts are used for health-related expenses (health spending account), other expenses (personal account), or executive expenses (perquisite account). Payments from a health spending account are non-taxable income to participants in all provinces except Quebec. Payments from a personal account are generally taxable. Taxability of payments from a personal perquisite account depends on the specific item being reimbursed.

Flexible Pension Plan Employees are permitted to make optional contributions to an ancillary account to purchase ancillary benefits. The employee contributions, subject to prescribed limits, are tax-deductible and do not reduce the individual's RRSP room. The contributing employee must use the account to purchase ancillary benefits from a menu that may include indexing, bridge benefits, and survivor benefits.

Focus Group A group of employees brought together to discuss their attitudes and perceptions toward a proposed company initiative. Focus groups are often used to test a flexible benefit program.

Forfeiture (Use-It-or-Lose-It) The insurance risk element imposed on health spending accounts by the Canada Revenue Agency. Funds allocated for use during a plan year are lost if not spent by the end of the year, or by the end of the second year, depending on program design.

Formulary A list of prescription drugs. In some supplemental medical plans, formulary drugs are reimbursed, while non-formulary drugs are not. In other plans, non-formulary drugs are reimbursed at a lower rate than those on the formulary.

Fringe Benefit Tax An Australian tax on benefit programs that eliminated many of the tax advantages of flexible benefits.

Frozen Formulary All prescription drugs available as of a given date are eligible for reimbursement, while new drugs released after that date will not be eligible under the plan.

Full Flex The earliest flexible benefit plans were full flex programs, often called "core plus credits" or "cafeteria plans." Under this type of plan, participants choose from a range of options in several benefit areas. The lowest option (core) is the minimum level of coverage that is permitted by the employer in each benefit. Participants pay for their selected benefit options using a combination of employer-provided flexible credits and after-tax payroll deductions.

Gain-Sharing (Profit-Related Approach) A method of contributing credits to a flexible benefit plan whereby flexible credits allotted to the plan are based on an employer's financial performance.

Generic Substitution A generic drug is a drug with the same active ingredients, strength, and effectiveness as the brand-name drug. Generic substitution refers to a supplemental medical plan provision that offers reimbursement for generic drugs only, or will pay up to the equivalent of the cost of the generic substitute.

Goods and Services Tax (GST) A federal excise tax imposed on the provision of most goods and services in Canada.

Grandfathering A term used in the insurance industry to signify that prior benefit levels or conditions will be continued for specified individuals despite changes in plan design or carrier.

Group Plans Employer-sponsored benefit plans that provide coverage to a group of employees or retirees.

Guaranteed Income Supplement A benefit payable under the federal *Old Age Security Act* to those whose income is below a certain threshold.

Health and Welfare Trust (H&WT) A vehicle, recognized by the Canada Revenue Agency, sometimes used by employers as a means of funding certain employee benefits. It can provide funding for the following insured benefits:
- Group sickness or accident;
- Private health services plan; and
- Group term life.

Health Reimbursement Arrangement (HRA) or Health Savings Account (HSA) A U.S. tax-sheltered trust or custodial account established to receive tax-favoured employer contributions on behalf of eligible individuals enrolled in high-deductible health plans. Amounts accumulate on a tax-free basis and are not subject to tax if they are used to pay for eligible medical expenses for the participant and dependants. Contributions made in one year may be used to pay eligible medical expenses in later years, including retirement.

Health Spending Account (HSA) Participants allocate flexible credits to this account. During the plan year, participants are reimbursed tax-free for health care expenses (in Quebec the payments are subject to provincial income tax). Expenses that can be covered by this account include those that could be covered by a private health services plan (as defined in the *Income Tax Act*), but are not covered by other private or provincial health insurance plans.

Hearing Care A health care plan that provides reimbursement for hearing aids. Usually included as a part of a supplemental medical plan.

High Option The richest option available in a flexible benefit plan.

Hospital Insurance and Diagnostic Services Act Provided the framework for the Canadian health care system. Provinces complying with federal standards received subsidies of about half the cost of providing hospital benefits. Replaced by the *Canada Health Act* in 1984.

Human Rights Code Provincial and federal legislation that includes definitions of prohibited grounds for employment discrimination. The legislation is administered by human rights commissions.

Income Tax Act (ITA) Legislation governing income tax for individuals and organizations. The *ITA* contains provisions addressing the taxation of benefit programs but does not specifically address flexible plans.

Indemnity Plans A benefit plan that provides reimbursement of a predetermined amount for designated covered services (e.g., health care, group-term life and disability). Payments can be made either to participants or, on assignment, directly to health care providers.

Information Circular A publication of the Canada Revenue Agency that provides information about administrative, enforcement, or procedural matters relating to income tax law. *See also* Interpretation Bulletin.

Insurance Carrier Reporting Production of group insurance reports showing the total coverage costs for each benefit.

Interpretation Bulletin A publication of the Canada Revenue Agency giving the agency's technical interpretation and position on certain provisions contained in income tax law. *See also* Information Circular.

Interpretation Bulletin IT-85R2 A Canada Revenue Agency document that describes health and welfare trusts.

Interpretation Bulletin IT-339R2 A Canada Revenue Agency document that sets out the criteria for a "Private Health Services Plan" as defined in the *Income Tax Act*.

Interpretation Bulletin IT-428 A Canada Revenue Agency document that describes the taxation of wage loss replacement (disability) plans.

Interpretation Bulletin IT-470R (Consolidated) A Canada Revenue Agency document that describes the taxation of perquisites or fringe benefits.

Interpretation Bulletins IT-502 and IT-502SR Canada Revenue Agency documents that describe employee benefit plans and employee trusts.

Interpretation Bulletin IT-519R2 (Consolidated) A Canada Revenue Agency document that describes which medical expenses may be used to claim a tax credit on an individual's income tax return. By extension, these expenses may be reimbursed tax-free (taxed provincially in Quebec) from a health spending account.

Interpretation Bulletin IT-529 A Canada Revenue Agency document that outlines the tax issues applying to flexible benefit programs.

Leave of Absence Time off from work that lasts for an extended period of time. Examples include educational leave, sabbatical leave, and maternity/paternity/adoption leave. Except for the last category, these types of leave typically require management approval.

Lifestyle Drugs Classes of prescription drugs, such as those used to treat obesity, erectile dysfunction (ED), male pattern baldness, infertility, smoking cessation, or cosmetic problems (e.g., Botox), which are not considered medically necessary by some employers. These classes of drugs are frequently excluded from the list of drugs covered by a formulary.

Long-Term Care An insurance plan that provides a benefit if an individual requires medical and support services for an extended period of time. This is usually a flat dollar amount provided per day and can cover nursing homes, home care, day care, and respite care.

Long-Term Disability (LTD) A plan that provides income protection in the event of time lost due to sickness or accident of a long-term nature. Benefits typically begin after six months, continue to age 65, and provide from 50 per cent of pay to 70 per cent of pay.

Low Option The lowest level of coverage available in a flexible benefit plan. This may be no coverage (i.e., participants are allowed to opt out of the plan), or some core level of coverage viewed as catastrophic protection, or a safety-net option.

Mail Order Pharmacy *See* Direct Delivery Pharmacy.

Maintenance of Benefits A co-ordination of benefits approach in which deductibles and co-payment amounts are preserved when the plan is secondary. The secondary plan defines its payment as the difference between what it would pay if it were the sole plan and what the other plan actually pays.

Maintenance Prescriptions Prescriptions that a person takes on an ongoing basis.

Managed Care A term used to describe an array of programs or initiatives designed to manage health care costs and quality of services delivered by intervening in the health care delivery system. Some examples include drug formularies, dental capitation plans, and utilization reviews.

Manual Intervention Information is entered manually into a carrier's administration system.

Medicare A term that refers to provincial government health insurance plans. These plans generally cover hospital ward care, hospital services, and physicians' fees.

Mock Enrolment An exercise aimed at anticipating what actual benefit enrolment patterns are likely to be. It is generally conducted using a subgroup of the employee population during focus group sessions when a new or altered flexible benefit plan is being introduced, and involves asking the participants which options they would enrol in, given the alternatives presented.

Modular A design structure for a flexible benefit program. Modules are created that include specific coverage levels in several benefit areas: for example, a rich set of options, a moderate set of options, and a core set of options. Participants must choose one module.

Money Purchase Pension Plan (MPPP) A type of defined contribution retirement plan. Employee contributions (if any) are typically expressed as a percentage of salary, with the employer making matching contributions. Contributions and investment earnings are used to provide income at the employee's retirement.

Multi-Process Outsourcing The broadest approach to outsourcing human resource administration, whereby an organization transfers most, if not all, of the following transactional and administrative activities to a third party:
- Flexible and traditional benefits administration;
- Pension administration;
- Payroll processing;
- HRIS management;
- Recruiting;
- Compensation administration;
- Disability management; and
- Participant interaction.

Net Contribution Pricing (Net Pricing) Under the net contribution approach, employers do not utilize the credits and price tag structure. Rather, participants are offered choices and see their net cost or net credit for each choice (equal to the price tag minus credit, but the specific amounts are not shown).

Newsletter 96-3 Canada Revenue Agency's requirements regarding flexible defined benefit pension plans are published in Newsletter 96-3.

Newsletter Plans Pension plans that comply with CRA's Newsletter 96-3.

No-Coverage Pricing The process of determining how many credits to give to someone opting out of coverage. *See also* Opt-Out Credits.

Old Age Security (OAS) Act Provides for a monthly pension to be paid out to qualified Canadian residents regardless of past earnings or current income. This pension is indexed to the Consumer Price Index. This benefit is taxed back wholly or partially for those with incomes over a certain level ($63,511 in 2007).

Ongoing Coverage Administration Administration of benefits for participants enrolled in the program and for new employees prior to their eligibility for the flexible program.

Online Enrolment *See* Web-Based Enrolment.

Open Enrolment A "window" or a period of time during which participants are allowed to select any level of coverage with no evidence requirements.

Options The choices available within each benefit area of a flexible benefit program.

Opt Out A plan member who chooses not to be covered for a certain option, for example, dental.

Opt-Out Credits Credits made available to a plan member who elects not to be covered in an option. These credits depend on the pricing structure of the plan and may be less than the credits available to members electing higher plan options.

Orthodontics A branch of dentistry that corrects the abnormal arrangement of teeth or jaws, straightens them, and keeps them in correct position.

Out-of-Canada Design Provides coverage only for emergency expenses incurred while outside Canada, or, in some cases, also within Canada but outside the participant's province of residence.

Out-of-Pocket Expense Payments by a participant for expenses not reimbursed under a group insurance plan.

Outsourcing (Plan and Participant Administration) Transferring the plan and participant administration activities to a third party. The outsourcing provider deals directly with the plan participants, leaving the employer with responsibility for strategic activities such as plan design and pricing.

Partial Insurance An arrangement whereby the employer self-insures the coverage up to a predetermined limit, after which the carrier's liability begins.

Pay Equity Requires equal pay for work of equal value, even where the jobs are not similar.

Payroll Deductions When an employer deducts after-tax dollars from an employee's paycheque; can be used to pay for benefit coverages.

Pending Feature Frequently incorporated into a health spending account administration system, allowing a claim that exceeds the amount available in the account to be partially paid. The balance is carried over ("pended") in the system and is automatically paid once funds become available. This feature eliminates the need to resubmit claims, or portions of claims, when sufficient funds aren't available in the account.

Pension Adjustment (PA) The value of pension benefits accruing to a plan member during a year, as defined in the *Income Tax Act*. The PA is subtracted from the member's comprehensive retirement contribution limit (18 per cent of pay, subject to specified dollar limits) to determine the maximum RRSP contribution for the following year.

Pension Adjustment Reversal (PAR) Reinstates RRSP room "lost" when a plan member terminates from an RPP or DPSP and receives a lower lump sum value than the aggregate PAs reported.

Perquisite A benefit provided for a specific executive-level job. Examples include a company car for personal use, a cell phone, financial counselling, or use of a company fitness facility.

Perquisite Account A discretionary personal spending account for executives. Participants are provided with an allowance they can use to purchase perquisites from a list of available choices. The employer determines the key plan features, namely the amount of the allowance for each executive and the types of perquisites that are available.

Personal Account Used to reimburse participants for specified expenses that are not eligible for payment under a health spending account. The employer determines the list of eligible expenses.

Personal Benefit Statement A statement included in flexible benefit enrolment materials that lists a participant's options, price tags, and credits. The statement is personalized, because the items are calculated based on factors such as the participant's age, pay, date of hire, family status, and sex.

Personal Days (Personal Time) A pool of paid time-off days an employee may choose to use for vacation, illness, and holidays.

Personal Information Protection and Electronic Documents Act (PIPEDA) Canadian federal privacy legislation.

Pharmacare The term refers to provincial prescription drug plans.

Plan Administration Outsourcing (Third-Party Administration) Transferring all day-to-day benefit administration activities to a third party. This includes the annual enrolment processing and the processing of new plan entries and terminations. The organization's administration department maintains all direct contact with participants and acts as a liaison between participants and the outsourcing provider.

Plan Maximum The highest dollar amount available for reimbursement under a plan. Eligible claims are reimbursed up to this amount. Maximums can be specified for the overall plan or for particular benefits within the plan (e.g., a vision maximum of $250 per 24 months).

Pooled Insurance Insured groups are placed in a pool with others sharing similar characteristics. The experience of the pool influences the rates members of the group are charged.

Prescription Drug Benefit Manager (PBM) An organization that administers the prescription drug benefits that may be a component of a supplemental medical plan. A PBM typically works in conjunction with an insurance company.

Prescription Drug Card Most employers who implement formularies, procedural limitations, or dispensing fee limitations use a prescription drug card. The card contains information about the drug benefits (e.g., formulary, deductible, co-insurance, etc.) available to the employee. The card allows the pharmacist to inform the participant of the financial implications of the purchase and to educate the participant at the point of sale about alternative products that might be available at a lower cost.

Premium The amount of money paid by an employer to an insurance company for an insurance policy or annuity.

Price Tag The dollar value paid by participants for a certain level of benefit coverage. May be different from the premium.

Pricing The process of determining the price paid by the participant for a benefit and the employer subsidy allocated to the participant for a flexible benefit program. Two common approaches are credit-based pricing and net contribution pricing.

Prior Authorization A process for determining who is allowed to have which prescription drugs and under what circumstances. Prior authorization processes usually work with a specified list of drugs.

Private Health Services Plan (PHSP) As defined by the *Income Tax Act*, a health care plan with the following elements:

1. It must be an undertaking of one person
2. To indemnify another person

3. For an agreed consideration

4. For a loss or liability in respect of an event

5. The happening of which is uncertain.

When a plan qualifies as a PHSP, the employer is entitled to deduct the plan's premiums as a business expense.

Provincial Formulary A list of drugs covered by a provincial drug plan. The prime consideration for inclusion on a provincial formulary is cost effectiveness of the prescription for the formulary's target population, namely seniors.

Provincial Health Insurance Each province has a health insurance plan. Provinces complying with the *Canada Health Act* are entitled to a transfer of federal tax revenues. The provincial health insurance plans vary from province to province, but in general they provide some degree of coverage for basic medical services such as hospital care, chronic care, pharmacare, the services of some medical practitioners, and the services provided by a medical doctor, surgeon, or nurse, if medically necessary.

Purposive Sample A method of selecting participants for a survey or focus group if reliable statistics are not required. Participants are hand-selected to represent key subgroups.

Qualitative Employee Listening A method of gathering employee perceptions and identifying employee needs that involves face-to-face discussions. These occur either one-on-one or in group meetings, usually with only a small cross-section of employees. Used to determine why employees have certain views or opinions. Does not produce reliable statistics on what portion of the group holds a specific viewpoint.

Quantitative Employee Listening A method of identifying employee needs and gathering employee perceptions that involves a written survey. Typically administered to all employees or a statistically reliable sample. Designed to produce statistics on what portion of a group holds a specific viewpoint. Does not explain why the employees have certain opinions.

Quebec Pension Plan (QPP) A retirement plan for Quebec residents that is almost identical to the Canada Pension Plan (CPP). The most notable differences in the QPP are that the maximum monthly pension of a surviving spouse is significantly higher prior to age 65 than in the CPP, and the children's supplement is significantly lower than in the CPP.

RAMQ The Régie de l'assurance maladie du Quebec. Responsible for administering the Quebec medicare and pharmacare programs.

Random Sample An unbiased method of selecting employees for a survey or focus group, usually accomplished by choosing a name randomly from a name roster and then selecting, say, every twentieth name after that.

Realistic Price Tags Prices that can reasonably be expected to support claims costs in aggregate. Realistic price tags do not reflect the impact of adverse selection and therefore will not match the pattern of claims expected for each option when several options are offered. However, aggregate claims should track closely with the total of all the option prices.

Re-enrolment *See* Enrolment.

Registered Education Savings Plan (RESP) An arrangement permitted under the *Income Tax Act* by which earnings on investments for education accrue tax-free. At maturity, the principal amount is repaid to the contributor and the investment income and any government grants are paid out to the student as taxable income.

Registered Pension Plan (RPP) A pension plan registered with the Canada Revenue Agency as well as the applicable provincial or federal pension regulator.

Registered Retirement Savings Plan (RRSP) An arrangement between an individual and an authorized insurer, trust company, or corporation for the purpose of providing a retirement income for the individual. These are covered under Section 146 of the *Income Tax Act*. At the plan's maturity, an annuity is purchased or the plan assets are transferred to a registered retirement income fund (RRIF). Subject to certain maximums, the individual's contributions to an RRSP are deductible for income tax purposes and the investment income is tax-deferred.

Relative Values A method of comparing option values to a base plan value:

$$\text{relative value} = \frac{\text{option premium}}{\text{base plan premium}}$$

This method compares characteristics of optional plans to a base plan, using actuarial methodology, and assists in setting option prices.

Renewals Proposed costs for the following year, prepared by insurance carrier. Renewal rates for flexible benefit plans are required four to six months prior to the plan anniversary date.

Repricing The process of determining new prices (and credits under credit-based structures) for the upcoming plan year for a flexible benefit plan based on claim experience, utilization levels, inflation trends, and design considerations.

Reserves Funds set aside by an insurer for the purpose of meeting any pending obligations. For example, this would include liabilities for unearned premiums and claims that have been incurred but have not yet been reported.

Retail Sales Tax A provincial tax imposed by many provinces on the sale of most goods in the province.

Retention The portion of the premium retained by the insurer for expenses, contingencies, profits, and contribution to surplus.

Retirement Compensation Arrangement (RCA) A funded plan to provide benefits for employees, typically on termination of employment or retirement.

Rollover A major consideration with health spending accounts is that expenses must be anticipated carefully, or the employee will have an unused account balance at year-end that may have to be forfeited to meet Canada Revenue

Agency requirements. There are two ways of handling the required forfeiture of year-end account balances. Plans can either employ a one-year rollover of unused balances or a one-year rollover of unpaid claims.

Roll Over Unpaid Claims Funds in the account can be used to reimburse eligible expenses incurred during the current year. In addition, unpaid claims from the prior year can also be paid from the current year's balance as long as the participant allocated funds to the previous year's health spending account. Any remaining funds in the account balances at the end of the year are forfeited.

Roll Over Unused Balances Funds in the account can be used to reimburse eligible expenses incurred during the year. Any balance remaining at year-end is rolled over to the next year's account to reimburse expenses incurred in the second year. At the end of the second year, any unused amounts from the first year are forfeited.

Sabbatical Leave An extended period of paid time off (more than six months), frequently for the purpose of study or pursuit of personal interests. Typically, an employee defers a portion of salary each year (subject to Canada Revenue Agency rules) in order to draw upon it while on sabbatical leave.

Salary Deferral Arrangements (SDA) Any funded or unfunded arrangement under which a taxpayer is intending to defer payment of income tax to a subsequent calendar year. Excluded from the SDA definition are disability insurance plans, group sickness or accident insurance plans, supplementary unemployment benefit plans, vacation pay trusts, certain education and training plans, and sabbatical plans.

Salary Reduction A U.S. mechanism whereby employee contributions for benefits are treated as employer payments, thus escaping federal income tax and most state and local taxes. Salary reduction is not tax-effective in Canada.

Salary Sacrifice A U.K. and Australian term for salary reduction.

Section 5(1) A section of the *Canadian Charter of Rights and Freedoms* that guarantees the rights and freedoms set out in it, subject only to reasonable limits prescribed by law that can be justified in a free and democratic society.

Section 15(1) A section of the *Canadian Charter of Rights and Freedoms* that states that every individual, regardless or race, origin, colour, religion, sex, age, or mental or physical disability, has the right to equal protection and benefit under the law.

Section 125 A section of the U.S. Tax Code that governs the taxation of benefits.

Section 401(k) A section of the U.S. Tax Code that permits trade-offs between cash and deferral of compensation into a retirement income vehicle.

Self-Insurance An arrangement whereby the employer pays claims and may administer a plan such as life insurance directly. In this arrangement, the employer assumes the risks and liabilities of an insurance carrier.

Short-Form Medical Questionnaire An abbreviated version of the evidence of insurability form, used to expedite the approval process for life insurance and long-term disability coverage. The questionnaires are submitted to the employer for approval and only those forms requiring further investigation are passed to the insurer. Some employers choose not to use the short form for confidentiality reasons.

Short-Term Disability (STD) A benefit plan that provides payment to a disabled person for the period of the disability before long-term disability benefits are payable. Typically covers the first six months of an employee absence and is paid by the employer.

Sick Leave Time off from work due to illness.

Simplified Flex Many newer flexible benefit plans give participants some choice over how to spend employer money but do not incorporate some of the more complex features of "core plus credits" flexible plans. Types of simplified flexible benefit plans include:
- Health spending accounts,
- Modular plans,
- Health care only plan, and
- Net pricing plans.

Spousal Life Insurance A life insurance plan that covers an employee's spouse. The amount of coverage is typically a flat amount, but may be related to the employee's pay. Price tags for spousal life may be a flat premium amount expressed as dollars per thousand dollars of coverage or may be graded according to age, gender, or smoker status of the spouse.

Staircase Rule A stipulation in a flexible benefit plan that restricts changes to one level (one stair) of coverage per year. For example, a participant electing Option 3 medical in the first year would be permitted to increase to Option 4 or decrease to Option 2 in the second year. The purpose of the rule is to reduce adverse selection costs. *See also* Up Staircase Rule.

Stop-Loss Limits An insurance contract provision that limits the out-of-pocket expenses paid by a participant during the period of coverage.

Stratified Random Sample A method of choosing an employee sample for a survey or focus group whereby employees are arranged by a factor such as job category and then chosen randomly within each category.

Subgroup Pricing A method of dividing the pricing structure into smaller groups with similar characteristics. The most common category is dependant coverage: for example, employee, employee-plus-one, and employee-plus-two-or-more dependants.

Subsidized Pricing This pricing method refers to any difference between the premiums determined by claims experience and the price tags the participant is charged.

Supplemental Medical Plan A medical plan that provides benefits not included in the various provincial health insurance plans. Typically, these plans include coverage for semi-private or private hospital rooms, prescription drugs, certain medical equipment, and health care practitioners that are not covered, or not covered in full, under the provincial plans.

Survivor's Income A form of group life insurance that provides a benefit in the form of a monthly life annuity, payable to the beneficiary of a deceased employee. The benefit amount is typically 25 to 30 per cent of the employee's monthly earnings at the date of death.

Task Force (Study Group) A group of employees, generally representing various work groups and personal situations, who work together in designing a flexible benefit program.

Term Life Insurance Life insurance payable to a beneficiary when the insured person dies. No cash value is developed.

Therapeutic Substitution Two prescription drugs are of the same therapeutic class if they have different active ingredients but can be substituted for one another to provide the same outcome. Under a formulary, the therapeutic substitution is normally the more cost-effective drug.

Third-Party Administration (TPA) *See* Plan Administration Outsourcing.

Traditional Benefit Plan Refers to a benefit plan that does not offer choice in how the employer's benefit subsidy is spent. Typically, this term is used to describe a plan that is not a flexible benefit plan.

Trial Prescriptions Participants who are prescribed a drug for the first time are encouraged to take a smaller amount (e.g., seven days instead of thirty days) when initially picking up the prescription. A participant who reacts well to the new medication and wishes to have the remainder of the prescription filled can return to the pharmacist after the initial supply runs out and receive the remainder.

Universal Life Insurance A life insurance policy under which the policyholder may change the death benefit from time to time and vary the amount or timing of premium payments. A policy account is set up from which premiums and expense charges are deducted and to which interest is credited.

Up Staircase Rule A variation of the staircase rule whereby a participant is permitted to increase by only one flex option per year, but is allowed to decrease to any level of coverage available.

Utilization The extent to which a group uses a service such as a medical or dental plan. Typically expressed as a number of claims per 100 or per 1,000 plan participants.

Vacation Banking A system under which employers allow participants to save unused vacation time for use at a later date.

Vacation Buying An option that allows employees to use flexible credits or payroll deductions to purchase vacation days. Typically, a vacation day is priced at the value of one day's salary for the employee.

Vacation Selling An option that allows employees to exchange a vacation day for taxable flexible credits. Typically, a vacation day is priced at the value of one day's salary for the employee.

Vesting An employee's right to receive a pension benefit whether or not the employee stays with the employer providing the benefit. Employee contributions to a pension plan are immediately vested, but employer-paid benefits may be vested after a number of years of service or plan participation.

Vision Care A health care plan that provides coverage for eyeglasses and/or contact lenses. May be included in supplemental medical plans or be set up as a stand-alone plan.

Wage Loss Replacement Plan An arrangement between an employer and employees under which benefits are provided if an employee loses employment income, as a result of sickness, maternity, or accident, for example.

Waiver of Coverage A provision allowing participants to elect no coverage in certain benefit areas.

Web-Based Enrolment (Online Enrolment) The most common approach for collecting and processing enrolment information. Web-based enrolment normally involves logging on, enrolling, reviewing, printing forms, and confirming.

Weekly Indemnity A weekly payment provided under an insurance policy to reimburse an employee for loss of earnings due to disability. Also known as disability income insurance. These plans pay a periodic cash amount such as 60 per cent of normal earnings for a limited period such as six or twelve months.

Whole Life Insurance Insurance payable to a beneficiary at the death of the insured person. A cash value builds up over time. Premiums may be payable for a specified number of years or for life.

Winners and Losers Analysis Comparison of benefit coverage before and after implementation of a flexible benefit program. Winners are those participants who can buy back the pre-flexible options with no additional cost to them. Losers have to pay more in credits or payroll deductions to buy back their previous coverage.

Workbook/Enrolment Guide A booklet that explains the options and pricing available in a flexible benefit program. This communication material is developed to assist participants in enrolling in the flexible benefit program.

Index